Merriam-Webster's

Japanese-English

Dictionary

Merriam-Webster's
Japanese-English
Dictionary

MERRIAM-WEBSTER, INCORPORATED

Springfield, Massachusetts, U.S.A

First Edition 2010

© HarperCollins Publishers 2010

Typeset by Lingea s.r.o

ISBN: 978-0-87779-861-3

MANAGING EDITOR
Gaëlle Amiot-Cadey

EDITOR
Susanne Reichert

CONTRIBUTORS
Eugene Benoit
Francesca Forrest

SERIES EDITOR
Rob Scriven

Printed in India

7th Printing   Thomson Press India Ltd.   April   2022

Contents

Preface

MERRIAM-WEBSTER'S JAPANESE-ENGLISH DICTIONARY
is a new dictionary designed to meet the needs of English and
Japanese speakers in a time of ever-expanding communication
among the countries of the world. It is intended for language
learners, teachers, office workers, tourists, and business trave-
lers – anyone who needs to communicate effectively in the Japanese and English languages as they are spoken and written today.

This dictionary provides accurate and up-to-date coverage of current vocabulary in both languages, as well as abun-
dant examples of words used in context to illustrate usage.
The dictionary includes Japanese words and phrases as they
are spoken in Japan. The English vocabulary and spellings
included here reflect American English usage. Entered words
that we have reason to believe are constitute trademarks have
been designated as such with the symbol ®. However, neither the presence nor absence of such designation should
be regarded as affecting the legal status of any trademark.

The front matter of this dictionary begins with an Explanatory
Notes section about how to use this dictionary followed by a
list of abbreviations used in the dictionary. The list includes
both Japanese and English abbreviations in a single list that
gives both the Japanese and the English meanings of all of
the abbreviations. This is followed by a listing of English
irregular verbs, a table explaining Japanese Romanization,
a comprehensive section on Japanese pronunciation and a
table showing the symbols from the International Phonetic
Alphabet (IPA) relating to English. The front matter
concludes with a section on numbers, days and months.

This dictionary is the result of a unique collaboration
between Collins and Merriam-Webster. It is based on the
Collins Japanese-English database and reflects the bilingual
lexicographical expertise of Collins editors and contributors. In addition, it has been thoroughly reviewed by editors at
Merriam-Webster to ensure its accurate treatment of American English spelling, vocabulary, and idioms. The editors of
Collins and Merriam-Webster offer this new dictionary in
the belief that it will serve well those who want a concise and
handy guide to the Japanese and English languages of today.

Explanatory Notes

Japanese-to-English section

Headwords

The words you look up in the dictionary – "headwords" – are listed alphabetically by their romanized spelling and set flush left with the left-hand margin of each column. The guidewords appearing at the top of each page indicate the first and last headword on that page. The guidewords show the word in both its romanized spelling and in Japanese characters. (For more information about the correspondence between the roman characters and their hiragana and katakana equivalents, see the section beginning on page 14a.)

If a headword can function as more than one part of speech, the different parts of speech are covered at the same entry, separated by an open triangle

Pronunciation

The romanized spelling is a guide to how the word is pronounced. To better understand the spelling and sound correspondence of the roman characters, see the section on Japanese Pronunciation, beginning on page 16a.

Grammatical Information

Part of speech labels are given in abbreviated form in italics following the romanized spelling. An explanation of the abbreviations used is found on page 9a.

Translations

Translations are shown in normal roman type, and where more than one meaning or usage exists, they are separated by a comma. If the translation word can have more than one meaning, it is followed by a word or short phrase in italics and parentheses to indicate which use of the translation word is appropriate.

Phrases and Related Words

Common phrases and compound words in which the headword appears are shown within the entry for the headword, separated by a semicolon. Closely related words are often similarly treated within the same entry (as the words for *investment*, *invest*, and *investor* at the entry for *toushi*).

English-to-Japanese Section

Headwords

Headwords are listed alphabetically and set flush left with the left-hand margin of each column. They are printed in **bold type** for easy identification. The guidewords appearing at the top of each page indicate the first and last headword on that page.

If a headword can function as more than one part of speech, the different parts of speech are covered at the same entry, separated by an open triangle.

Pronunciation

Where the phonetic spelling of headwords is given, it appears in square brackets immediately after the headword. The phonetic spelling is given in the International Phonetic Alphabet (IPA). A list and explanation of these symbols is given on page 18a.

Grammatical Information

Part of speech labels are given in abbreviated form in italics following the phonetic spelling. An explanation of the abbreviations used is found on page 9a.

Translations

Translations are given in both romanized spelling and Japanese characters. Where more than one meaning or usage exists, they are separated by a comma. If the translation word can have more than one meaning, it is followed by a word or short phrase in italics and parentheses to indicate which use of the translation word is appropriate.

Phrases and Related Words

Common phrases and compound words in which the headword appears are shown within the entry for the headword, separated by a semicolon.

ABBREVIATIONS　　略語

adjective	*adj*	形容詞
adverb	*adv*	副詞
conjunction	*conj*	接続詞
interjection	*intj*	感嘆詞
exclamation	*excl*	感嘆符
feminine	*f*	女性の言葉
masculine	*m*	男性の言葉
noun	*n*	名詞
plural	*pl*	複数形
preposition	*prep*	前置詞
pronoun	*pron*	代名詞
verb	*v*	動詞
intransitive verb	*vi*	自動詞
transitive verb	*vt*	他動詞

English Irregular Verbs

present	past tense	past participle
arise (arising)	arose	arisen
awake (awaking)	awoke	awaked
be (am, is, are; being)	was, were	been
bear	bore	born(e)
beat	beat	beaten
become (becoming)	became	become
begin (beginning)	began	begun
bend	bent	bent
bet (betting)	bet	bet
bid (bidding)	bid	bid
bind	bound	bound
bite (biting)	bit	bitten
bleed	bled	bled
blow	blew	blown
break	broke	broken
breed	bred	bred
bring	brought	brought
build	built	built
burn	burned (o burnt)	burned (o burnt)
burst	burst	burst
buy	bought	bought
can	could	(been able)
cast	cast	cast
catch	caught	caught
choose (choosing)	chose	chosen
cling	clung	clung
come (coming)	came	come
cost	cost	cost
creep	crept	crept
cut (cutting)	cut	cut
deal	dealt	dealt
dig (digging)	dug	dug
do (does)	did	done
draw	drew	drawn
dream	dreamed (o dreamt)	dreamed (o dreamt)
drink	drank	drunk
drive (driving)	drove	driven
eat	ate	eaten
fall	fell	fallen
feed	fed	fed

feel	felt	felt
fight	fought	fought
find	found	found
flee	fled	fled
fling	flung	flung
fly (flies)	flew	flown
forbid (forbidding)	forbade	forbidden
foresee	foresaw	foreseen
forget (forgetting)	forgot	forgotten
forgive (forgiving)	forgave	forgiven
freeze (freezing)	froze	frozen
get (getting)	got	got, (US) gotten
give (giving)	gave	given
go (goes)	went	gone
grind	ground	ground
grow	grew	grown
hang	hung (o hanged)	hung (o hanged)
have (has; having)	had	had
hear	heard	heard
hide (hiding)	hid	hidden
hit (hitting)	hit	hit
hold	held	held
hurt	hurt	hurt
keep	kept	kept
kneel	knelt (o kneeled)	knelt (o kneeled)
know	knew	known
lay	laid	laid
lead	led	led
lean	leaned (o leant)	leaned (o leant)
leap	leaped (o leapt)	leaped (o leapt)
learn	learned (o learnt)	learned (o learnt)
leave (leaving)	left	left
lend	lent	lent
let (letting)	let	let
lie (lying)	lay	lain
light	lit (o lighted)	lit (o lighted)
lose (losing)	lost	lost
make (making)	made	made
may	might	–
mean	meant	meant
meet	met	met
mow	mowed	mown (o mowed)
must	(had to)	(had to)
pay	paid	paid
put (putting)	put	put

quit (quitting)	quit (o quitted)	quit (o quitted)
read	read	read
rid (ridding)	rid	rid
ride (riding)	rode	ridden
ring	rang	rung
rise (rising)	rose	risen
run (running)	ran	run
saw	sawed	sawn
say	said	said
see	saw	seen
seek	sought	sought
sell	sold	sold
send	sent	sent
set (setting)	set	set
shake (shaking)	shook	shaken
shall	should	–
shine (shining)	shone	shone
shoot	shot	shot
show	showed	shown
shrink	shrank	shrunk
shut (shutting)	shut	shut
sing	sang	sung
sink	sank	sunk
sit (sitting)	sat	sat
sleep	slept	slept
slide (sliding)	slid	slid
sling	slung	slung
slit (slitting)	slit	slit
smell	smelled (o smelt)	smelled (o smelt)
sow	sowed	sown (o sowed)
speak	spoke	spoken
speed	sped (o speeded)	sped (o speeded)
spell	spelled (o spelt)	spelled (o spelt)
spend	spent	spent
spin (spinning)	spun	spun
spit (spitting)	spat	spat
split (splitting)	split	split
spoil	spoiled (o spoilt)	spoiled (o spoilt)
spread	spread	spread
spring	sprang	sprung
stand	stood	stood
steal	stole	stolen
stick	stuck	stuck
sting	stung	stung
stink	stank	stunk

12a

strike (striking)	struck	struck
strive (striving)	strove	striven
swear	swore	sworn
sweep	swept	swept
swell	swelled	swollen (o swelled)
swim (swimming)	swam	swum
swing	swung	swung
take (taking)	took	taken
teach	taught	taught
tear	tore	torn
tell	told	told
think	thought	thought
throw	threw	thrown
thrust	thrust	thrust
tread	trod	trodden
wake (waking)	woke (o waked)	woken (o waked)
wear	wore	worn
weave (weaving)	wove (o weaved)	woven (o weaved)
weep	wept	wept
win (winning)	won	won
wind	wound	wound
write (writing)	wrote	written

Japanese Romanization
日本語のローマ字表記

There are several systems for writing Japanese in Roman characters, but the most understandable for English speakers is the Hepburn system. The following table illustrates this system, with its hiragana and katakana equivalents, as it has been adopted in this dictionary.

	a	i	u	e	o
	あ	い	う	え	お
	ア	イ	ウ	エ	オ
k	ka	ki	ku	ke	ko
	か	き	く	け	こ
	カ	キ	ク	ケ	コ
s	sa	shi	su	se	so
	さ	し	す	せ	そ
	サ	シ	ス	セ	ソ
t	ta	chi	tsu	te	to
	た	ち	つ	て	と
	タ	チ	ツ	テ	ト
n	na	ni	nu	ne	no
	な	に	ぬ	ね	の
	ナ	ニ	ヌ	ネ	ノ
h	ha	hi	fu	he	ho
	は	ひ	ふ	へ	ほ
	ハ	ヒ	フ	ヘ	ホ
m	ma	mi	mu	me	mo
	ま	み	む	め	も
	マ	ミ	ム	メ	モ

	ya	**yu**		**yo**
y	や	ゆ		よ
	ヤ	ユ		ヨ
	ra	**ri**	**ru**	**re**	**ro**
r	ら	り	る	れ	ろ
	ラ	リ	ル	レ	ロ
	wa			**wo**
w	わ			を
	ワ			ヲ
				n
				ん
				ン

	ga	**gi**	**gu**	**ge**	**go**
g	が	ぎ	ぐ	げ	ご
	ガ	ギ	グ	ゲ	ゴ
z	**za**	**ji**	**zu**	**ze**	**zo**
	ざ	じ	ず	ぜ	ぞ
	ザ	ジ	ズ	ゼ	ゾ
d	**da**	**ji**	**zu**	**de**	**do**
	だ	ぢ	づ	で	ど
	ダ	ヂ	ヅ	デ	ド
b	**ba**	**bi**	**bu**	**be**	**bo**
	ば	び	ぶ	べ	ぼ
	バ	ビ	ブ	ベ	ボ
p	**pa**	**pi**	**pu**	**pe**	**po**
	ぱ	ぴ	ぷ	ぺ	ぽ
	パ	ピ	プ	ペ	ポ

Japanese Pronunciation

VOWELS

		Japanese example	Explanation
[a]	秋	[aki]	Like *a* in father
[e]	枝	[eda]	Like *e* in set
[i]	犬	[inu]	Like *i* in machine
[o]	音	[oto]	Like *o* in open
[u]	歌	[uta]	Like *oo* in soon

but generally the *u* at the end of syllables is barely pronounced. Common endings such as *-desu* and *-masu* are pronounced as "des" and "mas" respectively.

Doubled vowels such as *aa, ee, ii, oo,* and *uu* are pronounced as above but with twice the length. The dipthongs *ei* and *ou* are pronounced like the "ay" in say and the "ow" in crow respectively.

CONSONANTS

In Romanized Japanese, consonants are pronounced as in English but note the few differences.

		Japanese example	Explanation
[b]	晩	[ban]	Like *b* in bank
[d]	度	[do]	Like *d* in dog
[f]	藤	[fuji]	Like *f* in far or a cross between f and h
[g]	蛾	[ga]	Always like *g* in girl, never like in gin
[h]	葉	[ha]	Like *h* in happy
[j]	十	[juu]	Like *j* in jam
[k]	亀	[kame]	Like *k* in kettle
[m]	豆	[mame]	Like *m* in mother

[n]	名前	[namae]	Like *n* in not, but like *m* before b, m, p
[p]	パンク	[panku]	Like *p* in pie
[r]	例	[rei]	Like *r* in three or a cross between l and r
[s]	先生	[sensei]	Like *s* in sister
[t]	手紙	[tegami]	Like *t* in tell
[w]	ワイン	[wain]	Like *w* in wine
[y]	山	[yama]	Like *y* in yes
[z]	像	[zou]	Like *z* in zoo

[ch], [sh], [ts] -These are pronounced just as in English: *ch* as in chair, sh as in shout and *ts* as in hot soup.

Double consonants such as *kk, pp, ss, tt* are pronounced as double letters with a pause between each. Some sounds such as *ki, gi, ri,* etc. may combine with *ya, yu, yo* to form double consonant combinations such as *kya, kyu, gyo*, etc.

Phonetic Symbols

VOWELS

[ɑ]	**f**a**ther**
[ʌ]	**b**u**t, c**o**me**
[æ]	**m**a**n, c**a**t**
[ə]	**f**a**th**e**r, **a**go**
[ɜ]	**b**i**rd, h**ea**rd**
[ɛ]	**g**e**t, b**e**d**
[ɪ]	**i**t, b**i**g**
[i]	**t**ea**, s**ee**
[ɒ]	**h**o**t, w**a**sh**
[ɔ]	**s**aw**, **a**ll**
[ʊ]	**p**u**t, b**oo**k**
[u]	**t**oo**, y**ou**

DIPHTHONGS

[aɪ]	**fl**y**, h**igh**
[a]	**h**ow**, h**ou**se**
[ɛə]	**th**ere**, b**ear**
[eɪ]	**d**ay**, ob**ey**
[ɪə]	**h**ere**, h**ear**
[o]	**g**o**, n**o**te**
[ɔɪ]	**b**oy**, **oi**l**
[ə]	**p**oor**, s**ure**

CONSONANTS

[b]	**b**ig, lo**bb**y
[d]	men**d**e**d**
[g]	**g**o, **g**et, bi**g**
[dʒ]	**g**in, ju**dg**e
[ŋ]	si**ng**
[h]	**h**ouse, **h**e
[y]	**y**oung, **y**es
[k]	**c**ome, mo**ck**
[r]	**r**ed, t**r**ead
[s]	**s**and, ye**s**
[z]	ro**s**e, **z**ebra
[ʃ]	**sh**e, ma**ch**ine
[tʃ]	**ch**in, ri**ch**
[v]	**v**alley
[w]	**w**ater, **wh**ich
[ʒ]	vi**s**ion
[θ]	**th**ink, my**th**
[ð]	**th**is, **th**e

Numbers
数字

zero	0	ゼロ zero
one	1	一 ichi
two	2	二 ni
thee	3	三 san
four	4	四 shi, yon
five	5	五 go
six	6	六 roku
seven	7	七 shichi, nana
eight	8	八 hachi
nine	9	九 kyuu, kuu
ten	10	十 juu
eleven	11	十一 juuichi
twelve	12	十二 juuni
thirteen	13	十三 juusan
fourteen	14	十六 juuyon
fifteen	15	十五 juugo
sixteen	16	十六 juuroku
seventeen	17	十七 juunana
eighteen	18	十八 juuhachi
nineteen	19	十九 juukyuu
twenty	20	二十 nijuu
twenty one	21	二十一 nijuuichi
twenty two	22	二十二 nijuuni
twenty three	23	二十三 nijuusan
thirty	30	三十 sanjuu
thirty one	31	三十一 sanjuuichi
forty	40	四十 yonjuu

fifty	50	五十	gojuu
sixty	60	六十	rokujuu
seventy	70	七十	nanajuu, shichijuu
eighty	80	八十	hachijuu
ninety	90	九十	kyuujuu
one hundred	100	百	hyaku
one hundred ten	110	百十	hyakujuu
two hundred	200	二百	nihyaku
two hundred fifty	250	二百五十	nihyakugojuu
one thousand	1.000	千、一千	sen, issen
ten thousand	10.000	一万	ichiman
one million	1.000.000	十万	juuman

Days 曜日

Monday	月曜日 getsuyoobi
Tuesday	火曜日 kayoobi
Wednesday	水曜日 suiyoobi
Thursday	木曜日 mokuyoobi
Friday	金曜日 kinyoobi
Saturday	土曜日 doyoobi
Sunday	日曜日 nichiyoobi

Months 月

January	一月 ichigatsu
February	二月 nigatsu
March	三月 sangatsu
April	四月 shigatsu
May	五月 gogatsu
June	六月 rokugatsu
July	七月 sichigatsu
August	八月 hachigatsu
September	九月 kugatsu
October	十月 juugatsu
November	十一月 juuichigatsu
December	十二月 nigatsu

Japanese-English
Dictionary

A

アーチ [aachi] n arch

アーモンド [aamondo] n almond

アーティチョーク [aatichooku] n artichoke

アボカド [abokado] n avocado

アブダビ [abudabi] n Abu Dhabi

危ない [abunai] adj dangerous

油 [abura] n oil; 油で揚げた [abura de ageta] adj fried; 油で揚げる [abura de ageru] v deep-fry, fry; 油を差す [abura-o sasu] (注油) v oil

脂 [abura] 脂を含んだ [abura-o fukunda] adj greasy

脂っこい [aburakkoi] 食べ物がとても脂っこいです [tabemono ga totemo aburakkoi desu] The food is very greasy

あっち [acchi] あっちへ行ってください! [atchi e itte kudasai!] Go away!

あちこち [achikochi] prep around

あだ名 [adana] ···とあだ名をつけられた [... to adana-o tsukerareta] adj dubbed

アダプタ [adaputa] ソケットアダプタ [soketto adaputa] n adapter

アドレス [adoresu] n address; あなたのEメールアドレスは何ですか? [anata no ii-meeru-adoresu wa nan desu ka?] What's your e-mail address?

アドリア海 [adoriakai] n Adriatic Sea; アドリア海の [adoriakai no] adj Adriatic

亜鉛 [aen] n zinc

アフガニスタン [afuganisutan] n Afghani-stan; アフガニスタンの [afuganisutan no] adj Afghan

アフガニスタン人 [afuganisutanjin] n Afghan (person)

アフリカ [afurika] n Africa; 中央アフリカ共和国 [Chuuou Afurika Kyouwakoku] n Central African Republic; アフリカの [afurika no] adj African

アフリカーナー [afurikaanaa] n Afrikaner

アフリカーンス語 [afurikaansugo] n Afrikaans

アフリカ人 [afurikajin] n African (person)

上がる [agaru] v come up, go up

上げる [ageru] v raise; 速度を上げる [sokudo-o ageru] v speed up; 金切り声を上げる [kanagiri koe-o ageru] v scream

揚げる [ageru] 油で揚げた [abura de ageta] adj fried; 油で揚げる [abura de ageru] v deep-fry, fry

あご [ago] n chin, jaw

あごひげ [agohige] n beard; あごひげを生やした [agohige-o hayashita] adj bearded

アヒル [ahiru] n duck

愛 [ai] n love; 愛する [ai suru] v love; 私はあなたを愛しています [watashi wa anata o aishite imasu] I love you

愛着 [aichaku] n attachment

間 [aida] n while; ···の間に [... no aida ni] prep between

愛人 [aijin] n lover; 女性の愛人 [josei no aijin] n mistress

愛情 [aijou] 愛情のこもった [aijou no komotta] adj affectionate

愛国 [aikoku] 愛国的な [aikokuteki na] adj patriotic

愛国主義 [aikokushugi] 熱狂的愛国主義者 [nekkyoutekiaikokushugisha] n male chauvinist

曖昧 [aimai] 曖昧な [aimai na] adj vague

アイライナー [airainaa] n eyeliner

アイロン [airon] アイロンをかける [airon-o kakeru] v iron; アイロンをかけるべきもの [airon-o kakerubeki mono] n ironing; アイロン台 [airondai] n ironing board; どこでこれにアイロンをかけてもらえますか? [doko de kore ni airon o kakete moraemasu ka?] Where can I get this ironed?; 私はアイロンが必要です [watashi wa airon ga hitsuyou desu] I need an iron

アイルランド [airurando] n Eire, Ireland

アイルランド人 [airurandojin] n Irish, Irishman, Irishwoman

アイルランドの [airurando no] adj Irish

挨拶 [aisatsu] n greeting; 挨拶する [aisatsu suru] v salute; ···に挨拶する [... ni aisatsu suru] v greet

アイシャドウ [aishadou] n eye shadow

アイシング [aishingu] n icing

アイス [aisu] アイスキャンディー [aisu kyandii] n Popsicle®; アイスボックス [aisu bokkusu] n icebox

アイスホッケー [aisuhokkee] n hockey

アイスクリーム [aisukuriimu] n ice cream; 私はアイスクリームをいただきます [watashi wa aisukuriimu o itadakimasu] I'd like some ice cream

アイスキューブ [aisukyuubu] n ice cube

アイスランド [aisurando] n Iceland

アイスランド人 [aisurandojin] n Icelandic (person)

アイスランドの [aisurando no] adj Icelandic

アイススケート [aisusukeeto] n ice-skating

相手 [aite] n partner; 決まった相手がいる [kimatta aite ga iru] adj attached; 競争相手 [kyousouaite] n rival

合図 [aizu] n signal; 合図する [aizu suru] v signal

味 [aji] n flavor, taste; 味のない [aji no nai] adj tasteless; 味のよい [aji no yoi] adj tasty; 味をみる [aji-o miru] v taste; 味があまりよくありません [aji ga amari yoku arimasen] It doesn't taste very good

アジア [ajia] n Asia; アジアの [ajia no] adj Asian, Asiatic

アジア人 [ajiajin] n Asian (person)

赤ちゃん [akachan] n baby; どこで赤ちゃんに授乳できますか? [doko de akachan ni junyuu dekimasu ka?] Where can I breast-feed the baby?; どこで赤ちゃんのおしめを替えられますか? [doko de akachan no oshime o kaeraremasu ka?] Where can I change the baby?; 赤ちゃんがいる両親のための設備はありますか? [akachan ga iru ryoushin no tame no setsubi wa arimasu ka?] Are there facilities for parents with babies?

赤ちゃん用ウェットティシュー [akachanyou-uettotishuu] n baby wipe

赤毛 [akage] n redhead; 赤毛の [akage no] adj red-haired

赤い [akai] adj red; 赤十字社 [Sekijuujisha] n Red Cross

赤身 [akami] 赤身肉 [akaminiku] n red meat; 私は赤身肉を食べません [watashi wa akaminiku o tabemasen] I don't eat red meat

赤ん坊 [akanbou] n baby

明かり [akari] n light; 明かりがつきません [akari ga tsukimasen] The light doesn't work; 明かりをつけてもいいですか? [akari o tsukete mo ii desu ka?] May I turn on the light?; 明かりを消してもいいですか? [akari o keshite mo ii desu ka?] May I turn off the light?

明るい [akarui] adj bright, light (not dark); 明るいところに持っていってもいいですか? [akarui tokoro ni motte itte mo ii desu ka?] May I take it over to the light?

赤ワイン [akawain] よい赤ワインを教えてもらえますか? [yoi aka-wain o oshiete moraemasu ka?] Can you recommend a good red wine?

あける [akeru] 穴をあけた [ana-o aketa] adj pierced; 穴をあける [ana-o akeru] v bore, drill; 錠をあける [jou-o akeru] v unlock

空ける [akeru] いつ部屋を空けなければなりませんか? [itsu heya o akenakereba

narimasen ka?] When do I have to be out of the room?

開ける [akeru] v open; ファスナーを開ける [fasunaa-o hirakeru] v unzip; 窓を開けてもいいですか? [mado o akete mo ii desu ka?] May I open the window?; 窓を開けられません [mado o akeraremasen] I can't open the window

秋 [aki] n autumn

空き瓶 [akibin] 空き瓶回収ボックス [akikan kaishuu bokkusu] n glass recycling container

明らか [akiraka] 明らかな [akiraka na] adj apparent; 明らかに [akiraka ni] adv apparently, obviously; 明らかにする [akiraka ni suru] v clarify, disclose, reveal

明らかな [akiraka na] adj obvious

空き室 [akishitsu] n vacancy; 空き室はありますか? [akishitsu wa arimasu ka?] Do you have any vacancies?

悪化 [akka] 悪化する [akka suru] v deteriorate, worsen

あこがれる [akogareru] v adore

アコーディオン [akoodeion] n accordion

空く [aku] 空いている [aite iru] adj vacant; この席は空いていますか? [kono seki wa aite imasu ka?] Is this seat free?

あくび [akubi] v あくびをする [akubi-o suru] v yawn

悪意 [akui] n venom; 悪意のある [akui no aru] adj malicious, malignant

悪魔 [akuma] n devil

悪夢 [akumu] n nightmare

アクセル [akuseru] n accelerator

アクセス [akusesu] v アクセスする [akusesu suru] v access

悪臭 [akushuu] n stink; 悪臭を放つ [akushuu-o hanatsu] v stink

アクティビティ [akuteibeitei] 子供向けのアクティビティはありますか? [kodomo muke no akutibiti wa arimasu ka?] Do you have activities for children?

アクティブ [akuteibu] アクティブホリデー [akutibu horidee] n activity vacation

悪徳 [akutoku] n vice

悪党 [akutou] n villain

アマチュア [amachua] n amateur

甘い [amai] adj sweet (taste); 甘いもの [amai mono] n dessert

甘味 [amami] 甘味料 [kanmiryou] n sweetener

余り [amari] n surplus

雨 [ame] n rain; 酸性雨 [sanseiu] n acid rain; 雨の [ame no] adj rainy; 雨が降る [ame ga furu] v rain; 雨が降っています [ame ga futte imasu] It's raining; 雨が降ると思いますか? [ame ga furu to omoimasu ka?] Do you think it's going to rain?

アメニティー [ameniteii] n amenities

アメリカ [amerika] n America; 中央アメリカ [Chuuou Amerika] n Central America; アメリカの [amerika no] adj American

アメリカ人 [amerikajin] n American (person)

網 [ami] n net

編み [ami] 編み棒 [amibou] n knitting needle

編物 [amimono] n knitting

編む [amu] v knit

穴 [ana] n hole; 穴をあけた [ana-o aketa] adj pierced; 穴をあける [ana-o akeru] v bore, drill, pierce; 鼻の穴 [hana no ana] n nostril

アナグマ [anaguma] n badger

あなた [anata] n sir ▷ pron you; あなたの [anata no] adj your, yours; あなた自身 [anata jishin] pron yourself; あなたは? [anata wa?] And you?

あなた方 [anatagata] あなた方自身 [anatagata jishin] pron yourselves

アンチウイルス [anchiuirusu] n antivirus

アンチョビー [anchobii] n anchovy

アンダーパス [andaapasu] n underpass

アンダースカート [andaasukaato] n slip

アンデス [andesu] アンデス山脈 [andesu sanmyaku] n Andes

アンドラ [andora] n Andorra

アンゴラ [angora] n Angola; アンゴラの

[angora no] *adj* Angolan

アンゴラ人 [angorajin] *n* Angolan *(person)*

暗号 [angou] *n* code

アニシード [anishiido] *n* aniseed

アンケート [ankeeto] アンケート用紙 [ankeeto youshi] *n* questionnaire

案内 [annai] *n* information; 案内所 [annaijo] *n* information office, inquiries office; 案内書 [annaisho] *n* prospectus; 番号案内サービス [bangou annai saabisu] *n* directory assistance

アノラック [anorakku] *n* parka

アンパイア [anpaia] *n* umpire

アンペア [anpea] *n* ampere

アンプ [anpu] *n* amplifier

安楽 [anraku] *n* comfort; 安楽椅子 [anraku isu] *n* easy chair

安心 [anshin] *n* relief; 安心させる [anshin saseru] *v* reassure, relieve; 安心した [anshin shita] *adj* relieved

暗証 [anshou] 暗証番号 [anshobango] *n* personal identification number *(PIN)*

安息 [ansoku] 安息日 [ansokubi] *n* Sabbath

安定 [antei] *n* stability; 安定した [antei shita] *adj* stable; 公共職業安定所 [koukyoushokugyou anteisho] *n* employment office

アンテナ [antena] *n* antenna

安全 [anzen] *n* safety; 安全ピン [anzenpin] *n* safety pin; 安全ベルト [anzenberuto] *n* safety belt; 安全な [anzen na] *adj* secure

安全な [anzen na] *adj* safe

青々 [aoao] 青々とした [aoao to shita] *adj* lush

青い [aoi] *adj* blue

青緑色 [aomidoriiro] 青緑色の [aomidori iro no] *adj* turquoise

アパート [apaato] *n* apartment; ワンルームのアパート [wanruumu no apaato] *n* efficiency apartment

アパートメント [apaatomento] *n* apartment; アパートメントを案内していただけますか? [apaatomento o annai shite itadakemasu ka?] Could you show us around the apartment?; 私たちはアパートメントを探しています [watashi-tachi wa apaatomento o sagashite imasu] We're looking for an apartment; ・・・の名前でアパートメントを予約してあります [... no namae de apaatomento o yoyaku shite arimasu] We've reserved an apartment in the name of...

アペリチフ [aperichifu] *n* aperitif; アペリチフをいただきます [aperichifu o itadakimasu] We'd like an aperitif

アポストロフィ [aposutorofi] *n* apostrophe

アップグレード [appugureedo] *n* upgrade; 切符をアップグレードしたいのですが [kippu o appugureedo shitai no desu ga] I want to upgrade my ticket

アップル [appuru] アップルパイ [appurupai] *n* apple pie

アプリコット [apurikotto] *n* apricot

アブザイレン [apuzairen] 私はアブザイレンをしたいのですが [watashi wa apuzairen o shitai no desu ga] I'd like to go rappelling

アラビア [arabia] アラビアの [arabia no] *adj* Arab

アラビア語 [arabiago] *n* Arabic; アラビア語の [arabiago no] *adj* Arabic

アラビア人 [arabiajin] *n* Arab *(person)*

アラブ首長国連邦 [arabu shuchoukokuren-pou] *n* United Arab Emirates

洗える [araeru] 洗濯機で洗える [sentakuki de araeru] *adj* machine washable; それは洗えますか? [sore wa araemasu ka?] Is it washable?

粗い [arai] *adj* rough; きめの粗い [kime no komakai] *adj* coarse

アライグマ [araiguma] *n* racoon

粗い砂 [araisuna] *n* grit

あらかじめ [arakajime] *adv* beforehand

嵐 [arashi] *n* storm; 嵐の [arashi no] *adj* stormy; 嵐になると思いますか? [arashi ni naru to omoimasu ka?] Do you think there'll be a storm?

洗う [arau] *v* wash; ごしごし洗う [goshigoshi arau] *v* scrub; 洗って片付ける [aratte

katazukeru] v wash the dishes; 食器洗い
[shokkiarai] n washing the dishes; 食器洗い
機 [shokkiaraiki] n dishwasher; 車を洗いた
いのですが [kuruma o araitai no desu ga] I'd
like to wash the car

現れる [arawareru] v appear, show up

現す [arawasu] v signify; 姿を現す [sugata-o
arawasu] v turn up

表す [arawasu] v stand for; 感謝を表さない
[kansha-o arawasanai] adj ungrateful

アレチネズミ [arechinezumi] n gerbil

荒野 [areno] n moor

荒れる [areru] v deteriorate

アレルギー [arerugii] n allergy; アレルギーの
[arerugii no] adj allergic; 小麦アレルギー
[komugi arerugii] n wheat allergy

アリ [ari] n ant

アリバイ [aribai] n alibi

ありがとう [arigatou] Thank you; ありがとうご
ざいます [arigatou gozaimasu] Thank you
very much

ありがとう! [arigatou] excl thanks!

ありそうもない [arisou mo nai] adj unlikely

ありそうな [arisou na] adj probable

アロマセラピー [aromaserapii] n aromatherapy

アッラー [arraa] n Allah

ある [aru] v have

アルバム [arubamu] n album, photo album

アルバニア [arubania] n Albania; アルバニア
の [arubania no] adj Albanian

アルバニア語 [arubaniago] n Albanian
(language)

アルバニア人 [arubaniajin] n Albanian
(person)

あるべき所にない [aru beki tokoro ni nai] v
missing

アルファベット [arufabetto] n alphabet

アルジェリア [arujeria] n Algeria; アルジェリア
の [arujieria no] adj Algerian

アルジェリア人 [arujieriajin] n Algerian
(person)

歩き回る [arukimawaru] v wander

アルコール [arukooru] n alcohol; 低アルコー
ルの [tei arukooru no] adj low-alcohol; アル
コール中毒者 [arukooru chuudokusha] n
alcoholic; アルコールの [arukooru no] adj
alcoholic; アルコールを含まない [arukooru
wo fukumanai] adj alcohol-free; それにはア
ルコールが入っていますか? [sore ni wa
arukooru ga haitte imasu ka?] Does that
contain alcohol?; 私はアルコールを飲みま
せん [watashi wa arukooru o nomimasen] I
don't drink alcohol

アルコール中毒 [arukooru chuudoku] アルコ
ール中毒者 [arukooru chuudokusha] n
alcoholic

歩く [aruku] v walk; ぶらぶら歩き [burabura
aruki] n stroll; 足をひきずって歩く [ashi-o
hikizutte aruku] v shuffle; 夢遊病で歩く
[muyuubyou de aruku] v sleepwalk; そこま
で歩いて行けますか? [soko made aruite
ikemasu ka?] Can I walk there?

アルメニア [arumenia] n Armenia; アルメニ
アの [arumenia no] adj Armenian

アルメニア語 [arumeniago] n Armenian
(language)

アルメニア人 [arumeniajin] n Armenian (person)

アルミ [arumi] アルミ箔 [arumihaku] n tinfoil

アルミニウム [aruminiumu] n aluminum

アルプス [arupusu] アルプス山脈 [arupusu
sanmyaku] n Alps

アルゼンチン [aruzenchin] n Argentina; アル
ゼンチンの [aruzenchin no] adj Argentine

アルゼンチン人 [aruzenchinjin] n Argentine
(person)

朝 [asa] n morning; 朝寝坊 [asanebou] n
sleep late; 明日の朝 [asu no asa] tomorrow
morning

麻 [asa] n linen

浅い [asai] adj shallow; 子供用の浅いプール
はありますか? [kodomo-you no asai puuru
wa arimasu ka?] Is there a shallow pool
for the children?

あさって [asatte] the day after tomorrow

汗 [ase] n perspiration, sweat; 汗をかく [ase wo kaku] v sweat

汗だらけ [asedarake] 汗だらけの [ase darake no] adj sweaty

褪せる [aseru] v fade

足 [ashi] n feet, foot; 足の指 [ashi no yubi] n toe; 足治療医 [ashichiryoui] n podiatrist; 動物の足 [doubutsu no ashi] n paw; 私は足が痛みます [watashi wa ashi ga itamimasu] My feet are sore; 私の足は六号です [watashi no ashi wa roku-gou desu] My feet are a size seven

脚 [ashi] n leg; 私は脚がかゆみます [watashi wa ashi ga kayumimasu] My leg itches; 私は脚がつっています [watashi wa ashi ga tsutte imasu] I've got a cramp in my leg; 私は脚を動かせません [watashi wa ashi o ugokasemasen] I can't move my leg; 彼は脚を動かせません [kare wa ashi o ugokasemasen] He can't move his leg; 彼女は脚を痛めました [kanojo wa ashi o itamemashita] She's hurt her leg

アシ [ashi] n (植物) reed

足跡 [ashiato] n footprint

足場 [ashiba] n scaffolding

足取り [ashidori] n footstep

遊び [asobi] n fun; 遊び時間 [asobi jikan] n playtime

遊び場 [asobiba] n playground

遊ぶ [asobu] n play; 楽しく遊ぶ [tanoshiku asobu] v have fun

あそこ [asoko] adv over there; あそこです [asoko desu] It's over there

明日 [asu] adv tomorrow; 明日何かなさりたいですか? [asu nani ka nasaritai desu ka?] Would you like to do something tomorrow?; 明日の朝 [asu no asa] tomorrow morning; 明日の午後 [asu no gogo] tomorrow afternoon; 明日電話してもいいですか? [asu denwa shite mo ii desu ka?] May I call you tomorrow?; 私は明日の朝10時に出発します [watashi wa asu no asa jyuu-ji ni shuppatsu shimasu] I shall be

leaving tomorrow morning at ten a.m.; 私は明日出発します [watashi wa asu shuppatsu shimasu] I'm leaving tomorrow

アスパラガス [asuparagasu] n asparagus

アスピリン [asupirin] n aspirin; アスピリンが欲しいのですが [asupirin ga hoshii no desu ga] I'd like some aspirin; 私はアスピリンを飲めません [watashi wa asupirin o nomemasen] I can't take aspirin

与える [ataeru] v give; 不快感を与える [fukaikan-o ataeru] v offend; 権限を与える [kengen-o ataeru] v authorize; 衝撃を与える [shougeki-o ataeru] v shock; 食物を与える [tabemono o ataeru] v feed; 影響を与える [eikyou-o ataeru] v affect

値する [atai suru] v be worth; ···に値する [...ni atai suru] v deserve

頭 [atama] n head (body part); 頭のはげた [atama no hageta] adj bald; 頭のいい [atama no ii] adj brainy

新しい [atarashii] adj new; 全く新しいスタイルにしてください [mattaku atarashii sutairu ni shite kudasai] I want a completely new look

あたり [atari] あたりを見回す [atari-o miwatasu] v look around; 1時間あたりいくらですか? [ichi-jikan atari ikura desu ka?] How much is it per hour?

暖かい [atatakai] adj warm

暖まる [atatamaru] v warm up

温める [atatameru] これを温めてもらえますか? [kore o atatamete moraemasu ka?] Could you warm this up, please?

あて [ate] あてにならない [ate ni naranai] adj shifty; あてにする [ate ni suru] v depend, rely on

あてにならない [ate ni naranai] adj unreliable

跡 [ato] n trace; 汚れの跡 [yogore no ato] n stain; 汚れの跡をつける [yogore no ato-o tsukeru] v stain

あと [ato] あとで [ato de] adv later

あとで [ato de] あとでもう一度かけてもらえます

か? [ato de mou ichido kakete moraemasu ka?] Would you mind trying again later?; あとで出直ししましょうか? [ato de denaoshi-mashou ka?] Shall I come back later?

熱い [atsui] adj hot; 食べ物が熱すぎます [tabemono ga atsu-sugimasu] The food is too hot

暑い [atsui] adj hot; うだるように暑い [udaru youni atsui] adj sweltering; とても暑いです [totemo atsui desu] It's very hot; 暑くて眠れません [atsukute nemuremasen] I can't sleep because of the heat; 部屋が暑すぎます [heya ga atsu-sugimasu] The room is too hot; 少し暑すぎます [sukoshi atsu-sugimasu] It's a little too hot

厚い [atsui] adj thick; 厚さ [atsusa] n thickness

扱う [atsukau] v deal with, treat; 巧みに扱う [takumi ni atsukau] v manipulate

厚く [atsuku] 厚く切ったもの [atsuku kitta mono] n chunk

集まる [atsumaru] v get together

集める [atsumeru] v collect, gather

圧力 [atsuryoku] n pressure; 圧力を加える [atsuryoku-o kuwaeru] v pressure

アットマー [attomaa] アットマークが見つかりません [atto-maaku ga mitsukarimasen] I can't find the at sign

会う [au] vi meet; 〜に会う [~ ni au] vt meet; どこでお会いしましょうか? [doko de o-ai shimashou ka?] Where shall we meet?; どこでお会いできますか? [doko de o-ai dekimasu ka?] Where can we meet?; あとでお会いしましょうか? [ato de o-ai shimashou ka?] Shall we meet afterwards?; お会いできてうれしいです [o-ai dekite ureshii desu] Pleased to meet you; お会いできて光栄でした [o-ai dekite kouei deshita] It was a

pleasure to meet you; ロビーでお会いしましょう [robii de o-ai shimashou] I'll meet you in the lobby

合う [au] v fit; 分け合う [wakeau] v share out; 合った [atta] adj matching

アウトドア [autodoa] adv outdoors

泡 [awa] n bubble; 泡風呂 [awaburo] n bubble bath

泡立つ [awadatsu] シュシュと泡立つ [shushu to awadatsu] adj carbonated

哀れみ [awaremi] n pity

哀れむ [awaremu] v pity

哀れな [aware na] adj pitiful

合わせる [awaseru] v combine; 焦点を合わせる [shouten-o awaseru] v focus

泡立て器 [awatateki] n whisk

誤る [ayamaru] v err; 判断を誤る [handan-o ayamaru] v misjudge

謝る [ayamaru] v apologize

アヤメ [ayame] n iris

怪しげな [ayashige na] adj dubious

怪しむ [ayashimu] v wonder

歩み [ayumi] n step

あざける [azakeru] v mock, scoff

アザミ [azami] n thistle

アザラシ [azarashi] n seal (animal)

鮮やかな [azayaka na] adj vivid

アゼルバイジャン [azerubaijan] n Azerbaijan; アゼルバイジャンの [azerubai-jan no] adj Azerbaijani

アゼルバイジャン人 [azerubaijanjin] n Azerbaijani (person)

預かり所 [azukarisho] 手荷物一時預かり所 [tenimotsu ichiji azukarisho] n luggage storage office

預ける [azukeru] 預けた手荷物 [azuketa tenimotsu] n luggage storage

B

場 [ba] *n* place; 火葬場 [kasouba] *n* crematorium

バー [baa] *n* (酒場) bar (alcohol); どこかに感じの良いバーはありますか? [doko-ka ni kanji no yoi baa wa arimasu ka?] Where is there a nice bar?; バーはどこですか? [baa wa doko desu ka?] Where is the bar?

バーベキュー [baabekyuu] *n* barbecue; バーベキュー場はどこですか? [baabekyuu-jou wa doko desu ka?] Where is the barbecue area?

バーチャルリアリティー [baacharuriariteii] *n* virtual reality

バードウォッチング [baadowotchingu] *n* birdwatching

バーガー [baagaa] *n* burger; ビーフバーガー [biifu baagaa] *n* beefburger

場合 [baai] *n* case, occasion

バージ [baaji] *n* barge

バーナー [baanaa] CDバーナー [shiidii baanaa] *n* CD burner; DVDバーナー [diibuidii baanaa] *n* DVD burner

バーレーン [baareen] *n* Bahrain

バーテンダー [baatendaa] *n* bartender; 女性バーテンダー [josei baatendaa] *n* bartender

バチカン [bachikan] *n* Vatican

バドミントン [badominton] *n* badminton; バドミントンのシャトル [badominton no shatoru] *n* birdie, shuttlecock

バグパイプ [bagupaipu] *n* bagpipes

バハマ [bahama] *n* Bahamas

売買 [baibai] *n* buying and selling; 売買契約 [baibai keiyaku] *n* bargain

バイバイ! [baibai] *excl* bye-bye!

売機 [bai ki] 券売機 [kenbaiki] *n* ticket machine

バイオリン [baiorin] *n* violin; バイオリン奏者 [baiorinsousha] *n* violinist

バイパス [baipasu] *n* bypass

バイリンガル [bairingaru] バイリンガルの [bairingaru no] *adj* bilingual

バイロウ® [bairou] *n* ballpoint pen

陪審 [baishin] *n* jury

賠償 [baishou] *n* reparation; 賠償金 [baishoukin] *n* compensation

売春 [baishun] *n* prostitution; 売春婦 [baishunfu] *n* prostitute

買収 [baishuu] *n* buyout; 企業買収 [kigyou baishuu] *n* takeover

バジル [bajiru] *n* basil

バッジ [bajji] *n* button

ばか [baka] *n* idiot, fool; ばかな [baka na] *adj* foolish, idiotic

ばかげる [bakageru] ばかげた [bakageta] *adj* absurd, ridiculous

ばか者 [bakamono] *n* fool

バケツ [baketsu] *n* bucket, pail

罰金 [bakkin] *n* fine; どこで罰金を払うのですか? [doko de bakkin o harau no desu ka?] Where do I pay the fine?; 罰金はいくらですか? [bakkin wa ikura desu ka?] How much is the fine?

バックアップ [bakkuappu] *n* backup

バックミラー [bakkumiraa] *n* rearview mirror

バックパッカー [bakkupakkaa] *n* backpacker

バックパッキング [bakkupakkingu] backpacking

バックパック [bakkupakku] *n* backpack

バックル [bakkuru] *n* buckle

バックスラッシュ [bakkusurasshu] *n*

backslash

爆弾 [bakudan] n bomb; 時限爆弾 [jigenbakudan] n timebomb; 原子爆弾 [genshibakudan] n atom bomb

爆撃 [bakugeki] n bombing; 爆撃する [bakugeki suru] v bomb

爆破 [bakuha] n blast, explosion; 爆破する [bakuha suru] v blow up

爆発 [bakuhatsu] n blast, explosion; 爆発する [bakuhatsu suru] v explode

爆発物 [bakuhatsubutsu] n explosive

バクテリア [bakuteria] n bacteria

場面 [bamen] n scene

番 [ban] 二十番目の [nijuu banme no] adj twentieth; 七番目 [shichi banme] n seventh; 七番目の [shichi banme no] adj seventh; 三番目 [san banme] n third; 三番目の [san banme no] adj third; 六番目の [roku banme no] adj sixth; 十二番目の [juuni banme no] adj twelfth; 十七番目の [juushichi banme no] adj seventeenth; 十三番目の [juusan banme no] adj thirteenth; 十番目 [juu banme] n tenth; 十番目の [juu banme no] adj tenth; 十六番目の [juuroku banme no] adj sixteenth; 千番目 [sen banme] n thousandth; 千番目の [sen banme no] adj thousandth; 誰の番ですか? [dare no ban desu ka?] Whose turn is it?

晩 [ban] n evening; 晩に [ban ni] in the evening; 晩にできることは何がありますか? [ban ni dekiru koto wa nani ga arimasu ka?] What is there to do in the evenings?

バン [ban] n (自動車) van, (食べ物) bun

バナナ [banana] n banana

バンド [bando] n (音楽グループ) band (musical group); ブラスバンド [burasubando] n brass band; 腕時計のバンド [udedokei no bando] n watchband

バンドエイド [bandoeido] n Band-Aid®

ばね [bane] n spring (coil)

バンガロー [bangaroo] n bungalow

番号 [bangou] 携帯電話番号 [keitai denwa bangou] n cell phone number; 番号案内サービス [bangou annai saabisu] n directory assistance; 電話番号 [denwabangou] n phone number; 口座番号 [kouzabangou] n account number; あなたの携帯電話番号は何番ですか? [anata no keitai-denwa-bangou wa nan-ban desu ka?] What's your cell number?; 番号間違いです [bangou machigai desu] You have a wrong number; 私の携帯電話番号は・・・です [watashi no keitai-denwa-bangou wa... desu] My cellular number is...; 電話番号は何番ですか? [denwa-bangou wa nan-ban desu ka?] What's the telephone number?

番組 [bangumi] n program; リアリティーテレビ番組 [riaritii terebi bangumi] n reality TV

バングラデシュ [banguradeshu] n Bangladesh; バングラデシュの [Banguradeshu no] adj Bangladeshi

バングラデシュ人 [banguradeshujin] n Bangladeshi (person)

バニオン [banion] n bunion

バニラ [banira] n vanilla

バンジージャンプ [banjiijanpu] n bungee jumping

バンジョー [banjoo] n banjo

番人 [bannin] n watchman; 番人のいない [bannin no inai] adj unattended

バンパー [banpaa] n bumper

ばんそうこう [bansoukou] n (medical) plaster

万歳! [banzai] excl hooray!

バプテスト [baputesuto] n Baptist

バラ [bara] n (植物) rose

ばらばら [barabara] in pieces; ばらばらにする [barabara ni suru] v break up

バランス [baransu] n balance; バランスのとれた [baransu no toreta] adj balanced

バレエ [baree] n ballet; バレエシューズ [baree shuuzu] n ballet shoes; バレエダンサー [bareedansaa] n ballet dancer; どこでそのバレエのチケットを買えますか? [doko de sono baree no chiketto o kaemasu ka?] Where can I buy tickets for the ballet?

バレーボール [bareebooru] *n* volleyball

バレリーナ [bareriina] *n* ballerina

バルバドス [barubadosu] *n* Barbados

バルカン [barukan] バルカン諸国の [Barukan shokoku no] *adj* Balkan

バルコニー [barukonii] *n* balcony; バルコニー付きの部屋はありますか? [barukonii-tsuki no heya wa arimasu ka?] Do you have a room with a balcony?

場所 [basho] *n* location, place; 住む場所 [sumu basho] *n* accommodations; 屋外市を催す場所 [okugai ichi-o moyousu basho] *n* fairground; 待避場所 [taihi basho] *n* rest area; 今いる場所は···です [ima iru basho wa... desu] My location is....

バス [basu] *n* (乗り物) bus, (声楽) bass; バスの切符 [basu no kippu] *n* bus ticket; バスターミナル [basutaaminaru] *n* bus station; バス停 [basutei] *n* bus stop; 空港バス [kuukou basu] *n* airport bus; 長距離バス [choukyori basu] *n* bus (vehicle); すみません、···へ行くバスはどれですか? [sumimasen,... e iku basu wa dore desu ka?] Excuse me, which bus goes to...?; バスは二十分おきに出ています [basu wa nijup-pun oki ni dete imasu] The bus runs every twenty minutes; バスは何時に着きますか? [basu wa nan-ji ni tsukimasu ka?] What time does the bus arrive?; バスは何時に出ますか? [basu wa nan-ji ni demasu ka?] What time does the bus leave?; 最終のバスは何時ですか? [saishuu no basu wa nan-ji desu ka?] What time is the last bus?; ···へ行くバスはどのくらい出ていますか? [... e iku basu wa dono kurai dete imasu ka?] How often are the buses to...?; ···へ行く次のバスは何時ですか? [... e iku tsugi no basu wa nan-ji desu ka?] When is the next bus to...?; ···へ行く始発のバスは何時ですか? [... e iku shihatsu no basu wa nan-ji desu ka?] When is the first bus to...?; 長距離バスは朝何時に出ますか? [choukyori-basu wa asa nan-ji ni demasu ka?] When does the bus leave in

the morning?; 長距離バスが私を乗せずに出発してしまいました [choukyori-basu ga watashi o nosezu ni shuppatsu shite shimaimashita] The bus has left without me

バスドラム [basudoramu] *n* bass drum

バスケットボール [basukettobooru] *n* basketball

バスク地方 [basuku chihou] バスク地方の [Basuku chihou no] *adj* Basque

バスク語 [basuku go] *n* Basque (language)

バスク人 [basukujin] *n* Basque (person)

バスローブ [basuroobu] *n* bathrobe

バスルーム [basuruumu] *n* bathroom; その部屋に専用のバスルームはありますか? [sono heya ni senyou no basu-ruumu wa arimasu ka?] Does the room have a private bathroom?; バスルームに介助の手すりはありますか? [basu-ruumu ni kaijo no tesuri wa arimasu ka?] Are there support railings in the bathroom?; バスルームが水浸しになっています [basu-ruumu ga mizu-bitashi ni natte imasu] The bathroom is flooded

バスターミナル [basutaaminaru] バスターミナルはどこですか? [basu-taaminaru wa doko desu ka?] Where is the bus station?; バスターミナルまでどのくらいありますか? [basu-taaminaru made dono kurai arimasu ka?] How far are we from the bus station?

バス停 [basutei] 一番近いバス停はどこですか? [ichiban chikai basu-tei wa doko desu ka?] Where is the nearest bus stop?; バス停までどのくらいの距離ですか? [basu-tei made dono kurai no kyori desu ka?] How far away is the bus stop?

バスト [basuto] *n* bust

バター [bataa] *n* butter

罰 [batsu] *n* punishment; 罰する [bassuru] *v* penalize, punish

ばったり [battari] *adv* accidentally; ばったり出会う [battari deau] *v* bump into

バッテリー [batterii] *n* battery; バッテリーはありますか? [batterii wa arimasu ka?] Do you

have any batteries?; バッテリーが上がってし
まいました [batterii ga agatte shimaimashita].
The battery is dead; 私は新しいバッテリー
が必要です [watashi wa atarashii batterii ga
hitsuyou desu] I need a new battery

バット [batto] n bat (with ball)

ベビー [bebii] n baby; ベビーミルク [bebii
miruku] n formula

ベビーカー [bebiikaa] n stroller

ベビーシート [bebiishiito] n baby-seat

ベビーシッター [bebiishittaa] n babysitter; ベ
ビーシッターをする [bebiishittaa wo suru] v
babysit

ベッド [beddo] n bed; 二段ベッド [nidanbed-
do] n bunk beds; キングサイズのベッド
[kingu saizu no beddo] n king-size bed; キャ
ンプベッド [kyanpubeddo] n cot; ベッドサイド
ランプ [beddosaido ranpu] n bedside lamp;
ベッドカバー [beddokabaa] n bedspread; 持
ち運び用ベッド [mochihakobi you beddo] n
baby carrier; 日光浴用ベッド [nikkouyoku
you beddo] n sunbed; 小児用ベッド [shouni
you beddo] n crib; ベッドの寝心地がよくあり
ません [beddo no ne-gokochi ga yoku
arimasen] The bed is uncomfortable

ベッド＆ブレックファースト [beddo
burekkufaasuto] n bed and breakfast, B&B

ベッドリネン [beddorinen] n bed linen

ベッドサイド [beddosaido] n bedside; ベッド
サイドテーブル [beddosaido teeburu] n
nightstand

ベージュ [beeju] adj beige; ベージュの [beeju
no] adj beige

ベーキング [beekingu] n baking; ベーキング
パウダー [beekingupaudaa] n baking
powder

ベーコン [beekon] n bacon

ベークドポテト [beekudopoteto] n baked
potato

ベール [beeru] n veil

米国 [beikoku] n United States, US, USA

ベジタリアン [bejitarian] n vegetarian; ベジタ
リアンの [bejitarian no] adj vegetarian; ここ

にベジタリアン用のレストランはありますか?
[koko ni bejitarian-you no resutoran wa
arimasu ka?] Are there any vegetarian
restaurants here?; これはベジタリアン向きで
すか? [kore wa bejitarian muki desu ka?] Is
this suitable for vegetarians?; ベジタリアン
料理はありますか? [bejitarian-ryouri wa
arimasu ka?] Do you have any vegetarian
dishes?; 私はベジタリアンです [watashi wa
bejitarian desu] I'm a vegetarian

別館 [bekkan] n pavilion

別個 [bekko] 別個に [bekko ni] adv apart

ベンチ [benchi] n bench

ベネチアンブラインド [benechianburaindo] n
Venetian blind

ベネズエラ [benezuera] n Venezuela; ベネズ
エラ人 [Benezuera jin] n Venezuelan
(person); ベネズエラの [Benezuera no] adj
Venezuelan

弁護 [bengo] n (verbal) defense; 弁護士 [ben-
goshi] n attorney

弁護士 [bengoshi] n lawyer; 事務弁護士
[jimubengoshi] n lawyer

ベニバナインゲン [benibanaingen] n scarlet
runner bean

ベニヤ板 [beniyaita] n plywood

弁解 [benkai] n excuse; 弁解する [benkai
suru] v excuse

便器 [benki] n toilet; 幼児用の便器 [youjiyou
no benki] n potty

勉強 [benkyou] 勉強する [benkyou suru] v
study

便秘 [benpi] n constipation; 便秘した [benpi
shita] adj constipated

便利 [benri] 便利な [benri na] adj convenient

弁済 [bensai] 弁済する [bensai suru] v
reimburse

弁当 [bentou] n box lunch

ベラルーシ [beraruushi] n Belarus; ベラルー
シの [Beraruushi no] adj Belarussian

ベラルーシ語 [beraruushi go] n Belarussian
(language)

ベラルーシ人 [beraruushijin] n Belarussian

(person)

ベリー [berii] n berry

ベルギー [berugii] n Belgium; ベルギーの [berugii no] adj Belgian

ベルギー人 [berugiijin] n Belgian *(person)*

ベルクロ® [berukuro] n Velcro®

ベルト [beruto] n belt; 救命ベルト [kyuumei beruto] n life preserver; 安全ベルト [anzenberuto] n safety belt

別荘 [bessou] n summer home

ベストセラー [besutoseraa] n best seller

べたぼめ [betabome] n rave

べとべと [betobeto] べとべとした [betobeto shita] adj sticky

ベトナム [betonamu] n Vietnam; ベトナムの [betonamu no] adj Vietnamese; ベトナム語 [betonamugo] n Vietnamese *(language)*; ベトナム人 [betonamujin] n Vietnamese *(person)*

別 [betsu] 男女の別 [danjo no betsu] n sexuality; ・・・は別として [... wa betsu to shite] prep apart from; 別々に [betsubetsu ni] adv separately; これの別の色はありますか? [kore no betsu no iro wa arimasu ka?] Do you have this in another color?; 別のものが欲しいのですが [betsu no mono ga hoshii no desu ga] I'd like something different

別名 [betsumei] n alias; ・・・の別名で知られる [... no betsumei de shirareru] prep alias

別な [betsu na] adj another; 別なふうに [betsu na fuuni] adv otherwise

美貌 [bibou] 美貌の [bibou no] adj good-looking

ビデオ [bideo] n video

ビデオゲーム [bideogeemu] n video game; ビデオゲームができますか? [bideo-geemu ga dekimasu ka?] Can I play video games?

ビデオカメラ [bideokamera] n video camera; このビデオカメラ用のテープをいただけますか? [kono bideo-kamera-you no teepu o itadakemasu ka?] Can I have a tape for this video camera, please?

美顔術 [biganjutsu] n facial

ビーバー [biibaa] n beaver

ビーチ [biichi] n beach; ビーチサンダル [biichi sandaru] n flip-flops; この近くにいいビーチはありますか? [kono chikaku ni ii biichi wa arimasu ka?] Are there any good beaches near here?; この近くに静かなビーチはありますか? [kono chikaku ni shizuka na biichi wa arimasu ka?] Is there a quiet beach near here?; ビーチまでどのくらいの距離ですか? [biichi made dono kurai no kyori desu ka?] How far away is the beach?; ビーチまでどのくらいありますか? [biichi made dono kurai arimasu ka?] How far are we from the beach?; ビーチへ行くバスはありますか? [biichi e iku basu wa arimasu ka?] Is there a bus to the beach?; 私はビーチに行きます [watashi wa biichi ni ikimasu] I'm going to the beach

ビーフ [biifu] n beef; ビーフバーガー [biifu baagaa] n beefburger

ビーガン [biigan] n vegan; これはビーガン向きですか? [kore wa biigan muki desu ka?] Is this suitable for vegans?; ビーガン料理はありますか? [biigan-ryouri wa arimasu ka?] Do you have any vegan dishes?

ビール [biiru] n beer; ビールをもう一杯 [biiru o mou ippai] another beer

ビートルート [biitoruuto] n beet

ビーズ [biizu] n bead

ビジネス [bijinesu] n business; ビジネスクラス [bijinesu kurasu] n business class

ビジネスマン [bijinesuman] n businessman; 私はビジネスマンです [watashi wa bijinesu-man desu] I'm a businessman

ビジネスウーマン [bijinesuuuman] n businesswoman

ビジターセンター [bijitaasentaa] n visitor center

美術 [bijutsu] n art; 美術館 [bijutsukan] n art gallery; 美術品 [bijutsuhin] n work of art; 美術学校 [bijutsugakkou] n art school

ビキニ [bikini] n bikini

びっこ [bikko] びっこの [bikko no] *adj* lame

びっこをひく [bikko wo hiku] *v* limp

びっくり [bikkuri] びっくりさせる [bikkuri saseru] *v* surprise

微妙 [bimyou] 微妙な [bimyou na] *adj* subtle

便 [bin] *n* flight; チャーター便 [chaataa bin] *n* charter flight; 航空便 [koukuubin] *n* airmail; 定期便 [teikibin] *n* scheduled flight

瓶 [bin] *n* jar; ジャムの瓶 [jamu no bin] *n* jam jar; 哺乳瓶 [honyuubin] *n* baby bottle

ビンディング [bindeingu] *npl* bindings

ビネグレットドレッシング [binegurettodoresshingu] *n* vinaigrette

ビンゴ [bingo] *n* bingo

ビニール [biniiru] *n* vinyl; ビニール袋 [biniiru bukuro] *n* plastic bag

便箋 [binsen] *n* writing paper

ビオラ [biora] *n* viola

ビリヤード [biriyaado] *n* billiards

ビロード [biroodo] *n* velvet

ビルマ [biruma] *n* Burma; ビルマの [biruma no] *adj* Burmese

ビルマ語 [biruma go] *n* Burmese *(language)*

ビルマ人 [birumajin] *n* Burmese *(person)*

びしょぬれ [bishonure] びしょぬれにする [bishonure ni suru] *v* drench

微小 [bishou] 微小な [bishou na] *adj* minute

ビスケット [bisuketto] *n* cookie

ビタミン [bitamin] *n* vitamin

美容 [biyou] 美容外科 [biyou geka] *n* plastic surgery

美容院 [biyouin] *n* beauty parlor, hairdresser's

美容師 [biyoushi] *n* hairdresser

ビザ [biza] *n* visa; 私のビザです [watashi no biza desu] Here is my visa; 入国ビザを持っています [nyuukoku-biza o motte imasu] I have an entry visa

墓地 [bochi] *n* cemetery, graveyard

ボディービル [bodiibiru] *n* bodybuilding

ボディーガード [bodiigaado] *n* bodyguard

母音 [boin] *n* vowel

ボイラー [boiraa] *n* boiler

ボイスメール [boisumeeru] *n* voicemail

ボックス [bokkusu] *n* box; アイスボックス [aisu bokkusu] *n* icebox; グローブボックス [guroobubokkusu] *n* glove compartment; 空き瓶回収ボックス [akian kaishuu bokkusu] *n* glass recycling container; 電話ボックス [denwa bokkusu] *n* phone booth

母国 [bokoku] 母国語 [bokokugo] *n* native language

母国語 [bokokugo] 母国語とする人 [bokokugo to suru hito] *n* native speaker

ボクサー [bokusaa] *n* boxer; ボクサーショーツ [bokusaa shootsu] *n* boxer shorts

牧師 [bokushi] 教区牧師 [kyouku bokushi] *n* pastor

ボクシング [bokushingu] *n* boxing

牧草地 [bokusouchi] *n* meadow

牧羊 [bokuyou] 牧羊犬 [bokuyouken] *n* sheepdog

盆 [bon] *n (台所用品)* tray

ボンネット [bonnetto] *n* hood *(car)*

ぼんやり [bonyari] ぼんやりした [bonyari shita] *adj* absent minded

ボーイフレンド [booifurendo] *n* boyfriend; 私にはボーイフレンドがいます [watashi ni wa booifurendo ga imasu] I have a boyfriend

ボーナス [boonasu] *n* bonus

ボール [booru] *n* ball *(toy)*

ボール箱 [boorubako] *n* carton

ボール紙 [boorugami] *n* cardboard

ボールペン [boorupen] *n* ballpoint pen

ボート [booto] *n* boat; ボートを漕ぐこと [booto-o kogu koto] *n* rowing; 救命ボート [kyuumeibooto] *n* lifeboat

勃発 [boppatsu] *n* outbreak

ボリビア [boribia] *n* Bolivia; ボリビアの [Boribia no] *adj* Bolivian

ボリビア人 [boribiajin] *n* Bolivian *(person)*

ぼろきれ [borokire] *n* rag

ボルト [boruto] *n (電圧)* volt

ボリューム [boryuumu] *n* volume; ボリュームを上げてもいいですか? [boryuumu o agete mo ii desu ka?] May I turn up the volume?; ボリュームを下げてもらえますか? [boryuumu o sagete moraemasu ka?] Could you lower the volume, please?

母性 [bosei] 母性の [bosei no] adj maternal

没収 [bosshuu] 没収する [bosshuu suru] v confiscate

ボス [bosu] n boss

ボスニア [bosunia] n Bosnia; ボスニアの [Bosunia no] adj Bosnian

ボスニア・ヘルツェゴビナ [bosunia herutsuegobina] n Bosnia and Herzegovina

ボスニア人 [bosuniajin] n Bosnian (person)

ボタン [botan] n (服) button; どのボタンを押すのですか? [dono botan o osu no desu ka?] Which button do I press?

ボトル [botoru] n bottle; ボトルをもう1本持ってきてください [botoru o mou ippon motte kite kudasai] Please bring another bottle; ミネラルウォーターのボトル1本 [mineraru-uootaa no botoru 1 hon] a bottle of mineral water; 赤ワインのボトルを1本 [aka-wain no botoru o ippon] a bottle of red wine

ボツワナ [botsuwana] n Botswana

棒 [bou] n bar (strip), pole, rod, staff (stick or rod); 棒切れ [bou kire] n stick; 編み棒 [amibou] n knitting needle

膨張 [bouchou] 膨張性の [bouchou sei no] adj inflatable

暴動 [boudou] n riot; 暴動を起こす [boudou-o okosu] v riot

望遠 [bouen] 望遠鏡 [bouenkyou] n telescope

防護 [bougo] n security

防御 [bougyo] n defense; 防御する [bougyo suru] v defend; 防御者 [bougyosha] n defender

防火壁 [boukaheki] n firewall

傍観 [boukan] 傍観者 [boukansha] n bystander

冒険 [bouken] n adventure; 冒険好きな [bouken zuki na] adj adventurous

膀胱 [boukou] n bladder; 膀胱炎 [boukouen] n cystitis

亡命 [boumei] n asylum; 亡命者 [boumeisha] n asylum seeker

暴利 [bouri] n rip-off

ボウリング [bouringu] n bowling; ボウリング場 [bouringu jou] n bowling alley

ボウル [bouru] n bowl

暴力 [bouryoku] n violence; 暴力的な [bouryokuteki na] adj violent

帽子 [boushi] n hat; ベレー帽 [bereebou] n beret; 縁なし帽子 [fuchinashi boushi] n cap; 野球帽 [yakyuubou] n baseball cap

防水 [bousui] 防水の [bousui no] adj waterproof

防水布 [bousuifu] タール塗り防水布 [taaru nuri bousuifu] n tarpaulin

棒高跳び [bou taka tobi] n pole vault

部分 [bubun] n part, portion, section; 部分的な [bubunteki na] adj partial; 部分的に [bubunteki ni] adv partly

仏陀 [budda] n Buddha

ブドウ [budou] n grape; ブドウ園 [budouen] n vineyard

ブイ [bui] n buoy

侮辱 [bujoku] n insult; 侮辱する [bujoku suru] v insult

武器 [buki] n weapon

不器用 [bukiyou] 不器用な [bukiyou na] adj clumsy

仏教 [bukkyou] n Buddhism; 仏教の [Bukkyou no] adj Buddhist; 仏教徒 [Bukkyouto] n Buddhist

部門 [bumon] n category, department, sector

文 [bun] n (言葉) sentence (words); 引用文 [in-youbun] n quotation

ブナ [buna] n beech (tree)

無難な [bunan na] adj acceptable

分別 [bunbetsu] n discretion; 分別のない [funbetsu no nai] adj unwise; 分別のある [bunbetsu no aru] adj sensible

文房具 [bunbougu] n stationery; 文房具店

[bunbouguten] n office supply store

ブンブン [bunbun] n humming; ブンブンいう [bunbun iu] v hum

文学 [bungaku] n literature; 文学士 [bungakushi] n Bachelor of Arts *(person)*

文化 [bunka] n culture; 文化の [bunka no] *adj* cultural

分解 [bunkai] n dissolution; 生物分解性の [seibutsu bunkaisei no] *adj* biodegradable; 分解する [bunkai suru] v take apart

分割 [bunkatsu] n division; 分割払い [bunkatsu harai] n installment

文明 [bunmei] n civilization

分派 [bunpa] n sect

文法 [bunpou] n grammar; 文法の [bunpou no] *adj* grammatical

分裂 [bunretsu] n division; 分裂する [bunretsu suru] v split up

分離 [bunri] n separation

分離帯付き [bunritaitsuki] 中央分離帯付き道路 [chuuou bunritai tsuki douro] n divided highway

分類 [bunrui] n class; 分類広告 [bunruikoukoku] n classified ads

分量 [bunryou] どのくらいの分量を飲ませればよいのですか? [donokuraino bunryou wo noma serebayoinodesuka?] How much should I give?

分析 [bunseki] n analysis; 分析する [bunseki suru] v analyze

分子 [bunshi] n molecule

文書 [bunsho] n document

文書館 [bunshokan] n archive

文通 [buntsuu] n correspondence; 文通者 [buntsuusha] n correspondent

ぶらぶら [burabura] *adv* idly; ぶらぶら歩き [burabura aruki] n stroll

ブラインド [buraindo] n blind

ブラジャー [burajaa] n bra

ブラジル [burajiru] n Brazil; ブラジルの [burajiru no] *adj* Brazilian

ブラジル人 [burajirujin] n Brazilian *(person)*

ブラックベリー [burakkuberii] n blackberry

ブラックベリー® [burakkuberii] n BlackBerry®

ブラックチョコレート [burakku chokoreeto] n dark chocolate

ブランデー [burandee] n brandy; ブランデーをください [burandee o kudasai] I'll have a brandy

ブランド [burando] n brand; ブランド名 [burando mei] n brand name

ブラシ [burashi] n brush; ブラシをかける [burashi wo kakeru] v brush; 歯ブラシ [haburashi] n toothbrush

ブラス [burasu] n brass; ブラスバンド [burasubando] n brass band

ブラウス [burausu] n blouse

ブラウザ [burauza] n browser

ブレーキ [bureeki] n brake; ブレーキをかける [bureeki-o kakeru] v brake; ブレーキランプ [bureeki ranpu] n brake light; ブレーキがきません [bureeki ga kikimasen] The brakes aren't working, The brakes don't work

ブレンダー [burendaa] n blender

ブレサライザー® [buresaraizaa] n Breathalyzer®

ブレスレット [buresuretto] n bracelet

ブレザー [burezaa] n blazer

ブリーフィング [buriifingu] n briefing

ブリーフ [buriifu] n briefs

ブリーフケース [buriifukeesu] n briefcase

ブリザード [burizaado] n blizzard

ブログ [burogu] n blog; ブログを書く [burogu-o kaku] v blog

ブロッコリー [burokkorii] n broccoli

ブロック [burokku] n block *(buildings)*

ブロンド [burondo] ブロンドの [burondo no] *adj* blonde; 私は生まれつきブロンドです [watashi wa umaretsuki burondo desu] My hair is naturally blonde

ブロンズ [buronzu] n bronze

ブローチ [buroochi] n brooch

ブロードバンド [buroodobando] n broadband

ブロードライ [buroodorai] n blow-dry

ブローカー [burookaa] *n* broker

ブルドーザー [burudoozaa] *n* bulldozer

ブルガリア [burugaria] *n* Bulgaria; ブルガリアの [burugaria no] *adj* Bulgarian

ブルガリア語 [burugaria go] *n* Bulgarian *(language)*

ブルガリア人 [burugariajin] *n* Bulgarian *(person)*

ブルーベリー [buruuberii] *n* blueberry

ブルース [buruusu] *n* blues

武装 [busou] 武装した [busou shita] *adj* armed

物質 [busshitsu] *n* matter, substance; 抗生物質 [kousei busshitsu] *n* antibiotic

豚 [buta] *n* pig

豚肉 [butaniku] *n* pork; 私は豚肉を食べません [watashi wa butaniku o tabemasen] I don't eat pork

舞踏 [butou] 舞踏会 [butoukai] *n* ball *(dance)*

物理学 [butsurigaku] *n* physics

物理学者 [butsurigakusha] *n* physicist

物体 [buttai] 未確認飛行物体 [mikakunin hikoubuttai] *n* UFO

ブーケ [buuke] *n* bouquet

ブースターケーブル [buusutaakeeburu] *npl* jumper cables

ブースターコード [buusutaakoodo] *npl* jumper cables

ブーツ [buutsu] *n* boot

部族 [buzoku] *n* tribe

病 [byou] アルツハイマー病 [arutsuhaimaa byou] *n* Alzheimer's disease; 私は心臓病があります [watashi wa shinzou-byou ga arimasu] I have a heart condition

鋲 [byou] *n* stud

平等 [byoudou] *n* equality

病学 [byougaku] 老人病学の [roujinbyougaku no] *adj* geriatric

病院 [byouin] *n* hospital; 産科病院 [sanka byouin] *n* maternity hospital; 精神病院 [seishinbyouin] *n* mental hospital; その病院へはどう行けばいいのですか? [sono byouin e wa dou ikeba ii no desu ka?] How do I get to the hospital?; 病院はどこですか? [byouin wa doko desu ka?] Where is the hospital?; 私は病院で働いています [watashi wa byouin de hataraite imasu] I work in a hospital; 私たちは彼を病院に連れて行かなければなりません [watashi-tachi wa kare o byouin ni tsurete ikanakereba narimasen] We have to get him to a hospital; 彼は病院に行かなければなりませんか? [kare wa byouin ni ikanakereba narimasen ka?] Will he have to go to the hospital?; 彼女は病院に行かなければなりませんか? [kanojo wa byouin ni ikanakereba narimasen ka?] Will she have to go to the hospital?

病欠 [byouketsu] 病欠届け [byouketsu todoke] *n* sick note

病気 [byouki] *n* disease, illness, sickness; 病気休暇 [byoukikyuuka] *n* sick leave; 病気の [byouki no] *adj* ill

病人 [byounin] *n* invalid *(ill person)*

病棟 [byoutou] *n* ward *(hospital room)*; ···はどの病棟に入院していますか? [... wa dono byoutou ni nyuuin shite imasu ka?] Which ward is... in?

病棟 [byoutou] 救急病棟 [kyuukyuubyou-tou] *n* emergency room

ビュッフェ [byuffe] *n* snack bar; ビュッフェ車 [byuffesha] *n* dining car

C

チャージ [chaaji] n charge; カバーチャージ [kabaa chaaji] n cover charge

チャーター [chaataa] n charter; チャーター便 [chaataa bin] n charter flight

チャド [chado] n Chad

チャイブ [chaibu] n chives

茶色 [chairo] n brown; 茶色の [chairo no] adj brown

チャイルドマインダー [chairudomaindaa] n nanny

チャイルドシート [chairudoshiito] 2歳の子供用のチャイルドシートが欲しいのですが [ni-sai no kodomo-you no chairudo-shiito ga hoshii no desu ga] I'd like a child seat for a two-year-old child; チャイルドシートはありますか? [chairudo-shiito wa arimasu ka?] Do you have a child's seat?

着地 [chakuchi] n touchdown

着古す [chaku furusu] 着古した [kifurushita] adj worn

着陸 [chakuriku] 着陸する [chakuriku suru] v land; 緊急着陸 [kinkyuu chakuriku] n emergency landing

着席 [chakuseki] 着席する [chakuseki suru] v sit down

着信 [chakushin] 着信メロディ [chakushin merodi] n ringtone

着色 [chakushoku] n coloring

チャンネル [channeru] n channel

チャリティー [charitii] チャリティーショップ [charitii shoppu] n charity store

チャット [chatto] チャットルーム [chatto ruumu] n chatroom

チェア [chea] n chair; デッキチェア [dekkichea] n deck chair

チェアリフト [chearifuto] n chairlift; 最後のチェアリフトはいつ出ますか? [saigo no chea-rifuto wa itsu demasu ka?] When does the last chairlift go?; 最初のチェアリフトはいつ出ますか? [saisho no chea-rifuto wa itsu demasu ka?] When does the first chairlift go?

チェチェン [chechien] チェチェン共和国 [Chechen kyouwakoku] n Chechnya

チェッカー [chekkaa] n checkers

チェック [chekku] n check; チェックの [chekku no] adj checked; チェックする [chekku suru] v check off

チェックアウト [chekkuauto] n checkout; チェックアウトする [chekkuauto suru] v check out

チェックイン [chekkuin] n check-in; チェックインする [chekkuin suru] v check in

チェコ [cheko] チェコの [cheko no] adj Czech; チェコ共和国 [Cheko kyouwakoku] n Czech Republic

チェコ語 [cheko go] n Czech (language)

チェコ人 [chekojin] n Czech (person)

チェロ [chero] n cello

チェス [chesu] n chess

血 [chi] n blood; 血を見るスポーツ [chi-o miru supootsu] n blood sports; 血圧 [ketsuatsu] n blood pressure

地 [chi] 沼地 [numachi] n swamp

治安 [chian] n public order; 治安判事 [chian hanji] n magistrate

チベット [chibetto] n Tibet; チベットの [Chibetto no] adj Tibetan; チベット語 [Chibetto go] n Tibetan (language); チベット人 [Chibetto jin] n Tibetan (person)

乳房 [chibusa] *n* breast

乳 [chichi] *n* mother's milk; 乳を搾る [chichi-o shiboru] *v* milk; 脱脂乳 [dasshinyuu] *n* skim milk; 半脱脂乳 [han dasshi nyuu] *n* reduced-fat milk

父 [chichi] *n* father; 継父 [mama chichi] *n* stepfather

地中海 [chichuukai] *n* Mediterranean; 地中海の [chichuukai no] *adj* Mediterranean

チフス [chifusu] 腸チフス [chouchifusu] *n* typhoid

違い [chigai] *n* difference

違う [chigau] *adj* different

地平 [chihei] 地平線 [chiheisen] *n* horizon

地方 [chihou] *n* locality; 地方議会議員 [chihou gikai giin] *n* council member

地位 [chii] *n* job (*rank*)

地域 [chiiki] *n* area, region, territory; 地域の [chiiki no] *adj* regional; 地域社会 [chiiki shakai] *n* community; この地域ではどんなところを見物できますか? [kono chiiki de wa donna tokoro o kenbutsu dekimasu ka?] What can we visit in the area?

チーム [chiimu] *n* team

小い [chiisai] *adj* small; 小さくする [chiisaku suru] *v* turn down (*volume*)

小さな [chiisa na] *adj* tiny; 小さな袋 [chiisana fukuro] *n* sachet; 小さな包み [chiisana tsutsumi] *n* packet

小さい [chiisai] *adj* little, small; 小さい方の [chiisai hou no] *adj* minor; それは小さすぎます [sore wa chiisa-sugimasu] It's too small

チーズ [chiizu] *n* cheese; どんなチーズですか? [donna cheezu desu ka?] What kind of cheese?

縮む [chijimu] *v* shrink; 縮んだ [chijinda] *adj* shrunken

地下 [chika] 地下に [chika ni] *adv* underground; 地下運動 [chika undou] *n* underground movement

地下道 [chikadou] *n* underpass

近づきやすい [chikadukiyasui] *adj* accessible

近づく [chikaduku] *v* approach

誓い [chikai] *n* oath

近い [chikai] *adj* close, near

地階 [chikai] *n* basement

近く [chikaku] すぐ近くの [sugu chikaku no] *adj* close by; 近くに [chikaku ni] *adv* close, near, nearby; 近くの [chikaku no] *adj* nearby; すぐ近くです [sugu chikaku desu] It's very near; 近くに銀行はありますか? [chikaku ni ginkou wa arimasu ka?] Is there a bank nearby?

近道 [chikamichi] *n* shortcut

力 [chikara] *n* strength; 意志の力 [ishi no chikara] *n* willpower; 説得力のある [settokuryoku no aru] *adj* convincing

地下牢 [chikarou] *n* dungeon

地下室 [chikashitsu] *n* cellar

地下鉄 [chikatetsu] *n* subway; 地下鉄駅 [chikatetsu eki] *n* subway station; 一番近い地下鉄の駅はどこですか? [ichiban chikai chikatetsu no eki wa doko desu ka?] Where is the nearest subway station?; 一番近い地下鉄の駅へはどう行けばいいのですか? [ichiban chikai chikatetsu no eki e wa dou ikeba ii no desu ka?] How do I get to the nearest subway station?; 地下鉄のマップはありますか? [chikatetsu no mappu wa arimasu ka?] Do you have a map of the subway?; 地下鉄のマップをいただけますか? [chikatetsu no mappu o itadakemasu ka?] Could I have a map of the subway, please?

チケット [chiketto] *n* ticket; 今晩のチケットを2枚お願いします [konban no chiketto o nimai o-negai shimasu] Two tickets for tonight, please; どこでそのコンサートのチケットを買えますか? [doko de sono konsaato no chiketto o kaemasu ka?] Where can I buy tickets for the concert?; ここでそのチケットを買えますか? [koko de sono chiketto o kaemasu ka?] Can I buy the tickets here?; 私はチケットをなくしました [watashi wa chiketto o

nakushimashita] I've lost my ticket; 私たち
のためにそのチケットを予約してもらえますか?
[watashi-tachi no tame ni sono chiketto o
yoyaku shite moraemasu ka?] Could you
reserve the tickets for us?; 駐車チケットを
買わなければなりませんか? [chuusha-chiket-
to o kawanakereba narimasen ka?] Do I
need to buy a ticket to park?; 子供のチケッ
ト [kodomo no chiketto] a child's ticket

地区 [chiku] n district; 指定地区 [shitei chiku]
n pedestrian area

畜牛 [chikugyuu] n cattle

地球 [chikyuu] n earth; 地球の [chikyuu no]
adj global

地球儀 [chikyuugi] n globe

地球温暖化 [chikyuuondanka] n global
warming

血まみれ [chimamire] 血まみれの [chi mamire
no] adj bloody

致命 [chimei] n place name; 致命的な
[chimeiteki na] adj fatal

賃借り [chingari] n hire (rental); 賃借りする
[chingari suru] v hire (people)

賃金 [chingin] n wage

知能 [chinou] n intelligence; 知能指数
[chinoushisuu, IQ aikyuu] n IQ

チンパンジー [chinpanjii] n chimpanzee

チンピラ [chinpira] n punk

鎮静 [chinsei] 鎮静剤 [chinseizai] n sedative

賃借 [chinshaku] 賃借人 [chinshakunin] n
tenant

賃貸 [chintai] 賃貸する [chintai suru] v rent;
賃貸料 [chintairyou] n rent

賃貸借 [chintaishaku] 賃貸借する [chin-
taishaku suru] v lease; 賃貸借契約
[chintaishaku keiyaku] n lease

チップ [chippu] n (電子) chip (electronic), (心
づけ) tip (reward); チップをやる [chippu-o
yaru] (心づけ) v tip (reward); チップはいくら
渡せばよいですか? [chippu wa ikura
wataseba yoi desu ka?] How much should
I give as a tip?; チップを渡すのは一般的なこ
とですか? [chippu o watasu no wa

ippan-teki na koto desu ka?] Is it usual to
give a tip?

チップス [chippusu] npl chips; ポテトチップス
[potetochippusu] n potato chips

散らかす [chirakasu] v mess up; 散らかしたも
の [chirakashita mono] n clutter

散らかった [chira katta] v messy

ちらし [chirashi] n (印刷物) brochure

チリ [chiri] n Chile; チリの [chiri no] adj
Chilean

地理学 [chirigaku] n geography

チリ人 [chirijin] n Chilean (person)

ちり取り [chiritori] n dustpan

治療 [chiryou] n cure, remedy, treatment

治療医 [chiryoui] 足治療医 [ashichiryoui] n
podiatrist

治療室 [chiryoushitsu] 集中治療室
[shuuchuuchiryoushitsu, ICU aishiiyuu] n
intensive care unit

知識 [chishiki] n information, knowledge; 一
般知識 [ippan chishiki] n general
knowledge; 知識を与える [chishiki-o ataeru]
adj informative

知識人 [chishikijin] n intellectual

地質学 [chishitsugaku] n geology

窒素 [chisso] n nitrogen

窒息 [chissoku] 窒息する [chissoku suru] v
suffocate

地帯 [chitai] n zone

知的 [chiteki] adj intellectual; 知的な [chiteki
na] adj intellectual

地点 [chiten] n spot (place)

地図 [chizu] n map; 街路地図 [gairo chizu] n
street map; 地図帳 [chizuchou] n atlas; どこ
でその街の地図を買えますか? [doko de sono
machi no chizu o kaemasu ka?] Where can I
buy a map of the city?; どこでその国の地
図を買えますか? [doko de sono kuni no
chizu o kaemasu ka?] Where can I buy a
map of the country?; どこでその地方の地図
を買えますか? [doko de sono chihou no
chizu o kaemasu ka?] Where can I buy a
map of the region?; 道順を示す地図を書い

てもらえますか? [michijun o shimesu chizu o
kaite moraemasu ka?] Could you draw me
a map with directions?; 地図でそれがどこに
あるか教えてもらえますか? [chizu de sore ga
doko ni aru ka oshiete moraemasu ka?]
Could you show me where it is on the
map?; 地図で私たちがいる場所を教えてもらえ
ますか? [chizu de watashi-tachi ga iru basho
o oshiete moraemasu ka?] Could you show
me where we are on the map?

貯金 [chokin] n savings; 貯金箱 [chokinbako]
n piggy bank

直角 [chokkaku] n right angle

直感 [chokkan] n intuition

直径 [chokkei] n diameter

直行 [chokkou] 直行で [chokkou de] adv
non-stop

チョコレート [chokoreeto] n chocolate

直毛 [chokumou] 私は生まれつき直毛です
[watashi wa umaretsuki chokumou desu]
My hair is naturally straight

直接 [chokusetsu] 直接に [chokusetsu ni] adv
directly; 直接自分で [chokusetsu jibun de]
adv personally

直通 [chokutsuu] 直通のほうがいいのですが
[chokutsuu no hou ga ii no desu ga] I'd
prefer to go direct

チョーク [chooku] n (白墨) chalk

著者 [chosha] n author

貯水 [chosui] 貯水池 [chosuichi] n reservoir

ちょっと [chotto] adv little while; ちょっとの間
[chotto no aida] adv momentarily

腸 [chou] n bowels, gut; 腸チフス
[chouchifusu] n typhoid

長 [chou] n (統率) master, (統率) principal

帳 [chou] n book; メモ帳 [memochou] n
notepad; 電話帳 [denwachou] n telephone
directory

チョウ [chou] n butterfly

・・・長 [...chou] n chief, head

諜報 [chouhou] 諜報機関 [chouhou kikan] n
secret service

長方形 [chouhoukei] n rectangle; 長方形の

[chouhoukei no] adj oblong, rectangular

頂上 [choujou] n summit

超過 [chouka] n excess; 超過手荷物
[choukatenimotsu] n excess baggage; 超過
勤務 [chouka kinmu] n overtime

聴覚 [choukaku] 聴覚の [choukaku no] adj
acoustic

帳消す [choukesu] v cancel; 帳消しにする
[choukeshi ni suru] v cross out

彫刻 [choukoku] n sculpture; 彫刻家
[choukokuka] n sculptor

兆候 [choukou] n sign

長距離 [choukyori] n long distance bus; 長
距離バス [choukyori basu] n bus (vehicle)

調味 [choumi] 調味料 [choumiryou] n
seasoning

調味料 [choumiryou] n flavoring

蝶ネクタイ [chounekutai] n bow tie

超音波 [chouonpa] n ultrasound

調理 [chouri] n cooking; 調理法 [chourihou] n
recipe; 調理済みの [chouri zumi no] adj
ready-to-serve

長老派 [chourouha] 長老派の [chourouha no]
adj Presbyterian; 長老派の人 [chourouha
no hito] n Presbyterian

聴力 [chouryoku] n hearing

調査 [chousa] n investigation, research,
survey; 世論調査 [yoronchousa] n opinion
poll, poll; 調査する [chousa suru] v explore;
綿密な調査 [menmitsu na chousa] n scan;
国勢調査 [kokuzeichousa] n census; 市場調
査 [shijouchousa] n market research

調整 [chousei] n adjustment; 調整できる
[chousei dekiru] adj adjustable

挑戦 [chousen] n challenge; 挑戦する
[chousen suru] v challenge; 挑戦的な
[chousenteki na] adj challenging

朝鮮 [chousen] n Korea; 朝鮮の [chousen no]
adj Korean

朝鮮語 [chousengo] n Korean (language)

朝鮮人 [chousenjin] n Korean (person)

調子 [choushi] n pitch (sound)

超自然 [choushizen] 超自然の [choushizen

no] *adj* supernatural

朝食 [choushoku] *n* breakfast; ヨーロッパ大陸式の簡単な朝食 [Yooroppa tairikushiki no kantan na choushoku] *n* continental breakfast; 朝食付きで [choushoku-tsuki de] with breakfast; 朝食なしで [choushoku nashi de] without breakfast; 朝食には何を召し上がりますか? [choushoku ni wa nani o meshiagarimasu ka?] What would you like for breakfast?; 朝食は何時ですか? [choushoku wa nan-ji desu ka?] What time is breakfast?; 朝食はどこで取るのですか? [choushoku wa doko de toru no desu ka?] Where is breakfast served?; 朝食は含まれていますか? [choushoku wa fukumarete imasu ka?] Is breakfast included?; 自分の部屋で朝食を取ることができますか? [jibun no heya de choushoku o toru koto ga dekimasu ka?] Can I have breakfast in my room?

聴衆 [choushuu] *n* audience

調達 [choutatsu] *n* supply; 資金を調達する [shikin-o choutatsu suru] *v* finance

ちょうつがい [choutsugai] *n* hinge

調剤 [chouzai] 調剤師 [chouzaishi] *n* dispenser

チュニジア [chunijia] *n* Tunisia; チュニジア人 [Chunijia jin] *n* Tunisian *(person)*; チュニジアの [Chunijia no] *adj* Tunisian

チューブ [chuubu] *n* tube

中断 [chuudan] *n* interruption; 中断する [chuudan suru] *v* interrupt

中毒 [chuudoku] *n* poisoning; 中毒者 [chuudokusha] *n* addict; アルコール中毒者 [arukooru chuudokusha] *n* alcoholic

中学 [chuugaku] 中学校 [chuugakkou] *n* secondary school

中国 [chuugoku] *n* China; 中国の [chuugoku no] *adj* Chinese

中国語 [chuugokugo] *n* Chinese *(language)*

中国人 [chuugokujin] *n* Chinese *(person)*

中尉 [chuui] *n* lieutenant

注意 [chuui] *n* attention, care, caution, notice *(note)*; 注意をそらす [chuui-o sorasu]

v distract

注意深い [chuuibukai] *adj* careful

注意深く [chuuibukaku] *adv* carefully

チューインガム [chuuingamu] *n* chewing gum

注意せよ [chuui seyo] NB

忠実 [chuujitsu] 忠実な [chuujitsu na] *adj* faithful; 忠実に [chuujitsuni] *adv* faithfully

中間 [chuukan] 中間の [chuukan no] *adj* mid; 中間の [chuukan no] *adj* intermediate

中古 [chuuko] 中古の [chuuko no] *adj* secondhand, used

注文 [chuumon] *n* order; 注文用紙 [chuumon youshi] *n* order form; これは私が注文したものと違います [kore wa watashi ga chuumon shita mono to chigaimasu] This isn't what I ordered; 注文していいですか? [chuumon shite ii desu ka?] May I order now, please?

中年 [chuunen] 中年の [chuunen no] *adj* middle-aged

注入 [chuunyuu] ポンプで注入する [ponpu de chuunyuu suru] *v* pump

中央 [chuuou] *n* middle; 中央の [chuuou no] *adj* central; 中央アメリカ [Chuuou Amerika] *n* Central America; 中央アフリカ共和国 [Chuuou Afurika Kyouwakoku] *n* Central African Republic; 中央分離帯付き道路 [chuuou bunritai tsuki douro] *n* four-lane highway

チューリップ [chuurippu] *n* tulip

中立 [chuuritsu] 中立の [chuuritsu no] *adj* neutral; 中立国 [chuuritsukoku] *n* neutral

中流階級 [chuuryuu kaikyuu] 中流階級の [chuuryuu kaikyuu no] *adj* middle-class

仲裁 [chuusai] *n* arbitration

中世 [chuusei] *n* Middle Ages; 中世の [chuusei no] *adj* medieval

忠誠 [chuusei] *n* loyalty

注射 [chuusha] *n* injection; 注射する [chuusha suru] *v* inject; 注射器 [chuushaki] *n* syringe; 注射を打ってください [chuusha o utte kudasai] Please give me an injection; 私は痛み止めの注射は欲しくありません

[watashi wa itami-dome no chuusha wa hoshiku arimasen] I don't want an injection for the pain

駐車 [chuusha] *n* parking; 駐車する [chuusha suru] *v* park; 駐車違反切符 [chuushaihan kippu] *n* parking ticket

駐車場 [chuushajou] *n* parking lot; この近くに駐車場はありますか? [kono chikaku ni chuusha-jou wa arimasu ka?] Is there a parking lot near here?

中止 [chuushi] *n* stop

中心 [chuushin] *n* center; 街の中心部 [machi no chuushinbu] *n* downtown area; 町の中心部 [machi no chuushinbu] *n* downtown area

中心部 [chuushinbu] *n* downtown area; 街の中心部までどのくらいありますか? [machi no chuushinbu made dono kurai arimasu ka?] How far are we from the downtown area?; 街の中心部までお願いします [machi no chuushinbu made o-negai shimasu] Please take me to the downtown area

昼食 [chuushoku] *n* lunch; 昼食にはどこで停まりますか? [chuushoku ni wa doko de tomarimasu ka?] Where do we stop for lunch?; 昼食には時間があいています [chuushoku ni wa jikan ga aite imasu] I'm free for lunch; 昼食はいつ用意できますか? [chuushoku wa itsu youi dekimasu ka?] When will lunch be ready?; 昼食はすばらしかったです [chuushoku wa subarashikatta desu] The lunch was excellent; 昼食をご一緒できますか? [chuushoku o go-issho dekimasu ka?] Can we meet for lunch?

抽象 [chuushou] 抽象的な [chuushouteki na] *adj* abstract

虫垂炎 [chuusuien] *n* appendicitis

中東 [chuutou] *n* Middle East

中絶 [chuuzetsu] 妊娠中絶 [ninshinchuuzetsu] *n* abortion

鋳造 [chuuzou] 貨幣鋳造所 [kahei chuuzoujo] *n* mint *(coins)*

D

ダーツ [daatsu] n darts; ダーツ用の投げ矢 [daatsu you no nageya] n dart

打撲傷 [dabokushou] n bruise

だぶだぶ [dabudabu] だぶだぶの [dabudabu no] adj baggy

ダブル [daburu] ダブルルーム [dabururuumu] n double room; ダブルの部屋がいいのですが [daburu no heya ga ii no desu ga] I'd like a room with a double bed

ダブルベッド [daburubeddo] n double bed

ダブルルーム [dabururuumu] n double-room

ダチョウ [dachou] n ostrich

唾液 [daeki] n saliva

ダイビング [daibingu] n diving; ダイビングをしたいのですが [daibingu o shitai no desu ga] I'd like to go diving

大部分 [daibubun] n majority

台所 [daidokoro] n kitchen

ダイエット [daietto] n diet; ダイエットする [daietto suru] v diet; 私はダイエットしています [watashi wa daietto shite imasu] I'm on a diet

大学 [daigaku] n university; 大学の [daigaku no] adj academic; 大学の卒業生 [daigaku no sotsugyousei] n graduate; 大学卒業 [daigaku sotsugyou] n graduation

大学院 [daigakuin] n graduate school; 大学院生 [daigakuinsei] n graduate student

大虐殺 [daigyakusatsu] n massacre

代表 [daihyou] n delegate; 代表する [daihyou suru] v represent; 代表として派遣する [daihyou toshite haken suru] v delegate

第一 [daiichi] adj first; まず第一に [mazu daiichi ni] adv firstly; 第一の [daiichi no] adj primary

第一級 [daiikkyuu] 第一級の [daiikkyuu no] adj first-class

大臣 [daijin] n minister (government)

大丈夫 [daijoubu] adj all right; ぬれても大丈夫な [nurete mo daijoubu na] adj waterproof; 大丈夫ですか? [daijoubu desu ka?] Are you all right?

大工 [daiku] n carpenter; 大工仕事 [daikushigoto] n carpentry

題名 [daimei] n title

代名詞 [daimeishi] n pronoun

台無し [dainashi] 台無しにされた [dainashi ni sareta] adj ruined; 台無しにする [dainashi ni suru] v ruin

第二 [daini] 第二に [dai ni ni] adv secondly

ダイニング [dainingu] n dining; ダイニングルーム [dainingu ruumu] n dining room

代理 [dairi] n substitute; 代理母 [dairibo] n surrogate mother; 臨時代理の [rinji dairi no] adj acting

代理人 [dairinin] n agent

大理石 [dairiseki] n marble

代理店 [dairiten] n agency; 旅行代理店 [ryokoudairiten] n travel agency

大災害 [daisaigai] n catastrophe

第三 [daisan] 第三に [dai san ni] adv thirdly

第三者 [daisansha] n third party; 第三者賠償責任保険 [daisansha baishousekinin hoken] n liability insurance

大聖堂 [daiseidou] n cathedral; その大聖堂はいつ開きますか? [sono daiseidou wa itsu hirakimasu ka?] When is the cathedral open?

大集会 [daishuukai] n rally

大好き [daisuki] 大好きな [daisuki na] adj

favorite

大邸宅 [daiteitaku] *n* mansion

大統領 [daitouryou] *n* president

ダイヤモンド [daiyamondo] *n* diamond

ダイヤル [daiyaru] ダイヤルする [daiyaru suru] *v* dial

代用 [daiyou] *n* substitute; 代用する [daiyou suru] *v* substitute

大豆 [daizu] *n* soy bean

抱きしめる [dakishimeru] *v* cuddle, hug; 抱きしめること [dakishimeru koto] *n* hug

妥協 [dakyou] *n* compromise; 妥協する [dakyou suru] *v* compromise

黙る [damaru] *v* shut up

だます [damasu] *v* cheat, deceive, fool, trick

だめな [damena] *adj* lousy

ダム [damu] *n* dam

暖房 [danbou] *n* heating; 暖房器具 [danbou kigu] *n* heater; その部屋に暖房はありますか? [sono heya ni danbou wa arimasu ka?] Does the room have heating?; 暖房はどうやって使うのですか? [danbou wa dou-yatte tsukau no desu ka?] How does the heating work?; 暖房がつきません [danbou ga tsukimasen] The heating doesn't work

団地 [danchi] *n* complex; 工業団地 [kougyoudanchi] *n* industrial park

段地作り [dan chi tsukuri] 段地作りの [danchizukuri no] *adj* in a row (*row houses*)

弾丸 [dangan] *n* bullet

ダンガリー [dangarii] ダンガリーのオーバーオール [dangarii no oobaaooru] *n* dungarees

断言 [dangen] *n* assertion; 断言する [dangen suru] *v* declare

男女 [danjo] *adj* co-ed; 男女の別 [danjo no betsu] *n* sexuality

男女別 [danjobetsu] 男女別々の部屋はありますか? [danjo betsubetsu no heya wa arimasu ka?] Do you have any single-sex dorms?

段階 [dankai] *n* stage

断固 [danko] 断固とした [dan ko to shita] *adj* determined; ···に断固たる措置を取る [...

ni dankotaru sochi-o toru] *v* crack down on

ダンプリング [danpuringu] *n* dumpling

段落 [danraku] *n* paragraph

暖炉 [danro] *n* fireplace

ダンサー [dansaa] *n* dancer; バレエダンサー [bareedansaa] *n* ballet dancer

男性 [dansei] *n* male; 独身の男性 [dokushin no dansei] *n* bachelor; 男性の [dansei no] *adj* male; 男性用トイレ [dansei you toire] *n* men's room

弾性 [dansei] 弾性ゴム [dansei gomu] *n* rubber band

男子 [danshi] 男子生徒 [danshiseito] *n* schoolboy

ダンス [dansu] *n* dance; 社交ダンス [shakou dansu] *n* ballroom dancing; どこに行けばダンスができますか? [doko ni ikeba dansu ga dekimasu ka?] Where can we go dancing?; ダンスはいかがですか? [dansu wa ikaga desu ka?] Would you like to dance?

団体 [dantai] *n* group; 慈善団体 [jizen dantai] *n* charity; 団体割引はありますか? [dantai-waribiki wa arimasu ka?] Are there any discounts for groups?

弾薬 [dan-yaku] *n* ammunition, cartridge, magazine (*ammunition*)

男優 [danyuu] *n* actor

だらけ [darake] *prep* full of; しみだらけの [shimidarake no] *adj* spotty

堕落 [daraku] *n* depravity; 堕落した [daraku shita] *adj* vile

だらしのない [darashi no nai] *adj* untidy

誰 [dare] *pron* who; 誰の番ですか? [dare no ban desu ka?] Whose round is it?

誰でも [dare demo] *pron* anybody, anyone

脱脂 [dasshi] 脱脂乳 [dasshinyuu] *n* skim milk; 脱脂綿 [dasshimen] *n* cotton

ダッシュボード [dasshuboodo] *n* dashboard

脱水 [dassui] 脱水機 [dassuiki] *n* spin dryer

出す [dasu] *v* put forth; 煙を出す [kemuri wo dasu] *v* smoke; 金切り声を出す [kanakirigoe wo dasu] *v* shriek; 声を出して [koe wo dashite] *adv* aloud

脱退 [dattai] ・・・から脱退する [... kara dattai suru] *v* opt out

ダウン [daun] ダウン症候群 [Daun shoukougun] *n* Down syndrome

ダウンロード [daunroodo] *n* download; ダウンロードする [daunroodo suru] *v* download; ここに写真をダウンロードできますか? [koko ni shashin o daunroodo dekimasu ka?] Can I download photos to here?

出会う [deau] *v* encounter; ばったり出会う [battari deau] *v* bump into

デビット [debitto] *n* debit; デビットカードは使えますか? [debitto-kaado wa tsukaemasu ka?] Do you take debit cards?

デビットカード [debitto kaado] *n* debit card

データ [deeta] *n* data

データベース [deetabeesu] *n* database

出口 [deguchi] *n* exit; ・・・へ行く出口はどれですか? [... e iku deguchi wa dore desu ka?] Which is the exit for...?; 出口はどこですか? [deguchi wa doko desu ka?] Where is the exit?

で走る [de hashiru] ギャロップで走る [gyaroppu de hashiru] *v* gallop

ディーゼル [deiizeru] ディーゼルエンジン [diizeruenjin] *n* diesel

ディナー [deinaa] *n* dinner; ディナーの時刻 [dinaa no jikoku] *n* dinner time; ディナージャケット [dinaa jaketto] *n* dinner jacket; ディナーパーティー [dinaa paatii] *n* dinner party

ディンギー [deingii] *n* dinghy

ディスケット [deisuketto] *n* diskette

泥炭 [deitan] *n* peat

デジタル [dejitaru] デジタルの [dejitaru no] *adj* digital; デジタルカメラ [dejitaru kamera] *n* digital camera; デジタルラジオ [dejitaru rajio] *n* digital radio; デジタルテレビ [dejitaru terebi] *n* digital television; デジタル時計 [dejitaru tokei] *n* digital watch

デジタルカメラ [dejitaru kamera] このデジタルカメラ用のメモリカードをください [kono dejitaru-kamera-you no memori-kaado o kudasai] A memory card for this digital camera, please

出かける [dekakeru] *v* go out; 食事に出かけるのはいかがですか? [shokuji ni dekakeru no wa ikaga desu ka?] Would you like to go out for dinner?

出来事 [dekigoto] *n* event, incident, occurrence; 不幸な出来事 [fukou na dekigoto] *n* mishap; 悲惨な出来事 [hisan na dekigoto] *n* tragedy; 出来事の多い [dekigoto no oui] *adj* eventful

・・・できない [...dekinai] *adj* unable to

できる [dekiru] *v* be able; 読み書きのできない [yomikaki no dekinai] *adj* illiterate; ・・・ができる [... ga dekiru] *adj* able, capable; ・・・できる [... dekiru] *v* can; 利用できる [riyou dekiru] *adj* available

できるだけ [dekiru dake] できるだけ早く [dekiru dake hayaku] *adv* ASAP

溺死 [dekishi] 溺死する [dekishi suru] *v* drown

デッキ [dekki] *n* deck; デッキチェア [dekkichea] *n* deck chair; デッキに出られますか? [dekki ni deraremasu ka?] Can we go out on deck?

でこぼこ [dekoboko] でこぼこのある [dekoboko no aru] *adj* bumpy

デモ [demo] *n* demo, demonstration

デモンストレーター [demonsutoreetaa] *n* demonstrator

・・・でない [...denai] *adv* not

電圧 [den-atsu] *n* voltage; 電圧は何ボルトですか? [denatsu wa nan-boruto desu ka?] What's the voltage?

臀部 [denbu] *n* backside, behind, buttocks

電池 [denchi] *n* battery

伝言 [dengon] *n* message; 伝言をお願いできますか? [dengon o o-negai dekimasu ka?] May I leave a message?; 私あての伝言がありますか? [watashi ate no dengon ga arimasu ka?] Are there any messages for me?; 彼の秘書に伝言を残すことはできますか? [kare no hisho ni dengon o nokosu koto wa dekimasu ka?] May I leave a message with his secretary?

デニム [denimu] n denim

電荷 [denka] 電荷がもちません [denka ga mochimasen] It isn't holding its charge

伝記 [denki] n biography

電気 [denki] n electricity; 電気に関する [denki ni kansuru] adj electrical; 電気の [denki no] adj electric; 電気コード [denki koodo] n electric cord; 電気毛布 [denkimoufu] n electric blanket; 電気技師 [denki gishi] n electrician; 電気掃除機 [denki soujiki] n vacuum cleaner; 電気通信 [denkitsuushin] n telecommunications; 電気代は別に払わなければなりませんか? [denki-dai wa betsu ni harawanakereba narimasen ka?] Do we have to pay extra for electricity?; 電気代は含まれていますか? [denki-dai wa fukumarete imasu ka?] Is the cost of electricity included?; 電気のメーターはどこですか? [denki no meetaa wa doko desu ka?] Where's the electricity meter?; 電気がきていません [denki ga kite imasen] There's no electricity

電気系統 [denkikeitou] 電気系統に何か問題があります [denki-keitou ni nani ka mondai ga arimasu] There's something wrong with the electrical system

電球 [denkyuu] n bulb (electricity), light bulb

デンマーク [denmaaku] n Denmark; デンマークの [denmaaku no] adj Danish

デンマーク語 [denmaakugo] n Danish (language)

デンマーク人 [denmaakujin] n Dane

電報 [denpou] n telegram; どこで電報を送ることができますか? [doko de denpou o okuru koto ga dekimasu ka?] Where can I send a telegram?; ここから電報を送れますか? [koko kara denpou o okuremasu ka?] Can I send a telegram from here?; 私は電報を送りたいのですが [watashi wa denpou o okuritai no desu ga] I want to send a telegram

澱粉 [denpun] n starch

伝票 [denpyou] n slip (paper)

電流 [denryuu] n current (electricity)

伝染 [densen] 伝染性の [densensei no] adj contagious

伝染性 [densensei] 伝染性の [densensei no] adj catching

伝説 [densetsu] n legend

電車 [densha] n train; これは···行きの電車ですか? [kore wa... iki no densha desu ka?] Is this the train for...?; 次に乗れる電車をお願いします [tsugi ni noreru densha o o-negai shimasu] The next available train, please; ···へ行く次の電車は何時ですか? [... e iku tsugi no densha wa nan-ji desu ka?] When is the next train to...?; ···へ行く電車にはどこで乗れますか? [... e iku densha ni wa doko de noremasu ka?] Where can I get a train to...?; ···へ行く電車は何時ですか? [... e iku densha wa nan-ji desu ka?] What time is the train to...?; 電車は何時に出ますか? [densha wa nan-ji ni demasu ka?] What time does the train leave?; 電車は···に停まりますか? [densha wa... ni tomarimasu ka?] Does the train stop at...?; 電車は十分遅れています [densha wa jup-pun okurete imasu] The train is running ten minutes late

電子 [denshi] adj electronic; 電子の [denshi no] adj electronic; 電子メール [denshi meeru] n e-mail; 電子メールを送る [denshi meeru-o okuru] v e-mail; 電子メールアドレス [denshi meeru adoresu] n e-mail address; 電子書籍 [denshi shoseki] n e-book; 電子工学 [denshikougaku] n electronics

電子メール [denshi meeru] n e-mail

電子レンジ [denshi renji] n microwave oven

伝承 [denshou] 伝承童謡 [denshou douyou] n nursery rhyme; 民間伝承 [minkandenshou] n folklore

電卓 [dentaku] n pocket calculator

デンタル [dentaru] デンタルフロス [dentaru furosu] n dental floss

伝統 [dentou] n tradition; 伝統的な

[dentouteki na] *adj* classical, traditional

電灯 [dentou] *n* lamp; **懐中電灯** [kaichuuden-tou] *n* flashlight

電話 [denwa] *n* phone, telephone; **カメラ付き携帯電話** [kamera tsuki keitai denwa] *n* camera phone; **テレビ電話** [terebi denwa] *n* videophone; **携帯電話** [keitai denwa] *n* cell phone; **留守番電話** [rusubandenwa] *n* answering machine; **間違い電話** [machigai denwa] *n* wrong number; **電話交換台** [denwa koukandai] *n* switchboard; **電話しなおす** [denwa shinaosu] *v* call back; **電話セールス** [denwa seerusu] *n* telemarketing; **電話をかけなおす** [denwa-o kakenaosu] *v* call back; **電話をかける** [denwa-o kakeru] *v* phone; **電話を切る** [denwa wo kiru] *v* hang up; **電話番号** [denwabangou] *n* phone number; **電話帳** [denwachou] *n* phone-book, telephone directory; **公衆電話** [koushuudenwa] *n* payphone; **あなたは携帯電話をお持ちですか?** [anata wa keitai-denwa o o-mochi desu ka?] Do you have a cell phone?; **私は電話をかけなければなりません** [watashi wa denwa o kakenakereba narimasen] I have to make a phone call; **電話をお借りできますか?** [denwa o o-kari dekimasu ka?] May I use your phone, please?, May I use your phone?; **電話をかけたいのですが** [denwa o kaketai no desu ga] I want to make a phone call; **電話番号は何番ですか?** [denwa-bangou wa nan-ban desu ka?] What's the telephone number?; **家に電話していいですか?** [ie ni denwa shite ii desu ka?] May I phone home?; **国際電話用のテレホンカードを売っていますか?** [kokusai-denwa-you no terehon-kaado o utte imasu ka?] Do you sell international phone cards?

デオドラント [deodoranto] *n* deodorant

デパート [depaato] *n* department store

デリカテッセン [derikatessen] *n* delicatessen

出る [deru] *v* run/leave

です [desu]...is; **•••です** [...desu] It's..., This

is...

•••です [...desu] I'm from...

デスク [desuku] 照会デスク [shoukai desuku] *n* information desk

出て行く [deteiku] *adj* outgoing

ではまた [dewa mata] See you later

ではまた! [dewa mata] *excl* bye!

デザート [dezaato] *n* dessert; **デザートスプーン** [dezaato supuun] *n* dessert spoon; **デザートのメニューをください** [dezaato no menyuu o kudasai] The dessert menu, please; **私たちはデザートをいただきます** [watashi-tachi wa dezaato o itadakimasu] We'd like dessert

デザイン [dezain] *n* design; **デザインする** [dezain suru] *v* design

デザイナー [dezainaa] *n* designer

痔 [di] *n* hemorrhoids

DVD [dii bui dii] *n* DVD [dii bui dii]; **DVDバーナー** [diibuidii baanaa] *n* DVD burner; **DVDプレーヤー** [dibuidii pureiyaa] *n* DVD player

DNA [dii enu ee] *n* DNA [dii enu ee]

ディーラー [diiraa] *n* dealer; **麻薬ディーラー** [mayaku diiraa] *n* drug dealer

ディスコ [disuko] *n* disco

ディスク [disuku] *n* disc, disk; **ディスクドライブ** [disukudoraibu] *n* disk drive; **フロッピーディスク** [furoppi disuku] *n* floppy disk

ディスクジョッキー [disukujokkii] *n* disc jockey, DJ

度 [do] 度を超えた [do-o koeta] *adj* excessive

ドア [doa] *n* door; **ドアハンドル** [doahandoru] *n* door handle; **ドアに鍵がかかりません** [doa ni kagi ga kakarimasen] The door won't lock; **ドアの取っ手が外れました** [doa no totte ga hazuremashita] The door handle has come off; **ドアが閉まりません** [doa ga shimarimasen] The door won't close; **ドアが開きません** [doa ga akimasen] The door won't open

ドアマン [doaman] *n* doorman

ドブネズミ [dobunezumi] *n* rat

どちら [dochira] どちらさまでしょうか？ [dochira-sama deshou ka?] Who am I talking to?, Who's calling?

土台 [dodai] n base

どぎもを抜かれた [dogimo wo nukareta] adj stunned

ドイツ [doitsu] n Germany

ドイツ語 [doitsugo] n German (language)

ドイツ人 [doitsujin] n German (person)

ドイツの [doitsu no] adj German

ドイツスズラン [doitsusuzuran] n lily of the valley

どけち [dokechi] n miser

ドック [dokku] n dock

どこ [doko] adv where; 三十号車はどこですか？ [sanjuu-gou-sha wa doko desu ka?] Where is carriage number thirty?; どこに行けば・・・ができますか？ [doko ni ikeba... ga dekimasu ka?] Where can you go...?; どこで払うのですか？ [doko de harau no desu ka?] Where do I pay?; どこで電話をかけられますか？ [doko de denwa o kakeraremasu ka?] Where can I make a phone call?; ここはどこですか？ [koko wa doko desu ka?] Where are we?; エレベーターはどこですか？ [erebeetaa wa doko desu ka?] Where is the elevator?; ・・・はどこですか？ [... wa doko desu ka?] Where is...?

どこでも [dokodemo] adv anywhere, everywhere

どこにも・・・ない [dokonimo... nai] adv nowhere

毒 [doku] n poison; 毒を盛る [doku-o moru] v poison; 毒キノコ [doku kinoko] n toadstool

独立 [dokuritsu] n independence; 独立した [dokuritsu shita] adj independent

独裁 [dokusai] 独裁者 [dokusaisha] n dictator

独占 [dokusen] n monopoly

読者 [dokusha] n reader

独身 [dokushin] n loner; 独身の男性 [dokushin no dansei] n bachelor; 独身女性 [dokushinjosei] n spinster

独身女性 [dokushinjosei] n single woman; 独身女性の名字の前に付ける敬称 [dokushinjosei no myouji no mae ni tsukeru keishou] n Miss

読唇術 [dokushinjutsu] 読唇術で解する [dokushinjutsu de kaisuru] v lip-read

読書 [dokusho] n reading

独創 [dokusou] 独創的な [dokusouteki na] adj ingenious

独特 [dokutoku] 独特の [dokutoku no] adj unique

ドキュメンタリー [dokyumentarii] n documentary

ドキュメンテーション [dokyumenteeshon] n documentation

ドキュメント [dokyumento] n documents

ドミニカ [dominika] ドミニカ共和国 [Dominika kyouwakoku] n Dominican Republic

ドミノ [domino] n domino, dominoes

どもる [domoru] v stammer, stutter

ドナー [donaa] n donor

どなた [donata] pron who; どなたですか？ [donata desu ka?] Who is it?

どんぐり [donguri] n acorn

鈍感 [donkan] 鈍感な [donkan na] adj insensitive

どのように [dono you ni] adv how

ドーナツ [doonatsu] n doughnut

ドライ [dorai] adj dry; ドライシェリーをください [dorai-sherii o kudasai] A dry sherry, please

ドライバー [doraibaa] n (人) motorist, (道具) screwdriver

ドライブ [doraibu] n drive; ディスクドライブ [disukudoraibu] n disk drive

ドライクリーニング [doraikuriiningu] n dry-cleaning; ドライクリーニング屋 [doraikuriininguya] n dry-cleaner's

ドラマー [doramaa] n drummer

ドラム [doramu] n drum

どれでも [dore de mo] pron any

奴隷 [dorei] n slave; 奴隷のように働く [dorei no youni hataraku] v slave

D

ドレッシングガウン [doresshingugaun] *n* bathrobe

ドリル [doriru] *n* drill; 空気ドリル [kuukidoriru] *n* pneumatic drill

泥 [doro] *n* mud

泥棒 [dorobou] *n* thief; 泥棒に入る [dorobou ni hairu] *v* burgle; 個人情報泥棒 [kojin jouhou dorobou] *n* identity theft

泥だらけ [dorodarake] 泥だらけの [doro darake no] *adj* muddy

泥よけ [doroyoke] *n* fender

ドル [doru] *n* dollar; ドルを使えますか? [doru o tsukaemasu ka?] Do you take dollars?

努力 [doryoku] *n* effort, try

土砂降り [doshaburi] *n* downpour

どっしり [dosshiri] どっしりした [dosshiri shita] *adj* massive

土手 [dote] *n* bank *(ridge)*

銅 [dou] *n* copper

堂 [dou] 軽食堂 [keishokudou] *n* snack bar

どう [dou] *adv* how/what

動物 [doubutsu] *n* animal; 齧歯動物 [gesshi doubutsu] *n* rodent; 動物の一腹子 [doubutsu no ippukushi] *n* litter *(offspring)*; 動物の足 [doubutsu no ashi] *n* paw; 動物園 [doubutsuen] *n* zoo; 動物学 [doubutsugaku] *n* zoology; 哺乳動物 [honyuu doubutsu] *n* mammal

動物相 [doubutsusou] *n* fauna

道義心 [dougishin] *n* honor

道具 [dougu] *n* tool

胴衣 [doui] *n* vest; 救命胴衣 [kyuumeidoui] *n* life jacket

同意 [doui] *n* agreement

どういたしまして [douitashimashite] You're welcome

同一 [douitsu] 同一の [douitsu no] *adj* identical

同時 [douji] *n* pulse; 同時に [douji ni] *adv* simultaneously; 同時に起こる [douji ni okoru] *v* coincide; 同時の [douji no] *adj* simultaneous

同情 [doujou] *n* sympathy; 同情する [doujou suru] *v* sympathize; 同情的な [doujouteki na] *adj* sympathetic

動き [douki] *n* movement

動機 [douki] *n* motive; 動機づけ [douki zuke] *n* motivation; 動機づけられた [douki zukerareta] *adj* motivated

動悸 [douki] 動悸を打つ [douki-o utsu] *v* throb

瞳孔 [doukou] *n* pupil *(eye)*

同行 [doukou] 同行する [doukou suru] *v* accompany

同級生 [doukyuusei] *n* classmate

同盟 [doumei] 同盟国 [doumeikoku] *n* ally

動脈 [doumyaku] *n* artery

道路 [douro] *n* road; 中央分離帯付き道路 [chuuou bunritai tsuki douro] *n* divided highway; 環状道路 [kanjoudouro] *n* beltway; 高速道路 [kousokudouro] *n* expressway; 道路標識 [dourohyoushiki] *n* road sign, signpost; 道路封鎖 [douro fuusa] *n* roadblock; 道路工事 [dourokouji] *n* road work; この地域の道路マップはありますか? [kono chiiki no douro-mappu wa arimasu ka?] Do you have a road map of this area?; 私は・・・の道路マップが必要です [watashi wa... no douro-mappu ga hitsuyou desu] I need a road map of...; 道路は凍結していますか? [douro wa touketsu shite imasu ka?] Are the roads icy?

同僚 [douryou] *n* colleague

同棲 [dousei] 同棲する [dousei suru] *v* live together

動詞 [doushi] *n* verb

どうした [doushita] *adv* what; どうしたのですか? [dou shita no desu ka?] What's the matter?

同室者 [doushitsusha] *n* roommate

道徳 [doutoku] 不道徳な [fudoutoku na] *adj* immoral; 道徳の [doutoku no] *adj* moral

同等 [doutou] 同等のもの [doutou no mono] *n* equivalent

童謡 [douyou] *n* children's song; 伝承童謡 [denshou douyou] *n* nursery rhyme

土曜日 [doyoubi] *n* Saturday; 今週の土曜日に [konshuu no doyoubi ni] this Saturday; 毎週土曜日に [maishuu doyoubi ni] every Saturday; 毎土曜日に [mai-doyoubi ni] on Saturdays; 来週の土曜日に [raishuu no doyoubi ni] next Saturday; 先週の土曜日に [senshuu no doyoubi ni] last Saturday; 土曜日に [doyoubi ni] on Saturday

E

絵 [e] n picture; 絵のように美しい [e no youni utsukushii] adj picturesque; 絵を描く [e-o egaku] v paint; 開くと絵が飛び出す本 [hiraku to e ga tobidasu hon] n pop-up book

エアバッグ [eabaggu] n air bag

エアコン [eakon] n air conditioning; その部屋にエアコンはありますか? [sono heya ni eakon wa arimasu ka?] Does the room have air conditioning?; エアコンはついていますか? [eakon wa tsuite imasu ka?] Does it have air conditioning?; エアコンが動きません [eakon ga ugokimasen] The air conditioning doesn't work

エアロビクス [earobikusu] n aerobics

エアゾール [eazooru] n aerosol

エビ [ebi] 小エビ [koebi] n shrimp

エチオピア [echiopia] n Ethiopia; エチオピア人 [echiopiajin] n Ethiopian; エチオピアの [echiopia no] adj Ethiopian

枝 [eda] n branch

エーカー [eekaa] n acre

エープリルフール [eepurirufuuru] エープリルフールの日 [eepuriru fuuru no nichi] n April Fools' Day

エース [eesu] n ace

絵筆 [efude] n paintbrush

FAQ [efueekyuu] abbr FAQ [efueekyuu]

描く [egaku] v draw (sketch); スケッチを描く [suketchi-o egaku] v sketch; 絵を描く [e-o egaku] v paint

笑顔 [egao] n beam

エッグカップ [eggukappu] n eggcup

エグゼクティブ [eguzekuteibu] n executive

エホバ [ehoba] エホバの証人 [Ehoba no shounin] n Jehovah's Witness

永遠 [eien] 永遠の [eien no] adj eternal; 永遠性 [eiensei] n eternity

映画 [eiga] n movie; ホラー映画 [horaa eiga] n horror movie; 映画スター [eigasutaa] n movie star; どこに行けば映画を見られますか? [doko ni ikeba eiga o miraremasu ka?] Where can we go to see a movie?; 映画はいつ始まりますか? [eiga wa itsu hajimarimasu ka?] When does the movie start?; 英語の映画はありますか? [eigo no eiga wa arimasu ka?] Are there any movies in English?

映画館 [eigakan] n movie theater; その映画館で今晩何が上映されますか? [sono eigakan de konban nani ga jouei saremasu ka?] What's playing tonight at the movie theater?; その映画館で何が上映されていますか? [sono eigakan de nani ga jouei sarete imasu ka?] What's playing at the movie theater?; その映画館でどの映画が上映されていますか? [sono eigakan de dono eiga ga jouei sarete imasu ka?] Which film is playing at the movie theater?

英語 [eigo] n English; 英語のガイドブックはありますか? [eigo no gaidobukku wa arimasu ka?] Do you have a guide book in English?; 英語を話せるお医者さんはいらっしゃいますか? [eigo o hanaseru o-isha-san wa irasshaimasu ka?] Is there a doctor who speaks English?; 私は英語をほとんど話せません [watashi wa eigo o hotondo hanasemasen] I speak very little English; あなたは英語を話しますか? [anata wa eigo o hanashimasu ka?] Do you speak English?; 誰か英語を話せる人はいますか? [dare ka eigo o hanaseru hito wa imasu ka?] Does anyone speak English?; 私は英語を話せません [watashi wa eigo o hanasemasen] I don't speak English

営業 [eigyou] 自営業の [jieigyou no] adj self-employed; 営業時間 [eigyoujikan] n office hours, opening hours; 営業していますか? [eigyou shite imasu ka?] Are you open?

英貨 [eika] n pound sterling

英国 [eikoku] n Britain, UK, United Kingdom; 英国の [eikoku no] adj British

英国人 [eikokujin] n British (person)

影響 [eikyou] n effect, impact, influence; 影響を与える [eikyou-o ataeru] v affect, influence

永久 [eikyuu] 永久に [eikyuu ni] adv forever, permanently; 永久の [eikyuu no] adj permanent

衛生 [eisei] n hygiene

衛星 [eisei] 人工衛星 [jinkou eisei] n satellite; 衛星ナビゲーション [eisei nabigeeshon] n satellite navigation; 衛星放送用パラボラアンテナ [eisei housou you parabora antena] n satellite dish

栄誉 [eiyo] n glory

栄養 [eiyou] n nutrition; 栄養不良 [eiyou furyou] n malnutrition; 栄養物摂取 [eiyoubutsu sesshu] n nutrition; 栄養分 [eiyoubun] n nutrient

エイス [eizu] n AIDS

餌食 [ejiki] n prey

エジプト [ejiputo] n Egypt

エジプト人 [ejiputojin] n Egyptian (person)

エジプトの [ejiputo no] adj Egyptian

液 [eki] 不凍液 [futoueki] n antifreeze

駅 [eki] n station; 鉄道駅 [tetsudoueki] n train station; 地下鉄駅 [chikatetsu eki] n subway station; 鉄道駅へ行く一番よい方法は何ですか? [tetsudou-eki e iku ichiban yoi houhou wa nan desu ka?] What's the best way to get to the train station?

液体 [ekitai] n liquid

エキゾチック [ekizochikku] エキゾチックな [ekizochikku na] adj exotic

エキゾーストパイプ [ekizoosutopaipu] n exhaust pipe

エキゾースト [ekizoosuto] エキゾーストが壊れています [ekizoosuto ga kowarete imasu] The exhaust is broken

X線 [ekkusosen] n X-ray; X線写真を撮る [x-sen shashin-o toru] v X-ray

エコノミー [ekonomii] エコノミークラス [ekonomiikurasu] n economy class

エクアドル [ekuadoru] n Ecuador

エクスタシー [ekusutashii] n ecstasy

MP4プレーヤー [emu pi foa pyreeyaa] n MP4 player

MP3プレーヤー [emu pi surii pyreeyaa] n MP3 player

縁 [en] n rim

円 [en] n (丸) circle, round (circle)

エナメル [enameru] n enamel

延長 [enchou] n extension; サッカー・ラグビーなどで怪我の手当てなどに要した分の延長時間 [sakkaa / ragubii nado de kega no teate nado ni youshita bun no enchou jikan] n injury time-out; 延長コード [enchoukoodo] n extension cord

円柱 [enchuu] n column

演壇 [endan] n platform

エンドウ [endou] n peas

エネルギー [enerugii] n energy; 太陽エネルギー [taiyou enerugii] n solar power

沿岸 [engan] n coast; 沿岸警備隊 [engankeibitai] n coast guard

園芸 [engei] 園芸用品店 [engei youhinten] n garden center

演劇 [engeki] 演劇の [engeki no] adj dramatic

演技 [engi] n acting

縁組 [engumi] 養子縁組 [youshiengumi] n adoption

縁組み [engumi] n match (partnership)

円グラフ [engurafu] n pie chart

エンジン [enjin] n engine; ディーゼルエンジン

[diizeruenjin] *n* diesel; 検索エンジン
[kensaku enjin] *n* search engine; エンジンが
オーバーヒートしています [enjin ga
oobaahiito shite imasu] The engine is
overheating

援助 [enjo] *n* aid, assistance, help

円形 [enkei] 円形の [enkei no] *adj* circular

延期 [enki] 延期する [enki suru] *v* postpone,
put off

煙霧 [enmu] *n* fumes

縁日 [ennichi] *n* fair

鉛筆 [enpitsu] *n* pencil

鉛筆削り [enpitsukezuri] *n* pencil sharpener

遠慮 [enryo] 遠慮のない [enryo no nai] *adj*
outspoken

遠視 [enshi] 私は遠視です [watashi wa enshi
desu] I'm far-sighted

炎症 [enshou] *n* inflammation; 炎症を起こし
た [enshou-o okoshita] *adj* inflamed

塩素 [enso] *n* chlorine

遠足 [ensoku] *n* outing

演奏 [ensou] 演奏する [ensou suru] *v* play
(music); 演奏者 [ensousha] *n* player
(instrumentalist)

円錐形 [ensuikei] 円錐形のもの [ensuikei no
mono] *n* cone

エンターテイナー [entaateinaa] *n*
entertainer

煙突 [entotsu] *n* chimney

円筒 [entou] *n* cylinder

演説 [enzetsu] *n* address *(speech)*

エピソード [episoodo] *n* episode

エプロン [epuron] *n* apron, pinafore

選ぶ [erabu] *v* choose, pick, pick out, select;

選ばれた [erabareta] *adj* chosen

エラストプラスト® [erasutopurasuto] *n*
Band-Aid®

エレベーター [erebeetaa] *n* elevator *(up/
down)*; エレベーターはどこですか?
[erebeetaa wa doko desu ka?] Where is the
elevator?; エレベーターはありますか?
[erebeetaa wa arimasu ka?] Is there an
elevator?; 建物内にエレベーターはあります
か? [tatemono-nai ni erebeetaa wa arimasu
ka?] Is there an elevator in the building?

襟 [eri] *n* collar

エリア [eria] *n* area; 禁煙エリアはありますか?
[kin'en-eria wa arimasu ka?] Is there a
no-smoking area?; 喫煙エリアの席が欲しい
のですが [kitsuen-eria no seki ga hoshii no
desu ga] I'd like a seat in the smoking
area

エリトリア [eritoria] *n* Eritrea

エロチックな [erochikku na] *adj* erotic

得る [eru] *v* gain, get; 利益を得る [rieki wo
eru] *v* benefit; 勝利を得た [shouri-o eta] *adj*
winning

エッセイ [essei] *n* essay

エスカレーター [esukareetaa] *n* escalator

エステートカー [esuteetokaa] *n* station
wagon

エストニア [esutonia] *n* Estonia

エストニア語 [esutonia go] *n* Estonian
(language)

エストニア人 [esutoniajin] *n* Estonian
(person)

エストニアの [esutonia no] *adj* Estonian

E

F

ファーストネーム [faasutoneemu] n first name

ファゴット [fagotto] n bassoon

ファイル [fairu] n file (folder); ファイルする [fairu suru] v file (folder)

ファックス [fakkusu] n fax; ファックスを送る [fakkusu-o okuru] v fax; あなたのファックスに問題があります [anata no fakkusu ni mondai ga arimasu] There's a problem with your fax; あなたのファックスを再送信してください [anata no fakkusu o sai-soushin shite kudasai] Please resend your fax; ここからファックスを送れますか? [koko kara fakkusu o okuremasu ka?] Can I send a fax from here?; ファックスがありますか? [fakkusu ga arimasu ka?] Do you have a fax?; ファックスを送るのはいくらですか? [fakkusu o okuru no wa ikura desu ka?] How much does it cost to send a fax?; ファックス番号は何番ですか? [fakkusu-bangou wa nan-ban desu ka?] What is the fax number?; 私はファックスを送りたいのですが [watashi wa fakkusu o okuritai no desu ga] I want to send a fax; 私が使えるファックス機はありますか? [watashi ga tsukaeru fakkusuki wa arimasu ka?] Is there a fax machine I can use?

ファミリールーム [famiriiruumu] ファミリールームを予約したいのですが [famirii-ruumu o yoyaku shitai no desu ga] I want to reserve a family room, I'd like to reserve a family room

ファンベルト [fanberuto] n fan belt

ファスナー [fasunaa] n zipper; ファスナーを締める [fasunaa-o shimeru] v zip; ファスナーを開ける [fasunaa-o hirakeru] v unzip

ファウル [fauru] n foul

フェミニスト [feminisuto] n feminist

フェンネル [fenneru] n fennel

フェリー [ferii] n ferry; ···行きのフェリーはどこで乗るのですか? [... iki no ferii wa doko de noru no desu ka?] Where do we catch the ferry to...?; ···行きのフェリーはありますか? [... iki no ferii wa arimasu ka?] Is there a ferry to...?

フェロー [feroo] フェロー諸島 [Feroo shotou] n Faroe Islands

フェルト [feruto] n felt

フェルトペン [ferutopen] n felt-tip pen

フェスティバル [fesutibaru] n festival

フィジー [fijii] n Fiji

フィクション [fikushon] n fiction

フィンランド [finrando] n Finland

フィンランド人 [finrandojin] n Finn, Finnish (person)

フィンランドの [finrando no] adj Finnish

フィリピン [firipin] n Filipino; フィリピン人 [firipinjin] n Filipino (person); フィリピンの [firipin no] adj Filipino

フィルム [firumu] n film; このフィルムを現像していただけますか? [kono firumu o genzou shite itadakemasu ka?] Could you develop this film, please?; フィルムが動かなくなってしまいました [firumu ga ugokanaku natte shimaimashita] The film has jammed

フィットネス [fittonesu] n fitness; フィットネス運動 [fittonesu undou] n fitness program

フォグランプ [foguranpu] n fog light

フォーク [fooku] n fork; フォークミュージック [fooku myuujikku] n folk music; 新しいフォークをいただけますか? [atarashii fooku o

itadakemasu ka?] Could I have a clean
fork, please?

フォワードスラッシュ [fowaadosurasshu] *n*
forward slash

不 [fu] 不自然な [fushizen na] *adj* strained

符 [fu] 引用符 [in-youfu] *n* quotation marks

不安 [fuan] *n* uneasiness; 不安な [fuan na]
adj uneasy

不安定 [fuantei] *n* instability; 不安定な
[fuantei na] *adj* unstable, unsteady

不便 [fuben] *n* inconvenience; 不便な [fuben
na] *adj* inconvenient

吹雪 [fubuki] *n* snowstorm

縁石 [fuchiishi] *n* curb

不注意 [fuchuui] 不注意な [fuchuui na] *adj*
careless; 不注意で [fuchuui de] *adv*
inadvertently

不断 [fudan] *adj* casual; 優柔不断な [yuujuu
fudan na] *adj* indecisive

筆箱 [fudebako] *n* pencil case

不動産 [fudousan] 不動産屋 [fudousanya] *n*
real estate agent

不道徳 [fudoutoku] 不道徳な [fudoutoku na]
adj immoral

腐敗 [fuhai] *n* decay; 腐敗した [fuhai shita]
adj corrupt

腐敗行為 [fuhaikoui] *n* corruption

不平 [fuhei] *n* complaint, gripe *(complaint)*;
不平を言う [fuhei wo iu] *v* complain

不必要 [fuhitsuyou] 不必要な [fuhitsuyou na]
adj unnecessary

不法 [fuhou] 不法侵入者 [fuhou shinnyuusha]
n burglar; 不法な [fuhou na] *adj* illegal

不意 [fui] 不意に [fui ni] *adv* unexpectedly; 不
意の [fui no] *adj* unexpected

藤紫 [fujimurasaki] 藤紫色の [fuji murasaki iro
no] *adj* mauve

婦人 [fujin] *n* lady; 婦人警官 [fujinkeikan] *n*
policewoman

婦人科医 [fujinkai] *n* gynecologist

不十分 [fujuubun] 不十分な [fujuubun na] *adj*
inadequate, insufficient, skimpy

不従順 [fujuujun] 不従順な [fujuujun na] *adj*
disobedient

深い [fukai] *adj* deep; 思慮深い [shiryobukai]
adj thoughtful; 深さ [fukasa] *n* depth; 疑い
深い [utagaibukai] *adj* skeptical; 嫉妬深い
[shittobukai] *adj* jealous

不快感 [fukaikan] *n* insensitivity; 不快感を与
える [fukaikan-o ataeru] *v* offend

不快な [fukai na] *adj* obnoxious

付加価値税 [fukakachizei] 付加価値税は含ま
れていますか？ [fukakachi-zei wa fukumarete
imasu ka?] Are taxes included?

不可欠 [fukaketsu] 不可欠な [fukaketsu na]
adj indispensable

深く [fukaku] *adv* deeply

不確実 [fukakujitsu] *n* uncertainty; 不確実な
[fukakujitsu na] *adj* uncertain

不可能 [fukanou] 不可能な [fukanou na] *adj*
impossible

不完全 [fukanzen] 不完全な [fukanzen na] *adj*
incomplete

深さ [fukasa] *n* depth

ふけ [fuke] *n* dandruff

不健康 [fukenkou] 不健康な [fukenkou na] *adj*
unhealthy

不潔 [fuketsu] 不潔な [fuketsu na] *adj* filthy

吹き出物 [fukidemono] *n* pimple

不機嫌 [fukigen] 不機嫌な [fukigen na] *adj*
cross

噴きこぼれる [fukikoboreru] *v* boil over

布巾 [fukin] *n* dish towel, dishcloth

不吉 [fukitsu] 不吉な [fukitsu na] *adj* sinister

ふっかける [fukkakeru] *v* carry out; 法外な値
をふっかける [hougai na ne-o fukkakeru] *v*
rip off

復活 [fukkatsu] 復活する [fukkatsu suru] *v*
revive

復活祭 [fukkatsusai] *n* Easter; 復活祭の卵
[Fukkatsusai no tamago] *n* Easter egg

腹腔 [fukkou] 腹腔の [fukkou no] *adj* celiac

フック [fukku] *n* hook

不幸 [fukou] 不幸な [fukou na] *adj* unhappy;
不幸な出来事 [fukou na dekigoto] *n* mishap

不公平 [fukouhei] *n* injustice; 不公平な

[fukouhei na] *adj* unfair

服 [fuku] *n* clothes; 服を脱ぐ [fuku wo nugu] *v* undress; 服を着た [fuku-o kita] *adj* dressed; 服を着る [fuku wo kiru] *v* dress; 服のロッカーはどこですか? [fuku no rokkaa wa doko desu ka?] Where are the clothes lockers?; 服を干すところがありますか? [fuku o hosu tokoro ga arimasu ka?] Is there somewhere to dry clothes?; 私の服が湿っています [watashi no fuku ga shimette imasu] My clothes are damp

副 [fuku] 副作用 [fukusayou] *n* side effect

拭く [fuku] *v* wipe; 皿拭きをする [sarafuki-o suru] *v* wipe up

吹く [fuku] *v* blow; 口笛を吹く [kuchibue wo fuku] *v* whistle

腹部 [fukubu] *n* belly

複合 [fukugou] 複合の [fukugou no] *adj* complex

複合体 [fukugoutai] *n* complex

福音 [fukuin] *n* gospel

含まる [fukumaru] *v* include; 含まれた [fukumareta] *adj* included

含める [fukumeru] 含めた [fukumeta] *adj* inclusive

含む [fukumu] *v* contain, include; アルコールを含まない [arukooru wo fukumanai] *adj* alcohol-free; 脂を含んだ [abura-o fukunda] *adj* greasy; 付加価値税は含まれていますか? [fukakachi-zei wa fukumarete imasu ka?] Are taxes included?; 朝食は含まれていますか? [choushoku wa fukumarete imasu ka?] Is breakfast included?; 電気代は含まれていますか? [denki-dai wa fukumarete imasu ka?] Is the cost of electricity included?

膨らむ [fukuramu] *v* fill up; ポンプで膨らませる [ponpu de fukuramaseru] *v* pump up

袋 [fukuro] *n* bag; ビニール袋 [biniiru bukuro] *n* plastic bag; ポリエチレンの袋 [poriechiren no fukuro] *n* polyethylene bag; 買物袋 [kaimonobukuro] *n* shopping bag; 寝袋 [nebukuro] *n* sleeping bag; 小さな袋 [chiisana fukuro] *n* sachet; 余分に袋をいた

だけますか? [yobun ni fukuro o itadakemasu ka?] May I have an extra bag, please?; 袋は要りません [fukuro wa irimasen] I don't need a bag, thanks; 袋をいただけますか? [fukuro o itadakemasu ka?] May I have a bag, please?

フクロウ [fukurou] *n* owl

複製 [fukusei] *n* copy *(reproduction)*; 複製する [fukusei suru] *v* copy

復讐 [fukushuu] *n* revenge

服装 [fukusou] *npl* clothes; 服装倒錯 [fukusou tousaku] *n* transvestite; 服装の決まりがありますか? [fukusou no kimari ga arimasu ka?] Is there a dress code?

複層 [fukusou] 複層ガラス [fukusou garasu] *n* Thermopane®

複数 [fukusuu] *n* plural

複数回 [fukusuukai] 複数回乗車できる切符はありますか? [fukusuukai jousha dekiru kippu wa arimasu ka?] Do you have multitrip tickets?

服用 [fukuyou] 過量服用 [karyou fukuyou] *n* overdose

服用量 [fukuyouryou] *n* dose

複雑 [fukuzatsu] 複雑な [fukuzatsu na] *adj* complicated; 複雑な要因 [fukuzatsu na youin] *n* complication

不満 [fuman] *n* dissatisfaction; 不満な [fuman na] *adj* dissatisfied

不満足 [fumanzoku] 不満足な [fumanzoku na] *adj* unsatisfactory

不明 [fumei] *adj* missing; 私の息子が行方不明です [watashi no musuko ga yukue-fumei desu] My son is missing; 私の娘が行方不明です [watashi no musume ga yukue-fumei desu] My daughter is missing; 私の子供が行方不明です [watashi no kodomo ga yukue-fumei desu] My child is missing

不明瞭 [fumeiryou] 不明瞭な [fumeiryou na] *adj* unclear

不名誉 [fumeiyo] *n* disgrace; 不名誉な [fumeiyo na] *adj* disgraceful

踏切 [fumikiri] *n* railroad crossing

不眠症 [fuminshou] n insomnia

踏みつける [fumitsukeru] v stamp

踏む [fumu] v step on

不向き [fumuki] **不向きな** [fumuki na] adj unfit

分 [fun] n minute

船乗り [funanori] n seaman

不慣れ [funare] **不慣れの** [funare no] adj unfamiliar

船 [fune] n ship; **船に酔った** [fune ni yotta] adj seasick; **宇宙船** [uchuusen] n spacecraft; **定期船** [teikisen] n liner

舟 [fune] n boat; **漕ぎ舟** [kogibune] n rowboat

憤慨 [fungai] n indignation; **憤慨した** [fungai shita] adj resentful; **憤慨する** [fungai suru] v resent

噴火 [funka] n volcano; **噴火口** [funkakou] n volcano

粉末 [funmatsu] n powder; **粉末洗剤** [funmatsusenzai] n laundry detergent

粉末洗剤 [funmatsusenzai] **粉末洗剤はありますか?** [funmatsu-senzai wa arimasu ka?] Do you have laundry detergent?

噴霧 [funmu] n spray; **噴霧する** [funmu suru] v spray

紛失 [funshitsu] n misplaced item

噴水 [funsui] n fountain

フライ [furai] adj fried; **フライパン** [furaipan] n frying pan

フライドポテト [furaidopoteto] n french fries

フライト [furaito] n flight; **もっと早いフライトがいいのですが** [motto hayai furaito ga ii no desu ga] I'd rather have an earlier flight; **フライトは遅れています** [furaito wa okurete imasu] The flight has been delayed; **フライトをキャンセルしたいのですが** [furaito o kyanseru shitai no desu ga] I'd like to cancel my flight; **フライトを変更したいのですが** [furaito o henkou shitai no desu ga] I'd like to change my flight; **私はフライトに乗り遅れました** [watashi wa furaito ni noriokuremashita] I've missed my flight; **・・・からのフライトの手荷物はどこですか?** [... kara no furaito no tenimotsu wa doko desu ka?] Where is the luggage for the flight from...?; **・・・行きのフライトはどこでチェックインするのですか?** [... iki no furaito wa doko de chekku-in suru no desu ka?] Where do I check in for the flight to...?; **安いフライトはありますか?** [yasui furaito wa arimasu ka?] Are there any cheap flights?

フラミンゴ [furamingo] n flamingo

フラン [furan] n (食べ物) flan

フランス [furansu] n France

フランス人 [furansujin] n French (person), Frenchman, Frenchwoman

フランスの [furansuno] adj French

フラッシュ [furasshu] n flash; **フラッシュが働きません** [furasshu ga hatarakimasen] The flash isn't working

フラット [furatto] n apartment

フラットスクリーン [furattosukuriin] **フラットスクリーンの** [furatto sukuriin no] adj flat-screen

フレーバー [fureebaa] n flavor; **どんなフレーバーがありますか?** [donna fureebaa ga arimasu ka?] What flavors do you have?

フレックスタイム [furekkusutaimu] n flexitime

フレンチホルン [furenchihorun] n French horn

触れる [fureru] v touch

不利 [furi] n disadvantage

フリー [furii] adj free; **フリーキック** [furiikikku] n free kick

フリース [furiisu] n fleece

振替 [furikae] **自動振替** [jidoufurikae] n standing order

ふりをする [furi wo suru] v pretend

風呂 [furo] **泡風呂** [awaburo] n bubble bath

フロントガラス [furontogarasu] n windshield; **フロントガラスのワイパー** [furonto garasu no waipaa] n windshield wiper; **フロントガラスが割れています** [furonto-garasu ga warete imasu] The windshield is broken; **フロントガラスを拭いてもらえます**

か? [furonto-garasu o fuite moraemasu ka?] Could you clean the windshield?

フロントガラスのウォッシャー液 [furontogarasu no uossha eki] フロントガラスのウォッシャー液を補充してもらえますか? [furonto-garasu no wosshaa-eki o hojuu shite moraemasu ka?] Could you add some windshield wiper fluid?

フロッピー [furoppii] フロッピーディスク [furoppii disuku] n floppy disk

浮浪者 [furousha] n tramp (beggar)

振る [furu] vt shake; 手を振る [te wo furu] v wave

降る [furu] v fall; みぞれが降る [mizore ga furu] v sleet; 雪が降る [yuki ga furu] v snow

震える [furueru] v shiver, tremble

古い [furui] 古くなった [furuku natta] adj stale

ふるい [furui] n (ざる) sieve

振舞う [furumau] v behave

フルタイム [furutaimu] フルタイムの [furutaimu no] adj full-time; フルタイムで [furutaimu de] adv full-time

フルート [furuuto] n flute

フルーツ [furuutsu] n fruit; フルーツサラダ [furuutsusarada] n fruit salad; フルーツジュース [furuutsujuusu] n fruit juice

不良 [furyou] 消化不良 [shoukafuryou] n indigestion; 栄養不良 [eiyou furyou] n malnutrition

ふさ [fusa] n tuft; 髪のふさ [kami no fusa] n lock (hair)

ふさぐ [fusagu] v block, (じゃま) obstruct

防ぐ [fusegu] v prevent

不正 [fusei] adj improper; 不正を働く [fusei-o hataraku] v misbehave

不正確 [fuseikaku] 不正確な [fuseikaku na] adj inaccurate, incorrect

不成功 [fuseikou] 不成功に終わった [fuseikou ni owatta] adj unsuccessful

不詳 [fushou] 身元不詳の [mimoto fushou no] adj unidentified

不正直 [fushoujiki] 不正直な [fushoujiki na] adj crooked (dishonest)

不正直な [fushoujiki na] dishonest

不足 [fusoku] n shortage; 不足して [fusoku shite] adj scarce; 不足すること [fusoku suru koto] n shortfall

ふすま [fusuma] n (小麦外皮) bran

蓋 [futa] n lid

双子 [futago] n twin

双子座 [futagoza] n Gemini

再び [futatabi] adv again; 再び始められる [futatabi hajimerareru] adj renewable

不貞 [futei] 不貞な [futei na] adj unfaithful

不定詞 [futeishi] n infinitive

不適切 [futekisetsu] 不適切な [futekisetsu na] adj unsuitable

布団 [futon] n futon mattress; キルトの掛け布団 [kiruto no kakebuton] n comforter

太りすぎ [futorisugi] 太りすぎの [futori sugi no] adj overweight

太る [futoru] 丸々太った [marumaru futotta] adj chubby, plump; 太った [futotta] adj fat

不凍 [futou] 不凍液 [futoueki] n antifreeze

不当 [futou] 不当な [futou na] adj unreasonable

埠頭 [futou] n pier, quay

二日酔い [futsukayoi] n hangover

普通 [futsuu] 普通に [futsuu ni] adv normally; 普通は [futsuu wa] adv usually; 普通の [futsuu no] adj common, normal, ordinary, usual; 普通でない [futsuu de nai] adj unusual; 普通車 [futsuu-sha] a standard class cabin; 普通郵便でどのくらいの日数がかかりますか? [futsuu-yuubin de dono kurai no nissuu ga kakarimasu ka?] How long will it take by regular mail?

普通駆け足 [futsuu kakeashi] 普通駆け足で行く [futsuu kakeashi de iku] v canter

フットボール [futtobooru] n soccer; アメリカンフットボール [Amerikan futtobooru] n football; フットボールの試合 [futtobooru no shiai] n soccer game; フットボール選手 [futtobooru senshu] n soccer player

フットプリント [futtopurinto] n footprint; カーボンフットプリント [kaabon futtopurinto] n carbon footprint

沸騰 [futtou] 沸騰した [futtou shita] *adj* boiled; 沸騰する [futtou suru] *vi* boil

封 [fuu] 封をする [fuu-o suru] *v* seal

ふう [fuu] 別なふうに [betsu na fuuni] *adv* otherwise

フーバー® [fuubaa] *n* vacuum cleaner

フード [fuudo] *n* hood

フードプロセッサー [fuudopurosessaa] *n* food processor

風変わり [fuugawari] 風変わりな [fuugawari na] *adj* eccentric

封印 [fuuin] *n* seal *(mark)*

風景 [fuukei] *n* landscape, scenery

不運 [fuun] *n* misfortune

封鎖 [fuusa] *n* blockage; 道路封鎖 [douro fuusa] *n* roadblock; 封鎖された [fuusa sareta] *adj* blocked

風船 [fuusen] *n* balloon

風車 [fuusha] 風車小屋 [fuushagoya] *n* windmill

風疹 [fuushin] *n* German measles

風習 [fuushuu] *n* custom

封筒 [fuutou] *n* envelope

不和 [fuwa] *n* disagreement; 不和になる [fuwa ni naru] *v* fall out

冬 [fuyu] *n* winter

富裕 [fuyuu] *n* wealth; 富裕な [fuyuu na] *adj* wealthy

不愉快 [fuyuukai] 不愉快な [fuyukai na] *adj* unpleasant

不在 [fuzai] *n* absence; 不在の [fuzai no] *adj* absent

付属 [fuzoku] 付属物 [fuzokubutsu] *n* accessory

ふぞろい [fuzoroi] ふぞろいの [fuzoroi no] *adj* irregular

F

G

蛾 [ga] n moth

ガーナ [gaana] n Ghana; ガーナの [gaana no] adj Ghanaian

ガーナ人 [gaanajin] n Ghanaian (person)

ガーリック [gaarikku] n garlic; それにはガーリックが入っていますか？ [sore ni wa gaarikku ga haitte imasu ka?] Is there any garlic in it?

ガールフレンド [gaarufurendo] n girlfriend; 私にはガールフレンドがいます [watashi ni wa gaarufurendo ga imasu] I have a girlfriend

ガボン [gabon] n Gabon

画鋲 [gabyou] n tack, thumbtack

ガチョウ [gachou] n goose

害 [gai] 害する [gai suru] v harm

ガイアナ [gaiana] n Guyana

外部 [gaibu] 外部の [gaibu no] adj external

害虫 [gaichuu] n pest

ガイド [gaido] n guide; ガイドツアーは何時に始まりますか？ [gaido-tsuaa wa nan-ji ni hajimarimasu ka?] What time does the guided tour begin?; 英語を話すガイドはいますか？ [eigo o hanasu gaido wa imasu ka?] Is there a guide who speaks English?; 地元のウォーキングのガイドはいますか？ [jimoto no wookingu no gaido wa imasu ka?] Do you have a guide to local trails?

ガイドブック [gaidobukku] n guidebook

ガイドツアー [gaidotsuaa] n guided tour

外貨 [gaika] n foreign currency; 外貨両替所 [gaika ryougaesho] n currency exchange counter

外国 [gaikoku] 外国人 [gaikokujin] n foreigner; 外国の [gaikoku no] adj foreign

外国語 [gaikokugo] n foreign language; 外国語慣用句集 [gaikokugo kan'youku shuu] n phrasebook

外国人 [gaikokujin] n foreigner

外交 [gaikou] 外交上の [gaikoujou no] adj diplomatic; 外交官 [gaikoukan] n diplomat

街路 [gairo] 街路計画 [gairo keikaku] n street plan; 街路地図 [gairo chizu] n street map

外線電話 [gaisendenwa] n external call

外傷 [gaishou] 外傷性の [gaishou sei no] adj traumatic

外出 [gaishutsu] 外出する [gaishutsu suru] v go out

外出する [gaishutsu suru] 彼は外出しています [kare wa gaishutsu shite imasu] He's out

街灯 [gaitou] n streetlight; 街灯柱 [gaitouchuu] n lamppost

概要 [gaiyou] n outline

画家 [gaka] n painter

崖 [gake] n cliff

学会 [gakkai] n institute

がっかりする [gakkari suru] がっかりさせる [gakkari saseru] v let down; がっかりさせる [gakkari saseru] v disappointing

楽器 [gakki] n musical instrument

学期 [gakki] n term (division of year); 二学期制度の一学期 [nigakki seido no ichigakki] n semester; 学期中の中間休暇 [gakkichuu no chuukan kyuuka] n half-term (midterm vacation)

学校 [gakkou] n school; 語学学校 [gogaku gakkou] n language school; 美術学校 [bijutsugakkou] n art school; 寄宿学校 [kishuku gakkou] n boarding school; 夜間学校 [yakangakkou] n night school; 学校の制

服 [gakkou no seifuku] n school uniform; 小学校 [shougakkou] n elementary school

学 [gaku] 社会学 [shakaigaku] n sociology; 心理学 [shinrigaku] n psychology; 動物学 [doubutsugaku] n zoology

学部 [gakubu] 学部学生 [gakubu gakusei] n undergraduate

額縁 [gakubuchi] n picture frame

学童 [gakudou] n schoolchildren

楽譜 [gakufu nijuu] n score (of music)

岳救助隊 [gakukyuujotai] 一番近い山岳救助隊はどこですか? [ichiban chikai sangaku-kyuujo-tai wa doko desu ka?] Where is the nearest mountain rescue station?

学問 [gakumon] n scholarship

学年 [gakunen] n academic year

学生 [gakusei] n student; 成人学生 [seijin gakusei] n adult learner; 学生割引 [gakusei waribiki] n student discount; 学部学生 [gakubu gakusei] n undergraduate; 私は学生です [watashi wa gakusei desu] I'm a student; 学生割引はありますか? [gakusei-waribiki wa arimasu ka?] Are there any discounts for students?

楽節 [gakusetsu] n passage (musical)

学者 [gakusha] n scholar; 言語学者 [gengogakusha] n linguist; 経済学者 [keizaigakusha] n economist; 心理学者 [shinrigakusha] n psychologist

学士院 [gakushiin] n academy

学習者 [gakushuusha] n learner

がみがみ [gamigami] がみがみ小言を言う [gamigami kogoto-o iu] v nag

ガム [gamu] n gum; 風船ガム [fuusengamu] n bubble gum

癌 [gan] n cancer (illness)

がんばる [ganbaru] v bear up

ガンビア [ganbia] n Gambia

頑固 [ganko] 頑固な [ganko na] adj stubborn

頑固な [ganko na] adj obstinate, stubborn

丸薬 [ganyaku] n pill

合併 [gappei] n merger; 合併する [gappei suru] v merge

ガラガラヘビ [garagarahebi] n rattlesnake

ガラガラいう音 [garagara iu oto] n rattle

がらくた [garakuta] n junk

がらんとした [garan to shita] adj stark

ガラス [garasu] n glass; ガラス繊維 [garasu sen'i] n fiberglass; 複層ガラス [fukusou garasu] n Thermopane®; 窓ガラス [madogarasu] n windowpane

ガレージ [gareeji] n garage

ガリ勉 [gariben] ガリ勉する [gariben suru] v cram (study)

画廊 [garou] n art museum

餓死 [gashi] n starvation; 餓死する [gashi suru] v starve

画素 [gaso] n pixel

ガソリン [gasorin] n gasoline; 無鉛ガソリン [muen gasorin] n unleaded gasoline

ガソリンスタンド [gasorinsutando] n gas station

ガソリンタンク [gasorintanku] n gas tank; ガソリンタンクが漏れています [gasorin-tanku ga morete imasu] The gas tank is leaking

ガス [gasu] n gas; キャンプ用ガス [kyanpu you gasu] n portable gas cylinder; 排気ガス [haikigasu] n exhaust fumes; 催涙ガス [sairuigasu] n tear gas; 天然ガス [tennengasu] n natural gas; ガスのにおいがします [gasu no nioi ga shimasu] I can smell gas

ガスケット [gasuketto] n gasket

ガスレンジ [gasurenji] n gas stove

ガス点火器 [gasutenkaki] n gas lighter; ガス点火器用のカートリッジはありますか? [gasu-tenkaki-you no kaatorijji wa arimasu ka?] Do you have a refill for my gas lighter?

側 [gawa] n side

画像 [gazou] n graphics

ゲーム [geemu] n game; コンピューターゲーム [konpyuutaa geemu] n computer game; ゲームコンソール [geemu konsooru] n game console; ゲームセンター [geemu sentaa] n game arcade; ボードゲーム [boodo geemu]

n board game

ゲート [geeto] *n* gate; ・・・ゲートに行ってください [... geeto ni itte kudasai] Please go to gate...

芸術 [geijutsu] *n* art; 芸術的な [geijutsuteki na] *adj* artistic; 芸術家 [geijutsuka] *n* artist

芸人 [geinin] *n* performer; 大道芸人 [daidougeinin] *n* street musician

外科 [geka] 美容外科 [biyou geka] *n* plastic surgery; 外科医 [gekai] *n* surgeon; 形成外科 [keisei geka] *n* plastic surgery

劇 [geki] *n* drama, play

劇団 [gekidan] *n* theatrical troupe; レパートリー劇団 [repaatorii gekidan] *n* reperatory theater

激怒 [gekido] *n* rage; ドライバーが路上で激怒すること [doraibaa ga rojou de gekido suru koto] *n* road rage

激動 [gekidou] *n* turbulence

劇場 [gekijou] *n* theater; その劇場で何が上演されていますか? [sono gekijou de nani ga jouen sarete imasu ka?] What's on at the theater?

月経 [gekkei] *n* menstruation

現場 [genba] *n* site; 建設現場 [kensetsu genba] *n* construction site

現代 [gendai] 現代の [gendai no] *adj* contemporary, modern; 現代語 [gendaigo] *n* modern languages; 現代化する [gendaika suru] *v* modernize

言語 [gengo] *n* language; 言語の [gengo no] *adj* linguistic; 言語学者 [gengogakusha] *n* linguist

原因 [gen'in] *n* reason

現実 [genjitsu] *n* reality; 現実的な [genjitsuteki na] *adj* realistic

現実のものではない [genjitsu no mono dewa nai] *adj* unreal

現状 [genjou] *n* status quo

限界 [genkai] *n* limit

厳格 [genkaku] 厳格さ [genkakusa] *n* austerity

玄関 [genkan] *n* hallway; 玄関の呼び鈴

[genkan no yobisuzu] *n* doorbell

元気 [genki] *n* energy; 元気のよい [genki no yoi] *adj* lively

現金 [genkin] *n* cash; 現金自動支払い機 [genkin jidoushiharaiki] *n* ATM; 現金で払うと割引がありますか? [genkin de harau to waribiki ga arimasu ka?] Do you offer a discount for cash?; 私は現金がありません [watashi wa genkin ga arimasen] I don't have any cash; 私のカードを使って現金を引き出せますか? [watashi no kaado o tsukatte genkin o hikidasemasu ka?] Can I use my card to get cash?

現金化 [genkinka] *n* getting cash

げんこつ [genkotsu] *n* jab; げんこつをくらわす [genkotsu-o kurawasu] *v* punch

原稿 [genkou] *n* copy *(written text)*, manuscript

玄米 [genmai] *n* brown rice

原子 [genshi] *n* atom; 原子炉 [genshiro] *n* reactor; 原子爆弾 [genshibakudan] *n* atom bomb; 原子力の [genshiryoku no] *adj* atomic

原子力 [genshiryoku] 原子力の [genshiryoku no] *adj* atomic, nuclear

減少 [genshou] *n* decrease, reduction; 減少する [genshou suru] *v* decrease

厳守 [genshu] 時間厳守の [jikangenshu no] *adj* punctual

現在 [genzai] *n* present *(time being)*; 現在の [genzai no] *adj* current

現像 [genzou] *n* film developing

げっぷ [geppu] *n* (口) burp; げっぷをする [geppu wo suru] *v* burp

ゲレンデ [gerende] *n* ski hills; 初心者用ゲレンデ [shoshinshayou gerende] *n* bunny hill

下痢 [geri] *n* diarrhea; 私は下痢しています [watashi wa geri shite imasu] I have diarrhea

下船 [gesen] *n* disembarking

下宿人 [geshukunin] *n* lodger

下水 [gesui] *n* sewer

ゲストハウス [gesutohausu] *n* guesthouse

月曜 [getsuyou] *n* Monday; 私は月曜から具合が悪いです [watashi wa getsuyou kara guai ga warui desu] I've been sick since Monday

月曜日 [getsuyoubi] *n* Monday; 月曜日に [getsuyoubi ni] on Monday; 六月十五日の月曜日です [roku-gatsu juugo-nichi no getsuyoubi desu] It's Monday, June fifteenth

ギア [gia] *n* gear (*mechanism*); ギアがききません [gia ga kikimasen] The gears don't work

ギアボックス [giabokkusu] *n* transmission; ギアボックスが壊れています [gia-bokkusu ga kowarete imasu] The transmission is broken

ギアレバー [giarebaa] *n* gearshift

ギアシフト [giashifuto] *n* gearshift

義母 [gibo] *n* mother-in-law

議長 [gichou] *n* chairman

義父 [gifu] *n* father-in-law

ギフト [gifuto] *n* gift; ギフトショップ [gifuto shoppu] *n* gift shop; どこでギフトを買えますか? [doko de gifuto o kaemasu ka?] Where can I buy gifts?; それをギフト用にラッピングしていただけますか? [sore o gifuto-you ni rappingu shite itadakemasu ka?] Could you gift wrap it, please?

議員 [giin] *n* member; 地方議会議員 [chihou gikai giin] *n* council member

議事 [giji] 議事日程 [giji nittei] *n* agenda

技術 [gijutsu] *n* technology; 情報技術 [jouhou gijutsu] *n* IT; 技術的な [gijutsuteki na] *adj* technological; 専門技術 [senmon gijutsu] *n* technique; 専門技術者 [senmon gijutsusha] *n* technician

議会 [gikai] *n* parliament; 地方議会議員 [chihou gikai giin] *n* council member

義兄弟 [gikyoudai] *n* brother-in-law

疑問 [gimon] *n* query

疑問符 [gimonfu] *n* question mark

銀 [gin] *n* silver

ギニア [ginia] *n* Guinea; 赤道ギニア [Sekidou Ginia] *n* Equatorial Guinea

銀行 [ginkou] *n* bank (*finance*); 銀行の残高 [ginkou no zandaka] *n* bank balance; 銀行の手数料 [ginkou no tesuuryou] *n* bank charges; 銀行の明細書 [ginkou no meisaisho] *n* bank statement; 銀行家 [ginkouka] *n* banker; 銀行口座 [ginkoukouza] *n* bank account; ここに銀行はありますか? [koko ni ginkou wa arimasu ka?] Is there a bank here?; その銀行は今日開いていますか? [sono ginkou wa kyou hiraite imasu ka?] Is the bank open today?; その銀行はいつ閉まりますか? [sono ginkou wa itsu shimarimasu ka?] When does the bank close?; その銀行はいつ開きますか? [sono ginkou wa itsu hirakimasu ka?] When does the bank open?; 近くに銀行はありますか? [chikaku ni ginkou wa arimasu ka?] Is there a bank nearby?; ···にある取引銀行から送金したいのですが [... ni aru torihiki-ginkou kara soukin shitai no desu ga] I'd like to transfer some money from my bank in...; 銀行までどのくらいの距離ですか? [ginkou made dono kurai no kyori desu ka?] How far away is the bank?

儀礼 [girei] 儀礼的行為 [gireiteki koui] *n* formality

義理 [giri] 義理の姉妹 [giri no shimai] *n* sister-in-law

ギリシャ [girisha] *n* Greece

ギリシャ語 [girishago] *n* Greek (*language*)

ギリシャ人 [girishajin] *n* Greek (*person*)

ギリシャの [girisha no] *adj* Greek

犠牲 [gisei] *n* sacrifice, victim

議席 [giseki] *n* seat (*constituency*)

技師 [gishi] *n* engineer; 電気技師 [denki gishi] *n* electrician

儀式 [gishiki] *n* ceremony, ritual; 儀式の [gishiki no] *adj* ritual

偽証 [gishou] *n* perjury

ぎっしり [gisshiri] *adv* tightly; ぎっしり詰まった [gisshiri tsumatta] *adj* compact; ぎっしり詰め込んだ [gisshiri tsumekonda] *adj* jammed

G

ギター [gitaa] n guitar

偽造 [gizou] n forgery

五 [go] *number* five

五番目 [gobanme] 五番目の [go banme no] *adj* fifth

五分五分 [gobugobu] 五分五分の [gobugobu no] *adj* fifty-fifty; 五分五分で [gobugobu de] *adv* fifty-fifty

伍長 [gochou] n corporal

ゴッドファーザー [goddofaazaa] n godfather *(criminal leader)*

護衛 [goei] n stewardship; 護衛されている輸送車隊 [goei sareteiru yusoushatai] n convoy; 護衛する [goei suru] v escort

語学 [gogaku] n language study; 語学ラボ [gogaku rabo] n language laboratory; 語学学校 [gogaku gakkou] n language school

五月 [gogatsu] n May

午後 [gogo] n afternoon; 午後の [gogo no] *abbr* p.m.; 明日の午後 [asu no gogo] tomorrow afternoon; 午後に [gogo ni] in the afternoon

語彙 [goi] n vocabulary

ご一緒 [go issho] *adv* together; また近いうちにお仕事でご一緒できることを願っています [mata chikai uchi ni o-shigoto de go-issho dekiru koto o negatte imasu] I hope we can work together again soon

五時 [goji] 五時前に [go-ji mae ni] before five o'clock

五十 [gojuu] *number* fifty

誤解 [gokai] n misunderstanding; 誤解する [gokai suru] v misunderstand; 誤解を招きやすい [gokai-o manekiyasui] *adj* misleading; 誤解があります [gokai ga arimasu] There's been a misunderstanding

語形 [gokei] 語形変化 [gokei henka] n conjugation

ゴキブリ [gokiburi] n cockroach

ごめんなさい [gomen nasai] I'm sorry, Sorry; 本当にごめんなさい [hontou nigomennasai] I'm very sorry

ごめんなさい! [gomen nasai] *excl* sorry!

ごみ [gomi] n garbage, litter *(trash)*, refuse, trash; ごみ捨て場 [gomi suteba] n dump, landfill; ごみ収集人 [gomishuushuunin] n garbage collector; ごみはどこに出すのですか? [gomi wa doko ni dasu no desu ka?] Where do we leave the trash?

ごみ箱 [gomibako] n garbage can, wastebasket

ゴム [gomu] n rubber; ゴム手袋 [gomu tebukuro] n rubber gloves; 輪ゴム [wagomu] n rubber band; 弾性ゴム [dansei gomu] n rubber band

娯楽 [goraku] n pastime

ゴリラ [gorira] n gorilla

ゴルフ [gorufu] n golf; ゴルフ用クラブ [gorufu you kurabu] n golf club *(game)*; ゴルフ場 [gorufujou] n golf course; どこでゴルフができますか? [doko de gorufu ga dekimasu ka?] Where can I play golf?; この近くに公共のゴルフコースはありますか? [kono chikaku ni kookyou no gorufu-koosu wa arimasu ka?] Is there a public golf course near here?; ゴルフクラブを貸し出していますか? [gorufu-kurabu o kashidashite imasu ka?] Do they rent out golf clubs?

ゴルフクラブ [gorufukurabu] n golf club *(society)*

誤植 [goshoku] n misprint

ゴツン [gotsun] n whack; ゴツンと打つ [gotsun to utsu] v thump

強奪 [goudatsu] n mugging; 襲って強奪する [osotte goudatsu suru] v mug

合同 [goudou] 合同する [goudou suru] v chip in

ゴーグル [gouguru] n goggles; ゴーグルを借りたいのですが [googuru o karitai no desu ga] I want to rent goggles

合法 [gouhou] 合法的な [gouhouteki na] *adj* legal

合意 [goui] n agreement; 合意された [goui sareta] *adj* agreed

合格 [goukaku] n pass *(meets standard)*; 合格する [goukaku suru] v pass *(an exam)*

強姦 [goukan] 強姦者 [goukansha] n rapist

合計 [goukei] n sum, total; ···を合計する [...-o goukei suru] v add up

拷問 [goumon] n torture; 拷問にかける [goumon ni kakeru] v torture

合理 [gouri] 理にかなった [ri ni kanatta] adj rational

ゴール [gouru] n goal

ゴールキーパー [gourukiipaa] n goalkeeper

強盗 [goutou] n (人) mugger, (人) robber, (行為) robbery, (量・程度) hold-up

午前 [gozen] n morning; 午前の [gozen no] abbr a.m.; 午前中に [gozen-chuu ni] in the morning

具 [gu] n stand; 水彩絵の具 [suisai enogu] n watercolor

具合 [guai] n condition

グアテマラ [guatemara] n Guatemala

愚人 [gujin] n lunatic

グカード [gukaado] グリーティングカード [guriitingukaado] n greeting card

軍 [gun] 軍の [gun no] adj military; 空軍 [kuugun] n Air Force

軍人 [gunjin] n serviceman; 女性軍人 [josei gunjin] n servicewoman

群集 [gunshuu] n crowd

軍曹 [gunsou] n sergeant

軍隊 [guntai] n army, troops

グラフ [gurafu] n graph

グライダー [guraidaa] n glider; グライダー競技 [guraidaa kyougi] n gliding

グラム [guramu] n gram

グラウンド [guraundo] n playing field

グレービーソース [gureebiisoosu] n gravy

グレープフルーツ [gureepufuruutsu] n grapefruit

グレートブリテン [gureetoburiten] n Great Britain

グリッド [guriddo] n grid

グリーンランド [guriinrando] n Greenland

グリーティン [guriitin] n greeting; グリーティングカード [guriitingukaado] n greeting card

グリル [guriru] n grill; グリルで焼く [guriru de yaku] v broiler; 網焼きにする [amiyaki ni suru] adj broiled

グローバル [guroobaru] adj global; グローバル化 [guroobaruka] n globalization

グローバルポジショニングシステム [guroobarupojishoningushisutemu] n GPS; グローバルポジショニングシステムはついていますか? [guroobaru-pojishoningu-shisutemu wa tsuite imasu ka?] Does it have GPS?

グローブ [guroobu] n glove; グローブボックス [guroobubokkusu] n glove compartment

グルジア [gurujia] n Georgia (country); グルジアの [Gurujia no] adj Georgian (re Georgia)

グルジア人 [gurujiajin] n Georgian (inhabitant of Georgia)

グルコース [gurukoosu] n glucose

グルテン [guruten] n gluten; グルテンを使っていない料理はありますか? [guruten o tsukatte inai ryouri wa arimasu ka?] Do you have gluten-free dishes?; グルテンを使わずに食事を用意していただけますか? [guruten o tsukawazu ni shokuji o youi shite itadakemasu ka?] Could you prepare a meal without gluten?

グループ [guruupu] n group

グーグル® [guuguru] グーグル®で調べる [Guuguru® de shiraberu] v Google®

偶然 [guuzen] n coincidence; 偶然に [guuzen ni] adv accidentally, casually; 偶然の [guuzen no] adj accidental, casual

グーズベリー [guuzuberii] n gooseberry

逆 [gyaku] n reverse; 逆に [gyaku ni] adv vice versa; 逆にする [gyaku ni suru] v reverse

逆戻り [gyakumodori] n relapse

虐待 [gyakutai] n abuse; 虐待する [gyakutai suru] v abuse; 児童虐待 [jidou gyakutai] n child abuse

ギャンブラー [gyanburaa] n gambler

ギャンブル [gyanburu] n gambling

ギャング [gyangu] n gang; ギャングの一員 [gyangu no ichiin] n gangster

ギャロップ [gyaroppu] *n* gallop; ギャロップで走る [gyaroppu de hashiru] *v* gallop

漁業 [gyogyou] *n* fishing

魚介類 [gyokairui] 魚介類を使わずに食事を用意していただけますか? [gyokairui o tsukawazu ni shokuji o youi shite itadakemasu ka?] Could you prepare a meal without seafood?

漁船 [gyosen] *n* fishing boat

ぎょっとさせる [gyotto saseru] *v* frightening

業 [gyou] *n* industry; 旅行業 [ryokou gyou] *n* tourism

行儀 [gyougi] *n* manners; 行儀のよい [gyougi no yoi] *adj* well-behaved

業者 [gyousha] 旅行業者 [ryokougyousha] *n* tour operator, travel agent; 製造業者 [seizougyousha] *n* manufacturer; 建築業者 [kenchikugyousha] *n* building contractor; 密輸業者 [mitsuyu gyousha] *n* smuggler; 出版業者 [shuppan gyousha] *n* publisher; 印刷業者 [insatsu gyousha] *n* printer *(person)*; 卸売業者 [oroshiuri gyousha] *n* distributor; 小売業者 [kourigyousha] *n* retailer

牛肉 [gyuuniku] *n* beef

牛乳 [gyuunyuu] *n* milk; 超高温殺菌牛乳 [choukouon sakkin gyuunyuu] *n* UHT milk; あなたは牛乳を飲みますか? [anata wa gyuunyuu o nomimasu ka?] Do you drink milk?; それは低温殺菌していない牛乳を使って作られていますか? [sore wa teion-sakkin shite inai gyuunyuu o tsukatte tsukurarete imasu ka?] Is it made with unpasteurised milk?; 本物の牛乳はありますか? [honmono no gyuunyuu wa arimasu ka?] Do you have real milk?

H

歯 [ha] *n* tooth; 歯の [ha no] *adj* dental; 歯が
生える [ha ga haeru] *v* teethe; 歯ブラシ
[haburashi] *n* toothbrush; 練り歯ミガキ [neri
hamigaki] *n* toothpaste; 入れ歯 [ireba] *n*
dentures; この歯が痛みます [kono ha ga
itamimasu] This tooth hurts; 私は歯を折りま
した [watashi wa ha o orimashita] I've
broken a tooth

派 [ha] *n* group; 過激派 [kagekiha] *n*
extremist

葉 [ha] *n* leaf, leaves

刃 [ha] *n* blade; 安全かみそりの刃 [anzen
kamisori no ha] *n* razor blade

ハーブ [haabu] *n* herbs

ハーブティー [haabuteii] *n* herbal tea

ハードボード [haadoboodo] *n* hardboard

ハードディスク [haadodisuku] *n* hard disk

ハードコピー [haadokopii] *n* hard copy,
printout

ハードル [haadoru] *n* hurdle

ハードウェア [haadouea] *n* hardware

ハーフタイム [haafutaimu] *n* half-time

ハーモニカ [haamonika] *n* harmonica

ハープ [haapu] *n* harp

幅 [haba] *n* width

幅木 [habaki] *n* baseboard

幅跳び [habatobi] *n* long jump

省く [habuku] *v* leave out

ハブキャップ [habukyappu] *n* hubcap

鉢 [hachi] *n* flowerpot; 植木鉢 [uekibachi] *n*
planter; 鉢植え植物 [hachiue shokubutsu] *n*
potted plant

八 [hachi] *number* eight

ハチ [hachi] *n* (昆虫) bee

八番目 [hachibanme] *n* eighth; 八番目の

[hachi banme no] *adj* eighth

八月 [hachigatsu] *n* August

八時 [hachiji] *n* 8 o'clock

八十 [hachijuu] *number* eighty

蜂蜜 [hachimitsu] *n* honey

波長 [hachou] *n* wavelength

爬虫類 [hachuurui] *n* reptile

肌 [hada] *n* skin; 鳥肌 [torihada] *n* goose
pimples

肌着 [hadagi] *n* undershirt

裸 [hadaka] 裸の [hadaka no] *adj* naked,
nude

裸足 [hadashi] 裸足の [hadashi no] *adj*
barefoot; 裸足で [hadashi de] *adv* barefoot

派手な [hade na] *adj* gaudy

ハドック [hadokku] *n* haddock

ハエ [hae] *n* fly

生える [haeru] *vi* grow; 歯が生える [ha ga
haeru] *v* teethe

はがき [hagaki] *n* postcard; 郵便はがき
[yuubin hagaki] *n* postcard; どこで郵便はが
きを買えますか? [doko de yuubin-hagaki o o
kaemasu ka?] Where can I buy some
postcards?; 私は郵便はがきを探しています
[watashi wa yuubin-hagaki o sagashite
imasu] I'm looking for postcards; 郵便はが
きはありますか? [yuubin-hagaki wa arimasu
ka?] Do you have any postcards?

励み [hagemi] *n* encouragement; 励みになる
[hagemi ni naru] *adj* encouraging

はげる [hageru] *v* become bald; 頭のはげた
[atama no hageta] *adj* bald

ハゲワシ [hagewashi] *n* vulture

はぐ [hagu] *v* strip

歯ぐき [haguki] *n* gums

母 [haha] *n* mother; 代理母 [dairibo] *n* surrogate mother; 継母 [mama haha] *n* stepmother

破片 [hahen] *n* splinter

灰 [hai] *n* ash; 灰の水曜日 [hai no suiyoubi] *n* Ash Wednesday

肺 [hai] *n* lung

はい [hai] Yes ▷ *excl* yes!

配置 [haichi] *n* layout, placement

ハイチ [haichi] *n* Haiti

背泳 [haiei] *n* backstroke

肺炎 [haien] *n* pneumonia

ハイファイ [haifai] ハイファイ装置 [haifai souchi] *n* hi-fi

配布 [haifu] 配布する [haifu suru] *v* give out

ハイフン [haifun] *n* hyphen

配偶者 [haiguusha] *n* spouse

ハイヒール [haihiiru] *n* high heels; ハイヒールの [haihiiru no] *adj* high-heeled

灰色 [haiiro] 灰色の [hai iro no] *adj* gray

ハイジャック [haijakku] ハイジャックの犯人 [haijakku no hannin] *n* hijacker; ハイジャックする [haijakku suru] *v* hijack

排除 [haijo] 可能性を排除する [kanousei-o haijo suru] *v* rule out

ハイカー [haikaa] *n* hiker

配管 [haikan] *n* plumbing; 配管工 [haikankou] *n* plumber

背景 [haikei] *n* background

敗血症 [haiketsushou] *n* blood poisoning

排気 [haiki] 排気ガス [haikigasu] *n* exhaust fumes

廃棄 [haiki] 廃棄する [haiki suru] *v* scrap

ハイキング [haikingu] *n* hike, hiking

ハイライト [hairaito] *n* (やま場) highlight, (化粧品) highlighter; 私はハイライトを入れています [watashi wa hairaito o irete imasu] My hair is highlighted

入る [hairu] *v* come in, enter, go in; 中に入れない [naka ni irenai] *v* keep out; ひびの入った [hibi no haitta] *adj* cracked; お入りください! [o-hairi kudasai!] Come in!

敗者 [haisha] *n* loser

歯医者 [haisha] *n* dentist; 私は歯医者さんに診てもらわなければなりません [watashi wa haisha-san ni mite morawanakereba narimasen] I need a dentist

廃止 [haishi] *n* abolition; 廃止する [haishi suru] *v* abolish

排水 [haisui] 排水する [haisui suru] *v* drain; 排水管 [haisuikan] *n* drain, drainpipe; 排水口 [haisuikou] *n* drain

排水管 [haisuikan] *n* drain pipe

配達 [haitatsu] *n* delivery; 新聞配達 [shinbun haitatsu] *n* paper route; 郵便配達人 [yuubin haitatsunin] *n* mail deliverer; 配達する [haitatsu suru] *v* deliver; 女性郵便配達人 [josei yuubin haitatsunin] *n* femail mail deliverer

俳優 [haiyuu] *n* actor; 喜劇俳優 [kigeki haiyuu] *n* comedian

灰皿 [haizara] *n* ashtray; 灰皿をいただけますか? [haizara o itadakemasu ka?] May I have an ashtray?

始まる [hajimaru] *vi* start

初め [hajime] 初めは [hajime wa] *adv* originally; 六月の初めに [roku-gatsu no hajime ni] at the beginning of June

始め [hajime] *n* beginning

始める [hajimeru] *v* begin ▷ *vt* start

恥じて [hajite] *adj* ashamed

波状 [hajou] 波状の [hajou no] *adj* wavy

墓 [haka] *n* grave, tomb

破壊 [hakai] *n* break, destruction; 故意に破壊する [koi ni hakai suru] *v* sabotage, vandalize; 故意の破壊 [koi no hakai] *n* sabotage; 破壊する [hakai suru] *v* destroy; 破壊行為 [hakai koui] *n* vandalism; 破壊者 [hakaisha] *n* vandal

墓石 [hakaishi] *n* gravestone

測る [hakaru] *v* gauge

博士号 [hakasegou] *n* PhD

派遣 [haken] 代表として派遣する [daihyou toshite haken suru] *v* delegate

破棄 [haki] 破棄する [haki suru] *v* rip up

吐き出す [hakidasu] 息を吐き出す [iki-o

hakidasu] v breathe out

吐き気 [hakike] n nausea; つわりの時期の朝の吐き気 [tsuwari no jiki no asa no hakike] n morning sickness; 吐き気がする [hakike ga suru] v feel sick; 吐き気をもよおさせる [hakike-o moyousaseru] adj sickening

ハッカー [hakkaa] n hacker

発汗 [hakkan] 発汗抑制剤 [hakkan yokuseizai] n antiperspirant

発見 [hakken] n discovery; 発見する [hakken suru] v discover, find out

白血病 [hakketsubyou] n leukemia

はっきり [hakkiri] adv clearly

箱 [hako] n box; 貯金箱 [chokinbako] n piggy bank

運び去る [hakobi saru] v take away

運ぶ [hakobu] v carry

箔 [haku] アルミ箔 [arumihaku] n tinfoil

掃く [haku] v sweep

吐く [haku] v throw up, vomit; つばを吐く [tsuba wo haku] v spit

博物館 [hakubutsukan] n museum; その博物館はいつ開きますか? [sono hakubutsukan wa itsu hirakimasu ka?] When is the museum open?; その博物館は毎日開いていますか? [sono hakubutsukan wa mainichi hiraite imasu ka?] Is the museum open every day?; その博物館は日曜日は開いていますか? [sono hakubutsukan wa nichiyoubi wa hiraite imasu ka?] Is the museum open on Sundays?; その博物館は午後開いていますか? [sono hakubutsukan wa gogo hiraite imasu ka?] Is the museum open in the afternoon?; その博物館は午前中開いていますか? [sono hakubutsukan wa gozen-chuu hiraite imasu ka?] Is the museum open in the morning?

白鳥 [hakuchou] n swan

迫害 [hakugai] 迫害する [hakugai suru] v persecute

白状 [hakujou] n confession; すっかり白状する [sukkari hakujou suru] v own up

白内障 [hakunaishou] n cataract (eye)

白紙 [hakushi] 白紙の [hakushi no] adj blank

拍手 [hakushu] n applause; 拍手する [hakushu suru] v clap; 拍手を送る [hakushu-o okuru] v applaud

浜辺 [hamabe] n beach

葉巻き [hamaki] n cigar

ハム [hamu] n ham

ハムスター [hamusutaa] n hamster

版 [han] n edition, version

犯 [han] 凶悪犯 [kyouakuhan] n thug

班 [han] 交替班 [koutai han] n relay race

半 [han] n half

花 [hana] n blossom, flower; 花が咲く [hana ga saku] v blossom, flower; 花屋 [hanaya] n florist

鼻 [hana] n nose; 鼻の穴 [hana no ana] n nostril; 鼻で吸う [hana de suu] v sniff

花火 [hanabi] n fireworks

鼻血 [hanaji] n nosebleed

花婿 [hanamuko] n bridegroom

離れる [hanareru] v leave; 遠く離れて [touku hanarete] adv remotely; 遠く離れた [touku hanareta] adj remote; 離れて [hanarete] adv away; 離れて [hanarete] adv off; 離れた [hanareta] adj distant

離れわざ [hanarewaza] n stunt

話せる [hanaseru] v be able to speak

話 [hanashi] n tale, talk; 話に出す [hanashi ni dasu] v mention; 話がわかる [hanashi ga wakaru] adj understanding; 話好きな [hanashi zuki na] adj talkative

話し [hanashi] 話し中の信号音 [hanashichuu no shingouon] n busy signal; 話し手 [hanashite] n teller

話し合う [hanashiau] ···を話し合う [...-o hanashiau] v discuss

話し中 [hanashichuu] お話し中です [o-hanashi-chuu desu] It's busy

話しかける [hanashikakeru] ···に話しかける [... ni hanashikakeru] v talk to

話します [hanashimasu] 何語が話せますか? [nani-go ga hanasemasu ka?] What languages do you speak?; あなたは英語を

話しますか? [anata wa eigo o hanashimasu ka?] Do you speak English?; 誰か英語を話せる人はいますか? [dare ka eigo o hanaseru hito wa imasu ka?] Does anyone speak English?; 私は英語をほとんど話せません [watashi wa eigo o hotondo hanasemasen] I speak very little English; 私は英語を話せません [watashi wa eigo o hanasemasen] I don't speak English; 私は・・・を話します [watashi wa... go o hanashimasu] I speak...

話す [hanasu] v speak, talk; 話す人 [hanasu hito] n speaker; 遠慮なく話す [enryo naku hanasu] v speak up; あなたと個人的にお話ができますか? [anata to kojin-teki ni o-hanashi ga dekimasu ka?] May I speak to you in private?; お医者さんと話をしたいのですが [o-isha-san to hanashi o shitai no desu ga] I'd like to speak to a doctor; オーナーと話させていただけますか? [oonaa to hanasasete itadakemasu ka?] Could I speak to the owner, please?; もっと大きな声で話していただけますか? [motto ooki-na koe de hanashite itadakemasu ka?] Could you speak louder, please?; マネージャーと話させてください [maneejaa to hanasasete kudasai] I'd like to speak to the manager, please; 私は婦人警官と話したいのです [watashi wa fujin-keikan to hanashitai no desu] I want to speak to a policewoman

話す [hanasu] もっとゆっくり話していただけますか? [motto yukkuri hanashite itadakemasu ka?] Could you speak more slowly, please?

放つ [hanatsu] v release; 悪臭を放つ [akushuu-o hanatsu] v stink

花嫁 [hanayome] n bride

ハンバーガー [hanbaagaa] n hamburger

販売 [hanbai] n sale; 信用販売 [shinyou hanbai] n credit; 販売価格 [hanbai kakaku] n selling price; 販売スタッフ [hanbai sutaffu] n sales assistant; 販売期限 [hanbai kigen] n sell-by date; 販売員 [hanbaiin] n sales rep

販売機 [hanbaiki] 自動販売機 [jidouhanbaiki] n vending machine

販売店 [hanbaiten] n vendor; 乳製品販売店 [nyuuseihin hanbaiten] n dairy; 新聞販売店 [shinbunhanbaiten] n newsdealer

反駁 [hanbaku] n contradiction; 反駁する [hanbaku suru] v contradict

半分 [hanbun] n half; 半分の [hanbun no] adj half; 半分だけ [hanbun dake] adv half

判断 [handan] 判断する [handan suru] v believe; 判断を誤る [handan-o ayamaru] v misjudge

半脱脂 [handasshi] 半脱脂乳 [han dasshi nyuu] n reduced-fat milk

ハンディーキャップ [handiikyappu] あなたのハンディーキャップはどのくらいですか? [anata no handiikyappu wa dono kurai desu ka?] What's your handicap?; 私のハンディーキャップは・・・です [watashi no handiikyappu wa... desu] My handicap is...

ハンドバッグ [handobaggu] n handbag

ハンドボール [handobooru] n handball

ハンドブック [handobukku] n handbook

ハンドブレーキ [handobureeki] n emergency brake

判読しにくい [handokushinikui] adj illegible

ハンドメイド [handomeido] adj hand-made

ハンドル [handoru] n (自転車・バイク) handlebars, (取っ手) handle; ドアハンドル [doahandoru] n door handle; 右ハンドル [migi handoru] n right-hand drive

反動 [handou] n repercussions

羽 [hane] n feather

繁栄 [han-ei] n prosperity

はねかける [hanekakeru] v splash

ハネムーン [hanemuun] n honeymoon; 私たちはハネムーン中です [watashi-tachi wa hanemuun-chuu desu] We're on our honeymoon

半円 [han'en] n semicircle

跳ねる [haneru] v leap; 飛び跳ねる [tobihaneru] v skip

ハンガー [hangaa] n coat hanger, hanger

半額 [hangaku] 半額の [hangaku no] *adj* half-price; 半額で [hangaku de] *adv* half-price

ハンガリー [hangarii] *n* Hungary

ハンガリー人 [hangariijin] *n* Hungarian *(person)*

ハンガリーの [hangarii no] *adj* Hungarian

ハンググライディング [hanguguraideingu] *n* hang gliding

範囲 [han-i] *n* range *(limits)*

判事 [hanji] *n* judge; 治安判事 [chian hanji] *n* magistrate

繁華 [hanka] 繁華街へ [hankagai-e] *adv* downtown

ハンカチ [hankachi] *n* handkerchief, hankie

版権 [hanken] *n* copyright

判決 [hanketsu] 判決を下す [hanketsu-o kudasu] *v* sentence

反響 [hankyou] *n* echo

半狂乱 [hankyouran] 半狂乱の [hankyouran no] *adj* frantic

ハンマー [hanmaa] *n* hammer

ハンモック [hanmokku] *n* hammock

犯人 [hannin] *n* criminal; ハイジャックの犯人 [haijakku no hannin] *n* hijacker

反応 [hannou] *n* reaction; 反応する [hannou suru] *v* react

反復 [hanpuku] 反復性の [hanpuku sei no] *adj* repetitive

氾濫 [hanran] *n* flooding; 氾濫させる [hanran saseru] *vt* flood; 氾濫する [hanran suru] *vi* flood

伴る [hanru] 雷鳴を伴った [raimei-o tomonatta] *adj* thundery

ハンサム [hansamu] ハンサムな [hansamu na] *adj* handsome

反射 [hansha] *n* reflection; 反射作用 [hansha sayou] *n* reflex; 反射する [hansha suru] *v* reflect

繁殖 [hanshoku] *n* reproduction

繁殖力 [hanshokuryoku] *n* fertility; 繁殖力のない [hanshokuryoku no nai] *adj* infertile; 繁殖力のある [hanshokuryoku no aru] *adj* fertile

ハンター [hantaa] *n* hunter

反対 [hantai] *n* objection, opposition; 反対した [hantai shita] *adj* opposed; 反対する [hantai suru] *adj* oppose, opposing

半島 [hantou] *n* peninsula

犯罪 [hanzai] *n* crime; サイバー犯罪 [saibaa hanzai] *n* cybercrime; 犯罪の [hanzai no] *adj* criminal; 犯罪者 [hanzaisha] *n* criminal, culprit

ハンズフリー [hanzufurii] ハンズフリーの [hanzufurii no] *adj* hands-free; ハンズフリーキット [hanzu furii kitto] *n* hands-free kit

発砲 [happou] *n* shot

発表 [happyou] *n* announcement; 発表する [happyou suru] *v* announce

腹 [hara] *n* abdomen; 腹の減った [hara no hetta] *adj* hungry; 腹を立てた [hara-o tateta] *adj* mad *(angry)*

ハラール [haraaru] *adj* halal; ハラール料理はありますか? [haraaru-ryouri wa arimasu ka?] Do you have halal dishes?

腹立たしい [haradata shii] *adj* infuriating

払い戻し [haraimodoshi] *n* refund

払い戻す [haraimodosu] *v* pay back, refund; 払い戻してもらえますか? [haraimodoshite moraemasu ka?] Can I have a refund?

払う [harau] *v* pay/sweep; ほこりを払う [hokori-o harau] *v* dust; 分割払い [bunkatsu harai] *n* installment; 十分な額が払われていない [juubun na gaku ga harawarete inai] *adj* underpaid

晴れる [hareru] *v* be clear; 晴れています [harete imasu] It's sunny; 晴れますか? [haremasu ka?] Is the weather going to be good?

腫れる [hareru] swell; 腫れた [hareta] *adj* swollen

破裂 [haretsu] 破裂する [haretsu suru] *v* burst; タイヤが破裂しました [taiya ga haretsu shimashita] The tire has burst

針 [hari] *n* needle; 針と糸をお持ちですか? [hari to ito o o-mochi desu ka?] Do you have a needle and thread?

鍼 [hari] n acupuncture

針金 [harigane] n wire

ハリケーン [harikeen] n hurricane

ハリネズミ [harinezumi] n hedgehog

春 [haru] n spring *(season)*

張る [haru] v stretch; ぴんと張った [pin to hatta] adj tight; タイルを張った [tairu-o hatta] adj tiled; 虚勢を張る [kyosei-o haru] v bluff

はさみ [hasami] n clippers, scissors; 爪切りばさみ [tsume kiri basami] n nail scissors

破産 [hasan] 破産した [hasan shita] adj bankrupt, broke

端 [hashi] n edge

箸 [hashi] n chopsticks

橋 [hashi] n bridge

はしご [hashigo] n ladder

はしか [hashika] n measles; 私は最近はしかにかかりました [watashi wa saikin hashika ni kakarimashita] I had measles recently

柱 [hashira] n pillar, post *(stake)*; 街灯柱 [gaitouchuu] n lamppost

走り書き [hashirigaki] 走り書きする [hashirigaki suru] v scribble

走り高跳ぶ [hashiritakatobu] 走り高跳び [hashiri takatobi] n high jump

走る [hashiru] vi run; を走る [-o hashiru] vt run; 走ること [hashiru koto] n run; 全力で走る [zenryoku de hashiru] v sprint

破傷風 [hashoufuu] n tetanus

破損 [hason] n damage; 着いた私のスーツケースが破損しています [tsuita watashi no suutsukeesu ga hason shite imasu] My suitcase has arrived damaged; 私の手荷物が破損しています [watashi no tenimotsu ga hason shite imasu] My luggage has been damaged

発生する [hassei suru] v occur; 繰り返し発生する [kurikaeshi hassei suru] adj recurring

発信 [hasshin] 発信音 [hasshin-on] n dial tone

発疹 [hasshin] n rash; 私は発疹がでました

[watashi wa hasshin ga demashita] I have a rash

発送 [hassou] 発送する [hassou suru] v send out

旗 [hata] n flag

働く [hataraku] v work; 奴隷のように働く [dorei no youni hataraku] v slave away; 共同して働く [kyoudou shite hataraku] v collaborate; フラッシュが働きません [furasshu ga hatarakimasen] The flash isn't working; 私はオフィスで働いています [watashi wa ofisu de hataraite imasu] I work in an office; 私は病院で働いています [watashi wa byouin de hataraite imasu] I work in a hospital; 私は働いています [watashi wa hataraite imasu] I work; 私は工場で働いています [watashi wa koujou de hataraite imasu] I work in a factory

働く人 [hatarakuhito] n worker

果たす [hatasu] v fulfill

ハッチバック [hatchibakku] n hatchback

鳩 [hato] n pigeon

ハト [hato] n dove

発電機 [hatsudenki] n generator

ハツカネズミ [hatsukanezumi] n mouse

発明 [hatsumei] n invention; 発明する [hatsumei suru] v invent; 発明者 [hatsumeisha] n inventor

発音 [hatsuon] n pronunciation; 発音する [hatsuon suru] v pronounce

発展 [hatten] n development, evolution; 発展させる [hatten saseru] vt develop; 発展する [hatten suru] vi develop; 発展途上国 [hattentojoukoku] n developing country

這う [hau] v crawl

ハウスワイン [hausuwain] n house wine; ハウスワインのボトルを1本 [hausu-wain no botoru o ippon] a bottle of the house wine

速足 [hayaashi] 速足で駆ける [hayaashi de kakeru] v trot

早い [hayai] adj early; より早く [yori hayaku] adv sooner; もっと早いフライトがいいのですが [motto hayai furaito ga ii no desu ga] I'd rather have an earlier flight

速い [hayai] *adj* fast

早く [hayaku] *adv* early; できるだけ早く [dekiru dake hayaku] *adv* ASAP

速く [hayaku] *adv* fast

はやる [hayaru] *v* become popular; はやらない [hayaranai] *adj* unfashionable

速さ [hayasa] *n* speed

早瀬 [hayase] *n* rapids

恥ずかしい [hazukashii] *adj* embarassed; 恥ずかしい思い [hazukashii omoi] *n* shame

弾む [hazumu] *v* bounce

ヘア [hea] *n* hair; ヘアスタイル [heasutairu] *n* hairdo, hairstyle

ヘアバンド [heabando] *n* headband

ヘアブラシ [heaburashi] *n* hairbrush

ヘアドライヤー [headoraiyaa] *n* hair dryer

ヘアジェル [heajieru] *n* hair gel

ヘアカット [heakatto] *n* haircut

ヘアピン [heapin] *n* bobby pin

ヘアスプレー [heasupuree] *n* hair spray

ヘビ [hebi] *n* snake

ヘッドホン [heddohon] *n* headphones; ヘッドホンはついていますか? [heddohon wa tsuite imasu ka?] Does it have headphones?

ヘッドライト [heddoraito] *n* headlight

ヘッドランプ [heddoranpu] *n* headlight; ヘッドランプがつきません [heddoranpu ga tsukimasen] The headlights aren't working

ヘッドスカーフ [heddosukaafu] *n* headscarf

ヘーゼルナッツ [heezerunattsu] *n* hazelnut

兵 [hei] *n* soldier; 偵察兵 [teisatsuhei] *n* scout

平原 [heigen] *n* plain

平日 [heijitsu] *n* weekday

平価 [heika] 平価切下げ [heikakirisage] *n* devaluation

閉経 [heikei] 閉経期 [heikeiki] *n* menopause

平均 [heikin] *n* average; 平均の [heikin no] *adj* average

平行 [heikou] 平行の [heikou no] *adj* parallel

平面 [heimen] *n* plane *(surface)*

平穏 [heion] *n* peace

閉鎖 [heisa] *n* closure; 閉鎖する [heisa suru] *v* shut down

弊社 [heisha] *n* company; 弊社についての情報です [heisha ni tsuite no jouhou desu] Here's some information about my company

兵士 [heishi] *n* soldier

閉所 [heisho] *n* partition; 閉所恐怖症の [heisho kyoufushou no] *adj* claustrophobic

閉塞 [heisoku] 閉塞物 [heisokubutsu] *n* block *(obstruction)*

平坦な [heitan na] *adj* plain

閉店 [heiten] 閉店時刻 [heiten jikoku] *n* closing time

平和な [heiwa na] *adj* peaceful

へこみ [hekomi] *n* dent

へこむ [hekomu] *v* dent

変動 [hendou] 気候変動 [kikou hendo] *n* climate change

返事 [henji] *n* reply; 返事をする [henji-o suru] *v* reply

変化 [henka] *n* change, shift; 語形変化 [gokei henka] *n* conjugation; 変化する [henka suru] *v* range

偏見 [henken] *n* prejudice; 偏見をもった [henken-o motta] *adj* prejudiced

返金 [henkin] *n* refund

変更 [henkou] *n* modification; 変更する [henkou suru] *v* alter, modify

変な [hen na] *adj* odd, peculiar, weird

ヘンパーティー [henpaatii] *n* bachelorette party

返品 [henpin] これを返品したいのですが [kore o henpin shitai no desu ga] I'd like to return this

返済 [hensai] *n* repayment; 返済する [hensai suru] *v* repay

編成 [hensei] 再編成する [saihensei suru] *v* reorganize, restructure

編集 [henshuu] 編集者 [henshuusha] *n* editor

変装 [hensou] 変装する [hensou suru] *v*

disguise

扁桃 [hentou] n tonsils; 扁桃腺炎 [hentousen'en] n tonsillitis

返答 [hentou] n response; 返答する [hentou suru] v respond

変容 [henyou] 変容させる [hen'you saseru] v transform

片頭痛 [henzutsuu] n migraine

へら [hera] n spatula

減らす [herasu] v diminish, reduce

へり [heri] n margin

ヘリコプター [herikoputaa] n helicopter

ヘロイン [heroin] n heroin

減る [heru] v decrease; 腹の減った [hara no hetta] adj hungry

ヘルメット [herumetto] n helmet; ヘルメットをください [herumetto o kudasai] May I have a helmet?

ヘルニア [herunia] n hernia

ヘルプライン [herupurain] n helpline

へそ [heso] n navel

部屋 [heya] n room; 子供部屋 [kodomobeya] n nursery; 今晩部屋はありますか? [konban heya wa arimasu ka?] Do you have a room for tonight?; これがあなたの部屋です [kore ga anata no heya desu] This is your room; その部屋にテレビはありますか? [sono heya ni terebi wa arimasu ka?] Does the room have a TV?; その部屋はいくらですか? [sono heya wa ikura desu ka?] How much is the room?; ダブルの部屋がいいのですが [daburu no heya ga ii no desu ga] I'd like a room with a double bed; ツインの部屋がいいのですが [tsuin no heya ga ii no desu ga] I'd like a room with twin beds; 自分の部屋で朝食を取ることができますか? [jibun no heya de choushoku o toru koto ga dekimasu ka?] Can I have breakfast in my room?; 禁煙の部屋がいいのですが [kin'en no heya ga ii no desu ga] I'd like a no-smoking room; ･･･の名前で部屋を予約しました [... no namae de heya o yoyaku shimashita] I reserved a room in the name of...; 部屋に問題があります [heya ni mondai ga arimasu] There's a problem with the room; 部屋はありますか? [heya wa arimasu ka?] Do you have a room?; 部屋が狭すぎます [heya ga sema-sugimasu] The room is too small; 部屋を掃除してもらえますか? [heya o souji shite moraemasu ka?] Can you clean the room, please?; 部屋を替えることができますか? [heya o kaeru koto ga dekimasu ka?] Can I switch rooms?; 部屋を借りたいのですが [heya o karitai no desu ga] I'd like to rent a room; 山が見える部屋がいいのですが [yama ga mieru heya ga ii no desu ga] I'd like a room with a view of the mountains; 別の部屋がいいのですが [betsu no heya ga ii no desu ga] I'd like another room; 喫煙できる部屋がいいのですが [kitsuen dekiru heya ga ii no desu ga] I'd like a smoking room

ヘザー [hezaa] n heather

火 [hi] n fire; 火をもみ消す [hi-o momikesu] v stub out; 大かがり火 [oukagaribi] n bonfire

費 [hi] n expense; 生活費 [seikatsuhi] n cost of living

日当たり [hiatari] 日当たりのよい [hiatari no yoi] adj sunny

火花 [hibana] n spark

ひび [hibi] ひびの入った [hibi no haitta] adj cracked

ヒッチハイク [hicchihaiku] n hitchhiking; ヒッチハイクする [hitchihaiku suru] v hitchhike; ヒッチハイクをする人 [hitchihaiku wo suru hito] n hitchhiker

左 [hidari] n left; 左に [hidari ni] adv left; 左の [hidari no] adj left; 左に曲がってください [hidari ni magatte kudasai] Turn left

左側 [hidarigawa] 左側の [hidarigawa no] adj left-hand; 左側通行 [hidarigawa tsuukou] n left-hand drive

左利き [hidarikiki] 左利きの [hidarikiki no] adj left-handed

左回り [hidarimawari] 左回りに [hidari mawari ni] adv counterclockwise

日照り [hideri] n drought

ひどい [hidoi] adj awful, gross, terrible, vicious; ひどく [hidoku] adv terribly; 実にひどい [jitsu ni hidoi] adj horrible; なんてひどい天気でしょう! [nante hidoi tenki deshou!] What awful weather!; サービスがひどかったです [saabisu ga hidokatta desu] The service was terrible

ひどく [hidoku] adv awfully, grossly

日付 [hiduke] n date

冷える [hieru] v cool

飛越 [hietsu] n jumping; 障害飛越 [shougaihietsu] n show jumping

皮膚 [hifu] n skin

日帰り [higaeri] n one-day return; 日帰り往復割引切符 [higaeri oufuku waribiki kippu] n one-day round-trip ticket

東 [higashi] n east; 東の [higashi no] adj east, eastern; 東へ [higashi e] adv east

東行き [higashiiki] 東行きの [higashi yuki no] adj eastbound

ひげ [hige] n whiskers; ひげを剃っていない [hige-o sotte inai] adj unshaven; 口ひげ [kuchi hige] n mustache

非現実 [higenjitsu] 非現実的な [higenjitsuteki na] adj unrealistic

批判 [hihan] n criticism; 批判する [hihan suru] v criticize

批評 [hihyou] n review; 批評家 [hihyouka] n critic

ヒーロー [hiiroo] n hero

ひじ [hiji] n elbow

肘掛け [hijikake] adj reclining; 肘掛け椅子 [hijikakeke isu] n armchair

非常 [hijou] 非常に [hijou ni] adv very; 非常階段 [hijoukaidan] n fire escape

非常口 [hijouguchi] n emergency exit

控えめ [hikae me] 控えめの [hikaeme no] adj reserved

比較 [hikaku] n comparison; 比較する [hikaku suru] v compare; 比較的 [hikakuteki] adv comparatively, relatively

悲観 [hikan] n pessimism; 悲観主義者 [hikanshugisha] n pessimist; 悲観的な [hikanteki na] adj pessimistic

ひからびる [hikarabiru] v be parched; ひからびた [hikarabita] adj bone dry

光 [hikari] n light

光り [hikari] n light; 光り輝く [hikari kagayaku] adj brilliant

光る [hikaru] v shine; 光った [hikatta] adj shiny

引き出し [hikidashi] n drawer; 引き出しが動きません [hikidashi ga ugokimasen] The drawer is jammed

ヒキガエル [hikigaeru] n toad

引換 [hikikae] 引換券 [hikikaeken] n voucher

引き返す [hikikaesu] v turn back

挽肉 [hikiniku] n ground meat

引き起こす [hikiokosu] v cause

引き落とす [hikiotosu] 口座引き落とし [kouza hikiotoshi] n direct debit

引き裂く [hikisaku] v rip; ずたずたに引き裂く [zutazuta ni hikisaku] v tear up

引き継ぐ [hikitsugu] v take over

ひきつける [hikitsukeru] v attract

引き分ける [hikiwakeru] v tie (equal with)

ひきずる [hikizuru] v drag; 足をひきずって歩く [ashi-o hikizutte aruku] v shuffle

引っ掻く [hikkaku] v scratch

引っ込める [hikkomeru] 引っ込めること [hikkomeru koto] n withdrawal

引越し [hikkoshi] 引越しトラック [hikkoshi torakku] n moving van

ひっくり [hikkuri] ひっくり返す [hikkurigaesu] v overturn

被告 [hikoku] 被告人 [hikokunin] n accused

被告人 [hikokunin] n defendant

飛行 [hikou] n flight; 未確認飛行物体 [mikakunin hikoubuttai] n UFO

飛行機 [hikouki] n plane (airplane); 飛行機に酔った [hikouki ni yotta] adj airsick

飛行機搭 [hikoukitou] n flying clearance

非公認 [hikounin] n pilot; 非公認の [hikounin no] adj unofficial

飛行士 [hikoushi] 宇宙飛行士 [uchuuhikoushi]

n astronaut

挽く [hiku] *v* grind

轢く [hiku] *v* run over

引く [hiku] *v* pull, subtract; 下線を引く [kasen-o hiku] *v* underline; 綱引き [tsunahiki] *n* tug-of-war

低い [hikui] *adj* low; より低い [yori hikui] *adj* lower

低く [hikuku] *adv* low

暇 [hima] *n* leisure time

肥満 [himan] 肥満した [himan shita] *adj* obese

ヒマワリ [himawari] *n* sunflower

秘密 [himitsu] *n* confidence *(secret)*, secret; 秘密に [himitsu ni] *adv* secretly; 秘密の [himitsu no] *adj* secret

ひも [himo] *n* string; 革ひも [kawa himo] *n* strap; 靴ひも [kutsuhimo] *n* shoelace; 帯状のひも [obijou no himo] *n* band *(strip)*

品 [hin] *n* product; 記念品 [kinenhin] *n* souvenir; 貴重品 [kichouhin] *n* valuables; 美術品 [bijutsuhin] *n* work of art; 免税品 [menzeihin] *n* duty-free goods; 在庫品 [zaikohin] *n* stock

ヒナギク [hinagiku] *n* daisy

避難 [hinan] 避難させる [hinan saseru] *v* evacuate; 避難所 [hinanjo] *n* refuge, shelter; 避難者 [hinansha] *n* refugee

非難 [hinan] *n* accusation, blame; 非難する [hinan suru] *v* condemn

皮肉 [hiniku] *n* irony; 皮肉な [hiniku na] *adj* ironic

皮肉な [hiniku na] *adj* sarcastic

避妊 [hinin] *n* birth control, contraception; 私は避妊が必要です [watashi wa hinin ga hitsuyou desu] I need contraception

避妊具 [hiningu] *n* contraceptive

貧血 [hinketsu] 貧血の [hinketsu no] *adj* anemic

貧困 [hinkon] *n* poverty

品行 [hinkou] *n* morals

頻発 [hinpatsu] *n* frequency

品種 [hinshu] *n* breed; 品種改良する [hinshu kairyou suru] *v* breed

ヒント [hinto] *n* hint

ヒンズー [hinzuu] ヒンズー教徒 [Hinzuu kyouto] *n* Hindu

ヒンズー教 [hinzuukyou] *n* Hinduism; ヒンズー教の [Hinzuu kyou no] *adj* Hindu

引っ張る [hipparu] *v* drag

ひっぱたく [hippataku] *v* spank

ヒッピー [hippii] *n* hippie

開く [hiraku] 開いた [aita] *adj* open; いつ開きますか? [itsu hirakimasu ka?] When does it open?; その銀行はいつ開きますか? [sono ginkou wa itsu hirakimasu ka?] When does the bank open?; それは今日開いていますか? [sore wa kyou hiraite imasu ka?] Is it open today?; それは明日開きますか? [sore wa asu hirakimasu ka?] Is it open tomorrow?; ドアが開きません [doa ga akimasen] The door won't open; 窓が開きません [mado ga akimasen] The window won't open; 郵便局はいつ開きますか? [yuubinkyoku wa itsu hirakimasu ka?] When does the post office open?; 鍵が開きません [kagi ga akimasen] The key doesn't work

ヒラマメ [hiramame] *n* lentils

平泳ぎ [hiraoyogi] *n* breaststroke

ひれ足 [hireashi] *n* flippers

比例 [hirei] 比例した [hirei shita] *adj* proportional

ヒレ肉 [hireniku] *n* fillet; ···からヒレ肉を取る [… kara hireniku-o toru] *v* fillet

卑劣 [hiretsu] 卑劣な [hiretsu na] *adj* lousy

比率 [hiritsu] *n* proportion, ratio

広がり [hirogari] *n* extent

広がる [hirogaru] 広がること [hirogaru koto] *n* spread

広げる [hirogeru] *v* spread, spread out, unroll

拾い [hiroi] *adj* random; 拾い読みする [hiroiyomi suru] *v* browse

広い [hiroi] *adj* broad, extensive, wide; 広く [hiroku] *adv* wide

ヒロイン [hiroin] *n* heroine

広く [hiroku] *adv* extensively

広まる [hiromaru] *v* pervade; 広まった [hiromatta] *adj* widespread

ヒル [hiru] ヒルウォーキングに行きたいのですが [hiru-wookingu ni ikitai no desu ga] I'd like to go hiking

昼間 [hiruma] *n* daytime

ヒルウォーキング [hiruuookingu] *n* hiking

肥料 [hiryou] *n* fertilizer

悲惨 [hisan] 悲惨な [hisan na] *adj* tragic; 悲惨な出来事 [hisan na dekigoto] *n* tragedy

秘書 [hisho] *n* secretary; 個人秘書 [kojin hisho] *n* personal assistant, PA

被収 [hi shuu] *n* detainment; 被収容者 [hishuuyousha] *n* inmate

ひそめる [hisomeru] まゆをひそめる [mayu wo hisomeru] *v* frown

必死 [hisshi] 必死の [hisshi no] *adj* desperate; 必死で [hisshi de] *adv* desperately

ヒスタミン [hisutamin] 抗ヒスタミン剤 [kouhisutaminzai] *n* antihistamine

額 [hitai] *n (顔)* forehead; 十分な額が払われていない [juubun na gaku ga harawarete inai] *adj* underpaid

悲嘆 [hitan] *n* mourning

浸す [hitasu] *v* soak; ちょっと浸す [chotto hitasu] *v* dip

否定 [hitei] 否定の [hitei no] *adj* negative; 否定の答え [hitei no kotae] *n* negative; 否定する [hitei suru] *v* deny; 否定できない [hitei dekinai] *adj* undeniable

人 [hito] *n* person; 人の住んでいない [hito no sunde inai] *adj* uninhabited; 人を車に乗せてあげること [hito-o kuruma ni nosete ageru koto] *n* ride *(free ride)*; いとしい人 [itoshii hito] *n* beloved; 有名人 [yuumeijin] *n* celebrity; 食事する人 [shokuji suru hito] *n* diner

一晩 [hitoban] *adj* overnight; 私は一晩入院しなければなりませんか? [watashi wa hitoban nyuuin shinakereba narimasen ka?] Do I have to stay overnight

一晩駐車 [hitoban chuusha] *n* overnight parking

人々 [hitobito] *n* people

ひと針 [hitohari] *n* stitch

ひとひら [hitohira] ひとひらの雪 [hitohira no yuki] *n* snowflake

人質 [hitojichi] *n* hostage

ひと口 [hitokuchi] ひと口いただいてもいいですか? [hito-kuchi itadaite mo ii desu ka?] May I taste it?

ひと組 [hitokumi] *n* pair

HIV [hitomen'ekifuzenuirusu] 私はHIVに感染しています [watashi wa eichi-ai-vui ni kansen shite imasu] I'm HIV-positive

HIV陰性 [hitomenekizenuiruru negatibu] HIV陰性の [eichiaibui insei no] *adj* HIV-negative

HIV陽性 [hitomenekizenuiruru pojitibu] HIV陽性の [eichiaibui yousei no] *adj* HIV-positive

一人 [hitori] *n* one person

一人よがり [hitoriyogari] 一人よがりの [hitori yogari no] *adj* smug

ひとさじ [hitosaji] *n* spoonful

等しい [hitoshii] *adj* equal; 等しくする [hitoshiku suru] *v* equalize; 等しくすること [hitoshiku suru koto] *n* equation; ···に等しい [... ni hitoshii] *v* equal

一つ [hitotsu] *n* piece; 一つの [hitotsu no] *indef art* a, an; もう一つの [mou hitotsu no] *adj* another

ひと続き [hitotsuduki] *n* series

ひとつの···もない [hitotsuno... monai] *adjx* no

ひつぎ [hitsugi] *n* coffin

羊 [hitsuji] *n* sheep; 羊の毛皮 [hitsuji no kegawa] *n* sheepskin; 羊飼い [hitsujikai] *n* shepherd

必要 [hitsuyou] *n* need; 必要とする [hitsuyou to suru] *v* need, require; 必要性 [hitsuyousei] *n* necessity; 何か必要ですか? [nani ka hitsuyou desu ka?] Do you need anything?; 私は介助が必要です [watashi wa kaijo ga hitsuyou desu] I need assistance; 私は避妊が必要です [watashi wa hinin ga hitsuyou desu] I need contraception; 食器がもっと必要です [shokki ga motto hitsuyou desu] We need more dishes

必要な [hitsuyou na] *adj* necessary

ひったくる [hittakuru] *v* snatch

匹敵 [hitteki] 匹敵する [hitteki suru] *adj* comparable

ひっつかむ [hittsukamu] *v* grab

日焼け [hiyake] *n* sunburn, tan; 日焼けした [hiyake shita] *adj* sunburned; 日焼け色の [hiyake iro no] *adj* tanned; 小麦色の日焼け [komugi iro no hiyake] *n* suntan; 私は日焼けでヒリヒリします [watashi wa hiyake de hirihiri shimasu] I'm sunburned

日焼け止め [hiyakedome] *n* sunblock

ヒヤシンス [hiyashinsu] *n* hyacinth

冷やす [hiyasu] *v* chill

ひよこ [hiyoko] *n* chick

ヒヨコマメ [hiyokomame] *n* chickpea

費用 [hiyou] *n* cost; 参加費用はいくらですか? [sanka-hiyou wa ikura desu ka?] How much does it cost to get in?

ひざ [hiza] *n* knee, lap; ひざを曲げる [hiza-o mageru] *v* kneel

ひざがしら [hizagashira] *n* kneecap

ひざまずく [hizamazuku] *v* kneel down

帆 [ho] *n* sail

ホバークラフト [hobaakurafuto] *n* hovercraft

歩調 [hochou] *n* pace

補聴器 [hochouki] *n* hearing aid; 私は補聴器をつけています [watashi wa hochouki o tsukete imasu] I have a hearing aid

ほどく [hodoku] *v* undo, untie, unwind

歩道 [hodou] *n* sidewalk; 横断歩道 [oudanhodou] *n* pedestrian crossing

吠える [hoeru] *v* bark

保護 [hogo] *n* custody, protection; 保護する [hogo suru] *v* protect; 保護区 [hogoku] *n* preserve *(land)*

歩兵 [hohei] *n* infantry

ほほ笑み [hohoemi] *n* smile

ほほ笑む [hohoemu] *v* smile

ホイールがロック [hoiiru ga rokku] ホイールがロックします [hoiiru ga rokku shimasu] The wheels lock

保育園 [hoikuen] *n* nursery school

ホイップクリーム [hoippukuriimu] *n* whipped cream

ホイル [hoiru] *n* foil

補充 [hojuu] *n* supplement; 新人補充 [shinjin hojuu] *n* recruitment; 補充する [hojuu suru] *v* refill

ほか [hoka] ほかの [hoka no] *adj* other; ほかに何かありますか? [hoka ni nani ka arimasu ka?] Do you have anything else?; ほかの部屋はありますか? [hoka no heya wa arimasu ka?] Do you have any others?

保管 [hokan] *n* storage

補完 [hokan] 補完的な [hokanteki na] *adj* complementary

ほかに [hoka ni] そのほかに [sono hoka ni] *adv* other than that

保管所 [hokanjo] 死体保管所 [shitaihokanjo] *n* morgue

保険 [hoken] *n* insurance; 事故保険 [jiko hoken] *n* accident insurance; 保険に入った [hoken ni haitta] *adj* insured; 保険をかける [hoken-o kakeru] *v* insure; 旅行保険 [ryokou hoken] *n* travel insurance; 自動車保険 [jidousha hoken] *n* car insurance; 第三者賠償責任保険 [daisansha baishousekinin hoken] *n* liability insurance; 生命保険 [seimeihoken] *n* life insurance; 保険でそれが補償されますか? [hoken de sore ga hoshou saremasu ka?] Will the insurance pay for it?; あなたは保険に入っていますか? [anata wa hoken ni haitte imasu ka?] Do you have insurance?; あなたの保険の詳細を教えてください [anata no hoken no shousai o oshiete kudasai] Give me your insurance information, please; あなたの保険証書を見せていただけますか? [anata no hoken-shousho o misete itadakemasu ka?] May I see your insurance certificate, please?; 私

は保険に入っています [watashi wa hoken ni haitte imasu] I have insurance; 私は歯科保険に入っていません [watashi wa shika-hoken ni haitte imasen] I don't have dental insurance; 私の保険の詳細です [watashi no hoken no shousai desu] Here's my insurance information; 総合自動車保険に加入する追加料金はいくらですか? [sougou-jidousha-hoken ni kanyuu suru tsuika-ryoukin wa ikura desu ka?] How much extra is comprehensive insurance coverage?; 個人傷害保険をかけたいのですが [kojin-shougai-hoken o kaketai no desu ga] I'd like to arrange personal accident insurance

保険請求 [hokenseikyuu] 私は保険請求に警察の証明書が必要です [watashi wa hoken-seikyuu ni keisatsu no shoumeisho ga hitsuyou desu] I need a police report for my insurance

北海 [hokkai] n North Sea

ホッケー [hokkee] n field hockey

北極 [hokkyoku] n North Pole; 北極グマ [hokkyoguma] n polar bear; 北極海 [Hokkyokukai] n Arctic Ocean; 北極圏 [hokkyokuken] n Arctic Circle

誇り [hokori] n pride

ほこり [hokori] n (ごみ) dust; ほこりを払う [hokori-o harau] v dust

誇りに思う [hokori ni omou] adj proud

ほこりっぽい [hokorippoi] adj dusty

歩行 [hokou] n walking; 歩行者 [hokousha] n pedestrian; 歩行者用通路 [hokoushayou tsuuro] n walkway; 歩行者専用になった [hokousha sen'you ni natta] adj pedestrianized

歩行者 [hokousha] n pedestrian; 歩行者用の小道 [hokoushayou no komichi] n footpath

歩行者天国 [hokoushatengoku] n pedestrian area

ほくろ [hokuro] n mole (skin)

北西 [hokusei] n northwest

北東 [hokutou] n northeast

補給 [hokyuu] n refill; 燃料を補給する [nenryou wo hokyuu suru] v refuel

ほめことば [homekotoba] n compliment

ホメオパシー [homeopashii] n homeopathy; ホメオパシーの [homeopashii no] adj homeopathic

ほめる [homeru] v compliment, praise

本 [hon] n (書物) book; 漫画本 [mangabon] n comic book; 料理の本 [ryouri no hon] n cookbook; 開くと絵が飛び出す本 [hiraku to e ga tobidasu hon] n pop-up book

本箱 [honbako] n bookcase

本文 [honbun] n text

本棚 [hondana] n bookshelf

本土 [hondo] n mainland

骨 [hone] n bone; 頭蓋骨 [zugaikotsu] n skull

骨組み [honegumi] n frame

骨付き [honetsuki] 骨付き肉 [honetsuki niku] n joint (meat)

本位 [hon'i] 自己本位の [jiko hon'i no] adj self-centered

ホンジュラス [honjurasu] n Honduras

本管 [honkan] 本管で止めてください [honkan de tomete kudasai] Turn it off at the mains

本物 [honmono] 本物の [honmono no] adj authentic; 本物の [honmono no] adj genuine

ほんの [hon no] n mere

本能 [honnou] n instinct

ほのめかす [honomekasu] v hint

炎 [hono-o] n flame; 扁桃腺炎 [hentousen'en] n tonsillitis; 気管支炎 [kikanshien] n bronchitis; 膀胱炎 [boukouen] n cystitis; 喉頭炎 [koutouen] n laryngitis

本社 [honsha] n head office, headquarters, HQ

本当 [hontou] 本当の [hontou no] adj true

本当に [hontou ni] adv really

翻訳 [honyaku] n translation; 翻訳者 [hon'yakusha] n translator

哺乳 [honyuu] 哺乳瓶 [honyuubin] n baby bottle; 哺乳動物 [honyuu doubutsu] n mammal

H

ほお [hoo] *n* cheek

ほお紅 [hoobeni] *n* rouge

ほお骨 [hoobone] *n* cheekbone

ホーム [hoomu] *adj* home; ホームの試合 [hoomu no shiai] *n* home game

ホームページ [hoomupeeji] *n* home page

ホームシック [hoomushikku] ホームシックの [hoomushikku no] *adj* homesick

ホース [hoosu] *n* hose, hosepipe

洞 [hora] *n* sinus

ホラー [horaa] *adj* horror; ホラー映画 [horaa eiga] *n* horror movie

ほら穴 [horaana] *n* cave

濠 [hori] *n* moat

ホリデー [horidee] アクティブホリデー [akutibu horidee] *n* activite vacation

ほろ酔い [horoyoi] ほろ酔いの [horo yoi no] *adj* tipsy

掘る [horu] *v* dig

彫る [horu] *v* carve, engrave

ホルダー [horudaa] *n* folder

ホルモン [horumon] *n* hormone

保釈 [hoshaku] 保釈金 [hoshakukin] *n* bail

星 [hoshi] *n* star *(sky)*

干しブドウ [hoshibudou] 小粒の種なし干しブドウ [kotsubu no tanenashi hoshibudou] *n* currant

欲しい [hoshii] *v* want

干し草 [hoshikusa] *n* hay; 干し草の山 [hoshikusa no yama] *n* haystack

星占い [hoshiuranai] *n* horoscope

保証 [hoshou] *n* guarantee, warranty; 信用を保証するもの [shin'you-o hoshou suru mono] *n* credentials; 保証する [hoshou suru] *v* ensure, guarantee; まだ保証期間内です [mada hoshou-kikan nai desu] It's still under warranty; 車はまだ保証期間内です [kuruma wa mada hoshou-kikan nai desu] The car is still under warranty

保障 [hoshou] 社会保障 [shakaihoshou] *n* social security

補償 [hoshou] *n* compensation; 補償する [hoshou suru] *v* compensate

保証金 [hoshoukin] *n* deposit; 保証金はいくらですか? [hoshoukin wa ikura desu ka?] How much is the deposit?; 保証金を返していただけますか? [hoshoukin o kaeshite itadakemasu ka?] Can I have my deposit back, please?

保守 [hoshu] 保守的な [hoshuteki na] *adj* conservative

補足 [hosoku] *n* supplement

発作 [hossa] *n* fit, seizure; 癲癇の発作 [tenkan no hossa] *n* epileptic fit; 心臓発作 [shinzouhossa] *n* heart attack

ほっそり [hossori] ほっそりした [hossori shita] *adj* slender, slim

干す [hosu] *v* dry; 服を干すところがありますか? [fuku o hosu tokoro ga arimasu ka?] Is there somewhere to dry clothes?

ホステル [hosuteru] *n* hostel

ホスト [hosuto] *n* host *(entertains)*

ホタテガイ [hotategai] *n* scallop

ホテル [hoteru] *n* hotel; いいホテルを教えてもらえますか? [ii hoteru o oshiete moraemasu ka?] Could you recommend a hotel?; おたくのホテルは車椅子で利用できますか? [otaku no hoteru wa kuruma-isu de riyou dekimasu ka?] Is your hotel wheelchair accessible?; このホテルまでのタクシー料金はいくらですか? [kono hoteru made no takushii-ryoukin wa ikura desu ka?] How much is the taxi fare to this hotel?; このホテルへ行く一番よい方法は何ですか? [kono hoteru e iku ichiban yoi houhou wa nan desu ka?] What's the best way to get to this hotel?; 私はホテルに滞在しています [watashi wa hoteru ni taizai shite imasu] I'm staying at a hotel; 私のためにホテルの部屋を予約してもらえますか? [watashi no tame ni hoteru no heya o yoyaku shite moraemasu ka?] Could you make a hotel reservation for me?; 私たちはホテルを探しています [watashi-tachi wa hoteru o sagashite imasu] We're looking for a hotel; 彼がホテルの経営者です [kare ga hoteru no keieisha desu]

He runs the hotel

ほとんど [hotondo] adv almost, nearly; ほとんど・・・ない [hotondo... nai] adv hardly, scarcely

ホットドッグ [hottodokku] n hot dog

法 [hou] n method; 調理法 [chourihou] n recipe

法案 [houan] n bill (legislation)

報知器 [houchiki] n alarm; 火災報知器 [kasai houchiki] n fire alarm

法外 [hougai] 法外な [hougai na] adj extortionate; 法外な値をふっかける [hougai na ne-o fukkakeru] v rip off

方言 [hougen] n dialect

方法 [houhou] n manner, method, way; 組織的な方法 [soshikiteki na houhou] n system

放火 [houka] n arson

放棄 [houki] 放棄する [houki suru] v waive

ほうき [houki] n broom

報告 [houkoku] n report; 報告する [houkoku suru] v report

方向 [houkou] n direction; 方向転換する [houkoutenkan suru] v turn around

芳香 [houkou] n aroma

訪問 [houmon] n visit; 訪問者 [houmonsha] n visitor; 訪問する [houmon suru] v visit

法王 [houou] ローマ法王 [Rooma Houou] n pope

ほうれん草 [hourensou] n spinach

法律 [houritsu] n law; 法律制定 [houritsu seitei] n legislation

砲声 [housei] n bang

宝石 [houseki] n gem, jewel; 宝石類 [housekirui] n jewelry; 宝石商 [housekishou] n jeweler, jewelry store

放射 [housha] n radiation; 放射性のある [houshasei no aru] adj radioactive

報酬 [houshuu] n reward

法則 [housoku] 法則化する [housokuka suru] v generalize

放送 [housou] n broadcast; 放送する [housou suru] v broadcast

包装 [housou] n wrapping; 包装を解く [housou-o toku] v unwrap; 包装紙 [housoushi] n wrapping paper

包帯 [houtai] n bandage; 包帯をする [houtai-o suru] v bandage; 吊り包帯 [tsuri houtai] n sling; 新しい包帯をしてください [atarashii houtai o shite kudasai] I'd like a fresh bandage; 包帯をしてください [houtai o shite kudasai] I'd like a bandage

法廷 [houtei] n court

抱擁 [houyou] n cuddle

ホワイティング [howaitingu] n (魚) whiting

ホワイトボード [howaitoboodo] n whiteboard

保全 [hozen] n conservation

保存 [hozon] 保存料 [hozonryou] n preservative

百科 [hyakka] 百科事典 [hyakka jiten] n encyclopedia

百 [hyaku] number hundred

100万 [hyakuman] n million

百につき [hyaku ni tsuki] adv percent

雹 [hyou] n hail

ヒョウ [hyou] n (動物) leopard, (動物) panther

評判 [hyouban] n reputation

氷河 [hyouga] n glacier

表現 [hyougen] n expression; 表現する [hyougen suru] v express

漂白 [hyouhaku] 漂白した [hyouhaku shita] adj bleached; 漂白剤 [hyouhakuzai] n bleach

標準 [hyoujun] n standard; 標準の [hyoujun no] adj standard; 標準時間帯 [hyoujun jikantai] n time zone

評価 [hyouka] 評価する [hyouka suru] v rate; 高く評価する [takaku hyouka suru] v appreciate; 過大評価する [kadai hyouka suru] v overestimate

評決 [hyouketsu] n verdict

表面 [hyoumen] n surface; 表面的な [hyoumenteki na] adj superficial

漂流 [hyouryuu] 漂流する [hyouryuu suru] v drift

H

標識 [hyoushiki] **道路標識** [dourohyoushiki] *n* road sign, signpost

標的 [hyouteki] *n* target

氷山 [hyouzan] *n* iceberg

ヒューズ [hyuuzu] *n* fuse; ヒューズがとびました [hyuuzu ga tobimashita] A fuse has blown; ヒューズを直してもらえますか? [hyuuzu o naoshite moraemasu ka?] Can you fix a fuse?

ヒューズボックス [hyuuzubokkusu] *n* fuse box

I

胃 [i] n stomach

医 [i] n doctor; 一般医 [ippan'i] n family doctor; 外科医 [gekai] n surgeon

威張る [ibaru] v look down on; 威張った [ibatta] adj bossy

イベント [ibento] n event; 私たちはどのスポーツイベントに行けますか? [watashi-tachi wa dono supootsu-ibento ni ikemasu ka?] Which sporting events can we go to?

いびき [ibiki] n snoring; いびきをかく [ibiki wo kaku] v snore

いぼ [ibo] n wart

イブニングドレス [ibuningu doresu] n formal attire

いぶす [ibusu] いぶした [ibushita] adj smoked

遺物 [ibutsu] n remains

一致 [icchi] 満場一致の [manjouitchi no] adj unanimous

一 [ichi] number one

位置 [ichi] n position; 位置している [ichi shite iru] adj situated

市場 [ichiba] n market, marketplace; 株式市場 [kabushikishijou] n stock market; 市場調査 [shijouchousa] n market research

一番 [ichiban] adv most; 一番上の [ichiban ue no] adj top; 一番若い [ichiban wakai] adj youngest

一度 [ichido] adv once; 年に一度 [nen ni ichido] adv yearly; 年に一度の [nen ni ichido no] adj yearly

一月 [ichigatsu] n January

一語 [ichigo] 一語です [ichi-go desu] all one word

イチゴ [ichigo] n strawberry

一腹子 [ichi hara ko] 動物の一腹子 [doubutsu no ippukushi] n litter (offspring)

イチイ [ichii] n yew

一時 [ichiji] 一時の [ichiji no] adj temporary; 一時解雇する [ichiji kaiko suru] v lay off; 一時停止 [ichiji teishi] n suspension; 一時です [ichi-ji desu] It's one o'clock

一時間 [ichijikan] n hour; 一時間ごとに [ichijikan goto ni] adv hourly; 一時間ごとの [ichijikan goto no] adj hourly; 1時間あたりいくらですか? [ichi-jikan atari ikura desu ka?] How much is it per hour?

一時期 [ichijiki] n spell (time)

イチジク [ichijiku] n fig

著しい [ichijirushii] adj remarkable; 著しく [ichijirushiku] adv remarkably

一覧表 [ichiranhyou] n list; 一覧表を作る [ichiranhyou-o tsukuru] v list

一流の芸術作品 [ichiryuu no geijutsusakuhin] n classic

遺伝 [iden] n heredity; 遺伝的な [identeki na] adj hereditary

遺伝学 [idengaku] n genetics

遺伝子 [idenshi] n gene; 遺伝子の [idenshi no] adj genetic; 遺伝子組み換えの [idenshi kumikae no] adj genetically modified

遺伝子組み換え [idenshikumikae] 遺伝子組み換えの [idenshi kumikae no] adj genetically modified

イデオロギー [ideorogii] n ideology

井戸 [ido] n well

緯度 [ido] n latitude

移動 [idou] n move, removal; レッカー移動する [rekkaa idou suru] v tow away; 移動する [idou suru] v travel; 移動性の [idousei no] adj migrant; 移動可能な [idoukanou na] n mobile

家 [ie] *n* house; 住む家のない [sumu ie no nai] *adj* homeless; 家にいる [ie ni iru] *v* stay in; 専門家 [senmonka] *n* specialist; 家はかなり大きいです [ie wa kanari ookii desu] The house is quite big

絆創膏 [iedomo chimakemu] *n* bandage *(for wound)*

イエメン [iemen] *n* Yemen

イエローページ® [ieroopeeji] *n* Yellow Pages®

イエス [iesu] *n* Jesus

衣服 [ifuku] *n* garment

意外な [igai na] *adj* surprising

医学 [igaku] *n* medicine; 医学の [igaku no] *adj* medical

威厳 [igen] *n* dignity, majesty

異議 [igi] *n* objection; 異議のない [igi no nai] *adj* undisputed

違反 [ihan] *n* offense; 駐車違反切符 [chuushaihan kippu] *n* parking ticket

いい [ii] *adj* appropriate

Eチケット [iichiketto] *n* e-ticket

いいえ [iie] *adv* no

いい加減 [iikagen] いい加減な [iikagen na] *adj* irresponsible

Eコマース [iikomaasu] *n* e-commerce

Eメール [iimeeru] あなたのEメールアドレスは何ですか? [anata no ii-meeru-adoresu wa nan desu ka?] What's your e-mail address?; 私のEメールが届きましたか? [watashi no ii-meeru ga todokimashita ka?] Did you get my e-mail?; 私のEメールアドレスは・・・です [watashi no ii-meeru-adoresu wa... desu] My e-mail address is...; Eメールを送っていいですか? [ii-meeru o okutte ii desu ka?] Can I send an e-mail?; Eメールアドレスをお持ちですか? [ii-meeru-adoresu o o-mochi desu ka?] Do you have e-mail?; Eメールアドレスを教えてもらえますか? [ii-meeru-adoresu o oshiete moraemasu ka?] May I have your e-mail?

委員会 [iinkai] *n* committee; 裁定委員会

[saitei iinkai] *n* tribunal

EU [iiyuu] *abbr* EU [iiyuu]

維持 [iji] *n* maintenance; 維持する [iji suru] *v* keep up, maintain

意地 [iji] *n* stubbornness; 意地の悪い [iji no warui] *adj* spiteful

いじめる [ijimeru] *v* bully, pick on

意地悪 [ijiwaru] *n* spite; 意地悪をする [ijiwaru-o suru] *v* spite

以上 [ijou] *adv* not less than; それ以上の [sore ijou no] *adj* further

異常 [ijou] 異常な [ijou na] *adj* abnormal, extraordinary

移住 [ijuu] *n* immigration, migration; 移住する [ijuu suru] *v* emigrate; 移住者 [ijuusha] *n* immigrant, migrant

以下 [ika] 以下の [ika no] *(次の) adj* following

イカ [ika] *n* squid

いかだ [ikada] *n* raft

錨 [ikari] *n* anchor

怒り [ikari] *n* anger

池 [ike] *n* pond; 貯水池 [chosuichi] *n* reservoir

意見 [iken] *n* feedback, opinion, remark; 意見の相違 [iken no soui] *n* disagreement; 意見が異なる [iken ga kotonaru] *v* disagree

息 [iki] *n* breath; 息が詰まる [iki ga tsumaru] *v* choke; 息をする [iki-o suru] *v* breathe; 息を吐き出す [iki-o hakidasu] *v* breathe out; 息を吸い込む [iki-o suikomu] *v* breathe in

意気 [iki] *n* mood; 意気消沈した [ikishouchin shita] *adj* depressed

行き止まり [ikidomari] *n* dead end

行きづまる [ikidumaru] 行きづまった [ikizumatta] *adj* stuck

生き物 [ikimono] *n* creature

生き残る [ikinokoru] *v* survive

生きる [ikiru] *v* live; 生きている [ikite iru] *adj* live

行き渡る [ikiwataru] 皆に行き渡る [mina ni iki wataru] *v* go around

一か月 [ikkagetsu] *n* one month

一階 [ikkai] *n* first floor

一回 [ikkai] *adv* once; 一回限りのこと [ikkai kagiri no koto] *n* one-off; 年一回の [nen'ikkai no] *adj* annual

一貫 [ikkan] 一貫した [ikkan shita] *adj* consistent

一貫性 [ikkansei] 一貫性のない [ikkansei no nai] *adj* inconsistent

一戸建て [ikkodate] 土地付き一戸建て家屋 [tochi tsuki ikkodate kaoku] *n* house

一行 [ikkou] *n* (集まり) party *(group)*

移行 [ikou] *n* transition

行く [iku] *v* go; まっすぐ行ってください [massugu itte kudasai] Go straight ahead; もう行く時間ですか? [mou iku jikan desu ka?] Is it time to go?; 私は…へ行きます [watashi wa... e ikimasu] I'm going to...; 私たちは…に行きたいのですが [watashi-tachi wa... ni ikitai no desu ga] We'd like to go to...; 私たちは…へ行きます [watashi-tachi wa... e ikimasu] We're going to...; …に行けますか? [... ni ikemasu ka?] Can we go to...?

育児 [ikuji] *n* child rearing; 父親の育児休暇 [chichioya no ikuji kyuuka] *n* paternity leave

いくら [ikura] *adv* how much; 2食付きはいくらですか? [ni-shoku tsuki wa ikura desu ka?] How much is the modified American plan?; 3食付きはいくらですか? [san-shoku tsuki wa ikura desu ka?] How much is the American plan?; 一泊いくらですか? [ippaku ikura desu ka?] How much is it per night?; あれはいくらですか? [are wa ikura desu ka?] How much does that cost?; いくらでしょう? [ikura deshou?] How much will it be?; いくらですか? [ikura desu ka?] How much is it?; その部屋はいくらですか? [sono heya wa ikura desu ka?] How much is the room?; それは1週間あたりいくらですか? [sore wa isshuukan atari ikura desu ka?] How much is it per week?; それは一人あたりいくらですか? [sore wa hitori atari ikura desu ka?]

How much is it per person?; それは一泊いくらですか? [sore wa ippaku ikura desu ka?] How much is it per night?; それはいくらですか? [sore wa ikura desu ka?] How much does it cost?; それはいくら分ですか? [sore wa ikura-bun desu ka?] How much is it worth?; …に電話するのはいくらですか? [... ni denwa suru no wa ikura desu ka?] How much would it cost to telephone...?

いくつ [ikutsu] *adv* how old; おいくつですか? [o-ikutsu desu ka?] How old are you?

いくつか [ikutsuka] いくつかの [ikutsuka no] *adj* several

今 [ima] *adv* now; たった今 [tatta ima] *adv* just

居間 [ima] *n* living room

今はやり [imahayari] 今はやりの [ima hayari no] *adj* trendy

いまいましい [imaimashii] *adj* damn

今まで [ima made] 今までに [ima made ni] *adv* ever

イメージ [imeeji] *n* image

意味 [imi] *n* meaning; 意味する [imi suru] *v* mean; 無意味な [muimi na] *adj* senseless

イモムシ [imomushi] *n* caterpillar

イモリ [imori] *n* newt

陰 [in] *n* shade

員 [in] 乗務員 [joumuin] *n* cabin crew; 警備員 [keibiin] *n* security guard; 店員 [ten-in] *n* salesperson

イナゴ [inago] *n* grasshopper

田舎 [inaka] *n* countryside; 田舎の [inaka no] *adj* rural; 田舎屋 [inakaya] *n* cottage

いなくなる [inakunaru] *v* disappear; いなくなって [inaku natte] *adj* gone

インボイス [inboisu] *n* invoice; インボイスを送る [inboisu-o okuru] *v* invoice

陰謀 [inbou] *n* conspiracy

インチ [inchi] *n* inch

インド [indo] *n* India; インド洋 [indoyou] *n* Indian Ocean

インドア [indoa] *adv* indoors

インド人 [indojin] *n* Indian *(person)*

インドネシア [indoneshia] n Indonesia

インドネシア人 [indoneshiajin] n Indonesian (*person*)

インドネシアの [indoneshia no] *adj* Indonesian

インドの [indo no] *adj* Indian

居眠り [inemuri] n snooze; 居眠りをする [inemuri-o suru] *v* snooze

インフラストラクチャー [infurasutorakuchaa] n infrastructure

インフレーション [infureeshon] n inflation

インフルエンザ [infuruenza] n flu, influenza; 鳥インフルエンザ [tori infuruenza] n bird flu; 私はインフルエンザにかかりました [watashi wa infuruenza ni kakarimashita] I have the flu; 私は最近インフルエンザにかかりました [watashi wa saikin infuruenza ni kakarimashita] I had the flu recently

イングランド [ingurando] n England; イングランドの [inngurando no] *adj* English

イングランド人 [ingurandojin] イングランド人男性 [ingurandojin dansei] n Englishman; イングランド人女性 [ingurandojin josei] n Englishwoman

イニシアチブ [inishiachibu] n initiative

陰気 [inki] 陰気な [inki na] *adj* dismal

インク [inku] n ink

インナーチューブ [innaachuubu] n inner tube

祈り [inori] n prayer

祈る [inoru] *v* pray

飲料 [inryou] n (medical) treatment; 飲料水 [inryousui] n drinking water

印刷 [insatsu] 印刷する [insatsu suru] *v* print; 印刷業者 [insatsu gyousha] n printer (*person*); 印刷機 [insatsuki] n printer (*machine*); 印刷物 [insatsubutsu] n print; 印刷はいくらですか? [insatsu wa ikura desu ka?] How much is printing?

隕石 [inseki] n meteorite

姻戚 [inseki] n in-laws

印象 [inshou] n impression; 印象的な [inshouteki na] *adj* impressive

印象づける [inshoudukeru] 強く印象づける [tsuyoku inshou zukeru] *v* impress

飲酒 [inshu] n drinking; 飲酒運転 [inshu unten] n drunk driving

インシュリン [inshurin] n insulin

インターホン [intaahon] n entry phone

インターコム [intaakomu] n intercom

インターネット [intaanetto] n Internet; インターネットサービスプロバイダ [intaanetto saabisu purobaida] n ISP; インターネットカフェ [intaanetto kafe] n Internet café; インターネット利用者 [intaanetto riyousha] n Internet user; その部屋にインターネットの接続ポイントはありますか? [sono heya ni intaanetto no setsuzoku-pointo wa arimasu ka?] Is there an Internet connection in the room?

インターネットカフェ [intaanetto kafe] ここにインターネットカフェはありますか? [koko ni intaanetto-kafe wa arimasu ka?] Are there any Internet cafés here?

インテリアデザイナー [interiadezainaa] n interior designer

イントラネット [intouranetto] n intranet

犬 [inu] n dog; 牧羊犬 [bokuyouken] n sheepdog; 雑種の犬 [zasshu no inu] n mongrel

犬小屋 [inugoya] n kennel

引用 [inyou] 引用する [inyou suru] *v* quote; 引用文 [in-youbun] n quotation, quote; 引用符 [in-youfu] n quotation marks

引用符 [in-youfu] n quotation marks

iPod® [ipod] n iPod® [ipod]

一杯 [ippai] コップ一杯の水 [koppu ippai no mizu] a glass of water; 紅茶をもう一杯いただけますか? [koucha o mou ippai itadakemasu ka?] Could we have another cup of tea, please?; ビールをもう一杯 [biiru o mou ippai] another beer

いっぱい [ippai] *adj* full; いっぱいにする [ippai ni suru] *v* fill

一泊 [ippaku] n one night

一般 [ippan] 一般に [ippan ni] *adv* generally;

一般の [ippan no] *adj* general; 一般知識 [ippan chishiki] *n* general knowledge; 一般医 [ippan'i] *n* general practitioner

1本 [ippon] *n* one bottle

以来 [irai] その時以来 [sono toki irai] *adv* since

依頼 [irai] 制作依頼 [seisaku irai] *n* commission

依頼人 [irainin] *n* client

いらいら [iraira] いらいらさせる [iraira saseru] *adj* irritating

いらいらした [irairashita] *v* irritated

いらいらして [iraira shite] *adv* impatiently

いらいらしている [iraira shiteiru] *v* impatient

いらいらする [iraira suru] いらいらした [irairashita] *adj* irritated, impatient

イラク [iraku] *n* Iraq

イラク人 [irakujin] *n* Iraqi

イラクの [iraku no] *adj* Iraqi

イラクサ [irakusa] *n* nettle

イラン [iran] *n* Iran

イラン人 [iranjin] *n* Iranian *(person)*

イランの [iran no] *adj* Iranian

いらっしゃる [irassharu] *v* be

入れ [ire] *n* pouch; 洗面用具入れ [senmen yougu ire] *n* cosmetics bag

入れ歯 [ireba] *n* false teeth

入れる [ireru] *v* let in; 香辛料を入れた [koushinryou-o ireta] *adj* spicy; 入れ歯 [ireba] *n* dentures

入れ墨 [irezumi] *n* tattoo

入口 [iriguchi] *n* entrance, entry; 入口の廊下 [iriguchi no rouka] *n* hall; 車椅子で利用できる入口はどこですか? [kuruma-isu de riyou dekiru iriguchi wa doko desu ka?] Where's the wheelchair-accessible entrance?

炒り卵 [iritamago] *n* scrambled eggs

色 [iro] *n* color; クリーム色の [kuriimuiro no] *adj* cream; ライラック色の [rairakku iro no] *adj* lilac; 日焼け色の [hiyake iro no] *adj* tanned; この色でお願いします [kono iro de o-negai shimasu] This color, please; これの別の色はありますか? [kore no betsu no iro

wa arimasu ka?] Do you have this in another color?; 色が好きではありません [iro ga suki de wa arimasen] I don't like the color

色白 [irojiro] 色白の [irojiro no] *adj* fair *(light color)*

いる [iru] *v* be; 家にいる [ie ni iru] *v* stay in

居る [iru] *adj* present

衣類 [irui] *n* clothing; 毛織物衣類 [keorimono irui] *n* woolens

イルカ [iruka] *n* dolphin

医療 [iryou] *n* medical treatment

異性愛 [iseiai] 異性愛の [iseiai no] *adj* heterosexual

医者 [isha] *n* doctor; お医者さんの予約を取れますか? [o-isha-san no yoyaku o toremasu ka?] Can I have an appointment with the doctor?; お医者さんと話をしたいのですが [o-isha-san to hanashi o shitai no desu ga] I'd like to speak to a doctor; 英語を話せるお医者さんはいらっしゃいますか? [eigo o hanaseru o-isha-san wa irasshaimasu ka?] Is there a doctor who speaks English?; 私はお医者さんに診てもらわなければなりません [watashi wa o-isha-san ni mite morawanakereba narimasen] I need a doctor; 医者を呼んで! [isha o yonde!] Call a doctor!

石 [ishi] *n* stone

意志 [ishi] *n* will *(motivation)*; 意志の力 [ishi no chikara] *n* willpower

意識 [ishiki] *n* consciousness; 意識がある [ishiki ga aru] *adj* conscious; 意識を回復する [ishiki-o kaifuku suru] *v* come around; 意識を失った [ishiki wo ushinatta] *adj* unconscious; 意識を失う [ishiki-o ushinau] *v* pass out; 自意識の強い [jiishiki no tsuyoi] *adj* self-conscious

遺失物 [ishitsubutsu] *n* lost-and-found; 遺失物取扱所 [ishitsubutsu toriatsukaijo] *n* lost-and-found department

移植 [ishoku] *n* transplant

移植ごて [ishokugote] *n* trowel

衣装 [ishou] 衣装一式 [ishou isshiki] *n* outfit

忙しい [isogashii] adj busy; ごめんなさい、忙
しいのです [gomen nasai, isogashii no desu]
Sorry, I'm busy

急ぐ [isogu] v hurry, hurry up, rush; 大急ぎ
[ooisogi] n hurry; 私は急いでいます [watashi
wa isoide imasu] I'm in a hurry

急いで [isoide] adv hastily

一式 [isshiki] 用具一式 [yougu isshiki] n kit

一緒 [issho] adv together; 全部一緒にお勘定
をお願いします [zenbu issho ni o-kanjou o
o-negai shimasu] All together, please

一緒に [issho ni] adv together

一周 [isshuu] n circuit

一週間 [isshuukan] n one week

一層 [issou] 一層悪い [issou warui] adj
worse; 一層悪く [issou waruku] adv worse

椅子 [isu] n chair (furniture); 肘掛け椅子
[hijikakeke isu] n armchair; 安楽椅子
[anraku isu] n easy chair; 小児用の食事椅子
[shouni you no shokuji isu] n highchair; 子
供用の椅子はありますか? [kodomo-you no
isu wa arimasu ka?] Do you have a high
chair?

イスラエル [isuraeru] n Israel

イスラエル人 [isuraerujin] n Israeli (person)

イスラエルの [isuraeru no] adj Israeli

イスラム教 [isuramukyou] n Islam; イスラム
教の [isuramukyou no] adj Moslem,
Muslim; イスラム教の [isuramukyou no] adj
Islamic; イスラム教徒 [isuramukyouto] n
Muslim

板 [ita] n board (wood); 掲示板 [keijiban] n
bulletin board

イタチ [itachi] n weasel

痛い [itai] adj painful, sore; さわると痛いとこ
ろ [sawaru to itai tokoro] n sore

痛める [itameru] v hurt

痛み [itami] n ache, pain; 耳の痛み [mimi no
itami] n earache; 痛み止めに何かもらえます
か? [itami-dome ni nani ka moraemasu ka?]
Can you give me something for the pain?;
私はここが痛みます [watashi wa koko ga
itamimasu] I have a pain here; 私は胸に痛

みがあります [watashi wa mune ni itami ga
arimasu] I have a pain in my chest

痛み止め [itamidome] n painkiller

痛む [itamu] v ache

イタリア [itaria] n Italy

イタリア語 [itariago] n Italian (language)

イタリア人 [itariajin] n Italian (person)

イタリアの [itaria no] adj Italian

いたずら [itazura] n mischief; いたずら好きな
[itazura zuki na] adj mischievous

移転 [iten] n transfer

射手座 [iteza] n Sagittarius

糸 [ito] n thread; 針と糸をお持ちですか? [hari
to ito o o-mochi desu ka?] Do you have a
needle and thread?

意図 [ito] n intention; 意図的な [itoteki na]
adj intentional

いとこ [itoko] n cousin

営む [itonamu] v run (a business)

いとしい [itoshii] いとしい人 [itoshii hito] n
beloved

いとわない [itowanai] v willing

いつ [itsu] adv when; いつ仕上がりますか?
[itsu shiagarimasu ka?] When will it be
ready?

いつまでに [itsumadeni] それはいつまでに払
わなければならないのですか? [sore wa itsu
made ni harawanakereba naranai no desu
ka?] When is it due to be paid?

胃痛 [itsuu] n stomachache

偽り [itsuwari] 偽りの [itsuwari no] adj false

偽る [itsuwaru] 偽りなく [itsuwari naku] adv
truly

行って連れて来る [itte tsurete kuru] v fetch

言う [iu] v say; ブツブツ言う [butsubutsu iu] v
mutter; 冗談を言う [joudan wo iu] v joke; 大
げさに言う [oogesa ni iu] v exaggerate

岩 [iwa] n rock; 石灰岩 [sekkaigan] n
limestone

祝い [iwai] n celebration

いわせる [iwaseru] 世間をあっといわせるよう
な [seken-o atto iwaseru you na] adj
sensational

祝う [iwau] *v* celebrate, congratulate

いや [iya] いやな [iya na] *adj* foul, grim; いや
だと思う [iyadato omou] *v* mind

いやがらせ [iyagarase] *n* harassment

イヤホン [iyahon] *n* earphones

いやいや [iyaiya] *adv* reluctantly; いやいや
ながらの [iyaiya nagara no] *adj* reluctant

嫌な [iya na] *adj* nasty, offensive, repellent;
実に嫌な [jitsu ni iya na] *adj* revolting

いやな [iya na] *adj* disgusting; いやなにおい
のする [iya na nioino suru] *adj* smelly

イヤリング [iyaringu] *n* earring

以前 [izen] 以前に [izen ni] *adv* before; 以前
は [izen wa] *adv* formerly; 以前の [izen no]
adj former

以前に [izen ni] *adv* previously

以前の [izen no] *adj* previous

I

J

ジャージー [jaajii] *n* jersey

邪悪 [jaaku] 邪悪な [jaaku na] *adj* wicked

ジャーナリスト [jaanarisuto] *n* journalist

ジャーナリズム [jaanarizumu] *n* journalism

ジャガイモ [jagaimo] *n* potato

ジャグ [jagu] *n* jug

ジャケット [jaketto] *n* jacket; ディナージャケット [dinaa jaketto] *n* dinner jacket

ジャッキ [jakki] *n* jack

邪魔 [jama] *n* burden; 邪魔をする [jama-o suru] *v* disturb

ジャマイカ人 [jamaikajin] *n* Jamaican (*person*)

ジャマイカの [jamaika no] *adj* Jamaican

ジャム [jamu] *n* jam; ジャムの瓶 [jamu no bin] *n* jam jar

ジャンボジェット [janbojetto] *n* jumbo jet

ジャングル [janguru] *n* jungle

ジャンク [janku] *n* junk; ジャンクメール [janku meeru] *n* junk mail

ジャンクション [jankushon] *n* junction

砂利 [jari] *n* gravel

ジャズ [jazu] *n* jazz

ジェル [jeru] *n* gel

自爆 [jibaku] 自爆者 [jibakusha] *n* suicide bomber

自分 [jibun] 直接自分で [chokusetsu jibun de] *adv* personally

自分自身 [jibunjishin] 自分自身の [jubunjishin no] *adj* own

自治 [jichi] 自治権のある [jichiken no aru] *adj* autonomous; 自治国家 [jichi kokka] *n* autonomy

時代 [jidai] *n* era; 青春時代 [seishun jidai] *n* youth; 子供時代 [kodomo jidai] *n* childhood

時代遅れ [jidaiokure] 時代遅れの [jidaiokure no] *adj* old-fashioned, out-of-date

自動 [jidou] *adj* automatic; 自動振替 [jidoufurikae] *n* standing order; 自動販売機 [jidouhanbaiki] *n* vending machine; 自動的な [jidouteki na] *adj* automatic; 自動的に [jidouteki ni] *adv* automatically

児童 [jidou] 児童虐待 [jidou gyakutai] *n* child abuse; 児童養護 [jidou yougo] *n* childcare

自動券売機 [jidoukenbaiki] *n* ticket machine; 自動券売機はどうやって使うのですか? [jidou-kenbaiki wa dou-yatte tsukau no desu ka?] How does the ticket machine work?; 自動券売機はどこですか? [jidou-kenbaiki wa doko desu ka?] Where is the ticket machine?; 自動券売機が故障しています [jidou-kenbaiki ga koshou shite imasu] The ticket machine isn't working

自動車 [jidousha] *n* car; 自動車保険 [jidousha hoken] *n* car insurance; 自動車整備士 [jidousha seibishi] *n* auto mechanic

自動車教習 [jidoushakyoushuu] *n* driving lesson; 自動車教習指導員 [jidousha kyoushuu shidouin] *n* driving instructor

自衛 [jiei] *n* self-defense

自営業 [jieigyou] 私は自営業です [watashi wa jieigyou desu] I'm self-employed

ジェット [jietto] ジェット機 [jettoki] *n* jet

時限 [jigen] 時限爆弾 [jigenbakudan] *n* timebomb

地獄 [jigoku] *n* hell

ジグソーパズル [jigusoo pazuru] *n* jigsaw puzzle

事業 [jigyou] *n* enterprise; 政府の社会福祉事業 [seifu no shakai fukushi jigyou] *n* social services

自白 [jihaku] *n* confession; **自白する** [jihaku suru] *v* confess

自発 [jihatsu] **自発的な** [jihatsuteki na] *adj* spontaneous, voluntary; **自発的に** [jihatsuteki ni] *adv* voluntarily; **自発的に申し出る** [jihatsuteki ni moushideru] *v* volunteer

慈悲 [jihi] *n* mercy

寺院 [jiin] *n* temple; **その寺院は一般公開されていますか？** [sono jiin wa ippan-koukai sarete imasu ka?] Is the temple open to the public?; **その寺院はいつ開きますか？** [sono jiin wa itsu hirakimasu ka?] When is the temple open?

ジーンズ [jiinzu] *n* jeans

時事 [jiji] **時事的な** [jijiteki na] *adj* topical; **時事問題** [jiji mondai] *n* current affairs

事実 [jijitsu] *n* fact, truth

自叙 [jijo] **自叙伝** [jijoden] *n* autobiography

事情 [jijou] *n* circumstances

時間 [jikan] *n* time; **サッカー・ラグビーなどで怪我の手当てなどに要した分の延長時間** [sakkaa / ragubii nado de kega no teate nado ni youshita bun no enchou jikan] *n* injury time-out; **コマーシャルの時間** [komaasharu no jikan] *n* commercial break; **欠勤時間** [kekkin jikan] *n* time off; **時間厳守の** [jikangenshu no] *adj* punctual; **標準時間帯** [hyoujun jikantai] *n* time zone; **超過勤務** [chouka kinmu] *n* overtime; **食事時間** [shokuji jikan] *n* mealtime; **遊び時間** [asobi jikan] *n* playtime; **面会時間** [menkaijikan] *n* visiting hours; **営業時間** [eigyoujikan] *n* office hours, opening hours; **もう行く時間ですか？** [mou iku jikan desu ka?] Is it time to go?; **時間がかかりますか？** [jikan ga kakarimasu ka?] Will it take long?

自家製 [jikasei] **自家製の** [jikasei no] *adj* homemade

磁器 [jiki] *n* china

時期 [jiki] *n* time period; **時期尚早の** [jikishousou no] *adj* premature

実験 [jikken] *n* experiment

実験台 [jikkendai] *n* guinea pig *(for experiment)*

実験室 [jikkenshitsu] *n* laboratory

実行 [jikkou] **実行する** [jikkou suru] *v* carry out; **実行可能な** [jikkoukanou na] *adj* feasible

実況 [jikkyou] **実況解説** [jikkyou kaisetsu] *n* commentary

事故 [jiko] *n* accident; **事故保険** [jiko hoken] *n* accident insurance; **事故にあったらどうすればいいのですか？** [jiko ni attara dou sureba ii no desu ka?] What do I do if I have an accident?; **事故がありました！** [jiko ga arimashita!] There's been an accident!; **私は事故にあいました** [watashi wa jiko ni aimashita] I've been in an accident, I've had an accident

自己 [jiko] **自己本位の** [jiko hon'i no] *adj* self-centered; **自己訓練** [jiko kunren] *n* self-discipline

時刻 [jikoku] *n* time; **ディナーの時刻** [dinaa no jikoku] *n* dinnertime; **時刻表** [jikokuhyou] *n* timetable; **閉店時刻** [heiten jikoku] *n* closing time; **就寝時刻** [shuushin jikoku] *n* bedtime; **電車は時刻どおりですか？** [densha wa jikoku doori desu ka?] Is the train on time?

時刻表 [jikokuhyou] *n* time table

ジマー [jimaa] *n* walker

字幕 [jimaku] *n* subtitles; **字幕を入れた** [jimaku-o ireta] *adj* subtitled

自慢 [jiman] **自慢する** [jiman suru] *v* boast

地面 [jimen] *n* ground; **地面に置く** [jimen ni oku] *v* ground

事務 [jimu] *n* office work; **事務弁護士** [jimubengoshi] *n* lawyer; **机上事務** [kijou jimu] *n* paperwork

ジム [jimu] *n* gym; **ジムはどこですか？** [jimu wa doko desu ka?] Where's the gym?

地虫 [jimushi] *n* grub

事務所 [jimusho] *n* office

ジン [jin] *n* gin

J

ジンバブウェ [jinbabuue] *n* Zimbabwe; ジンバブウェ人 [Jinbabuue jin] *n* Zimbabwean; ジンバブウェの [Jinbabuue no] *adj* Zimbabwean

人道主義 [jindoushugi] 人道主義の [jindou shugi no] *adj* humanitarian

人員 [jin-in] *n* personnel

人権 [jinken] *n* human rights

人口 [jinkou] *n* population

人工 [jinkou] 人工の [jinkou no] *adj* artificial; 人工衛星 [jinkou eisei] *n* satellite

人類 [jinrui] *n* mankind; 人類学 [jinruigaku] *n* anthropology

人種 [...jinshu...] *n* race *(origin)*; 人種の [jinshu no] *adj* racial; 人種差別 [jinshusabetsu] *n* racism

人種差別 [jinshusabetsu] 人種差別主義者 [jinshusabetsushugisha] *n* racist; 人種差別主義者の [jinshu sabetsu shugisha no] *adj* racist

ジントニック [jintonikku] *n* gin and tonic; ジントニックをお願いします [jin-tonikku o o-negai shimasu] I'll have a gin and tonic, please

地主 [jinushi] *n* landowner

人造 [jinzou] 人造の [jinzou no] *adj* man-made

腎臓 [jinzou] *n* kidney

ジプシー [jipushii] *n* gypsy

事例 [jirei] *n* instance

ジレンマ [jirenma] *n* dilemma

時差ぼけ [jisaboke] *n* jetlag

自殺 [jisatsu] *n* suicide

時制 [jisei] *n* tense

自制 [jisei] *n* self-control

磁石 [jishaku] *n* magnet; 磁石の [jishaku no] *adj* magnetic

自信 [jishin] *n* confidence *(self-assurance)*; 自信のある [jishin no aru] *adj* self-assured

自身 [jishin] *n* oneself; あなた方自身 [anatagata jishin] *pron* yourselves; あなた自身 [anata jishin] *pron* yourself

地震 [jishin] *n* earthquake

辞書 [jisho] *n* dictionary

地所 [jisho] *n* estate

辞職 [jishoku] 辞職する [jishoku suru] *v* resign

実際 [jissai] 実際に [jissai ni] *adv* actually, practically; 実際の [jissai no] *adj* actual; 実際的な [jissaiteki na] *adj* practical; 実際的でない [jissaiteki denai] *adj* impractical

実施 [jisshi] レッスンを実施していますか? [ressun o jisshi shite imasu ka?] Do you give lessons?

実質 [jisshitsu] *n* substance; 実質上の [jisshitsujou no] *adj* virtual

地すべり [jisuberi] *n* landslide

自炊 [jisui] *n* with kitchen *(lodging)*

事態 [jitai] *n* situation; 緊急事態 [kinkyuujitai] *n* emergency

自宅 [jitaku] *n* home; 自宅住所 [jitaku juusho] *n* home address

事典 [jiten] *n* dictionary; 百科事典 [hyakka jiten] *n* encyclopedia

次点 [jiten] 次点者 [jitensha] *n* runner-up

自転車 [jitensha] *n* bicycle, bike; タンデム自転車 [tandemu jitensha] *n* tandem bicycle *v* 自転車に乗る [jitensha ni noru] *v* ride a bike; 自転車ポンプ [jitensha ponpu] *n* bicycle pump; 一番近い自転車修理店はどこですか? [ichiban chikai jitensha shuuri-ten wa doko desu ka?] Where is the nearest bike repair shop?; どこで自転車をレンタルできますか? [doko de jitensha o rentaru dekimasu ka?] Where can I rent a bike?; ここに自転車を置いておけますか? [koko ni jitensha o oite okemasu ka?] Can I keep my bike here?; 自転車はいつ返すことになっていますか? [jitensha wa itsu kaesu koto ni natte imasu ka?] When is the bike due back?; 自転車はコースターブレーキ付きですか? [jitensha wa koosutaa-bureeki tsuki desu ka?] Does the bike have coaster brakes?; 自転車はギア付きですか? [jitensha wa gia tsuki desu ka?] Does the bike have gears?; 自転車はライト付きですか? [jitensha wa raito tsuki desu ka?] Does the bike have lights?; 自転車はブレーキ付きですか?

[jitensha wa bureeki tsuki desu ka?] Does the bike have brakes?; 自転車を借りたいのですが [jitensha o karitai no desu ga] I want to rent a bike; ···へ行く自転車道はどこですか? [... e iku jitensha-dou wa doko desu ka?] Where's the bicycle path to...?

実在 [jitsuzai] 実在の [jitsuzai no] *adj* real

じっと [jitto] *adv* still; じっと見つめる [jitto mitsumeru] *v* stare

滋養 [jiyou] 滋養のある [jiyou no aru] *adj* nutritious

自由 [jiyuu] *n* freedom; 自由な [jiyuu na] *adj* free *(no restraint)*; 自由契約の [jiyuu keiyaku no] *adj* freelance; 自由契約で [jiyuu keiyaku de] *adv* freelance; ···を自由にする [...-o jiyuu ni suru] *v* free

自由選択 [jiyuusentaku] 自由選択の [jiyuusentakuno] *adj* optional

事前 [jizen] *adv* beforehand; 事前予約 [jizen yoyaku] *n* advance reservation

慈善 [jizen] 慈善団体 [jizen dantai] *n* charity

持続 [jizoku] 持続性の [jizokusei no] *adj* persistent; 持続期間 [jizoku kikan] *n* duration

除外 [jogai] 除外する [jogai suru] *v* exclude

助言 [jogen] *n* advice, tip *(suggestion)*; 助言する [jogen suru] *v* advise

ジョギング [jogingu] *n* jogging; ジョギングする [jogingu suru] *v* jog; どこに行けばジョギングができますか? [doko ni ikeba jogingu ga dekimasu ka?] Where can I go jogging?

除氷 [johyou] 除氷装置 [johyou souchi] *n* deicer

女医 [joi] *n* female physician

徐々 [jojo] 徐々に [jojo ni] *adv* gradually; 徐々の [jojo no] *adj* gradual

抒情 [jojou] 抒情詩 [jojoushi] *n* lyrics

除光液 [jokoueki] *n* nail-polish remover

除去 [jokyo] 除去する [jokyo suru] *v* eliminate

ジョージア [joojia] *n* Georgia *(US state)*

女王 [joou] *n* queen

助産婦 [josanpu] *n* midwife

女性 [josei] *n* female, woman; 独身女性 [dokushinjosei] *n* spinster; 女性の [josei no] *adj* female; 女性バーテンダー [josei baatendaa] *n* female bartender; 女性軍人 [josei gunjin] *n* servicewoman; 女性用トイレ [joseiyou toire] *n* ladies' room; 女性店員 [josei ten'in] *n* saleslady

助成金 [joseikin] *n* grant, subsidy; 助成金を支給する [joseikin-o shikyuu suru] *v* subsidize

除雪 [josetsu] 除雪車 [josetsusha] *n* snowplow

女子 [joshi] 女子修道院 [joshishuudouin] *n* convent; 女子生徒 [joshiseito] *n* schoolgirl

助手 [joshu] *n* assistant; 教室助手 [kyoushitsu joshu] *n* teacher's aide

除草 [josou] *n* girl; 除草剤 [josouzai] *n* weedkiller

錠 [jou] *n* lock *(door)*; 錠をあける [jou-o akeru] *v* unlock; 錠剤 [jouzai] *n* pill

乗馬 [jouba] *n* horseback riding, riding; 乗馬に行きましょう [jouba ni ikimashou] Let's go horseback riding; 乗馬に行けますか? [jouba ni ikemasu ka?] Can we go horseback riding?

丈夫 [joubu] 丈夫な [joubu na] *adj* strong, durable

冗談 [joudan] *n* joke; 冗談を言う [joudan wo iu] *v* joke

上演 [jouen] *n* performance

定規 [jougi] *n* ruler *(measure)*

じょうご [jougo] *n* funnel

譲歩 [jouho] *n* concession

情報 [jouhou] *n* information; 情報技術 [jouho gijutsu] *n* IT; 個人情報泥棒 [kojin jouhou dorobou] *n* identity theft; 会社についての情報を教えていただきたいのですが [kaisha ni tsuite no jouhou o oshiete itadakitai no desu ga] I'd like some information about the company; ···に関する情報が欲しいのですが [... ni kansuru jouhou ga hoshii no desu ga] I'd like some information about...; 弊社についての情報です [heisha ni tsuite no jouhou desu] Here's some information about my company

浄化槽 [joukasou] *n* septic tank

条件付き [joukentsuki] 条件付きの [joukentsuki no] *adj* conditional

蒸気 [jouki] *n* steam

条項 [joukou] *n* clause

乗客 [joukyaku] *n* passenger

状況 [joukyou] *n* context, situation

上級官吏 [joukyuu kanri] *n* mandarin *(official)*

錠前屋 [joumaeya] *n* locksmith

乗務 [joumu] 乗務員 [joumuin] *n* cabin crew

乗務員 [joumuin] *n* crew member; 客室乗務員 [kyakushitsu joumuin] *n* flight attendant

静脈 [joumyaku] *n* vein

じょうろ [jouro] *n* watering can

蒸留 [jouryuu] 蒸留所 [jouryuujo] *n* distillery

乗車 [jousha] *n* boarding

常識 [joushiki] *n* common sense

上昇 [joushou] *n* rise

常習 [joushuu] 常習的な [joushuuteki na] *adj* addicted

状態 [joutai] *n* condition, state; 乱雑な状態 [ranzatsu na joutai] *n* shambles; 混乱状態 [konranjoutai] *n* confusion

条約 [jouyaku] *n* treaty

常用 [jouyou] 麻薬常用者 [mayaku jouyousha] *n* drug addict

醸造 [jouzou] 醸造所 [jouzoujo] *n* brewery

女優 [joyuu] *n* actress

授業 [jugyou] *n* lesson, tuition; 授業料 [jugyouryou] *n* tuition fees

受験 [juken] *n* taking an exam; 再受験する [saijuken suru] *v* retake

熟 [juku] 熟した [juku shita] *adj* ripe

熟練 [jukuren] *n* skill; 熟練していない [jukuren shite inai] *adj* unskilled; 熟練した [jukuren shita] *adj* skilled, skillful; 熟練職業 [jukuren shokugyou] *n* craft

受給 [jukyuu] 老齢年金受給者 [rourei nenkin jukyuusha] *n* old-age pensioner

受給者 [jukyuusha] 年金受給者 [nenkin

jukyuusha] *n* senior

呪文 [jumon] *n* spell *(magic)*

準… [jun...] *adj* associate

順番 [junban] 順番待ち名簿 [junbanmachi meibo] *n* waiting list

準備 [junbi] *n* preparation; 準備する [junbi suru] *v* prepare, provide for

順序 [junjo] *n* sequence

準々決勝 [junjunkesshou] *n* quarter final

循環 [junkan] *n* circulation

準決勝 [junkesshou] *n* semifinal

巡航 [junkou] *n* cruise

殉教 [junkyou] 殉教者 [junkyousha] *n* martyr

順応 [junnou] 順応する [junnou suru] *v* adjust

巡礼 [junrei] *n* pilgrimage; 巡礼者 [junreisha] *n* pilgrim

巡礼の旅 [junrei no tabi] *n* pilgrimage

純粋な [junsui na] *adj* pure

授乳 [junyuu] 授乳する [junyuu suru] *v* breast-feed; どこで赤ちゃんに授乳できますか? [doko de akachan ni junyuu dekimasu ka?] Where can I breast-feed the baby?; ここで授乳できますか? [koko de junyuu dekimasu ka?] Can I breast-feed here?

受領証 [juryoushou] *n* receipt

樹脂 [jushi] *n* resin

受信 [jushin] *n* reception; 受信機 [jushinki] *n* receiver *(electronic)*

授賞 [jushou] 授賞式 [jushoushiki] *n* prize-giving

受賞 [jushou] 受賞者 [jushousha] *n* prizewinner

十歳 [jussai] *n* 10 years old

十進法 [jusshinhou] 十進法の [jusshinhou no] *adj* decimal

銃 [juu] *n* gun; ライフル銃 [raifuru juu] *n* rifle; 散弾銃 [sandanjuu] *n* shotgun

十 [juu] *number* ten; 十番目 [juu banme] *n* tenth; 十番目の [juu banme no] *adj* tenth

十分 [juubun] *adj* enough; 不十分な [fujuubun na] *adj* inadequate, insufficient; 十分な [juubun na] *adj* enough; 十分に [juubun ni] *adv* fully

重大 [juudai] adj serious; きわめて重大な [kiwamete juudai na] adj momentous, vital; 重大な [juudai na] adj critical, crucial; 重大局面 [juudai kyokumen] n crisis

十代 [juudai] n teens

充電 [juuden] n charge (electricity); 充電する [juuden suru] v charge (electricity); 再充電する [saijuuden suru] v recharge; どこで携帯電話を充電できますか? [doko de keitai-denwa o juuden dekimasu ka?] Where can I charge my cell phone?; 充電されません [juuden saremasen] It isn't charging

充電器 [juudenki] n charger

柔道 [juudou] n judo

十月 [juugatsu] n October; 十月三日の日曜日です [juu-gatsu mik-ka no nichiyoubi desu] It's Sunday, October third

十五 [juugo] number fifteen

十五番目 [juugobanme] 十五番目の [juugo banme no] adj fifteenth

十五分 [juugofun] 二時十五分です [ni-ji juugo-fun desu] It's two-fifteen

従業員 [juugyouin] n employee

十八 [juuhachi] number eighteen

十八番目 [juuhachibanme] 十八番目の [juuhachi banme no] adj eighteenth

獣医 [juui] n vet

十一 [juuichi] number eleven

十一番目 [juuichibanme] 十一番目の [juuichi banme no] adj eleventh

十一月 [juuichigatsu] n November

十字 [juuji] 赤十字社 [Sekijuujisha] n Red Cross; 十字形 [juujigata] n cross

十字架 [juujika] n crucifix

従順 [juujun] adj obedient; 不従順な [fujuujun na] adj disobedient

従順な [juujun na] adj obedient

住居 [juukyo] n residence; 住居侵入罪 [juukyoshinnyuuzai] n burglary

十九 [juukyuu] number nineteen

十九番目 [juukyuubanme] 十九番目の [juukyuu banme no] adj nineteenth

十七 [juunana] number seventeen; 十七番目の [juushichi banme no] adj seventeenth

柔軟剤 [juunanzai] n fabric softener; 柔軟剤はありますか? [juunan-zai wa arimasu ka?] Do you have fabric softener?

十年間 [juunenkan] n decade

十二 [juuni] number twelve; 十二番目の [juuni banme no] adj twelfth

十二月 [juunigatsu] n December; 十二月三十一日の金曜日に [juuni-gatsu sanjuuichi-nichi no kinyoubi ni] on Friday, December thirty-first

十二時 [juuniji] n 12 o'clock

12個 [juuniko] n dozen

十二宮 [juunikyuu] n zodiac

住人 [juunin] n inhabitant

10億 [juuoku] n billion

十六 [juuroku] number sixteen; 十六番目の [juuroku banme no] adj sixteenth

重量挙げ [juuryouage] n weightlifting; 重量挙げ選手 [juuryouage senshu] n weight-lifter

十三 [juusan] number thirteen; 十三番目の [juusan banme no] adj thirteenth

獣脂 [juushi] n grease

住所 [juusho] n address (location); 住所氏名録 [juusho shimei roku] n directory; 住所録 [juushoroku] n address book; 自宅住所 [jitaku juusho] n home address; 私あての郵便物をこの住所に回送してください [watashi ate no yuubinbutsu o kono juusho ni kaisou shite kudasai] Please forward my mail to this address

重症 [juushou] n serious condition; 重症ですか? [juushou desu ka?] Is it serious?

ジュース [juusu] n juice; フルーツジュース [furuutsujuusu] n fruit juice

渋滞 [juutai] 交通渋滞 [koutsuujuutai] n traffic jam; この渋滞の原因は何ですか? [kono juutai no gen'in wa nan desu ka?] What is causing this hold-up?

住宅 [juutaku] n residence; 公営住宅 [koueijuutaku] n government-subsidized

housing
住宅地 [juutakuchi] **住宅地の** [juutakuchi no] *adj* residential

重炭酸ソーダ [juutansansooda] *n* bicarbonate of soda

十四 [juuyon] *number* fourteen

十四番目 [juuyonbanme] **十四番目の** [juuyon banme no] *adj* fourteenth

重要 [juuyou] *n* importance; **最も重要な** [mottomo juuyou na] *adj* essential; **重要な** [juuyou na] *adj* important, significant; **重要でない** [juuyou de nai] *adj* unimportant; **重要である** [juuyou de aru] *v* matter; **重要性** [juuyousei] *n* importance, significance

K

科 [ka] 精神科の [seishinka no] *adj* psychiatric; 精神科医 [seishinka-i] *n* psychiatrist

課 [ka] 貴社には広報報道課がありますか? [kisha ni wa kouhou-houdou-ka ga arimasu ka?] Do you have a press office?

蚊 [ka] *n* mosquito

カーボン [kaabon] カーボンフットプリント [kaabon futtopurinto] *n* carbon footprint

カーデッキ [kaadekki] カーデッキへはどう行けばいいのですか? [kaa-dekki e wa dou ikeba ii no desu ka?] How do I get to the car deck?

カーディガン [kaadigan] *n* cardigan

カード [kaado] *n* card; カード式公衆電話 [kaado shiki koushuu denwa] *n* cardphone; クリスマスカード [kurisumasu kaado] *n* Christmas card; このカードをどこで投函できますか? [kono kaado o doko de toukan dekimasu ka?] Where can I mail these cards?; この現金自動支払い機で私のカードを使えますか? [kono genkin-jidou-shiharaiki de watashi no kaado o tsukaemasu ka?] Can I use my card with this ATM?; クレジットカードは使えますか? [kurejitto-kaado wa tsukaemasu ka?] Do you take credit cards?; クレジットカードで支払えますか? [kurejitto-kaado de shiharaemasu ka?] Can I pay by credit card?; デビットカードは使えますか? [debitto-kaado wa tsukaemasu ka?] Do you take debit cards?; バスのカードはどこで買えますか? [basu no kaado wa doko de kaemasu ka?] Where can I buy a bus card?; 現金自動支払い機が私のカードを吸い込んでしまいました [genkin-jidou-shiharaiki ga watashi no kaado o suikonde shimaimashita] The ATM swallowed my card; 私はカードをキャンセルしなければなりません [watashi wa kaado o kyanseru shinakereba narimasen] I need to cancel my card; 私のカードが盗まれました [watashi no kaado ga nusuma remashita] My card has been stolen; 私のカードです [watashi no kaado desu] Here's my card; 私のカードを使って現金を引き出せますか? [watashi no kaado o tsukatte genkin o hikidasemasu ka?] Can I use my card to get cash?

カーフェリー [kaaferii] *n* car ferry

カーネーション [kaaneeshon] *n* carnation

カーニバル [kaanibaru] *n* carnival

カーペット [kaapetto] *n* carpet

カーラー [kaaraa] *n* curler

カーソル [kaasoru] *n* cursor

カーステレオ [kaasutereo] *n* car stereo; 車にカーステレオはついていますか? [kuruma ni kaa-sutereo wa tsuite imasu ka?] Is there a stereo in the car?

カーテン [kaaten] *n* curtain

カート [kaato] 手荷物カート [tenimotsu kaato] *n* baggage cart

カートリッジ [kaatorijji] *n* cartridge

樺 [kaba] *n* birch

カバ [kaba] *n* (動物) hippo, (動物) hippopotamus

カバー [kabaa] カバーチャージ [kabaa chaaji] *n* cover charge; ベッドカバー [beddokabaa] *n* bedspread; 枕カバー [makurakabaa] *n* pillowcase

カバブ [kababu] *n* kebab

かばん [kaban] *n* briefcase; 一泊旅行用かば

ん [ippaku ryokou you kaban] n overnight bag; 肩掛けかばん [katakake kaban] n backpack; 通学かばん [tsuugaku kaban] n schoolbag; 大型の旅行かばん [ougata no ryokou kaban] n duffel bag; 誰かが私のかばんを盗みました [dare ka ga watashi no kaban o nusumimashita] Someone's stolen my briefcase; 私はタクシーにかばんを置き忘れました [watashi wa takushii ni kaban o okiwasuremashita] I left my briefcase in the taxi

壁 [kabe] n wall

壁紙 [kabegami] n wallpaper

カビ [kabi] n mold (fungus)

花瓶 [kabin] n vase

過敏な [kabin na] 神経過敏な [shinkeikabin na] adj neurotic

かびる [kabiru] かびた [kabita] adj moldy

カボチャ [kabocha] n pumpkin

カブ [kabu] n (食べ物) turnip

株主 [kabunushi] n shareholder, stockholder

株式 [kabushiki] 株式仲買人 [kabushikinakagainin] n stockbroker; 株式市場 [kabushikishijou] n stock market

カブトムシ [kabutomushi] n beetle

価値 [kachi] n value; 価値のない [kachi no nai] adj worthless

カチカチ [kachikachi] カチッという音 [kachitto iu oto] n click; カチッと鳴る [kachitto naru] v click

家畜 [kachiku] 迷い出た家畜 [mayoideta kachiku] n stray

課長補佐 [kachouhosa] n assistant principal

過大 [kadai] 過大評価する [kadai hyouka suru] v overestimate

過大な [kadai na] 過大請求する [kadai seikyuu suru] v overcharge

角¹ [kado] n corner; 2番目の角を左に曲がってください [ni-ban-me no kado o hidari ni magatte kudasai] Take the second turn on your left; その角です [sono kado desu] It's

on the corner; その角を曲がったところです [sono kado o magatta tokoro desu] It's around the corner; 最初の角を右に曲がってください [saisho no kado o migi ni magatte kudasai] Take the first turn on your right

角² [kado] (数学) angle

カエデ [kaede] n maple

火炎 [kaen] n blaze

変えられる [kaerareru] v convertible

帰る [kaeru] 帰ること [kaeru koto] n return (coming back); あなたが帰ってくるころには私たちは寝ています [anata ga kaette kuru koro ni wa watashi-tachi wa nete imasu] We'll be in bed when you get back; いつお国へお帰りになりますか? [itsu o-kuni e o-kaeri ni narimasu ka?] When are you returning to your country?; 私は家に帰りたいです [watashi wa ie ni kaeritai desu] I'd like to go home

カエル [kaeru] n frog

変える [kaeru] v convert, switch ▷ vt change; 向きを変える [muki wo kaeru] v turn

返す [kaesu] v give back; ひっくり返す [hikkurigaesu] v knock over; もとへ返す [moto-e kaesu] v put back; 送り返す [okurikaesu] v send back

カフェ [kafe] n café; インターネットカフェ [intaanetto kafe] n Internet café

カフェイン [kafein] n caffeine

カフェイン抜き [kafein nuki] カフェイン抜きの [kafein nuki no] adj decaffeinated; カフェイン抜きのコーヒー [kafein nuki no koohii] n decaffeinated coffee

カフェテリア [kafeteria] n cafeteria

カフカス [kafukasu] カフカス山脈 [Kafukasu sanmyaku] n Caucasus

花粉 [kafun] n pollen

花粉症 [kafunshou] n hay fever

カフスリンク [kafusurinku] n cufflinks

科学 [kagaku] n science; コンピューター科学 [konpyuutaa kagaku] n computer science; 科学の [kagaku no] adj scientific; 科学者 [kagakusha] n scientist

化学 [kagaku] n chemistry; 化学薬品 [kagakuyakuhin] n chemical

鏡 [kagami] n mirror; 望遠鏡 [bouenkyou] n telescope

かがむ [kagamu] v bend down, bend over

輝く [kagayaku] 光り輝く [hikari kagayaku] adj brilliant

影 [kage] n shadow

過激 [kageki] 過激主義 [kageki shugi] n extremism; 過激派 [kagekiha] n extremist

鍵 [kagi] n key (for lock); 車の鍵 [kuruma no kagi] n car keys; 鍵をかける [kagi-o kakeru] v lock; 202号室の鍵 [nihyaku-ni-gou-shitsu no kagi] the key for room number two hundred and two; このドアの鍵はどれですか? [kono doa no kagi wa dore desu ka?] Which is the key to this door?; この鍵は何のためですか? [kono kagi wa nan no tame desu ka?] What's this key for?; 正面玄関の鍵はどれですか? [shoumen-genkan no kagi wa dore desu ka?] Which is the key to the front door?; 裏口の鍵はどれですか? [uraguchi no kagi wa dore desu ka?] Which is the key to the back door?; 車庫の鍵はどれですか? [shako no kagi wa dore desu ka?] Which is the key to the garage?; 私は鍵を置き忘れました [watashi wa kagi o okiwasuremashita] I've forgotten the key; 私の鍵は開きません [watashi no kagi wa akimasen] My key doesn't work; ···の鍵はどこでもらえばいいのですか? [... no kagi wa doko de moraeba ii no desu ka?] Where do we get the key...?; 鍵に問題があります [kagi ni mondai ga arimasu] I'm having trouble with the key; 鍵がもう一つ必要です [kagi ga mou hitotsu hitsuyou desu] We need a second key; 鍵が開きません [kagi ga akimasen] The key doesn't work; 鍵をお願いします [kagi o o-negai shimasu] The key, please; 鍵をもらえますか? [kagi o moraemasu ka?] May I have a key?

かぎ針編み [kagibariami] かぎ針編みをする [kagiamibari-o suru] v crochet

限り [kagiri] 一回限りのこと [ikkai kagiri no koto] n one-off

かぎり [kagiri] できるかぎりの [dekiru kagiri no] adj as much as you can do

かぎづめ [kagizume] n claw

かご [kago] n basket, cage

家具 [kagu] n furniture; 家具付きの [kagu tsuki no] adj furnished

嗅ぐ [kagu] においを嗅ぐ [nioi-o kagu] vt smell

カグール [kaguuru] n raincoat

貨幣 [kahei] 貨幣鋳造所 [kahei chuuzoujo] n mint (coins)

貝 [kai] n shellfish

階 [kai] それは何階ですか? [sore wa nan-kai desu ka?] What floor is it on?

怪物 [kaibutsu] n monster

懐中 [kaichuu] 懐中電灯 [kaichuudentou] n flashlight

懐中電灯 [kaichuudentou] n flashlight

階段 [kaidan] n staircase, stairs; 非常階段 [hijoukaidan] n fire escape

回復 [kaifuku] n recovery; 意識を回復する [ishiki-o kaifuku suru] v come around; 回復する [kaifuku suru] v recover, regain

絵画 [kaiga] n painting

海外 [kaigai] 海外に [kaigai ni] adv abroad, overseas

海岸 [kaigan] n seashore, seaside; 海岸の遊歩道 [kaigan no yuuhodou] n promenade

会議 [kaigi] n conference, meeting

海軍 [kaigun] n navy; 海軍の [kaigun no] adj naval

解放 [kaihou] n liberation, release; 解放する [kaihou suru] v release

会員 [kaiin] n member; 会員でないといけないのですか? [kaiin de nai to ikenai no desu ka?] Do you have to be a member?; 会員でなければなりませんか? [kaiin de nakereba narimasen ka?] Do I have to be a member?

海事 [kaiji] 海事の [kaiji no] adj maritime

介助 [kaijo] 私は介助が必要です [watashi wa

K

kaijo ga hitsuyou desu] I need assistance

会場 [kaijou] n venue

階下 [kaika] 階下の [kaika no] adj downstairs; 階下へ [kaika-e] adv downstairs

会計 [kaikei] n accountancy; 会計係 [kaikeigakari] n cashier, treasurer; 会計監査人 [kaikei kansanin] n auditor; 会計士 [kaikeishi] n accountant

会計年度 [kaikeinendo] n fiscal year

会見 [kaiken] 記者会見 [kishakaiken] n press conference

解決 [kaiketsu] n solution; 解決する [kaiketsu suru] v settle, solve, sort out

会期 [kaiki] n session

解雇 [kaiko] n dismissal; 一時解雇する [ichiji kaiko suru] v lay off; 余剰人員の解雇 [yojou jin'in no kaiko] n layoff; 余剰人員として解雇された [yojou jin'in to shite kaiko sareta] adj laid off; 解雇する [kaiko suru] v dismiss

開口部 [kaikoubu] n aperture

階級 [kaikyuu] n rank (status); 労働者階級の [roudoushakaikyuu no] adj working-class

買物 [kaimono] n shopping; 買物袋 [kaimonobukuro] n shopping bag

飼いならす [kainarasu] 飼いならされた [kainarasareta] adj tame

貝類 [kairui] 私は貝類のアレルギーがあります [watashi wa kairui no arerugii ga arimasu] I'm allergic to shellfish

改良 [kairyou] 品種改良する [hinshu kairyou suru] v breed

海流 [kairyuu] 海流がありますか? [kairyuu ga arimasu ka?] Are there currents?

改札 [kaisatsu] 改札係 [kaisatsugakari] n ticket collector; 改札口 [kaisatsuguchi] n ticket barrier; 回転式改札口 [kaitenshiki kaisatsuguchi] n turnstile

回線 [kaisen] n telephone line

解説 [kaisetsu] 解説者 [kaisetsusha] n commentator; 実況解説 [jikkyou kaisetsu] n commentary

会社 [kaisha] n company, firm; 航空会社 [koukuu gaisha] n airline; 子会社 [kogaisha] n subsidiary; 会社についての情報を教えていただきたいのですが [kaisha ni tsuite no jouhou o oshiete itadakitai no desu ga] I'd like some information about the company

解釈 [kaishaku] 解釈する [kaishaku suru] v interpret

開始 [kaishi] n start

快速 [kaisoku] 快速モーターボート [kaisoku mootaabooto] n speedboat

海藻 [kaisou] n seaweed

改装 [kaisou] 改装する [kaisou suru] v redecorate

回送 [kaisou] 私あての郵便物をこの住所に回送してください [watashi ate no yuubinbutsu o kono juusho ni kaisou shite kudasai] Please forward my mail to this address

海水 [kaisui] n sea water; 海水面 [kaisui men] n sea level

解する [kai suru] 読唇術で解する [dokushin-jutsu de kaisuru] v lip-read

回数 [kaisuu] 回数券をください [kaisuuken o kudasai] A book of tickets, please

快適 [kaiteki] 快適な [kaiteki na] adj comfortable

回転 [kaiten] 回転木馬 [kaitenmokuba] n merry-go-round; 回転式乾燥機 [kaitenshiki kansouki] n (clothes) dryer; 回転式改札口 [kaitenshiki kaisatsuguchi] n turnstile

会話 [kaiwa] n conversation

海洋 [kaiyou] n ocean

潰瘍 [kaiyou] n ulcer

改善 [kaizen] n improvement; 改善する [kaizen suru] v improve

海賊 [kaizoku] n pirate

改造 [kaizou] n makeover

火事 [kaji] 火事だ! [kaji da!] Fire!

家事 [kaji] n housework

カジノ [kajino] n casino

果樹 [kaju] 果樹園 [kajuen] n orchard

価格 [kakaku] n price; 価格表 [kakakuhyou] n price list; 販売価格 [hanbai kakaku] n selling price; 小売価格 [kourikakaku] *n* retail price

係 [kakari] *n* person in charge; 会計係 [kaikeigakari] *n* cashier, treasurer; 改札係 [kaisatsugakari] *n* ticket collector; 検札係 [kensatsugakari] *n* ticket inspector

係官 [kakarikan] 税関係官 [zeikan kakarikan] *n* customs officer

かかる [kakaru] *v* (費用) cost

掛かる [kaka ru] *vi* hang

かかし [kakashi] *n* scarecrow

かかと [kakato] *n* heel

かかわる [kakawaru] *v* be connected; 個人に かかわらない [kojin ni kakawaranai] *adj* impersonal

賭け [kake] *n* bet; 賭け事 [kakegoto] *n* betting; 賭け屋 [kakeya] *n* betting shop

···掛け [...kake] *n* (帽子や洋服) rack

かけなおす [kakenaosu] 電話をかけなおす [denwa-o kakenaosu] *v* call back; あとでか けなおします [ato de kakenaoshimasu] I'll call back later; かけなおしてください [kakenaoshite kudasai] Please call me back; 明日かけなおします [asu kakenaoshi-masu] I'll call back tomorrow

かけら [kakera] *n* chip (small piece)

かけられる [kakerareru] ここから電話をかけら れますか? [koko kara denwa o kakerar-emasu ka?] Can I call from here?

かける [kakeru] 保険をかける [hoken-o kakeru] *v* insure; やすりをかける [yasuri-o kakeru] *v* file (smoothing); アイロンをかける [airon-o kakeru] *v* iron; アイロンをかけるべき もの [airon-o kakerubeki mono] *n* ironing; 拷問にかける [goumon ni kakeru] *v* torture; 疑いをかける [utagai-o kakeru] *v* suspect; ご 迷惑をかけてすみません [go-meiwaku o kakete sumimasen] I'm sorry to bother you; 私は電話をかけなければなりません [watashi wa denwa o kakenakereba narimasen] I have to make a phone call; 電話をかけたいのですが [denwa o kaketai no desu ga] I want to make a phone call

掛ける [kakeru] *vt* hang

賭ける [kakeru] *v* bet; 賭け事をする [kakegoto-o suru] *v* gamble

駆ける [kakeru] 速足で駆ける [hayaashi de kakeru] *v* trot

掛け算 [kakezan] *n* multiplication

牡蠣 [kaki] *n* oyster

夏季 [kaki] *n* summertime

かき集める [kakiatsumeru] *v* round up

かき傷 [kakikizu] *n* scratch

かき混ぜる [kakimazeru] *v* stir

垣根 [kakine] *n* hedge

書留 [kakitome] *n* registered mail; 簡易書留 [kan-i kakitome] *n* certified mail

書き留める [kakitomeru] *v* make a note of, write down; ちょっと書き留める [chotto kakitodomeru] *v* jot down

括弧 [kakko] *n* parentheses (round)

かっこいい [kakkoii] *adj* cool (stylish)

カッコウ [kakkou] *n* cuckoo

過去 [kako] *n* past

囲い [kakoi] *n* fold

囲む [kakomu] *v* surround

過越し [ka koshi] 過越しの祭 [Sugikoshi no matsuri] *n* Passover

角² [kaku] *n* (場所) corner

かく [kaku] 汗をかく [ase wo kaku] *v* sweat

書く [kaku] *v* write; ブログを書く [burogu-o kaku] *v* blog; 書いたもの [kaita mono] *n* writing; その住所を紙に書いてもらえますか? [sono juusho o kami ni kaite moraemasu ka?] Could you write down the address, please?; それを書いていただけますか? [sore o kaite itadakemasu ka?] Could you write it down, please?; それを紙に書いていただけ ませんか? [sore wo kami ni kaite itadakemasen ka?] Could you write that down, please?; 値段を書いてください [nedan o kaite kudasai] Please write down the price

拡大 [kakudai] *n* enlargement

拡大鏡 [kakudaikyou] *n* magnifying glass

確実 [kakujitsu] 確実なこと [kakujitsu na koto]

n certainty

革命 [kakumei] *n* revolution

革命的な [kakumeiteki na] *adj* revolutionary

確認 [kakunin] *n* confirmation; 確認する [kakunin suru] *v* confirm

隠れん坊 [kakurenbou] *n* hide-and-seek

隠れる [kakureru] *vi* hide

隠される [kakusareru] 隠された [kakusareta] *adj* hidden

確信 [kakushin] *n* confidence; 確信のない [kakushin no nai] *adj* unsure; 確信させる [kakushin saseru] *v* convince; 確信して [kakushin shite] *adj* confident; 確信している [kakushin shite iru] *adj* certain, positive; 確信している [kakushin shite iru] *adj* sure

革新 [kakushin] *n* innovation; 革新的な [kakushinteki na] *adj* innovative

各種 [kakushu] 各種取り合わせ [kakushu toriawase] *n* assortment

隠す [kakusu] *vt* hide

カクテル [kakuteru] *n* cocktail; カクテルはありますか? [kakuteru wa arimasu ka?] Do you sell cocktails?

確約 [kakuyaku] 確約する [kakuyaku suru] *v* assure

下級 [kakyuu] 下級の [kakyuu no] *adj* junior

かまう [kamau] *v* care about

カメ [kame] *n (動物)* tortoise, *(動物)* turtle

カメラ [kamera] *n* camera; カメラ付き携帯電話 [kamera tsuki keitai denwa] *n* camera phone; カメラマン [kameraman] *n* cameraman; デジタルカメラ [dejitaru kamera] *n* digital camera; このカメラ用のバッテリーはありますか? [kono kamera-you no batterii wa arimasu ka?] Do you have batteries for this camera?; 私はこのカメラ用のカラーフィルムが必要です [watashi wa kono kamera-you no karaa-firumu ga hitsuyou desu] I need a color film for this camera; 私のカメラが動きません [watashi no kamera ga ugokimasen] My camera is sticking

カメルーン [kameruun] *n* Cameroon

神 [kami] *n* god

紙 [kami] *n* paper; 包装紙 [housoushi] *n* wrapping paper

髪 [kami] *n* hair; 髪のふさ [kami no fusa] *n* lock of hair; 私のようなタイプの髪をカットしたことがありますか? [watashi no you na taipu no kami o katto shita koto ga arimasu ka?] Have you cut my type of hair before?; 私の髪には何がいいと思いますか? [watashi no kami ni wa nani ga ii to omoimasu ka?] What do you recommend for my hair?; 私の髪は乾性です [watashi no kami wa kansei desu] I have dry hair; 私の髪は脂性です [watashi no kami wa aburashou desu] I have oily hair; 髪をまっすぐにしてもらえますか? [kami o massugu ni shite moraemasu ka?] Can you straighten my hair?; 髪を染めていただけますか? [kami o somete itadakemasu ka?] Could you color my hair, please?

紙ばさみ [kamibasami] *n* portfolio

紙吹雪 [kamifubuki] *n* confetti

かみ傷 [kamikizu] このかみ傷は感染しています [kono kami-kizu wa kansen shite imasu] This bite is infected

紙巻きタバコ [kamimakitabako] *n* cigarette

雷 [kaminari] *n* lightning

かみそり [kamisori] *n* razor; 安全かみそりの刃 [anzen kamisori no ha] *n* razor blade

寡黙な [kamoku na] *adj* silent

カモメ [kamome] *n* seagull

貨物 [kamotsu] *n* cargo; 貨物輸送 [kamotsu yusou] *n* freight

かむ [kamu] *v (歯)* bite; かむこと [kamu koto] *(歯) n* bite; 私はかまれました [watashi wa kamaremashita] I've been bitten

噛む [kamu] *v* chew

カムコーダー [kamukoodaa] *n* camcorder

缶 [kan] 缶詰にした [kanzume ni shita] *adj* canned; 缶切り [kankiri] *n* can opener

管 [kan] *n* tube; 排水管 [haisuikan] *n* drain, drainpipe; 試験管 [shikenkan] *n* test tube

艦 [kan] 潜水艦 [sensuikan] *n* submarine

官 [kan] 検査官 [kensakan] n inspector; 裁判官 [saibankan] n judge; 外交官 [gaikoukan] n diplomat

カナダ [kanada] n Canada; カナダの [kanada no] adj Canadian

カナダ人 [kanadajin] n Canadian (person)

金切り声 [kanakirigoe] n scream; 金切り声を上げる [kanagiri koe-o ageru] v scream; 金切り声を出す [kanakirigoe wo dasu] v shriek

金物 [kanamono] 金物屋 [kanamonoya] n hardware store

必ず [kanarazu] adv necessarily

かなり [kanari] adv pretty, quite, rather; かなり遠いです [kanari tooi desu] It's quite a long way

カナリア [kanaria] n canary

カナリア諸島 [kanaria shotou] n Canaries

悲しい [kanashii] adj sad

悲しみ [kanashimi] 深い悲しみ [fukai kanashimi] n grief

悲しむ [kanashimu] 悲しんで [kanashinde] adv sadly

カンボジア [kanbojia] n Cambodia; カンボジアの [kanbojia no] adj Cambodian

カンボジア人 [kanbojiajin] n Cambodian (person)

寛大 [kandai] n generosity

感電 [kanden] n electric shock

感動 [kandou] 感動させる [kandou saseru] adj moving; 感動した [kandou shita] adj impressed, moved; 感動的な [kandouteki na] adj moving

鐘 [kane] n bell; 鐘の音 [kane no oto] n toll

金遣い [kanedukai] 金遣いが荒い [kanezukai ga arai] adj extravagant

金持ち [kanemochi] 金持ちの [kanemochi no] adj rich

肝炎 [kanen] n hepatitis

可燃 [kanen] 可燃性の [kanensei no] adj flammable

加熱 [kanetsu] 加熱する [kanetsu suru] v heat up

考え [kangae] n idea

考え出す [kangaedasu] v work out

考え直す [kangaenaosu] v reconsider

考える [kangaeru] v think

管楽器 [kangakki] 木管楽器 [mokkangakki] n woodwind

カンガルー [kangaruu] n kangaroo

歓迎 [kangei] n welcome; 歓迎する [kangei suru] v welcome

観劇 [kangeki] n theatrical play

緩下剤 [kangezai] n laxative

看護 [kango] 看護師 [kangoshi] n nurse

看護師 [kangoshi] n nurse; 看護師さんと話をしたいのですが [kangoshi-san to hanashi o shitai no desu ga] I'd like to speak to a nurse

カニ [kani] n crab

蟹座 [kaniza] n Cancer (horoscope)

患者 [kanja] n patient; 老人病患者 [roujinbyou kanja] n geriatric; 糖尿病患者 [tounyoubyoukanja] n diabetic; 癲癇患者 [tenkan kanja] n epileptic

感じ [kanji] ぞくぞくする感じ [zokuzoku suru kanji] n thrill; 空虚な感じ [kuukyo na kanji] n void

感じる [kanjiru] v feel

環状 [kanjou] 環状交差路 [kanjou kousaro] n rotary; 環状道路 [kanjoudouro] n beltway

感情 [kanjou] n emotion; 感情の [kanjou no] adj emotional

勘定 [kanjou] n bill; それを私の勘定につけておいてください [sore o watashi no kanjou ni tsukete oite kudasai] Put it on my bill

感覚 [kankaku] n sense; 感覚に訴える [kankaku ni uttaeru] adj sensuous; 感覚のない [kankaku no nai] adj numb

間隔 [kankaku] n interval

関係 [kankei] n connection, relation, relationship; 無関係な [mukankei na] adj irrelevant; 関係している [kankei shiteiru] adj concerned; 婚姻関係の有無 [kon'in kankei no umu] n marital status

簡潔 [kanketsu] 簡潔な [kanketsu na] adj concise

K

缶切り [kankiri] *n* can opener

韓国 [kankoku] *n* South Korea

観光 [kankou] *n* sightseeing

観客 [kankyaku] *n* spectator

環境 [kankyou] *n* environment, surroundings; 環境にやさしい [kankyou ni yasashii] *adj* ecofriendly, environmentally friendly; 環境の [kankyou no] *adj* environmental

甘味料 [kanmiryou] 甘味料はありますか? [kanmiryou wa arimasu ka?] Do you have any artificial sweetener?

かんな [kanna] *n* (道具) plane *(tool)*

かんぬき [kannuki] *n* bolt

可能 [kanou] 不可能な [fukanou na] *adj* impossible; 実行可能な [jikkoukanou na] *adj* feasible; 可能な [kanou na] *adj* possible; 可能性 [kanousei] *n* possibility, potential; 可能性のある [kanousei no aru] *adj* potential; 可能性を排除する [kanousei-o haijo suru] *v* rule out

乾杯 [kanpai] *n* toast *(tribute)*

乾杯! [kanpai] *excl* cheers!

完璧 [kanpeki] *n* perfection; 完璧に [kanpeki ni] *adv* perfectly

完璧な [kanpeki na] *adj* perfect

歓楽街 [kanrakugai] 歓楽街での夜の楽しみ [kanrakugai deno yoru no tanoshimi] *n* nightlife

慣例 [kanrei] *n* custom; 慣例にのっとった [kanrei ni nottotta] *adj* conventional; 慣例に従わない [kanrei ni shitagawanai] *adj* unconventional

関連 [kanren] 関連する [kanren suru] *adj* relevant

管理 [kanri] *n* administration; 管理上の [kanrijou no] *adj* administrative; 管理者 [kanrisha] *n* director, warden

管理人 [kanrinin] *n* caretaker

官僚主義 [kanryoushugi] *n* bureaucracy

監査 [kansa] *n* audit; 会計監査人 [kaikei kansanin] *n* auditor; 監査する [kansa suru] *v* audit

観察 [kansatsu] 観察する [kansatsu suru] *v* observe; 観察者 [kansatsusha] *n* observer

観察力 [kansatsuryoku] 観察力の鋭い [kansatsuryoku no surudoi] *adj* observant

感染 [kansen] *n* infection; 感染性の [kansensei no] *adj* infectious

幹線道路 [kansendouro] *n* main road

間接 [kansetsu] 間接的な [kansetsuteki na] *adj* indirect

関節 [kansetsu] 関節炎 [kansetsuen] *n* arthritis

関節炎 [kansetsuen] *n* arthritis; 私は関節炎をわずらっています [watashi wa kansetsuen o wazuratte imasu] I suffer from arthritis

感謝 [kansha] *n* gratitude; 感謝している [kansha shite iru] *adj* grateful; 感謝する [kansha suru] *v* thank; 感謝を表さない [kansha-o arawasanai] *adj* ungrateful

かんしゃく [kanshaku] *n* tantrum, temper

監視 [kanshi] 交通監視員 [koutsuu kanshiin] *n* parking enforcement officer

監視員 [kanshiin] 監視員はいますか? [kanshi-in wa imasu ka?] Is there a lifeguard?

感心 [kanshin] *n* admiration; 感心する [kanshin suru] *v* admire

関心 [kanshin] *n* concern

感傷 [kanshou] 感傷的な [kanshouteki na] *adj* sentimental

看守 [kanshu] *n* corrections officer

観測所 [kansokujo] *n* observatory

乾燥 [kansou] 乾燥の [kansou no] *adj* dehydrated; 乾燥させた [kansou saseta] *adj* dried; 乾燥させる [kansou saseru] *v* dry; 乾燥した [kansou shita] *adj* dry; 乾燥機 [kansouki] *n* dryer

乾燥機 [kansouki] 回転式乾燥機 [kaitenshiki kansouki] *n* (clothes) dryer

関する [kan suru] 電気に関する [denki ni kansuru] *adj* electrical

歓待 [kantai] *n* hospitality, treat

艦隊 [kantai] *n* fleet

簡単 [kantan] 簡単な [kantan na] *adj* easy, simple; 簡単に [kantan ni] *adv* briefly, simply; 簡単にする [kantan ni suru] v simplify; 一番簡単なスロープはどれですか? [ichiban kantan na suroopu wa dore desu ka?] Which are the easiest runs?

感嘆符 [kantanfu] n exclamation point

鑑定 [kantei] 鑑定士 [kanteishi] n surveyor

観点 [kanten] n perspective, viewpoint

監督 [kantoku] n oversight (supervision); 試験監督者 [shiken kantokusha] n exam proctor; 監督する [kantoku suru] v direct, supervise; 監督者 [kantokusha] n supervisor; 監督生 [kantokusei] n prefect

カヌー [kanuu] n canoe; カヌー漕ぎ [kanuu kogi] n canoeing; どこに行けばカヌーをこげますか? [doko ni ikeba kanuu o kogemasu ka?] Where can we go canoeing?

慣用 [kanyou] 慣用句 [kan'youku] n phrase

寛容 [kanyou] 寛容な [kan'you na] adj tolerant

慣用句集 [kanyoukushuu] 外国語慣用句集 [gaikokugo kan'youku shuu] n phrasebook

加入 [kanyuu] 免責補償制度に加入したいのですが [menseki-hoshou-seido ni kanyuu shitai no desu ga] I'd like to arrange a collision damage waiver

関税 [kanzei] n customs; 関税率 [kanzeiritsu] n tariff

完全 [kanzen] adj perfect; 不完全な [fukanzen na] adj incomplete; 完全な [kanzen na] adj total; 完全に [kanzen ni] adv totally

肝臓 [kanzou] n liver

缶詰め [kanzume] 缶詰めにした [kanzume ni shita] adj canned

顔 [kao] n face; 顔の [kao no] adj facial

顔立ち [kaodachi] n feature

顔色 [kaoiro] n complexion

家屋 [kaoku] 土地付き一戸建て家屋 [tochi tsuki ikkodate kaoku] n house

カップ [kappu] n cup

カップル [kappuru] n couple

カプセル [kapuseru] n capsule

殻 [kara] n shell

から [kara] ・・・だから [... dakara] conj because

カラー [karaa] カラーテレビ [karaaterebi] n color television; このカラーコピーをお願いします [kono karaa-kopii o o-negai shimasu] I'd like a color photocopy of this, please; カラーで [karaa de] in color

カラーフィルム [karaafirumu] カラーフィルムをください [karaa-firumu o kudasai] Color film, please

カラープリンター [karaapurintaa] カラープリンターはありますか? [karaa-purintaa wa arimasu ka?] Is there a color printer?

体 [karada] n body

カラフ [karafu] n carafe

からかう [karakau] v tease

カラオケ [karaoke] n karaoke

カラス [karasu] n crow, raven

空手 [karate] n karate

カラット [karatto] n carat

カレー [karee] カレー料理 [karee ryouri] n curry; カレー粉 [kareeko] n curry powder

華麗 [karei] 華麗な [karei na] adj gorgeous

カレッジ [karejji] n college

カレンダー [karendaa] n calendar

仮 [kari] 仮の詰め物をしてもらえますか? [kari no tsumemono o shite moraemasu ka?] Can you do a temporary filling?

狩り [kari] n hunting; 狩りをする [kari-o suru] v hunt

借り [kari] 借りがある [kari ga aru] v owe

カリブ人 [karibujin] n Caribbean (person)

カリブ海 [karibukai] カリブ海の [karibukai no] adj Caribbean

カリフラワー [karifurawaa] n cauliflower

借方 [karikata] n debit; 借方に記入する [karikata ni kinyuu suru] v debit

刈り込み [karikomi] n clip

カリキュラム [karikyuramu] n curriculum

借りる [kariru] v borrow

カロリー [karorii] n calorie

かろうじて [karoujite] adv barely

刈る [karu] v mow

軽い [karui] *adj* light *(not heavy)*

軽く [karuku] 軽くたたくこと [karuku tataku koto] *n* tap

カルシウム [karushiumu] *n* calcium

軽業 [karuwaza] 軽業師 [karuwazashi] *n* acrobat

過量 [karyou] 過量服用 [karyou fukuyou] *n* overdose

傘 [kasa] *n* umbrella

火災 [kasai] 火災報知器 [kasai houchiki] *n* fire alarm

かさむ [kasamu] *v* pile up

カササギ [kasasagi] *n* magpie

稼ぐ [kasegu] *v* earn

下線 [kasen] 下線を引く [kasen-o hiku] *v* underline

カセット [kasetto] *n* cassette

貨車 [kasha] 無蓋貨車 [mugai kasha] *n* truck

呵責 [kashaku] 良心の呵責 [ryoushin no kashaku] *n* remorse

華氏 [kashi] 華氏温度 [kashi ondo] *n* degree Fahrenheit

菓子 [kashi] *n* layer cake

賢い [kashikoi] *adj* clever, wise

カシミヤ [kashimiya] *n* cashmere

頭文字 [kashiramoji] *n* initials; 頭文字で署名する [atamamoji de shomei suru] *v* initial

貸し付ける [kashitsukeru] *v* lend; 貸し付け [kashizuke] *n* loan

過食症 [kashokushou] *n* bulimia

過小評価する [kashouhyouka suru] *v* underestimate

歌手 [kashu] *n* singer

カシューナッツ [kashuunattsu] *n* cashew

加速 [kasoku] *n* acceleration; 加速する [kasoku suru] *v* accelerate

火葬 [kasou] 火葬場 [kasouba] *n* crematorium

仮装服 [kasoufuku] *n* costume *(party)*

喝采 [kassai] *n* cheer

滑走 [kassou] 滑走路 [kassouro] *n* runway

貸す [kasu] *v* lend; お金をいくらか貸していただけますか? [o-kane o ikura ka kashite itadakemasu ka?] Could you lend me some money?; タオルを貸していただけますか? [taoru o kashite itadakemasu ka?] Could you lend me a towel?

かすか [kasuka] かすかな [kasuka na] *adj* faint

カスタード [kasutaado] *n* custard sauce

カスタマイズ [kasutamaizu] カスタマイズされた [kasutamaizu sareta] *adj* customized

肩 [kata] *n* shoulder; 肩をすくめる [kata wo sukumeru] *v* shrug; 肩掛けかばん [katakake kaban] *n* satchel; 肩甲骨 [kenkoukotsu] shoulder blade; 私は肩を痛めました [watashi wa kata o itamemashita] I've hurt my shoulder

型 [kata] *n* mold *(shape)*; 内蔵型の [naizougata no] *adj* self-contained

カタール [kataaru] *n* Qatar

片足 [kataashi] 片足スケート [kataashi sukeeto] *n* scooter

形 [katachi] *n* form, shape; 十字形 [juujigata] *n* cross

固い [katai] *adj* firm; 固く縛る [kataku shibaru] *v* tie up

堅い [katai] *adj* hard *(firm, rigid)*, stiff

塊 [katamari] *n* block *(solid piece)*, lump; パンのひと塊 [pan no hitokatamari] *n* loaf

片道 [katamichi] 片道切符 [katamichi kippu] *n* one-way ticket; 片道切符はいくらですか? [katamichi-kippu wa ikura desu ka?] How much is a one-way ticket?; ···行き片道 [... iki katamichi] a one-way ticket to...

傾ける [katamukeru] *v* tip *(incline)*

片親 [kataoya] 片親で子育てをする人 [kataoya de kosodate-o suru hito] *n* single parent

カタログ [katarogu] *n* catalog; カタログが欲しいのですが [katarogu ga hoshii no desu ga] I'd like a catalog

カタル [kataru] *n* catarrh

カタツムリ [katatsumuri] *n* snail

偏らない [katayoranai] *adj* impartial

偏る [katayoru] 偏った [katayotta] *adj* biased

片付ける [katazukeru] *v* clear up, tidy; 洗っ

て片付ける [aratte katazukeru] v wash the dishes

仮定 [katei] n supposition; もし…と仮定するならば [moshi… to katei surunaraba] conj supposing

過程 [katei] n course, process

カトリック [katorikku] カトリックの [katorikku no] adj Catholic; カトリック教徒 [katorikkukyouto] n Catholic

勝つ [katsu] v win; …に勝つ [… ni katsu] v beat (outdo)

活動 [katsudou] n action, activity; 活動的な [katsudouteki na] adj active, dynamic

かつら [katsura] n toupee, wig

カッテージチーズ [katteeji chiizu] n cottage cheese

カット [katto] n haircut

買う [kau] v buy; 買い手 [kaite] n buyer; どこでその地域の地図を買えますか？ [doko de sono chiiki no chizu o kaemasu ka?] Where can I buy a map of the area?; どこでテレホンカードを買えますか？ [doko de terehon-kaado o kaemasu ka?] Where can I buy a phone card?

飼う [kau] v keep (a pet)/raise (cattle); 羊飼い [hitsujikai] n shepherd

カウボーイ [kaubooi] n cowboy

カウチソファー [kauchisofaa] n couch

カウンター [kauntaa] n counter

皮 [kawa] n (果物・野菜) peel; 皮むき器 [kawamukiki] n potato peeler; 皮をむく [kawa-o muku] v peel

革 [kawa] n leather; 革ひも [kawa himo] n strap

川 [kawa] n river; その川の遊覧ツアーはありますか？ [sono kawa no yuuran-tsuaa wa arimasu ka?] Are there any boat trips on the river?; その川で泳げますか？ [sono kawa de oyogemasu ka?] Can you swim in the river?

かわいい [kawaii] adj cute

渇く [kawaku] v become dry; のどの渇き [nodo no kawaki] n thirst; のどが渇いた [nodo ga kawaita] adj thirsty

代わり [kawari] 代わりに [kawari ni] adv otherwise; 代わりの [kawari no] adj alternative

代わりに [kawari ni] その代わりに [sono kawari ni] adv instead

変わる [kawaru] v vary ▷ vi change; 変わりやすい [kawariyasui] adj changeable, variable

為替 [kawase] n exchange; 為替レート [kawase reeto] n exchange rate, foreign-exchange rate; 郵便為替 [yuubin kawase] n postal money order; 為替レートはいくらですか？ [kawase-reeto wa ikura desu ka?] What's the exchange rate?

カワセミ [kawasemi] n kingfisher

変わっていない [kawatteinai] adj unchanged

カワウソ [kawauso] n otter

火曜日 [kayoubi] n Tuesday; 告解火曜日 [Kokkai Kayoubi] n Mardi Gras; 火曜日に [kayoubi ni] on Tuesday

かよわい [kayowai] adj frail

かゆい [kayui] adj itchy ▷ v itch

かゆむ [kayumu] 私は脚がかゆみます [watashi wa ashi ga kayumimasu] My leg itches

カザフスタン [kazafusutan] n Kazakhstan

風 [kaze] n wind; 風の強い [kaze no tsuyoi] adj windy

風邪 [kaze] n cold; おたふく風邪 [otafuku-kaze] n mumps; 私は風邪をひきました [watashi wa kaze o hikimashita] I have a cold; 風邪に効くものが欲しいのですが [kaze ni kiku mono ga hoshii no desu ga] I'd like something for a cold

風通し [kazetooshi] n ventilation; 風通しの悪い [kazetoushi no warui] adj stuffy

数える [kazoeru] v count

家族 [kazoku] n family, household; 私は家族と来ています [watashi wa kazoku to kite imasu] I'm here with my family

数 [kazu] n number

毛深い [kebukai] adj hairy

ケチャップ [kechappu] n ketchup

K

けち [kechi] けちな [kechi na] *adj* stingy

ケーブル [keeburu] *n* cable; ケーブルテレビ [keeburu terebi] *n* cable television

ケーブルカー [keeburukaa] *n* cable car

ケーキ [keeki] *n* cake

ケース [keesu] *n* case; パンケース [pan keesu] *n* breadbox

ケータリング [keetaringu] *n* catering

怪我 [kega] *n* injury; サッカー・ラグビーなどで怪我の手当てなどに要した分の延長時間 [sakkaa / ragubii nado de kega no teate nado ni youshita bun no enchou jikan] *n* injury time-out

怪我人 [keganin] 怪我人がいます [keganin ga imasu] There are some injured people

毛皮 [kegawa] *n* fur; 羊の毛皮 [hitsuji no kegawa] *n* sheepskin

毛皮コート [kegawa kooto] 毛皮のコート [kegawa no kooto] *n* fur coat

系 [kei] 太陽系 [taiyoukei] *n* solar system

継 [kei] 継母 [mama haha] *n* stepmother; 継父 [mama chichi] *n* stepfather; 継兄弟 [mama kyoudai] *n* stepbrother; 継姉妹 [mama shimai] *n* stepsister; 継娘 [mama musume] *n* stepdaughter; 継子 [mamako] *n* stepson

計 [kei] 温度計 [ondokei] *n* thermometer; 速度計 [sokudokei] *n* speedometer

競馬 [keiba] *n* horse racing; 競馬騎手 [keiba kishu] *n* jockey; 競馬場 [keibajou] *n* racetrack

刑罰 [keibatsu] *n* penalty, sentence *(punishment)*

軽蔑 [keibetsu] *n* contempt; 軽蔑する [keibetsu suru] *v* despise

警備 [keibi] *n* guard; 沿岸警備隊 [engankeibitai] *n* coast guard; 警備員 [keibiin] *n* security guard

経度 [keido] *n* longitude

経営 [keiei] *n* management; 最高経営責任者 [saikou keiei sekininsha] *n* CEO; 経営者 [keieisha] *n* manager; 経営陣 [keieijin] *n* management; 女性経営者 [josei keieisha] *n* manager

経営者 [keieisha] *n* manager

経費 [keihi] *n* expenses; 諸経費 [shokeihi] *n* overhead

警報 [keihou] *n* alarm; 警報を出す [keihou-o dasu] *v* alert; 盗難警報機 [tounankeihouki] *n* burglar alarm; 間違い警報 [machigai keihou] *n* false alarm

警報器 [keihouki] 煙警報器 [kemuri keihouki] *n* smoke detector

敬意 [keii] *n* regard

掲示 [keiji] *n* notice; 掲示板 [keijiban] *n* bulletin board

刑事 [keiji] *n* detective

警戒 [keikai] 油断なく警戒して [yudan naku keikai shite] *adj* alert; 警戒心をいだかせる [keikaishin-o idakaseru] *adj* alarming

計画 [keikaku] *n* plan, planning; 街路計画 [gairo keikaku] *n* street plan; 計画する [keikaku suru] *v* plan; 都市計画 [toshikeikaku] *n* town planning

警官 [keikan] *n* cop, policeman; 婦人警官 [fujinkeikan] *n* policewoman

経験 [keiken] *n* experience; 経験のない [keiken no nai] *adj* inexperienced; 経験のある [keiken no aru] *adj* experienced; 経験する [keiken suru] *v* go through, undergo

景気 [keiki] *n* economic situation; 景気後退 [keikikoutai] *n* recession

計器 [keiki] *n* gauge

警告 [keikoku] *n* warning; 故障警告灯 [koshou keikokutou] *n* hazard warning lights; 警告する [keikoku suru] *v* warn

蛍光 [keikou] 蛍光性の [keikousei no] *adj* fluorescent

傾向 [keikou] *n* tendency, trend; 傾向がある [keikou ga aru] *v* tend

刑務所 [keimusho] *n* jail, prison

痙攣 [keirei] *n* spasm

計算 [keisan] *n* calculation, computing; 計算して出す [keisan shite dasu] *v* figure out; 計算する [keisan suru] *v* calculate; 計算機 [keisanki] *n* calculator

警察 [keisatsu] n police; 警察署 [keisatsu-sho] n police station; 警察官 [keisatsukan] n police officer; 警察を! [keisatsu o!] Police!; 警察を呼んでください [keisatsu o yonde kudasai] Call the police; 警察署はどこですか? [keisatsusho wa doko desu ka?] Where's the police station?; 私たちはそれを警察に届け出なければなりません [watashi-tachi wa sore o keisatsu ni todokedenakereba narimasen] We'll have to report it to the police

警察署 [keisatsusho] n police station; 私は警察署をさがしています [watashi ha keisatsusho wosagashiteimasu] I need to find a police station

形成 [keisei] 形成外科 [keisei geka] n plastic surgery

傾斜面 [keishamen] n ramp

形式 [keishiki] 形式ばらない [keishikibaranai] adj informal; 形式を定める [keishiki-o sadameru] v format

軽食 [keishoku] n refreshments, snack; 軽食堂 [keishokudou] n snack bar

敬称 [keishou] n honorific (title); 既婚女性の名字の前に付ける敬称 [kikonjosei no myouji no mae ni tsukeru keishou] n Mrs.; 未婚・既婚にかかわらず、女性に対する敬称 [mikon / kikon ni kakawarazu, josei ni taisuru keishou] n Ms.; 独身女性の名字の前に付ける敬称 [dokushin josei no myouji no mae ni tsukeru keishou] n Miss; 男性の名字の前に付ける敬称 [dansei no myouji no mae ni tsukeru keishou] n Mr.

景勝地 [keishouchi] n scenic area

携帯 [keitai] n cellphone; カメラ付き携帯電話 [kamera tsuki keitai denwa] n camera phone; 携帯電話 [keitai denwa] n cell phone; あなたは携帯電話をお持ちですか? [anata wa keitai-denwa o o-mochi desu ka?] Do you have a cell phone?; 携帯電話番号 [keitai denwa bangou] n cell phone number; あなたの携帯電話番号は何番ですか? [anata no keitai-denwa-bangou wa

nan-ban desu ka?] What's your cell number?; 私の携帯電話番号は・・・です [watashi no keitai-denwa-bangou wa... desu] My cell number is...

形態 [keitai] n shape; 図書形態 [tosho keitai] n format

契約 [keiyaku] n contract; 保険契約書 [hoken keiyakusho] n insurance certificate; 賃貸借契約 [chintaishaku keiyaku] n lease; 自由契約の [jiyuu keiyaku no] adj freelance; 自由契約で [jiyuu keiyaku de] adv freelance; 契約人 [keiyakunin] n contractor; 売買契約 [baibai keiyaku] n bargain

形容 [keiyou] 形容詞 [keiyoushi] n adjective

軽油 [keiyu] n light oil

経済 [keizai] n economy; 経済の [keizai no] adj economic; 経済的な [keizaiteki na] adj economical; 経済学者 [keizaigakusha] n economist

経済学 [keizaigaku] n economics

継続 [keizoku] 継続教育 [keizoku kyouiku] n higher education (lower-level); 継続的な [keizokuteki na] adj continual; 継続的に [keizokuteki ni] adv continually

結果 [kekka] n consequence, outcome, result; 結果として生じる [kekka toshite shoujiru] v result

結核 [kekkaku] n tuberculosis, TB

欠陥 [kekkan] n defect; 欠陥のある [kekkan no aru] adj faulty

欠勤 [kekkin] n absence; 欠勤時間 [kekkin jikan] n time off

結婚 [kekkon] n marriage; 結婚している [kekkon shite iru] adj married; 結婚する [kekkon suru] v marry; 結婚指輪 [kekkon yubiwa] n wedding ring; 結婚証明書 [kekkonshoumeisho] n marriage certificate; 結婚記念日 [kekkon kinenbi] n wedding anniversary; 結婚式 [kekkonshiki] n wedding; 女性の結婚前の旧姓 [josei no kekkonmae no kyuusei] n maiden name

結構 [kekkou] adj adequate

煙 [kemuri] n smoke; 煙を出す [kemuri wo

dasu] v smoke; 煙警報器 [kemuri keihouki]
n smoke detector

権 [ken] 拒否権 [kyohiken] n veto; 優先権
[yuusenken] n right of way

券 [ken] n ticket; 搭乗券 [toujouken] n
boarding pass; 引換券 [hikikaeken] n
voucher; 定期券 [teikiken] n season ticket;
券売機 [kenbaiki] n ticket machine; 回数券
をください [kaisuuken o kudasai] A book of
tickets, please

ケナガイタチ [kenagaitachi] n ferret

けなす [kenasu] v lambaste

顕微鏡 [kenbikyou] n microscope

見物 [kenbutsu] n sightseeing

見地 [kenchi] n standpoint

建築 [kenchiku] n architecture; 高層建築
[kousou kenchiku] n high-rise; 建築業者
[kenchikugyousha] n building contractor;
建築様式 [kenchikuyoushiki] n architecture;
建築家 [kenchikuka] n architect

検疫 [ken'eki] 検疫期間 [ken'eki kikan] n
quarantine

懸念 [kenen] n reservation

権限 [kengen] 権限を与える [kengen-o ataeru]
v authorize

ケニア [kenia] n Kenya

ケニア人 [keniajin] n Kenyan

ケニアの [kenia no] n Kenyan

喧嘩 [kenka] n quarrel (argument); 喧嘩する
[kenka suru] v quarrel (to argue)

けんか [kenka] n (争い) scrap (dispute)

見解 [kenkai] n view

健康 [kenkou] n health; 健康な [kenkou na]
adj healthy; 健康診断 [kenkoushindan] n
physical

謙虚 [kenkyo] 謙虚な [kenkyo na] adj
humble, modest

研究者 [kenkyuusha] n researcher; 自然誌研
究者 [shizenshi kenkyuusha] n naturalist

懸命 [kenmei] 懸命に [kenmei ni] adv hard

賢明 [kenmei] n wisdom; 賢明な [kenmei na]
adj advisable

憲法 [kenpou] n constitution

権利 [kenri] n right

検査 [kensa] n checkup; 検査する [kensa
suru] v inspect; 検査官 [kensakan] n
inspector; 血液検査 [ketsuekikensa] n
blood test; 身体検査 [shintai kensa] n
physical; 塗沫検査 [tomatsu kensa] n
smear test

検索 [kensaku] n 検索エンジン [kensaku enjin]
n search engine

検札 [kensatsu] 検札係 [kensatsugakari] n
ticket inspector

建設 [kensetsu] n construction; 建設する
[kensetsu suru] v construct; 建設現場
[kensetsu genba] n construction site; 建設
的な [kensetsuteki na] adj constructive

検死 [kenshi] 検死審問 [kenshi shinmon] n
inquest

献身 [kenshin] n dedication; 献身的な
[kenshinteki na] adj devoted

倹約 [kenyaku] 倹約な [kenyaku na] adj
thrifty

健全 [kenzen] 健全な [kenzen na] adj sound

毛織り [keori] 毛織りの [keori no] adj woolen

毛織物 [keorimono] 毛織物衣類 [keorimono
irui] n woolens

潔白 [keppaku] 潔白な [keppaku na] adj
innocent

蹴り [keri] n kick

蹴る [keru] v kick

今朝 [kesa] this morning; 私は今朝から具合
が悪いです [watashi wa kesa kara guai ga
warui desu] I've been sick since this morning

ケシ [keshi] n poppy

消印 [keshiin] n postmark

化粧 [keshou] 洗面化粧用品 [senmen keshou
youhin] n toiletries; 化粧着 [keshougi] n
negligee

化粧品 [keshouhin] n cosmetics

傑作 [kessaku] n masterpiece

決心 [kesshin] 決心がついていない [kesshin
ga tsuite inai] adj undecided

決勝 [kesshou] n final

傑出 [kesshutsu] 傑出した [kesshutsu shita] *adj* outstanding

欠損 [kesson] *n* deficit

消す [kesu] *v* (消去) erase, (切る) turn out

ケトル [ketoru] *n* teakettle

欠乏 [ketsubou] *n* lack

血液 [ketsueki] *n* blood; 血液検査 [ketsuekikensa] *n* blood test

血液型 [ketsuekigata] *n* blood type; 私の血液型はO型Rhプラスです [watashi no ketsueki-gata wa oo-gata aaru-eichi-purasu desu] My blood type is O positive

結合 [ketsugou] *n* conjunction, union; 結合する [ketsugou suru] *v* combine, unite

決意 [ketsui] *n* resolution

欠員 [ketsuin] *n* vacancy

結末 [ketsumatsu] *n* ending

結露 [ketsuro] *n* condensation

結論 [ketsuron] *n* conclusion; 結論を出す [ketsuron-o dasu] *v* conclude

決定 [kettei] *n* decision; 決定する [kettei suru] *v* decide; 決定的な [ketteiteki na] *adj* decisive; 決定的にする [ketteiteki ni suru] *v* finalize; 有罪と決定する [yuuzai to kettei suru] *v* convict

欠点 [ketten] *n* drawback, shortcoming

血統の明らかな [kettou no akiraka na] *adj* pedigree

険しい [kewashii] *adj* steep; それはとても険しいですか? [sore wa totemo kewashii desu ka?] Is it very steep?

機 [ki] *n* device; 洗濯機 [sentakuki] *n* washing machine; 洗車機 [senshaki] *n* car wash; 脱水機 [dassuiki] *n* spin dryer; 盗難警報機 [tounankeihouki] *n* burglar alarm; 受信機 [jushinki] *n* receiver (*electronic*); 私が使えるファックス機はありますか? [watashi ga tsukaeru fakkusuki wa arimasu ka?] Is there a fax machine I can use?

木 [ki] *n* tree; 木管楽器 [mokkangakki] *n* woodwind; 添え木 [soegi] *n* splint

気 [ki] 気がついて [ki ga tsuite] *adj* aware; 気をもむ [ki-o momu] *v* fret

厳しい [kibishii] *adj* harsh, strict; 要求の厳しい [youkyuu no kibishii] *adj* demanding; 厳しく [kibishiku] *adv* strictly

希望 [kibou] *n* desire, hope; 希望が持てる [kibou ga moteru] *adj* hopeful; 希望する [kibou suru] *v* desire; 希望を持って [kibou-o motte] *adv* hopefully; 希望を失って [kibou-o ushinatte] *adj* hopeless

気分 [kibun] *n* mood; 気分のすぐれない [kibun no sugurenai] *adj* unwell

気分が悪い [kibun ga warui] 私は気分が悪いのです [watashi wa kibun ga warui no desu] I don't feel well

機知 [kichi] *n* wit; 機知に富んだ [kichi ni tonda] *adj* witty

気違い [kichigai] *n* nut case; 気違いのように [kichigai no youni] *adv* crazily; 気違い男 [kichigai otoko] *n* lunatic

きちんと [kichin to] *adv* neatly; きちんとした [kichin to shita] *adj* neat; きちんとした [kichin to shita] *adj* tidy

貴重 [kichou] 貴重品 [kichouhin] *n* valuables

貴重品 [kichouhin] *npl* valuables; 貴重品はどこに置いておけますか? [kichouhin wa doko ni oite okemasu ka?] Where can I leave my valuables?; 私は貴重品を金庫に入れたいのですが [watashi wa kichohin o kinko ni iretai no desu ga] I'd like to put my valuables in the safe

貴重な [kichou na] *adj* precious

気だてのよい [kidate no yoi] *adj* good-natured

消える [kieru] *v* vanish

寄付 [kifu] *n* contribution; 寄付する [kifu suru] *v* contribute, donate

着替える [kigaeru] *v* change

気がもめる [ki ga momeru] *v* worrying

喜劇 [kigeki] 喜劇俳優 [kigeki haiyuu] *n* comic

紀元 [kigen] *n* term; 紀元前 [kigenzen] *prep* BC

機嫌 [kigen] 機嫌の悪い [kigen no warui] *adj* bad-tempered

期限 [kigen] 使用期限 [shiyou kigen] *n*

expiration date; 期限が切れる [kigen ga kireru] v expire; 賞味期限 [shoumikigen] n best-if-used-by date; 販売期限 [hanbai kigen] n sell-by date; 締切り期限 [shimekiri kigen] n deadline

起源 [kigen] n origin

器具 [kigu] n apparatus, appliance, instrument; 暖房器具 [danbou kigu] n heater

木靴 [kigutsu] n clog

企業 [kigyou] 企業買収 [kigyou baishuu] n takeover; 多国籍企業 [takokuseki kigyou] n multinational

樹林 [ki hayashi] 土地の植物と樹木を見たいのですが [tochi no shokubutsu to jumoku o mitai no desu ga] We'd like to see local plants and trees

基本 [kihon] n basics; 基本的な [kihonteki na] adj basic; 基本的に [kihonteki ni] adv basically

キー [kii] n key (music/computer)

キーボード [kiiboodo] n keyboard

キーリング [kiiringu] n keyring

黄色 [kiiro] 黄色の [ki iro no] adj yellow

キーウィ [kiiui] n kiwi

キジ [kiji] n pheasant

生地 [kiji] n (料理) pastry

記事 [kiji] n article; トップ記事 [toppu kiji] n lead (position); 死亡記事 [shiboukiji] n obituary

机上 [kijou] 机上事務 [kijou jimu] n paperwork

基準 [kijun] n criterion

記述 [kijutsu] n description; 記述する [kijutsu suru] v describe

機会 [kikai] n opportunity

機械 [kikai] n machine; 乾燥機 [kansouki] n dryer; ジェット機 [jettoki] n jet; 機械の [kikai no] adj mechanical; 機械類 [kikairui] n machinery; 機械工 [kikaikou] n mechanic; 掘削機 [kussakuki] n digger; 食器洗い機 [shokkiaraiki] n dishwasher

企画 [kikaku] n project

機関 [kikan] n (組織) institution; 諜報機関 [chouhou kikan] n secret service; 公共交通機関 [koukyou koutsuu kikan] n public transportation

期間 [kikan] n period; 持続期間 [jizoku kikan] n duration; 検疫期間 [ken'eki kikan] n quarantine; 試用期間 [shiyou kikan] n trial period

気管支 [kikan shi] 気管支炎 [kikanshien] n bronchitis

危険 [kiken] n danger, risk; 危険な [kiken na] adj dangerous, risky; 危険にさらす [kiken ni sarasu] v endanger, risk; なだれの危険はありますか? [nadare no kiken wa arimasu ka?] Is there a danger of avalanches?

飢饉 [kikin] n famine

聞き手 [kikite] n listener

聞き取る [kikitoru] v hear

キック [kikku] フリーキック [furiikikku] n free kick

キックオフ [kikkuofu] n kickoff; キックオフする [kikkuofu suru] v kick off

聞こえる [kikoeru] v be audible

機構 [kikou] n (機械) mechanism

気候 [kikou] n climate; 気候変動 [kikou hendo] n climate change

帰航 [kikou] いつ帰航しますか? [itsu kikou shimasu ka?] When do we leave for home?

きく [kiku] 機転のきく [kiten no kiku] adj tactful

キク [kiku] n chrysanthemum

聞く [kiku] v hear, listen; 耳の聞こえない [mimi no kikoenai] adj deaf; …を聞く [...o kiku] v listen to

気前 [kimae] 気前のよい [kimae no yoi] adj generous

決めきる [kimarikiru] 決まりきった仕事 [kimarikitta shigoto] n routine

決まった [kimatta] 決まった相手がいる [kimatta aite ga iru] adj attached

きめ [kime] きめの粗い [kime no komakai] adj coarse

気味 [kimi] 気味の悪い [kimi no warui] adj

spooky

黄身 [kimi] 卵の黄身 [tamago no kimi] n egg yolk, yolk

機密 [kimitsu] n secret; 最高機密の [saikou kimitsu no] adj top-secret

気密 [kimitsu] 気密の [kimitsu no] adj airtight

気味悪い [kimiwarui] 薄気味悪い [usukimiwarui] adj spooky, creepy

気持ち [kimochi] n feeling

気むずかしい [kimuzukashii] adj grumpy

奇妙 [kimyou] 奇妙な [kimyou na] adj strange

金 [kin] n (金属) gold; 賠償金 [baishoukin] n compensation

緊張 [kinchou] n tension; 極度の緊張 [kyokudo no kinchou] n strain; 緊張させる [kinchou saseru] v strain; 緊張しきった [kinchou shikitta] adj uptight; 緊張した [kinchou shita] adj tense

禁煙 [kin'en] 禁煙の [kin'en no] adj no-smoking; 禁煙の部屋がいいのですが [kin'en no heya ga ii no desu ga] I'd like a no-smoking room; 禁煙エリアはありますか? [kin'en-eria wa arimasu ka?] Is there a no-smoking area?

記念 [kinen] n commemoration; 100周年記念祭 [hyakushuunen kinensai] n centenary; 記念日 [kinenbi] n anniversary; 記念碑 [kinenhi] n monument; 記念銘板 [kinen meiban] n plaque; 記念品 [kinenhin] n souvenir

記念日 [kinenbi] n anniversary; 結婚記念日 [kekkon kinenbi] n wedding anniversary

記念碑 [kinenhi] n memorial

禁煙席 [kin'enseki] 禁煙席が欲しいのですが [kin'en-seki ga hoshii no desu ga] I'd like a no-smoking seat

禁煙車 [kin'ensha] 禁煙車の席を予約したいのですが [kin'en-sha no seki o yoyaku shitai no desu ga] I want to reserve a seat in a no-smoking compartment; 禁煙席をお願いします [kin'en-seki o o-negai shimasu] No-smoking, please

キングサイズ [kingusaizu] キングサイズのベッ

ド [kingu saizu no beddo] n king-size bed

金魚 [kingyo] n goldfish

気に入る [ki ni iru] v …が気に入る [... ga ki ni iru] v like

近似 [kinji] 近似の [kinji no] adj approximate

禁じる [kinjiru] v forbid; 禁じられた [kinjirareta] adj forbidden

近所 [kinjo] n neighborhood, vicinity; 近所の人 [kinjo no hito] n neighbor

金庫 [kinko] n safe; それを金庫に入れてください [sore o kinko ni irete kudasai] Put that in the safe, please; 私はジュエリーを金庫に入れたいのですが [watashi wa juerii o kinko ni iretai no desu ga] I'd like to put my jewelry in the safe; 私は貴重品を金庫に入れたいのですが [watashi wa kichohin o kinko ni iretai no desu ga] I'd like to put my valuables in the safe; 金庫に入れたものがあります [kinko ni ireta mono ga arimasu] I have some things in the safe

筋骨 [kinkotsu] 筋骨たくましい [kinkotsu takumashii] adj muscular

緊急 [kinkyuu] n urgency; 緊急事態 [kinkyuujitai] n emergency; 緊急の [kinkyuu no] adj urgent; 緊急着陸 [kinkyuu chakuriku] n emergency landing

金めっき [kinmekki] 金めっきの [kinmekki no] adj gold-plated

筋肉 [kinniku] n muscle

キノコ [kinoko] 毒キノコ [doku kinoko] n toadstool

昨日 [kinou, sakujitsu] adv yesterday

キンポウゲ [kinpouge] n buttercup

金製 [kinsei] 金製の [kinsei no] adj golden

金銭 [kinsen] n money

近接 [kinsetsu] n proximity; 近接した [kinsetsu shita] adj adjacent

禁止 [kinshi] n ban; 禁止された [kinshi sareta] adj banned, prohibited; 禁止する [kinshi suru] v ban, prohibit

近視 [kinshi] 近視の [kinshi no] adj nearsighted; 私は近視です [watashi wa kinshi desu] I'm nearsighted

近親 [kinshin] 近親者 [kinshinsha] *n* next-of-kin

禁酒 [kinshu] 絶対禁酒の [zettai kinshu no] *adj* teetotal

絹 [kinu] *n* silk

金曜日 [kin-youbi] *n* Friday; 金曜日に [kinyoubi ni] on Friday; 十二月三十一日の金曜日に [juuni-gatsu sanjuuichi-nichi no kinyoubi ni] on Friday, December thirty-first

記入 [kinyuu] 記入する [kinyuu suru] *v* fill out, fill up; 借方に記入する [karikata ni kinyuu suru] *v* debit

金属 [kinzoku] *n* metal; 装飾用のぴかぴか光る金属片や糸 [soushoku you no pikapika hikaru kinzokuhen ya ito] *n* tinsel

記憶 [kioku] *n* memory; 記憶する [kioku suru] *v* memorize

気温 [kion] 気温は何度ですか? [kion wa nan-do desu ka?] What's the temperature?

キオスク [kiosuku] *n* kiosk

キッパー [kippaa] *n* smoked herring

切符 [kippu] *n* ticket; キャンセル待ちの切符 [kyanserumachi no kippu] *n* stand-by ticket; バスの切符 [basu no kippu] *n* bus ticket; 日帰り往復割引切符 [higaeri oufuku waribiki kippu] *n* one-day round-trip ticket; 片道切符 [katamichi kippu] *n* one-way ticket; 往復切符 [oufuku kippu] *n* round-trip ticket; 切符売場 [kippu uriba] *n* box office, ticket office; 今夜の切符を2枚ください [kon'ya no kippu o nimai kudasai] I'd like two tickets for tonight; 来週の金曜の切符を2枚ください [raishuu no kinyou no kippu o nimai kudasai] I'd like two tickets for next Friday; 片道切符はいくらですか? [katamichi-kippu wa ikura desu ka?] How much is a one-way ticket?; ・・・行き往復切符2枚 [... iki oufuku-kippu nimai] two round-trip tickets to...; 往復切符はいくらですか? [oufuku-kippu wa ikura desu ka?] How much is a round-trip ticket?; 切符はどこで買うのですか? [kippu wa doko de kau no desu ka?] Where do I buy a ticket?; 切符はどこで買えますか? [kippu wa doko de kaemasu ka?] Where can I get tickets?, Where can we get tickets?; 切符を2枚ください [kippu o nimai kudasai] I'd like two tickets, please; 切符をください [kippu o kudasai] A ticket, please; 切符をアップグレードしたいのですが [kippu o appugureedo shitai no desu ga] I want to upgrade my ticket; 切符を変更したいのですが [kippu o henkou shitai no desu ga] I want to change my ticket

キプロス [kipurosu] *n* Cyprus; キプロスの [kipurosu no] *adj* Cypriot

キプロス人 [kipurosujin] *n* Cypriot *(person)*

嫌い [kirai] *adj* distasteful

嫌う [kirau] *v* dislike; ひどく嫌う [hidoku kirau] *v* loathe

きれい [kirei] *adj* clean; 部屋がきれいではありません [heya ga kirei de wa arimasen] The room isn't clean

きれいな [kirei na] *adj* pretty

きれいに [kirei ni] *adv* prettily

切れる [kireru] *v* cut; 棒切れ [bou kire] stick; 期限が切れる [kigen ga kireru] *v* expire

霧 [kiri] *n* fog; 霧の立ちこめた [kiri no tachikometa] *adj* foggy

切り離す [kirihanasu] *v* cut off

キリン [kirin] *n* giraffe

切り抜き [kirinuki] *n* clipping

切下げる [kirisageru] *v* devalue; 平価切下げ [heikakirisage] *n* devaluation

霧雨 [kirisame] *n* drizzle

キリスト [kirisuto] *n* Christ

キリスト教 [kirisutokyou] *n* Christianity; キリスト教の [kirisutokyou no] *adj* Christian; キリスト教徒 [kirisutokyouto] *n* Christian

伐り倒す [kiritaosu] *v* cut down

起立 [kiritsu] 起立する [kiritsu suru] *v* stand up

規律 [kiritsu] *n* discipline

切り分ける [kiriwakeru] *v* cut up

キロ [kiro] n kilo; 毎時…キロ [maiji… kiro] adv km/h

記録 [kiroku] n record; 記録係 [kirokugakari] n recorder (scribe); 記録する [kiroku suru] v record; テープに記録する [teepu ni kiroku suru] v tape

キロメートル [kiromeetoru] n kilometer

着る [kiru] v put on; 服を着た [fuku-o kita] adj dressed; 服を着る [fuku wo kiru] v dress; 何を着ればよいですか? [nani o kireba yoi desu ka?] What should I wear?

切る [kiru] v cut, turn off; 薄く切る [usuku kiru] v slice; 厚く切ったもの [atsuku kitta mono] n chunk; あまりたくさん切らないでください [amari takusan kiranaide kudasai] Don't cut too much off; 暖房を切ることができません [danbou o kiru koto ga dekimasen] I can't turn the heat off

キルギスタン [kirugisutan] n Kyrgyzstan

キルト [kiruto] n (タータン) kilt, (ベッドの上掛け) quilt; キルトの掛け布団 [kiruto no kakebuton] n comforter

既製 [kisei] 既製の [kisei no] adj bought

規制 [kisei] n regulation

奇跡 [kiseki] n miracle

季節 [kisetsu] n season; 季節の [kisetsu no] adj seasonal

記者 [kisha] 記者会見 [kishakaiken] n press conference; 取材記者 [shuzai kisha] n reporter

希釈 [kishaku] 希釈した [kishaku shita] adj diluted; 希釈する [kishaku suru] v dilute

岸 [kishi] n shore

きしる [kishiru] v squeak

騎手 [kishu] 競馬騎手 [keiba kishu] n jockey

寄宿 [kishuku] 寄宿生 [kishukusei] n boarder; 寄宿学校 [kishuku gakkou] n boarding school

起訴 [kiso] 起訴する [kiso suru] v prosecute

基礎 [kiso] n basis, foundations

規則 [kisoku] n rule; 交通規則集 [koutsuu kisokushuu] n traffic code

キス [kisu] n (口) kiss; キスする [kisu suru] v kiss

北 [kita] n north; 北に [kita ni] adv north; 北の [kita no] adj north, northern

北アフリカ [kitaafurika] n North Africa; 北アフリカ人 [Kita Afurika jin] n North African; 北アフリカの [Kita Afurika no] adj North African

北アイルランド [kita airurando] n Northern Ireland

北アメリカ [kitaamerika] n North America; 北アメリカ人 [Kita Amerika jin] n North American; 北アメリカの [Kita Amerika no] adj North American

北朝鮮 [kitachousen] n North Korea

期待 [kitai] 期待する [kitai suru] v expect

帰宅 [kitaku] 好きな時間に帰宅していいですよ [suki na jikan ni kitaku shite ii desu yo] Come home whenever you like; 午後11時までに帰宅してください [gogo juuichi-ji made ni kitaku shite kudasai] Please come home by eleven p.m.

北大西洋条約機構 [kitataiseiyou jouyaku kikou] n NATO

北行き [kitayuki] 北行きの [kitayuki no] adj northbound

機転 [kiten] n tact; 機転のきかない [kiten no kikanai] adj tactless; 機転のきく [kiten no kiku] adj tactful

喫煙 [kitsuen] n smoking; 非喫煙者 [hikitsuensha] n no-smoker; 喫煙者 [kitsuensha] n smoker; 喫煙できる部屋がいいのですが [kitsuen dekiru heya ga ii no desu ga] I'd like a smoking room; 喫煙エリアの席が欲しいのですが [kitsuen-eria no seki ga hoshii no desu ga] I'd like a seat in the smoking area

喫煙席 [kitsuenseki] n smoking seat

キツネ [kitsune] n fox

切手 [kitte] n stamp; どこで切手を買えますか? [doko de kitte o kaemasu ka?] Where can I buy stamps?; …あての郵便はがき四枚分の切手をもらえますか? [… ate no yuubin-hagaki yonmai-bun no kitte o moraemasu ka?] May I have stamps for four postcards to...; 切手を売っていますか? [kitte o utte imasu ka?] Do you sell stamps?; 切手を売っている一番近い店はどこですか? [kitte o utte iru ichiban chikai mise wa doko desu ka?] Where is the nearest place to buy stamps?

キット [kitto] 修理キット [shuuri kitto] n repair kit; ハンズフリーキット [hanzu furii kitto] n hands-free kit; 救急処置キット [kyuukyuu shochi kitto] n first-aid kit

気をつける [ki wo tsukeru] v be careful

器用 [kiyou] 不器用な [bukiyou na] adj awkward

気絶 [kizetsu] 気絶する [kizetsu suru] v faint; 彼女は気絶しました [kanojo wa kizetsu shimashita] She's fainted

傷 [kizu] n wound; 刺し傷 [sashi kizu] n sting

きず [kizu] n (損傷) flaw

傷痕 [kizuato] n scar

気づく [kizuku] v notice

傷つける [kizutsukeru] v hurt, injure, wound

傷つく [kizutsuku] 傷ついた [kizutsuita] adj hurt, injured; 傷つきやすい [kizutsukiyasui] adj sensitive, vulnerable

子 [ko] 継子 [mamako] n stepson; 馬の子 [uma no ko] n foal; 野獣の子 [yajuu no ko] n cub; 子会社 [kogaisha] n subsidiary; 子守り [komori] n babysitting

個別 [kobetsu] 個別指導 [kobetsu shidou] n tutorial; 個別指導教官 [kobetsu shidou kyoukan] n tutor

小人 [kobito] n dwarf

こぼす [kobosu] v (漏らす) spill

こぶし [kobushi] 握りこぶし [nigiri kobushi] n fist

誇張 [kochou] n exaggeration

孤独 [kodoku] n loneliness; 孤独の [kodoku no] adj lonely, lonesome

子供 [kodomo] n child, kid; 子供時代 [kodomo jidai] n childhood; 子供用プール [kodomoyou puuru] n wading pool; 子供部屋 [kodomobeya] n nursery; 一人前を子供

用の量にできますか? [ichinin-mae o kodomo-you no ryou ni dekimasu ka?] Do you have children's portions?; それは子供にも安全ですか? [sore wa kodomo ni mo anzen desu ka?] Is it safe for children?; それは子供に安全ですか? [sore wa kodomo ni anzen desu ka?] Is it safe for children?; 私には子供が一人います [watashi ni wa kodomo ga hitori imasu] I have a child; 私には子供が三人います [watashi ni wa kodomo ga sannin imasu] I have three children; 私には子供がいません [watashi ni wa kodomo ga imasen] I have no children; 私の子供が病気です [watashi no kodomo ga byouki desu] My child is ill; 子供ができることは何がありますか? [kodomo ga dekiru koto wa nani ga arimasu ka?] What is there for children to do?; 子供たちが車の中にいます [kodomo-tachi ga kuruma no naka ni imasu] My children are in the car; 子供を連れて行っても大丈夫ですか? [kodomo o tsurete itte mo daijoubu desu ka?] Is it OK to take children?

子供じみた [kodomojimita] v childish

子供用 [kodomoyou] 子供用のプールはありますか? [kodomo-you no puuru wa arimasu ka?] Is there a children's pool?

声 [koe] n voice; 泣き叫ぶ声 [nakisakebu koe] n cry; 笑い声 [waraigoe] n laughter; 声を出して [koe wo dashite] adv aloud

超える [koeru] v exceed; 度を超えた [do-o koeta] adj excessive

古風 [kofuu] 古風で趣のある [kofuu de omomuki no aru] adj quaint

小型 [kogata] 小型タクシー [kogata takushii] n private taxi

こげる [kogeru] どこに行けばカヌーをこげますか? [doko ni ikeba kanuu o kogemasu ka?] Where can we go canoeing?

漕げる [kogeru] v row

小切手 [kogitte] n check; 旅行者用小切手 [ryokousha you kogitte] n traveler's check; 白地小切手 [shiraji kogitte] n blank check;

小切手帳 [kogittechou] n checkbook; 小切手で支払えますか? [kogitte de shiharaemasu ka?] Can I pay by check?; 小切手を現金化してください [kogitte o genkinka shite kudasai] I want to cash a check, please; 小切手を現金化できますか? [kogitte o genkinka dekimasu ka?] Can I cash a check?

凍える [kogoeru] v be cold

小言 [kogoto] がみがみ小言を言う [gamigami kogoto-o iu] v nag

漕ぐ [kogu] v row (in boat); カヌー漕ぎ [kanuu kogi] n canoeing; パドルで漕ぐ [padoru de kogu] v paddle; ボートを漕ぐこと [booto-o kogu koto] n rowing; 漕ぎ舟 [kogibune] n rowboat

琥珀 [kohaku] 琥珀色 [kohaku iro] n amber

子羊 [kohitsuji] n lamb

故意 [koi] 故意に [koi ni] adv deliberately; 故意に破壊する [koi ni hakai suru] v sabotage, vandalize; 故意の [koi no] adj deliberate; 故意の破壊 [koi no hakai] n sabotage; 故意でない [koi de nai] adj unintentional

コイン [koin] n coin; コインロッカー [koinrokkaa] n luggage locker; 電話に使うコインをいくらかお願いします [denwa ni tsukau koin o ikura ka o-negai shimasu] I'd like some coins for the phone, please

コインランドリー [koinrandorii] この近くにコインランドリーはありますか? [kono chikaku ni koin-randorii wa arimasu ka?] Is there a Laundromat near here?

コインロッカー [koinrokkaa] コインロッカーはありますか? [koin-rokkaa wa arimasu ka?] Are there any luggage lockers?

子犬 [koinu] n puppy

小石 [koishi] n pebble

恋をもてあそぶ [koi wo moteasobu] v flirt

孤児 [koji] n orphan

乞食 [kojiki] n beggar

個人 [kojin] n individual; 個人にかかわらない [kojin ni kakawaranai] adj impersonal; 個人の所有物 [kojin no shoyuubutsu] n private property; 個人情報泥棒 [kojin jouhou dorobou] n identity theft; 個人的な [kojinteki na] adj personal, private; 個人秘書 [kojin hisho] n personal assistant, PA

コカイン [kokain] n cocaine

コカコーラ® [kokakoora] n Coke®

コケ [koke] n moss

こき使う [kokitsukau] v boss around

国歌 [kokka] n anthem, national anthem

国家 [kokka] n nation; 自治国家 [jichi kokka] n autonomy; 国家主義 [kokkashugi] n nationalism; 国家主義者 [kokkashugisha] n nationalist

告解 [kokkai] 告解火曜日 [Kokkai Kayoubi] n Mardi Gras

骨格 [kokkaku] n skeleton

コックピット [kokkupitto] n cockpit

国境 [kokkyou] n frontier

ここ [koko] ここに [koko ni] adv here

個々 [koko] 個々の [koko no] adj individual

ココア [kokoa] n cocoa

心地 [kokochi] 居心地のよい [igokochi no yoi] adj cozy; 心地よくない [kokochi yokunai] adj uncomfortable

ココナツ [kokonatsu] n coconut

心 [kokoro] n mind, heart; 心の広い [kokoro no hiroi] adj broad-minded; 心から [kokoro kara] adv sincerely; 心からの [kokoro kara no] adj sincere

試み [kokoromi] n attempt

試みる [kokoromiru] v attempt

心を強くとらえる [kokoro wo tsuyoku toraeru] vx gripping

快い [kokoroyoi] adj sweet (pleasing)

黒板 [kokuban] n blackboard

国営 [kokuei] 国営にする [kokuei ni suru] v nationalize

克服 [kokufuku] 克服する [kokufuku suru] v overcome

国外 [kokugai] 国外退去させる [kokugai taikyo saseru] v deport

穀草 [koku kusa] n cereal crops

国民 [kokumin] n nation; 国民の [kokumin

no] *adj* national

国内 [kokunai] 国内の [kokunai no] *adj* domestic

国立 [kokuritsu] 国立公園 [kokuritsu kouen] *n* national park

穀類 [kokurui] *n* cereals

国際 [kokusai] 国際的な [kokusaiteki na] *adj* international; 国際連合 [kokusairengou] *n* UN; どこで国際電話をかけられますか? [doko de kokusai-denwa o kakeraremasu ka?] Where can I make an international phone call?; ここから国際電話をかけられますか? [koko kara kokusai-denwa o kakeraremasu ka?] Can I call internationally from here?; 国際電話用のテレホンカードをください [kokusai-denwa-you no terehon-kaado o kudasai] An international phone card, please; 国際電話用のテレホンカードを売っていますか? [kokusai-denwa-you no terehon-kaado o utte imasu ka?] Do you sell international phone cards?

国際連合 [kokusairengou] *n* United Nations

国勢 [kokusei] 国勢調査 [kokuzeichousa] *n* census

国籍 [kokuseki] *n* nationality

告訴 [kokuso] *n* charge (accusation); 告訴する [kokuso suru] *v* charge (accuse)

穀粒 [kokutsubu] *n* grain

顧客 [kokyaku] *n* customer

呼吸 [kokyuu] *n* breathing

コマーシャル [komaasharu] *n* commercial; コマーシャルの時間 [komaasharu no jikan] *n* commercial break

コマドリ [komadori] *n* robin

細かい [komakai] 細かく調べる [komakaku shiraberu] *v* scan

細かいお金 [komakai okane] *n* small change

鼓膜 [komaku] *n* eardrum

困らせる [komaraseru] *adj* puzzling

困る [komaru] 困った [komatta] *adj* puzzled

米 [kome] *n* rice

コメディアン [komedian] *n* comedian

コメディー [komedii] *n* comedy

小道 [komichi] *n* path, track; 歩行者用の小道 [hokoushayou no komichi] *n* footpath

込み合う [komi gou ru] 込み合った [komiatta] *adj* crowded

小文字 [komoji] すべて小文字です [subete ko-moji desu] all lower case

顧問医 [komon-i] *n* specialist (physician)

子守 [komori] *n* baby-sitter; 子守歌 [komoriuta] *n* lullaby

こもる [komoru] 愛情のこもった [aijou no komotta] *adj* affectionate

小麦 [komugi] *n* wheat; 小麦アレルギー [komugi arerugii] *n* wheat allergy

小麦粉 [komugiko] *n* flour

コミュニケーション [komyunikeeshon] *n* communication

根 [kon] *n* root

粉 [kona] *n* powder; カレー粉 [kareeko] *n* curry powder; パン粉 [panko] *n* breadcrumbs, crumb; 粉石鹸 [kona sekken] *n* laundry detergent; 粉砂糖 [konazatou] *n* confectioners' sugar

コンバーター [konbaataa] 触媒コンバーター [shokubai konbaataa] *n* catalytic converter

コンバーティブル [konbaateiburu] *n* convertible

今晩 [konban] *n* this evening/tonight

こんばんは [konban wa] Good evening

コンベヤベルト [konbeyaberuto] *n* conveyor belt

棍棒 [konbou] *n* club (weapon)

コンチェルト [koncheruto] *n* concerto

昆虫 [konchuu] *n* insect

コンディショナー [kondeishonaa] *n* conditioner; コンディショナーを売っていますか? [kondishonaa o utte imasu ka?] Do you sell conditioner?

コンドーム [kondoomu] *n* condom

混同 [kondou] *n* confusion, mix-up; 混同する [kondou suru] *v* mix up

子猫 [koneko] *n* kitten

コンファレンスセンター [konfarensusentaa] コンファレンスセンターまでお願いします

[konfarensu-sentaa made o-negai shimasu] Please take me to the conference center

懇願 [kongan] *n* appeal; 懇願する [kongan suru] *v* appeal

コンゴ [kongo] *n* Congo

混合 [kougou] *n* mixture; 混合物 [kougoubutsu] *n* mix, mixture

混合する [kougou suru] 混合した [kougou shita] *adj* mixed

婚姻 [kon'in] 婚姻関係の有無 [kon'in kankei no umu] *n* marital status

コンクリート [konkuriito] *n* concrete

コンマ [konma] *n* comma

困難 [konnan] *n* difficulty, trouble; 困難な [konnan na] *adj* difficult, hard *(difficult)*

こんにちは [konnichi wa] Good afternoon

こんにちは! [konnichi wa] *excl* hello!

この [kono] このバスは・・・へ行きますか? [kono basu wa... e ikimasu ka?] Does this bus go to...?

このごろは [konogoro wa] *adv* nowadays

好ましい [konomashii] 好ましくない [konomashikunai] *adj* unfavorable

好み [konomi] *n* preference

好む [konomu] *v* like; ・・・の方を好む [...no hou wo konomu] *v* prefer

好んで [kononde] *adv* preferably

コンパートメント [konpaatomento] *n* compartment

コンパクトディスク [konpakuto disuku] *n* compact disc

コンパス [konpasu] *n* compass

コンピューター [konpyu taa] コンピューターゲーム [konpyuutaa geemu] *n* computer game

コンピューター [konpyuutaa] *n* computer; コンピューター科学 [konpyuutaa kagaku] *n* computer science; あなたのコンピューターをお借りできますか? [anata no konpyuutaa o o-kari dekimasu ka?] May I use your computer?; このコンピューターでCDを作成できますか? [kono konpyuutaa de shii-dii o sakusei dekimasu ka?] Can I make CDs at

this computer?; 私のコンピューターがフリーズしました [watashi no konpyuutaa ga furiizu shimashita] My computer has frozen

コンピューター室 [konpyuutaa shitsu] コンピューター室はどこですか? [konpyuutaa-shitsu wa doko desu ka?] Where is the computer room?

混乱 [konran] 混乱させる [konran saseru] *v* disrupt; 混乱状態 [konranjoutai] *n* confusion; 大混乱 [daikonran] *n* chaos; 大混乱した [daikonran shita] *adj* chaotic

コンサーバトリー [konsaabatorii] *n* conservatory

コンサート [konsaato] *n* concert; 何かよいコンサートがありますか? [nani ka yoi konsaato ga arimasu ka?] Are there any good concerts?; どこでそのコンサートのチケットを買えますか? [doko de sono konsaato no chiketto o kaemasu ka?] Where can I buy tickets for the concert?

コンサートホール [konsaatohooru] *n* concert hall; コンサートホールでは今晩何をやっていますか? [konsaato-hooru de wa konban nani o yatte imasu ka?] What's on tonight at the concert hall?

コンセンサス [konsensasu] *n* consensus

コンセント [konsento] *n* socket; 電気カミソリのコンセントはどこですか? [denki-kamisori no konsento wa doko desu ka?] Where's the socket for my electric razor?

今週 [konshuu] 今週の土曜日に [konshuu no doyoubi ni] this Saturday

コンソール [konsooru] ゲームコンソール [geemu konsooru] *n* game console

昏睡 [konsui] *n* coma

コンタクト [kontakuto] コンタクトレンズ [kontakutorenzu] *n* contact lenses

コンタクトレンズ [kontakutorenzu] *n* contact lens; コンタクトレンズの洗浄液 [kontakuto-renzu no senjou-eki] cleansing solution for contact lenses; 私はコンタクトレンズをはめています [watashi wa kontakuto-renzu o hamete imasu] I wear contact lenses

K

コントラバス [kontorabasu] n double bass

困惑 [konwaku] n embarrassment; 困惑させる [konwaku saseru] adj confuse, confusing; 困惑した [konwaku shita] adj baffled, bewildered

今夜 [konya] adv tonight; 今夜は寒くなりますか? [kon'ya wa samuku narimasu ka?] Will it be cold tonight?; 今夜の切符を2枚ください [kon'ya no kippu o nimai kudasai] I'd like two tickets for tonight

婚約 [konyaku] 婚約中の男性 [kon'yakuchuu no dansei] n fiancé; 婚約中の女性 [kon'yakuchuu no josei] n fiancée; 婚約している [konyaku shiteiru] adj engaged; 婚約指輪 [konyaku yubiwa] n engagement ring

コーチ [koochi] n coach (trainer), trainer

コーデュロイ [koodeyuroi] n corduroy

コード [koodo] 電気コード [denki koodo] n electric cord; 延長コード [enchoukoodo] n extension cord

コードレス [koodoresu] コードレスの [koodoresu no] adj cordless

コーヒー [koohii] n coffee; コーヒーテーブル [koohii teeburu] n coffee table; コーヒーポット [koohiipotto] n coffeepot; コーヒー豆 [koohiimame] n coffee bean; カフェイン抜きのコーヒー [kafein nuki no koohii] n decaffeinated coffee; ブラックコーヒー [burakku koohii] n black coffee; コーヒーをください [koohii o kudasai] Coffee, please; コーヒーをもう一杯いただけますか? [koohii o mou ippai itadakemasu ka?] Could we have another cup of coffee, please?; ラウンジでコーヒーをいただけますか? [raunji de koohii o itadakemasu ka?] Could we have coffee in the lounge?; ミルク入りコーヒーをください [miruku-iri koohii o kudasai] Coffee with milk, please; 挽きたてのコーヒーはありますか? [hikitate no koohii wa arimasu ka?] Do you have fresh coffee?; 本物のコーヒーはありますか? [honmono no koohii wa arimasu ka?] Do you have real coffee?

コーンフラワー [koonfurawaa] n cornstarch

コーンフレーク [koonfureeku] n cornflakes

コーラン [kooran] n Koran

コオロギ [koorogi] n cricket (insect)

コール [kooru] コールセンター [kooru sentaa] n call center

コールスロー [koorusuroo] n coleslaw

コーシャ [koosha] コーシャ料理はありますか? [koosha-ryouri wa arimasu ka?] Do you have kosher dishes?

コース [koosu] n course; 再教育コース [saikyouiku koosu] n refresher course; この近くに公共のゴルフコースはありますか? [kono chikaku ni kookyou no gorufu-koosu wa arimasu ka?] Is there a public golf course near here?

コート [kooto] n (洋服) coat

コピー [kopii] n (複写) photocopy; コピーする [kopii suru] v photocopy; どこでコピーを取ってもらえますか? [doko de kopii o totte moraemasu ka?] Where can I get some photocopying done?; このコピーをお願いします [kono kopii o o-negai shimasu] I'd like a photocopy of this, please; このカラーコピーをお願いします [kono karaa-kopii o o-negai shimasu] I'd like a color photocopy of this, please

コピー機 [kopiiki] n photocopier

コップ [koppu] n glass, cup

これ [kore] これには何が入っていますか? [kore ni wa nani ga haitte imasu ka?] What is in this?; 私はこれをいただきます [watashi wa kore o itadakimasu] I'll have this

コレクション [korekushon] n collection

コレクトコール [korekutokooru] コレクトコールをかけたいのですが [korekuto-kooru o kaketai no desu ga] I'd like to make a collect call

コレステロール [koresuterooru] n cholesterol

コリアンダー [koriandaa] n coriander (seed)

コリー [korii] n collie

孤立 [koritsu] 孤立した [koritsu shita] adj isolated

ころぶ [korobu] 彼女はころびました [kanojo wa korobimashita] She fell

転がる [korogaru] v roll; 転がり [korogari] n roll

ころも [koromo] (料理用の)ころも [(ryouriyou no) koromo] n batter

コロン [koron] n colon

コロンビア [koronbia] n Colombia

コロンビア人 [koronbiajin] n Colombian (person)

コロンビアの [koronbia no] adj Colombian

殺す [korosu] v kill

コルク [koruku] n cork; コルク栓抜き [koruku sennuki] n corkscrew

コルネット [korunetto] n cornet

個性 [kosei] n personality

腰 [koshi] n hip

腰掛け [koshikake] 窓下の腰掛け [mado shita no koshikake] n window seat

故障 [koshou] n breakdown; 故障した [koshou shita] adj broken down; 故障する [koshou suru] v break down; 故障警告灯 [koshou keikokutou] n hazard warning lights; 故障時緊急修理サービスを呼んでください [koshou-ji kinkyuu-shuuri-saabisu o yonde kudasai] Call the breakdown service, please

コショウ [koshou] n pepper

コショウひき [koshou hiki] n peppermill

コショウソウ [koshousou] n cress

コソボ [kosobo] n Kosovo

子育て [kosodate] 片親で子育てをする人 [kataoya de kosodate-o suru hito] n single parent; 私は子育てをしています [watashi wa kosodate o shite imasu] I'm a full-time parent

骨折 [kossetsu] n fracture

こする [kosuru] v rub

コスタリカ [kosutarika] n Costa Rica

コスト [kosuto] n cost

答え [kotae] n answer; 否定の答え [hitei no kotae] n negative

答える [kotaeru] v answer

固体 [kotai] 固体の [kotai no] adj solid

固定 [kotei] adj 固定した [kotei shita] adj fixed; 固定する [kotei suru] v fix

こと [koto] 電話をかけること [denwa-o kakeru koto] n phone call

言葉 [kotoba] n word, speech

事柄 [kotogara] n affair

異なる [kotonaru] v differ; 意見が異なる [iken ga kotonaru] v disagree

ことによると [koto ni yoru to] adv perhaps, possibly

今年 [kotoshi] this year

ことわざ [kotowaza] n proverb, saying

骨盤 [kotsuban] n pelvis

小粒の種なし [kotsubu no tane nashi] 小粒の種なし干しブドウ [kotsubu no tanenashi hoshibudou] n currant

骨髄 [kotsuzui] n marrow

骨董 [kottou] adj 骨董屋 [kottou ya] n antique store; 骨董品 [kottouhin] n antique

抗 [kou] 抗ヒスタミン剤 [kouhisutaminzai] n antihistamine; 抗生物質 [kousei busshitsu] n antibiotic; 抗鬱剤 [kouutsuzai] n antidepressant

校 [kou] 中学校 [chuugakkou] n secondary school

腱 [kou] n tendon

考案 [kouan] 考案する [kouan suru] v devise

酵母菌 [koubokin] n yeast

鉱物 [koubutsu] n mineral; 鉱物の [koubutsu no] adj mineral

紅茶 [koucha] n black tea

校長 [kouchou] n principal

甲冑 [kouchuu] n armor

高度 [koudo] n (海抜) altitude

購読 [koudoku] 定期購読 [teiki koudoku] n subscription

行動 [koudou] 行動する [koudou suru] v act

公営 [kouei] 公営住宅 [koueijuutaku] n government-subsidized housing

光栄 [kouei] n honor

後援 [kouen] n sponsorship; 後援者 [kouensha] n sponsor; 後援者となる

[kouensha to naru] v sponsor

公演 [kouen] n performance; 公演は何時に終わりますか? [kouen wa nan-ji ni owarimarimasu ka?] When does the performance end?; 公演は何時に始まりますか? [kouen wa nan-ji ni hajimarimasu ka?] When does the performance begin?; 公演時間はどのくらいの長さですか? [kouen-jikan wa dono kurai no nagasa desu ka?] How long does the performance last?

公園 [kouen] n park; 国立公園 [kokuritsu kouen] n national park

公布 [koufu] 公布する [koufu suru] v issue

降伏 [koufuku] 降伏する [koufuku suru] v surrender

幸福 [koufuku] n happiness; 幸福な [koufuku na] adj happy; 幸福に [koufuku ni] adv happily

興奮 [koufun] 興奮させる [koufun saseru] adj exciting; 興奮した [koufun shita] adj excited

郊外 [kougai] n outskirts, suburb; 郊外の [kougai no] adj suburban; 郊外の大型スーパー [kougai no ougata suupaa] n hypermarket

工学 [kougaku] n engineering; 電子工学 [denshikougaku] n electronics

攻撃 [kougeki] n attack; テロリストによる攻撃 [terorisuto niyoru kougeki] n terrorist attack; 攻撃する [kougeki suru] v attack; 攻撃的な [kougekiteki na] adj aggressive

抗議 [kougi] n protest; 抗議する [kougi suru] v protest

講義 [kougi] n lecture; 講義をする [kougi-o suru] v lecture

交互 [kougo] 交互の [kougo no] adj alternate

鉱業 [kougyou] n mining

工業 [kougyou] 工業団地 [kougyoudanchi] n industrial park

荒廃 [kouhai] n ruin; 荒廃させる [kouhai saseru] v ruin

口辺ヘルペス [kouhenherupesu] n cold sore

候補 [kouho] 選抜候補者リスト [senbatsu kouhosha risuto] n short list; 候補者 [kouhosha] n candidate

広報 [kouhou] n public relations

後方 [kouhou] 後方に [kouhou ni] adv backwards

行為 [koui] n act; スパイ行為 [supai koui] n espionage, spying; 破壊行為 [hakai koui] n vandalism; 儀礼的行為 [gireiteki koui] n formality

更衣室 [kouishitsu] n changing room

工事 [kouji] 道路工事 [dourokouji] n road work

口実 [koujitsu] n pretext

工場 [koujou] n factory; 製造工場 [seizou koujou] n plant (site/equipment); 私は工場で働いています [watashi wa koujou de hataraite imasu] I work in a factory

口述 [koujutsu] n dictation

硬貨 [kouka] n coin

高価 [kouka] 高価な [kouka na] adj expensive, valuable

効果 [kouka] 効果的な [koukateki na] adj effective; 効果的に [koukateki ni] adv effectively

狡猾 [koukatsu] 狡猾な [koukatsu na] adj cunning

紅海 [koukai] n Red Sea

航海 [koukai] n sailing; 航海する [koukai suru] v sail

後悔 [koukai] n regret; 後悔する [koukai suru] v regret

交換 [koukan] 交換する [koukan suru] v trade; これを交換したいのですが [kore o koukan shitai no desu ga] I'd like to exchange this; ・・・を交換できますか? [... o koukan dekimasu ka?] Can you replace....?

高価な [kouka na] adj pricey (expensive)

交換台 [koukandai] 電話交換台 [denwa koukandai] n switchboard

後継 [koukei] 後継者 [koukeisha] n successor

考古学 [koukogaku] n archaeology; 考古学者 [koukogakusha] n archaeologist

広告 [koukoku] n ad, advertisement; 広告す

る [koukoku suru] v advertise; 広告すること [koukoku suru koto] n advertising; 分類広告 [bunruikoukoku] n classified ads

甲骨 [koukotsu] 肩甲骨 [kenkoukotsu] n shoulder blade

航空 [koukuu] 航空会社 [koukuu gaisha] n airline; 航空便 [koukuubin] n airmail; 航空機 [koukuuki] n aircraft; 航空管制官 [koukuu kanseikan] n air-traffic controller

航空便 [koukuubin] n airmail

公共 [koukyou] 公共職業安定所 [koukyoushokugyou anteisho] n employment office

交響曲 [koukyoukyoku] n symphony

高慢ちき [koumanchiki] 高慢ちきな [koumanchiki na] adj stuck-up

公民権 [kouminken] n civil rights

項目 [koumoku] n item

コウモリ [koumori] n (動物) bat (mammal)

公務員 [koumuin] n civil servant

被る [koumuru] v suffer

購入 [kounyuu] 購入する [kounyuu suru] v purchase

行楽 [kouraku] 行楽地 [kourakuchi] n resort

高齢 [kourei] 高齢者 [koureisha] n senior citizen

氷 [kouri] n ice; 路面の薄い透明な氷 [romen no usui toumei na kouri] n black ice; 氷を入れてください [koori o irete kudsai] With ice, please

小売 [kouri] 小売価格 [kourikakaku] n retail price; 小売業者 [kourigyousha] n retailer

小売り [kouri] n retail; 小売りする [kouri suru] v retail

効率 [kouritsu] 効率の悪い [kouritsu no warui] adj inefficient; 効率的な [kouritsuteki na] adj efficient

口論 [kouron] n argument, quarrel; つまらないことで口論する [tsumaranai koto de kouron suru] v squabble; 口論する [kouron suru] v quarrel

凍る [kouru] v freeze; 凍った [koutta] adj frozen; 凍るような [kouru you na] adj freezing

荒涼 [kouryou] 荒涼とした [kouryou to shita] adj bleak

拘留 [kouryuu] n detention

交差 [kousa] 環状交差路 [kanjou kousaro] n roundabout

交際 [kousai] ごめんなさい、交際している人がいます [gomen nasai, kousai shite iru hito ga imasu] Sorry, I'm in a relationship

交差路 [kousaro] n crossroads

交差点 [kousaten] n crossing

構成 [kousei] n composition; 構成している [kousei shite iru] adj component; 構成要素 [kousei youso] n component

公正 [kousei] n fairness; 公正な [kousei na] adj fair (reasonable); 公正に [kousei ni] adv fairly

校正刷り [kouseizuri] n proof (for checking)

鉱泉 [kousen] n spa

講師 [koushi] n assistant professor

子牛 [koushi] n calf; 子牛の肉 [koushi no niku] n veal

公式 [koushiki] n formula

更新 [koushin] 更新する [koushin suru] v update

行進 [koushin] n march, procession; 行進する [koushin suru] v march

香辛料 [koushinryou] n spice; 香辛料を入れた [koushinryou-o ireta] adj spicy

交渉 [koushou] n negotiations; 交渉する [koushou suru] v negotiate; 交渉者 [koushousha] n negotiator

公衆 [koushuu] n public; 公衆の [koushuu no] adj public; 公衆電話 [koushuudenwa] n payphone

公衆電話 [koushuudenwa] n public phone; カード式公衆電話 [kaado shiki koushuu denwa] n cardphone; 公衆電話ボックス [koushuu denwa bokkusu] n phone booth

拘束 [kousoku] n curb

高速 [kousoku] 高速進行 [kousoku shinkou] n speeding; 高速道路 [kousokudouro] n expressway

K

高速道路 [kousokudourou] *n* highway; 高速道路の進入退出路 [kousoku douro no shinnyuu taishutsuro] *n* highway ramp

高層 [kousou] 高層建築 [kousou kenchiku] *n* high-rise

降霜 [kousou] *n* frosting

香水 [kousui] *n* perfume

交替 [koutai] 交替班 [koutai han] *n* relay race

抗体 [koutai] *n* antibody

後退 [koutai] 景気後退 [keikikoutai] *n* recession

後退する [koutai suru] 後退させる [koutai saseru] *v* back

皇帝 [koutei] *n* emperor

鋼鉄 [koutetsu] *n* steel

高等 [koutou] 高等教育 [koutoukyouiku] *n* higher education

口頭 [koutou] 口頭の [koutou no] *adj* oral; 口頭試験 [koutou shiken] *adj* oral

喉頭 [koutou] 喉頭炎 [koutouen] *n* laryngitis

交通 [koutsuu] *n* traffic; 交通信号 [koutsuu shingou] *n* traffic lights; 交通渋滞 [koutsuujuutai] *n* traffic jam; 交通規則集 [koutsuu kisokushuu] *n* traffic code; 交通監視員 [koutsuu kanshiin] *n* parking enforcement officer; 公共交通機関 [koukyou koutsuu kikan] *n* public transportation

幸運 [kouun] 幸運な [kouun na] *adj* fortunate; 幸運にも [kouun nimo] *adv* fortunately

口座 [kouza] *n* account; 銀行口座 [ginkoukouza] *n* bank account; 預金口座 [yokin kouza] *n* account *(in bank)*; 共同預金口座 [kyoudou yokin kouza] *n* joint account; 口座番号 [kouzabangou] *n* account number; 口座引き落とし [kouza hikiotoshi] *n* direct debit; 私の口座から送金したいのですが [watashi no kouza kara soukin shitai no desu ga] I would like to transfer some money from my account

鉱山 [kouzan] *n* mine

構造 [kouzou] *n* structure

洪水 [kouzui] *n* flood

怖がる [kowagaru] 怖がらせる [kowagaraseru] *v* frighten

怖い [kowai] *adj* scary; 怖がった [kowagatta] *adj* scared, terrified; 怖がらせる [kowagaraseru] *v* scare, terrify; ・・・が怖い [... ga kowai] *adj* afraid of...

壊れる [kowareru] これは壊れています [kore wa kowarete imasu] This is broken; ギアボックスが壊れています [gia-bokkusu ga kowarete imasu] The transmission is broken; エキゾーストが壊れています [ekizoosuto ga kowarete imasu] The exhaust is broken; メーターが壊れています [meetaa ga kowarete imasu] The meter is broken; 鍵が壊れています [kagi ga kowarete imasu] The lock is broken

壊れやすい [kowareyasui] *adj* fragile

壊る [kowaru] 壊れた [kowareta] *adj* broken

壊す [kowasu] *v* break

壊すことのできない [kowasu koto no dekinai] *adj* unbreakable

小屋 [koya] *n* hut, shed; 馬小屋 [umagoya] *n* stable; 風車小屋 [fuushagoya] *n* windmill; 一番近い山小屋はどこですか? [ichiban chikai yama-goya wa doko desu ka?] Where is the nearest mountain hut?

雇用 [koyou] *n* employment; 雇用主 [koyounushi] *n* employer; 雇用する [koyou suru] *v* employ

小銭 [kozeni] *n* change; すみません、小銭がありません [sumimasen, kozeni ga arimasen] Sorry, I don't have any change; ・・・の小銭をいただけますか? [... no kozeni o itadakemasu ka?] Could you give me change for...?; 小銭がありますか? [kozeni ga arimasu ka?] Do you have any small change?; 小銭をいくらかいただけますか? [kozeni o ikura ka itadakemasu ka?] Could you give me some change, please?

小包 [kozutsumi] *n* package; この小包を送りたいのですが [kono kozutsumi o okuritai no desu ga] I'd like to send this package; この

小包を送るのにいくらかかりますか? [kono kozutsumi o okuru no ni ikura kakarimasu ka?] How much will it cost to send this package?

区 [ku] n ward (area); 保護区 [hogoku] n preserve (land); 選挙区 [senkyoku] n constituency

句 [ku] 慣用句 [kan'youku] n phrase

配る [kubaru] v distribute

区別 [kubetsu] n distinction; 区別する [kubetsu suru] v distinguish

首 [kubi] n (体) neck; 首にする [kubi ni suru] v fire (employee)

口 [kuchi] n mouth; 改札口 [kaisatsuguchi] n ticket barrier; 口に出す [kuchi ni dasu] v refer; 口のきけない [kuchi no kikenai] adj speechless; 口ひげ [kuchi hige] n mustache

くちばし [kuchibashi] n beak

口紅 [kuchibeni] n lipstick

口火 [kuchibi] n pilot light

唇 [kuchibiru] n lip

口笛 [kuchibue] n whistle; 口笛を吹く [kuchibue wo fuku] v whistle

口汚い [kuchi kitanai] adj abusive

口のきけない [kuchi no kikenai] adj mute

果物 [kudamono] n fruit

くだらないこと [kudaranai koto] n trash

下さる [kudasaru] ・・・をください [... o kudasai] I'd like..., please

下す [kudasu] 判決を下す [hanketsu-o kudasu] v sentence

クエーカー [kueekaa] n Quaker

九月 [kugatsu] n September

釘 [kugi] n nail

クイズ [kuizu] n quiz

クジャク [kujaku] n peacock

くじ [kuji] n (抽選) draw

くじく [kujiku] v sprain; ・・・の勇気をくじく [... no yuuki-o kujiku] v discourage

クジラ [kujira] n whale

苦情 [kujou] n complaint; 誰に苦情を言えばいいのですか? [dare ni kujou o ieba ii no desu ka?] Where can I make a com-

plaint?; 苦情があるのですが [kujou ga aru no desu ga] I'd like to make a complaint

区画 [kukaku] 小区画 [shou kukaku] n plot (piece of land)

クマ [kuma] n (動物) bear; 北極グマ [hokkyokuguma] n polar bear

熊手 [kumade] n rake

組合 [kumiai] 労働組合 [roudoukumiai] n labor union

組み合わせ [kumiawase] n combination

組み換える [kumikaeru] v modify; 遺伝子組み換えの [idenshi kumikae no] adj genetically modified

組み込む [kumikomu] v fit in

クミン [kumin] n cumin

雲 [kumo] n cloud

クモ [kumo] n (動物) spider; クモの巣 [kumo no su] n spiderweb

苦悶 [kumon] n agony

くもの巣 [kumo no su] n cobweb

曇る [kumoru] 曇った [kumotta] adj cloudy, overcast; 曇っています [kumotte imasu] It's cloudy

国 [kuni] n country; 発展途上国 [hattentojou-koku] n developing country; どこでその国の地図を買えますか? [doko de sono kuni no chizu o kaemasu ka?] Where can I buy a map of the country?

国番号 [kunibangou] 英国の国番号は何番ですか? [eikoku no kuni-bangou wa nan-ban desu ka?] What's the country code for the UK?

訓練 [kunren] 自己訓練 [jiko kunren] n self-discipline; 訓練された [kunren sareta] adj trained; 訓練する [kunren suru] v train; 訓練を受けている人 [kunren-o ukete iru hito] n trainee

君主 [kunshu] n monarch; 君主制 [kunshusei] n monarchy

屈服 [kuppuku] 屈服する [kuppuku suru] v give in

クラブ [kurabu] n (集団) club (group); ゴルフ用クラブ [gorufu you kurabu] n golf club *(game)*; どこかによいクラブはありますか? [doko-ka ni yoi kurabu wa arimasu ka?] Where is there a good club?; ゴルフクラブを貸し出していますか? [gorufu-kurabu o kashidashite imasu ka?] Do they rent out golf clubs?

クラゲ [kurage] *n* jellyfish; ここにクラゲはいますか? [koko ni kurage wa imasu ka?] Are there jellyfish here?

暗い [kurai] *adj* dark; 暗いです [kurai desu] It's dark

クライマー [kuraimaa] *n* climber

クライミング [kuraimingu] *n* climbing; 私はクライミングをしたいのですが [watashi wa kuraimingu o shitai no desu ga] I'd like to go climbing

クラッカー [kurakkaa] *n* cracker

クラック [kurakku] *n* crack *(cocaine)*

クランベリー [kuranberii] *n* cranberry

クラリネット [kurarinetto] *n* clarinet

暗さ [kurasa] *n* darkness

クラス [kurasu] *n* class; エコノミークラス [ekonomiikurasu] *n* economy class; ビジネスクラス [bijinesu kurasu] *n* business class; 夜間クラス [yakan kurasu] *n* night class

暮らす [kurasu] ···にたよって暮らす [... ni tayotte kurasu] *v* live on

クラッチ [kuratchi] *n* clutch

くらわす [kurawasu] げんこつをくらわす [genkotsu o kurawasu] *v* punch

クレームフォーム [kureemufoomu] *n* claim form

クレーン [kureen] *n* crane *(for lifting)*

クレジット [kurejitto] *n* credit; クレジットカードは使えますか? [kurejitto-kaado wa tsukaemasu ka?] Do you take credit cards?

クレジットカード [kurejittokaado] *n* credit card; 私のクレジットカードでキャッシングが利用できますか? [watashi no kurejitto-kaado de kyasshingu ga riyou dekimasu ka?] Can I get a cash advance with my credit card?

クレメンタイン [kurementain] *n* clementine

クレンジングローション [kurenjingurooshon] *n* cleansing lotion

クレンザー [kurenzaa] *n* cleanser

クレソン [kureson] *n* watercress

クレヨン [kureyon] *n* crayon

クリ [kuri] *n* chestnut

クリーム [kuriimu] *n* cream; クリーム色の [kuriimuiro no] *adj* cream

クリーニング [kuriiningu] *n* cleaning

栗色 [kuriiro] 栗色の [kuri iro no] *adj* maroon

繰り返し [kurikaeshi] *n* repeat; 繰り返し発生する [kurikaeshi hassei suru] *adj* recurring

繰り返す [kurikaesu] *v* repeat; 繰り返して [kurikaeshite] *adv* repeatedly

クリケット [kuriketto] *n* cricket *(game)*

クリスマス [kurisumasu] *n* Christmas, Xmas; クリスマスカード [kurisumasu kaado] *n* Christmas card; メリークリスマス! [merii kurisumasu!] Merry Christmas!

クリスマスイブ [kurisumasu ibu] *n* Christmas Eve

クリスマスツリー [kurisumasu tsurii] *n* Christmas tree

クロアチア [kuroachia] *n* Croatia; クロアチアの [kuroachia no] *adj* Croatian

クロアチア語 [kuroachiago] *n* Croatian *(language)*

クロアチア人 [kuroachiajin] *n* Croatian *(person)*

黒い [kuroi] *adj* black

クロッカス [kurokkasu] *n* crocus

クロム [kuromu] *n* chrome

クローブ [kuroobu] *n* clove

クローク [kurooku] *n* cloakroom

クローン [kuroon] *n* clone; クローンを作る [kuroon-o tsukuru] *v* clone

クロスグリ [kurosuguri] *n* black currant

クロスカントリー [kurosukantorii] *n* cross-country

クロスカントリースキー [kurosukantoriisukii] クロスカントリースキーに行くことは可能ですか? [kurosukantorii-sukii ni iku koto wa kanou desu ka?] Is it possible to go cross-country skiing?; **クロスカントリースキーの板を借りたいのですが** [kurosukantorii-sukii no ita o karitai no desu ga] I want to rent cross-country skis

クロスワードパズル [kurosuwaadopazuru] n crossword puzzle

クロウタドリ [kuroutadori] n blackbird

繰る [kuru] **繰り上げる** [kuriageru] v bring forward

来る [kuru] v come

くるぶし [kurubushi] n ankle

車 [kuruma] n car; **人を車に乗せてあげること** [hito-o kuruma ni nosete ageru koto] n give a ride to; **ビュッフェ車** [byuffesha] n dining car; **車の鍵** [kuruma no kagi] n car keys; **社用車** [shayousha] n company car; **食堂車** [shokudousha] n dining car; **除雪車** [josetsusha] n snowplow; **寝台車** [shindaisha] n sleeping car; **寝台車コンパートメントの寝台** [shindaisha konpaatomento no shindai] n sleeping berth; **あなたの車を動かしていただけますか?** [anata no kuruma o ugokashite itadakemasu ka?] Could you move your car, please?; **車はいつ直りますか?** [kuruma wa itsu naorimasu ka?] When will the car be ready?; **車を5日間借りたいのですが** [kuruma o itsuka-kan karitai no desu ga] I want to rent a car for five days; **車を洗いたいのですが** [kuruma o araitai no desu ga] I'd like to wash the car; **車を週末借りたいのですが** [kuruma o shuumatsu karitai no desu ga] I want to rent a car for the weekend; **車を借りたいのですが** [kuruma o karitai no desu ga] I want to rent a car; **私は車に鍵を置き忘れました** [watashi wa kuruma ni kagi o okiwasuremashita] I left the keys in the car; **私の車が故障しました** [watashi no kuruma ga koshou shimashita] My car has broken down; **私の車が壊されて侵入されました** [watashi no kuruma ga kowasarete shinnyuu saremashita] My car has been broken into; **私を車で連れて行ってもらえますか?**

[watashi o kuruma de tsurete itte moraemasu ka?] Could you take me by car?; **子供たちが車の中にいます** [kodomo-tachi ga kuruma no naka ni imasu] My children are in the car

クルマエビ [kurumaebi] n scampi, shrimp

車椅子 [kurumaisu] n wheelchair; **おたくには車椅子がありますか?** [otaku ni wa kuruma-isu ga arimasu ka?] Do you have wheelchairs?; **おたくのホテルは車椅子で利用できますか?** [otaku no hoteru wa kuruma-isu de riyou dekimasu ka?] Is your hotel accessible to wheelchairs?; **車椅子で・・・を訪れることができますか?** [kuruma-isu de... o otozureru koto ga dekimasu ka?] Can you visit... in a wheelchair?; **車椅子で利用できる入口はどこですか?** [kuruma-isu de riyou dekiru iriguchi wa doko desu ka?] Where's the wheelchair-accessible entrance?; **車椅子用のエレベーターはありますか?** [kuruma-isu-you no erebeetaa wa arimasu ka?] Do you have a wheelchair elevator?; **私は車椅子で入れる部屋が必要です** [watashi wa kuruma-isu de haireru heya ga hitsuyou desu] I need a room with wheelchair access; **私は車椅子を使っています** [watashi wa kuruma-isu o tsukatte imasu] I use a wheelchair; **・・・へ行くのに車椅子で利用しやすい交通手段はありますか?** [... e iku no ni kuruma-isu de riyou shiyasui koutsuu-shudan wa arimasu ka?] Is there wheelchair-friendly transportation available to...?; **電車は車椅子で乗れますか?** [densha wa kuruma-isu de noremasu ka?] Is the train wheelchair-accessible?

クルミ [kurumi] n walnut

苦しい [kurushii] **苦しい体験** [kurushii taiken] n ordeal

狂う [kuruu] **怒り狂った** [ikarikurutta] adj furious; **気の狂った** [kino kurutta] adj crazy (insane)

クルーカット [kuruukatto] n crew cut

草 [kusa] n grass (plant)

K

草刈り [kusakari] 草刈り機 [kusakariki] *n* mower

鎖 [kusari] *n* chain

腐る [kusaru] *v* rot; 腐った [kusatta] *adj* rotten

癖 [kuse] *n* habit

くせ毛 [kuseke] 私は生まれつきくせ毛です [watashi wa umaretsuki kusege desu] My hair is naturally curly

くしゃみ [kushami] くしゃみをする [kushami wo suru] *v* sneeze

櫛 [kushi] *n* comb; 櫛でとかす [kushi de tokasu] *v* comb

掘削 [kussaku] 掘削機 [kussakuki] *n* digger; 掘削装置 [kussaku souchi] *n* rig

掘削装置 [kussaku souchi] 石油掘削装置 [sekiyu kussakusouchi] *n* oil rig

クッション [kusshon] *n* cushion

くすぐる [kusuguru] *v* tickle; くすぐったがる [kusuguttagaru] *adj* ticklish

薬 [kusuri] *n* drug, medicine; 目薬 [megusuri] *n* eyedrops; 睡眠薬 [suimin-yaku] *n* sleeping pill; 局所麻酔薬 [kyokusho masuiyaku] *n* local anesthetic; 咳止め薬 [sekidomegusuri] *n* cough syrup; 私はすでにこの薬を飲んでいます [watashi wa sudeni kono kusuri o nonde imasu] I'm already taking this medicine

苦闘 [kutou] *n* struggle; 苦闘する [kutou suru] *v* struggle

句読 [kutou] *n* punctuation

靴 [kutsu] *n* shoe; スケート靴 [sukeeto kutsu] *n* skates; ローラースケート靴 [rooraa sukeeto kutsu] *n* rollerskates; 靴ひも [kutsuhimo] *n* shoelace; 靴屋 [kutsuya] *n* shoe store; 靴墨 [kutsuzumi] *n* shoe polish; この靴のヒールを付け直すことができますか? [kono kutsu no hiiru o tsukenaosu koto ga dekimasu ka?] Can you reheel these shoes?; この靴を修理できますか? [kono kutsu o shuuri dekimasu ka?] Can you repair these shoes?; 靴に穴があきました [kutsu ni ana ga akimashita] I have a hole

in my shoe; 靴は何階にありますか? [kutsu wa nan-kai ni arimasu ka?] Which floor are shoes on?

くつがえす [kutsugaesu] *v* overrule

くつろぐ [kutsurogu] *v* relax; くつろいだ [kutsuroida] *adj* laid-back, relaxed; くつろがせる [kutsurogaseru] *adj* relaxing; くつろぎ [kutsurogi] *n* relaxation

靴下 [kutsushita] 靴下留め [kutsushitadome] *n* garters

空調 [kuuchou] *n* air conditioning; 空調された [kuuchou sareta] *adj* air-conditioned

空洞 [kuudou] 空洞の [kuudou no] *adj* hollow

クウェート [kuueeto] *n* Kuwait

クウェート人 [kuueetojin] *n* Kuwaiti *(person)*

クウェートの [kuueeto no] *adj* Kuwaiti

空腹 [kuufuku] *n* hunger

空間 [kuukan] *n* space

空気 [kuuki] *n* air

空気圧 [kuukiatsu] *n* air pressure

空港 [kuukou] *n* airport; 空港バス [kuukou basu] *n* airport bus; 空港までのタクシーはいくらですか? [kuukou made no takushii wa ikura desu ka?] How much is the taxi to the airport?; 空港へはどう行けばいいのですか? [kuukou e wa dou ikeba ii no desu ka?] How do I get to the airport?; 空港へ行くバスはありますか? [kuukou e iku basu wa arimasu ka?] Is there a bus to the airport?

空虚 [kuukyo] 空虚な感じ [kuukyo na kanji] *n* void

空欄 [kuuran] *n* blank

加わる [kuwawaru] *v* join

くず紙 [kuzugami] *n* scrap paper

くずかご [kuzukago] *n* wastepaper basket

崩れる [kuzureru] *v* collapse

キャベツ [kyabetsu] *n* cabbage; 芽キャベツ [mekyabetsu] *n* Brussels sprouts

キャビン [kyabin] *n* cabin; 5番のキャビンはどこですか? [go-ban no kyabin wa doko desu ka?] Where is cabin number five?

キャビネット [kyabinetto] *n* cabinet

キャブレター [kyaburetaa] *n* carburetor

客 [kyaku] n guest, customer

脚本 [kyakuhon] 脚本家 [kyakuhonka] n playwright

客車 [kyakusha] n car (train)

客室 [kyakushitsu] n guest room; 客室乗務員 [kyakushitsu joumuin] n flight attendant; 客室係のメイド [kyakushitsugakari no meido] n maid; 客室番号 [kyakushitsu bangou] n room number

キャンバス [kyanbasu] n canvas

キャンデー [kyandee] n candy; 棒付きキャンデー [boutsuki kyandee] n lollipop

キャンディー [kyandii] アイスキャンディー [aisu kyandii] n Popsicle®

キャニスター [kyanisutaa] n canister

キャンパス [kyanpasu] n campus

キャンピングカー [kyanpingukaa] n camper; 4人用のキャンピングカーでいくらですか？ [yonin-you no kyanpingukaa de ikura desu ka?] How much is it for a camper with four people?

キャンプ [kyanpu] n camp; キャンプする [kyanpu suru] v camp; キャンプする人 [kyanpu suru nin] n camper; キャンプベッド [kyanpubeddo] n cot; キャンプ生活 [kyanpu seikatsu] n camping; キャンプ用ガス [kyanpu you gasu] n portable gas cylinder; キャンプ場 [kyanpujou] n campsite; トレーラーハウスキャンプ場 [toreeraa hausu kyanpu jou] n trailer park; ここで一晩キャンプできますか？ [koko de hitoban kyanpu dekimasu ka?] Can we camp here overnight?

キャンプ場 [kyanpujou] キャンプ場にレストランはありますか？ [kyanpu-jou ni resutoran wa arimasu ka?] Is there a restaurant on the campsite?

キャンセル [kyanseru] n cancellation; キャンセル待ちの切符 [kyanserumachi no kippu] n stand-by ticket; キャンセルされたフライトはありますか？ [kyanseru sareta furaito wa arimasu ka?] Are there any cancellations?

キャンティーン [kyantiin] n canteen

キャプション [kyapushon] n caption

キャラメル [kyarameru] n caramel

キャリア [kyaria] n career

キャロル [kyaroru] n carol

キャセロール [kyaserooru] n casserole

キャッシング [kyasshingu] n advanced cash payment

キャスト [kyasuto] n cast

脚立 [kyatatsu] n stepladder

巨大 [kyodai] 巨大な [kyodai na] adj enormous, giant, gigantic, huge, mammoth, tremendous

拒否 [kyohi] n refusal; 拒否する [kyohi suru] v refuse, reject, throw out; 拒否権 [kyohiken] n veto

巨人 [kyojin] n giant

居住 [kyojuu] 居住者 [kyojuusha] n resident

許可 [kyoka] n permission; 許可証 [kyokashou] n pass (permit), permit; 入場許可 [nyuujou kyoka] n admittance; 労働許可証 [roudou kyokashou] n work permit

極 [kyoku] 北極 [hokkyoku] n Arctic; 南極 [nankyoku] n Antarctic

曲 [kyoku] n tune

局 [kyoku] ラジオ局 [rajio kyoku] n radio station; 郵便局 [yuubinkyoku] n post office

局番 [kyokuban] n area code

局部 [kyokubu] 局部の [kyokubu no] adj local

極地 [kyokuchi] 極地の [kyokuchi no] adj polar

極度 [kyokudo] adv 極度に [kyokudo ni] adv extremely; 極度の [kyokudo no] adj extreme; 極度の緊張 [kyokudo no kinchou] n strain

局面 [kyokumen] n aspect; 重大局面 [juudai kyokumen] n crisis

局所 [kyokusho] 局所麻酔薬 [kyokusho masuiyaku] n local anesthetic

極東 [kyokutou] n Far East

去年 [kyonen] last year

距離 [kyori] n distance; 短距離走者 [tankyori sousha] n sprinter; 短距離競走 [tankyorikyousou] n sprint

虚勢 [kyosei] n bluff; 虚勢を張る [kyosei-o

K

haru] v bluff

拒食症 [kyoshokushou] 拒食症的な
[kyoshokushouteki na] adj anorexic

興 [kyou] 人の興をそぐ人 [hito no kyou-o sogu
hito] n spoilsport

今日 [kyou] adv today; 今日は何日ですか?
[kyou wa nan-nichi desu ka?] What is
today's date?; 今日は何曜日ですか? [kyou
wa nani-youbi desu ka?] What day is it
today?

凶悪 [kyouaku] 凶悪犯 [kyouakuhan] n thug

競売 [kyoubai] n auction

教母 [kyoubo] n godmother

凶暴 [kyoubou] 凶暴な [kyoubou na] adj
fierce

強調 [kyouchou] 強調する [kyouchou suru] v
emphasize, highlight, stress

強打 [kyouda] n bash, blow; 強打する
[kyouda suru] v bash

鏡台 [kyoudai] n dressing table

兄弟 [kyoudai] n brother; 継兄弟 [mama
kyoudai] n stepbrother

兄弟姉妹 [kyoudaishimai] n siblings

郷土料理 [kyoudoryouri] n local cuisine

共同 [kyoudou] 共同の [kyoudou no] adj
joint; 共同して働く [kyoudou shite hataraku]
v collaborate; 共同資金 [kyoudou shikin] n
pool (resources); 共同預金口座 [kyoudou
yokin kouza] n joint account; 共同寝室
[kyoudoushinshitsu] n dormitory (large
bedroom); 共同部屋がいいのですが
[kyoudou-beya ga ii no desu ga] I'd like a
dorm bed

共同所有権 [kyoudoushoyuuken] 休暇施設の
共同所有権 [kyuuka shisetsu no kyoudou
shoyuuken] n timeshare

恐怖 [kyoufu] n alarm, fright, horror, scare;
恐怖症 [kyoufushou] n phobia

教父 [kyoufu] n (名づけ親) godfather
(baptism)

恐怖症 [kyoufushou] 閉所恐怖症の [heisho
kyoufushou no] adj claustrophobic

強風 [kyoufuu] n gale

競技 [kyougi] 五種競技 [goshu kyougi] n
pentathlon; グライダー競技 [guraidaa
kyougi] n gliding; 競技を行う [kyougi-o
okonau] (in sport) v play; 陸上競技 [rikujou
kyougi] n track-and-field

共犯者 [kyouhansha] n accomplice

教育 [kyouiku] n education; 教育の [kyouiku
no] adj educational; 教育のある [kyouiku no
aru] adj educated; 継続教育 [keizoku
kyouiku] n higher education (lower-level);
生涯教育 [shougai kyouiku] n adult
education; 高等教育 [koutoukyouiku] n
higher education; 再教育コース [saikyouiku
koosu] n refresher course

教員 [kyouin] 臨時教員 [rinji kyouin] n
substitute teacher

狂人 [kyoujin] n maniac

教女 [kyoujo] n goddaughter

教授 [kyouju] n professor

教会 [kyoukai] n church; ローマカトリック教会
の [Rooma Katorikku kyoukai no] adj
Roman Catholic; 私たちがその教会を訪れる
ことはできますか? [watashi-tachi ga sono
kyoukai o otozureru koto wa dekimasu ka?]
Can we visit the church?

協会 [kyoukai] n association

境界 [kyoukai] n border, boundary

教会区 [kyoukaiku] n parish

教科書 [kyoukasho] n schoolbook, textbook

恐喝 [kyoukatsu] n blackmail; 恐喝する
[kyoukatsu suru] v blackmail

狂犬病 [kyoukenbyou] n rabies

狂気 [kyouki] n madness

教子 [kyouko] n (男女) godchild, (男子)
godson

峡谷 [kyoukoku] n ravine

教区 [kyouku] 教区牧師 [kyouku bokushi] n
rector

教訓 [kyoukun] n moral

供給 [kyoukyuu] n supply; 供給する
[kyoukyuu suru] v provide, supply; 供給者
[kyoukyuusha] n supplier

興味 [kyoumi] n interest (curiosity); 興味が

ある [kyoumi ga aru] *adj* interested; 興味を起こさせる [kyoumi-o okosaseru] *v* interest

興味深い [kyoumibukai] *adj* interesting

強烈 [kyouretsu] 強烈な [kyouretsu na] *adj* intense

協力 [kyouryoku] *n* cooperation

強力な [kyouryoku na] *adj* powerful

恐竜 [kyouryuu] *n* dinosaur

共産主義 [kyousanshugi] *n* communism; 共産主義の [kyousanshugi no] *adj* communist; 共産主義者 [kyousanshugisha] *n* communist

強制的な [kyouseiteki na] *adj* compulsory

教師 [kyoushi] *n* teacher; 学校教師 [gakkou kyoushi] *n* schoolteacher; 私は教師です [watashi wa kyoushi desu] I'm a teacher

教室 [kyoushitsu] *n* classroom; 教室助手 [kyoushitsu joshu] *n* teacher's aide

競争 [kyousou] *n* competition, contest, rivalry; 競争する [kyousou suru] *adj* compete, race, rival; 競争者 [kyousousha] *n* competitor, contestant; 競争的な [kyousouteki na] *adj* competitive; 競争相手 [kyousouaite] *n* rival

競走 [kyousou] 短距離競走 [tankyorikyousou] *n* sprint

強壮 [kyousou] 強壮剤 [kyousouzai] *n* tonic

競走馬 [kyousouba] *n* racehorse

教徒 [kyouto] *n* adherent; カトリック教徒 [katorikkukyouto] *n* Catholic (person); シーク教徒 [Shiiku kyouto] *n* Sikh (person); ヒンズー教徒 [Hinzuu kyouto] *n* Hindu (person); ローマカトリック教徒 [Rooma Katorikku kyouto] *n* Roman Catholic (person)

共和 [kyouwa] 共和政体 [kyouwa seitai] *n* republic

共和国 [kyouwakoku] 中央アフリカ共和国 [Chuuou Afurika Kyouwakoku] *n* Central African Republic; チェコ共和国 [Cheko kyouwakoku] *n* Czech Republic; チェチェン共和国 [Chechen kyouwakoku] *n* Chechnya; ドミニカ共和国 [Dominika kyouwakoku] *n* Dominican Republic

強要 [kyouyou] 強要する [kyouyou suru] *v* insist

共有 [kyouyuu] *n* communion

許容 [kyoyou] 無料手荷物許容量 [muryou tenimotsu kyoyouryou] *n* baggage allowance

九 [kyuu] *number* nine

急 [kyuu] 急にそれる [kyuu ni soreru] *v* swerve

キュー [kyuu] *n* cue

キューバ [kyuuba] *n* Cuba

キューバ人 [kyuubajin] *n* Cuban (person)

九番目 [kyuubanme] *n* ninth; 九番目の [kyuu banme no] *adj* ninth

キューバの [kyuuba no] *adj* Cuban

宮殿 [kyuuden] *n* palace; その宮殿は一般公開されていますか? [sono kyuuden wa ippan-koukai sarete imasu ka?] Is the palace open to the public?; その宮殿はいつ開きますか? [sono kyuuden wa itsu hirakimasu ka?] When is the palace open?

臼砲 [kyuuhou] *n* mortar (military)

給仕 [kyuuji] 給仕する人 [kyuuji suru hito] *n* server (person)

休日 [kyuujitsu] *n* vacation day; 休日の仕事 [kyuujitsu no shigoto] *n* vacation job

救助 [kyuujo] *n* rescue

救助員 [kyuujoin] 水泳場の救助員 [suieijou no kyuujoin] *n* lifeguard; 救助員を呼んで! [kyuujoin o yonde!] Get the lifeguard!

救助艇 [kyuujotei] 救助艇を呼んで! [kyuujotei o yonde!] Call out the lifeboat!

九十 [kyuujuu] *number* ninety

休暇 [kyuuka] *n* vacation; 父親の育児休暇 [chichioya no ikuji kyuuka] *n* paternity leave; 病気休暇 [byoukikyuuka] *n* sick leave; 病気休暇中の手当て [byouki kyuukachuu no teate] *n* sick pay; 出産休暇 [shussan kyuuka] *n* maternity leave; 夏の休暇 [natsu no kyuuka] *n* summer vacation; 学期中の中間休暇 [gakkuchuu no chuukan kyuuka] *n* midterm vacation; 楽しい休暇を! [tanoshii kyuuka o!] Have a good

K

vacation!; 私は休暇で来ています [watashi wa kyuuka de kite imasu] I'm here on vacation, I'm on vacation here

吸血鬼 [kyuuketsuki] *n* vampire

球根 [kyuukon] *n* bulb *(plant)*

救急 [kyuukyuu] 救急救命士 [kyuukyuu kyuumeishi] *n* paramedic; 救急車 [kyuukyuusha] *n* ambulance; 救急病棟 [kyuukyuubyoutou] *n* emergency room; 救急処置 [kyuukyuu shochi] *n* first aid; 救急処置キット [kyuukyuu shochi kitto] *n* first-aid kit

救急病棟 [kyuukyuubyoutou] 救急病棟はどこですか? [kyuukyuu-byoutou wa doko desu ka?] Where is the emergency room?; 私は救急病棟に行かなければなりません [watashi wa kyuukyuu-byoutou ni ikanakereba narimasen] I need to go to the emergency room

救急医 [kyuukyuui] 救急医を呼んでください [kyuukyuu-i o yonde kudasai] Please call the emergency doctor

救急車 [kyuukyuusha] 救急車を呼んでください [kyuukyuu-sha o yonde kudasai] Call an ambulance

救命 [kyuumei] 救命救急士 [kyuukyuu kyuumeishi] *n* paramedic; 救命の [kyuumei no] *adj* life-saving; 救命ベルト [kyuumei beruto] *n* life preserver; 救命ボート [kyuumeibooto] *n* lifeboat; 救命胴衣 [kyuumeidoui] *n* life jacket

急な [kyuu na] *adj* (傾斜) steep

救難 [kyuunan] 救難信号 [kyuunan shingou] *n* SOS

吸入器 [kyuunyuuki] *n* inhaler

キュウリ [kyuuri] *n* cucumber

給料 [kyuuryou] *n* pay, salary; 給料のよい [kyuuryou no yoi] *adj* well-paid

旧姓 [kyuusei] 女性の結婚前の旧姓 [josei no kekkonmae no kyuusei] *n* maiden name

休戦 [kyuusen] *n* truce

急使 [kyuushi] *n* courier

M

マーチャントバンク [maachantobanku] *n* merchant bank

マーガリン [maagarin] *n* margarine

マーケティング [maaketeingu] *n* marketing

マーケット [maaketto] *n* market; マーケットが立つのはいつですか? [maaketto ga tatsu no wa itsu desu ka?] When is the market?

マーマレード [maamareedo] *n* marmalade

まばたき [mabataki] まばたきする [mabataki suru] *v* blink

まぶた [mabuta] *n* eyelid

マッチ [macchi] マッチさせる [matchi saseru] *v* match

町 [machi] *n* town; 町の中心部 [machi no chuushinbu] *n* downtown area

街 [machi] *n* shopping district; スラム街 [suramugai] *n* slum; 街の中心部 [machi no chuushinbu] *n* downtown area; 繁華街へ [hankagai-e] *adv* downtown

待ち合わせ [machiawase] 待合室 [machiaishitsu] *n* waiting room

待ち合わせる [machiawaseru] *v* meet

待ち伏せ [machifuse] *n* ambush

間違える [machigaeru] *v* mistake; 間違えた [machigaeta] *adj* mistaken

間違い [machigai] *n* error, mistake, slip (*mistake*), slip-up; 間違い警報 [machigai keihou] *n* false alarm; 間違い電話 [machigai denwa] *n* wrong number

間違う [machigau] *v* slip up; 間違って [machigatte] *adv* mistakenly, wrong; 間違った [machigatta] *adj* wrong

まだ [mada] *adv* still, yet

マダガスカル [madagasukaru] *n* Madagascar

窓 [mado] *n* window; 窓下の腰掛け [mado shita no koshikake] *n* window seat; 窓の下枠 [mado no shitawaku] *n* windowsill; 窓ガラス [madogarasu] *n* windowpane; 窓が開きません [mado ga akimasen] The window won't open; 窓を閉めてもいいですか? [mado o shimete mo ii desu ka?] May I close the window?; 窓を開けてもいいですか? [mado o akete mo ii desu ka?] May I open the window?; 窓を開けられません [mado o akeraremasen] I can't open the window; 私は窓を壊してしまいました [watashi wa mado o kowashite shimaimashita] I've broken the window

窓側 [madogawa] 窓側の席をお願いします [mado-gawa no seki o o-negai shimasu] I'd like a window seat

まどろむ [madoromu] *v* doze off

前 [mae] *n* front; ···の前に [... no mae ni] *prep* before; ···する前に [... suru mae ni] *conj* before; 前に [mae ni] *adv* ahead; 前に [mae ni] *adv* earlier; 前の [mae no] *adj* preceding; 前の [mae no] *adj* front

前髪 [maegami] 切下げ前髪 [kirisagemaegami] *n* bangs (*hair*)

前かがみ [maekagami] 前かがみになる [maekagami ni naru] *v* lean forward

マフラー [mafuraa] *n* scarf

まがい [magai] まがいの [magai no] *adj* mock

曲がる [magaru] *v* turn; 曲がった [magatta] *adj* bent (*not straight*); 曲がり [magari] *n* bend

曲げる [mageru] *v* bend; ひざを曲げる [hiza-o mageru] *v* kneel

曲げやすい [mageyasui] *adj* flexible

孫 [mago] *n* grandchild, grandchildren

孫息子 [magomusuko] *n* grandson

孫娘 [magomusume] *n* granddaughter

マグ [magu] *n* mug

マグロ [maguro] *n* tuna

麻痺 [mahi] 麻痺した [mahi shita] *adj* paralyzed

真昼 [mahiru] *n* noon

マホガニー [mahoganii] *n* mahogany

魔法 [mahou] *n* magic; 魔法使い [mahoutsu-kai] *n* sorcerer; 魔法の [mahou no] *adj* magic

魔法瓶 [mahoubin] *n* thermos

毎 [mai] 毎土曜日に [mai-doyoubi ni] on Saturdays

毎時 [maiji] 毎時…キロ [maiji... kiro] *adv* km/h

マイク [maiku] *n* mike

マイクロバス [maikurobasu] *n* minibus

マイクロチップ [maikurochippu] *n* microchip, silicon chip

マイクロホン [maikurohon] *n* microphone; マイクロホンはついていますか? [maikurohon wa tsuite imasu ka?] Does it have a microphone?

毎日 [mainichi] *adv* daily; 毎日の [mainichi no] *adj* daily

マイル [mairu] *n* mile; 毎時…マイル [maiji... mairu] *adv* mph; 走行マイル計 [soukou mairu kei] *n* odometer; 総マイル数 [sou mairu suu] *n* mileage

マイルドな [mairudo na] *adj* mild

毎週 [maishuu] 毎週土曜日に [maishuu doyoubi ni] every Saturday

埋葬 [maisou] 埋葬する [maisou suru] *v* bury

毎月 [maitsuki] 毎月の [maitsuki no] *adj* monthly

マジパン [majipan] *n* marzipan

魔女 [majo] *n* witch

魔術 [majutsu] *n* magic; 魔術的な [majutsuteki na] *adj* magical; 魔術師 [majutsushi] *n* magician

マカロニ [makaroni] *n* macaroni

負かす [makasu] *v* defeat; 打ち負かす [uchimakasu] *v* knock out

負け [make] *n* defeat

負ける [makeru] *vi* lose

巻き毛 [makige] *n* curl; 巻き毛の [makige no] *adj* curly

巻尺 [makijaku] *n* tape measure

巻き戻す [makimodosu] *v* rewind

末期 [makki] 末期の [makki no] (終わりの時期) *adj* terminal; 末期的に [makkiteki ni] *adv* terminally

巻く [maku] *v* wind *(coil around)*

枕 [makura] *n* pillow; 枕カバー [makurakabaa] *n* pillowcase; 追加の枕を持ってきてください [tsuika no makura o motte kite kudasai] Please bring me an extra pillow

まま [mama] …のままである [...no mama de aru] *v* remain

ママ [mama] *n* mom, mommy *(mother)*

豆 [mame] *n* bean; コーヒー豆 [koohiimame] *n* coffee bean; 豆もやし [mame moyashi] *n* bean sprouts

豆類 [mamerui] *n* legumes

まもなく [mamonaku] *adv* shortly, soon

守る [mamoru] 子守り [komori] *n* babysitting

学ぶ [manabu] *v* learn

万引き [manbiki] *n* shoplifting

マンダリンオレンジ [mandarin orenji] *n* mandarin orange

マネーベルト [maneeberuto] *n* money belt

マネージャー [maneejaa] マネージャーと話させてください [maneejaa to hanasasete kudasai] I'd like to speak to the manager, please

マネキン [manekin] *n* dummy, mannequin

招く [maneku] 誤解を招きやすい [gokai-o manekiyasui] *adj* misleading

漫画 [manga] *n* cartoon; コマ割り漫画 [komawari manga] *n* comic strip; 漫画本 [mangabon] *n* comic book

満月 [mangetsu] *n* full moon

マンゴー [mangou] *n* mango

マニキュア [manikyua] n manicure; マニキュアを塗る [manikyua-o nuru] v do one's nails; マニキュア液 [manikyua eki] n nail polish

満場 [manjou] 満場一致の [manjouitchi no] adj unanimous

マンモス [manmosu] n mammoth

万年筆 [mannenhitsu] n fountain pen

満腹 [manpuku] adj satiated

慢性 [mansei] 慢性の [mansei no] adj chronic

満タン [mantan] 満タンにしてください [mantan ni shite kudasai] Fill it up, please

マントルピース [mantorupiisu] n mantel

マニュアル [manyuaru] n manual

マニュアル車 [manyuarusha] n manual (transmission) car

満足 [manzoku] n satisfaction; 満足のいく [manzoku no iku] adj satisfactory; 満足した [manzoku shita] adj satisfied

マオリ [maori] マオリの [Maori no] adj Maori; マオリ族 [Maori zoku] n Maori (person); マオリ語 [Maori go] n Maori (language)

マップ [mappu] n map; この地域のサイクルマップはありますか? [kono chiiki no saikuru-mappu wa arimasu ka?] Is there a bicycling map of this area?; この地域の道路マップはありますか? [kono chiiki no douro-mappu wa arimasu ka?] Do you have a road map of this area?; その街のストリートマップが欲しいのですが [sono machi no sutoriito-mappu ga hoshii no desu ga] I want a street map of the city; ゲレンデのマップはありますか? [gerende no mappu wa arimasu ka?] Do you have a map of the ski runs?; マップをください [mappu o kudasai] May I have a map?; 私は・・・の道路マップが必要です [watashi wa... no douro-mappu ga hitsuyou desu] I need a road map of...; 地下鉄のマップはありますか? [chikatetsu no mappu wa arimasu ka?] Do you have a map of the subway?; 地下鉄のマップをいただけますか? [chikatetsu no mappu o

itadakemasu ka?] Could I have a map of the subway, please?

マラリア [mararia] n malaria

マラソン [marason] n marathon

マラウィ [maraui] n Malawi

マレーシア [mareeshia] n Malaysia; マレーシア人 [Mareeshia jin] n Malaysian (person); マレーシアの [Mareeshia no] adj Malaysian

マリファナ [marifana] n marijuana

マリーゴールド [mariigourudo] n marigold

マリーナ [mariina] n marina

マリネ [marine] n marinade; マリネにする [marine ni suru] v marinate

マルチメディアメッセージングサービス [maruchimedia messeejingu saabisu] n multimedia messaging service

マルハナバチ [maruhanabachi] n bumblebee

丸い [marui] adj round

マルクス [marukusu] マルクス主義 [marukusushugi] n Marxism

丸太 [maruta] n log

マルタ [maruta] n Malta; マルタ人 [marutajin] n Maltese (person); マルタ語 [Maruta go] n Maltese (language); マルタの [maruta no] adj Maltese

マシンガン [mashingan] n machine gun

マッサージ [massaaji] n massage

マッシュポテト [masshu poteto] n mashed potatoes

マッシュルーム [masshuruumu] n mushroom

まっすぐ [massugu] adv straight ahead; まっすぐ上に [massugu ueni] adv straight up; まっすぐな [massugu na] adj straight; まっすぐに [massugu ni] adv straight ahead; まっすぐ行ってください [massugu itte kudasai] Go straight ahead

マス [masu] n (魚) trout

増す [masu] v increase, multiply

麻酔 [masui] 麻酔薬 [masuiyaku] n anesthetic; 局所麻酔薬 [kyokusho masuiyaku] n local anesthetic; 全身麻酔 [zenshin masui] n general anesthetic

M

マスカラ [masukara] *n* mascara

マスク [masuku] *n* mask; マスクをした [masuku-o shita] *adj* masked

ますます [masumasu] *adv* increasingly

マスメディア [masumedia] *n* media

マスタード [masutaado] *n* mustard

マスト [masuto] *n* mast

また [mata] *adv* (おなじく) too

また近いうちに [mata chikai uchi ni] See you soon

摩天楼 [matenrou] *n* skyscraper

マトン [maton] *n* mutton

マツ [matsu] *n* pine

待つ [matsu] *v* wait, wait for; そのまま待つ [sono mama matsu] *v* hang on; 寝ないで待つ [nenaide matsu] *v* wait up; ここで数分待ってもらえますか? [koko de suu-fun matte moraemasu ka?] Could you wait here for a few minutes?; 私が待っているあいだにできますか? [watashi ga matte iru aida ni dekimasu ka?] Can you do it while I wait?; 私たちはとても長いあいだ待っています [watashi-tachi wa totemo nagai aida matte imasu] We've been waiting for a very long time; 私たちは応対してもらうのをまだ待っています [watashi-tachi wa outai shite morau no wo mada matte imasu] We're still waiting to be served; 私を待っていてください [watashi o matte ite kudasai] Please wait for me

松葉杖 [matsubadue] *n* crutch

まつげ [matsuge] *n* eyelash

祭 [matsuri] 過越しの祭 [Sugikoshi no matsuri] *n* Passover

全く [mattaku] *adv* absolutely, altogether, completely, entirely, indeed; 全くの [mattaku no] *adj* complete; 全くの [mattaku no] *adj* sheer

マット [matto] *n* mat

マットレス [mattoresu] *n* mattress

マウンテンバイク [mauntenbaiku] *n* mountain bike

マウスパッド [mausupaddo] *n* mouse pad

マウスウォッシュ [mausu uosshu] *n* mouthwash

周り [mawari] 周りに [mawari ni] *adv* around

回り道 [mawarimichi] *n* detour

麻薬 [mayaku] *n* narcotic; 麻薬ディーラー [mayaku diiraa] *n* drug dealer; 麻薬常用者 [mayaku jouyousha] *n* drug addict

迷い出る [mayoideru] 迷い出た家畜 [mayoideta kachiku] *n* stray

真夜中 [mayonaka] *n* midnight

マヨネーズ [mayoneezu] *n* mayonnaise

マヨラナ [mayorana] *n* marjoram

迷う [mayou] *v* become confused

眉 [mayu] *n* eyebrow

まゆ [mayu] まゆをひそめる [mayu wo hisomeru] *v* frown

混ぜる [mazeru] *v* mix

まず [mazu] first of all; まず第一に [mazu daiichi ni] *adv* firstly

貧しい [mazushii] *adj* poor

目 [me] *n* eye; 目に見えない [me ni mienai] *adj* invisible; 目が覚める [me ga sameru] *v* awake, wake up; 目薬 [megusuri] *n* eyedrops; 私は目に何か入っています [watashi wa me ni nani ka haitte imasu] I have something in my eye; 私は目が痛みます [watashi wa me ga itamimasu] My eyes are sore

芽 [me] 芽キャベツ [mekyabetsu] *n* Brussels sprouts

メダル [medaru] *n* medal; 大メダル [dai medaru] *n* medallion

目立つ [medatsu] *adj* noticeable ▷ *v* striking

メーキャップ [meekyappu] *n* makeup

メーリングリスト [meeringurisuto] *n* mailing list

メール [meeru] *n* mail; ジャンクメール [janku meeru] *n* junk mail; 電子メール [denshi meeru] *n* e-mail; 電子メールを送る [denshi meeru-o okuru] *v* e-mail

メールアドレス [meeruadoresu] 電子メールアドレス [denshi meeru adoresu] *n* e-mail address

メーター [meetaa] n meter; パーキングメーター [paakingumeetaa] n parking meter; それではメーター料金より高いです [sore de wa meetaa-ryoukin yori takai desu] It's more than on the meter; メーターはありますか? [meetaa wa arimasu ka?] Do you have a meter?; メーターが壊れています [meetaa ga kowarete imasu] The meter is broken; メーターを使ってください [meetaa o tsukatte kudasai] Please use the meter; 電気のメーターはどこですか? [denki no meetaa wa doko desu ka?] Where's the electricity meter?

メートル [meetoru] n meter; メートル法の [meetoruhou no] adj metric

眼鏡 [megane] n glasses, specs, spectacles; 眼鏡士 [meganeshi] n optician

メガネ [megane] 遠近両用メガネ [enkin ryouyou megane] n bifocals; 私のメガネを修理できますか? [watashi no megane o shuuri dekimasu ka?] Can you repair my glasses?

雌羊 [mehitsuji] n ewe

銘 [mei] n inscription

姪 [mei] n niece

名簿 [meibo] 順番待ち名簿 [junbanmachi meibo] n waiting list

メイド [meido] 客室係のメイド [kyakushitsu-gakari no meido] n maid

明白 [meihaku] 明白な [meihaku na] adj clear

明確 [meikaku] 明確な [meikaku na] adj definite; 明確に [meikaku ni] adv definitely

明記 [meiki] 明記する [meiki suru] v specify

メインコース [meinkoosu] n main course

命令 [meirei] n command, order; 命令する [meirei suru] n order

迷路 [meiro] n maze

明細 [meisai] 請求書の明細をもらえますか? [seikyuusho no meisai o moraemasu ka?] May I have an itemized bill?

明細書 [meisaisho] 銀行の明細書 [ginkou no meisaisho] n bank statement

名声 [meisei] n fame, prestige; 名声のある [meisei no aru] adj prestigious

名詞 [meishi] n noun

名刺 [meishi] n business card; お名刺をお持ちですか? [o-meishi o o-mochi desu ka?] Do you have a business card?

迷信 [meishin] 迷信的な [meishinteki na] adj superstitious

名所 [meisho] n famous place

瞑想 [meisou] n meditation

迷惑 [meiwaku] n trouble

名誉 [meiyo] 不名誉な [fumeiyo na] adj disgraceful

メカジキ [mekajiki] n swordfish

目隠し [mekakushi] 目隠しする [mekakushi suru] v blindfold; 目隠し布 [mekakushi nuno] n blindfold

メキシコ [mekishiko] n Mexico; メキシコ人 [mekishikojin] n Mexican (person); メキシコの [mekishiko no] adj Mexican; メキシコ湾岸諸州 [Mekishiko wangan shoshuu] n Gulf States

メッカ [mekka] n Mecca

滅菌 [mekkin] 滅菌した [mekkin shita] adj sterile; 滅菌する [mekkin suru] v sterilize

めまい [memai] n vertigo; めまいがする [memai ga suru] adj dizzy; 私はめまいがします [watashi wa memai ga shimasu] I suffer from vertigo

メモ [memo] n memo, note (message); メモ用紙 [memoyoushi] n notepaper; メモ帳 [memochou] n notepad

メモパッド [memopaddo] n notepad

メモリカード [memorikaado] n memory card; このデジタルカメラ用のメモリカードをください [kono dejitaru-kamera-you no memori-kaado o kudasai] A memory card for this digital camera, please

綿 [men] n cotton; 脱脂綿 [dasshimen] n cotton; 綿菓子 [watagashi] n cotton candy

面 [men] n surface; 海水面 [kaisui men] n sea level

メンバー [menbaa] n (会員) member, (会員資格) membership

M

メンバーカード [menbaakaado] *n*
membership card

綿棒 [menbou] *n* cotton swab

麺棒 [menbou] *n* rolling pin

めんどり [mendori] *n* hen

面倒 [mendou] *n* annoyance

免疫系 [men'ekikei] *n* immune system

免状 [menjou] *n* diploma

面会 [menkai] *n* interview; 面会時間
[menkaijikan] *n* visiting hours

免許 [menkyo] *n* license; 運転免許証
[untenmenkyoshou] *n* driver's license; 酒類
販売免許 [sakerui hanbai menkyo] *n* liquor
license

免許証 [menkyoshou] *n* license; 私の運転免
許証です [watashi no unten-menkyoshou
desu] Here is my driver's license; 私の運
転免許証番号は…です [watashi no
unten-menkyoshou bangou wa... desu] My
driver's license number is...

綿密 [menmitsu] 綿密な調査 [menmitsu na
chousa] *n* scan

目の見えない [me no mienai] *adj* blind

免責補償制度 [mensekihoshouseido] 免責補
償制度に加入したいのですが [menseki-
hoshou-seido ni kanyuu shitai no desu ga]
I'd like to arrange a collision damage
waiver

面接 [mensetsu] *n* interview; 面接する
[mensetsu suru] *v* interview; 面接者
[mensetsusha] *n* interviewer

メニュー [menyuu] *n* menu; セットメニューを
ください [setto-menyuu o kudasai] We'll
take the set menu; メニューをください
[menyuu o kudasai] The menu, please; デザ
ートのメニューをください [dezaato no
menyuu o kudasai] The dessert menu,
please; 子供用のメニューはありますか?
[kodomo-you no menyuu wa arimasu ka?]
Do you have a children's menu?

免税 [menzei] 免税の [menzei no] *adj*
duty-free; 免税品 [menzeihin] *n* duty-free
goods

免税店 [menzeiten] 免税店はどこですか?
[menzei-ten wa doko desu ka?] Where is
the duty-free shopping?

メレンゲ [merenge] *n* meringue

メロディ [merodi] 着信メロディ [chakushin
merodi] *n* ringtone

メロディー [merodii] *n* melody

メロン [meron] *n* melon

召し上がる [meshiagaru] *v* eat, drink

目下 [meshita] *adv* (今) currently; 目下の者
[meshita no mono] *n* inferior

メソジスト派 [mesojisutoha] メソジスト派の
[Mesojisuto ha no] *adj* Methodist

メッセンジャー [messenjaa] メッセンジャープ
ログラムを使えますか? [messenjaa-progura-
mu o tsukaemasu ka?] Can I use
messenger programs?

雌 [mesu] 雌ライオン [mesuraion] *n* lioness

雌犬 [mesuinu] *n* bitch *(female dog)*

目つき [metsuki] *n* look

めったに [mettani] めったに…しない
[mettani... shinai] *adv* rarely, seldom

雌馬 [meuma] *n* mare

雌牛 [meushi] *n* cow

目覚まし [mezamashi] 目覚まし時計
[mezamashi tokei] *n* alarm clock

珍しい [mezurashii] *adj* rare *(uncommon)*

身 [mi] *n* one's body; …から身を乗り出す [...
kara mi-o noridasu] *v* lean out

見当たる [miataru] 息子の姿が見当たりません
[musuko no sugata ga miatarimasen] My
son is lost; 娘の姿が見当たりません
[musume no sugata ga miatarimasen] My
daughter is lost

未払 [mibarai] 未払金 [miharaikin] *n* arrears

未亡人 [miboujin] *n* widow

身分 [mibun] *n* status; 身分証明 [mibun
shoumei] *n* identification; 身分証明書
[mibunshomeisho] *n* ID card

身振り [miburi] *n* gesture

身震い [miburui] 身震いする [miburui suru] *v*
shudder

路 [michi] ドライバーが路上で激怒すること

[doraibaa ga rojou de gekido suru koto] n
road rage; 滑走路 [kassourou] n runway

道 [michi] n road; 小道 [komichi] n lane; この
道はどこにつながっていますか? [kono michi
wa doko ni tsunagatte imasu ka?] Where
does this path lead?; 混雑を避けられる道は
ありますか? [konzatsu o sakerareru michi
wa arimasu ka?] Is there a route that
avoids the traffic?; ···へ行くにはどの道を
走ればいいのですか? [... e iku ni wa dono
michi o hashireba ii no desu ka?] Which
road do I take for...?; ···へ行く自転車道は
どこですか? [... e iku jitensha-dou wa doko
desu ka?] Where's the bicycle path to...?;
道に沿って進んでください [michi ni sotte
susunde kudasai] Keep to the path; 彼女は
道を譲りませんでした [kanojo wa michi o
yuzurimasen deshita] She didn't yield

未知 [michi] 未知の [michi no] adj unknown

導く [michibiku] v lead

満ちる [michiru] 満ちた [michita] adj full

満ち潮 [michishio] n high-tide

見出し [midashi] n headline

三重 [mie] 三重の [mie no] adj triple

見えなくなる [mienaku naru] 見えなくなること
[mienaku naru koto] n disappearance

見える [mieru] v be visible; 見えなくなる
[mienaku naru] v disappear; 目に見えない
[me ni mienai] adj invisible; 目に見える [me
ni mieru] adj visible; 透けて見える [sukete
mieru] adj see-through

ミガキ [migaki] v polish; 練り歯ミガキ [neri
hamigaki] n toothpaste

右 [migi] 右の [migi no] adj right (not left); 右
ハンドル [migi handoru] n right-hand drive;
右に曲がってください [migi ni magatte
kudasai] Turn right

右側 [migigawa] 右側の [migigawa no] adj
right-hand

右利き [migikiki] 右利きの [migikiki no] adj
right-handed

右回り [migimawari] 右回りに [migimawari ni]
adv clockwise

見事 [migoto] 見事な [migoto na] adj fine; 見
事に [migoto ni] adv fine

見張り [mihari] n guard

見張る [miharu] v guard, spy

見本 [mihon] n sample

ミイラ [miira] n mummy (body)

ミーティング [miitingu] n meeting; ···さんと
のミーティングを設定したいのですが [... san
to no miitingu o settei shitai no desu ga] I'd
like to arrange a meeting with...

ミートボール [miitobooru] n meatball

短い [mijikai] adj brief, short

惨めな [mijime na] adj miserable

惨めさ [mijimesa] n misery

未熟 [mijuku] adj unripe; 未熟な [mijuku na]
(経験不足) adj green (inexperienced)

みかげ石 [mikageishi] n granite

未開 [mikai] 未開の [mikai no] adj uncivilized

幹 [miki] n trunk

ミキサー [mikisaa] n blender, mixer

密告 [mikkoku] 密告者 [mikkokusha]
(informer) n police informant (informer)

ミックスサラダ [mikkususarada] n mixed
salad

見込み [mikomi] n chance, probability

未婚 [mikon] 未婚の [mikon no] adj
unmarried

見回す [mimawasu] あたりを見回す [atari-o
miwatasu] v look around

耳 [mimi] n ear; 耳の聞こえない [mimi no
kikoenai] adj deaf; 耳の痛み [mimi no itami]
n earache; 耳を聾するような [mimi-o rousuru
you na] adj deafening

耳栓 [mimisen] n earplugs

身元 [mimoto] n identity; 身元不詳の
[mimoto fushou no] adj unidentified

南 [minami] n south; 南に [minami ni] adv
south; 南の [minami no] adj south,
southern

南アフリカ [minami afurika] n South Africa;
南アフリカ人 [minami afurikajin] n South
African (person); 南アフリカの [minami
afurika no] adj South African

M

南アメリカ [minamiamerika] *n* South America; 南アメリカ人 [Minami Amerika jin] *n* South American *(person)*; 南アメリカの [Minami Amerika no] *adj* South American

南行き [minamiyuki] 南行きの [minami yuki no] *adj* southbound

見習う [minarau] 見習い [minarai] *n* apprentice

身なり [minari] *n* costume

みなす [minasu] *v* consider, regard

港 [minato] *n* harbor, port *(ships)*

民営 [min'ei] 民営化する [min'eika suru] *v* privatize

ミネラルウォーター [mineraru uootaa] *n* mineral water; ミネラルウォーターのボトル1本 [mineraruuootaa no botoru 1 hon] a bottle of mineral water; 炭酸なしミネラルウォーターのボトル1本 [tansan-nashi mineraru-wootaa no botoru ippon] a bottle of still mineral water; 炭酸入りミネラルウォーターのボトル1本 [tansan-iri mineraru-wootaa no botoru ippon] a bottle of sparkling mineral water

ミニバー [minibaa] *n* minibar

ミニチュア [minichua] *n* miniature; ミニチュアの [minichua no] *adj* miniature

醜い [minikui] *adj* ugly

ミニスカート [minisukaato] *n* miniskirt

身に着ける [mi ni tsukeru] 身に着けている [mi ni tsukete iru] *v* wear

民間 [minkan] 民間伝承 [minkandenshou] *n* folklore; 民間の [minkan no] *adj* civilian

民間人 [minkanjin] *n* civilian

ミンク [minku] *n* mink

見逃す [minogasu] *v* miss

身代金 [minoshirokin] *n* ransom

民主 [minshu] *n* the people; 民主主義 [minshushugi] *n* democracy; 民主主義の [minshu shugi no] *adj* democratic

ミント [minto] *n* mint *(herb/sweet)*

民族 [minzoku] 民族の [minzoku no] *adj* ethnic

見落とし [miotoshi] *n* oversight *(mistake)*

見落とす [miotosu] *v* overlook

未来 [mirai] *n* future; 未来の [mirai no] *adj* future

ミリメートル [mirimeetoru] *n* millimeter

みる [miru] 試してみる [tameshite miru] *v* try out

見る [miru] *v* look, see; ちらっと見る [chiratto miru] *v* glance; ちらっと見ること [chiratto miru koto] *n* glance; じっと見る [jitto miru] *v* stare; 見る人 [miru hito] *n* viewer; …をよく見る [...-o yoku miru] *v* look at; 夢を見る [yume wo miru] *v* dream; ちょっと見ているだけです [chotto mite iru dake desu] I'm just looking

ミルク [miruku] *n* milk; ベビーミルク [bebii miruku] *n* formula; ミルクは別にください [miruku wa betsu ni kudasai] with the milk on the side

ミルクチョコレート [mirukuchokoreeto] *n* milk chocolate

ミルク入り [miruku iri] ミルク入りコーヒーをください [miruku-iri koohii o kudasai] Coffee with milk, please

ミルクシェイク [mirukusheiku] *n* milkshake

魅力 [miryoku] *n* attraction, charm; 魅力的な [miryokuteki na] *adj* attractive, glamorous

魅力的な [miryokuteki na] *adj* attractive, appealing

ミサ [misa] *n* mass *(church)*; ミサはいつですか? [misa wa itsu desu ka?] When is mass?

ミサイル [misairu] *n* missile

店 [mise] *n* store; 文房具店 [bunbouguten] *n* office supply store; 店主 [tenshu] *n* store owner; 店員 [ten-in] *n* salesperson; お店は何時に閉まりますか? [o-mise wa nan-ji ni shimarimasu ka?] What time do the stores close?

見せびらかす [misebirakasu] *v* show off; 見せびらかし [misebirakashi] *n* show-off

未成年 [miseinen] 未成年の [miseinen no] *adj* underage; 未成年者 [miseinensha] *n* minor

見せる [miseru] *v* show; 見せていただけます

か? [misete itadakemasu ka?] Could you show me, please?

ミシン [mishin] *n* sewing machine

ミソサザイ [misosazai] *n* wren

密集 [misshuu] *n* congestion, density; 密集した [misshuu shita] *adj* dense

みすぼらしい [misuborashii] *adj* shabby

見捨てる [misuteru] *v* abandon

認める [mitomeru] *v* admit *(confess)*

ミトン [miton] *n* mitten

見通し [mitoushi] *n* outlook, prospect

三つ子 [mitsugo] *n* triplets

見つかる [mitsukaru] *v* be found

見つけ出す [mitsukedasu] 跡をたどって見つけ出す [ato-o tadotte mitsukedasu] *v* track down

見つける [mitsukeru] *v* find, spot

見つめる [mitsumeru] *v* gaze; じっと見つめる [jitto mitsumeru] *v* stare

見積もり [mitsumori] *n* estimate

見積もる [mitsumoru] *v* estimate

密漁 [mitsuryou] 密漁した [mitsuryou shita] *adj* poached *(caught illegally)*

密輸 [mitsuyu] *n* smuggling; 密輸する [mitsuyu suru] *v* smuggle; 密輸業者 [mitsuyu gyousha] *n* smuggler

魅惑 [miwaku] 魅惑的な [miwakuteki na] *adj* fascinating

溝 [mizo] *n* ditch; 深くて細長い溝 [fukakute hosonagai mizo] *n* trench

みぞれ [mizore] *n* sleet; みぞれが降る [mizore ga furu] *v* sleet

水 [mizu] *n* water; 水上スキー [suijousukii] *n* water-skiing; 水をやる [mizu-o yaru] *v* water; 飲料水 [inryousui] *n* drinking water; 水をもっと持ってきてください [mizu o motto motte kite kudasai] Please bring more water; 水差し一杯の水 [mizusashi ippai no mizu] a jug of water

水疱瘡 [mizubousou] *n* chickenpox

水ぶくれ [mizubukure] *n* blister

水瓶座 [mizugameza] *n* Aquarius

水着 [mizugi] *n* bathing suit, swimsuit

水切り [mizukiri] *n* colander

水切り板 [mizukiriban] *n* drainboard

水たまり [mizutamari] *n* puddle

湖 [mizu-umi] *n* lake

・・・も [...mo] *adv* also

モビールハウス [mobiiruhausu] *n* mobile home

持ち上げる [mochiageru] *v* lift, pick up

持ち運び [mochihakobi] 持ち運びできる [mochihakobi dekiru] *adj* portable

持ち運ぶ [mochihakobu] 持ち運び用ベッド [mochihakobi you beddo] *n* portable baby bed

持ちこたえる [mochikotaeru] *v* hold up

持ち続ける [mochitsudukeru] *v* keep

モデム [modemu] *n* modem

戻る [modoru] *v* get back, go back ▷ *vi* return; 戻ってくる [modotte kuru] *v* come back

戻す [modosu] *v* bring back ▷ *vt* return

モグラ [mogura] *n* mole *(mammal)*

模範 [mohan] *n* example; 模範的な [mohanteki na] *adj* model

模倣 [mohou] 模倣する [mohou suru] *v* imitate

モイスチャライザー [moisucharaizaa] *n* moisturizer

文字 [moji] *n* letter *(a, b, c)*; 文字どおりに [mojidouri ni] *adv* literally

モジュール [mojuuru] *n* module

模型 [mokei] *n* model; 模型を作る [mokei-o tsukuru] *v* model

木工 [mokkou] 木工部 [mokkoubu] *n* woodwork

木馬 [mokuba] 揺り木馬 [yurimokuba] *n* rocking horse

目撃 [mokugeki] 目撃者 [mokugekisha] *n* witness

目撃者 [mokugekisha] *n* witness; 私の目撃者になってもらえますか? [watashi no mokugekisha ni natte moraemasu ka?] Can you be a witness for me?

目次 [mokuji] *n* contents

目録 [mokuroku] *n* inventory; 目録に載ってい
ない [mokuroku ni notte inai] *adj* unlisted

木製 [mokusei] 木製の [mokusei no] *adj*
wooden

木炭 [mokutan] *n* charcoal

目的 [mokuteki] *n* aim, objective, purpose

目的地 [mokutekichi] *n* destination

木曜日 [mokuyoubi] *n* Thursday; 木曜日に
[mokuyoubi ni] on Thursday

···もまた···でない [...momata...denai]
neither

もめごと [momegoto] もめごとを起こす人
[momegoto-o okosu hito] *n* troublemaker

モミ [momi] *n* fir (tree)

もみ消す [momikesu] 火をもみ消す [hi-o
momikesu] *v* stub out

腿 [momo] *n* thigh

モモ [momo] *n* peach

門 [mon] *n* gate

モナコ [monako] *n* Monaco

問題 [mondai] *n* problem; 時事問題 [jiji
mondai] *n* current affairs; あなたのファック
スに問題があります [anata no fakkusu ni
mondai ga arimasu] There's a problem
with your fax; 問題があったときに誰に連絡
すればいいのですか? [mondai ga atta toki ni
dare ni renraku sureba ii no desu ka?] Who
do we contact if there are problems?

門限 [mongen] *n* curfew; 門限はありますか?
[mongen wa arimasu ka?] Is there a
curfew?

モンゴル [mongoru] *n* Mongolia; モンゴル人
[Mongoru jin] *n* Mongolian *(person)*; モンゴ
ルの [mongoru no] *adj* Mongolian; モンゴル
語 [Mongoru go] *n* Mongolian *(language)*

モニター [monitaa] *n* monitor

物 [mono] *n* object, thing; 洗濯物
[sentakumono] *n* laundry, washing

者 [mono] 目下の者 [meshita no mono] *n*
inferior

もの [mono] *n* (材料) stuff; ···のものである
[... no mono de aru] *v* belong to

物語 [monogatari] *n* story, tale

物乞い [monogoi] 物乞いをする [monogoi-o
suru] *v* beg

物干し [monohoshi] 物干し綱 [monohoshi
tsuna] *n* clothesline

物まね [monomane] 物まねをする [mono-
mane-o suru] *v* mimic

ものすごい [monosugoi] *adj* terrific

モンスーン [monsuun] *n* monsoon

モーニング [mooningu] モーニングコール
[mooningukooru] *n* wake-up call

モーニングコール [mooningukooru] *n*
morning/wakeup call

モーリシャス [moorishasu] *n* Mauritius

モーリタニア [mooritania] *n* Mauritania

モールス [moorusu] モールス信号 [moorusu
shingou] *n* Morse code

モーター [mootaa] *n* motor

モーターバイク [mootaabaiku] *n* motorcycle

モーターボート [mootaabooto] *n* motorboat;
快速モーターボート [kaisoku mootaabooto] *n*
speedboat

モーターレース [mootaareesu] *n* auto racing

モーテル [mooteru] *n* motel

モペッド [mopeddo] *n* moped

モペット [mopetto] モペットを借りたいのですが
[mopetto o karitai no desu ga] I want to
rent a moped

もっぱら [moppara] *adv* exclusively

モップ [moppu] *n* mop; モップでぬぐい取る
[moppu de nuguitoru] *v* mop up

漏れ口 [moreguchi] *n* leak

漏れる [moreru] *v* leak; ガソリンタンクが漏れ
ています [gasorin-tanku ga morete imasu]
The gas tank is leaking; ラジエーターに漏
れがあります [rajieetaa ni more ga arimasu]
There's a leak in the radiator

森 [mori] *n* forest, woods

モロッコ [morokko] *n* Morocco; モロッコ人
[Morokko jin] *n* Moroccan *(person)* ▷ *adj* モロ
ッコの [Morokko no] *adj* Moroccan

漏る [moru] *v* leak

モルドバ [morudoba] *n* Moldova; モルドバ人
[Morudoba jin] *n* Moldovan *(person)* ▷ *adj* モ

ルドバの [Morudoba no] adj Moldovan

モルヒネ [moruhine] n morphine

モルモット [morumotto] n (動物) guinea pig (rodent)

モルタル [morutaru] n mortar (plaster)

モルトウイスキー [moruto uisukii] n malt whisky

もしかしたら [moshikashitara] adv maybe

モスク [mosuku] n mosque; どこかにモスクはありますか? [doko-ka ni mosuku wa arimasu ka?] Where is there a mosque?

もたれる [motareru] v (寄りかかる) lean; ···にもたれて [... ni motarete] prep against

素 [moto] n cause; 固形スープの素 [kokei suupu no moto] n bouillon cube

求める [motomeru] ···を求める [...-o motomeru] v ask for

基づく [motozuku] ···に基づく [... ni motozuku] adj based

持つ [motsu] 手に持つ [te ni motsu] v hold; 持っている [motte iru] v have; 持ってくる [motte kuru] v bring; 希望が持てる [kibou ga moteru] adj hopeful; 希望を持って [kibou-o motte] adv hopefully; これを持っていていただけますか? [kore o motte ite itadakemasu ka?] Could you hold this for me?; それはどのくらい日持ちしますか? [sore wa dono kurai himochi shimasu ka?] How long will it stay fresh?

最も [mottomo] 最もよい [mottomo yoi] adj best; 最もよく [mottomo yoku] adv best; 最も重要な [mottomo juuyou na] adj essential; 最も少ない [mottomo sukunai] adj least

最も多い [mottomo ooi] adj most; 最も多く [mottomo ouku] adv most

もっとのんびりする [motto nonbiri suru] v slow down

もう [mou] もう一つの [mou hitotsu no] adj another

盲導犬 [moudouken] n Seeing-Eye® dog

毛布 [moufu] n blanket; 電気毛布 [denkimoufu] n electric blanket; 毛布がもっと必要です [moufu ga motto hitsuyou desu] We need more blankets; 追加の毛布を持ってきてください [tsuika no moufu o motte kite kudasai] Please bring me an extra blanket

もう一度 [mou ichido] あとでもう一度かけてもらえますか? [ato de mou ichido kakete moraemasu ka?] Would you mind trying again later?; もう一度言っていただけますか? [mou ichido itte itadakemasu ka?] Could you repeat that, please?; もう一度言ってください [mou ichido itsutte kudasai] Pardon?

儲かる [moukaru] v lucrative

猛禽 [moukin] n bird of prey

申し分 [moushibun] 申し分ない [moushibun nai] adj well; 申し分なく [moushibun naku] adv all right, well

申し出る [moushideru] 自発的に申し出る [jihatsuteki ni moushideru] v volunteer

申込 [moushikomi] 申込書 [moushikomisho] n application form

申し込む [moushikomu] v apply; 申し込み [moushikomi] n application

申し立て [moushitate] n allegation

申し立てられた [moushitaterareta] v alleged

申し訳ない [moushiwakenai] 大変申し訳ありません、規則を知りませんでした [taihen moushiwake arimasen, kisoku o shirimasen deshita] I'm very sorry, I didn't know the rules

もや [moya] n mist; もやの立ち込めた [moya no tachikometa] adj misty

もやし [moyashi] 豆もやし [mame moyashi] n bean sprouts

燃やす [moyasu] v burn

催す [moyoosu] 屋外市を催す場所 [okugai ichi-o moyousu basho] n fairground

模様 [moyou] n pattern

モザイク [mozaiku] n mosaic

モザンビーク [mozanbiiku] n Mozambique

模造 [mozou] 模造の [mozou no] adj fake

模造品 [mozouhin] n fake, imitation

無 [mu] 無意味な [muimi na] adj senseless

無茶な [mucha na] adj crazy

M

鞭 [muchi] n whip

無知 [muchi] n ignorance; 無知の [muchi no] adj ignorant

無鉛 [muen] 無鉛の [muen no] adj lead-free; 無鉛ガソリン [muen gasorin] n unleaded gasoline; ···分の無鉛プレミアムガソリンをお願いします [... bun no muen-puremiamu-gasorin o o-negai shimasu]... worth of unleaded, please

無蓋 [mugai] 無蓋貨車 [mugai kasha] n truck

無害 [mugai] 無害な [mugai na] adj harmless

麦 [mugi] 大麦 [oumugi] n barley

麦わら [mugiwara] n straw

謀反 [muhon] 謀反の [muhon no] adj rebellious

無為 [mui] 無為に過ごす [mui ni sugosu] v mess around

無意味な [muimi na] adj pointless

無慈悲な [mujihi na] adj ruthless

無人 [mujin] 無人島 [mujintou] n desert island

無条件 [mujouken] 無条件の [mujouken no] adj unconditional

向かい側 [mukaigawa] 向かい側に [mukaigawa ni] adv across the street; 向かい側の [mukaigawa no] adj opposite

無関係 [mukankei] 無関係な [mukankei na] adj irrelevant

むかつく [mukatsuku] n (腹が立つ) disgusted; むかつくような [mukatsuku you na] (腹が立つ) adj repulsive; むかむかする [mukamuka suru] (腹が立つ) adj disgusting

向かう [mukau] ···に向かう [... ni mukau] (方角) v face

向き [muki] 向きを変える [muki wo kaeru] v turn

むき出す [mukidasu] むき出しにする [mukidashi ni suru] v bare; むき出しの [mukidashi no] adj bare

無効 [mukou] 無効の [mukou no] adj void

向こう [mukou] ···の向こうに [... no mukou ni] prep beyond

むこうずね [mukouzune] n shin

向く [muku] v face

報い [mukui] 報いのある [mukui no aru] adj rewarding

無給 [mukyuu] 無給の [mukyuu no] adj unpaid

胸 [mune] n chest (body part); 私は胸に痛みがあります [watashi wa mune ni itami ga arimasu] I have a pain in my chest

胸焼け [muneyake] n heartburn

無能 [munou] 無能な [munou na] adj incompetent

村 [mura] n village

紫色 [murasakiiro] 紫色の [murasakiiro no] adj purple

群れ [mure] n flock, group

無料 [muryou] 無料の [muryou no] adj free (no cost)

無線 [musen] n, adj wireless; 無線制御の [musen seigyo no] adj radio-controlled; その部屋で無線インターネット接続を利用できますか? [sono heya de musen-intaanetto-setsuzoku o riyou dekimasu ka?] Does the room have wireless internet access?

虫 [mushi] n bug, worm; 私の部屋に虫がいます [watashi no heya ni mushi ga imasu] There are bugs in my room

無視 [mushi] 無視する [mushi suru] v ignore

蒸し暑い [mushiatsui] 蒸し暑いです [mushiatsui desu] It's muggy

無神論 [mushinron] 無神論者 [mushinronsha] n atheist

無思慮 [mu shiryo] adv rather; 無思慮な [mushiryo na] adj thoughtless

虫よけ [mushiyoke] n insect repellent

結び目 [musubime] n knot

息子 [musuko] n son; 息子の妻 [musuko no tsuma] n daughter-in-law; 息子の姿が見当たりません [musuko no sugata ga miatarimasen] My son is lost; 私の息子が行方不明です [watashi no musuko ga yukue-fumei desu] My son is missing

娘 [musume] n daughter; おてんば娘 [otemba musume] n tomboy; 継娘 [mama musume] n stepdaughter; 娘の夫 [musume no otto] n son-in-law; 私の娘が行方不明です [watashi no musume ga yukue-fumei desu] My daughter is missing; 娘の姿が見当たりません [musume no sugata ga miatari-masen] My daughter is lost

むっとする [muttosuru] v (息詰まる) stifling

むっつり [muttsuri] むっつりした [muttsuri shita] adj moody

ムール貝 [muurugai] n mussel

ムース [muusu] n mousse

夢遊病 [muyuubyou] 夢遊病で歩く [muyuubyou de aruku] v sleepwalk

脈拍 [myakuhaku] n pulse

ミャンマー [myanmaa] n Myanmar

ミュージカル [myuujikaru] n musical

ミュージック [myuujikku] フォークミュージック [fooku myuujikku] n folk music

ミューズリー [myuuzurii] n muesli

M

N

ナビゲーション [nabigeeshon] 衛星ナビゲーション [eisei nabigeeshon] n satellite navigation

なだれ [nadare] n avalanche; なだれの危険はありますか? [nadare no kiken wa arimasu ka?] Is there a danger of avalanches?

なでる [naderu] v stroke; なでること [naderu koto] n stroke

など [nado] …など [… nado] adv etc.

長い [nagai] adj long; ひょろ長い [hyoro nagai] adj lanky; 長さ [nagasa] n length; 私たちはとても長いあいだ待っています [watashi-tachi wa totemo nagai aida matte imasu] We've been waiting for a very long time

長椅子 [nagaisu] 背付きの長椅子 [setsuki no nagaisu] n couch

長く [nagaku] adv long; より長く [yori nagaku] adv longer

眺め [nagame] n view; 壮観な眺めを見たいのですが [soukan na nagame o mitai no desu ga] We'd like to see spectacular views

流れ [nagare] n current (flow)

流れる [nagareru] v flow

長さ [nagasa] この長さでお願いします [kono nagasa de o-negai shimasu] This length, please

流す [nagasu] v pour

投げる [nageru] v pitch, throw; 投げ飛ばす [nagetobasu] v fling; 軽く投げる [karuku nageru] v toss

投げ捨てる [nagesuteru] v dump

投げ矢 [nageya] ダーツ用の投げ矢 [daatsu you no nageya] n dart

投げ槍 [nageyari] n javelin

内部 [naibu] 内部の [naibu no] adj internal

ナイフ [naifu] n knife

ナイジェリア [naijeria] n Nigeria; ナイジェリア人 [naijeriajin] n Nigerian (person); ナイジェリアの [naijeria no] adj Nigerian

内密 [naimitsu] 内密の [naimitsu no] adj confidential

ナイロン [nairon] n nylon

内線 [naisen] 内線番号 [naisen-bangou] extension

内戦 [naisen] n civil war

ナイトクラブ [naitokurabu] n nightclub

内蔵 [naizou] 内蔵型の [naizougata no] adj self-contained

中 [naka] 中に入れない [naka ni irenai] v keep out; 中くらいの [naka kurai no] adj medium (between extremes); …の中で [… no naka de] prep among; 午前中に [gozen-chuu ni] in the morning

仲買人 [nakagainin] 株式仲買人 [kabushikinakagainin] n stockbroker

中程 [nakahodo] 中程で [nakahodo de] adv halfway

仲間 [nakama] n buddy, companion

中身 [nakami] n content

中庭 [nakaniwa] n courtyard

泣きじゃくる [nakijakuru] v sob

泣き叫ぶ [nakisakebu] 泣き叫ぶ声 [nakisakebu koe] n cry

泣く [naku] v cry, weep

なくす [nakusu] vt lose

生ビール [namabiiru] 生ビールをください [nama-biiru o kudasai] A draft beer, please

名前 [namae] n name; 洗礼名 [senreimei] n first name; あなたのお名前は? [anata no o-namae wa?] What's your name?; 私の名前は・・・です [watashi no namae wa... desu] My name is...

生意気 [namaiki] 生意気な [namaiki na] *adj* sassy

生の [nama no] *n* raw

なまぬるい [namanurui] *adj* lukewarm

鉛 [namari] *n* lead *(metal)*

生卵 [namatamago] *n* raw egg; 私は生卵を食べられません [watashi wa nama-tamago o taberaremasen] I can't eat raw eggs

生焼け [namayake] 生焼けの [namayake no] *adj* rare *(undercooked)*

ナメクジ [namekuji] *n* slug

滑らかな [nameraka na] *adj* smooth

なめる [nameru] *v* (舌) lick

波 [nami] *n* wave; 打ち寄せる波 [uchiyoseru nami] *n* surf

涙 [namida] *n* tear *(from eye)*

何 [nan] *adv* what; これには何が入っていますか? [kore ni wa nani ga haitte imasu ka?] What is in this?; それは何ですか? [sore wa nan desu ka?] What is it?; ・・・は何といいますか? [... wa nan to iimasu ka?] What is the word for...?

ナナフシ [nanafushi] *n* stick insect

ナンバープレート [nanbaapureeto] *n* license plate; ナンバープレートの番号は・・・ [nanbaa-pureeto no bangou wa...] License plate number...

何でも [nandemo] *pron* anything

何語 [nanigo] 何語が話せますか? [nani-go ga hanasemasu ka?] What languages do you speak?

何も [nanimo] 何もしない [nanimo shinai] *adj* idle

何曜日 [naniyoubi] 今日は何曜日ですか? [kyou wa nani-youbi desu ka?] What day is it today?

何時 [nanji] 今何時か教えていただけますか? [ima nan-ji ka oshiete itadakemasu ka?] What time is it, please?; 何時に終わりますか? [nan-ji ni owarimasu ka?] When will you have finished?; ・・・へ行く電車は何時にありますか? [... e iku densha wa nan-ji ni arimasu ka?] What times are the trains to...?; ・・・へ行く電車は何時ですか? [... e iku densha wa nan-ji desu ka?] What time is the train to...?; 電車は・・・に何時に着きますか? [densha wa... ni nan-ji ni tsukimasu ka?] What time does the train arrive in...?

南京錠 [nankinjou] *n* padlock

軟膏 [nankou] *n* ointment

南極 [nankyoku] *n* South Pole; 南極大陸 [Nankyoku tairiku] *n* Antarctic

難問 [nanmon] *n* puzzle

何日 [nannichi] 今日は何日ですか? [kyou wa nan-nichi desu ka?] What is today's date?; 何日ですか? [nan-nichi desu ka?] What is the date?

難破 [nanpa] *n* shipwreck; 難破した [nanpa shita] *adj* shipwrecked

南西 [nansei] *n* southwest

ナンセンス [nansensu] *n* nonsense

なんてことを! [nantekoto wo] *excl* no!

何とおっしゃいましたか? [nan to osshaimashita ka] *excl* pardon?

南東 [nantou] *n* southeast

治る [naoru] *v* heal

直す [naosu] *v* repair, fix

治す [naosu] *v* cure

直す [naosu] 天気がもち直すといいですね [tenki ga mochinaosu to ii desu ne] I hope the weather improves

ナプキン [napukin] *n* napkin; 生理用ナプキン [seiriyou napukin] *n* sanitary napkin

並べる [naraberu] *v* set out

鳴らす [narasu] *v* ring; ゴロゴロとのどを鳴らす [gorogoro to nodo-o narasu] *v* purr; 鳴らすこと [narasu koto] *n* ring

なる [naru] ・・・になる [... ni naru] *v* become; それはいくらになりますか? [sore wa ikura ni narimasu ka?] How much does that come to?

成る [naru] ・・・から成る [... kara naru] *v* consist of

鳴る [naru] カチッと鳴る [kachitto naru] v click

なさる [nasaru] v do; 今日は何をなさりたいですか? [kyou wa nani o nasaritai desu ka?] What would you like to do today?

なし [nashi] n pear; 袖なしの [sode nashi no] adj sleeveless

ナス [nasu] n eggplant

夏 [natsu] n summer; 夏の休暇 [natsu no kyuuka] n summer vacation; 夏に [natsu ni] in summer; 夏の間 [natsu no aida] during the summer; 夏の後に [natsu no ato ni] after summer; 夏の前に [natsu no mae ni] before summer

ナツメグ [natsumegu] n nutmeg

ナット [natto] n natto, fermented soybeans, nut (device)

ナッツ [nattsu] n nut (food); ナッツを使わずに食事を用意していただけますか? [nattsu o tsukawazu ni shokuji o youi shite itadakemasu ka?] Could you prepare a meal without nuts?

ナッツアレルギー [nattsuarerugii] n nut allergy

納屋 [naya] n barn

悩ます [nayamasu] v bother; 神経を悩ます [shinkei-o nayamasu] adj nerve-racking

悩む [nayamu] 悩ませる [nayamaseru] v pester; 私は時差ぼけに悩んでいます [watashi wa jisaboke ni nayande imasu] I'm suffering from jet lag

謎 [nazo] n mystery

謎めく [nazomeku] 謎めいた [nazomeita] adj mysterious

寝坊 [nebou] 朝寝坊 [asanebou] n sleep late

値段 [nedan] 値段を書いてください [nedan o kaite kudasai] Please write down the price

願い [negai] n wish

願う [negau] v wish

ネギ [negi] n leek, scallion

値切る [negiru] うるさく値切る [urusaku negiru] v haggle

ネグリジェ [negurije] n nightgown

ねじ [neji] n screw; ねじを緩める [neji-o yurumeru] v unscrew; ねじがゆるくなっています [neji ga yuruku natte imasu] The screw has come loose

ねじる [nejiru] v twist, wrench; ねじり [nejiri] n wrench

ネックレス [nekkuresu] n necklace

熱狂 [nekkyou] 熱狂者 [nekkyousha] n fanatic; 熱狂的な愛国主義者 [nekkyoutekiaikokushugisha] n chauvinist

猫 [neko] n cat

ネクタイ [nekutai] n tie

ネクタリン [nekutarin] n nectarine

ねまき [nemaki] n nightclothes

眠い [nemui] adj drowsy, sleepy

眠らずに [nemurazu ni] v awake

眠り [nemuri] n sleep

眠る [nemuru] v sleep; 眠って [nemutte] adj asleep; うるさくて眠れません [urusakute nemuremasen] I can't sleep for the noise; よく眠れましたか? [yoku nemuremashita ka?] Did you sleep well?; 暑くて眠れません [atsukute nemuremasen] I can't sleep for the heat

年 [nen, toshi] n year; うるう年 [uruudoshi] n leap year; 年一回の [nen'ikkai no] adj annual; 年に一度 [nen ni ichido] adv yearly

粘土 [nendo] n clay

年一回 [nen'ikkai] adv annually

念入 [nen'iri] 念入りな [nen'iri na] adj conscientious

年次 [nenji] adj annual

年金 [nenkin] n pension; 年金受給者 [nenkin jukyuusha] n old-age pensioner

年配 [nenpai] 年配の [nenpai no] adj elderly

年齢 [nenrei] n age; 年齢制限 [nenreiseigen] n age limit

燃料 [nenryou] n fuel; 燃料を補給する [nenryou wo hokyuu suru] v refuel

粘性ゴム [nenseigomu] n gum

捻挫 [nenza] n sprain

ネオン [neon] n neon

ネパール [nepaaru] n Nepal

ねらう [nerau] v aim

寝る [neru] v sleep; いっしょに寝る [issho ni neru] v sleep together; 誰とでも寝る [dare todemo neru] v sleep around

熱心 [nesshin] 熱心な [nesshin na] adj enthusiastic

寝過ごす [nesugosu] v oversleep, sleep in

ねたみ [netami] n envy

熱 [netsu] n fever, heat; 熱する [nessuru] v heat; ···熱 [... netsu] (熱狂) n mania; 彼は熱があります [kare wa netsu ga arimasu] He has a fever

熱意 [netsui] n enthusiasm

熱情 [netsujou] n passion

熱帯 [nettai] 熱帯の [nettai no] adj tropical

熱帯雨林 [nettai urin] n rainforest

ネットボール [nettobooru] n netball

ネットワーク [nettowaaku] n network; ネットワークにつながりません [nettowaaku ni tsunagarimasen] I can't get a network

二 [ni] num two

荷 [ni] n load; 荷を解く [ni-o toku] v unpack; 荷を積む [ni-o tsumu] v load; 荷を降ろす [ni-o orosu] v unload

···に [...ni] prep at

似合う [niau] v suit

2倍 [nibai] 2倍にする [nibai ni suru] v double; 2倍の [nibai no] adj double

二番目 [nibanme] n second; 二番目の [ni banme no] adj second

荷馬車 [nibasha] n cart

鈍い [nibui] adj blunt

日 [nichi] n day; 日の出 [hi no de] n sunrise; なんてすばらしい日でしょう! [nante subarashii hi deshou!] What a beautiful day!

日没 [nichibotsu] n sunset

日曜日 [nichiyoubi] n Sunday; 日曜日に [nichiyoubi ni] on Sunday; 十月三日の日曜日です [juu-gatsu mik-ka no nichiyoubi desu] It's Sunday, October third

日曜大工 [nichiyoudaiku] n do-it-yourself

二段 [nidan] 二段ベッド [nidanbeddo] n bunk beds

煮出し汁 [nidashijiru] n broth

二度 [nido] adv twice

荷造り [nidukuri] 荷造りをする [nizukuri wo suru] v pack

にがい [nigai] adj bitter

二月 [nigatsu] n February

逃げ出す [nigedasu] v run away

逃げる [nigeru] v escape, flee, get away, get out

二泊 [nihaku] 二泊したいのですが [nihaku shitai no desu ga] I'd like to stay for two nights

日本 [nihon(nippon)] n Japan

日本語 [nihongo] n Japanese (language)

日本人 [nihon(nippon)jin] n Japanese (person)

日本の [nihon(nippon) no] adj Japanese

虹 [niji] n rainbow

二時 [niji] 二時です [ni-ji desu] It's two o'clock; 二時十五分です [ni-ji juugo-fun desu] It's a quarter past two; 二時半です [ni-ji-han desu] It's two-thirty; もうすぐ二時半です [mousugu niji han desu] It's almost two-thirty

ニジェール [nijieeru] n Niger

二十 [nijuu] number twenty; 二十番目の [nijuu banme no] adj twentieth

ニカラグア [nikaragua] n Nicaragua; ニカラグア人 [Nikaragua jin] n Nicaraguan (person); ニカラグアの [Nikaragua no] adj Nicaraguan

にきび [nikibi] n acne, zit

日記 [nikki] n datebook (appointments)

日光 [nikkou] n sunlight, sunshine

日光浴 [nikkouyoku] 日光浴をする [nikkouyoku wo suru] v sunbathe; 日光浴用ベッド [nikkouyoku you beddo] n sunbed

ニックネーム [nikkuneemu] n nickname

ニコチン [nikochin] n nicotine

二戸建て住宅 [nikodate juutaku] n duplex

肉 [niku] n meat; 赤身肉 [akaminiku] n red meat; 肉屋 [nikuya] n butcher; 骨付き肉 [honetsuki niku] n joint (meat); 子牛の肉

[koushi no niku] n veal; この肉はいたんでいます [kono niku wa itande imasu] This meat is spoiled; これは肉のストックで料理してありますか? [kore wa niku no sutokku de ryouri shite arimasu ka?] Is this cooked in meat stock?; 肉が冷たいです [niku ga tsumetai desu] The meat is cold; 私は肉が好きではありません [watashi wa niku ga suki de wa arimasen] I don't like meat; 私は肉を食べません [watashi wa niku o tabemasen] I don't eat meat

憎む [nikumu] v hate

憎しみ [nikushimi] n hatred

肉体労働者 [nikutairoudousha] workman

荷物 [nimotsu] n baggage; 超過手荷物 [choukatenimotsu] n excess baggage; これから荷物を詰めなければなりません [kore kara nimotsu o tsumenakereba narimasen] I need to pack now

人間 [ningen] n human being; 人間の [ningen no] adj human

人魚 [ningyo] n mermaid

人形 [ningyou] n doll; あやつり人形 [ayatsuri ningyou] n puppet

ニンジン [ninjin] n carrot

人気 [ninki] n (評判) popularity; 人気のない [hitoke no nai] adj unpopular; 人気のある [ninki no aru] adj popular

任命する [ninmei suru] v appoint

任者 [nin mono] 前任者 [zenninsha] n predecessor

任務 [ninmu] n duty, task

ニンニク [ninniku] n garlic

認識 [ninshiki] 認識できる [ninshiki dekiru] adj recognizable

妊娠 [ninshin] n pregnancy; 妊娠中絶 [ninshinchuuzetsu] n abortion; 妊娠した [ninshin shita] adj pregnant

忍耐 [nintai] n patience

忍耐強い [nintaizuyoi] adj patient

におい [nioi] n odor, scent, smell; においがする [nioi ga suru] vi smell; においを嗅ぐ [nioi-o kagu] vt smell; ガスのにおいがします

[gasu no nioi ga shimasu] I can smell gas

にらみつける [niramitsukeru] v glare

ニレ [nire] n elm

似る [niru] 似ている [niteiru] v resemble; ···に似る [... ni niru] v look like

煮る [niru] v cook; 弱火でとろとろ煮る [yowabi de torotoro niru] v simmer

二流 [niryuu] 二流の [niryuu no] adj second-rate

西 [nishi] n west; 西に [nishi ni] adv west; 西の [nishi no] adj west, western

西インド諸島 [nishiindoshotou] n West Indies; 西インド諸島の人 [nishiindoshotou no hito] n West Indian (person); 西インド諸島の [nishiindoshotou no] adj West Indian

ニシン [nishin] n herring

西行き [nishiyuki] 西行きの [nishi yuki no] adj westbound

二食付き [nishokutsuki] n modified American plan

二週間 [nishuukan] n two weeks

尼僧 [nisou] n nun

日射病 [nisshabyou] n sunstroke

ニス [nisu] n varnish; ニスを塗る [nisu-o nuru] v varnish

日常の食べ物 [nitchijou no tabemono] n diet

二等 [nitou] n second class; 二等の [nitou no] adj second-class

···について [...nitsuite] prep about

について行く [ni tsuiteiku] ···について行く [... ni tsuite iku] v follow

日程 [nittei] 議事日程 [giji nittei] n agenda

庭 [niwa] n garden, yard (enclosure); 庭仕事 [niwa shigoto] n gardening

庭師 [niwashi] n gardener

鶏 [niwatori] n chicken

荷造りをする [nizukuri wo suru] 荷造りが済んで [nizukuri ga sunde] adj packed

述べる [noberu] v state

伸びる [nobiru] v stretch, stretchy

登る [noboru] v climb

昇る [noboru] 最後に昇るのはいつですか? [saigo ni noboru no wa itsu desu ka?] When is the last ascent?

のぼる [noboru] v climb

ノブ [nobu] n knob

後 [nochi] ・・・の後に [... no nochi ni] prep after; ・・・した後に [... shita nochi ni] conj after; 後で [ato de] adv afterwards

のど [nodo] n throat; のどの渇き [nodo no kawaki] n thirst; のどが渇いた [nodo ga kawaita] adj thirsty; ゴロゴロとのどを鳴らす [gorogoro to nodo-o narasu] v purr

野原 [nohara] n field

のこぎり [nokogiri] n saw

残り [nokori] 残りの [nokori no] adj remaining

蚤 [nomi] n flea

飲み込む [nomikomu] vi swallow; を飲み込む [-o nomikomu] vt swallow

飲み物 [nomimono] n drink; お飲み物はいかがですか？ [o-nomimono wa ikaga desu ka?] Would you like a drink?; お飲み物を持ってきましょうか？ [o-nomimono o motte kimashou ka?] Can I get you a drink?; 飲み物は私のおごりです [nomimono wa watashi no ogori desu] The drinks are on me

ノミの市 [nomi no ichi] n flea market

飲む [nomu] v drink; 飲み騒ぐこと [nomisawagu koto] n binge drinking; 何をお飲みになりますか？ [nani o o-nomi ni narimasu ka?] What would you like to drink?

ののしり [nonoshiri] n curse, swearword

ののしる [nonoshiru] v swear

ノート [nooto] n notebook

乗り場 [noriba] タクシー乗り場 [takushii noriba] n taxi stand; タクシー乗り場はどこですか？ [takushii-noriba wa doko desu ka?] Where is the taxi stand?

乗り出す [noridasu] ・・・から身を乗り出す [... kara mi-o noridasu] v lean out

乗り換え [norikae] n transfer; あなたは・・・で乗り換えなければなりません [anata wa... de norikaenakereba narimasen] You have to transfer at...

乗り換える [norikaeru] v transfer

乗組員 [norikumiin] n crew

乗り物 [norimono] n vehicle

乗り遅れる [noriokureru] v be late for (sth)

乗り手 [norite] n rider

乗り継ぎ [noritsugi] 私は乗り継ぎを逃しました [watashi wa noritsugi o nogashimashita] I've missed my connection

乗る [noru] v get in, get on, ride

載る [noru] 目録に載っていない [mokuroku ni notte inai] adj unlisted

ノルウェー [noruuee] n Norway; ノルウェー人 [noruueejin] n Norwegian (person); ノルウェーの [noruuee no] adj Norwegian; ノルウェー語 [noruueego] n Norwegian (language)

乗せる [noseru] v give (sb) a ride; 人を車に乗せてあげること [hito-o kuruma ni nosete ageru koto] n give a ride to; 自動車修理工場まで私を乗せていってもらえますか？ [jidousha-shuuri-koujou made watashi o nosete itte moraemasu ka?] Could you give me a ride to the repair shop?

のっとる [nottoru] 慣例にのっとった [kanrei ni nottotta] adj conventional

脳 [nou] n brain; 脳震盪 [noushintou] n concussion

農業 [nougyou] n agriculture, farming; 農業の [nougyou no] adj agricultural

ノウハウ [nouhau] n know-how

嚢胞 [nouhou] n cyst

農場 [noujou] n farm

農場主 [noujoushu] n farmer

農家 [nouka] n farmhouse

濃紺 [noukon] 濃紺の [noukon no] adj navy-blue

能力 [nouryoku] n ability, power

農薬 [nouyaku] n pesticide

膿瘍 [nouyou] n abscess; 私は膿瘍があります [watashi wa nouyou ga arimasu] I have an abscess

納税 [nouzei] 納税者 [nouzeisha] n tax payer

望む [nozomu] v hope

脱ぐ [nugu] v take off; 服を脱ぐ [fuku wo

N

nugu] v undress

ぬぐい取る [nuguitoru] モップでぬぐい取る [moppu de nuguitoru] v mop up

縫い合わせる [nuiawaseru] v sew up

縫い針 [nuihari] n needle

縫い目 [nuime] n seam

ぬかるみ [nukarumi] n slush

抜き取る [nukitoru] v withdraw

抜く [nuku] v pull out; プラグを抜いて電源を断つ [puragu-o nuite dengen-o tatsu] v unplug

沼 [numa] n bog, marsh; 沼地 [numachi] n swamp

布 [nuno] 目隠し布 [mekakushi nuno] n blindfold

布地 [nunoji] n cloth

ぬれる [nureru] ぬれても大丈夫な [nurete mo daijoubu na] adj waterproof

濡れる [nureru] v get wet; 濡れた [nureta] adj wet

塗る [nuru] v paint; ニスを塗る [nisu-o nuru] v varnish; マニキュアを塗る [manikyua-o nuru] v do one's nails; 漆喰を塗る [shikkui-o nuru] v whitewash

盗み [nusumi] n theft

盗む [nusumu] v steal; 誰かが私のトラベラーズチェックを盗みました [dare ka ga watashi no toraberaazu-chekku o nusumimashita] Someone's stolen my traveler's checks; 私のカードが盗まれました [watashi no kaado ga nusuma remashita] My card has been stolen

縫う [nuu] v sew, stitch

ヌードル [nuudoru] n noodles

尿 [nyou] n urine

入院 [nyuuin] n hospitalization

ニュージーランド [nyuujiirando] n New Zealand; ニュージーランド人 [nyuujiirandojin] n New Zealander

入場 [nyuujou] n admission; 入場を許す [nyuujou-o yurusu] v admit (allow in); 入場料 [nyuujouryou] n admission charge; 入場許可 [nyuujou kyoka] n admittance

入場料 [nyuujouryou] n admission fee

入札 [nyuusatsu] n bid; 入札する [nyuusatsu suru] v bid (at auction)

乳製品 [nyuuseihin] n dairy products; 乳製品販売店 [nyuuseihin hanbaiten] n dairy

ニュース [nyuusu] n news; ニュースはいつですか? [nyuusu wa itsu desu ka?] When is the news?

ニュースキャスター [nyuusukyasutaa] n newscaster

O

尾 [o] *n* tail

オアシス [oashisu] *n* oasis

おば [oba] *n* (伯母・叔母) aunt; おばちゃん [obachan] *n* auntie

おばあちゃん [obaachan] *n* grandma, granny

おべっか [obekka] *n* lip balm

帯 [obi] 帯状のひも [obijou no himo] *n* band (strip)

おびえる [obieru] おびえた [obieta] *adj* frightened

おぼれる [oboreru] *v* drown; 誰かおぼれています! [dare ka oborete imasu!] Someone is drowning!

汚物 [obutsu] *n* dirt

お茶 [o-cha] *n* tea

落ちる [ochiru] *v* drop, fall

落ち着く [ochitsuku] *v* (住居) settle down, (気分) calm down; 落ち着いた [ochitsuita] *adj* calm; 落ち着かない [ochitsukanai] *adj* restless

おだてる [odateru] *v* flatter; おだてられた [odaterareta] *adj* flattered

踊り場 [odoriba] *n* landing

驚き [odoroki] *n* surprise

驚く [odoroku] 驚いた [odoroita] *adj* surprised; 驚かす [odorokasu] *v* astonish; 驚くべき [odorokubeki] *adj* amazing

踊る [odoru] *v* dance; ワルツを踊る [warutsu wo odoru] *v* waltz; 踊ること [odoru koto] *n* dancing; 私は本当に踊りません [watashi wa hontou ni odorimasen] I really don't dance; 私は踊りたい気分です [watashi wa odoritai kibun desu] I feel like dancing

脅す [odosu] *v* threaten; 脅し [odoshi] *n* threat; 脅すような [odosu you na] *adj* threatening

終える [oeru] *v* finish; 終えた [oeta] *adj* finished

オフィス [ofisu] *n* office; 予約オフィス [yoyaku ofisu] *n* ticket office; 貴社のオフィスへ伺うにはどう行けばいいでしょうか? [kisha no ofisu e ukagau ni wa dou ikeba ii deshou ka?] How do I get to your office?; 私はオフィスで働いています [watashi wa ofisu de hataraite imasu] I work in an office

オフ [ofu] シーズンオフ [shiizun'ofu] *n* off season

オフサイド [ofusaido] オフサイドの [ofusaido no] *adj* offside

おがくず [ogakuzu] *n* sawdust

小川 [ogawa] *n* stream

おごり [ogori] *n* treat

おはよう [ohayou] おはようございます [ohayou gozaimasu] Good morning

おへそ [oheso] *n* belly button

雄羊 [ohitsuji] 去勢していない雄羊 [kyosei shite inai ohitsuji] *n* ram

牡羊座 [ohitsujiza] *n* Aries

甥 [oi] *n* nephew

追い出す [oidasu] *v* expel

追い払う [oiharau] *v* send off

追い越す [oikosu] *v* pass (on road)

オイル警告灯 [oiru keikokutou] オイル警告灯が消えません [oiru keikoku-tou ga kiemasen] The oil warning light won't go off

おいしい [oishii] *adj* delicious; おいしかったです [oishikatta desu] That was delicious; とてもおいしいです [totemo oishii desu] It's pretty good; 食事はおいしかったです

[shokuji wa oishikatta desu] The meal was delicious; 夕食はおいしかったです [yuushoku wa oishikatta desu] The dinner was delicious

美味しい [oishii] *adj* delicious

置いて来る [oitekuru] 私は車を・・・に置いてきたいのですが [watashi wa kuruma o... ni oite kitai no desu ga] I'd like to leave the car in... and be right back

追いつく [oitsuku] *v* catch up

おじ [oji] *n* (伯父・叔父) uncle

お辞儀 [ojigi] *n* bow; お辞儀をする [ojigi-o suru] *v* bow

おじいちゃん [ojiichan] *n* granddad, grandpa

おじけづかせる [ojikedukaseru] *v* intimidate

丘 [oka] *n* hill

おかげ [okage] thanks to

お菓子 [okashi] 綿菓子 [watagashi] *n* cotton candy

犯す [okasu] *v* commit (a crime)

桶 [oke] かいば桶 [kaibaoke] *n* trough

置場 [okiba] 食料置場 [shokuryou okiba] *n* pantry

置き換え [okikae] *n* replacement

お金 [okin] どこでお金を両替できますか? [doko de o-kane o ryougae dekimasu ka?] Where can I exchange some money?; お金をいくらか至急送ってもらうように手配してもらえますか? [o-kane o ikura ka shikyuu okutte morau you ni tehai shite moraemasu ka?] Can you arrange to have some money sent over quickly?; お金をいくらか貸していただけますか? [o-kane o ikura ka kashite itadakemasu ka?] Could you lend me some money?; 私はお金がありません [watashi wa o-kane ga arimasen] I have no money; 私はお金を使い果たしてしまいました [watashi wa o-kane o tsukaihatashite shimaimashita] I've run out of money

お気に入り [o-kiniiri] *n* favorite

起きる [okiru] *v* get up; 起きている [okite iru] *v* getting up; あなたは何時に起きますか? [anata wa nan-ji ni okimasu ka?] What time

do you get up?

置き去り [okizari] 私は置き去りにされました [watashi wa okizari ni saremashita] I've been left behind

オッケー! [okkee] OK!

行う [okonau] *v* conduct, perform

怒りっぽい [okorippoi] *adj* irritable

怒る [okoru] 怒ってうなる [ikatte unaru] *v* growl; 怒った [okotta] *adj* angry; 怒りっぽい [okorippoi] *adj* touchy; 怒り狂った [ikarikurutta] *adj* furious

起こる [okoru] *v* happen, occur; いつ起こったのですか? [itsu okotta no desu ka?] When did it happen?

起こす [okosu] 興味を起こさせる [kyoumi-o okosaseru] *v* interest; 炎症を起こした [enshou-o okoshita] *adj* inflamed; 起こしてあげましょうか? [okoshite agemashou ka?] Shall I wake you up?

置く [oku] *v* lay, place, put; 置き忘れる [okiwasureru] *v* mislay; 在庫を置く [zaiko-o oku] *v* stock; 地面に置く [jimen ni oku] *v* ground; そこへ置いてください [soko e oite kudasai] Put it down over there, please

臆病 [okubyou] 臆病な [okubyou na] *adj* cowardly; 臆病者 [okubyoumono] *n* coward

屋外 [okugai] 屋外の [okugai no] *adj* outdoor; 屋外で [okugai de] *adv* outdoors

屋外市 [okugaiichi] 屋外市を催す場所 [okugai ichi-o moyousu basho] *n* fairground

屋内 [okunai] 屋内の [okunai no] *adj* indoor; 屋内で [okunai de] *adv* indoors

遅れ [okure] *n* delay

遅れる [okureru] *v* delay, lag behind; 遅れた [okureta] *adj* late (delayed); フライトは遅れています [furaito wa okurete imasu] The flight has been delayed

遅れずに [okurezu ni] *adv* on time

贈り物 [okurimono] *n* gift

送る [okuru] *v* send; インボイスを送る [inboisu-o okuru] *v* invoice; テキストメッセージを送る [tekisuto messeeji-o okuru] *v* text; ファックスを送る [fakkusu-o okuru] *v* fax; 送

り主 [okurinushi] *n* sender; 送り返す [okurikaesu] *v* send back; 電子メールを送る [denshi meeru-o okuru] *v* e-mail; ここからフ ァックスを送れますか? [koko kara fakkusu o okuremasu ka?] Can I send a fax from here?; 私は荷物を前もって送りました [watashi ha nimotsu wo mae motte okuri mashita] I sent my luggage on ahead

奥様 [okusama] *n* madam

オマーン [omaan] *n* Oman

おめでとう [omedetou] *n* congratulations

お目にかかる [ome ni kakaru] *v* meet; ついに お目にかかれて光栄です [tsuini o-me ni kakarete kouei desu] I'm delighted to meet you at last

おみごと! [omigoto] *excl* well done!

おみやげ [omiyage] *n* souvenirs

おもちゃ [omocha] *n* toy

思い [omoi] 恥ずかしい思い [hazukashii omoi] *n* shame

重い [omoi] *adj* heavy; 重さ [omosa] *n* weight; 重さが・・・ある [omosa ga... aru] *v* weigh; これは重すぎます [kore wa omo-sugimasu] This is too heavy

思い出す [omoidasu] *v* remember; 思い出さ せる [omoidasaseru] *v* remind; 思い出させる もの [omoidasaseru mono] *n* reminder

思い出 [omoide] *n* recollection; 思い出の品 [omoide no shina] *n* memento

思い描く [omoiegaku] *v* visualize

思いがけなく [omoigakenaku] *adv* unexpectedly

思い切る [omoikiru] 思い切ったスタイルにした くありません [omoikitta sutairu ni shitaku arimasen] I don't want anything drastic

思い切った [omoikitta] 思い切って・・・する [omoikitte... suru] *v* dare

思い切って [omoikitte] 思い切った [omoikitta] *adj* daring

思いやり [omoiyari] 思いやりのある [omoiyari no aru] *adj* considerate

思いやりのある [omoiyari no aru] *v* caring

重く [omoku] *adv* heavily

趣 [omomuki] 古風で趣のある [kofuu de omomuki no aru] *adj* quaint

主な [omo na] *adj* principal

面白い [omoshiroi] *adj* funny, interesting; 面 白くない [omoshirokunai] *adj* boring

おもしろい [omoshiroi] どこかおもしろい場所を 教えてもらえますか? [doko-ka omoshiroi basho o oshiete moraemasu ka?] Could you suggest somewhere interesting to go?

表 [omote] *n* (作表) table *(chart)*; 価格表 [kakakuhyou] *n* price list; 時刻表 [jikokuhyou] *n* timetable; 通知表 [tsuuchihyou] *n* report card

思うに [omou ni] *adv* presumably

オムレツ [omuretsu] *n* omelette

おむつ [omutsu] *n* diaper

同じ [onaji] *adj* same; ・・・と同じくらい [... to onaji kurai] *adv* as; 私にも同じものをください [watashi ni mo onaji mono o kudasai] I'll have the same

おなか [onaka] *n* tummy, stomach

温度 [ondo] *n* temperature; 摂氏温度 [sesshi ondo] *n* degree centigrade; 温度計 [ondokei] *n* thermometer; 華氏温度 [kashi ondo] *n* degree Fahrenheit

おんどり [ondori] *n* rooster; 若いおんどり [wakai ondori] *n* cockerel

お願い [onegai] お願いします [o-negai shimasu] Please!; 喫煙席をお願いします [kitsuen-seki o o-negai shimasu] Smoking, please

お願い! [onegai] *excl* please!

音楽 [ongaku] *n* music; 音楽の [ongaku no] *adj* musical; 音楽家 [ongakuka] *n* musician

女らしい [onnarashii] *adj* feminine

女相 [onna sou] 女相続人 [onna souzokunin] *n* heiress

斧 [ono] *n* ax

音符 [onpu] *n* note *(music)*

オンライン [onrain] オンラインの [onrain no] *adj* online; オンラインで [onrain de] *adv* online

音節 [onsetsu] *n* syllable

O

温室 [onshitsu] *n* greenhouse

オンス [onsu] *n* ounce

温水 [onsui] プールは温水ですか? [puuru wa onsui desu ka?] Is the pool heated?

温水器 [onsuiki] 温水器はどうやって使うのですか? [onsuiki wa dou-yatte tsukau no desu ka?] How does the water heater work?

オーバー [oobaa] *n* overcoat

オーバーヘッドプロジェクター [oobaahed-dopurojekutaa] *n* overhead projector

オーバーヒート [oobaahiito] エンジンがオーバーヒートしています [enjin ga oobaahiito shite imasu] The engine is overheating

オーバーオール [oobaaooru] *n* overalls; ダンガリーのオーバーオール [dangarii no oobaaooru] *n* dungarees

オーボエ [ooboe] *n* oboe

大袋 [oobukuro] *n* sack *(container)*

オーブン [oobun] *n* oven; オーブン耐熱性の [oobun tainetsusei no] *adj* ovenproof

オーブンミット [oobunmitto] *n* oven mitt

オーディション [oodishon] *n* audition

大金持ち [ooganemochi] *n* millionaire

大型 [oogata] 大型の旅行かばん [oogata no ryokou kaban] *n* duffel bag; 大型輸送車 [ougata yusousha] *n* semi *(truck)*

オーガズム [oogazumu] *n* orgasm

大げさ [oogesa] 大げさに言う [oogesa ni iu] *v* exaggerate

大声 [oogoe] 大声の [ougoe no] *adj* loud; 大声で [ougoe de] *adv* loudly

多い [ooi] さらに多い [sarani oui] *adj* more; 出来事の多い [dekigoto no oui] *adj* eventful; 多くの [ouku no] *adj* many, much; それには···が多すぎます [sore ni wa... ga oo-sugimasu] There's too much... in it

大い [ooi] 大いに [ooi ni] *adv* much

大かがり [ookagari] 大かがり火 [oukagaribi] *n* bonfire

オオカミ [ookami] *n* wolf

オーケー [ookee] *excl* okay!, OK!

オーケストラ [ookesutora] *n* orchestra

大きい [ookii] *adj* big, large; より大きい [yori oukii] *adj* bigger; 大きな [ooki na] *adj* great; 大きい方の [oukii hou no] *adj* major; これより大きな部屋はありますか? [kore yori ooki-na heya wa arimasu ka?] Do you have a bigger one?; それは大きすぎます [sore wa ooki-sugimasu] It's too big

オーク [ooku] *n* oak

大昔 [oomukashi] 大昔の [oumukashi no] *adj* ancient

オーナー [oonaa] *n* owner; オーナーと話させていただけますか? [oonaa to hanasasete itadakemasu ka?] Could I speak to the owner, please?

オーペア [oopea] *n* au pair

オール [ooru] *n* oar

オーストラレーシア [oosutorareeshia] *n* Australasia

オーストラリア [oosutoraria] *n* Australia; オーストラリアの [oosutoraria no] *adj* Australian

オーストラリア人 [oosutorariajin] *n* Australian *(person)*

オーストリア [oosutoria] *n* Austria; オーストリアの [oosutoria no] *adj* Austrian

オーストリア人 [oosutoriajin] *n* Austrian *(person)*

オートバイ [ootobai] *n* motorcycle

オートバイ乗り [ootobainori] *n* motorcyclist

オートマ車 [ootomasha] それはオートマ車ですか? [sore wa ootoma-sha desu ka?] Is it an automatic car?; オートマ車をお願いします [ootoma-sha o o-negai shimasu] An automatic, please

オートミール [ootomiiru] *n* oatmeal

オート麦 [ooto mugi] *n* oats

覆う [oou] *v* cover

公になる [ooyake ni naru] *v* come out

大雪 [ooyuki] 大雪です [ooyuki desu] The snow is very heavy

オペラ [opera] *n* opera

オペレーター [opereetaa] *n* operator

オランダ [oranda] *n* Holland, Netherlands

オランダ人 [orandajin] *n* Dutch; オランダ人男性 [orandajin dansei] *n* Dutchman; オランダ

人女性 [orandajin josei] n Dutchwoman

オランダの [oranda no] n Dutch

オレガノ [oregano] n oregano

オレンジ [orenji] n orange

オレンジ色 [orenjiiro] オレンジ色の [orenjiiro no] adj orange

オレンジジュース [orenjijuusu] n orange juice

オリーブ [oriibu] n olive, olive tree; オリーブ油 [oriibuyu] n olive oil

折り目 [orime] n crease; 折り目をつけた [orime-o tsuketa] adj creased

織物 [orimono] n fabric, textile

降りる [oriru] v descend, get off; 降りてくる [orite kuru] v come down; いつ降りればいいのか教えてください [itsu orireba ii no ka oshiete kudasai] Please tell me when to get off

折りたたみ [oritatami] 折りたたみの [oritatami no] adj folding

折りたたむ [oritatamu] v fold

愚かな [oroka na] adj silly, stupid

卸売 [oroshiuri] 卸売業者 [oroshiuri gyousha] n distributor

卸売り [oroshiuri] n wholesale; 卸売りの [oroshiuri no] adj wholesale

おろそか [orosoka] おろそかにされた [orosoka ni sareta] adj neglected; おろそかにする [orosoka ni suru] v neglect

降ろす [orosu] 荷を降ろす [ni-o orosu] v unload; 降ろしてください [oroshite kudasai] Please let me off

折る [oru] ポキッと折る [pokitto oru] v snap

オルガン [orugan] n organ (music)

おさげ [osage] n braid, pigtail

収める [osameru] 勝利を収める [shouri-o osameru] v triumph

オセアニア [oseania] n Oceania

汚染 [osen] n pollution; 汚染された [osen sareta] adj polluted; 汚染する [osen suru] v pollute

おしゃべり [o-shaberi] n chat

教える [oshieru] v teach; 教えること [oshieru koto] n teaching

押し入る [oshiiru] v break in; 押し入ること [oshiiru koto] n break-in

おしめ [oshime] どこで赤ちゃんのおしめを替えられますか? [doko de akachan no oshime o kaeraremasu ka?] Where can I change the baby?

押し流される [oshinagasareru] 押し流されるもの [oshinagasareru mono] n drift

お尻 [oshiri] n butt

押しつぶす [oshitsubusu] v crush, squash

御しやすい [o shiyasui] adj manageable

遅い [osoi] adj slow; 接続がとても遅いようです [setsuzoku ga totemo osoi you desu] The connection seems very slow

遅く [osoku] adv slowly

おそらく [osoraku] adv supposedly

恐れる [osoreru] v fear

恐ろしい [osoroshii] adj dreadful, horrendous

遅すぎる [ososugiru] 遅すぎます [oso-sugi-masu] It's too late

襲う [osou] vi strike; 襲って強奪する [osotte goudatsu suru] v mug

押す [osu] v press, push; 強く押す [tsuyoku osu] v squeeze; 押してもらえますか? [oshite moraemasu ka?] Could you give me a push?

おすすめ [osusume] 何がおすすめですか? [nani ga osusume desu ka?] What do you recommend?; おすすめの郷土料理はありますか? [osusume no kyoudo-ryouri wa arimasu ka?] Can you recommend a local dish?

おたふく [otafuku] おたふく風邪 [otafukukaze] n mumps

お玉 [otama] n ladle

オタマジャクシ [otamajakushi] n tadpole

おてんば [otenba] おてんば娘 [otenba musume] n tomboy

お手伝い [otetsudai] n (使用人) maid

音 [oto] n sound; カチッという音 [kachitto iu oto] n click; やかましい音 [yakamashii oto] n din; 発信音 [hasshin-on] n dial tone; 鐘の音 [kane no oto] n toll

おとぎ話 [otogibanashi] n fairy tale

男 [otoko] n guy, man; 男らしい [otokorashii] adj masculine

男やもめ [otokoyamome] n widower

乙女座 [otomeza] n Virgo

大人 [otona] n adult; 大人になる [otona ni naru] v grow up

衰える [otoroeru] v decay

劣る [otoru] 劣った [ototta] adj inferior

落とす [otosu] v drop

おととい [ototoi] the day before yesterday

訪れる [otozureru] 車椅子で・・・を訪れることができますか? [kuruma-isu de... o otozureru koto ga dekimasu ka?] Can you visit... in a wheelchair?; 私たちがその街を訪れる時間はありますか? [watashi-tachi ga sono machi o otozureru jikan wa arimasu ka?] Do we have time to visit the town?

お釣り [otsuri] n change; お釣りはとっておいてください [o-tsuri wa totte oite kudasai] Keep the change; お釣りが間違っていると思います [o-tsuri ga machigatte iru to omoimasu] I think you've given me the wrong change; この紙幣でお釣りがありますか? [kono shihei de o-tsuri ga arimasu ka?] Do you have change for this bill?

夫 [otto] n husband; 娘の夫 [musume no otto] n son-in-law; 私は夫へのプレゼントを探しています [watashi wa otto e no purezento o sagashite imasu] I'm looking for a present for my husband; 私の夫です [watashi no otto desu] This is my husband

王 [ou] n king

追う [ou] ・・・を追う [...-o ou] v pursue..., follow...

応募 [oubo] 応募者 [oubosha] n applicant

横断 [oudan] 横断歩道 [oudanhodou] n crosswalk

黄疸 [oudan] n jaundice

横断歩道 [oudanhodou] 太い白線の縞模様で示した横断歩道 [futoi hakusen no

shimamoyou de shimeshita oudanhodou] n zebra crossing (crosswalk)

往復 [oufuku] n round trip; 日帰り往復割引切符 [higaeri oufuku waribiki kippu] n one-day round-trip ticket; 往復切符 [oufuku kippu] n round-trip ticket; 定期往復便 [teiki oufuku bin] n shuttle; ・・・行き1等車往復 [...iki ittou-sha oufuku] a first-class round trip to...

横柄な [ouhei na] adj arrogant

覆い [oui] n cover

王子 [ouji] n prince

応じる [oujiru] v comply with; それに応じて [sore ni oujite] adv accordingly

王女 [oujo] n princess

王冠 [oukan] n crown

王国 [oukoku] n kingdom

オウム [oumu] n parrot

牡牛 [oushi] 牡牛座 [oushiza] n Taurus

雄牛 [oushi] n bull

王室 [oushitsu] 王室の [oushitsu no] adj royal

欧州 [oushuu] 欧州連合 [OUshuu Rengou] n European Union

応対 [outai] 私たちは応対してもらうのをまだ待っています [watashi-tachi wa outai shite morau no wo mada matte imasu] We're still waiting to be served

王座 [ouza] n throne

終わり [owari] n end, finish; 六月の終わりに [roku-gatsu no owari ni] at the end of June

終わりから2番目の [owari kara ni banme no] n second to last

終わりのない [owari no nai] adj endless

終わる [owaru] v end; 終わって [owatte] adj over

親 [oya] n parent

親知らず [oyashirazu] n wisdom tooth

親指 [oyayubi] n thumb

泳ぐ [oyogu] v swim; どこに行けば泳げますか? [doko ni ikeba oyogemasu ka?] Where can I go swimming?; ここで泳いで安全ですか? [koko de oyoide anzen desu ka?] Is it safe to swim here?; ここで泳げますか?

[koko de oyogemasu ka?] Can you swim here?; その川で泳げますか? [sono kawa de oyogemasu ka?] Can you swim in the river?; 泳ぎに行きましょう [oyogi ni ikimashou] Let's go swimming

泳ぐ人 [oyogu hito] *n* swimmer

およそ [oyoso] *adv* about, approximately, roughly

お湯 [oyu] *n* hot water; お湯は料金に含まれていますか? [o-yu wa ryoukin ni fukumarete imasu ka?] Is hot water included in the price?; お湯がありません [o-yu ga arimasen] There's no hot water

オゾン [ozon] *n* ozone; オゾン層 [ozonsou] *n* ozone layer

O

P

パーキング [paakingu] パーキングメーター [paakingumeetaa] n parking meter

パーキングメーター [paakingumeetaa] パーキングメーターが壊れています [paakingu-meetaa ga kowarete imasu] The parking meter is broken; パーキングメーター用の小銭をお持ちですか? [paakingu-meetaa-you no kozeni o o-mochi desu ka?] Do you have change for the parking meter?

パーマ [paama] n perm; 私はパーマをかけています [watashi wa paama o kakete imasu] My hair is permed

パーセンテージ [paasenteeji] n percentage

パーソナルステレオ [paasonarusutereo] n personal stereo

パースニップ [paasunippu] n parsnip

パーティー [paateii] n party (social gathering); ディナーパーティー [dinaa paatii] n dinner party

パートナー [paatonaa] n partner; 私にはパートナーがいます [watashi ni wa paatonaa ga imasu] I have a partner; 私のパートナーです [watashi no paatonaa desu] This is my partner

パートタイム [paatotaimu] パートタイムの [paatotaimu no] adj part-time; パートタイムで [paatotaimu de] adv part-time

パーツ [paatsu] n parts; トヨタ車のパーツはありますか? [toyota-sha no paatsu wa arimasu ka?] Do you have parts for a Toyota?

パブ [pabu] n pub; パブの主人 [pabu no shujin] n pub owner

パブリックスクール [paburikkusukuuru] n private school

パッド [paddo] n pad

パドル [padoru] n paddle; パドルで漕ぐ [padoru de kogu] v paddle

パフペースト [pafupeesuto] n puff pastry

パイ [pai] n pie; アップルパイ [appurupai] n apple pie

パイナップル [painappuru] n pineapple

パイント [painto] n pint

パイプ [paipu] n pipe

パイプライン [paipurain] n pipeline

パイロット [pairotto] n pilot

パジャマ [pajama] n pajamas

パキスタン [pakisutan] n Pakistan; パキスタン人 [pakisutanjin] n Pakistani (person); パキスタンの [pakisutan no] adj Pakistani

パッケージ [pakkeeji] n packaging

パック [pakku] パック旅行 [pakku ryokou] n vacation package

パン [pan] n bread; パンのひと塊 [pan no hitokatamari] n loaf; パンケース [pan keesu] n breadbox; パン粉 [panko] n bread-crumbs, crumb; パン屋 [pan-ya] n bakery; パン屋の主人 [pan ya no shujin] n baker; フライパン [furaipan] n frying pan; 黒パン [kuropan] n brown bread; パンはいかがですか? [pan wa ikaga desu ka?] Would you like some bread?; パンをもっと持ってきてください [pan o motto motte kite kudasai] Please bring more bread

パナマ [panama] n Panama

パンチ [panchi] n (殴打) punch (blow), (飲み物) punch (hot drink)

パンダ [panda] n panda

パンフレット [panfuretto] n brochure, pamphlet

パニック [panikku] n panic

パンケーキ [pankeeki] n pancake

パン生地 [pankiji] n dough

パンク [panku] n flat tire; タイヤがパンクして います [taiya ga panku shite imasu] I have a flat tire; タイヤがパンクしました [taiya ga panku shimashita] I have a flat tire

パンティー [pantii] n (women's) underpants

パントマイム [pantomaimu] n pantomime

パンツ [pantsu] n underpants

パパ [papa] n dad, daddy

パプリカ [papurika] n paprika

パラボラアンテナ [paraboraantena] 衛星放送 用パラボラアンテナ [eisei housou you parabora antena] n satellite dish

パラフィン [parafin] n paraffin

パラグアイ [paraguai] n Paraguay; パラグアイ 人 [Paraguai jin] n Paraguayan (person); パ ラグアイの [Paraguai no] adj Paraguayan

パラグライディング [paraguraidingu] どこに行 けばパラグライディングができますか? [doko ni ikeba paraguraidingu ga dekimasu ka?] Where can you go paragliding?

パラセーリング [paraseeringu] どこでパラセー リングができますか? [doko de paraseeringu ga dekimasu ka?] Where can you go parasailing?

パラセンディング [parasendeingu] 私はパラセ ンディングをしたいのですが [watashi wa parasendingu o shitai no desu ga] I'd like to go parascending

パラセタモール [parasetamooru] パラセタモ ールが欲しいのですが [parasetamooru ga hoshii no desu ga] I'd like some Tylenol®

パラシュート [parashuuto] n parachute

パレード [pareedo] n parade

パレスチナ [paresuchina] n Palestine; パレス チナ人 [paresuchinajin] n Palestinian (person); パレスチナの [paresuchina no] adj Palestinian

バリバリ [paripari] バリバリした [paripari shita] adj crisp; バリバリする [paripari suru] adj crispy

パセリ [paseri] n parsley

パッションフルーツ [passhonfuruutsu] n passion fruit

パス [pasu] n path; サイクルパス [saikuru pasu] n bicycle path; スキー場のパス [sukii jou no pasu] n ski pass

パスポート [pasupooto] n passport; パスポー ト審査窓口 [pasupooto shinsa madoguchi] n passport control; 私はパスポートをなくしま した [watashi wa pasupooto o nakushimashita] I've lost my passport; 私はパスポート を置き忘れました [watashi wa pasupooto o okiwasuremashita] I've forgotten my passport; 私のパスポートが盗まれました [watashi no pasupooto ga nusumaremashita] My passport has been stolen; 私のパ スポートです [watashi no pasupooto desu] Here is my passport; 私のパスポートを返し てください [watashi no pasupooto o kaeshite kudasai] Please give me my passport back; 子供はこのパスポートに載っています [kodomo wa kono pasupooto ni notte imasu] The child is on this passport

パスタ [pasuta] n pasta; スターターにパスタを いただきます [sutaataa ni pasuta o itadakimasu] I'd like pasta as an appetizer

パスワード [pasuwaado] n password

パタパタ動かす [patapata ugokasu] v flap

パティオ [pateio] n patio

パトロール [patorooru] n patrol

パトロールカー [patoroorukaa] n patrol car

パッと発火する [patsu to hakka suru] v flash

パウダー [paudaa] n powder; ベーキングパウ ダー [beekingupaudaa] n baking powder

ペダル [pedaru] n pedal

ページ [peeji] n page; 次ページへ続く [jipeji he tsuduku] PTO

ペーパー [peepaa] トイレットペーパーがありま せん [toiretto-peepaa ga arimasen] There's no toilet paper

ペーパーバック [peepaabakku] n paperback

ペーパークリップ [peepaakurippu] n paperclip

ペーパーウェイト [peepaaueito] n

paperweight

ペースメーカー [peesumeekaa] n
pacemaker

ペースト [peesuto] n paste

ペグ [pegu] n peg

北京 [pekin] n Beijing

ペキニーズ [pekiniizu] n Pekinese

ペン [pen] n pen; ペンをお借りできますか?
[pen o o-kari dekimasu ka?] Do you have a
pen I could borrow?

ペンダント [pendanto] n pendant

ペンギン [pengin] n penguin

ペニー [penii] n penny

ペニシリン [penishirin] n penicillin

ペンキ [penki] n paint

ペンナイフ [pennaifu] n penknife

ペンネーム [penneemu] n pseudonym

ペンパル [penparu] n pen pal

ペパーミント [pepaaminto] n peppermint

ペリカン [perikan] n pelican

ペルシャ [perusha] ペルシャの [Perusha no]
adj Persian

ペルー [peruu] n Peru; ペルー人 [peruujin] n
Peruvian (person); ペルーの [peruu no] adj
Peruvian

ペット [petto] n pet

ピアニスト [pianisuto] n pianist

ピアノ [piano] n piano

ピアス [piasu] n piercing

ピエロ [piero] n clown

PDF [piidiiefu] n PDF [piidiiefu]

ピーク時 [piikuji] n peak hours; ピーク時でな
く [piikuji denaku] adv off-peak

ピーナッツ [piinattsu] n peanut; それにはピー
ナッツが入っていますか? [sore ni wa
piinattsu ga haitte imasu ka?] Does that
contain peanuts?; 私はピーナッツのアレル
ギーがあります [watashi wa piinattsu no
arerugii ga arimasu] I'm allergic to
peanuts

ピーナッツアレルギー [piinattsu arerugii] n
peanut allergy

ピーナッツバター [piinattsubataa] n peanut

butter

PC [piishii] n PC [piishii]

ピクニック [pikunikku] n picnic

ピン [pin] n pin; 安全ピン [anzenpin] n safety
pin; 私は安全ピンが必要です [watashi wa
anzen-pin ga hitsuyou desu] I need a
safety pin

ピンク色 [pinkuiro] ピンク色の [pinkuiro no]
adj pink

ピンセット [pinsetto] n tweezers

ピラミッド [piramiddo] n pyramid

ピル [piru] n pill; 私はピルを飲んでいます
[watashi wa piru o nonde imasu] I'm on the
pill; 私はピルを飲んでいません [watashi wa
piru o nonde imasen] I'm not on the pill

ピストン [pisuton] n piston

ピストル [pisutoru] n pistol

ピッチ [pitchi] n (競技場) pitch (sport)

ぴったり [pittari] adj tightly; ぴったり体に合う
[pittari karada ni au] adj skin-tight; ぴったり
と [pittarito] adv closely; ぴったり合うように敷
かれたカーペット [pittari au youni shikareta
kaapetto] n wall-to-wall carpeting; マットレ
スにぴったり合うシーツ [mattoresu ni pittari
au shiitsu] n fitted sheet

ピザ [piza] n pizza

ポッドキャスト [poddokyasuto] n podcast

ポケット [poketto] n pocket

ポケットベル [poketto beru] n beeper, pager;
ポケットベルで呼び出す [poketto beru de
yobidasu] v page

ポケットマネー [pokettomanee] n pocket
money

ポンド [pondo] n pound; 英貨ポンド [Eika
pondo] n pound sterling

ポニー [ponii] n pony

ポニーテール [poniiteeru] n ponytail

ポニートレッキング [poniitorekkingu] n trail
riding

ポンプ [ponpu] n pump; ポンプで注入する
[ponpu de chuunyuu suru] v pump; ポンプで
膨らませる [ponpu de fukuramaseru] v pump
up; 自転車ポンプ [jitensha ponpu] n bicycle

pump; 3番のポンプをお願いします [san-ban
no ponpu o o-negai shimasu] Pump
number three, please

ポーチ [poochi] n porch

ポーチする [poochi suru] ポーチした [poochi
shita] adj poached (simmered gently)

ポーカー [pookaa] n poker

ポーク [pooku] n pork

ポークチョップ [pookuchoppu] n pork chop

ポーランド [poorando] n Poland; ポーランド
人 [poorandojin] n Pole, Polish (person); ポ
ーランドの [poorando no] adj Polish

ポーター [pootaa] n porter

ポートワイン [pootowain] n port (wine)

ポップコーン [poppukoon] n popcorn

ポプラ [popura] n poplar

ポリエチレン [poriechiren] ポリエチレンの袋
[poriechiren no fukuro] n polyethylene bag

ポリッジ [porijji] n oatmeal

ポリネシア [porineshia] n Polynesia; ポリネシ
ア人 [Porineshia jin] n Polynesian (person);
ポリネシア語 [Porineshia go] n Polynesian
(language); ポリネシアの [Porineshia no] adj
Polynesian

ポリオ [porio] n polio

ポロシャツ [poroshatsu] n polo shirt

ポルノ [poruno] n porn, pornography; ポルノ
の [poruno no] adj pornographic

ポルトガル [porutogaru] n Portugal; ポルトガ
ル人 [porutogarujin] n Portuguese (person);
ポルトガル語 [porutogarugo] n Portuguese
(language); ポルトガルの [porutogaru no]
adj Portuguese

ポスター [posutaa] n poster

ポテト [poteto] n potato; ジャケットポテト
[jaketto poteto] n baked potato; ポテトチッ
プス [potetochippusu] n potato chips

ポット [potto] n pot; コーヒーポット
[koohiipotto] n coffeepot

ポットホール [pottohooru] n pothole

プディング [pudingu] n dessert

プエルトリコ [puerutoriko] n Puerto Rico

プラチナ [purachina] n platinum

プラグ [puragu] n plug; プラグで接続する
[puragu de setsuzoku suru] v plug in; プラグ
を抜いて電源を断つ [puragu-o nuite
dengen-o tatsu] v unplug

プライバシー [puraibashii] n privacy

プライヤー [puraiyaa] n pliers

プラム [puramu] n plum

プラスチック [purasuchikku] n plastic; プラス
チックの [purasuchikku no] adj plastic

プラズマスクリーン [purazumasukuriin] n
plasma screen

プラズマテレビ [purazumaterebi] n plasma
TV

プレーパーク [pureepaaku] n playground; こ
の近くにプレーパークはありますか? [kono
chikaku ni puree-paaku wa arimasu ka?] Is
there a playground near here?

プレーヤー [pureeyaa] CDプレーヤー [shiidii
pureiyaa] n CD player; DVDプレーヤー
[diibuidii pureiyaa] n DVD player

プレイグループ [pureiguruupu] n playgroup

プレイステーション® [pureisuteeshon] n
PlayStation®

プレス機 [puresuki] n press

プレゼンター [purezentaa] n host

プレゼント [purezento] n present (gift); 私は
子供へのプレゼントを探しています [watashi
wa kodomo e no purezento o sagashite
imasu] I'm looking for a present for a
child

プリペイド [puripeido] プリペイドの [puripeido
no] adj prepaid

プロバイダ [purobaida] インターネットサービ
スプロバイダ [intaanetto saabisu purobaida]
n ISP

プロデューサー [purodyuusaa] n producer

プログラマー [puroguramaa] n programmer

プログラム [puroguramu] n program; プログ
ラム作成 [puroguramu sakusei] n
programming; プログラムを作成する
[puroguramu-o sakusei suru] v program; メ
ッセンジャープログラムを使えますか?
[messenjaa-puroguramu o tsukaemasu ka?]

Can I use messenger programs?
プロジェクター [purojekutaa] *n* projector
プロパガンダ [puropaganda] *n* propaganda
プロテスタント [purotesutanto] *n* Protestant;
　プロテスタントの [purotesutanto no] *adj*
　Protestant
プルオーバー [puruoobaa] *n* pullover
プルーン [puruun] *n* prune
プードル [puudoru] *n* poodle
プール [puuru] *n (水泳)* pool *(water)*; 子供用

プール [kodomoyou puuru] *n* wading pool;
それは屋外プールですか? [sore wa
okugai-puuru desu ka?] Is it an outdoor
pool?; スイミングプールはありますか?
[suimingu-puuru wa arimasu ka?] Is there a
swimming pool?; プールは温水ですか?
[puuru wa onsui desu ka?] Is the pool
heated?; 子供用のプールはありますか?
[kodomo-you no puuru wa arimasu ka?] Is
there a children's pool?

R

ラバ [raba] *n* mule

ラベンダー [rabendaa] *n* lavender

ラベル [raberu] *n* label

ラビ [rabi] *n* rabbi

ラボ [rabo] *n* lab; 語学ラボ [gogaku rabo] *n* language laboratory

ラディッシュ [radisshu] *n* radish

ラガー [ragaa] *n* lager beer

ラグ [ragu] *n* rug

ラグビー [ragubii] *n* rugby

ライブミュージック [raibumyuujikku] *n* live music; どこでライブミュージックを聴けますか? [doko de raibu-myuujikku o kikemasu ka?] Where can we hear live music?

ライチョウ [raichou] *n* grouse *(game bird)*

ライフル [raifuru] ライフル銃 [raifuru juu] *n* rifle

ライフスタイル [raifusutairu] *n* lifestyle

雷鳴 [raimei] *n* thunder; 雷鳴を伴った [raimei-o tomonatta] *adj* thundery

ライム [raimu] *n* lime *(fruit)*

ライ麦 [raimugi] *n* rye

来年 [rainen] next year

ライオン [raion] *n* lion; 雌ライオン [mesuraion] *n* lioness

ライラック [rairakku] *n* lilac; ライラック色の [rairakku iro no] *adj* lilac

ライロー® [rairoo] *n* floating pool mattress

来週 [raishuu] next week; 再来週 [saraishuu] the week after next

ライター [raitaa] *n* lighter; シガレットライター [shigaretto raitaa] *n* cigarette lighter

雷雨 [raiu] *n* thunderstorm

ラジエーター [rajieetaa] *n* radiator; ラジエーターに漏れがあります [rajieetaa ni more ga arimasu] There's a leak in the radiator

ラジオ [rajio] *n* radio; ラジオ局 [rajio kyoku] *n* radio station; デジタルラジオ [dejitaru rajio] *n* digital radio; ラジオをつけてもいいですか? [rajio o tsukete mo ii desu ka?] May I turn on the radio?; ラジオを消してもいいですか? [rajio o keshite mo ii desu ka?] May I turn off the radio?

ラケット [raketto] *n* racket; どこでラケットを借りられますか? [doko de raketto o kariraremasu ka?] Where can I rent a racket?; ラケットを貸し出していますか? [raketto o kashidashite imasu ka?] Do they rent out rackets?

落下 [rakka] *n* fall

ラッカー [rakkaa] *n* lacquer

楽観主義 [rakkanshugi] *n* optimism

ラクダ [rakuda] *n* camel

楽園 [rakuen] *n* paradise

落書き [rakugaki] *n* graffiti

楽観 [rakukan] 楽観主義者 [rakkan shugisha] *n* optimist; 楽観的な [rakkanteki na] *adj* optimistic

ラマダーン [ramadaan] *n* Ramadan

ラム [ramu] *n (酒)* rum

ラン [ran] *n* orchid

ランチタイム [ranchitaimu] *n* lunchtime

ランドマーク [randomaaku] *n* landmark

ランドリーサービス [randoriisaabisu] ランドリーサービスはありますか? [randorii-saabisu wa arimasu ka?] Is there a laundry service?

ランジェリー [ranjerii] *n* lingerie; ランジェリー売り場はどこですか? [ranjerii-uriba wa doko desu ka?] Where is the lingerie department?

卵形 [rankei] 卵形の [tamagogata no] *adj* oval

ランク付け [rankuzuke] ランク付けする [ranku zuke suru] *v* rank

ランナー [rannaa] *n* runner

ランニング [ranningu] *n* running

ランプ [ranpu] *n* lamp; ブレーキランプ [bureeki ranpu] *n* brake light; ランプがつきません [ranpu ga tsukimasen] The lamp isn't working

ランプシェード [ranpusheedo] *n* lampshade

ランプステーキ [ranpusuteeki] *n* round steak

卵巣 [ransou] *n* ovary

濫用 [ranyou] 濫用する [ran'you suru] *v* abuse

乱雑 [ranzatsu] 乱雑な状態 [ranzatsu na joutai] *n* shambles

ラオス [raosu] *n* Laos

ラッパズイセン [rappazuisen] *n* daffodil

ラッピング [rappingu] *n* wrapping

ラップトップ [rapputoppu] *n* laptop; ここで自分のラップトップを使えますか? [koko de jibun no rappu-toppu o tsukaemasu ka?] Can I use my own laptop here?

ラッシュアワー [rasshuawaa] *n* rush hour

ラスク [rasuku] *n* zwieback toast

裸体 [ratai] *n* nude; 裸体主義者 [rataishugisha] *n* nudist

ラテンアメリカ [ratenamerika] *n* Latin America

ラテンアメリカの [ratenamerika no] *adj* Latin American

ラテン語 [ratengo] *n* Latin

ラトビア [ratobia] *n* Latvia

ラトビア語 [ratobia go] *n* Latvian *(language)*

ラトビア人 [ratobiajin] *n* Latvian *(person)*

ラトビアの [ratobia no] *adj* Latvian

ラウンジ [raunji] *n* family room; 通過ラウンジ [tsuuka raunji] *n* transit lounge; 出発ラウンジ [shuppatsu raunji] *n* departure lounge

ラズベリー [razuberii] *n* raspberry

レバー [rebaa] *n* (操作ハンドル) lever

レバノン [rebanon] *n* Lebanon

レバノン人 [rebanonjin] *n* Lebanese *(person)*

レバノンの [rebanon no] *adj* Lebanese

レーダー [reedaa] *n* radar

レーサー [reesaa] *n* racer

レーシングドライバー [reeshingudoraibaa] *n* racecar driver

レーシングカー [reeshingukaa] *n* racecar

レース [reesu] *n* (競争) race *(contest)*, (布) lace

レーストラック [reesutorakku] *n* racetrack

レート [reeto] *n* rate; 為替レート [kawase reeto] *n* exchange rate, foreign-exchange rate; 為替レートはいくらですか? [kawase-reeto wa ikura desu ka?] What's the exchange rate?; …を…に替える為替レートはいくらですか? [... o... ni kaeru kawase-reeto wa ikura desu ka?] What is the rate for... to...?

レーザー [reezaa] *n* laser

レーズン [reezun] *n* raisin

レフェリー [referii] *n* referee

レギングス [regingusu] *n* leggings

例 [rei] *n* example

零 [rei] *n* nothing, zero

霊廟 [reibyou] *n* shrine

例外 [reigai] *n* exception; 例外的な [reigaiteki na] *adj* exceptional

礼拝 [reihai] 礼拝する [reihai suru] *v* worship

礼拝堂 [reihaidou] *n* chapel

冷却水 [reikyakusui] *n* coolant

レインコート [reinkooto] *n* raincoat

レイプ [reipu] *n* rape *(sexual attack)*; レイプする [reipu suru] *v* canola; 私はレイプされました [watashi wa reipu saremashita] I've been raped

冷凍庫 [reitouko] *n* freezer

レイヨウ [reiyou] *n* antelope

冷蔵庫 [reizouko] *n* fridge, refrigerator

レジャー [rejaa] レジャーセンター [rejaasen-taa] *n* leisure center

レジ [reji] *n* cash register

レジスターオフィス [rejisutaaofisu] *n* county

clerk's office

歴史 [rekishi] *n* history; 歴史上の [rekishijou no] *adj* historical; 歴史家 [rekishika] *n* historian

レッカー [rekkaa] レッカー移動する [rekkaa idou suru] *v* tow away; レッカー車を手配してもらえますか? [rekkaa-sha o tehai shite moraemasu ka?] Could you send a tow truck?

レッカー車 [rekkaasha] *n* tow truck

レモン [remon] *n* lemon; レモン入りで [remon-iri de] with lemon

レモネード [remoneedo] *n* lemonade; コップ一杯のレモネードをください [koppu ippai no remoneedo o kudasai] A glass of lemonade, please

レモンゼスト [remonzesuto] *n* lemon zest

恋愛 [ren-ai] *n* love

煉瓦 [renga] *n* brick; 煉瓦職人 [renga shokunin] *n* bricklayer

連合 [rengou] 欧州連合 [OUshuu Rengou] *n* European Union; 国際連合 [kokusairengou] *n* UN

レンジ [renji] 料理用レンジ [ryouri you renji] *n* stove

連盟 [renmei] *n* league

連絡 [renraku] *n* contact; 連絡を取る [renraku-o toru] *v* contact; どこであなたに連絡を取れますか? [doko de anata ni renraku o toremasu ka?] Where can I contact you?; 問題があったときに誰に連絡すればいいのですか? [mondai ga atta toki ni dare ni renraku sureba ii no desu ka?] Who do we contact if there are problems?

練習 [renshuu] *n* practice; 練習する [renshuu suru] *v* practice

連隊 [rentai] *n* regiment

レンタカー [rentakaa] *n* car rental, rental car, rented car

レンタル [rentaru] *n* rental

レンタルDVD [rentaru dvd] レンタルDVDはありますか? [rentaru dii-vui-dii wa arimasu ka?] Do you have DVDs for rent?

連続 [renzoku] *n* round (series); 連続する [renzoku suru] *adj* successive; 連続もの [renzokumono] *n* serial; 連続的な [renzokuteki na] *adj* consecutive, continuous

レンズ [renzu] *n* lens; コンタクトレンズ [kontakutorenzu] *n* contact lenses; ズームレンズ [zuumurenzu] *n* zoom lens

レオタード [reotaado] *n* leotard

レパートリー [repaatorii] レパートリー劇団 [repaatorii gekidan] *n* representative

レプリカ [repurika] *n* replica

レシート [reshiito] *n* receipt; レシートをください [reshiito o kudasai] I need a receipt, please; 私は保険請求のためにレシートが必要です [watashi wa hoken-seikyuu no tame ni reshiito ga hitsuyou desu] I need a receipt for the insurance

列車 [ressha] *n* train

レッスン [ressun] *n* lesson; スキーのレッスンを企画していますか? [sukii no ressun o kikaku shite imasu ka?] Do you organise skiing lessons?; スノーボードのレッスンを企画していますか? [sunooboodo no ressun o kikaku shite imasu ka?] Do you organise snowboarding lessons?; レッスンを実施していますか? [ressun o jisshi shite imasu ka?] Do you give lessons?; レッスンを受けられますか? [ressun o ukeraremasu ka?] Can we take lessons?

レスラー [resuraa] *n* wrestler

レスリング [resuringu] *n* wrestling

レストラン [resutoran] *n* restaurant; ここにベジタリアン用のレストランはありますか? [koko ni bejitarian-you no resutoran wa arimasu ka?] Are there any vegetarian restaurants here?; よいレストランを教えてもらえますか? [yoi resutoran o oshiete moraemasu ka?] Can you recommend a good restaurant?; キャンプ場にレストランはありますか? [kyanpu-jou ni resutoran wa arimasu ka?] Is there a restaurant on the campsite?

レタス [retasu] *n* lettuce

R

列 [retsu] n line, rank (line), row (line); 列を作る [retsu wo tsukuru] v wait in line; ここが列の最後ですか? [koko ga retsu no saigo desu ka?] Is this the end of the line?

リベート [ribeeto] n rebate

リベラル [riberaru] リベラルな [riberaru na] adj liberal

リベリア [riberia] n Liberia

リベリア人 [riberiajin] n Liberian (person)

リベリアの [riberia no] adj Liberian

リビア [ribia] n Libya

リビア人 [ribiajin] n Libyan (person)

リビアの [ribia no] adj Libyan

リボン [ribon] n ribbon

リボルバー [riborubaa] n revolver

利益 [rieki] n (もうけ) benefit; 利益を得る [rieki wo eru] v benefit

リフト [rifuto] スキー場のリフト [sukii jou no rifuto] n ski lift

理学 [rigaku] 理学療法 [rigaku ryouhou] n physiotherapy; 理学療法士 [rigaku ryouhoushi] n physiotherapist

リハーサル [rihaasaru] n rehearsal; リハーサルをする [rihaasaru-o suru] v rehearse

リヒテンシュタイン [rihitenshutain] n Liechtenstein

リーダー [riidaa] n leader

リードシンガー [riidoshingaa] n lead singer

リーフレット [riifuretto] n leaflet; リーフレットはありますか? [riifuretto wa arimasu ka?] Do you have any brochures?; 英語のリーフレットはありますか? [eigo no riifuretto wa arimasu ka?] Do you have a brochure in English?; ···に関するリーフレットはありますか? [... ni kansuru riifuretto wa arimasu ka?] Do you have any brochures on...?

リール [riiru] n reel

理解 [rikai] n comprehension; 理解する [rikai suru] v understand; 理解できる [rikai dekiru] adj understandable; 十分に理解する [juubun ni rikai suru] v realize

利己 [riko] 利己的な [rikoteki na] adj selfish

離婚 [rikon] n divorce; 私は離婚しています [watashi wa rikon shite imasu] I'm divorced

離婚する [rikon suru] 離婚した [rikonshita] adj divorced

リコーダー [rikoodaa] n recorder (music)

利口 [rikou] 利口な [rikou na] adj intelligent

陸 [riku] n land

陸上 [rikujou] 陸上競技 [rikujou kyougi] n track-and-field

リクライニング式 [rikurainingu shiki] リクライニング式の [rikurainingu shiki no] adj reclining

リキュール [rikyuuru] n liqueur; どんなリキュールがありますか? [donna rikyuuru ga arimasu ka?] What liqueurs do you have?

リメイク [rimeiku] n remake

リモコン [rimokon] n remote control

リムジン [rimujin] n limousine

りんご [ringo] りんご酒 [ringoshu] n hard cider

リンゴ [ringo] n apple

リングバインダー [ringubaindaa] n ring binder

理にかなう [ri ni kanau] 理にかなって [ri ni kanatte] adv reasonably; 理にかなった [ri ni kanatta] adj reasonable

臨時 [rinji] 臨時代理の [rinji dairi no] adj acting; 臨時教員 [rinji kyouin] n substitute teacher; 臨時職員 [rinjishokuin] n temp

リンク [rinku] スケートリンク [sukeetorinku] n ice rink

リノリウム [rinoriumu] n linoleum

倫理 [rinri] 倫理的な [rinriteki na] adj ethical

立方 [rippou] 立方の [rippou no] adj cubic

立方体 [rippoutai] n cube

履歴書 [rirekisho] n résumé, CV

離陸 [ririku] n takeoff

利率 [riritsu] n interest rate

理論 [riron] n theory

リサイクル [risaikuru] n recycling

利息 [risoku] n interest (income)

理想 [risou] 理想的な [risouteki na] adj ideal; 理想的に [risouteki ni] adv ideally

立証 [risshou] 立証する [risshou suru] v

argue, demonstrate, prove

リス [risu] n squirrel

リトアニア [ritoania] n Lithuania

リトアニア語 [ritoania go] n Lithuanian (*language*)

リトアニア人 [ritoaniajin] n Lithuanian (*person*)

リトアニアの [ritoania no] *adj* Lithuanian

利得 [ritoku] n gain

率 [ritsu] 関税率 [kanzeiritsu] n tariff

率的 [ritsu teki] 効率的に [kouritsuteki ni] *adv* efficiently

立体 [rittai] 立体的な [rittaiteki na] *adj* three-dimensional

リットル [rittoru] n liter

リウマチ [riumachi] n rheumatism

利用 [riyou] n use; 自動車の道路利用税 [jidousha no douro riyou zei] n highway tax; 再生利用する [saisei riyou suru] v recycle; 利用する [riyou suru] v exploit; 利用できる [riyou dekiru] *adj* available

利用者 [riyousha] インターネット利用者 [intaanetto riyousha] n Internet user

理由 [riyuu] n cause (*reason*), reason

リズム [rizumu] n rhythm

炉 [ro] 原子炉 [genshiro] n reactor

ロバ [roba] n donkey

ロビー [robii] ロビーでお会いしましょう [robii de o-ai shimashou] I'll meet you in the lobby

ロボット [robotto] n robot

ロブスター [robusutaa] n lobster

ロゴ [rogo] n logo

ログアウト [roguauto] ログアウトする [roguauto suru] v log out

ログイン [roguin] ログインする [roguin suru] v log in

ログオフ [roguofu] ログオフする [roguofu suru] v log off

ログオン [roguon] ログオンする [roguon suru] v log on; 1時間ログオンするのにいくらですか？ [ichi-jikan roguon suru no ni ikura desu ka?] How much does it cost to log on for

an hour?; ログオンできません [roguon dekimasen] I can't log on

路地 [roji] n alley

濾過 [roka] 濾過する [roka suru] v filter

濾過器 [rokaki] n filter

路肩 [rokata] n hard shoulder

ロケット [roketto] n locket, rocket

ロッカー [rokkaa] n locker; コインロッカー [koinrokkaa] n luggage locker; どれが私のロッカーですか？ [dore ga watashi no rokkaa desu ka?] Which locker is mine?; 服のロッカーはどこですか？ [fuku no rokkaa wa doko desu ka?] Where are the clothes lockers?

ロッキングチェア [rokkinguchea] n rocking chair

肋骨 [rokkotsu] n rib

ロック [rokku] n lock; ドアをロックしておいてください [doa o rokku shite oite kudasai] Keep the door locked; ロックをください [rokku o kudasai] May I have a lock?

ロッククライミング [rokkukuraimingu] n rock climbing

露骨 [rokotsu] 露骨な [rokotsu na] *adj* blatant

六 [roku] *number* six; 六番目の [roku banme no] *adj* sixth

六月 [rokugatsu] n June; 六月の終わりに [roku-gatsu no owari ni] at the end of June; 六月の初めに [roku-gatsu no hajime ni] at the beginning of June; 六月いっぱい [roku-gatsu ippai] all through June; 六月十五日の月曜日です [roku-gatsu juugo-nichi no getsuyoubi desu] It's Monday, June fifteenth

六時 [rokuji] 六時です [roku-ji desu] It's six o'clock

六十 [rokujuu] *number* sixty

録音 [rokuon] n recording

ロマンチックな [romanchikku na] *adj* romantic

ロマネスク [romanesuku] ロマネスク様式の [Romanesuku youshiki no] *adj* Romanesque

路面 [romen] 路面電車 [romendensha] n
streetcar

ロンドン [rondon] n London

論評 [ronpyou] n comment; 論評する
[ronpyou suru] v comment

論理 [ronri] 論理的な [ronriteki na] adj logical

論争 [ronsou] 論争の [ronsou no] adj
controversial

論点 [ronten] n issue

ロードマップ [roodomappu] n road map

ローマ [rooma] ローマの [rooma no] adj
Roman

ローマカトリック [roomakatorikku] ローマカト
リック教会の [Rooma Katorikku kyoukai no]
adj Roman Catholic; ローマカトリック教徒
[Rooma Katorikku kyouto] n Roman
Catholic

ローンドレット® [roondoretto] n Laundro-
mat®

ロープ [roopu] n rope; 洗濯ロープ [sentaku
roopu] n clothesline

ローラー [rooraa] n roller

ローラーコースター [rooraakoosutaa] n
roller coaster

ローラースケート [rooraasukeeto] n
rollerskating; ローラースケート靴 [rooraa
sukeeto kutsu] n rollerskates

ローリエ [roorie] n bay leaf

ロールパン [roorupan] n roll

ローション [rooshon] n lotion; アフターサンロ
ーション [afutaasan rooshon] n aftersun
lotion; アフターシェーブローション
[afutaasheeburooshon] n aftershave

ロースクール [roosukuuru] n law school

ローズマリー [roozumarii] n rosemary

路線 [rosen] n route

ロシア [roshia] n Russia; ロシア人 [roshiajin]
n Russian (person); ロシアの [roshia no] adj
Russian; ロシア語 [roshiago] n Russian
(language)

聾 [rou] 耳を聾するような [mimi-o rousuru you
na] adj deafening

蝋 [rou] n wax

狼狽 [roubai] 狼狽した [roubai shita] adj
upset

労働 [roudou] n labor, work; 労働体験
[roudou taiken] n work experience; 労働許
可証 [roudou kyokashou] n work permit; 労
働組合 [roudoukumiai] n labor union; 労働
組合主義者 [roudoukumiai shugisha] n
union member; 労働力 [roudouryoku] n
manpower

労働者 [roudousha] n laborer; 肉体労働者
[nikutairoudousha] n workman; 炭坑労働者
[tankou roudousha] n miner; 労働者階級の
[roudoushakaikyuu no] adj working-class

浪費 [rouhi] n waste; 浪費する [rouhi suru] v
squander, waste

老人 [roujin] adj 老人ホーム [roujin hoomu] n
nursing home; 老人病患者 [roujinbyou
kanja] n geriatric; 老人病学の [roujinbyou-
gaku no] adj geriatric

廊下 [rouka] n corridor; 入口の廊下 [iriguchi
no rouka] n hall

老齢年金 [roureinenkin] 老齢年金受給者
[rourei nenkin jukyuusha] n old-age
pensioner

老練 [rouren] 老練な [rouren na] adj veteran;
老練な人 [rouren na hito] n veteran

ろうそく [rousoku] n candle

ろうそく立て [rousokutate] n candlestick

ロゼワイン [rozewain] n rosé; よいロゼワイン
を教えてもらえますか? [yoi roze-wain o
oshiete moraemasu ka?] Can you
recommend a good rosé wine?

ルバーブ [rubaabu] n rhubarb

類 [rui] 機械類 [kikairui] n machinery; 宝石類
[housekirui] n jewelry

類似 [ruiji] n resemblance, similarity; 類似し
た [ruiji shita] adj similar

ルクセンブルク [rukusenburuku] n
Luxembourg

留守番 [rusuban] 留守番電話 [rusubandenwa]
n answering machine

ルーフラック [ruufurakku] n roof rack

ルーマニア [ruumania] n Romania; ルーマニ

ア人 [ruumaniajin] n Romanian *(person)*; ルーマニア語 [ruumaniago] n Romanian *(language)*; ルーマニアの [ruumania no] *adj* Romanian

ルーム [ruumu] ダイニングルーム [dainingu ruumu] n dining room; ダブルルーム [dabururuumu] n double room; チャットルーム [chatto ruumu] n chatroom

ルームメート [ruumumeeto] n roommate

ルームサービス [ruumusaabisu] n room service; ルームサービスはありますか? [ruumu-saabisu wa arimasu ka?] Is there room service?

ルーレット [ruuretto] n roulette

ルート [ruuto] n route

略語 [ryakugo] n abbreviation

旅行 [ryokou] n journey, tour, travel, traveling, trip; パック旅行 [pakku ryokou] n vacation package; 旅行代理店 [ryokoudairiten] n travel agency; 旅行保険 [ryokou hoken] n travel insurance; 旅行する [ryokou suru] v tour; 旅行業 [ryokou gyou] n tourism; 旅行業者 [ryokougyousha] n tour operator, travel agent; 旅行者 [ryokousha] n tourist, traveler; 旅行者用小切手 [ryokousha you kogitte] n traveler's check; 徒歩旅行 [tohoryokou] n hike *(long walk)*; 大型の旅行かばん [ougata no ryokou kaban] n duffel bag; よいご旅行を! [yoi go-ryokou o!] Have a good trip!; 私は一人で旅行しています [watashi wa hitori de ryokou shite imasu] I'm traveling alone; 私は旅行保険に入っていません [watashi wa ryoko-hoken ni haitte imasen] I don't have travel insurance; ・・・への旅行はこれが初めてです [... e no ryokou wa kore ga hajimete desu] This is my first trip to...

緑色 [ryokushoku] n green; 緑色の [midori iro no] *adj* green *(color)*

旅程 [ryotei] n itinerary

料 [ryou] n fee; サービス料 [saabisuryou] n service charge; 授業料 [jugyouryou] n tuition fees; 賃貸料 [chintairyou] n rent; 調味料 [choumiryou] n seasoning; 甘味料 [kanmiryou] n sweetener; 送金料がかかりますか? [soukin-ryou ga kakarimasu ka?] Is there a transfer charge?

量 [ryou] n amount, quantity; 量を決める [ryou-o kimeru] v quantify

両替 [ryougae] 外貨両替所 [gaika ryougaesho] n currency exchange counter; どこでお金を両替できますか? [doko de o-kane o ryougae dekimasu ka?] Where can I exchange some money?; ここに外貨両替所はありますか? [koko ni gaika ryougae-jo wa arimasu ka?] Is there a foreign exchange counter here?; 百・・・を・・・に両替したいのですが [hyaku... o... ni ryougae shitai no desu ga] I'd like to exchange a hundred... for...; 私は外貨両替所をさがしています [watashi ha gaikaryougae tokoro wosagashiteimasu] I need to find a place to exchange money; ・・・を・・・に両替したいのですが [... o... ni ryougae shitai no desu ga] I want to exchange some... for...

両替所 [ryougaejo] その外貨両替所はいつ開きますか? [sono gaika ryougae-jo wa itsu hirakimasu ka?] When is the foreign exchange counter open?

両方 [ryouhou] *pron* both; 両方の [ryouhou no] *adj* both

療法 [ryouhou] n therapy; 理学療法 [rigaku ryouhou] n physiotherapy; 理学療法士 [rigaku ryouhoushi] n physiotherapist; 心理療法 [shinri ryouhou] n psychotherapy

領事 [ryouji] n consul

領事館 [ryoujikan] n consulate

了見 [ryouken] 了見の狭い [ryouken no semai] *adj* narrow-minded

料金 [ryoukin] n charge *(price)*, fee; 追加料金 [tsuikaryoukin] n surcharge; 郵便料金 [yuubin ryoukin] n postage; 予約料金がかかりますか? [yoyaku-ryoukin ga kakarimasu ka?] Is there a service charge to pay?; サービスに料金がかかりますか? [saabisu ni

R

ryoukin ga kakarimasu ka?] Is there a charge for the service?; 走行距離に対して料金がかかりますか? [soukou-kyori ni taishite ryoukin ga kakarimasu ka?] Is there a mileage charge?

領空 [ryoukuu] n airspace

料理 [ryouri] n cooking; カレー料理 [karee ryouri] n curry; 料理の本 [ryouri no hon] n cookbook; 料理用レンジ [ryouri you renji] n stove; 料理する [ryouri suru] v cook

料理法 [ryourihou] n cookery

料理人 [ryourinin] n cook

両立 [ryouritsu] 両立できる [ryouritsu dekiru]

adj compatible

漁師 [ryoushi] n fisherman

両親 [ryoushin] n parents

良心 [ryoushin] n conscience; 良心の呵責 [ryoushin no kashaku] n remorse

リュックサック [ryukkusakku] n backpack

竜 [ryuu] n dragon

流暢 [ryuuchou] 流暢な [ryuuchou na] adj fluent

流行 [ryuukou] n fashion; 流行の [ryuukou no] adj fashionable

流行病 [ryuukoubyou] n epidemic

流産 [ryuuzan] n miscarriage

S

サーバー [saabaa] n server (computer)

サービス [saabisu] n service; サービスを提供
する [saabisu-o teikyou suru] v service; サー
ビス料 [saabisuryou] n service charge; イン
ターネットサービスプロバイダ [intaanetto
saabisu purobaida] n ISP; 番号案内サービス
[bangou annai saabisu] n directory
assistance; サービスに料金がかかりますか?
[saabisu ni ryoukin ga kakarimasu ka?] Is
there a charge for the service?; サービスが
ひどかったです [saabisu ga hidokatta desu]
The service was terrible; 故障時緊急修理
サービスを呼んでください [koshou-ji
kinkyuu-shuuri-saabisu o yonde kudasai]
Call the breakdown service, please; 託児
サービスはありますか? [takuji saabisu wa arimasu ka?] Is there childcare service?; 私
はサービスについて苦情があります [watashi
wa saabisu ni tsuite kujou ga arimasu] I
want to complain about the service

サービスエリア [saabisu eria] n service area

サービス料 [saabisuryou] サービス料は入って
いますか? [saabisu-ryou wa haitte imasu
ka?] Is service included?

サーブ [saabu] n serve

サーディン [saadein] n sardine

サーファー [saafaa] n surfer

サーフィン [saafin] n surfing; サーフィンをす
る [saafin-o suru] v surf; どこでサーフィンが
できますか? [doko de saafin ga dekimasu
ka?] Where can you go surfing?

サーフボード [saafuboodo] n surfboard

サーカス [saakasu] n circus

サーモス® [saamosu] n thermos

サーモスタット [saamosutatto] n thermostat

サバ [saba] n mackerel

砂漠 [sabaku] n desert; サハラ砂漠 [sahara
sabaku] n Sahara

差別 [sabetsu] n discrimination; 人種差別
[jinshusabetsu] n racism; 性差別主義
[seisabetsu shugi] n sexism; 性差別主義の
[seisabetsu shugi no] adj sexist

さび [sabi] n (腐食) rust

さびる [sabiru] さびた [sabita] adj rusty

サボる [saboru] v play hooky; 仕事をサボる
[shigoto-o saboru] v avoid work

サボテン [saboten] n cactus

定める [sadameru] v set; 形式を定める
[keishiki-o sadameru] v format

サドル [sadoru] n saddle

サドルバッグ [sadorubaggu] n saddlebag

さえ [sae] ···でさえ [... de sae] adv even

さえない [saenai] v drab

サファイア [safaia] n sapphire

サファリ [safari] n safari

サフラン [safuran] n saffron

砂岩 [sagan] n sandstone

下がる [sagaru] v go down; 後ろに下がる
[ushiro ni sagaru] v move back

捜す [sagasu] v seek

探す [sagasu] 私は警察署をさがしています
[watashi ha keisatsusho wosagashiteimasu]
I need to find a police station; 私は外貨両
替所をさがしています [watashi ha
gaikaryougae tokoro wosagashiteimasu] I
need to find a place to exchange money;
私たちはアパートメントを探しています
[watashi-tachi wa apaatomento o sagashite
imasu] We're looking for an apartment; 私
たちは···を探しています [watashi-tachi wa...

o sagashite imasu] We're looking for...
探す [sagasu] 私はスーパーマーケットをさが
しています [watashi ha suupaamaaketto
wosagashiteimasu] I need to find a
supermarket

さがす [sagasu] v find; ···をさがす [...-o
sagasu] v look for

下げる [sageru] v lower

サギ [sagi] n (鳥) heron

詐欺 [sagi] n fraud, scam

詐欺師 [sagishi] n cheat

作業 [sagyou] n operation (undertaking); 作
業スペース [sagyou supeesu] n workspace;
作業要員 [sagyou youin] n workforce

左派 [saha] 左派の [saha no] adj left-wing

サハラ [sahara] サハラ砂漠 [sahara sabaku] n
Sahara

再 [sai] pref re-; 再使用する [saishiyou suru] v
reuse; 再編成する [saihensei suru] v
reorganize, restructure; 再受験する
[saijuken suru] v retake

最悪 [saiaku] 最悪の [saiaku no] adj worst

サイバー [saibaa] サイバー犯罪 [saibaa
hanzai] n cybercrime

サイバーカフェ [saibaakafe] n cybercafé

裁判 [saiban] n trial; 裁判官 [saibankan] n
judge

細胞 [saibou] n cell

細部 [saibu] n detail

最大 [saidai] 最大の [saidai no] adj maximum

最大限 [saidaigen] n maximum

祭壇 [saidan] n altar

サイドミラー [saidomiraa] n side-view
mirror

サイドランプ [saidoranpu] ベッドサイドランプ
[beddosaido ranpu] n bedside lamp

サイエンスフィクション [saiensu fikushon] n
sci-fi, science fiction

財布 [saifu] n coin purse, wallet; 私は財布を
なくしました [watashi wa saifu o nakushi-
mashita] I've lost my wallet; 私の財布が盗
まれました [watashi no saifu ga nusumare-
mashita] My wallet has been stolen

災害 [saigai] n disaster; 大災害の [daisaigai
no] adj disastrous

最後 [saigo] 最後に [saigo ni] adv last, lastly;
最後の [saigo no] adj last; 最後通牒 [saigo
tsuuchou] n ultimatum

裁縫 [saihou] n sewing

祭日 [saijitsu] 聖バレンタインの祭日 [sei
barentain no saijitsu] n Valentine's Day; 祝
祭日 [shukusaijitsu] n public holiday

最盛 [saijou] 最盛期 [saiseiki] n peak season

再会 [saikai] n reunion

再開 [saikai] 再開する [saikai suru] v renew,
resume

再建 [saiken] 再建する [saiken suru] v
rebuild

細菌 [saikin] n germ

最近 [saikin] adv lately, recently; 最近の
[saikin no] adj recent

再婚 [saikon] 再婚する [saikon suru] v
remarry

さいころ [saikoro] n dice

最高 [saikou] 最高機密の [saikou kimitsu no]
adj top-secret; 最高経営責任者 [saikou keiei
sekininsha] n CEO

サイクリング [saikuringu] n cycling; サイクリン
グに行きましょう [saikuringu ni ikimashou]
Let's go cycling; 私たちはサイクリングに行き
たいのですが [watashi-tachi wa saikuringu ni
ikitai no desu ga] We'd like to go cycling

サイクリスト [saikurisuto] n cyclist

サイクロン [saikuron] n cyclone

サイクル [saikuru] サイクルパス [saikuru pasu]
n bicycle path; この地域のサイクルマップは
ありますか? [kono chiiki no saikuru-mappu
wa arimasu ka?] Is there a cycle map of
this area?

サイクルレーン [saikurureen] n bicycle lane

サイン [sain] n autograph

最年長 [sainenchou] 最年長の [sainenchou
no] adj eldest

才能 [sainou] n talent; 才能のある [sainou no
aru] adj talented; 生まれつき才能のある
[umaretsuki sainou no aru] adj gifted

サイレン [sairen] *n* siren

催涙 [sairui] 催涙ガス [sairuigasu] *n* tear gas

再生 [saisei] *n* replay; 再生する [saisei suru] *v* replay; 再生利用する [saisei riyou suru] *v* recycle

採石 [saiseki] 採石場 [saisekijou] *n* quarry

最新 [saishin] 最新の [saishin no] *adj* up-to-date; 最新設備 [saishin setsubi] *n* modern conveniences

最初 [saisho] *n* outset; 最初に [saisho ni] *adv* first, initially; 最初の [saisho no] *adj* first, original; 最初の [saisho no] *adj* initial; 最初のもの [saisho no mono] *n* first

最小 [saishou] 最小の [saishou no] *adj* minimum

最小限 [saishougen] *n* minimum; 最小限の [saishougen no] *adj* minimal; 最小限度にする [saishougendo ni suru] *v* minimize

最終 [saishuu] 最終の [saishuu no] *adj* final; 最終的な [saishuuteki na] *adj* ultimate; 最終的に [saishuuteki ni] *adv* ultimately; 最終のバスは何時ですか? [saishuu no basu wa nan-ji desu ka?] What time is the last bus?; 最終の船は何時ですか? [saishuu no fune wa nan-ji desu ka?] When is the last boat?; ・・・へ行く最終のバスは何時ですか? [... e iku saishuu no basu wa nan-ji desu ka?] When is the last bus to...?; ・・・へ行く最終の電車は何時ですか? [... e iku saishuu no densha wa nan-ji desu ka?] When is the last train to...?

裁定 [saitei] 裁定委員会 [saitei iinkai] *n* tribunal

採点 [saiten] 採点する [saiten suru] *v* grade

サイト [saito] テント用のサイトが欲しいのですが [tento-you no saito ga hoshii no desu ga] We'd like a site for a tent

サイズ [saizu] *n* measurements, size; 中サイズの [naka saizu no] *adj* medium-sized; これの大きなサイズはありますか? [kore no ooki-na saizu wa arimasu ka?] Do you have this in a larger size?; これの小さなサイズはありますか? [kore no chiisa-na saizu wa arimasu ka?] Do you have this in a smaller size?; 私のサイズは十六号です [watashi no saizu wa jyuuroku-gou desu] I'm a size twelve

坂 [saka] *n* slope

魚 [sakana] *n* fish; 魚を捕る [sakana-o toru] *v* fish; 魚釣り [sakana tsuri] *n* fishing; 魚屋 [sakanaya] *n* fish dealer; 私はこの魚をいただきます [watashi wa kono sakana o itadakimasu] I'll have the fish; 私は魚を食べません [watashi wa sakana o tabemasen] I don't eat fish; 魚は生鮮品ですか、それとも冷凍品ですか? [sakana wa seisen-hin desu ka, sore tomo reitou-hin desu ka?] Is the fish fresh or frozen?; 魚を使わずに食事を用意していただけますか? [sakana o tsukawazu ni shokuji o youi shite itadakemasu ka?] Could you prepare a meal without fish?; これは魚のストックで料理してありますか? [kore wa sakana no sutokku de ryouri shite arimasu ka?] Is this cooked in fish stock?

魚料理 [sakanaryouri] *n* fish dish; どんな魚料理がありますか? [donna sakana-ryouri ga arimasu ka?] What fish dishes do you have?

魚を釣る人 [sakana wo tsuru hito] *n* fisherman

坂の上 [saka no ue] 坂の上へ [saka no ue-e] *adv* uphill

逆さま [sakasama] 逆さまに [sakasama ni] *adv* upside down

酒 [sake] *n* rice wine, liquor; りんご酒 [ringoshu] *n* hard cider

サケ [sake] *n* (魚) salmon

叫び [sakebi] *n* shout

叫ぶ [sakebu] *v* shout, yell

避ける [sakeru] *v* avoid; さっと身をかわして避ける [satto mi-o kawashite sakeru] *v* dodge; 避けられない [sakerarenai] *adj* inevitable, unavoidable

作家 [sakka] *n* writer

サッカー [sakkaa] *n* soccer; サッカーをしましょ

S

う [sakkaa o shimashou] Let's play soccer; 私はサッカーの試合が観たいのですが [watashi wa sakkaa no shiai ga mitai no desu ga] I'd like to see a soccer game

錯覚 [sakkaku] n illusion

殺菌 [sakkin] 低温殺菌した [teion sakkin shita] adj pasteurized; 殺菌剤 [sakkinzai] n antiseptic; 超高温殺菌牛乳 [choukouon sakkin gyuunyuu] n UHT-treated milk

作曲 [sakkyoku] 作曲家 [sakkyokuka] n composer

鎖骨 [sakotsu] n collarbone

柵 [saku] n barrier, fence

鑿 [saku] n chisel

咲く [saku] 花が咲く [hana ga saku] v blossom, flower

索引 [sakuin] n index (list)

削除 [sakujo] 削除する [sakujo suru] v delete

サクランボ [sakuranbo] n cherry

サクラソウ [sakurasou] n primrose

策略 [sakuryaku] n trick

作成 [sakusei] n プログラム作成 [puroguramu sakusei] n programming; プログラムを作成 する [puroguramu-o sakusei suru] v program; このコンピューターでCDを作成でき ますか? [kono konpyuutaa de shii-dii o sakusei dekimasu ka?] Can I make CDs at this computer?

搾取 [sakushu] n exploitation

サクソフォーン [sakusofoon] n saxophone

昨夜 [sakuya] last night

砂丘 [sakyuu] n sand dune

さま [sama] どちらさまでしょうか? [dochira-sama deshou ka?] Who am I talking to?, Who's calling?

妨げる [samatageru] 妨げ [samatage] n setback

さまざま [samazama] さまざまな [samazama na] adj varied, various

サメ [same] n shark

覚める [sameru] 目が覚める [me ga sameru] v awake, wake up

寒い [samui] adj chilly, cold; 今夜は寒くなり

ますか? [kon'ya wa samuku narimasu ka?] Will it be cold tonight?; 部屋が寒すぎます [heya ga samu-sugimasu] The room is too cold; 寒いです [samui desu] I'm cold

寒気 [samuke] 私は寒気がします [watashi wa samuke ga shimasu] I feel cold

寒さ [samusa] n cold

三 [san] number three; 三番目 [san banme] n third; 三番目の [san banme no] adj third; 第三世界 [dai san sekai] n Third World

酸 [san] n acid; 酸性雨 [sanseiu] n acid rain

三倍 [sanbai] 三倍にする [sanbai ni suru] v triple

賛美 [sanbi] 賛美歌 [sanbika] n hymn

産物 [sanbutsu] 主要産物 [shuyou sanbutsu] n staple (commodity)

散弾 [sandan] 散弾銃 [sandanjuu] n shotgun

サンダル [sandaru] n sandal; ビーチサンダル [biichi sandaru] n flip-flops

サンドイッチ [sandoicchi] n sandwich; どんな サンドイッチがありますか? [donna sandoitchi ga arimasu ka?] What kinds of sandwiches do you have?

サンドペーパー [sandopeepaa] n sandpaper

三月 [sangatsu] n March

珊瑚 [sango] n coral

サングラス [sangurasu] n sunglasses

産業 [sangyou] n industry; 産業の [sangyou no] adj industrial

三時 [sanji] 三時に [san-ji ni] at three o'clock; 三時です [san-ji desu] It's three o'clock

三十分 [sanjuppun] n half hour

三十 [sanjuu] number thirty

産科 [sanka] 産科病院 [sanka byouin] n maternity hospital

参加 [sanka] n participation; ストライキ参加 者 [sutoraiki sankasha] n striker; 参加する [sanka suru] v participate

三角形 [sankakkei] n triangle

参考 [sankou] n reference

サンクリーム [sankuriimu] n sunscreen

サンマリノ [sanmarino] n San Marino

山脈 [sanmyaku] n range *(mountains)*; カフカス山脈 [Kafukasu sanmyaku] n Caucasus; アンデス山脈 [andesu sanmyaku] n Andes; アルプス山脈 [arupusu sanmyaku] n Alps

散歩 [sanpo] n walk

散乱 [sanran] n mess

三輪車 [sanrinsha] n tricycle

サンルーフ [sanruufu] n sunroof

賛成 [sansei] n favor; 賛成する [sansei suru] v agree

酸性 [sansei] 酸性雨 [sanseiu] n acid rain

参照 [sanshou] 参照番号 [sanshou bangou] n reference number

酸素 [sanso] n oxygen

サンスクリーン [sansukuriin] n sunscreen

サンタンオイル [santan oiru] n suntan oil

サンタンローション [santanrooshon] n suntan lotion

さんざん [sanzan] さんざんな [sanzan na] adj devastating

サンザシ [sanzashi] n hawthorn

皿 [sara] n dish; 皿拭きをする [sarafuki-o suru] v wipe up

さらば! [saraba] excl farewell!

サラダ [sarada] n salad; グリーンサラダ [guriin sarada] n green salad; フルーツサラダ [furuutsusarada] n fruit salad

サラダドレッシング [saradadoresshingu] n salad dressing

サラミ [sarami] n salami

さらに [sara ni] adv further

さらに多く [sara ni ooku] adv more

さらす [sarasu] 危険にさらす [kiken ni sarasu] v risk

サル [saru] n monkey

去る [saru] 飛び去る [tobisaru] v fly away

支え [sasae] n support

支える [sasaeru] v (支持) bear, (支持) support

些細 [sasai] 些細な [sasai na] adj trivial

ささやく [sasayaku] v whisper

左遷 [sasen] 左遷する [sasen suru] v relegate

刺し穴 [sashiana] n puncture

挿絵 [sashie] n illustration

差し引く [sashihiku] v deduct

指し示す [sashishimesu] v point

誘い込む [sasoikomu] 人を誘い込む [hito-o sasoi komu] v rope in

サソリ [sasori] n scorpion

蠍座 [sasoriza] n Scorpio

誘う [sasou] v invite

早速 [sassoku] adv immediately; 早速の [sassoku no] adj immediate

刺す [sasu] v sting; チクリと刺す [chikuri to sasu] v prick; 刺し傷 [sashi kizu] n sting; 私は虫に刺されました [watashi wa mushi ni sasaremashita] I've been stung

差す [sasu] 人差し指 [hitosashi yubi] n index finger; 油を差す [abura-o sasu] (注油) v oil

里子 [satogo] n foster child

砂糖 [satou] n sugar; 砂糖を含まない [satou-o fukumanai] adj sugar-free; 粉砂糖 [konazatou] n confectioners' sugar; 砂糖なしで [satou nashi de] no sugar

撮影 [satsuei] 撮影する [satsuei suru] v photograph; 写真撮影 [shashinsatsuei] n photography

殺害 [satsugai] 殺害する [satsugai suru] v murder

殺人 [satsujin] n murder; 殺人者 [satsujin-sha] n murderer

殺人者 [satsujinsha] n killer

サウジアラビア [saujiarabia] n Saudi Arabia; サウジアラビア人 [Saujiarabia jin] n Saudi, Saudi Arabian *(person)*; サウジアラビアの [saujiarabia no] adj Saudi, Saudi Arabian

サウナ [sauna] n sauna

サウンドトラック [saundotorakku] n soundtrack

騒ぎ [sawagi] n racket

騒ぐ [sawagu] 大騒ぎ [ousawagi] n fuss

さわる [sawaru] さわると痛いところ [sawaru to itai tokoro] n sore

さわやかな [sawayaka na] adj refreshing

サヤエンドウ [sayaendou] n snow peas

サヤインゲン [saya ingen] *n* green beans

さよなら! [sayonara] *excl* bye!

作用 [sayou] 副作用 [fukusayou] *n* side effect; 反射作用 [hansha sayou] *n* reflex

さようなら [sayounara] Goodbye

さようなら! [sayounara] *excl* goodbye!

背骨 [sebone] *n* backbone

世代 [sedai] *n* generation

セダン [sedan] *n* sedan

セールス [seerusu] 電話セールス [denwa seerusu] *n* telemarketing

セールスマン [seerusuman] *n* salesman

セーター [seetaa] *n* sweater; とっくり襟のセーター [tokkuri eri no seetaa] *n* turtleneck sweater

性 [sei] *n* gender; 性差別主義 [seisabetsu shugi] *n* sexism; 性差別主義の [seisabetsu shugi no] *adj* sexist

姓 [sei] *n* family name

···製 [...sei] *n* brand

聖バレンタイン [seibarentain] 聖バレンタインの祭日 [sei barentain no saijitsu] *n* Valentine's Day

性別 [seibetsu] *n* sex

整備士 [seibishi] 自動車整備士 [jidousha seibishi] *n* auto mechanic

生物 [seibutsu] 生物分解性の [seibutsu bunkaisei no] *adj* biodegradable; 野生生物 [yaseiseibutsu] *n* wildlife

生物学 [seibutsugaku] *n* biology; 生物学の [seibutsugaku no] *adj* biological

生物測定 [seibutsusokutei] 生物測定の [seibutsu sokutei no] *adj* biometric

成長 [seichou] *n* growth

成長する [seichou suru] *vi* grow

声援 [seien] 声援する [seien suru] *v* cheer

政府 [seifu] *n* government

征服 [seifuku] 征服する [seifuku suru] *v* conquer

制服 [seifuku] *n* uniform; 学校の制服 [gakkou no seifuku] *n* school uniform

製粉所 [seifunjou] *n* mill

制限 [seigen] 年齢制限 [nenreiseigen] *n* age limit; 制限する [seigen suru] *v* restrict; 制限速度 [seigensokudo] *n* speed limit

制限速度 [seigensokudo] *n* speed limit; この道の制限速度はどうなっていますか? [kono michi no seigen-sokudo wa dou natte imasu ka?] What's the speed limit on this road?

正義 [seigi] *n* justice

制御 [seigyo] 無線制御の [musen seigyo no] *adj* radio-controlled

制御できない [seigyodekinai] *adj* uncontrollable

制御装置 [seigyosouchi] *npl* controls

正反対 [seihantai] *n* contrary

製品 [seihin] *n* product

正方形 [seihoukei] *n* square; 正方形の [seihoukei no] *adj* square

誠意 [seii] 誠意のない [seii no nai] *adj* insincere

政治 [seiji] *n* politics; 政治の [seiji no] *adj* political; 政治家 [seijika] *n* politician

成人 [seijin] *n* grown-up; 成人学生 [seijin gakusei] *n* adult learner

聖人 [seijin] *n* saint

清浄 [seijou] ユダヤ教の掟に従って料理された清浄な [Yudaya kyou no okite ni shitagatte ryouri sareta seijou na] *adj* kosher

成熟 [seijuku] 成熟した [seijuku shita] *adj* mature; 未成熟の [miseijuku no] *adj* immature

生化学 [seikagaku] *n* biochemistry

正確 [seikaku] *adj* accurate; 不正確な [fuseikaku na] *adj* inaccurate, incorrect; 正確な [seikaku na] *adj* accurate; 正確に [seikaku ni] *adv* accurately, exactly, precisely; 正確さ [seikakusa] *n* accuracy

正確な [seikaku na] *adj* exact, precise

聖歌隊 [seikatai] *n* choir

生活 [seikatsu] *n* living; キャンプ生活 [kyanpu seikatsu] *n* camping; 生活水準 [seikatsusuijun] *n* standard of living; 生活費 [seikatsuhi] *n* cost of living

清潔 [seiketsu] 清潔な [seiketsu na] *adj* clean

世紀 [seiki] *n* century

聖金曜日 [seikinyoubi] n Good Friday

性交 [seikou] n sexual intercourse

成功 [seikou] n success; 成功した [seikou shita] adj successful; 成功する [seikou suru] v succeed

請求 [seikyuu] 請求する [seikyuu suru] v charge (price); 過大請求する [kadai seikyuu suru] v overcharge; なぜそんなにたくさん請求するのですか? [naze sonna ni takusan seikyuu suru no desu ka?] Why are you charging me so much?; 私は余分に請求されています [watashi wa yobun ni seikyuu sarete imasu] I've been overcharged

請求書 [seikyuusho] n bill (account); 電話の請求書 [denwa no seikyuusho] n phone bill; 請求書の明細をもらえますか? [seikyuusho no meisai o moraemasu ka?] May I have an itemized bill?; 請求書が間違っています [seikyuusho ga machigatte imasu] The bill is wrong; 請求書を用意してください [seikyuusho o youi shite kudasai] Please prepare the bill

生命 [seimei] n life; 生命保険 [seimeihoken] n life insurance

声明 [seimei] n statement

西暦 [seireki] n AD

生理 [seiri] 生理用ナプキン [seiriyou napukin] n sanitary napkin

整理 [seiri] 整理だんす [seiridansu] n bureau

精力 [seiryoku] 精力的な [seiryokuteki na] adj energetic

制作 [seisaku] 制作依頼 [seisaku irai] n commission

生産 [seisan] n production; 生産する [seisan suru] v produce; 生産性 [seisansei] n productivity

精製 [seisei] 石油精製所 [sekiyu seiseijo] n oil refinery; 精製所 [seiseijo] n refinery

精子 [seishi] n sperm

正式 [seishiki] 正式の [seishiki no] adj formal

精神 [seishin] n spirit; 精神の [seishin no] adj mental; 精神構造 [seishin kouzou] n mentality; 精神病院 [seishinbyouin] n mental hospital; 精神的な [seishinteki na] adj spiritual; 精神科の [seishinka no] adj psychiatric; 精神科医 [seishinka-i] n psychiatrist; 精神安定剤 [seishin anteizai] n tranquilizer

聖書 [seisho] n Bible

聖職 [seishoku] n ministry (religion); 聖職者 [seishokusha] n minister (clergy)

青春 [seishun] 青春時代 [seishun jidai] n youth

盛装 [seisou] 盛装する [seisou suru] v dress up

精巣 [seisou] n testicle

清掃人 [seisounin] n cleaner

政体 [seitai] 共和政体 [kyouwa seitai] n republic

生態学 [seitaigaku] n ecology; 生態学の [seitaigaku no] adj ecological

制定 [seitei] 法律制定 [houritsu seitei] n legislation

性的 [seiteki] 性的な [seiteki na] adj sexual

生徒 [seito] n cadet, pupil (learner); 男子生徒 [danshiseito] n schoolboy; 女子生徒 [joshiseito] n schoolgirl

整頓 [seiton] 整頓する [seiton suru] v tidy up

正当 [seitou] 正当な [seitou na] adj valid; 正当化する [seitouka suru] v justify

精通 [seitsuu] ···に精通している [... ni seitsuu shiteiru] adj knowledgeable

セイウチ [seiuchi] n walrus

性欲 [seiyoku] n lust

セイヨウアブラナ [seiyouaburana] n rape (plant)

セイヨウヒイラギ [seiyouhiiragi] n holly

西洋ナシ [seiyounashi] n pear

セイヨウワサビ [seiyouwasabi] n horseradish

生存 [seizon] n survival; 生存者 [seizonsha] n survivor

製造 [seizou] n production; 製造する [seizou suru] v manufacture; 製造業者 [seizougyousha] n manufacturer; 製造工場 [seizou koujou] n plant (site/equipment)

聖像 [seizou] n icon

世界 [sekai] n world; 第三世界 [dai san sekai] n Third World

咳 [seki] n cough; 咳をする [seki-o suru] v cough; 咳止め薬 [sekidomegusuri] n cough syrup; 私は咳がでます [watashi wa seki ga demasu] I have a cough

席 [seki] 通路側の席 [tsuurogawa no seki] n aisle seat; この席には誰か座っていますか? [kono seki ni wa dare ka suwatte imasu ka?] Is this seat taken?; この席は空いています か? [kono seki wa aite imasu ka?] Is this seat free?; すみません、それは私の席です [sumimasen, sore wa watashi no seki desu] Excuse me, that's my seat; 進行方向に向い た席をお願いします [shinkou-houkou ni muita seki o o-negai shimasu] Facing the front, please

赤道 [sekidou] n equator; 赤道ギニア [Sekidou Ginia] n Equatorial Guinea

潟湖 [sekiko] n lagoon

赤面 [sekimen] n flush; 赤面する [sekimen suru] v blush, flush

責任 [sekinin] n fault, responsibility; 最高経 営責任者 [saikou keiei sekininsha] n CEO; 説明する責任がある [setsumei suru sekinin ga aru] adj accountable; それは私の責任で はありません [sore wa watashi no sekinin de wa arimasen] It wasn't my fault

責任がある [sekinin ga aru] adj responsible

セキセイインコ [sekiseiinko] n parakeet

積雪 [sekisetsu] ・・・へ行く道は積雪しています か? [... e iku michi wa sekisetsu shite imasu ka?] Is the road to... covered with snow?

石炭 [sekitan] n coal

脊椎 [sekitsui] n spine

石油 [sekiyu] 石油掘削装置 [sekiyu kussakusouchi] n oil rig; 石油精製所 [sekiyu seiseijo] n oil refinery

脊髄 [sekizui] n spinal cord

石灰 [sekkai] n lime (compound); 石灰岩 [sekkaigan] n limestone

せっかく [sekkaku] adv kindly

赤褐色 [sekkasshoku] 赤褐色の [akakass-hoku no] adj auburn

石鹸 [sekken] n soap; 石鹸入れ [sekken ire] n soap dish; 粉石鹸 [kona sekken] n laundry detergent; 石鹸がありません [sekken ga arimasen] There's no soap

接近 [sekkin] n access

説教 [sekkyou] n sermon

セクシー [sekushii] セクシーな [sekushii na] adj sexy

狭い [semai] adj narrow; 了見の狭い [ryouken no semai] adj narrow-minded

セメント [semento] n cement

責める [semeru] v blame

セミコロン [semikoron] n semicolon

線 [sen] n line; 地平線 [chiheisen] n horizon

栓 [sen] n plug

腺 [sen] n gland

千 [sen] number thousand; 千番目 [sen banme] n thousandth; 千番目の [sen banme no] adj thousandth

背中 [senaka] n back; 私は背中が痛みます [watashi wa senaka ga itamimasu] I have a bad back, My back is sore; 私は背中を痛め ました [watashi wa senaka o itamemashita] I've hurt my back

選抜 [senbatsu] 選抜候補者リスト [senbatsu kouhosha risuto] n short list

センチメートル [senchimeetoru] n centimeter

センチメンタル [senchimentaru] いやにセンチ メンタルな [iya ni senchimentaru na] adj schmaltzy

船長 [senchou] n captain

宣伝 [senden] n publicity

セネガル [senegaru] n Senegal; セネガル人 [Senegaru jin] n Senegalese (person); セネ ガルの [Senegaru no] adj Senegalese

繊維 [sen-i] n fiber; ガラス繊維 [garasu sen'i] n fiberglass

船員 [sen'in] n sailor

戦術 [senjutsu] n tactics

戦艦 [senkan] n battleship

閃光 [senkou] n flash

選挙 [senkyo] n election; 総選挙 [sousenkyo] n general election; 選挙する [senkyo suru] v elect; 選挙区 [senkyoku] n constituency

選挙人 [senkyonin] n electorate

宣教 [senkyou] 宣教師 [senkyoushi] n missionary

洗面 [senmen] 洗面用タオル [senmen you taoru] n washcloth; 洗面用具バッグ [senmen yougu baggu] n toiletries bag; 洗面用具入れ [senmen yougu ire] n cosmetics bag; 洗面化粧用品 [senmen keshou youhin] n toiletries; 洗面台 [senmendai] n sink

洗面台 [senmendai] 洗面台が汚れています [senmendai ga yogorete imasu] The sink is dirty

洗面器 [senmenki] n basin

洗面する [senmen suru] v freshen up

専門 [senmon] n specialty; 専門にする [senmon ni suru] v specialize; 専門技術 [senmon gijutsu] n technique; 専門技術者 [senmon gijutsusha] n technician; 専門的な [senmonteki na] adj technical; 専門家 [senmonka] n expert, professional, specialist

船内 [sennai] 船内にトイレはありますか? [sennai ni toire wa arimasu ka?] Is there a restroom on board?; 船内で何か食べられるところはありますか? [sennai de nani ka taberareru tokoro wa arimasu ka?] Is there somewhere to eat on the boat?

千年間 [sennenkan] n millennium

栓抜き [sennuki] n bottle-opener; コルク栓抜き [koruku sennuki] n corkscrew

先輩 [senpai] 先輩の [senpai no] adj senior

先夫 [senpu] n ex-husband

扇風機 [senpuuki] n fan; その部屋に扇風機はありますか? [sono heya ni senpuuki wa arimasu ka?] Does the room have a fan?

洗礼 [senrei] n baptism; 洗礼名 [senreimei] n christian name

先例 [senrei] 先例のない [senrei no nai] adj unprecedented

洗練 [senren] 洗練された [senren sareta] adj sophisticated

戦略 [senryaku] n strategy; 戦略的な [senryakuteki na] adj strategic

染料 [senryou] n dye

占領 [senryou] n occupation (invasion)

先妻 [sensai] n ex-wife

詮索 [sensaku] 詮索する [sensaku suru] v pry; 詮索好きな [sensaku zuki na] adj inquisitive, nosy

占星術 [senseijutsu] n astrology

戦車 [sensha] n tank (combat vehicle)

洗車 [sensha] 洗車機 [senshaki] n car wash; 洗車機はどう使うのですか? [senshaki wa dou tsukau no desu ka?] How do I use the car wash?

選手 [senshu] n player (of a sport); テニス選手 [tenisusenshu] n tennis player; フットボール選手 [futtobooru senshu] n soccer player; 運動選手 [undousenshu] n athlete; 重量挙げ選手 [juuryouage senshu] n weightlifter

選手権 [senshuken] n championship

先週 [senshuu] last week; 先々週 [sensenshuu] the week before last

戦争 [sensou] n war

センス [sensu] ユーモアのセンス [yuumoa no sensu] n sense of humor

潜水 [sensui] 潜水艦 [sensuikan] n submarine

潜水夫 [sensuifu] n diver

センター [sentaa] n center; コールセンター [kooru sentaa] n call center; レジャーセンター [rejaasentaa] n leisure center

船体 [sentai] n hull

洗濯 [sentaku] n laundry; 洗濯ロープ [sentaku roopu] n clothesline; 洗濯機 [sentakuki] n washing machine; 洗濯物 [sentakumono] n laundry; どこで洗濯ができますか? [doko de sentaku ga dekimasu ka?] Where can I do some laundry?; この近くにコインランドリーはありますか? [kono chikaku ni koin-randorii wa arimasu ka?] Is there a

Laundromat near here?; これを洗濯して欲しいのですが [kore o sentaku shite hoshii no desu ga] I'd like to get these things cleaned; ランドリーサービスはありますか? [randorii-saabisu wa arimasu ka?] Is there a laundry service?

選択 [sentaku] n choice, option, pick, selection; 選択肢 [sentakushi] n alternative

洗濯ばさみ [sentakubasami] n clothespin

洗濯機 [sentakuki] 洗濯機で洗える [sentakuki de araeru] adj machine washable; 洗濯機はどうやって使うのですか? [sentakuki wa dou-yatte tsukau no desu ka?] How does the washing machine work?; 洗濯機はどこですか? [sentakuki wa doko desu ka?] Where are the washing machines?

先端 [sentan] n tip (end of object)

尖端 [sentan] n peak

セント [sento] n cent

セントラルヒーティング [sentoraruhiitingu] n central heating

戦闘 [sentou] n battle

先頭 [sentou] ···の先頭に立つ [... no sentou ni tatsu] v lead

尖塔 [sentou] n spire, steeple

専用 [senyou] 歩行者専用になった [hokousha sen'you ni natta] adj reserved for pedestrians; 専用の [sen'you no] adj dedicated

洗剤 [senzai] n detergent; 粉末洗剤 [funmatsusenzai] n laundry detergent; 食器洗い用液体洗剤 [shokkiarai you ekitai senzai] n dishwashing liquid

先祖 [senzo] n ancestor

セラミック [seramikku] セラミックの [seramikku no] adj ceramic

セロリ [serori] n celery

セロテープ® [seroteepu] n Scotch® tape

セルビア [serubia] n Serbia; セルビア人 [Serubia jin] n Serbian (person); セルビアの [Serubia no] adj Serbian; セルビア語 [Serubia go] n Serbian (language)

セルフサービス [serufusaabisu] セルフサービスの [serufusaabisu no] adj self-service

摂氏 [sesshi] 摂氏温度 [sesshi ondo] n degree centigrade

接種 [sesshu] 予防接種 [yobou sesshu] n vaccination; 予防接種をする [yobou sesshu-o suru] v vaccinate; 私は予防接種が必要です [watashi wa yobou-sesshu ga hitsuyou desu] I need a vaccination

摂取 [sesshu] 栄養物摂取 [eiyoubutsu sesshu] n nutrition

接着剤 [setchakuzai] n glue; 接着剤でつける [setchakuzai de tsukeru] v glue

設備 [setsubi] n facilities; 最新設備 [saishin setsubi] n modern conveniences

切望 [setsubou] 切望する [setsubou suru] v long

切断 [setsudan] n cut

説明 [setsumei] n account (report), explanation; 説明する [setsumei suru] v explain; ···の説明がつく [... no setsumei ga tsuku] v account for

節約 [setsuyaku] 節約する [setsuyaku suru] v economize

接続 [setsuzoku] 接続を断つ [setsuzoku-o tatsu] v disconnect; その部屋にインターネットの接続ポイントはありますか? [sono heya ni intaanetto no setsuzoku-pointo wa arimasu ka?] Is there an Internet connection in the room?; 接続がとても遅いようです [setsuzoku ga totemo osoi you desu] The connection seems very slow

接続する [setsuzoku suru] プラグで接続する [puragu de setsuzoku suru] v plug in

設定 [settei] ···さんとのミーティングを設定したいのですが [... san to no miitingu o settei shitai no desu ga] I'd like to arrange a meeting with...

説得 [settoku] 説得する [settoku suru] v persuade; 説得力のある [settokuryoku no aru] adj convincing, persuasive

セットメニュー [settomenyuu] セットメニューはありますか? [setto-menyuu wa arimasu ka?]

Do you have a set-price menu?; セットメニューはいくらですか? [setto-menyuu wa ikura desu ka?] How much is the set menu?

世話 [sewa] …の世話をする [... no sewa-o suru] v take care of

しゃべり [shaberi] おしゃべりする [o-shaberi suru] v chat

シャベル [shaberu] n shovel

社長 [shachou] n president (business)

車道 [shadou] n driveway

射撃 [shageki] n shooting

車軸 [shajiku] n axle

社会 [shakai] n society; 社会保障 [shakaihoshou] n social security; 社会主義 [shakaishugi] n socialism; 社会の [shakai no] adj social; 社会学 [shakaigaku] n sociology; 地域社会 [chiiki shakai] n community

社会福祉 [shakaifukushi] 政府の社会福祉事業 [seifu no shakai fukushi jigyou] n social services

社会主義 [shakaishugi] adj 社会主義の [shakaishugi no] adj socialist; 社会主義者 [shakaishugisha] n socialist

車検 [shaken] n Ministry of Transport test (vehicle safety)

借金 [shakkin] n debt

しゃっくり [shakkuri] n hiccups

社交 [shakou] 社交ダンス [shakou dansu] n ballroom dancing; 社交的な [shakouteki na] adj sociable

尺度 [shakudo] n scale (measure)

釈放 [shakuhou] 仮釈放 [kari shakuhou] n parole

シャンパン [shanpan] n champagne

シャンプー [shanpuu] n shampoo; シャンプーを売っていますか? [shanpuu o utte imasu ka?] Do you sell shampoo?

車輪 [sharin] n wheel

車両 [sharyou] n vehicle; 私の車両書類です [watashi no sharyou-shorui desu] Here are my vehicle documents

車線 [shasen] 車線から出る [shasen kara deru] v pull out; あなたは間違った車線にいます [anata wa machigatta shasen ni imasu] You're in the wrong lane

斜視 [shashi] 斜視である [shashi de aru] v squint

写真 [shashin] n photo, photograph; スナップ写真 [sunappu shashin] n snapshot; 写真撮影 [shashinsatsuei] n photography; 写真家 [shashinka] n photographer; X線写真を撮る [x-sen shashin-o toru] v X-ray; この写真をCDに焼き付けていただけますか? [kono shashin o shii-dii ni yakitsukete itadakemasu ka?] Could you put these photos on CD, please?; ここに写真をダウンロードできますか? [koko ni shashin o daunroodo dekimasu ka?] Can I download photos to here?; 写真代はいくらですか? [shashin-dai wa ikura desu ka?] How much do the photos cost?; 写真はいつできますか? [shashin wa itsu dekimasu ka?] When will the photos be ready?; 写真はマット仕上げにしてください [shashin wa matto-shiage ni shite kudasai] I'd like the photos matt; 写真は光沢仕上げにしてください [shashin wa koutaku-shiage ni shite kudasai] I'd like the photos glossy

写真用品 [shashinyouhin] 写真用品を売っている一番近い店はどこですか? [shashin-youhin o utte iru ichiban chikai mise wa doko desu ka?] Where is the nearest place to buy photography equipment?

車掌 [shashou] バスの車掌 [basu no shashou] n bus conductor; 車掌を見ましたか? [shashou wo mimashita ka?] Have you seen the guard?

シャトル [shatoru] バドミントンのシャトル [badominton no shatoru] n birdie (badminton)

シャッター [shattaa] n shutters

シャワー [shawaa] n shower; シャワーはどこですか? [shawaa wa doko desu ka?] Where are the showers?; シャワーはありますか? [shawaa wa arimasu ka?] Are there showers?; シャワーが汚れています [shawaa

ga yogorete imasu] The shower is dirty; シ
ャワーが冷たいです [shawaa ga tsumetai
desu] The showers are cold; シャワーが出ま
せん [shawaa ga demasen] The shower
doesn't work

シャワージェル [shawaajieru] *n* shower gel

シャワーキャップ [shawaakyappu] *n* shower
cap

社用 [shayou] 社用車 [shayousha] *n*
company car

シェービングクリーム [sheebingukuriimu] *n*
shaving cream

死 [shi] *n* death

詩 [shi] *n* poem; 抒情詩 [jojoushi] *n* lyrics

詞 [shi] 副詞 [fukushi] *n* adverb; 形容詞
[keiyoushi] *n* adjective

四 [shi] *number* four

仕上がる [shiagaru] いつ仕上がりますか?
[itsu shiagarimasu ka?] When will it be
ready?

試合 [shiai] *n* match *(sport)*; アウェーの試合
[auee no shiai] *n* away game; フットボールの
試合 [futtobooru no shiai] *n* soccer game; ホ
ームの試合 [hoomu no shiai] *n* home game

芝生 [shibafu] *n* lawn

芝刈り機 [shibakariki] *n* lawnmower

縛る [shibaru] *v* tie; 縛るもの [shibaru mono]
n bond; 固く縛る [kataku shibaru] *v* tie up

しばしば [shibashiba] *adv* often

シベリア [shiberia] *n* Siberia

死別 [shibetsu] 私は配偶者と死別しました
[watashi wa haiguusha to shibetsu
shimashita] I'm widowed

搾る [shiboru] 乳を搾る [chichi-o shiboru] *v*
milk

死亡 [shibou] 死亡記事 [shiboukiji] *n* obituary

脂肪 [shibou] *n* fat; 低脂肪の [teishibou no]
adj low-fat

試着 [shichaku] 試着する [shichaku suru] *v*
try on; 試着室 [shichakushitsu] *n* changing
room; このズボンを試着していいですか?
[kono zubon o shichaku shite ii desu ka?]
May I try on these pants?; このワンピース

を試着していいですか? [kono wanpiisu o
shichaku shite ii desu ka?] May I try on
this dress?; それを試着していいですか?
[sore o shichaku shite ii desu ka?] May I try
it on?

試着室 [shichakushitsu] 試着室はどこですか?
[shichaku-shitsu wa doko desu ka?] Where
are the fitting rooms?

七 [shichi] *number* seven; 七番目 [shichi
banme] *n* seventh; 七番目の [shichi banme
no] *adj* seventh

七月 [shichigatsu] *n* July

七十 [shichijuu] *number* seventy

七面鳥 [shichimenchou] *n* turkey

質屋 [shichiya] *n* pawnbroker

市長 [shichou] *n* mayor

シチュエーションコメディー [shichuees-
honkomedii] *n* sitcom

シチュー [shichuu] *n* stew

シダ [shida] *n* fern

指導 [shidou] 指導者 [shidousha] *n*
instructor; 個別指導 [kobetsu shidou] *n*
tutorial; 個別指導教官 [kobetsu shidou
kyoukan] *n* tutor

始動 [shidou] 車が始動しません [kuruma ga
shidou shimasen] The car won't start

指導員 [shidouin] 自動車教習指導員 [jidousha
kyoushuu shidouin] *n* driving instructor

シェーバー [shieebaa] *n* shaver

シェービングフォーム [shieebingufoomu] *n*
shaving foam

シェフ [shiefu] *n* chef; シェフの得意料理は何
ですか? [shefu no tokui-ryouri wa nan desu
ka?] What is the chef's specialty?

支援 [shien] *n* backing; 支援する [shien suru]
v back up

シェリー [shierii] *n* sherry; ドライシェリーをく
ださい [dorai-sherii o kudasai] A dry sherry,
please

シェルスーツ [shierusuutsu] *n* jogging suit

至福 [shifuku] *n* bliss

志願者 [shigansha] *n* volunteer

シガレット [shigaretto] シガレットライター

[shigaretto raitaa] n cigarette lighter

四月 [shigatsu] n April

茂み [shigemi] n bush (thicket)

資源 [shigen] n resource; 天然資源 [tennenshigen] n natural resources

仕事 [shigoto] n work; 仕事をサボる [shigoto-o saboru] v avoid work; 仕事場 [shigotoba] n workshop; 休日の仕事 [kyuujitsu no shigoto] n vacation job; つまらない仕事 [tsumaranai shigoto] n boring task; 決まりきった仕事 [kimarikitta shigoto] n routine; また近いうちにお仕事でご一緒できることを願っています [mata chikai uchi ni o-shigoto de go-issho dekiru koto o negatte imasu] I hope we can work together again soon; 私は仕事で来ています [watashi wa shigoto de kite imasu] I'm here for work

支配 [shihai] n control; 支配する [shihai suru] v control, master; 支配者 [shihaisha] n ruler (commander)

支払い [shiharai] n payment; 支払い済みの [shiharaizumi no] adj paid

支払い機 [shiharaiki] n ATM; 現金自動支払い機が私のカードを吸い込んでしまいました [genkin-jidou-shiharaiki ga watashi no kaado o suikonde shimaimashita] The ATM swallowed my card

支払い機 [shiharai ki] 一番近い現金自動支払い機はどこですか? [ichiban chikai genkin-jidou-shiharaiki wa doko desu ka?] Where is the nearest ATM?; この現金自動支払い機で私のカードを使えますか? [kono genkin-jidou-shiharaiki de watashi no kaado o tsukaemasu ka?] Can I use my card with this ATM?; ここに現金自動支払い機がありますか? [koko ni genkin-jidou-shiharaiki ga arimasu ka?] Is there an ATM here?

支払う [shiharau] v pay; 現金自動支払い機 [genkin jidoushiharaiki] n ATM; 私は支払わなければなりませんか? [watashi wa shiharawanakereba narimasen ka?] Will I have to pay?

支払うべき [shiharaubeki] adj payable

始発 [shihatsu] ···へ行く始発のバスは何時ですか? [... e iku shihatsu no basu wa nan-ji desu ka?] When is the first bus to...?; ···へ行く始発の電車は何時ですか? [... e iku shihatsu no densha wa nan-ji desu ka?] When is the first train to...?; 始発の船は何時ですか? [shihatsu no fune wa nan-ji desu ka?] When is the first boat?

紙幣 [shihei] n bill, bill (banknote); この紙幣でお釣りがありますか? [kono shihei de o-tsuri ga arimasu ka?] Do you have change for this bill?

資本主義 [shihonshugi] n capitalism

指標 [shihyou] n indicator

シーア派 [shiiaha] シーア派の信徒の [Shiia ha no shinto no] adj Shiite

シーフード [shiifuudo] n seafood; シーフードはお好きですか? [shii-fuudo wa o-suki desu ka?] Do you like seafood?

詩歌 [shiika] n poetry

飼育係 [shiikugakari] 馬の飼育係 [uma no shiikugakari] n groom

シーク教 [shiikukyou] adj シーク教の [Shiiku kyou no] adj Sikh; シーク教徒 [Shiiku kyouto] n Sikh

子音 [shiin] n consonant

仕入れる [shiireru] v stock up on

強いる [shiiru] v force

シーソー [shiisoo] n seesaw

シート [shiito] n seat; シートが低すぎます [shiito ga hiku-sugimasu] The seat is too low; シートが高すぎます [shiito ga taka-sugimasu] The seat is too high

シートベルト [shiitoberuto] n seatbelt

シーツ [shiitsu] n sheet; シーツがもっと必要です [shiitsu ga motto hitsuyou desu] We need more sheets; シーツが汚れています [shiitsu ga yogorete imasu] The sheets are dirty; 私のシーツは汚れています [watashi no shiitsu wa yogorete imasu] My sheets are dirty

シーズン [shiizun] シーズンオフ [shiizun'ofu] n off season

S

シーズンオフ [shiizun'ofu] シーズンオフに [shiizun'ofu ni] *adv* off-season; シーズンオフの [shiizun'ofu no] *adj* off-season

指示 [shiji] *n* directions, instructions; 指示する [shiji suru] *v* instruct

支持 [shiji] 支持者 [shijisha] *n* supporter

詩人 [shijin] *n* poet

四旬節 [shijunsetsu] *n* Lent

四十 [shijuu] *number* forty

四重奏 [shijuusou] *n* quartet

シカ [shika] *n* deer

歯科 [shika] *n* dentistry

視界 [shikai] *n* visibility

司会 [shikai] 司会者 [shikaisha] *n* master of ceremonies

歯科医 [shikai] *n* dentist

資格 [shikaku] *n* qualification; 資格を取る [shikaku wo toru] *v* qualify; ・・・の資格を取り上げる [… no shikaku-o toriageru] *v* disqualify

視覚 [shikaku] 視覚の [shikaku no] *adj* visual; 私は視覚障害があります [watashi wa shikaku-shougai ga arimasu] I'm visually impaired

資格のある [shikaku no aru] *adj* qualified

士官 [shikan] *n* officer

鹿肉 [shika niku] *n* venison

しかる [shikaru] *v* scold, tell off

死刑 [shikei] *n* capital punishment

試験 [shiken] *n* exam, examination, test; 試験する [shiken suru] *v* examine, test; 試験管 [shikenkan] *n* test tube; 試験監督者 [shiken kantokusha] *n* exam proctor; 運転免許試験 [untenmenkyoshiken] *n* driver's test; 口頭試験 [koutou shiken] *n* oral

試験官 [shikenkan] *n* examiner

式 [shiki] 授賞式 [jushoushiki] *n* awards ceremony; 結婚式 [kekkonshiki] *n* wedding

士気 [shiki] *n* morale

識別 [shikibetsu] 識別する [shikibetsu suru] *v* identify

敷地 [shikichi] *n* site

色盲 [shikimou] 色盲の [shikimou no] *adj* colorblind

資金 [shikin] *n* funds; 資金を調達する [shikin-o choutatsu suru] *v* finance; 共同資金 [kyoudou shikin] *n* pool *(resources)*

仕切り [shikiri] 仕切りをする [shikiri-o suru] *v* screen

色彩 [shikisai] 色彩に富んだ [shikisai ni tonda] *adj* colorful

指揮者 [shikisha] *n* conductor

しっかり [shikkari] しっかりした [shikkari shita] *adj* steady

湿気 [shikke] *n* humidity, moisture; 湿気のある [shikke no aru] *adj* damp; 湿気の多い [shikke no oui] *adj* humid

漆喰 [shikkui] *n* plaster *(for wall)*; 漆喰を塗る [shikkui-o nuru] *v* whitewash

思考 [shikou] *n* thought

支給 [shikyuu] 助成金を支給する [joseikin-o shikyuu suru] *v* subsidize

至急 [shikyuu] *adv* immediately

縞 [shima] *n* stripe; 縞のある [shima no aru] *adj* striped; 縞の入った [shima no haitta] *adj* striped

島 [shima] *n* island; 無人島 [mujintou] *n* desert island

姉妹 [shimai] *n* sister; 継姉妹 [mama shimai] *n* stepsister; 義理の姉妹 [giri no shimai] *n* sister-in-law

閉まる [shimaru] 閉まっている [shimatte iru] *adj* closed; 何時に閉まりますか? [nan-ji ni shimarimasu ka?] What time do you close?; いつ閉まりますか? [itsu shimarimasu ka?] When does it close?; お店は何時に閉まりますか? [o-mise wa nan-ji ni shimarimasu ka?] What time do the stores close?; その銀行はいつ閉まりますか? [sono ginkou wa itsu shimarimasu ka?] When does the bank close?; ドアが閉まりません [doa ga shimarimasen] The door won't close

シマウマ [shimauma] *n* zebra

締め出す [shimedasu] *v* lock out

指名 [shimei] *n* nomination; 指名する [shimei suru] *v* nominate

締切り [shimekiri] 締切り期限 [shimekiri kigen] n deadline

絞め殺す [shimekorosu] v strangle

湿る [shimeru] 湿った [shimetta] adj moist

締める [shimeru] v tighten; ファスナーを締める [fasunaa-o shimeru] v zip

閉める [shimeru] v close, shut; バタンと閉める [batan to shimeru] v slam; 窓を閉めてもいいですか? [mado o shimete mo ii desu ka?] May I close the window?

占める [shimeru] v occupy

示す [shimesu] v indicate

しみ [shimi] n spot (blemish), stain; しみのない [shimi no nai] adj spotless; しみがつく [shimi ga tsuku] v stain; しみだらけの [shimidarake no] adj stained; このしみはコーヒーです [kono shimi wa koohii desu] This stain is coffee; このしみはワインです [kono shimi wa wain desu] This stain is wine; このしみは油です [kono shimi wa abura desu] This stain is oil; このしみは血です [kono shimi wa chi desu] This stain is blood; このしみを落とすことができますか? [kono shimi o otosu koto ga dekimasu ka?] Can you remove this stain?

市民 [shimin] n citizen

市民権 [shiminken] n citizenship

しみ抜き [shiminuki] しみ抜き剤 [shiminuki zai] n stain remover

霜 [shimo] n frost

指紋 [shimon] n fingerprint

霜の降りる [shimo no oriru] adj frosty

芯 [shin] n core

シナゴーグ [shinagoogu] n synagogue; どこかにシナゴーグはありますか? [doko-ka ni shinagoogu wa arimasu ka?] Where is there a synagogue?

親愛 [shin'ai] 親愛な [shin'ai na] adj dear (loved)

しなければならない [shinakereba naranai] …しなければならない [… shinakereba naranai] v have to, must

シナモン [shinamon] n cinnamon

シンバル [shinbaru] n cymbals

辛抱 [shinbou] 辛抱する [shinbou suru] v persevere

新聞 [shinbun] n newspaper; 新聞販売店 [shinbunhanbaiten] n newsdealer; 新聞配達 [shinbun haitatsu] n paper route; どこで新聞を買えますか? [doko de shinbun o kaemasu ka?] Where can I buy a newspaper?; 新聞はありますか? [shinbun wa arimasu ka?] Do you have newspapers?; 新聞をください [shinbun o kudasai] I'd like a newspaper; 新聞を売っている一番近い店はどこですか? [shinbun o utte iru ichiban chikai mise wa doko desu ka?] Where is the nearest place to buy newspapers?

慎重 [shinchou] 慎重な [shinchou na] adj cautious; 慎重に [shinchou ni] adv cautiously

身長 [shinchou] あなたの身長はどのくらいありますか? [anata no shinchou wa dono kurai arimasu ka?] How tall are you?

真鍮 [shinchuu] n brass

寝台 [shindai] n berth; 作り付け寝台 [tsukuri zuke shindai] n bunk; 寝台車 [shindaisha] n sleeping car; 寝台車コンパートメントの寝台 [shindaisha konpaatomento no shindai] n sleeping berth

寝台車 [shindaisha] …行きの寝台車を予約したいのですが [… iki no shindai-sha o yoyaku shitai no desu ga] I want to reserve a sleeper to...; 寝台車を予約できますか? [shindai-sha o yoyaku dekimasu ka?] Can I reserve a sleeper?

診断 [shindan] n diagnosis; 健康診断 [kenkoushindan] n physical

診断書 [shindansho] n medical certificate

神学 [shingaku] n theology

審議会 [shingikai] n council

信号 [shingou] 交通信号 [koutsuu shingou] n traffic lights; 救難信号 [kyuunan shingou] n SOS; 話し中を示す信号 [hanashichuu-o shimesu shingou] n busy signal

信号音 [shingouon] 話し中の信号音

[hanashichuu no shingouon] n busy signal

寝具 [shingu] n bedding; 予備の寝具はありますか? [yobi no shingu wa arimasu ka?] Is there any spare bedding?

シングル [shinguru] n single

シングルベッド [shingurubeddo] n single bed

シングルルーム [shingururuumu] n single room; シングルルームを予約したいのですが [shinguru-ruumu o yoyaku shitai no desu ga] I want to reserve a single room, I'd like to reserve a single room

シングルス [shingurusu] n singles

新人 [shinjin] 新人補充 [shinjin hojuu] n recruitment; 最近来た人 [saikin kita hito] n newcomer

信じられない [shinjirarenai] adj incredible, unbelievable

信じる [shinjiru] vt believe; 信じている [shinjite iru] adj trusting

真珠 [shinju] n pearl

神経 [shinkei] n nerve (to/from brain); 神経を悩ます [shinkei-o nayamasu] adj nerve-racking; 神経衰弱 [shinkeisuijaku] n nervous breakdown; 神経過敏な [shinkeikabin na] adj neurotic

神経質な [shinkeishitsu na] adj nervous

申告 [shinkoku] 所得申告 [shotoku shinkoku] n tax return; 申告するスピリッツが1本あります [shinkoku suru supirittsu ga ippon arimasu] I have a bottle of liquor to declare; 申告するものは何もありません [shinkoku suru mono wa nani mo arimasen] I have nothing to declare; 申告する免税範囲のタバコがあります [shinkoku suru menzei-han'i no tabako ga arimasu] I have the allowed amount of cigarettes to declare

深刻 [shinkoku] 深刻な [shinkoku na] adj serious; 深刻に [shinkoku ni] adv seriously

信仰 [shinkou] 信仰する [shinkou suru] vi believe

進行 [shinkou] n proceedings; 高速進行 [kousoku shinkou] n speeding

進行方向 [shinkouhoukou] 進行方向に向いた

席をお願いします [shinkou-houkou ni muita seki o o-negai shimasu] Facing the front, please

シンク [shinku] n sink

深紅色 [shinku shoku] 深紅色の [shinkoush-oku no] adj scarlet

新芽 [shinme] n sprouts

審問 [shinmon] 検死審問 [kenshi shinmon] n inquest

深鍋 [shin nabe] n pot

信念 [shinnen] n faith

新年 [shinnen] n New Year

侵入 [shinnyuu] n invasion; 侵入者 [shinnyuusha] n intruder; 不法侵入者 [fuhou shinnyuusha] n burglar; 住居侵入罪 [juukyoshinnyuuzai] n burglary

心配 [shinpai] n anxiety, concern; 心配して [shinpai shite] adj apprehensive; 心配している [shinpai shite iru] adj worried; 心配する [shinpai suru] v care, worry

新品 [shinpin] 新品の [shinpin no] adj brand-new

進歩 [shinpo] n progress; 進歩した [shinpo shita] adj advanced

新婦 [shinpu] 新婦の付添い役 [shinpu no tsukisoiyaku] n bridesmaid

信頼 [shinrai] n belief, confidence (trust), trust; 信頼する [shinrai suru] v trust; 信頼できる [shinrai dekiru] adj reliable, reputable

心理 [shinri] 心理療法 [shinri ryouhou] n psychotherapy; 心理的な [shinriteki na] adj psychological; 心理学 [shinrigaku] n psychology; 心理学者 [shinrigakusha] n psychologist

新郎 [shinrou] 新郎の付添い役 [shinrou no tsukisoiyaku] n best man

親類 [shinrui] 親類の [shinrui no] adj related

侵略 [shinryaku] 侵略する [shinryaku suru] v invade

診療 [shinryou] 診療所 [shinryoujo] n clinic, doctor's office (doctor's), infirmary

審査 [shinsa] パスポート審査窓口 [pasupooto shinsa madoguchi] n passport control; 審査

する [shinsa suru] v judge

神聖 [shinsei] 神聖な [shinsei na] adj holy

神聖な [shinsei na] adj sacred

親戚 [shinseki] n relative

新鮮 [shinsen] 新鮮な [shinsen na] adj fresh

親切 [shinsetsu] n kindness; 不親切な [fushinsetsu na] adj unfriendly; 親切な [shinsetsu na] adj kind; 親切に [shinsetsu ni] adv kindly

紳士 [shinshi] n gentleman

紳士気取りの俗物 [shinshi kidori no zokubutsu] n snob

寝室 [shinshitsu] n bedroom; 予備の寝室 [yobi no shinshitsu] n spare room; 共同寝室 [kyoudoushinshitsu] n dormitory (large bedroom)

進水 [shinsui] 進水させる [shinsui saseru] v launch

身体 [shintai] adj 体の不自由な [karada no fujiyuu na] adj disabled; 身体の [shintai no] adj physical; 身体検査 [shintai kensa] n physical; 身体障害 [shintaishougai] n disability; 身体障害者 [shintaishougaisha] n disabled

身体障害者 [shintaishougaisha] n handicapped person

信徒 [shinto] シーア派の信徒の [Shiia ha no shinto no] adj Shiite

死ぬ [shinu] v die; 死んだ [shinda] adj dead

神話 [shinwa] n myth; 神話体系 [shinwa taikei] n mythology

信用 [shinyou] 信用できる [shinyou dekiru] adj credible; 信用を保証するもの [shin'you-o hoshou suru mono] n credentials; 信用販売 [shinyou hanbai] n credit

針葉樹 [shin-youju] n conifer

心臓 [shinzou] n heart; 心臓発作 [shin-zouhossa] n heart attack; 私は心臓病があります [watashi wa shinzou-byou ga arimasu] I have a heart condition

潮 [shio] n tide

塩 [shio] n salt; 塩を取っていただけますか? [shio o totte itadakemasu ka?] Pass the salt, please

塩味 [shioaji] 塩味の [shioaji no] adj savory; 食べ物に塩味がききすぎています [tabemono ni shioaji ga kiki-sugite imasu] The food is too salty

塩気 [shioke] 塩気のある [shioke no aru] adj salty

塩水 [shiomizu] 塩水の [shiomizu no] adj saltwater

しおれる [shioreru] v wilt

しおり [shiori] n bookmark

失敗 [shippai] n failure, flop; 失敗する [shippai suru] v fail; 大失敗 [daishippai] n blunder

調べる [shiraberu] v check, look up; グーグル®で調べる [Guuguru® de shiraberu] v Google®; 細かく調べる [komakaku shiraberu] v scan

しらふ [shirafu] しらふの [shirafu no] adj sober

白髪 [shiraga] 白髪のある [shiraga no aru] adj gray-haired

シラミ [shirami] n lice

知らない人 [shiranai hito] n stranger

知らせる [shiraseru] v inform

シリア [shiria] n Syria; シリア人 [shiriajin] n Syrian (person); シリアの [shiria no] adj Syrian

知りたがる [shiritagaru] v curious

城 [shiro] n castle; 砂のお城 [suna no oshiro] n sand castle; その城は一般公開されていますか? [sono shiro wa ippan-koukai sarete imasu ka?] Is the castle open to the public?; 私たちがその城を訪れることはできますか? [watashi-tachi ga sono shiro o otozureru koto wa dekimasu ka?] Can we visit the castle?

シロホン [shirohon] n xylophone

白い [shiroi] adj white

白黒 [shirokuro] 白黒で [shiro-kuro de] in black and white

白目 [shirome] n pewter

白身 [shiromi] 卵の白身 [tamago no shiromi]

n egg white

シロップ [shiroppu] *n* syrup

白ワイン [shirowain] *n* white wine; よい白ワインを教えてもらえますか? [yoi shiro-wain o oshiete moraemasu ka?] Can you recommend a good white wine?

知る [shiru] *v* know; よく知られている [yoku shirarete iru] *adj* well-known, familiar; 知っている [shitte iru] *v* know; 知られている [shirarete iru] *adj* known; これのやり方をご存知ですか? [kore no yarikata o go-zonji desu ka?] Do you know how to do this?

しるし [shirushi] *n* (現れ) token

思慮 [shiryo] 思慮深い [shiryobukai] *adj* thoughtful

視力 [shiryoku] *n* eyesight, sight

司祭 [shisai] *n* priest

資産 [shisan] *n* worth

施設 [shisetsu] *n* facility; どんなスポーツ施設がありますか? [donna supootsu-shisetsu ga arimasu ka?] What sports facilities are there?

使者 [shisha] *n* messenger

獅子座 [shishiza] *n* Leo

支障 [shishou] 道はいつ支障がなくなるのですか? [michi wa itsu shishou ga nakunaru no desu ka?] When will the road be clear?

死傷 [shishou] 死傷者 [shishousha] *n* casualty

思春期 [shishunki] *n* adolescence

支出 [shishutsu] *n* expenditure

刺繍 [shishuu] *n* embroidery; 刺繍する [shishuu suru] *v* embroider

湿疹 [shisshin] *n* eczema

システムアナリスト [shisutemu anarisuto] *n* systems analyst

システムコンポ [shisutemukonpo] *n* stereo

指数 [shisuu] *n* index (numerical scale); 知能指数 [chinoushisuu, IQ aikyuu] *n* IQ

下 [shita] 下に [shita ni] *adv* below, underneath; 下へ [shita e] *adv* down; ···の下に [...no shita ni] *prep* beneath; ···より下に [... yori shitani] *prep* below

舌 [shita] *n* tongue

下書き [shitagaki] *n* draft

従って [shitagatte] ···に従って [... ni shitagatte] *prep* according to

従う [shitagau] *v* obey; ···に従って [... ni shitagatte] *prep* according to; ···に従わない [... ni shitagawanai] *v* disobey

下着 [shitagi] *n* underwear

死体 [shitai] *n* corpse; 死体保管所 [shitaihokanjo] *n* morgue

···したことがない [...shita koto ga nai] *adv* never

親しい [shitashii] *adj* friendly, intimate

したたり [shitatari] *n* drop

したたる [shitataru] *v* drip

指定 [shitei] 指定地区 [shitei chiku] *n* pedestrian area; 8時指定で2人分 [hachi-ji shitei de futari-bun] two for the eight o'clock show

指摘 [shiteki] 指摘する [shiteki suru] *v* point out

質 [shitsu] *n* quality

室 [shitsu] *n* 手術室 [shujutsushitsu] *n* operating room; 試着室 [shichakushitsu] *n* changing room; 職員室 [shokuinshitsu] *n* staff room; 待合室 [machiaishitsu] *n* waiting room

失望 [shitsubou] *n* disappointment; 失望させる [shitsubou saseru] *v* disappoint; 失望した [shitsubou shita] *adj* disappointed

失読症 [shitsudokushou] *n* dyslexia; 失読症の [shitsudokushou no] *adj* dyslexic; 失読症の人 [shitsudokushou no hito] *n* dyslexic

室外 [shitsugai] それは屋外プールですか? [sore wa okugai-puuru desu ka?] Is it an outdoor pool?

失業 [shitsugyou] *n* unemployment; 失業中の [shitsugyouchuu no] *adj* jobless; 失業している [shitsugyou shite iru] *adj* unemployed; 失業手当 [shitsugyouteate] *n* welfare; 失業登録をする [shitsugyou touroku-o suru] *v* sign up for unemployment

しつけ [shitsuke] *n* upbringing

質問 [shitsumon] *n* question; 質問する [shitsumon suru] *v* interrogate, question

室内 [shitsunai] 室内装飾家 [shitsunai soushokuka] *n* painter *(in house)*

失礼 [shitsurei] 失礼な [shitsurei na] *adj* rude

失恋 [shitsuren] 失恋した [shitsuren shita] *adj* heartbroken

歯痛 [shitsuu] *n* toothache

知ったかぶりをする人 [shitta kaburi wo suru hito] *n* know-it-all

嫉妬 [shitto] 嫉妬深い [shittobukai] *adj* jealous

しわ [shiwa] *n* wrinkle; しわの寄った [shiwa no yotta] *adj* wrinkled

使用 [shiyou] *n* use; 使用人 [shiyounin] *n* servant; 使用する [shiyou suru] *v* use; 使用期限 [shiyou kigen] *n* expiration date; 使用者 [shiyousha] *n* user; 再使用する [saishiyou suru] *v* reuse

試用 [shiyou] 試用期間 [shiyou kikan] *n* trial period

自然 [shizen] *n* nature; 不自然な [fushizen na] *adj* unnatural; 自然食品 [shizen shokuhin] *n* whole foods

自然誌 [shizen shi] 自然誌研究者 [shizenshi kenkyuusha] *n* naturalist

静か [shizuka] 静かな [shizuka na] *adj* still; 一日中自分たちだけになれる静かなところがいいのですが [ichinichi-juu jibun-tachi dake ni nareru shizuka na tokoro ga ii no desu ga] We'd like to see nobody but ourselves all day!; 静かな部屋がいいのですが [shizuka na heya ga ii no desu ga] I'd like a quiet room

静かな [shizuka na] *adj* quiet

静かに [shizuka ni] *adv* quietly

静けさ [shizukesa] *n* silence

しずく [shizuku] *n* drop

沈む [shizumu] *v* sink

暑 [sho] 暑すぎます [atsu-sugimasu] I'm too hot

諸 [sho] 諸経費 [shokeihi] *n* overhead

処罰 [shobatsu] *n* punishment

処置 [shochi] 救急処置 [kyuukyuu shochi] *n* first aid; 救急処置キット [kyuukyuu shochi kitto] *n* first-aid kit

初演 [shoen] *n* premiere

処方 [shohou] 処方する [shohou suru] *v* prescribe; 処方箋 [shohousen] *n* prescription

処方箋 [shohousen] *n* prescription; どこでこの処方箋の薬を出してもらえますか? [doko de kono shohousen no kusuri o dashite moraemasu ka?] Where can I have this prescription filled?

所持 [shoji] 所持品 [shojihin] *n* belongings

処女 [shojo] *n* virgin

処刑 [shokei] *n* execution; 処刑する [shokei suru] *v* execute

初期 [shoki] 初期の [shoki no] *adj* primitive

食器 [shokki] *n* tableware; 食器棚 [shokkidana] *n* cupboard, hutch; 食器洗い [shokkiarai] *n* washing the dishes; 食器洗い機 [shokkiaraiki] *n* dishwasher; 食器洗い用液体洗剤 [shokkiarai you ekitai senzai] *n* dishwashing liquid

ショッキング [shokkingu] ショッキングな [shokkingu na] *adj* shocking

職 [shoku] *n* job; 職場 [shokuba] *n* workplace

触媒 [shokubai] 触媒コンバーター [shokubai konbaataa] *n* catalytic converter

植物 [shokubutsu] *n* plant *(vegetable organism)*; つる植物 [tsuru shokubutsu] *n* vine; 鉢植え植物 [hachiue shokubutsu] *n* potted plant; 土地の植物と樹木を見たいのですが [tochi no shokubutsu to jumoku o mitai no desu ga] We'd like to see local plants and trees

植物相 [shokubutsusou] *n* flora

食中毒 [shokuchuudoku] *n* food poisoning

食堂 [shokudou] 食堂車 [shokudousha] *n* dining car

職業 [shokugyou] *n* occupation *(work)*, profession; 職業上の [shokugyou jou no] *adj* vocational; 職業的な [shokugyouteki na] *adj* professional; 職業的に [shokugyouteki

S

ni] *adv* professionally; 熟練職業 [jukuren shokugyou] *n* craft; 公共職業安定所 [koukyoushokugyou anteisho] *n* employment office

食品 [shokuhin] 自然食品 [shizen shokuhin] *n* whole foods

職員 [shokuin] *n* staff *(workers)*; 職員室 [shokuinshitsu] *n* staff room; 臨時職員 [rinjishokuin] *n* temp

食事 [shokuji] *n* meal; 食事する人 [shokuji suru hito] *n* diner; 食事時間 [shokuji jikan] *n* mealtime; 小児用の食事椅子 [shouni you no shokuji isu] *n* high chair; お食事をお楽しみください! [o-shokuji o o-tanoshimi kudasai!] Enjoy your meal!; グルテンを使わずに食事を用意していただけますか? [guruten o tsukawazu ni shokuji o youi shite itadakemasu ka?] Could you prepare a meal without gluten?; ナッツを使わずに食事を用意していただけますか? [nattsu o tsukawazu ni shokuji o youi shite itadakemasu ka?] Could you prepare a meal without nuts?; 食事はおいしかったです [shokuji wa oishikatta desu] The meal was delicious; 魚介類を使わずに食事を用意していただけますか? [gyokairui o tsukawazu ni shokuji o youi shite itadakemasu ka?] Could you prepare a meal without seafood?; 魚を使わずに食事を用意していただけますか? [sakana o tsukawazu ni shokuji o youi shite itadakemasu ka?] Could you prepare a meal without fish?; 卵を使わずに食事を用意していただけますか? [tamago o tsukawazu ni shokuji o youi shite itadakemasu ka?] Could you prepare a meal without eggs?

職務 [shokumu] 職務上の [shokumujou no] *adj* official

職人 [shokunin] *n* craftsman; 煉瓦職人 [renga shokunin] *n* bricklayer

食糧 [shokuryou] *n* supplies

食料 [shokuryou] 食料置場 [shokuryou okiba] *n* pantry; 食料雑貨類 [shokuryou zakkarui] *n* groceries; 食料雑貨店 [shokuryou zakkaten] *n* grocery store; 食料雑貨商 [shokuryou zakkashou] *n* grocer

食卓用ナイフ・フォーク・スプーン類 [shokutaku yoo naifu. fouku. supuun rui] *n* flatware

食欲 [shokuyoku] *n* appetite

署名 [shomei] *n* signature; 署名する [shomei suru] *v* sign; 頭文字で署名する [atamamoji de shomei suru] *v* initial

ショー [shoo] *n* show; どこに行けばショーを見られますか? [doko ni ikeba shoo o miraremasu ka?] Where can we go to see a show?

ショービジネス [shoobijinesu] *n* show business

ショール [shooru] *n* shawl

ショートクラスト [shootokurasuto] *n* shortcrust pastry

ショートメッセージサービス [shootomesseejisaabisu] *n* SMS

ショーツ [shootsu] *n* underpants; ボクサーショーツ [bokusaa shootsu] *n* boxer shorts

ショーウィンドウ [shoouindou] *n* store window

ショッピングカート [shoppingukaato] *n* shopping cart

ショッピングセンター [shoppingu sentaa] *n* shopping center

ショップ [shoppu] ギフトショップ [gifuto shoppu] *n* gift shop; チャリティーショップ [charitii shoppu] *n* charity store

書類 [shorui] *n* document; この書類のコピーを取りたいのですが [kono shorui no kopii o toritai no desu ga] I want to copy this document; 私の車両書類です [watashi no sharyou-shorui desu] Here are my vehicle documents

書類受け [shoruiuke] *n* in-box

書籍 [shoseki] 電子書籍 [denshi shoseki] *n* e-book

初心者 [shoshinsha] *n* beginner; 初心者用ゲレンデ [shoshinshayou gerende] *n* bunny hill

諸州 [shoshuu] メキシコ湾岸諸州 [Mekishiko wangan shoshuu] n Gulf Coast states

書店 [shoten] n bookstore

所得 [shotoku] n earnings, income; 所得申告 [shotoku shinkoku] n tax return; 所得税 [shotokuzei] n income tax

諸島 [shotou] フェロー諸島 [Feroo shotou] n Faroe Islands

章 [shou] n chapter

症 [shou] 拒食症 [kyoshokushou] n anorexia; 狭心症 [kyoushinshou] n angina

省 [shou] n ministry (government)

賞 [shou] n award, prize

商 [shou] 宝石商 [housekishou] n jeweler, jewelry store

商売 [shoubai] n trade

消防士 [shouboushi] n fireman

消防隊 [shouboutai] n fire department; 消防隊を呼んでください [shoubou-tai o yonde kudasai] Please call the fire department

消沈 [shouchin] 意気消沈した [ikishouchin shita] adj depressed

象徴 [shouchou] n symbol

消毒剤 [shoudokuzai] n disinfectant

収益 [shoueki] n proceeds, profit, return (yield); 収益の多い [shuueki no oui] adj profitable

ショウガ [shouga] n ginger; ショウガ色の [shouga iro no] adj redheaded

生涯 [shougai] 生涯教育 [shougai kyouiku] n adult education

障害 [shougai] n hitch; 体の不自由な [karada no fujiyuu na] adj disabled; 身体障害 [shintaishougai] n disability; 身体障害者 [shintaishougaisha] n disabled; 障害のある [shougai no aru] adj handicapped; 障害飛越 [shougaihietsu] n show jumping

傷害 [shougai] n accident; 個人傷害保険をかけたいのですが [kojin-shougai-hoken o kaketai no desu ga] I'd like to arrange personal accident insurance

障害物 [shougaibutsu] n obstacle

衝撃 [shougeki] n shock; 衝撃を与える [shougeki-o ataeru] v shock

正午 [shougo] n noon; 正午に [shougo ni] at noon; 正午です [shougo desu] It's twelve noon

照合 [shougou] n check

照合の印 [shougou no in] n check mark; 照合の印をつける [shougou no in-o tsukeru] v check

将軍 [shougun] n general

小片 [shouhen] n bit, scrap (small piece)

消費 [shouhi] 消費者 [shouhisha] n consumer

商品 [shouhin] n goods

商品券 [shouhinken] n gift certificate

商標 [shouhyou] n trademark

正直 [shoujiki] n honesty; 不正直な [fushoujiki na] adj dishonest; 正直な [shoujiki na] adj honest, truthful; 正直に [shoujiki ni] adv honestly

生じる [shoujiru] 結果として生じる [kekka toshite shoujiru] v result

少女 [shoujo] n girl

症状 [shoujou] n symptom

消化 [shouka] n digestion; 消化不良 [shoukafuryou] n indigestion; 消化する [shouka suru] v digest

照会 [shoukai] 照会デスク [shoukai desuku] n information desk

紹介 [shoukai] n introduction, presentation; 紹介する [shoukai suru] v introduce, present

消火器 [shoukaki] n extinguisher, fire extinguisher

証券 [shouken] 証券取引所 [shouken torihikijo] n stock exchange

正気 [shouki] 正気でない [shouki de nai] adj insane

賞金 [shoukin] 多額の賞金 [tagaku no shoukin] n jackpot

証拠 [shouko] n evidence, proof (evidence)

症候群 [shoukougun] ダウン症候群 [Daun shoukougun] n Down syndrome

小球 [shoukyuu] n pellet

小休止 [shoukyuushi] *n* pause

照明 [shoumei] *n* lighting; 投光照明 [toukou shoumei] *n* floodlight

証明 [shoumei] 身分証明 [mibun shoumei] *n* identification

証明書 [shoumeisho] *n* certificate; 身分証明書 [mibunshomeisho] *n* ID card; 結婚証明書 [kekkonshoumeisho] *n* marriage certificate; 出生証明書 [shusshou (shussei) shoumeisho] *n* birth certificate; 私は「飛行機搭乗の適性」証明書が必要です [watashi wa "hikouki-toujou no tekisei" shoumei-sho ga hitsuyou desu] I need a 'fit to fly' certificate

正味 [shoumi] *n* Net

賞味 [shoumi] 賞味期限 [shoumikigen] *n* best-if-used-by date

小虫 [shou mushi] *n* midge

少年 [shounen] *n* boy

小児 [shouni] *n* enfant; 小児用の食事椅子 [shouni you no shokuji isu] *n* high chair; 小児用ベッド [shouni you beddo] *n* crib

小児科医 [shounikai] *n* pediatrician; いい小児科医を教えてもらえますか? [ii shounika-i o oshiete moraemasu ka?] Can you recommend a pediatrician?

承認 [shounin] *n* acknowledgment, approval; 承認する [shounin suru] *v* approve

証人 [shounin] エホバの証人 [Ehoba no shounin] *n* Jehovah's Witness

小児性愛者 [shouniseiaimono] *n* pedophile

消音 [shouon] 消音装置 [shouon souchi] *n* silencer

将来 [shourai] 将来有望な [shourai yuubou na] *adj* promising

奨励 [shourei] *n* encouragement, incentive

勝利 [shouri] *n* triumph, victory; 勝利を得た [shouri-o eta] *adj* winning; 勝利を収める [shouri-o osameru] *v* triumph

詳細 [shousai] 詳細な [shousai na] *adj* detailed; 私の保険の詳細です [watashi no hoken no shousai desu] Here is my insurance information

称賛 [shousan] *n* admiration; 称賛の [shousan no] *adj* complimentary

小冊子 [shousasshi] *n* booklet

小説 [shousetsu] *n* novel; 短篇小説 [tanpen shousetsu] *n* short story; 小説家 [shousetsuka] *n* novelist

勝者 [shousha] *n* winner

証書 [shousho] *n* certificate; 保険証書 [hokenshousho] *n* insurance policy; あなたの保険証書を見せていただけますか? [anata no hoken-shousho o misete itadakemasu ka?] May I see your insurance certificate, please?

少々 [shoushou] 少々お待ちください [shoushou o-machi kudasai] Just a moment, please

尚早 [shousou] 時期尚早の [jikishousou no] *adj* premature

少数 [shousuu] 少数派 [shousuuha] *n* minority

招待 [shoutai] *n* invitation

焦点 [shouten] *n* focus; 焦点を合わせる [shouten-o awaseru] *v* focus

衝突 [shoutotsu] *n* bump, collision, conflict, hit, percussion, wreck; 衝突させる [shoutotsu saseru] *v* wreck; 衝突する [shoutotsu suru] *vi* collide, crash; 私は自分の車を衝突させました [watashi wa jibun no kuruma o shoutotsu sasemashita] I've wrecked my car

衝突する [shoutotsu suru] *v* clash

醤油 [shouyu] *n* soy sauce

肖像画 [shouzouga] *n* portrait

所要 [shoyou] 所要時間は二時間です [shoyou-jikan wa ni-jikan desu] The trip takes two hours; 所要時間はどのくらいですか? [shoyou-jikan wa dono kurai desu ka?] How long is the trip?, How long will it take?

所有 [shoyuu] *n* possession; 所有する [shoyuu suru] *v* own, possess; 所有者 [shoyuusha] *n* owner; 所有物 [shoyuubutsu]

n property; 個人の所有物 [kojin no shoyuubutsu] *n* private property

所属 [shozoku] 所属する [shozoku suru] *v* belong

種 [shu] *n* (果実) seed

種[1] [shu] *n* (生物) species

主張 [shuchou] *n* claim; 主張する [shuchou suru] *v* claim

主題 [shudai] *n* subject

手段 [shudan] *n* means

主演 [shuen] 主演する [shuen suru] *v* star

主婦 [shufu] *n* housewife

主義 [shugi] *n* principle; 性差別主義 [seisabetsu shugi] *n* sexism; 性差別主義の [seisabetsu shugi no] *adj* sexist; 民主主義 [minshushugi] *n* democracy; 民主主義の [minshu shugi no] *adj* democratic; 社会主義 [shakaishugi] *n* socialism; 過激主義 [kageki shugi] *n* extremism; 国家主義 [kokkashugi] *n* nationalism

主義者 [shugisha] *n* 人種差別主義者 [jinshusabetsushugisha] *n* racist; 人種差別主義者の [jinshu sabetsu shugisha no] *adj* racist; 楽観主義者 [rakkan shugisha] *n* optimist; 悲観主義者 [hikanshugisha] *n* pessimist; 裸体主義者 [rataishugisha] *n* nudist; 労働組合主義者 [roudoukumiai shugisha] *n* union member; 国家主義者 [kokkashugisha] *n* nationalist

主人 [shujin] パン屋の主人 [pan ya no shujin] *n* baker; パブの主人 [pabu no shujin] *n* pub owner

手術 [shujutsu] *n* operation *(surgery)*, surgery *(operation)*; 手術する [shujutsu suru] *v* operate *(to perform surgery)*; 手術室 [shujutsushitsu] *n* operating room

出血 [shukketsu] 出血する [shukketsu suru] *v* bleed

出航 [shukkou] いつ出航しますか? [itsu shukkou shimasu ka?] When do we sail?; ···行きの次の出航は何時ですか? [... iki no tsugi no shukkou wa nan-ji desu ka?] When is the next sailing to...?; ···行きの最終の

出航は何時ですか? [... iki no saishuu no shukkou wa nan-ji desu ka?] When is the last sailing to...?

宿題 [shukudai] *n* homework

祝福 [shukufuku] 祝福する [shukufuku suru] *v* bless

宿泊 [shukuhaku] 月曜から水曜まで宿泊したいのですが [getsuyou kara suiyou made shukuhaku shitai no desu ga] I want to stay from Monday till Wednesday

祝日 [shukujitsu] 祝祭日 [shukusaijitsu] *n* public holiday

祝祭 [shukusai] 祝祭日 [shukusaijitsu] *n* public holiday

縮小 [shukushou] *n* cutback

主教 [shukyou] *n* bishop; 大主教 [dai shukyou] *n* archbishop

趣味 [shumi] *n* hobby; 趣味のよい [shumi no yoi] *adj* tasteful; 趣味が悪い [shumi ga warui] *adj* unstylish

瞬間 [shunkan] *n* moment; 瞬間の [shunkan no] *adj* momentary

春季 [shunki] *n* springtime; 春季の大掃除 [shunki no ousouji] *n* spring-cleaning

シュノーケリング [shunookeringu] シュノーケリングをしたいのですが [shunookeringu o shitai no desu ga] I'd like to go snorkeling

シュノーケル [shunookeru] *n* snorkel

主 [shu/nushi] 主な [omo na] *adj* main; 主に [omo ni] *adv* mainly; 主として [shutoshite] *adv* largely; 送り主 [okurinushi] *n* sender; 雇用主 [koyounushi] *n* employer; 店主 [tenshu] *n* store owner

出版 [shuppan] *n* publication; 出版する [shuppan suru] *v* publish; 出版業者 [shuppan gyousha] *n* publisher

出発 [shuppatsu] *n* departure; 出発する [shuppatsu suru] *v* depart, leave, set off; 出発ラウンジ [shuppatsu raunji] *n* departure lounge

種類 [shurui] *n* kind, sort, type

酒類販売 [shuruihanbai] 酒類販売免許 [sakerui hanbai menkyo] *n* liquor license

S

首相 [shushou] *n* prime minister

出産 [shussan] 出産休暇 [shussan kyuuka] *n* maternity leave; 出産前の [shussanmae no] *adj* prenatal; 私は五か月後に出産予定です [watashi wa gokagetsu-go ni shussan yotei desu] I'm due in five months

出生地 [shusseichi] 出生地の [shusseichi no] *adj* native

出席 [shusseki] *n* attendance; 出席する [shusseki suru] *v* attend

出身 [shushin] *n* birthplace; ···の出身である [… no shusshin de aru] *v* come from

出生 [shusshou] 出生証明書 [shusshou (shussei) shoumeisho] *n* birth certificate; 出生地 [shusseichi] *n* birthplace, place of birth

出張 [shutchou] *n* business trip

首都 [shuto] *n* capital

主として [shutoshite] *adv* primarily

出没 [shutsubotsu] 幽霊が出没する [yuurei ga shutsubotsu suru] *adj* haunted

出現 [shutsugen] *n* advent, appearance

週 [shuu] *n* week; 1週間パスはいくらですか？ [isshuukan pasu wa ikura desu ka?] How much is a pass per week?; 再来週 [saraishuu] the week after next

執着 [shuuchaku] *n* obsession; 執着した [shuuchaku shita] *adj* obsessed

集中 [shuuchuu] *n* concentration; 集中する [shuuchuu suru] *v* concentrate; 集中治療室 [shuuchuuchiryoushitsu, ICU aishiiyuu] *n* intensive care unit; 集中的な [shuuchu-uteki na] *adj* intensive

集団 [shuudan] *n* collective; 集団の [shuudan no] *adj* collective

修道 [shuudou] 修道院 [shuudouin] *n* monastery; 修道士 [shuudoushi] *n* monk

修道院 [shuudouin] 女子修道院 [joshishu-udouin] *n* convent; その修道院は一般公開されていますか？ [sono shuudouin wa ippan-koukai sarete imasu ka?] Is the monastery open to the public?

修復 [shuufuku] 修復する [shuufuku suru] *v* restore

襲撃 [shuugeki] *n* raid; 襲撃する [shuugeki suru] *v* raid

囚人 [shuujin] *n* prisoner

集会 [shuukai] *n* assembly

収穫 [shuukaku] *n* crop, harvest; 収穫する [shuukaku suru] *v* harvest

週間 [shuukan] 1週間でいくらですか？ [isshuukan de ikura desu ka?] How much is it for a week?; それは1週間あたりいくらですか？ [sore wa isshuukan atari ikura desu ka?] How much is it per week?

周期 [shuuki] *n* cycle *(recurring period)*

宗教 [shuukyou] *n* religion; 宗教の [shuukyou no] *adj* religious

週末 [shuumatsu] *n* weekend

周年 [shuunen] 100周年記念祭 [hyakushu-unen kinensai] *n* centenary

収納箱 [shuunoubako] *n* chest *(storage)*

収入 [shuunyuu] *n* receipts *(money)*, revenue

修理 [shuuri] *n* repair; 修理する [shuurisuru] *v* repair; 修理キット [shuuri kitto] *n* repair kit; 修理にどのくらいの時間がかかりますか？ [shuuri ni dono kurai no jikan ga kakarimasu ka?] How long will it take to repair?; 修理してもらえますか？ [shuuri shite moraemasu ka?] Can you repair it?; 修理する価値がありますか？ [shuuri suru kachi ga arimasu ka?] Is it worth repairing?; 一番近くの車椅子修理店はどこですか？ [ichiban chikaku no kuruma-isu shuuri-ten wa doko desu ka?] Where's the nearest repair shop for wheelchairs?; どこでこれを修理してもらえますか？ [doko de kore o shuuri shite moraemasu ka?] Where can I get this repaired?; この近くに自動車修理工場はありますか？ [kono chikaku ni jidousha-shuuri-koujou wa arimasu ka?] Is there a repair shop near here?; この靴を修理できますか？ [kono kutsu o shuuri dekimasu ka?] Can you repair these shoes?; これを修理できますか？ [kore o shuuri dekimasu ka?] Can you repair this?; それを修理できますか? [sore o shuuri dekimasu ka?] Can you repair it?; 自動車修理工場までけん引してもらえますか? [jidousha-shuuri-koujou made ken'in shite moraemasu ka?] Could you tow me to a repair shop?; 自動車修理工場まで私を乗せていってもらえますか? [jidousha-shuuri-koujou made watashi o nosete itte moraemasu ka?] Could you give me a ride to the repair shop?; 私のメガネを修理できますか? [watashi no megane o shuuri dekimasu ka?] Can you repair my glasses?; 私の時計を修理できますか? [watashi no tokei o shuuri dekimasu ka?] Can you repair my watch?; 私の入れ歯を修理してもらえますか? [watashi no ireba o shuuri shite moraemasu ka?] Can you repair my dentures?

修理代 [shuuridai] 修理代はいくらかかりますか? [shuuri-dai wa ikura kakarimasu ka?] How much will the repairs cost?

修理キット [shuuri kitto] 修理キットはありますか? [shuuri-kitto wa arimasu ka?] Do you have a repair kit?; 修理キットをください [shuuri-kitto o kudasai] May I have a repair kit?

修理工 [shuurikou] n mechanic; 修理工を手配してもらえますか? [shuuri-kou o tehai shite moraemasu ka?] Could you send a mechanic?

修理店 [shuuriten] n repair shop; 一番近い自転車修理店はどこですか? [ichiban chikai jitensha shuuri-ten wa doko desu ka?] Where is the nearest bike repair shop?

終了 [shuuryou] 終了した [shuuryou shita] adj done

修正 [shuusei] n revision; 修正する [shuusei suru] v rectify, revise

終止符 [shuushifu] n period (punctuation)

就寝 [shuushin] 就寝時刻 [shuushin jikoku] n bedtime

収集 [shuushuu] ごみ収集人 [gomishuushuunin] n garbage collector; 収

集家 [shuushuuka] n collector

収容 [shuuyou] 収容力 [shuuyouryoku] n capacity

修繕 [shuuzen] 修繕する [shuuzen suru] v renovate

シューズ [shuuzu] バレエシューズ [baree shuuzu] n ballet shoes

手話 [shuwa] n sign language

主役 [shuyaku] n lead (in play/film)

主要 [shuyou] 主要産物 [shuyou sanbutsu] n staple (commodity)

腫瘍 [shuyou] n tumor

主要な [shuyou na] adj chief

取材 [shuzai] 取材記者 [shuzai kisha] n reporter

CD [siidii] n CD [siidii]; CDバーナー [shiidii baanaa] n CD burner; CDプレーヤー [shiidii pureiyaa] n CD player; CDはいつできますか? [shii-dii wa itsu dekimasu ka?] When will the CD be ready?

CD-ROM [siidii romu] n CD-ROM [siidii romu]

そば [soba] ···のそばに [... no soba ni] prep beside

そばかす [sobakasu] n freckles

祖母 [sobo] n grandmother

率直 [socchoku] 率直な [sotchoku na] adj direct, straightforward; 率直に [sotchoku ni] adv frankly

育てる [sodateru] v bring up ▷ vt grow

袖 [sode] n sleeve; 袖なしの [sode nashi no] adj sleeveless; 半袖の [hansode no] adj short-sleeved

祖伝来 [sodenrai] 先祖伝来のもの [senzo denrai no mono] n heritage

添える [soeru] 添え木 [soegi] n splint

ソファー [sofaa] n sofa

ソファーベッド [sofaabeddo] n sofa bed

祖父 [sofu] n grandfather

祖父母 [sofubo] n grandparents

ソフトドリンク [sofutodorinku] n soft drink

ソフトウェア [sofutouea] n software

そぐ [sogu] 人の興をそぐ人 [hito no kyou-o

S

sogu hito] *n* spoilsport

ソケット [soketto] ソケットアダプタ [soketto adaputa] *n* adapter

速記 [sokki] *n* shorthand

ソックス [sokkusu] *n* sock

底 [soko] *n* bottom; 底の [soko no] *adj* bottom

そこ [soko] そこに [soko ni] *adv* there

祖国 [sokoku] *n* homeland

損なわれていない [sokonawareteinai] *adj* intact

速度 [sokudo] 速度を上げる [sokudo-o ageru] *v* speed up; 速度計 [sokudokei] *n* speedometer; 制限速度 [seigensokudo] *n* speed limit

促進 [sokushin] *n* promotion; 促進する [sokushin suru] *v* promote

測定 [sokutei] *n* measure; 測定する [sokutei suru] *v* measure

側灯 [sokutou] *n* parking light

即座 [sokuza] 即座に [sokuza ni] *adv* instantly; 即座の [sokuza no] *adj* instant

即座に [sokuza ni] *adv* promptly

即座の [sokuza no] *n* prompt

ソマリア [somaria] *n* Somalia; ソマリア人 [Somaria jin] *n* Somali *(person)*; ソマリアの [Somaria no] *adj* Somali; ソマリア語 [Somaria go] *n* Somali *(language)*

染める [someru] *v* dye

備える [sonaeru] 備えた [sonaeta] *adj* equipped

尊重 [sonchou] *n* respect; 尊重する [sonchou suru] *v* respect

尊敬 [sonkei] 尊敬すべき [sonkeisubeki] *adj* respectable

園 [sono] 果樹園 [kajuen] *n* orchard; 動物園 [doubutsuen] *n* zoo

その間 [sono aida] その間に [sono aida ni] *adv* meantime, meanwhile

そのほか [sonohoka] そのほかに [sono hoka ni] *adv* other than that

その時 [sono toki] *adv* then

その上 [sono ue] *adv* besides

損傷 [sonshou] *n* damage; 損傷する [sonshou suru] *v* damage

存在 [sonzai] *n* presence; 存在する [sonzai suru] *v* exist

ソーダ割り [soodawari] ウイスキーのソーダ割り [uisukii no sooda wari] a whiskey and soda

ソープオペラ [soopuopera] *n* soap opera

ソーセージ [sooseeji] *n* sausage

ソーシャルワーカー [soosharuwaakaa] *n* social worker

ソース [soosu] *n* sauce; ディップソース [dippu sousu] *n* dip *(food/sauce)*

ソースパン [soosupan] *n* saucepan

ソプラノ [sopurano] *n* soprano

空 [sora] *n* (天) sky; 空にする [kara ni suru] *v* empty; 空の [kara no] *adj* empty

ソラマメ [soramame] *n* fava bean

そらす [sorasu] 注意をそらす [chuui-o sorasu] *v* distract

それ [sore] それは何ですか? [sore wa nan desu ka?] What is it?

それる [soreru] 急にそれる [kyuu ni soreru] *v* swerve

逸れる [soreru] 逸れること [soreru koto] *n* turn

それぞれ [sorezore] *adv* respectively

そり [sori] *n* sled; どこに行けばそりに乗れますか? [doko ni ikeba sori ni noremasu ka?] Where can we go sledding?

ソリスト [sorisuto] *n* soloist

ソロ [soro] *n* solo

そろい [soroi] ひとそろい [hitosoroi] *n* set

剃る [soru] *v* shave

ソルベ [sorube] *n* sorbet

組織 [soshiki] *n* (生物) tissue, (団体) organization; 組織する [soshiki suru] *v* organize; 組織的な方法 [soshikiteki na houhou] *n* system

外 [soto] 外に [hoka ni] *adv* out; 外の [hoka no] *adj* out

外側 [sotogawa] *n* outside; 外側に [sotogawa ni] *adv* outside; 外側の [sotogawa no] *adj* outside; 外側の [sotogawa no] *adj* exterior

卒業 [sotsugyou] *n* 大学卒業 [daigaku sotsugyou] *n* graduation

卒業生 [sotsugyousei] 大学の卒業生 [daigaku no sotsugyousei] *n* graduate

層 [sou] *n* layer; オゾン層 [ozonsou] *n* ozone layer

沿う [sou] …に沿って […: ni sotte] *prep* along; 道に沿って進んでください [michi ni sotte susunde kudasai] Keep to the path

装置 [souchi] *n* device, equipment; ハイファイ装置 [haifai souchi] *n* hi-fi; 消音装置 [shouon souchi] *n* silencer; 掘削装置 [kussaku souchi] *n* rig; 点火装置 [tenkasouchi] *n* ignition; 除氷装置 [johyou souchi] *n* deicer

壮大 [soudai] 壮大な [sodai na] *adj* grand, magnificent

相談 [soudan] 相談する [soudan suru] *v* consult

双眼鏡 [sougankyou] *n* binoculars

葬儀 [sougi] 葬儀屋 [sougiya] *n* funeral director

葬儀場 [sougiba] *n* funeral home

相互 [sougo] 相互の [sougo no] *adj* mutual

総合 [sougou] 総合的な [sougouteki na] *adj* comprehensive

相違 [soui] *n* contrast; 意見の相違 [iken no soui] *n* disagreement

僧院 [souin] *n* abbey

掃除 [souji] *n* cleaning; 掃除する [souji suru] *v* clean; 掃除機で掃除する [soujiki de souji suru] *v* vacuum; 春季の大掃除 [shunki no ousouji] *n* spring-cleaning; 電気掃除機で掃除する [denki souji suru] *v* vacuum

掃除婦 [soujifu] *n* cleaning lady

掃除機 [soujiki] 掃除機で掃除する [soujiki de souji suru] *v* vacuum; 電気掃除機で掃除する [denki soujiki de souji suru] *v* vacuum; 電気掃除機 [denki soujiki] *n* vacuum cleaner

操縦桿 [soujuukan] *n* joystick

壮観 [soukan] 壮観な [soukan na] *adj* spectacular

送金 [soukin] *n* remittance

倉庫 [souko] *n* warehouse

走行 [soukou] 走行マイル計 [soukou mairu kei] *n* odometer

草木 [soumoku] *n* vegetation

騒音 [souon] *n* noise

騒る [sou ru] 騒ぎたてる [sawagitateru] *adj* fussy

操作 [sousa] 操作する [sousa suru] *v* operate *(to function)*

捜索 [sousaku] *n* search; 捜索する [sousaku suru] *v* search; 捜索隊 [sousakutai] *n* search party

走者 [sousha] 短距離走者 [tankyori sousha] *n* sprinter

奏者 [sousha] バイオリン奏者 [baiorinsousha] *n* violinist

葬式 [soushiki] *n* funeral

喪失 [soushitsu] *n* loss

装飾 [soushoku] 装飾する [soushoku suru] *v* decorate; 装飾用のぴかぴか光る金属片や糸 [soushoku you no pikapika hikaru kinzokuhen ya ito] *n* tinsel; 室内装飾家 [shitsunai soushokuka] *n* painter *(in house)*

装飾品 [soushokuhin] *n* ornament

曾祖母 [sousobo] *n* great-grandmother

曾祖父 [sousofu] *n* great-grandfather

想定 [soutei] 想定する [soutei suru] *v* assume, suppose

総売上高 [souuriagedaka] *n* turnover

相続 [souzoku] *n* inheritance; 相続する [souzoku suru] *v* inherit

相続人 [souzokunin] *n* heir

想像 [souzou] *n* imagination; 想像の [souzou no] *adj* imaginary; 想像する [souzou suru] *v* imagine

創造 [souzou] *n* creation; 創造する [souzou suru] *v* create; 創造的な [souzouteki na] *adj* creative

そよ風 [soyokaze] *n* breeze

粗雑 [sozatsu] 粗雑な [sozatsu na] *adj* crude

酢 [su] *n* vinegar

S

巣 [su] n nest; クモの巣 [kumo no su] n web

すばらしい [subarashii] adj excellent, fabulous, fantastic, glorious, marvelous, splendid, stunning, super, superb, terrific, wonderful; 昼食はすばらしかったです [chuushoku wa subarashikatta desu] The lunch was excellent

素早い [subayai] adj quick; 素早く [subayaku] adv quickly

滑る [suberu] v slide, slip; 滑りやすい [suberiyasui] adj slippery; 滑ること [suberu koto] n slide

スチュワーデス [suchuwaadesu] n flight attendant

スチュワード [suchuwaado] n steward

すでに [sude ni] adv already

スエード [sueedo] n suede

スエットシャツ [suettoshatsu] n sweatshirt

姿 [sugata] 姿を現す [sugata-o arawasu] v turn up

過ぎ [sugi] 八時過ぎに [hachi-ji sugi ni] after eight o'clock

過ぎる [sugiru] vi pass; ···を過ぎる [...-o sugiru] v go past

過ぎ去る [sugisaru] 過ぎ去った [sugisatta] adj past

過ごす [sugosu] 無為に過ごす [mui ni sugosu] v mess around; 私たちは楽しい時を過ごしています [watashi-tachi wa tanoshii toki wo sugoshite imasu] We're having a nice time

すぐ [sugu] adv immediately

すぐに [sugu ni] adv readily

優れる [sugureru] 優れた [sugureta] adj superior

スグリ [suguri] 赤スグリ [aka suguri] n red currant

垂直 [suichoku] 垂直の [suichoku no] adj vertical

水中 [suichuu] 水中に [suichuu ni] adv underwater

水泳 [suiei] n swimming

水泳場 [suieijou] 水泳場の救助員 [suieijou no kyuujoin] n lifeguard

水銀 [suigin] n mercury

水牛 [suigyuu] n buffalo

水平 [suihei] n level; 水平な [suihei na] adj horizontal; 水平の [suihei no] adj level

スイート [suiito] n suite

衰弱 [suijaku] 神経衰弱 [shinkeisuijaku] n nervous breakdown

水上スキー [suijousukii] どこで水上スキーができますか? [doko de suijou-sukii ga dekimasu ka?] Where can you go waterskiing?; ここで水上スキーはできますか? [koko de suijou-sukii wa dekimasu ka?] Is it possible to water-ski here?

水準 [suijun] 生活水準 [seikatsusuijun] n standard of living

スイカ [suika] n watermelon

スイカズラ [suikazura] n honeysuckle

吸い込む [suikomu] 息を吸い込む [iki-o suikomu] v breathe in; 現金自動支払い機が私のカードを吸い込んでしまいました [genkin-jidou-shiharaiki ga watashi no kaado o suikonde shimaimashita] The ATM swallowed my card

遂行 [suikou] n performance

睡眠 [suimin] 睡眠薬 [suimin-yaku] n sleeping pill

スイミング [suimingu] スイミングプールはありますか? [suimingu-puuru wa arimasu ka?] Is there a swimming pool?

スイミングプール [suimingupuuru] n swimming pool; スイミングプールはありますか? [suimingu-puuru wa arimasu ka?] Is there a swimming pool?; 公共のスイミングプールはどこですか? [koukyou no suimingu-puuru wa doko desu ka?] Where is the public swimming pool?

スイミングトランクス [suimingutorankusu] n swimming trunks

水彩絵 [suisaie] 水彩絵の具 [suisai enogu] n watercolor

彗星 [suisei] n comet

水晶 [suishou] n crystal

水素 [suiso] n hydrogen

推測 [suisoku] n guess; 推測する [suisoku suru] v guess, speculate

水槽 [suisou] n aquarium

スイス [suisu] n Switzerland; スイス人 [suisujin] n Swiss (person); スイスの [suisu no] adj Swiss

スイッチ [suitchi] n switch

推定 [suitei] 推定する [suitei suru] v presume

水曜日 [suiyoubi] n Wednesday; 灰の水曜日 [hai no suiyoubi] n Ash Wednesday; 水曜日に [suiyoubi ni] on Wednesday

スカーフ [sukaafu] n scarf

スカート [sukaato] n skirt

スカンジナビア [sukanjinabia] n Scandinavia; スカンジナビアの [Sukanjinabia no] adj Scandinavian

スカッシュ [sukasshu] n squash

スケート [sukeeto] n skating; スケートをする [sukeeto wo suru] v skate; スケートリンク [sukeetorinku] n ice rink; スケート靴 [sukeeto kutsu] n skates; 片足スケート [kataashi sukeeto] n scooter

スケートボーディング [sukeetoboodeingu] n skateboarding

スケートボード [sukeetoboodo] n skateboard; 私はスケートボードをしたいのですが [watashi wa sukeetoboodo o shitai no desu ga] I'd like to go skateboarding

スケートリンク [sukeetorinku] n rink, skating rink

透ける [sukeru] 透けて見える [sukete mieru] adj see-through

スケッチ [suketchi] n sketch; スケッチを描く [suketchi-o egaku] v sketch

鋤 [suki] n plow, spade

好き [suki] n fondness; スポーツ好きの [supootsuzuki no] adj sporty; 話好きな [hanashi zuki na] adj talkative; 詮索好きな [sensaku zuki na] adj inquisitive; ···が好きになる [... ga suki ni naru] v fall for

スキー [sukii] n ski, skiing; スキーをする [sukii wo suru] v ski; 水上スキー [suijousukii] n waterskiing; 1日スキーパスが欲しいのですが [ichinichi sukii-pasu ga hoshii no desu ga] I'd like a ski pass for a day; 1週間スキーパスが欲しいのですが [isshuukan sukii-pasu ga hoshii no desu ga] I'd like a ski pass for a week; どこでスキーパスを買えますか? [doko de sukii-pasu o kaemasu ka?] Where can I buy a ski pass?; どこでスキー用具を借りられますか? [doko de sukii-yougu o kariraremasu ka?] Where can I rent skiing equipment?; スキーに行きたいのですが [sukii ni ikitai no desu ga] I'd like to go skiing; スキーのレッスンを企画していますか? [sukii no ressun o kikaku shite imasu ka?] Can you arrange for skiing lessons?; スキースクールはありますか? [sukii-sukuuru wa arimasu ka?] Is there a ski school?; スキーパスはいくらですか? [sukii-pasu wa ikura desu ka?] How much is a ski pass?; ダウンヒルスキーの板を借りたいのですが [daunhiru-sukii no ita o karitai no desu ga] I want to rent downhill skis

スキー板 [sukiiita] ここでスキー板を借りられますか? [koko de sukii-ita o kariraremasu ka?] Can we rent skis here?; スキー板を借りたいのですが [sukii-ita o karitai no desu ga] I want to rent skis

スキー場 [sukiijou] スキー場のリフト [sukii jou no rifuto] n ski lift; スキー場のパス [sukii jou no pasu] n ski pass

スキーヤー [sukiiyaa] n skier

隙間 [sukima] n gap

隙間風 [sukimakaze] n draft

好きな [suki na] 詮索好きな [sensaku zuki na] adj nosy

スキンヘッド [sukinheddo] n skinhead

すっかり [sukkari] すっかり白状する [sukkari hakujou suru] v own up

少し [sukoshi] 少しの [sukoshi no] adj few

スコットランド [sukottorando] n Scotland; スコットランド人 [sukottorandojin] n Scot (person); スコットランド人男性 [Sukottorando jin dansei] n Scotsman; スコットランド人女性 [Sukottorando jin josei] n Scotswoman; スコ

S

ットランドの [sukottorando no] adj Scots, Scottish

すく [suku] 私はおなかがすいています [watashi wa onaka ga suite imasu] I'm hungry; 私はおなかがすいていません [watashi wa onaka ga suite imasen] I'm not hungry

すくめる [sukumeru] 肩をすくめる [kata wo sukumeru] v shrug

すくむ [sukumu] adj petrified

少ない [sukunai] 最も少ない [mottomo sukunai] adj least

少なく [sukunaku] adv less

少なくとも [sukunakutomo] adv at least

スクラップブック [sukurappubukku] n scrapbook

スクリーン [sukuriin] n screen

スクリーンセーバー [sukuriinseebaa] n screen saver

救う [sukuu] v rescue, save

スクール [sukuuru] スキースクールはあります か? [sukii-sukuuru wa arimasu ka?] Is there a ski school?

スキャナー [sukyanaa] n scanner

スキャンダル [sukyandaru] n scandal

スキューバダイビング [sukyuubadaibingu] n scuba diving

スマート [sumaato] スマートな [sumaato na] adj smart

スマートフォン [sumaatofon] n smart phone

スマイリー [sumairii] n smiley

済ます [sumasu] ···なしで済ます [... nashide sumasu] v do without

済み [sumi] 支払い済みの [shiharaizumi no] adj paid; 調理済みの [chouri zumi no] adj ready-to-serve

すみません [sumimasen] Excuse me

住む [sumu] v live; 人の住んでいない [hito no sunde inai] adj uninhabited; 住む家のない [sumu ie no nai] adj homeless; 住む場所 [sumu basho] n accommodations

砂 [suna] n sand; 砂のお城 [suna no oshiro] n sand castle

砂場 [sunaba] n sandbox

スナップ [sunappu] スナップ写真 [sunappu shashin] n snapshot

すなわち [sunawachi] conj i.e.

すねる [suneru] v sulk; すねた [suneta] adj sulky

スニーカー [suniikaa] n sneakers

スノーボード [sunooboodo] スノーボードのレ ッスンを企画していますか? [sunooboodo no ressun o kikaku shite imasu ka?] Do you plan on having snowboarding lessons?

スノーボート [sunoobooto] スノーボードを借 りたいのですが [sunooboodo o karitai no desu ga] I want to rent a snowboard

スノーチェーン [sunoocheen] スノーチェーン は必要ですか? [sunoo-cheen wa hitsuyou desu ka?] Do I need snow chains?

寸法 [sunpou] n dimension

スヌーカー [sunuukaa] n snooker

スパークプラグ [supaakupuragu] n spark plug

スパゲッティ [supagetti] n spaghetti

スパイ [supai] n mole (infiltrator), spy; スパ イ行為 [supai koui] n espionage, spying

スパムメール [supamumeeru] n spam

スパナ [supana] n wrench

スパニエル [supanieru] n spaniel

スペアホイール [supeahoiiru] n spare wheel

スペアパーツ [supeapaatsu] n spare part

スペアタイヤ [supeataiya] n spare tire

スペース [supeesu] n space; 作業スペース [sagyou supeesu] n workspace; 頭上スペー ス [zujou supeesu] n clearance

スペイン [supein] n Spain; スペイン人 [supeinjin] n Spaniard, Spanish (person); ス ペインの [supein no] adj Spanish

スペルチェッカー [superuchekkaa] n spell checker

スピード [supiido] n speed

スピーカー [supiikaa] n loudspeaker

スピリッツ [supirittsu] n spirits

スポンジ [suponji] n sponge (for washing)

スポンジケーキ [suponji keeki] n sponge

cake

スポーク [supooku] n spoke

スポークスマン [supookusuman] n spokesman

スポークスパーソン [supookusupaason] n spokesperson

スポークスウーマン [supookusuuuman] n spokeswoman

スポーツ [supootsu] n sport; スポーツ好きの [supootsuzuki no] adj sporty; 血を見るスポーツ [chi-o miru supootsu] n blood sports; どんなスポーツ施設がありますか? [donna supootsu-shisetsu ga arimasu ka?] What sports facilities are there?; 私たちはどのスポーツイベントに行けますか? [watashi-tachi wa dono supootsu-ibento ni ikemasu ka?] Which sporting events can we go to?

スポーツマン [supootsuman] n sportsman

スポーツウェア [supootsuuea] n sportswear

スポーツウーマン [supootsuuuman] n sportswoman

スポットライト [supottoraito] n spotlight

酸っぱい [suppai] adj sour

スプレッドシート [supureddoshiito] n spreadsheet

スプリンクラー [supurinkuraa] n sprinkler

スプーン [supuun] n spoon; デザートスプーン [dezaato supuun] n dessert spoon; 新しいスプーンをいただけますか? [atarashii supuun o itadakemasu ka?] Could I have a clean spoon, please?

スラム [suramu] スラム街 [suramugai] n slum

スレート [sureeto] n slate

スレッジング [surejjingu] n sledding

スリ [suri] n pickpocket

すりおろす [suriorosu] v grate

スリッパ [surippa] n slipper

スリップ [surippu] n (下着) slip (underwear)

スリラー [suriraa] n thriller

スリランカ [suriranka] n Sri Lanka

スロバキア [surobakia] n Slovakia; スロバキア人 [Surobakia jin] n Slovak (person); スロバキアの [Surobakia no] adj Slovak; スロバキア語 [Surobakia go] n Slovak (language)

スロベニア [surobenia] n Slovenia; スロベニア人 [Surobenia jin] n Slovenian (person); スロベニアの [Surobenia no] adj Slovenian; スロベニア語 [Surobenia go] n Slovenian (language)

スロープ [suroopu] n slope; このスロープはどのくらい難しいですか? [kono suroopu wa dono kurai muzukashii desu ka?] How difficult is this slope?; 初心者用のスロープはどこですか? [shoshinsha-you no suroopu wa doko desu ka?] Where are the beginners' slopes?

スロット [surotto] n slot

スロットマシン [surottomashin] n slot machine, vending machine

する [suru] v do; ···させる [... saseru] v let; ···しそうな [... shisou na] adj likely; ···をする [...-o suru] v do; 今日は何をなさりたいですか? [kyou wa nani o nasaritai desu ka?] What would you like to do today?

鋭い [surudoi] adj sharp; 観察力の鋭い [kansatsuryoku no surudoi] adj observant

スルタナ [surutana] n golden raisin

···するつもりだ [...suru tsumori da] v intend to

すす [susu] n soot

すすぐ [susugu] v rinse; すすぎ [susugi] n rinse

勧め [susume] n recommendation

勧める [susumeru] v recommend

進む [susumu] v advance; 先へ進む [saki-e susumu] v go ahead; 前へ進む [mae-e susumu] v move forward

進んで [susunde] adv willingly

スター [sutaa] n star (person); 映画スター [eigasutaa] n movie star

スターター [sutaataa] n starter

スタッフ [sutaffu] 販売スタッフ [hanbai sutaffu] n sales assistant

スタッグパーティー [sutaggupaateii] n bachelor party

スタイリング [sutairingu] スタイリング用品を売

っていますか? [sutairingu youhin o utte imasu ka?] Do you sell styling products?

スタイリスト [sutairisuto] *n* stylist

スタイル [sutairu] *n* style; ヘアスタイル [heasutairu] *n* hairdo, hairstyle; このスタイルでお願いします [kono sutairu de o-negai shimasu] This style, please; 全く新しいスタイルにしてください [mattaku atarashii sutairu ni shite kudasai] I want a completely new style

スタジアム [sutajiamu] *n* stadium; そのスタジアムにはどうやって行くのですか? [sono sutajiamu ni wa dou-yatte iku no desu ka?] How do we get to the stadium?

スタジオ [sutajio] *n* studio

スタジオフラット [sutajiofuratto] *n* studio apartment

スタミナ [sutamina] *n* stamina

スタンド [sutando] *n* stands

スタントマン [sutantoman] *n* stuntman

すたれる [sutareru] すたれた [sutareta] *adj* obsolete

ステアリング [sutearingu] *n* steering

ステアリングホイール [sutearinguhoiiru] *n* steering wheel

ステーキ [suteeki] *n* steak

ステープラー [suteepuraa] *n* stapler

ステープル [suteepuru] *n* staple (*wire*); ステープルで留める [suteepuru de todomeru] *v* staple

ステイルメイト [suteirumeito] *n* stalemate

すてきな [sutekina] *adj* nice

ステッカー [sutekkaa] *n* sticker

ステッキ [sutekki] *n* cane

ステンドグラス [sutendogurasu] *n* stained glass

ステンレススチール [sutenresusuchiiru] *n* stainless steel

ステレオ [sutereo] *n* stereo

ステレオタイプ [sutereotaipu] *n* stereotype

ステロイド [suteroido] *n* steroid

捨てる [suteru] *v* ditch, throw away; 使い捨ての [tsukaisute no] *adj* disposable; ごみ捨て場 [gomi suteba] *n* dump, landfill

スティック [sutikku] ディップスティック [dippu sutikku] *n* dipstick

ストッキング [sutokkingu] *n* stocking

ストック [sutokku] *n* ski pole; ストックを借りたいのですが [sutokku o karitai no desu ga] I want to rent ski poles

ストップウォッチ [sutoppuuocchi] *n* stopwatch

ストライキ [sutoraiki] *n* strike; ストライキ参加者 [sutoraiki sankasha] *n* striker; ストライキがあったからです [sutoraiki ga atta kara desu] because there was a strike

ストライキをする [sutoraiki wo suru] strike (*suspend work*)

ストレイトナー [sutoreitonaa] *n* straighteners

ストレス [sutoresu] *n* stress; ストレスの多い [sutoresu no oui] *adj* stressful; ストレスがたまった [sutoresu ga tamatta] *adj* stressed

ストリート [sutoriito] *n* street; その街のストリートマップが欲しいのですが [sono machi no sutoriito-mappu ga hoshii no desu ga] I want a street map of the city

ストリッパー [sutorippaa] *n* stripper

ストリップ [sutorippu] *n* strip

スツール [sutsuuru] *n* stool

吸う [suu] *v* suck; 鼻で吸う [hana de suu] *v* sniff

スーダン [suudan] *n* Sudan; スーダン人 [Suudan jin] *n* Sudanese (*person*); スーダンの [Suudan no] *adj* Sudanese

スウェーデン [suueeden] *n* Sweden; スウェーデン人 [suueedenjin] *n* Swede, Swedish (*person*); スウェーデンの [suueeden no] *adj* Swedish

スウェーデンカブ [suueedenkabu] *n* rutabaga

数分 [suufun] ここで数分待ってもらえますか? [koko de suu-fun matte moraemasu ka?] Could you wait here for a few minutes?

数学 [suugaku] *n* math, mathematics; 数学の [suugaku no] *adj* mathematical

数字 [suuji] *n* figure

スーパー [suupaa] *adj* super; 郊外の大型スーパー [kougai no ougata suupaa] *n* hypermarket

スーパーマーケット [suupaamaaketto] *n* supermarket; 私はスーパーマーケットをさがしています [watashi ha suupaamaaketto wosagashiteimasu] I need to find a supermarket

スープ [suupu] *n* soup; 固形スープの素 [kokei suupu no moto] *n* bouillon cube; 今日のおすすめスープは何ですか? [kyou no osusume suupu wa nan desu ka?] What is the soup of the day?

スーツ [suutsu] *n* suit

スーツケース [suutsukeesu] *n* suitcase

スワジランド [suwajirando] *n* Swaziland

すわり心地 [suwarigokochi] すわり心地がよくありません [suwari-gokochi ga yoku arimasen] The seat is uncomfortable

座る [suwaru] *v* sit; どこに座ればいいですか? [doko ni suwareba ii desu ka?] Where can I sit down?; どこか座れる場所がありますか? [doko-ka suwareru basho ga arimasu ka?] Is there somewhere I can sit down?; ここに座ってもいいですか? [koko ni suwatte mo ii desu ka?] May I sit here?

錫 [suzu] *n* tin

スズメ [suzume] *n* sparrow

スズメバチ [suzumebachi] *n* wasp

涼しい [suzushii] *adj* cool *(cold)*

T

ターミナル [taaminaru] n terminal; バスター
ミナル [basutaaminaru] n bus station

タールマカダム [taarumakadamu] n
blacktop

タータン [taatan] タータンの [taatan no] adj
tartan

束 [taba] n (ひとまとめ) bunch

タバコ [tabako] n cigarette; タバコ屋
[tabakoya] n tabaconist

食物 [tabemono] 食物を与える [tabemono o
ataeru] v feed

食べ物 [tabemono] n food; 食べ物に香辛料が
ききすぎています [tabemono ni koushinryou
ga kiki-sugite imasu] The food is too spicy;
食べ物に塩味がききすぎています [tabemono
ni shioaji ga kiki-sugite imasu] The food is
too salty; 食べ物はありますか? [tabemono
wa arimasu ka?] Do you have food?; 食べ
物がとても脂っこいです [tabemono ga totemo
aburakkoi desu] The food is very greasy;
食べ物が熱すぎます [tabemono ga atsu-sugi-
masu] The food is too hot; 食べ物が冷たす
ぎます [tabemono ga tsumeta-sugimasu]
The food is too cold

食べ残し [tabenokoshi] n leftovers

食べる [taberu] v eat; 食べられる [taberareru]
adj edible; 何を召し上がりますか? [nani o
meshiagarimasu ka?] What would you like
to eat?; テラスで食べられますか? [terasu de
taberaremasu ka?] Can I eat on the
terrace?; 私は肉を食べません [watashi wa
niku o tabemasen] I don't eat meat

食付き [tabetsuki] n mean plan

旅 [tabi] 苦難に満ちた旅 [kunan ni michita
tabi] n trek; 苦難に耐えつつ旅をする [kunan

ni taetsutsu tabi-o suru] v trek

旅立つ [tabidatsu] v start off

たびたび [tabitabi] たびたびの [tabitabi no]
adj frequent

多分 [tabun] adv probably

タブー [tabuu] n taboo; タブーとなっている
[tabuu to natte iru] adj taboo

タッチパッド [tacchipaddo] n touch pad

タッチライン [tacchirain] n touchline

立ち上がる [tachiagaru] v rise

立ち直る [tachinaoru] v get over

立ち往生 [tachioujou] 立ち往生した
[tachioujou shita] adj stranded

立ち去る [tachisaru] v go away

立ち退く [tachishirizoku] v vacate

太刀打ち [tachiuchi] 太刀打ちできない
[tachiuchi dekinai] adj unbeatable

立ち寄る [tachiyoru] 立ち寄ること [tachiyoru
koto] n stopover

ただ [tada] ただ一人の [tada hitori no] adj
alone

正しい [tadashii] adj correct, right (correct);
正しく [tadashiku] adv correctly

正しく [tadashiku] adv correctly, rightly

たどりなおす [tadorinaosu] v retrace

たどる [tadoru] 跡をたどって見つけ出す [ato-o
tadotte mitsukedasu] v track down

耐える [taeru] 耐えられない [taerarenai] adj
intolerant, unbearable

絶えず [taezu] v constantly; 絶えず続く
[taezu tsuzuku] adj constant

多額 [tagaku] 多額の賞金 [tagaku no shoukin]
n jackpot

耕す [tagayasu] v plow

多発性硬化症 [tahatsusei koukashou] n

multiple sclerosis, MS

タヒチ [tahichi] n Tahiti

多方面 [tahoumen] 多方面の [tahoumen no] adj versatile

隊 [tai] n group; 捜索隊 [sousakutai] n search party; 沿岸警備隊 [engankeibitai] n coast guard

タイ [tai] n (国) Thailand; タイ人 [Tai jin] n Thai (person); タイの [Tai no] adj Thai; タイ語 [taigo] n Thai (language)

体調 [taichou] 体調が悪い [taichou ga warui] adj unwell

怠惰 [taida] 怠惰な [taida na] adj lazy

態度 [taido] n attitude, behavior

大義 [taigi] n cause (ideals)

大破 [taiha] n wreck; 大破する [taiha suru] v wreck

太平洋 [taiheiyou] n Pacific

大変 [taihen] adv extremely

待避 [taihi] 待避場所 [taihi basho] n rest area

堆肥 [taihi] n manure

逮捕 [taiho] n arrest; 逮捕する [taiho suru] v arrest

退院 [taiin] 私はいつ退院できますか? [watashi wa itsu taiin dekimasu ka?] When will I be discharged?; 彼はいつ退院できますか? [kare wa itsu taiin dekimasu ka?] When will he be discharged?

胎児 [taiji] n fetus

体重 [taijuu] あなたの体重はどのくらいありますか? [anata no taijuu wa dono kurai arimasu ka?] How much do you weigh?

対角 [taikaku] 対角の [taikaku no] adj diagonal

体系 [taikei] 体系的な [taikeiteki na] adj systematic; 神話体系 [shinwa taikei] n mythology

体刑 [taikei] n corporal punishment

体験 [taiken] 苦しい体験 [kurushii taiken] n ordeal; 労働体験 [roudou taiken] n work experience

大気 [taiki] n atmosphere

大金 [taikin] n fortune

退屈 [taikutsu] n boredom; 退屈な [taikutsu na] adj boring; 退屈した [taikutsu shita] adj bored

退去 [taikyo] 国外退去させる [kokugai taikyo saseru] v deport

大麻 [taima] n cannabis

タイマー [taimaa] n timer

怠慢 [taiman] n neglect

タイム [taimu] n thyme

耐熱 [tainetsu] オーブン耐熱性の [oobun tainetsusei no] adj ovenproof

タイピスト [taipisuto] n typist

タイプ [taipu] タイプする [taipu suru] v type

タイプライター [taipuraitaa] n typewriter

平 [taira] 平らな [taira na] adj flat

平らな [taira na] adj even

平なべ [taira nabe] n pan

平皿 [taira sara] n plate

大陸 [tairiku] n continent; 南極大陸 [Nankyoku tairiku] adj Antarctic

タイル [tairu] n tile; タイルを張った [tairu-o hatta] adj tiled

大量 [tairyou] n mass (amount)

大佐 [taisa] n colonel

大西洋 [taiseiyou] n Atlantic

代謝 [taisha] n metabolism

貸借 [taishaku] 貸借対照表 [taishakutaishouhyou] n balance sheet

大使 [taishi] n ambassador

大使館 [taishikan] n embassy; 私は大使館に電話したいのですが [watashi wa taishikan ni denwa shitai no desu ga] I'd like to phone my embassy; 私は大使館に電話をしなければなりません [watashi wa taishikan ni denwa o shinakereba narimasen] I need to call my embassy

対処 [taisho] うまく対処する [umaku taisho suru] v cope

退職 [taishoku] n retirement; 退職した [taishoku shita] adj retired; 退職する [taishoku suru] v retire

対称 [taishou] 左右対称の [sayuu taishou no] adj symmetrical

体操 [taisou] *n* gymnastics; 体操家 [taisouka] *n* gymnast

たいてい [taitei] *adv* mostly

タイツ [taitsu] *n* tights

対話 [taiwa] *n* dialogue

台湾 [taiwan] *n* Taiwan; 台湾人 [Taiwan jin] *n* Taiwanese *(person)*; 台湾の [Taiwan no] *adj* Taiwanese

タイヤ [taiya] *n* tire; タイヤがパンクしています [taiya ga panku shite imasu] I have a flat tire; タイヤがパンクしました [taiya ga panku shimashita] I have a flat tire; タイヤが破裂しました [taiya ga haretsu shimashita] The tire has burst; タイヤを点検してもらえますか? [taiya o tenken shite moraemasu ka?] Could you check the tires, please?

タイヤ圧 [taiyaatsu] *n* tire pressure; 適正なタイヤ圧はどのくらいですか? [tekisei na taiya-atsu wa dono kurai desu ka?] What should the tire pressure be?

太陽 [taiyou] *n* sun; 太陽の [taiyou no] *adj* solar; 太陽エネルギー [taiyou enerugii] *n* solar power; 太陽系 [taiyoukei] *n* solar system

滞在 [taizai] *n* stay; 私はホテルに滞在しています [watashi wa hoteru ni taizai shite imasu] I'm staying at a hotel

タジキスタン [tajikisutan] *n* Tajikistan

高い [takai] *adj* (高低) high, (高低) tall

高く [takaku] *adv* high

高まる [takamaru] 高まり [takamari] *n* surge

高める [takameru] *v* boost

宝くじ [takarakuji] *n* lottery

高さ [takasa] *n* height

竹 [take] *n* bamboo

滝 [taki] *n* waterfall; 大きな滝 [ouki na taki] *n* cataract *(waterfall)*

タキシード [takishiido] *n* tuxedo

タックル [takkuru] *n* tackle

卓球 [takkyuu] *n* table tennis

凧 [tako] *n* kite

タコ [tako] *n* (動物) octopus

多国籍 [takokuseki] 多国籍企業 [takokuseki kigyou] *n* multinational; 多国籍の [takokuseki no] *adj* multinational

宅配 [takuhai] これを宅配便で送りたいのですが [kore o takuhai-bin de okuritai no desu ga] I want to send this by courier

託児 [takuji] 託児所 [takujisho] *n* day care center; 託児サービスはありますか? [takuji saabisu wa arimasu ka?] Is there child care service?

たくましい [takumashii] 筋骨たくましい [kinkotsu takumashii] *adj* muscular

巧む [takumu] 巧みに扱う [takumi ni atsukau] *v* manipulate

たくらむ [takuramu] *v* plot *(secret plan)*

タクシー [takushii] *n* cab, taxi; タクシー乗り場 [takushii noriba] *n* taxi stand; タクシー運転手 [takushii untenshu] *n* taxi driver; 小型タクシー [kogata takushii] *n* private taxi; どこでタクシーに乗れますか? [doko de takushii ni noremasu ka?] Where can I get a taxi?; タクシー乗り場はどこですか? [takushii-noriba wa doko desu ka?] Where is the taxi stand?; タクシーを呼んでください [takushii o yonde kudasai] Please order me a taxi; 街までのタクシー料金はいくらですか? [machi made no takushii-ryoukin wa ikura desu ka?] How much is the taxi fare into town?; 荷物をタクシーに運んでください [nimotsu o takushii ni hakonde kudasai] Please take my luggage to a taxi; 私はタクシーにかばんを置き忘れました [watashi wa takushii ni kaban o okiwasuremashita] I left my bags in the taxi; 私はタクシーが必要です [watashi wa takushii ga hitsuyou desu] I need a taxi; 私たちはタクシーを相乗りすることもできます [watashi-tachi wa takushii o ainori suru koto mo dekimasu] We could share a taxi; 八時にタクシーを呼んでください [hachi-ji ni takushii o yonde kudasai] Please order me a taxi for eight o'clock

蓄え [takuwae] *n* reserve *(retention)*

蓄える [takuwaeru] *v* save up, store

卵 [tamago] *n* egg; ゆで卵 [yudetamago] *n*

hard-boiled egg; 復活祭の卵 [Fukkatsusai no tamago] n Easter egg; 卵の白身 [tamago no shiromi] n egg white; 卵の黄身 [tamago no kimi] n egg yolk, yolk; 卵を使わずに食事を用意していただけますか? [tamago o tsukawazu ni shokuji o youi shite itadakemasu ka?] Could you prepare a meal without eggs?

タマネギ [tamanegi] n onion

たまる [tamaru] ストレスがたまった [sutoresu ga tamatta] adj stressed

魂 [tamashii] n soul

ため息 [tameiki] n sigh; ため息をつく [tameiki wo tsuku] v sigh

ためらう [tamerau] v hesitate

試しす [tameshi su] 試してみる [tameshite miru] v try out

試す [tamesu] v test

単 [tan] 単に [tan ni] adv only

棚 [tana] n shelf; 手荷物置き棚 [tenimotsu okidana] n luggage rack; 食器棚 [shokkidana] n cupboard, hutch

単調 [tánchou] adj 単調な [tanchou na] adj monotonous

タンデム [tandemu] タンデム自転車 [tandemu jitensha] n tandem bicycle

単独 [tandoku] 単独の [tandoku no] adj separate

種² [tane] n (植物) seed

嘆願 [tangan] 嘆願書 [tangansho] n petition

単語 [tango] n word

谷間 [taniai] n valley

単一体 [tan'itsutai] n unit

タンジェリン [tanjierin] n tangerine

誕生 [tanjou] n birth

誕生日 [tanjoubi] n birthday; お誕生日おめでとう! [o-tanjoubi omedetou!] Happy birthday!

担架 [tanka] n stretcher

タンカー [tankaa] n tanker

探検 [tanken] n expedition; 探検家 [tankenka] n explorer

短気 [tanki] n impatience

炭鉱 [tankou] n colliery

炭坑 [tankou] 炭坑労働者 [tankou roudousha] n miner

タンク [tanku] n tank (large container)

胆嚢 [tannou] n gall bladder

頼み [tanomi] n request

頼む [tanomu] v request

楽しい [tanoshii] adj delightful, enjoyable, fun, pleasant; 楽しく遊ぶ [tanoshiku asobu] v have fun

楽しみ [tanoshimi] n fun, pleasure; 歓楽街での夜の楽しみ [kanrakugai deno yoru no tanoshimi] n nightlife

楽む [tanoshimu] 楽しませる [tanoshimaseru] v amuse

楽しむ [tanoshimu] v enjoy; 楽しませる [tanoshimaseru] v entertain; お食事をお楽しみください! [o-shokuji o o-tanoshimi kudasai!] Enjoy your meal!

蛋白質 [tanpakushitsu] n protein

短篇 [tanpen] 短篇小説 [tanpen shousetsu] n short story

タンポン [tanpon] n tampon

タンポポ [tanpopo] n dandelion

炭酸 [tansan] 炭酸なしミネラルウォーターのボトル1本 [tansan-nashi mineraru-wootaa no botoru ippon] a bottle of still mineral water

たんさん [tansan] たんさんすい [tansansui] n sparkling water

胆石 [tanseki] n gallstone

炭素 [tanso] n carbon

たんす [tansu] 整理だんす [seiridansu] n bureau

淡水魚 [tansuigyo] n freshwater fish

炭水化物 [tansuikabutsu] n carbohydrate

単数 [tansuu] n singular

タンザニア [tanzania] n Tanzania; タンザニア人 [Tanzania jin] n Tanzanian (person); タンザニアの [Tanzania no] adj Tanzanian

鍛造 [tanzou] 鍛造する [tanzou suru] v forge

倒れる [taoreru] v fall down

タオル [taoru] n towel; バスタオル

T

[basutaoru] n bath towel; 浴用タオル

[yokuyou taoru] n washcloth; 洗面用タオル

[senmen you taoru] n washcloth; タオルが
補充されていません [taoru ga hojuu sarete
imasen] There are no more towels; タオル
をもっと持ってきてください [taoru o motto
motte kite kudasai] Please bring me more
towels; タオルを貸していただけますか?
[taoru o kashite itadakemasu ka?] Could
you lend me a towel?

倒す [taosu] 打ち倒す [uchitaosu] v knock
down

タップダンス [tappudansu] n tap-dancing

たっぷり [tappuri] n plenty

タラ [tara] n cod

タラゴン [taragon] n tarragon

樽 [taru] n barrel

タルカムパウダー [tarukamupaudaa] n
talcum powder

たるむ [tarumu] たるんだ [tarunda] adj flabby

タルト [taruto] n tart

確かに [tashika ni] adv certainly, surely

達成 [tassei] n achievement; 達成する [tassei
suru] v achieve

足す [tasu] v add

助ける [tasukeru] v help; すぐに助けを呼んで!
[sugu ni tasuke o yonde!] Get help
quickly!; 助けていただけますか? [tasukete
itadakemasu ka?] Can you help me,
please?; 助けてもらえますか? [tasukete
moraemasu ka?] Can you help me?; 助け
て! [tasukete!] Help!

助けて! [tasukete] excl help!

タスマニア [tasumania] n Tasmania

多数 [tasuu] n host (multitude); 多数の
[tasuu no] adj numerous

戦い [tatakai] n fight, fighting

戦う [tatakau] v fight

たたき切る [tatakikiru] v chop, hack; たたき切
ること [tatakikiru koto] n chop

たたく [tataku] v knock; たたくこと [tataku
koto] n knock; 軽くたたくこと [karuku tataku
koto] n tap

盾 [tate] n shield

建具 [tategu] 建具屋 [tateguya] n carpenter

建物 [tatemono] n building; 土地建物 [tochi
tatemono] n premises

立てる [tateru] 腹を立てた [hara-o tateta] adj
mad (angry)

建てる [tateru] v build, put up

たとえば [tatoeba] adv for example

立つ [tatsu] v stand; ・・・の先頭に立つ [... no
sentou ni tatsu] v head

断つ [tatsu] 接続を断つ [setsuzoku-o tatsu] v
disconnect

竜巻 [tatsumaki] n tornado

たった一つ [tatta hitotsu] たった一つの [tatta
hitotsu no] adj single

タウンホール [taunhooru] n town hall

たわごと [tawagoto] たわごとを並べる
[tawagoto-o naraberu] v waffle

戯れ [tawamure] n prank

頼る [tayoru] v resort to; ・・・に頼る [... ni
tayoru] v count on

たよる [tayoru] ・・・にたよって暮らす [... ni
tayotte kurasu] v live on

多様 [tayou] 多様性 [tayousei] n variety

手綱 [tazuna] n reins

訪ねる [tazuneru] v visit; 私たちは・・・を訪れ
たいのですが [watashi-tachi wa... o
otozuretai no desu ga] We'd like to visit...;
友人を訪ねるために来ました [yuujin o
tazuneru tame ni kimashita] I'm here
visiting friends

尋ねる [tazuneru] v ask, inquire, query

手 [te] n hand; 手に持つ [te ni motsu] v hold;
手に入れる [te ni ireru] v obtain; 手を振る [te
wo furu] v wave; 話し手 [hanashite] n
speaker; どこで手を洗えばいいのですか?
[doko de te o araeba ii no desu ka?] Where
can I wash my hands?

手当たり次第 [teatarishidai] 手当たり次第の
[teatari shidai no] adj random

手当 [teate] 失業手当 [shitsugyouteate] n
welfare

手当て [teate] 病気休暇中の手当て [byouki

kyuukachuu no teate] n sick pay

手放す [tebanasu] ···を手放す [...-o tebanasu] v part with

手袋 [tebukuro] n glove; ゴム手袋 [gomu tebukuro] n rubber gloves

手帳 [techou] システム手帳 [shisutemu techou] n personal organizer

テディーベア [tedeiibea] n teddy bear

テーブル [teeburu] n table (furniture); コーヒーテーブル [koohii teeburu] n coffee table; ベッドサイドテーブル [beddosaido teeburu] n nightstand; 今晩九時にテーブルを予約しました [konban ku-ji ni teeburu o yoyaku shimashita] The table is reserved for nine o'clock this evening; 今晩三人用のテーブルを予約したいのですが [konban sannin-you no teeburu o yoyaku shitai no desu ga] I'd like to reserve a table for three people for tonight; 明日の晩二人用のテーブルを予約したいのですが [asu no ban futari-you no teeburu o yoyaku shitai no desu ga] I'd like to reserve a table for two people for tomorrow night; 四人用のテーブルをお願いします [yonin-you no teeburu o o-negai shimasu] A table for four people, please

テーブルチャージ [teeburuchaaji] テーブルチャージがかかりますか? [teeburu-chaaji ga kakarimasu ka?] Is there a cover charge?

テーブルクロス [teeburukurosu] n tablecloth

テーブルスプーン [teeburusupuun] n tablespoon

テーブルワイン [teeburuwain] n table wine

テークアウト [teekuauto] n takeout

テーマ [teema] n theme

テーマパーク [teemapaaku] n theme park

テープ [teepu] n tape; テープに記録する [teepu ni kiroku suru] v tape; このビデオカメラ用のテープをいただけますか? [kono bideo-kamera-you no teepu o itadakemasu ka?] Can I have a tape for this video camera, please?

テープレコーダー [teepurekoodaa] n tape recorder

テーラー [teeraa] n tailor

手がかり [tegakari] n clue

手書き [tegaki] n handwriting

手紙 [tegami] n letter (message); この手紙を送りたいのですが [kono tegami o okuritai no desu ga] I'd like to send this letter

手ごろな [tegoro na] adj affordable

手配 [tehai] n arrangement; 手配する [tehai suru] v arrange

低 [tei] 低アルコールの [tei arukooru no] adj low-alcohol; 低脂肪の [teishibou no] adj low-fat

提案 [teian] n proposal, suggestion; 提案する [teian suru] v propose, suggest

低木 [teiboku] n bush, shrub

堤防 [teibou] n embankment

停電 [teiden] n power outage

程度 [teido] n degree

庭園 [teien] n garden; 私たちがその庭園を訪れることはできますか? [watashi-tachi ga sono teien o otozureru koto wa dekimasu ka?] Can we visit the gardens?

定義 [teigi] n definition; 定義する [teigi suru] v define

停泊 [teihaku] 停泊させる [teihaku saseru] v moor

提携 [teikei] n alliance; 提携者 [teikeisha] n associate

定期 [teiki] n, adj routine; 定期便 [teikibin] n scheduled flight; 定期購読 [teiki koudoku] n subscription; 定期船 [teikisen] n liner; 定期的な [teikiteki na] adj regular; 定期的に [teikiteki ni] adv regularly; 定期往復便 [teiki oufuku bin] n shuttle; 定期券 [teikiken] n season ticket

帝国 [teikoku] n empire

抵抗 [teikou] n resistance; 抵抗する [teikou suru] v resist

提供 [teikyou] n offer; サービスを提供する [saabisu-o teikyou suru] v service; 提供する [teikyou suru] v offer

丁寧 [teinei] n politeness

T

丁寧な [teinei na] *adj* polite

丁寧に [teinei ni] *adv* politely

定年 [teinen] 私は定年退職しています [watashi wa teinen-taishoku shite imasu] I'm retired

低温 [teion] 低温殺菌した [teion sakkin shita] *adj* pasteurized

停留所 [teiryuusho] バス停 [basutei] *n* bus stop

偵察 [teisatsu] 偵察兵 [teisatsuhei] *n* scout

訂正 [teisei] *n* correction; 訂正する [teisei suru] *v* correct

停戦 [teisen] *n* cease-fire

停車 [teisha] ···に停車しますか? [... ni teisha shimasu ka?] Do we stop at...?

停止 [teishi] *n* halt; 一時停止 [ichiji teishi] *n* suspension

定食 [teishoku] *n* set menu

提唱 [teishou] 提唱する [teishou suru] *v* put forward

邸宅 [teitaku] 大邸宅 [daiteitaku] *n* mansion, villa

蹄鉄 [teitetsu] *n* horseshoe

抵当 [teitou] *n* mortgage; 抵当に入れる [teitou ni ireru] *v* mortgage

低俗 [teizoku] 低俗な [teizoku na] *adj* vulgar

手品 [tejina] *n* sleight of hand

手品師 [tejinashi] *n* conjurer, juggler, stage, magician

手錠 [tejou] *n* handcuffs

敵 [teki] *n* enemy; 敵にまわす [teki ni mawasu] *v* antagonize

適度 [tekido] *n* moderation; 適度の [tekido no] *adj* moderate

適合 [tekigou] 適合させる [tekigou saseru] *v* adapt

敵意 [tekii] 敵意のある [teki-i no aru] *adj* hostile

的な [teki na] 活動的な [katsudouteki na] *adj* dynamic

適性 [tekisei] 私は「飛行機搭乗の適性」証明書が必要です [watashi wa "hikouki-toujou no tekisei" shoumei-sho ga hitsuyou desu] I need a 'fit to fly' certificate

適切 [tekisetsu] 適切な [tekisetsu na] *adj* appropriate, suitable; 適切に [tekisetsu ni] *adv* properly

適切な [tekisetsu na] *adj* proper

適する [teki suru] *v* fit; 適した [tekishita] *adj* fit

テキストメッセージ [tekisutomesseeji] *n* text message; テキストメッセージを送る [tekisuto messeeji-o okuru] *v* text

敵対 [tekitai] 敵対者 [tekitaisha] *n* adversary, opponent

摘要 [tekiyou] *n* syllabus

手首 [tekubi] *n* wrist

テクノポップ [tekunopoppu] *n* techno (*music*)

点 [ten] *n* (符号) dot; 点を取る [ten-o toru] *v* score

天秤 [tenbin] *n* scales

天秤座 [tenbinza] *n* Libra

天国 [tengoku] *n* heaven

手荷物 [tenimotsu] *n* baggage, carry-on baggage, luggage; 手荷物一時預かり所 [tenimotsu ichiji azukarisho] *n* luggage storage office; 手荷物カート [tenimotsu kaato] *n* baggage cart; 手荷物置き棚 [tenimotsu okidana] *n* luggage rack; 手荷物受取所 [tenimotsu uketorisho] *n* baggage claim; 無料手荷物許容量 [muryou tenimotsu kyouyouryou] *n* baggage allowance; 預けた手荷物 [azuketa tenimotsu] *n* luggage storage; 手荷物に保険をかけられますか? [tenimotsu ni hoken o kakeraremasu ka?] Can I insure my luggage?; 手荷物のチェックインはどこでするのですか? [tenimotsu no chekku-in wa doko de suru no desu ka?] Where do I check in my luggage?; 無料手荷物許容量はどう規定されていますか? [muryou-tenimotsu-kyouyouryou wa dou kitei sarete imasu ka?] What is the baggage allowance?; 私の手荷物が着いていません [watashi no tenimotsu ga tsuite imasen] My luggage hasn't arrived; 私の手荷物が破損しています [watashi no tenimotsu ga hason shite imasu] My luggage has been damaged; 私の手荷物が紛失しました [watashi no tenimotsu ga funshitsu shimashita] My luggage has been lost; 私たちの手荷物が着いていません [watashi-tachi no tenimotsu ga tsuite imasen] Our luggage hasn't arrived; ···からのフライトの手荷物はどこですか? [... kara no furaito no tenimotsu wa doko desu ka?] Where is the luggage for the flight from...?

店員 [ten-in] n salesperson; 女性店員 [josei ten'in] n saleslady

テニス [tenisu] n tennis; テニス選手 [tenisusenshu] n tennis player; どこでテニスができますか? [doko de tenisu ga dekimasu ka?] Where can I play tennis?; 私たちはテニスがしたいのですが [watashi-tachi wa tenisu ga shitai no desu ga] We'd like to play tennis

テニスコート [tenisukooto] n tennis court; テニスコートを借りるのはいくらですか? [tenisu-kooto o kariru no wa ikura desu ka?] How much does it cost to use a tennis court?

テニスラケット [tenisuraketto] n tennis racket

手に取る [te ni toru] v take

展示 [tenji] n display, exhibition, showing; 展示する [tenji suru] v display

天井 [tenjou] n ceiling

点火 [tenka] 点火装置 [tenkasouchi] n ignition

添加 [tenka] 添加剤 [tenkazai] n additive

癲癇 [tenkan] 癲癇の発作 [tenkan no hossa] n epileptic seizure; 癲癇患者 [tenkan kanja] n epileptic

転換 [tenkan] 方向転換する [houkoutenkan suru] v turn around

典型 [tenkei] 典型的な [tenkeiteki na] adj classic, typical

点検 [tenken] n inspection

天気 [tenki] n weather; 天気予報 [tenkiyohou] n forecast, weather forecast; なんてひどい天気でしょう! [nante hidoi tenki deshou!]

What awful weather!; 明日はどんな天気でしょう? [asu wa donna tenki deshou?] What will the weather be like tomorrow?; 天気予報はどうですか? [tenki-yohou wa dou desu ka?] What's the weather forecast?; 天気は変わりますか? [tenki wa kawarimasu ka?] Is the weather going to change?; 天気がこのまま続いてくれるといいですね [tenki ga kono-mama tsuzuite kureru to ii desu ne] I hope the weather stays like this; 天気がもち直すといいですね [tenki ga mochinaosu to ii desu ne] I hope the weather improves

点呼 [tenko] n roll call

転居 [tenkyo] ···に転居する [... ni tenkyo suru] v move in

天文学 [tenmongaku] n astronomy

天然 [tennen] 天然ガス [tennengasu] n natural gas; 天然資源 [tennenshigen] n natural resources

手のひら [tenohira] n palm (part of hand)

テノール [tenooru] n tenor

テンピンボウリング [tenpinbouringu] n bowling

転覆 [tenpuku] 転覆する [tenpuku suru] v capsize

天才 [tensai] n genius

天使 [tenshi] n angel

転送 [tensou] 転送する [tensou suru] v forward

テント [tento] n tent; ここにテントを張ってもいいですか? [koko ni tento o hatte mo ii desu ka?] Can we pitch our tent here?; テント一つにつき1週間でいくらですか? [tento hitotsu ni tsuki isshuukan de ikura desu ka?] How much is it per week for a tent?; テント一つにつき一晩でいくらですか? [tento hitotsu ni tsuki hitoban de ikura desu ka?] How much is it per night for a tent?; テント用のサイトが欲しいのですが [tento-you no saito ga hoshii no desu ga] We'd like a site for a tent

テントペグ [tentopegu] n tent peg

テントポール [tentopooru] n tent pole

テントウムシ [tentoumushi] n ladybug

手押し車 [teoshiguruma] n wheelbarrow

テラス [terasu] n terrace; テラスで食べられますか? [terasu de taberaremasu ka?] Can I eat on the terrace?

テラスハウス [terasuhausu] n row house

テレビ [terebi] n television, TV; ケーブルテレビ [keeburu terebi] n cable television; カラーテレビ [karaaterebi] n color television; リアリティーテレビ番組 [riariti terebi bangumi] n reality TV; テレビ電話 [terebi denwa] n videophone; デジタルテレビ [dejitaru terebi] n digital television; 閉回路テレビ [heikairo terebi] n CCTV; その部屋にテレビはありますか? [sono heya ni terebi wa arimasu ka?] Does the room have a TV?; テレビはどこですか? [terebi wa doko desu ka?] Where is the TV set?

テレビラウンジ [terebiraunji] テレビラウンジはありますか? [terebi-raunji wa arimasu ka?] Is there a television lounge?

テレホンカード [terehon kaado] n phone card

テリア [teria] n terrier

テロリスト [terorisuto] n terrorist; テロリストによる攻撃 [terorisuto niyoru kougeki] n terrorist attack

テロリズム [terorizumu] n terrorism

手探り [tesaguri] 手探りする [tesaguri suru] v grope

手製 [tesei] 手製の [tesei no] adj handmade

鉄線 [tessen] 有刺鉄線 [yuushitessen] n barbed wire

手すり [tesuri] n banister, rail, railings

手数料 [tesuuryou] n handling fee; 銀行の手数料 [ginkou no tesuuryou] n bank charges

鉄 [tetsu] n iron

手伝う [tetsudau] v help

鉄道 [tetsudou] n railroad; 鉄道駅 [tetsudoueki] n train station; 鉄道割引証 [tetsudou waribikishou] n railcard

哲学 [tetsugaku] n philosophy

徹底 [tettei] 徹底的な [tetteiteki na] adj thorough; 徹底的に [tetteiteki ni] adv thoroughly

鉄塔 [tettou] n electrical tower

手渡す [tewatasu] v hand

ティー [tii] n (ゴルフ) tee

ティーバッグ [tiibaggu] n tea bag

ティーカップ [tiikappu] n teacup

ティーンエージャー [tiineejaa] n teenager

ティーポット [tiipotto] n teapot

Tシャツ [tiishatsu] n T-shirt

ティースプーン [tiisupuun] n teaspoon

ティータイム [tiitaimu] n teatime

･･･と･･･ [...to...] conj and

飛ばす [tobasu] 投げ飛ばす [nagetobasu] v fling

跳びはねる [tobihaneru] v jump

飛込台 [tobikomidai] n diving board

飛び込む [tobikomu] v dive; 飛び込み [tobikomi] n dive, diving

トボガン [tobogan] n toboggan, tobogganing

飛ぶ [tobu] v fly; 飛び跳ねる [tobihaneru] v skip; 飛び去る [tobisaru] v fly away

土地 [tochi] n land; 土地建物 [tochi tatemono] n premises

土地付き [tochitsuki] 土地付き一戸建て家屋 [tochi tsuki ikkodate kaoku] n house

途中 [tochuu] on the way

戸棚 [todana] n cupboard

届け [todoke] 病欠届け [byouketsu todoke] n sick note

届け出る [todokede ru] 私は盗難の届出をしたいのです [watashi wa tounan no todokede o shitai no desu] I want to report a theft; 私たちはそれを警察に届け出なければなりません [watashi-tachi wa sore o keisatsu ni todokedenakereba narimasen] We'll have to report it to the police

届く [todoku] v be received

とどまる [todomaru] v stay

留める [todomeru] ステープルで留める [suteepuru de todomeru] v staple

トフィー [tofii] n toffee

とげ [toge] *n* thorn

戸口の上がり段 [toguchi no agaridan] *n* doorstep

徒歩 [toho] 徒歩旅行 [tohoryokou] *n* hike (*long walk*)

問い合わせ [toiawase] *n* inquiry

問い合わせる [toiawaseru] *v* inquire

トイレ [toire] *n* bathroom, toilet, washroom; 男性用トイレ [dansei you toire] *n* men's room; 女性用トイレ [joseiyou toire] *n* ladies' room; トイレが流れません [toire ga nagaremasen] The toilet won't flush

トイレット [toiretto] トイレットペーパーがありません [toiretto-peepaa ga arimasen] There's no toilet paper

トイレットペーパー [toirettopeepaa] *n* toilet paper

トイレットペーパーロール [toirettopeepaa-rooru] *n* roll of toilet paper

トカゲ [tokage] *n* lizard

とかす [tokasu] 櫛でとかす [kushi de tokasu] *v* comb

溶かす [tokasu] *v* dissolve ▷ *vt* melt

時計 [tokei] *n* clock; デジタル時計 [dejitaru tokei] *n* digital watch; 腕時計 [udedokei] *n* watch; 目覚まし時計 [mezamashi tokei] *n* alarm clock

溶ける [tokeru] *adj* soluble ▷ *vi* melt

解ける [tokeru] 雪解けしています [yukidoke shite imasu] It's thawing out

時 [toki] …している時 [... shite iru toki] *conj* as; 何時に閉まりますか? [nan-ji ni shimarimasu ka?] What time do you close?; 何時までにですか? [nan-ji made ni desu ka?] By what time?

とき [toki] *n* time; すばらしいときを過ごせました [subarashii toki o sugosemashita] I've had a great time

時折 [tokiori] *n* occasionally; 時折の [tokiori no] *adj* occasional

特権 [tokken] *n* privilege

所 [tokoro] 案内所 [annaijo] *n* information booth; 蒸留所 [jouryuujo] *n* distillery; 診療所 [shinryoujo] *n* clinic, doctor's office (*doctor's*), infirmary; 託児所 [takujisho] *n* day care center; 造船所 [zousenjo] *n* shipyard; 避難所 [hinanjo] *n* refuge, shelter; ここでの見どころは何がありますか? [koko de no midokoro wa nani ga arimasu ka?] What is there to see here?

ところ [tokoro] *n* place; よいところをご存知ですか? [yoi tokoro o go-zonji desu ka?] Do you know a good place to go?

床屋 [tokoya] *n* barber

解く [toku] 荷を解く [ni-o toku] *v* unpack; 包装を解く [housou-o toku] *v* unwrap; 荷物を解かなければなりません [nimotsu o tokanakereba narimasen] I have to unpack

特別 [tokubetsu] 特別に [tokubetsu ni] *adv* specially; 特別の [tokubetsu no] *adj* particular; 特別の [tokubetsu no] *adj* special; 特別売り出し [tokubetsu uridashi] *n* special offer

特徴 [tokuchou] *n* characteristic; 特徴的な [tokuchouteki na] *adj* distinctive

特大 [tokudai] 特大の [tokudai no] *adj* plus-size

得意料理 [tokuiryouri] レストランの得意料理は何ですか? [resutoran no tokui-ryouri wa nan desu ka?] What is the house specialty?

匿名 [tokumei] 匿名の [tokumei no] *adj* anonymous

特に [toku ni] *adv* especially, particularly, specifically

特質 [tokushitsu] *n* character

特定 [tokutei] 特定の [tokutei no] *adj* specific

得点 [tokuten] *n* score (*game/match*)

泊まる [tomaru] *v* stay; どちらにお泊まりですか? [dochira ni o-tomari desu ka?] Where are you staying?

止まる [tomaru] *v* go off ▷ *vi* stop; 私の時計が止まってしまいました [watashi no tokei ga tomatte shimaimashita] My watch has stopped

停まる [tomaru] *vi* stop

トマト [tomato] *n* tomato

トマトソース [tomatosoosu] n tomato sauce

塗沫 [tomatsu] 塗沫検査 [tomatsu kensa] n smear test

留め [tome] 靴下留め [kutsushitadome] n garters

留め金 [tomegane] n clasp

止める [tomeru] v pull up ▷ vt stop

停める [tomeru] vt stop

富くじ [tomikuji] n raffle

友だち [tomodachi] n friend, pal; 私は友だちと来ています [watashi wa tomo-dachi to kite imasu] I'm here with my friends

伴う [tomonau] v involve

灯 [tomoshibi] 故障警告灯 [koshou keikokutou] n hazard warning lights

ともす [tomosu] v light

富む [tomu] 機知に富んだ [kichi ni tonda] adj witty; 色彩に富んだ [shikisai ni tonda] adj colorful

トン [ton] n ton

トナカイ [tonakai] n reindeer

トンボ [tonbo] n dragonfly

とんでもない [tonde mo nai] adj outrageous

トンガ [tonga] n Tonga

とにかく [tonikaku] adv anyhow, anyway

トンネル [tonneru] n tunnel

遠吠えする [tooboe suru] v howl

トーゴ [toogo] n Togo

遠く [tooku] 遠くに [touku ni] adv far; かなり遠いです [kanari tooi desu] It's quite a long way; 遠くありません [tooku arimasen] It's not far away

トークショー [tookushoo] n talk show

トーナメント [toonamento] n tournament

とおりに [toorini] 文字どおりに [mojidouri ni] adv literally

通す [toosu] 通してください [tooshite kudasai] Please let me through

トースター [toosutaa] n toaster

トースト [toosuto] n toast (grilled bread)

トップ [toppu] トップ記事 [toppu kiji] n lead (position)

トップアップカード [toppuappukaado] どこでト

ップアップカードを買えますか? [doko de toppu-appu-kaado o kaemasu ka?] Where can I buy a top-up card?

突風 [toppuu] n gust

トラ [tora] n tiger

トラベラーズチェック [toraberaazu chekku] n traveler's check

捕える [toraeru] v capture

トラック [torakku] n truck; トラック運転手 [torakku untenshu] n truck driver, trucker; 引越しトラック [hikkoshi torakku] n moving van

トラックスーツ [torakkusuutsu] n jogging suit

トラクター [torakutaa] n tractor

トランジスター [toranjisutaa] n transistor

トランクス [torankusu] n trunks

トランペット [toranpetto] n trumpet

トランポリン [toranporin] n trampoline

トランプ [toranpu] n playing card

トランシーバー [toranshiibaa] n walkie-talkie

トレーニング [toreeningu] n training

トレーニングコース [toreeningukoosu] n training course

トレーニングシューズ [toreeningushuuzu] n gym shoes

トレーラー [toreeraa] n trailer

トレーラーハウス [toreeraahausu] n trailer; トレーラーハウスキャンプ場 [toreeraa hausu kyanpu jou] n trailer park; ここにトレーラーハウスを駐車してもいいですか? [koko ni toreeraa-hausu o chuusha shite mo ii desu ka?] Can we park our trailer here?; トレーラーハウスのサイトが欲しいのですが [toreeraa-hausu no saito ga hoshii no desu ga] We'd like a site for a trailer

トレース紙 [toreesushi] n tracing paper

トレッキング [torekkingu] n trekking

鳥 [tori] n bird; 鳥インフルエンザ [tori infuruenza] n bird flu; 鳥肌 [torihada] n goose bumps

取り上げる [toriageru] v take up; ···の資格

を取り上げる [... no shikaku-o toriageru] v disqualify

取扱所 [toriatsukaijo] 遺失物取扱所 [ishitsubutsu toriatsukaijo] n lost-and-found department

取り扱う [toritsukau] v handle

取り合わせ [toriawase] 各種取り合わせ [kakushu toriawase] n assortment

砦 [toride] n fort

取り外す [torihazusu] 取り外せる [torihazuse-ru] adj removable

取引 [torihiki] n deal, transaction

取引所 [torihikijo] 証券取引所 [shouken torihikijo] n stock exchange

取り交わす [torikawasu] v exchange

取り消す [torikesu] v cancel, take back; 約束を取り消す [yakusoku-o torikesu] v back out

取り壊す [torikowasu] v demolish, pull down

取り組む [torikumu] v tackle

トリニダード・トバゴ [torinidaado tobago] n Trinidad and Tobago

取り付ける [toritsukeru] v attach

取りやめる [toriyameru] v call off

トロフィー [torofii] n trophy

トロンボーン [toronboon] n trombone

捕る [toru] 魚を捕る [sakana-o toru] v fish

取る [toru] ···からヒレ肉を取る [... kara hireniku-o toru] v fillet; 連絡を取る [renraku-o toru] v contact

トルコ [toruko] n Turkey; トルコ人 [torukojin] n Turk; トルコの [toruko no] adj Turkish; トルコ語 [torukogo] n Turkish (language)

歳 [toshi] 私は五十歳です [watashi wa gojus-sai desu] I'm fifty years old; 彼女は十二歳です [kanojo wa juuni-sai desu] She's twelve years old

都市 [toshi] n city; 都市計画 [toshikeikaku] n town planning

年老いる [toshioiru] 年老いた [toshi oita] adj aged

年下 [toshishita] 年下の方の [toshishita no hou no] adj younger

···として [...toshite] prep as

年取った [toshitotta] v old

年上 [toshiue] 年上の [toshiue no] adj elder

図書 [tosho] 図書形態 [tosho keitai] n format

図書館 [toshokan] n library

図書館員 [toshokan-in] n librarian

突進 [tosshin] n rush; 突進する [tosshin suru] v dash

突出 [tosshutsu] 突出する [tosshutsu suru] v stand out

とても [totemo] とてもおいしいです [totemo oishii desu] It's delicious

とても大きい [totemo ookii] adj mega

十時 [totoki] 十時です [juu-ji desu] It's ten o'clock

整える [totonoeru] v trim; 髪を整えてもらえますか? [kami o totonoete moraemasu ka?] Could I have a trim?

取っ手 [totsu] ドアの取っ手が外れました [doa no totte ga hazuremashita] The door handle has come off; 取っ手が外れました [totte ga hazuremashita] The handle has come off

突然 [totsuzen] 突然に [totsuzen ni] adv suddenly; 突然の [totsuzen no] adj sudden

突堤 [tottei] n jetty

取って代わる [tottekawaru] v replace

取っておく [totteoku] v put away, reserve, save (money)

塔 [tou] n tower

逃亡 [toubou] n escape

到着 [touchaku] n arrival; ···に到着する [... ni touchaku suru] v get into

灯台 [toudai] n lighthouse

トウガラシ [tougarashi] n red pepper, cayenne pepper

峠 [touge] n pass (in mountains)

討議 [tougi] n discussion

投獄 [tougoku] 投獄する [tougoku suru] v jail

統合失調症 [tougoushicchoushou] 統合失調症の [tougou shitchoushou no] adj schizophrenic

投光 [touhikari] 投光照明 [toukou shoumei] n floodlight

投票 [touhyou] n vote; 投票する [touhyou
suru] v vote; 投票を頼んで回る [touhyou-o
tanonde mawaru] n canvass

遠い [toui] adj far; 遠く離れて [touku
hanarete] adv remotely; 遠く離れた [touku
hanareta] adj remote; 遠いですか? [tooi
desu ka?] Is it far away?

頭字語 [toujigo] n acronym

搭乗 [toujou] n boarding; 搭乗券 [toujouken]
n boarding pass; 搭乗はいつ始まりますか?
[toujou wa itsu hajimarimasu ka?] When
does boarding begin?

搭乗券 [toujouken] 私の搭乗券です [watashi
no toujou-ken desu] Here is my boarding
pass

灯火管制 [toukakansei] n blackout

投函 [toukan] このカードをどこで投函できます
か? [kono kaado o doko de toukan
dekimasu ka?] Where can I mail these
cards?

統計 [toukei] n statistics

凍結 [touketsu] 道路は凍結していますか?
[douro wa touketsu shite imasu ka?] Are
the roads icy?

凍結した [touketsu shita] v icy

陶器 [touki] n pottery

等級 [toukyuu] n grade

透明 [toumei] 透明な [toumei na] adj
transparent

糖蜜 [toumitsu] n molasses

トウモロコシ [toumorokoshi] n corn

盗難 [tounan] 盗難警報機 [tounankeihouki] n
burglar alarm; 私は盗難の届出をしたいので
す [watashi wa tounan no todokede o shitai
no desu] I want to report a theft

糖尿病 [tounyoubyou] n diabetes; 糖尿病の
[tounyoubyou no] adj diabetic; 糖尿病患者
[tounyoubyoukanja] n diabetic

投入 [tounyuu] 投入する [tounyuu suru] v put
in

通り [touri] n street; 大通り [oudouri] n
avenue

登録 [touroku] n registration; 登録した

[touroku shita] adj registered; 登録する
[touroku suru] v register; 登録簿 [tourokubo]
n register

討論 [touron] n debate; 討論する [touron
suru] v debate

倒錯 [tousaku] 服装倒錯 [fukusou tousaku] n
transvestite

等車 [tousha] 1等車 [ittou-sha] a first-class
cabin; ・・・行き1等車往復 [... iki ittou-sha
oufuku] a first-class round trip to...

投資 [toushi] n investment; 投資する [toushi
suru] v invest; 投資者 [toushisha] n
investor

当惑 [touwaku] 当惑させるような [touwaku
saseru you na] adj embarrassing; 当惑した
[touwaku shita] adj confused; 当惑した
[touwaku shita] adj embarrassed

東洋 [touyou] n Far East; 東洋の [touyou no]
adj far-eastern

灯油 [touyu] n kerosene

当座 [touza] 当座預金 [touzayokin] n
checking account

当座借越し [touzakarikoshi] n overdraft; 当
座借越しをした [touza karikoshi-o shita] adj
overdrawn

当然 [touzen] n naturally; 当然の [touzen no]
adj natural

・・・とはいえ [...towaie] conj although

トヨタ車 [toyotasha] トヨタ車のパーツはありま
すか? [toyota-sha no paatsu wa arimasu
ka?] Do you have parts for a Toyota?

登山 [tozan] n mountaineering; 登山者
[tozansha] n mountaineer

ツアー [tsuaa] n tour; その街のバスツアーは
いつですか? [sono machi no basu-tsuaa wa
itsu desu ka?] When is the bus tour of the
town?; その街の観光ツアーはありますか?
[sono machi no kankou-tsuaa wa arimasu
ka?] Are there any sightseeing tours of
the town?; ガイドツアーは何時に始まります
か? [gaido-tsuaa wa nan-ji ni hajimarimasu
ka?] What time does the guided tour
begin?; ツアーは楽しかったです [tsuaa ha

tanoshi kattadesu] I enjoyed the tour; ツアーは···時頃に始まります [tsuaa wa... ji goro ni hajimarimasu] The tour starts at about...; ツアーの所要時間はどのくらいですか? [tsuaa no shoyou-jikan wa dono kurai desu ka?] How long does the tour take?

ツアーガイド [tsuaagaido] n tour guide

つば [tsuba] n (唾液) spit; つばを吐く [tsuba wo haku] v spit

翼 [tsubasa] n wing

土 [tsuchi] n soil

つづる [tsuduru] v spell; それはどうつづりますか? [sore wa dou tsuzurimasu ka?] How do you spell it?

告げる [tsugeru] v tell

次 [tsugi] 次の [tsugi no] adj next; 次の駅はどこですか? [tsugi no eki wa doko desu ka?] What is the next stop?; ···へ行く次のバスは何時ですか? [... e iku tsugi no basu wa nan-ji desu ka?] When is the next bus to...?

つぎ [tsugi] n (布きれ) patch; つぎを当てた [tsugi-o ateta] adj patched

継ぎ目 [tsugime] n joint (junction)

次に [tsugi ni] adv next

都合 [tsugou] 都合のよい [tsugou no yoi] adj convenient

ツグミ [tsugumi] n thrush

つい [tsui] ついに [tsuini] adv eventually

追放 [tsuihou] n exile

追加 [tsuika] n addition; 追加の [tsuika no] adj additional; 追加料金 [tsuikaryoukin] n surcharge

追加カード [tsuikakaado] 度数追加カード [dosuu tsuika kaado] n top-up card

椎間板ヘルニア [tsuikanban herunia] n slipped disc

ツイン [tsuin] ツインの部屋がいいのですが [tsuin no heya ga ii no desu ga] I'd like a room with twin beds

ツインベッド [tsuinbeddo] n twin beds

ツインベッドルーム [tsuinbeddoruumu] n room with twin beds

ついに [tsuini] adv finally

対になる [tsui ni naru] 対になった [tsui ni natta] adj twinned

ツインルーム [tsuinruumu] n twin room

追跡 [tsuiseki] n chase, pursuit; 追跡する [tsuiseki suru] v chase, pursue

一日 [tsuitachi] n the first (day of the month)

費やす [tsuiyasu] v spend

仕える [tsukaeru] v serve

使い果たす [tsukaihatasu] v use up; ···を使い果たす [...-o tsukaihatasu] v run out of

使い残り [tsukainokori] npl scraps, remains

つかまえる [tsukamaeru] v catch

つかまる [tsukamaru] しっかりつかまる [shikkari tsukamaru] v hold on

つかむ [tsukamu] ぐいとつかむ [guito tsukamu] v seize; しっかりつかむ [shikkari tsukamu] v grasp, grip

疲れる [tsukareru] v tiring; 疲れきった [tsukarekitta] adj exhausted; 疲れた [tsukareta] adj tired

使う [tsukau] v use; 使いやすい [tsukaiyasui] adj user-friendly; 使い捨ての [tsukaisute no] adj disposable; 賄賂を使う [wairo-o tsukau] v bribe

つける [tsukeru] v (スイッチ) turn on; 折り目をつけた [orime-o tsuketa] adj creased; 接着剤でつける [setchakuzai de tsukeru] v glue; 照合の印をつける [shougou no in-o tsukeru] v check; ···とあだ名をつけられた [... to adana-o tsukerareta] adj nicknamed; どうやってつけるのですか? [dou-yatte tsukeru no desu ka?] How do you turn it on?; ラジオをつけてもいいですか? [rajio o tsukete mo ii desu ka?] May I turn on the radio?; 明かりをつけてもいいですか? [akari o tsukete mo ii desu ka?] May I turn on the light?

付け札 [tsuke satsu] n tag

月 [tsuki] n (暦) month, (天体) moon

突き [tsuki] n jab

突き出す [tsukidasu] v stick out

突き刺す [tsukisasu] v stab; 突き刺さる

T

[tsukisasaru] v prick

付添 [tsukisoi] 新郎の付添い役 [shinrou no tsukisoiyaku] n best man

付添う [tsukisoiu] 新婦の付添い役 [shinpu no tsukisoiyaku] n bridesmaid

突っ込む [tsukkomu] v plunge

つく [tsuku] しみがつく [shimi ga tsuku] v stain; つきません [tsukimasen] It won't turn on

着く [tsuku] v arrive, reach; バスは何時に着きますか? [basu ga nan-ji ni tsukimasu ka?] What time does the bus arrive?; 着いた私のスーツケースが破損しています [tsuita watashi no suutsukeesu ga hason shite imasu] My suitcase has arrived damaged; 私は着いたばかりです [watashi wa tsuita bakari desu] I've just arrived; 私たちは早く／遅く着きました [watashi-tachi wa hayaku / osoku tsukimashita] We arrived early / late; 私たちの手荷物が着いていません [watashi-tachi no tenimotsu ga tsuite imasen] Our luggage hasn't arrived

机 [tsukue] n desk; あなたの机をお借りできますか? [anata no tsukue o o-kari dekimasu ka?] May I use your desk?

造り主 [tsukurinushi] n maker (God)

造り付けのキッチン [tsukuritsuke no kicchin] n built-in kitchen

作り付け [tsukurizuke] 作り付け寝台 [tsukuri zuke shindai] n bunk

作る [tsukuru] v make; 一覧表を作る [ichiranhyou-o tsukuru] v list

尽くす [tsukusu] 売り尽くす [uritsukusu] v sell out

妻 [tsuma] n wife; 息子の妻 [musuko no tsuma] n daughter-in-law; 私は妻へのプレゼントを探しています [watashi wa tsuma e no purezento o sagashite imasu] I'm looking for a present for my wife; 私の妻です [watashi no tsuma desu] This is my wife

つまらない [tsumaranai] つまらない仕事 [tsumaranai shigoto] n boring task; つまらな

いもの [tsumaranai mono] n trifle

詰まる [tsumaru] v be full; ぎっしり詰まった [gisshiri tsumatta] adj compact; 息が詰まる [iki ga tsumaru] v choke

つまさき [tsumasaki] n tiptoe

つま楊枝 [tsuma youji] n toothpick

つまずく [tsumazuku] v stumble, trip

爪 [tsume] 指の爪 [yubi no tsume] n fingernail; 爪切りばさみ [tsume kiri basami] n nail scissors

詰 [tsume] 缶詰にした [kanzume ni shita] adj canned

爪ブラシ [tsumeburashi] n nail brush

詰め込む [tsumekomu] v cram; ぎっしり詰め込んだ [gisshiri tsumekonda] adj jammed; 詰め込んだ [tsumekonda] adj crammed

詰め物 [tsumemono] 仮の詰め物をしてもらえますか? [kari no tsumemono o shite moraemasu ka?] Can you do a temporary filling?; 詰め物がとれてしまいました [tsumemono ga torete shimaimashita] A filling has fallen out

詰める [tsumeru] v stuff

冷たい [tsumetai] adj cold; シャワーが冷たいです [shawaa ga tsumetai desu] The showers are cold; 食べ物が冷たすぎます [tabemono ga tsumeta-sugimasu] The food is too cold

爪やすり [tsumeyasuri] n nail file

罪 [tsumi] n (宗教・道徳) sin

積み重なる [tsumikasanaru] 積み重なったもの [tsumikasanatta mono] n heap

積み重ね [tsumikasane] n pile, stack

積み荷 [tsumini] n shipment

積む [tsumu] 荷を積む [ni-o tsumu] v load

綱 [tsuna] 綱引き [tsunahiki] n tug-of-war; 物干し綱 [monohoshi tsuna] n clothesline

つなぐ [tsunagu] v link

津波 [tsunami] n tsunami

常 [tsune] 常に [tsune ni] adv always

つねる [tsuneru] v pinch

角³ [tsuno] n (動物) horn

突っ張り [tsuppari] n brace

連れる [tsureru] v take (sb) along

釣り [tsuri] n fishing; どこに行けば釣りができますか? [doko ni ikeba tsuri ga dekimasu ka?] Where can I go fishing?; ここで釣りができますか? [koko de tsuri ga dekimasu ka?] Can we fish here?; ここで釣りをしていいのですか? [koko de tsuri o shite ii no desu ka?] Am I allowed to fish here?; 釣りの許可が要りますか? [tsuri no kyoka ga irimasu ka?] Do you need a fishing license?

吊り [tsuri] 吊り包帯 [tsuri houtai] n sling

吊橋 [tsuribashi] n suspension bridge

釣具 [tsurigu] n fishing tackle

釣竿 [tsurizao] n fishing rod

ツル [tsuru] n (鳥) crane (bird)

釣る [tsuru] 魚釣り [sakana tsuri] n fishing

剣 [tsurugi] n sword

つるす [tsurusu] v suspend

ツタ [tsuta] n ivy

伝える [tsutaeru] v communicate

努める [tsutomeru] v try

勤める [tsutomeru] v work

つつく [tsutsuku] v poke

包み [tsutsumi] 小さな包み [chiisana tsutsumi] n packet

包む [tsutsumu] v do up, wrap, wrap up

通知 [tsuuchi] 通知する [tsuuchi suru] v notify; 通知表 [tsuuchihyou] n report card

通牒 [tsuuchou] 最後通牒 [saigo tsuuchou] n ultimatum

通学 [tsuugaku] 通学かばん [tsuugaku kaban] n schoolbag

通貨 [tsuuka] n currency; 通貨の [tsuuka no] adj monetary

通過 [tsuuka] 通過する [tsuuka suru] vt go by, pass; 通過ラウンジ [tsuuka raunji] n transit lounge

通勤 [tsuukin] 通勤する [tsuukin suru] v commute; 通勤者 [tsuukinsha] n commuter

通告 [tsuukoku] n (解雇) notice (termination)

通行 [tsuukou] 左側通行 [hidarigawa tsuukou] n left-hand drive

ツーリストオフィス [tsuurisutoofisu] n tourist office

通路 [tsuuro] n aisle, passage (route); 歩行者用通路 [hokoushayou tsuuro] n walkway

通路側 [tsuurogawa] 通路側の席をお願いします [tsuuro-gawa no seki o o-negai shimasu] I'd like an aisle seat

通信 [tsuushin] 電気通信 [denkitsuushin] n telecommunications

通訳 [tsuuyaku] n interpretation; 通訳者 [tsuuyakusha] n interpreter

つわり [tsuwari] つわりの時期の朝の吐き気 [tsuwari no jiki no asa no hakike] n morning sickness

つや [tsuya] つやを出す [tsuya-o dasu] v polish

つや出し [tsuyadashi] つや出し剤 [tsuyadashi zai] n polish

強い [tsuyoi] adj strong; うぬぼれの強い [unubore no tsuyoi] adj vain; 自意識の強い [jiishiki no tsuyoi] adj self-conscious; 風の強い [kaze no tsuyoi] adj windy; 強み [tsuyomi] n asset; 強く [tsuyoku] adv strongly; 強くする [tsuyoku suru] v strengthen; 強さ [tsuyosa] n strength; 私はもっと強い薬が必要です [watashi wa motto tsuyoi kusuri ga hitsuyou desu] I need something stronger

強く [tsuyoku] 強く印象づける [tsuyoku inshou zukeru] v impress

続ける [tsuzukeru] v carry on, go on ▷ vt continue

続く [tsuzuku] v last ▷ vi continue; 絶えず続く [taezu tsuzuku] adj constant

つづり [tsuzuri] n spelling

T

U

乳母 [uba] n nanny

乳母車 [ubaguruma] n baby carriage, stroller

奪う [ubau] v rob

うぶな [ubuna] adj naive

内側 [uchigawa] n inside, interior; 内側に [uchigawa ni] adv inside; 内側の [uchigawa no] adj inner; 内側です [uchigawa desu] It's inside

打ち固める [uchikatameru] v ram

内気な [uchiki na] adj shy

打ち砕く [uchikudaku] v smash

打ちのめされる [uchinomesareru] 打ちのめされた [uchinomesareta] adj devastated

打ち寄せる [uchiyoseru] 打ち寄せる波 [uchiyoseru nami] n surf

宇宙 [uchuu] n universe; 宇宙船 [uchuusen] n spacecraft; 宇宙飛行士 [uchuuhikoushi] n astronaut

腕 [ude] n arm; 腕時計 [udedokei] n watch; 私は腕を動かせません [watashi wa ude o ugokasemasen] I can't move my arm; 彼は腕を痛めました [kare wa ude o itamemashita] He's hurt his arm

腕時計 [udedokei] 腕時計のバンド [udedokei no bando] n watchband

腕立て伏せ [udetatefuse] n push-up

上 [ue] n top; 一番上の [ichiban ue no] adj top; 上の [ue no] adj upper; 上へ [ue-e] adv up; まっすぐ上に [massugu ueni] adv upright; 物の上に載って [mono no ueni notte] adv on; ···の上に [... no ue ni] prep above

ウェブアドレス [uebuadoresu] n Web address

ウェブブラウザ [uebuburauza] n Web browser

ウェブジン [uebujin] n webzine

ウェブカム [uebu kamu] n webcam

ウェブマスター [uebumasutaa] n Webmaster

ウェブサイト [uebu saito] n Web site

ウェブサイトアドレス [uebusaitoadoresu] ウェブサイトアドレスは···です [webu-saito-adoresu wa... desu] The Web site address is...

ウェブ2.0 [uebu tsuu] n Web 2.0

ウェディングドレス [uedeingudoresu] n wedding dress

ウェールズ [ueeruzu] n Wales; ウェールズの [ueeruzu no] adj Welsh; ウェールズ語 [ueeruzugo] n Welsh (language)

ウエハース [uehaasu] n wafer

上へ向かって [ue he mukatte] adv upward

ウェイター [ueitaa] n waiter

ウェイトレス [ueitoresu] n waitress

植木 [ueki] 植木鉢 [uekibachi] n planter

上の階 [ue no kai] 上の階に [ueno kai ni] adv upstairs

ウェリントンブーツ [uerintonbuutsu] n rubber boots

植える [ueru] v plant

飢える [ueru] 飢えた [ueta] adj ravenous

ウェスタン [uesutan] n western

ウエスト [uesuto] n waist

ウエストバッグ [uesutobaggu] n fanny pack

ウエストコート [uesutokooto] n vest

ウェットスーツ [uettosuutsu] n wetsuit

ウガンダ [uganda] n Uganda; ウガンダ人 [Uganda jin] n Ugandan (person); ウガンダの [Uganda no] adj Ugandan

動かない [ugokanai] 動かなくなりました [ugokanaku narimashita] It's stuck

動かなくなる [ugokanakunaru] 動かなくなりました [ugokanaku narimashita] It's stuck

動かす [ugokasu] vt move; 彼は脚を動かせません [kare wa ashi o ugokasemasen] He can't move his leg; 彼を動かさないでください [kare o ugokasanaide kudasai] Don't move him

動く [ugoku] vi move; 動かない [ugokanai] adj motionless; あなたの車を動かしていただけますか? [anata no kuruma o ugokashite itadakemasu ka?] Could you move your car, please?; 彼女は動けません [kanojo wa ugokemasen] She can't move

右派 [uha] 右派の [uha no] adj right-wing

ウインドサーフィン [uindosaafin] n windsurfing

ウインク [uinku] ウインクする [uinku suru] v wink

ウィンタースポーツ [uintaasupootsu] n winter sports

ウイルス [uirusu] n virus

ウイスキー [uisukii] n whiskey

うじ [uji] n (虫) maggot

迂回路 [ukairo] n detour (road); 迂回路はありますか? [ukairo wa arimasu ka?] Is there a detour?

受け入れる [ukeireru] v accept

受身 [ukemi] 受身の [ukemi no] adj passive

受ける [ukeru] レッスンを受けられますか? [ressun o ukeraremasu ka?] Can we take lessons?

受取人 [uketorinin] n receiver (person), recipient

受け取る [uketoru] v receive; 手荷物受取所 [tenimotsu uketorisho] n baggage claim

受付 [uketsuke] n reception; 受付係 [uketsukegakari] n receptionist

受け皿 [ukezara] n saucer

浮き [uki] n flotation device

浮く [uku] v float

ウクライナ [ukuraina] n Ukraine; ウクライナ人 [Ukuraina jin] n Ukrainian (person); ウクライナの [Ukuraina no] adj Ukrainian; ウクライナ語 [Ukuraina go] n Ukrainian (language)

馬 [uma] n horse; 馬の飼育係 [uma no shiikugakari] n groom; 馬の子 [uma no ko] n foal; 馬小屋 [umagoya] n stable

うまく [umaku] adv successfully; うまく···する [umaku... suru] v manage; うまく対処する [umaku taisho suru] v cope

生まれながら [umarenagara] 生まれながらの [umare nagara no] adj born

生まれたばかり [umaretabakari] 生まれたばかりの [umareta bakari no] adj newborn

生る [umaru] v be born; 生きている [ikite iru] adj alive

埋め合わせる [umeawaseru] v make up

うめく [umeku] v moan

海 [umi] n sea; 北極海 [Hokkyokukai] n Arctic Ocean; 今日は海が荒れていますか? [kyou wa umi ga arete imasu ka?] Is the sea rough today?; 海が見える部屋がいいのですが [umi ga mieru heya ga ii no desu ga] I'd like a room with a view of the sea

膿 [umi] n pus

生む [umu] v (利益) yield

運 [un] n luck; 運のよい [un no yoi] adj lucky; 運の悪い [un no warui] adj unlucky; 運悪く [unwaruku] adv unfortunately

ウナギ [unagi] n eel

うなる [unaru] v groan; 怒ってうなる [ikatte unaru] v growl; 歯をむきだしてうなる [ha-o mukidashite unaru] v snarl

うなずく [unazuku] v nod

運賃 [unchin] n fare

運動 [undou] n (行動) campaign, (身体) exercise; フィットネス運動 [fittonesu undou] n fitness program; 運動選手 [undousenshu] n athlete; 地下運動 [chika undou] n underground

運動選手 [undousenshu] 運動選手らしい [undou senshu rashii] adj athletic

運河 [unga] n canal

U

運命 [unmei] n destiny, fate

運転 [unten] n driving; 仮免許運転者 [karimenkyo untensha] n student driver; 飲酒運転 [inshu unten] n drunk driving; 運転する [unten suru] v drive; 運転免許試験 [untenmenkyoshiken] n driver's test; 運転免許証 [untenmenkyoshou] n driver's license

運転免許証 [untenmenkyoshou] n driver's license

運転手 [untenshu] n driver; おかかえ運転手 [okakae untenshu] n chauffeur; タクシー運転手 [takushii untenshu] n taxi driver; トラック運転手 [torakku untenshu] n truck driver, trucker

うぬぼれ [unubore] うぬぼれの強い [unubore no tsuyoi] adj vain

うぬぼれた [unuboreta] adj conceited

運よく [un yoku] adv luckily

うんざりする [unzari suru] うんざりして [unzari shite] adj fed up

ウォッカ [uokka] n vodka

ウォーキング [uookingu] n walking

魚座 [uoza] n Pisces

裏 [ura] 屋根裏 [yaneura] n attic

裏切る [uragiru] v betray

裏地 [uraji] n lining

裏目 [urame] 裏目に出る [urame ni deru] v backfire

恨み [urami] n grudge

ウラニウム [uraniumu] n uranium

うらやましそうな [urayamashisouna] adj envious

うらやむ [urayamu] v envy

嬉しい [ureshii] adj glad, pleased

うれしい [ureshii] adj happy

売場 [uriba] 切符売場 [kippu uriba] n box office, ticket office

売り出し [uridashi] 特別売り出し [tokubetsu uridashi] n special offer

売切れ [urikire] 売切れの [urikire no] adj sold out

うろこ [uroko] n scale (tiny piece)

うろたえる [urotaeru] v panic

売る [uru] v sell; 売り払う [uriharau] v sell off; 売り尽くす [uritsukusu] v sell out; 売る人 [uru hito] n vendor; テレホンカードを売っていますか? [terehon-kaado o utte imasu ka?] Do you sell phone cards?

ウルグアイ [uruguai] n Uruguay; ウルグアイ人 [Uruguai jin] n Uruguayan (person); ウルグアイの [Uruguai no] adj Uruguayan

うるさがらせる [urusagaraseru] v annoy

うるさい [urusai] adj annoying

うるう [uruu] うるう年 [uruudoshi] n leap year

ウサギ [usagi] n rabbit; 野ウサギ [nousagi] n hare

失う [ushinau] 意識を失った [ishiki wo ushinatta] adj unconscious; 意識を失う [ishiki-o ushinau] v pass out; 失った [utta] adj lost; 希望を失って [kibou-o ushinatte] adj hopeless

後ろ [ushiro] n rear; ···の後ろに [... no ushiro ni] prep behind; 後ろに [ushiro ni] adv back, behind; 後ろに下がる [ushiro ni sagaru] v move back; 後ろの [ushiro no] adj back, rear

嘘 [uso] n lie; 嘘をつく [uso-o tsuku] v lie

嘘つき [usotsuki] n liar

薄切り [usugiri] n slice

薄暗い [usugurai] adj dim

薄い [usui] adj (住居) pale, (厚み) thin; 薄く色を着けた [usuku iro-o tsuketa] adj tinted; 薄く切る [usuku kiru] v slice

薄い肉片 [usui nikuhen] n cutlet

歌 [uta] n song; 賛美歌 [sanbika] n hymn; 子守歌 [komoriuta] n lullaby

疑い [utagai] n doubt; 疑いなく [utagainaku] adv undoubtedly; 疑いをかける [utagai-o kakeru] v suspect

疑う [utagau] v doubt; 疑い深い [utagaibukai] adj skeptical

疑わしい [utagawashii] adj doubtful, suspicious

うたたね [utatane] n nap

うたた寝 [utatane] うたた寝する [utatane suru]

v doze

歌う [utau] *v* sing; **歌うこと** [utau koto] *n* singing

鬱 [utsu] **抗鬱剤** [kouutsuzai] *n* antidepressant

ウッ [utsu] *excl* ugh!

打つ [utsu] *v* hit ▷ *vt* strike; **ゴツンと打つ** [gotsun to utsu] *v* thump; **バンと打つ** [ban to utsu] *v* bang; **ピシャリと打つ** [pishari to utsu] *v* slap, smack, swat; **打ち負かす** [uchimakasu] *v* knock out; **打ち倒す** [uchitaosu] *v* knock down; **打つこと** [utsu koto] *n* beat; **続けざまに打つ** [tsuzukezama ni utsu] *v* beat (*strike*); **動悸を打つ** [douki-o utsu] *v* throb

撃つ [utsu] *v* shoot

美しい [utsukushii] *adj* beautiful, lovely; **絵のように美しい** [e no youni utsukushii] *adj* picturesque; **美しさ** [utsukushisa] *n* beauty

美しく [utsukushiku] *adv* beautifully

写し [utsushi] *n* transcript

移す [utsusu] *v* move, remove

器 [utsuwa] **注射器** [chuushaki] *n* syringe; **皮むき器** [kawamukiki] *n* potato peeler

訴える [uttaeru] *v* accuse, sue; **感覚に訴える** [kankaku ni uttaeru] *adj* sensuous

浮気 [uwaki] **浮気者** [uwakimono] *n* flirt, playboy

うわさ [uwasa] *n* rumor

うわさ話 [uwasabanashi] *n* gossip ▷ **うわさ話をする** [uwasabanashi-o suru] *v* gossip

上役 [uwayaku] *n* superior

ウズベキスタン [uzubekisutan] *n* Uzbekistan

うずくまる [uzukumaru] *v* crouch

ウズラ [uzura] *n* quail

U

V

ヴィラ [vira] *n* villa; **ヴィラを借りたいのですが**
[vira o karitai no desu ga] I'd like to rent a
villa

W

輪 [wa] *n* ring; 輪ゴム [wagomu] *n* rubber band

ワークステーション [waakusuteeshon] *n* work station, workstation

ワールドカップ [waarudokappu] *n* World Cup

詫び [wabi] *n* apology

話題 [wadai] *n* topic

ワッフル [waffuru] *n* waffle

我が [waga] 我が家へ [wagaya-e] *adv* home

輪ゴム [wagomu] *n* rubber band

ワゴン [wagon] *n* cart

ワイファイ [waifai] *n* Wi-Fi

ワイン [wain] *n* wine; 赤ワイン [akawain] *n* red wine; このワインは冷えていません [kono wain wa hiete imasen] This wine isn't chilled; よいワインを教えてもらえますか? [yoi wain o oshiete moraemasu ka?] Can you recommend a good wine?; ワインは冷えていますか? [wain wa hiete imasu ka?] Is the wine chilled?; ハウスワインをカラフで1本 [hausu-wain o karafu de ippon] a carafe of the house wine; 赤ワインのボトルを1本 [aka-wain no botoru o ippon] a bottle of red wine; 赤ワインをカラフで1本 [aka-wain o karafu de ippon] a carafe of red wine; 白ワインのボトルを1本 [shiro-wain no botoru o ippon] a bottle of white wine; 白ワインをカラフで1本 [shiro-wain o karafu de ippon] a carafe of white wine; 私はワインは全く飲みません [watashi wa wain wa mattaku nomimasen] I never drink wine

ワイングラス [waingurasu] *n* wineglass

ワインリスト [wainrisuto] *n* wine list; ワインリストをください [wain-risuto o kudasai] The wine list, please

ワイパー [waipaa] フロントガラスのワイパー [furonto garasu no waipaa] *n* windshield wiper

賄賂 [wairo] 賄賂を使う [wairo-o tsukau] *v* bribe

猥褻な [waisetsu] *adj* obscene

ワイシャツ [waishatsu] *n* shirt

若い [wakai] *adj* young; 一番若い [ichiban wakai] *adj* youngest; 若いおんどり [wakai ondori] *n* cockerel

若者 [wakamono] *n* adolescent

別れ [wakare] *n* parting

分かれ道 [wakaremichi] *n* turnoff

わかります [wakarimasu] I understand; わかりません [wakarimasen] I don't understand

わかる [wakaru] 話がわかる [hanashi ga wakaru] *adj* understanding

分かる [wakaru] *v* recognize

沸かす [wakasu] *vt* boil

分け前 [wakemae] *n* share

分ける [wakeru] *v* divide, separate, share; 分け合う [wakeau] *v* share out

腋 [waki] 腋の下 [waki no shita] *n* armpit

わき道 [wakimichi] わき道へ入る [wakimichi-e hairu] *v* turn off

枠 [waku] 窓の下枠 [mado no shitawaku] *n* windowsill

沸く [waku] 沸き立つ [wakitatsu] *adj* boiling

惑星 [wakusei] *n* planet

わめく [wameku] *v* rave

湾 [wan] *n* bay

わな [wana] *n* trap

湾岸 [wangan] メキシコ湾岸諸州 [Mekishiko wangan shoshuu] *n* Gulf Coast states

ワニ [wani] *n* alligator, crocodile

湾曲 [wankyoku] *n* crook

腕白 [wanpaku] 腕白な [wanpaku na] *adj* mischievous

ワンピース [wanpiisu] *n* dress; このワンピースを試着していいですか? [kono wanpiisu o shichaku shite ii desu ka?] May I try on this dress?

ワンルーム [wanruumu] *n* studio (apartment); ワンルームのアパート [wanruumu no apaato] *n* studio apartment

笑う [warau] *v* laugh; にこにこ笑い [nikoniko warai] *n* grin; にやにや笑う [niyaniya warau] *v* snicker; くすくす笑う [kusukusu warau] *v* giggle; 歯を見せてにっこり笑う [ha-o misete nikkori warau] *v* grin; 笑い [warai] *n* laugh; 笑い声 [waraigoe] *n* laughter

割れ目 [wareme] *n* crack *(fracture)*

割れる [wareru] *v* crack

割合 [wariai] *n* rate

割当て [wariate] *n* quota

割り当て [wariate] *n* assignment

割引 [waribiki] *n* discount; 日帰り往復割引切符 [higaeri oufuku waribiki kippu] *n* one-day round-trip ticket; 鉄道割引証 [tetsudou waribikishou] *n* railcard; 学生割引 [gakusei waribiki] *n* student discount; このパスで割引がありますか? [kono pasu de waribiki ga arimasu ka?] Is there a discount with this pass?; 身体障害者用の割引がありますか? [shintai-shougaisha-you no waribiki ga arimasu ka?] Is there a discount for disabled people?; 現金で払うと割引がありますか? [genkin de harau to waribki ga arimasu ka?] Do you offer a discount for cash?; 高齢者割引はありますか? [koureisha-waribiki wa arimasu ka?] Are there any discounts for senior citizens?; 団体割引はありますか? [dantai-waribiki wa arimasu ka?] Are there any discounts for groups?; 学生割引はありますか? [gakusei-waribiki wa arimasu ka?] Are there any discounts for students?; 子供割引はありますか? [kodomo-waribiki wa arimasu ka?] Are there any discounts for children?

割り込む [warikomu] *v* squeeze in

割る [waru] *v* break, split

悪がき [warugaki] *n* brat

悪い [warui] *adj* bad, evil; 一層悪い [issou warui] *adj* worse; 一層悪く [issou waruku] *adv* worse; 機嫌の悪い [kigen no warui] *adj* bad-tempered; 意地の悪い [iji no warui] *adj* spiteful; 気味の悪い [kimi no warui] *adj* spooky; 運悪く [unwaruku] *adv* unfortunately; 風通しの悪い [kazetoushi no warui] *adj* stuffy; 効率の悪い [kouritsu no warui] *adj* inefficient

悪く [waruku] *adv* badly

ワルツ [warutsu] *n* waltz; ワルツを踊る [warutsu wo odoru] *v* waltz

ワシ [washi] *n* eagle

忘れる [wasureru] *v* forget; 置き忘れる [okiwasureru] *v* misplace; 忘れられない [wasurerarenai] *adj* unforgettable; 忘れられた [wasurerareta] *adj* forgotten

渡す [watasu] *v* hand (in)

わずか [wazuka] わずかな [wazuka na] *adj* slight; わずかに [wazuka ni] *adv* slightly

Y

矢 [ya] *n* arrow

屋 [ya] タバコ屋 [tabakoya] *n* tabaconist; 葬儀屋 [sougiya] *n* funeral director

やあ! [yaa] *excl* hi!

ヤード [yaado] *n* yard (*measurement*)

野蛮 [yaban] 野蛮な [yaban na] *adj* barbaric

破れる [yabureru] 破れ目 [yabureme] *n* tear (*split*)

破る [yaburu] *v* tear

宿 [yado] 宿を提供する [yado-o teikyou suru] *v* accommodate; 宿屋 [yadoya] *n* inn

ヤドリギ [yadorigi] *n* mistletoe

やがて [yagate] *adv* soon

ヤギ [yagi] *n* goat

ヤギが子を産む [yagi ga ko wo umu] *v* kid

山羊座 [yagiza] *n* Capricorn

野獣 [yajuu] 野獣の子 [yajuu no ko] *n* cub

やかましい [yakamashii] *adj* noisy; やかましい音 [yakamashii oto] *n* din

夜間 [yakan] 夜間クラス [yakan kurasu] *n* night class; 夜間学校 [yakangakkou] *n* night school

夜間外出禁止令 [yakan gaishutsu kinshirei] *n* curfew

火傷 [yakedo] *n* burn

焼け落ちる [yakeochiru] *v* burn down

焼き串 [yakigushi] *n* skewer

夜勤 [yakin] *n* night shift

厄介 [yakkai] 厄介なもの [yakkai na mono] *n* nuisance

薬局 [yakkyoku] *n* pharmacy; どの薬局が夜間休日サービスを実施していますか? [dono yakkyoku ga yakan-kyuujitsu-saabisu o jisshi shite imasu ka?] Which pharmacy provides emergency service?

焼く [yaku] *v* bake; グリルで焼く [guriru de yaku] *v* broiler; 網焼きにする [amiyaki ni suru] *adj* broiled; 焼いた [yaita] *adj* baked, roast

薬品 [yakuhin] 化学薬品 [kagakuyakuhin] *n* chemical

役員 [yakuin] 役員会 [yakuinkai] *n* board (*meeting*)

役に立たない [yaku ni tatanai] *adj* unhelpful, useless

役に立つ [yaku ni tatsu] *adj* helpful, useful

約束 [yakusoku] *n* engagement, promise; 会う約束 [au yakusoku] *n* rendezvous; 約束する [yakusoku suru] *v* promise; 約束を取り消す [yakusoku-o torikesu] *v* back out

訳す [yakusu] *v* translate; これを訳してもらえますか? [kore o yakushite moraemasu ka?] Can you translate this for me?; これを私に訳していただけませんか? [kore o watashi ni yakushite itadakemasen ka?] Could you translate this for me?

役割 [yakuwari] *n* role

薬剤 [yakuzai] *n* medicine, drugs

薬剤師 [yakuzaishi] *n* pharmacist

野球 [yakyuu] *n* baseball; 野球帽 [yakyuubou] *n* baseball cap

山 [yama] *n* mountain; 山の多い [yama no oui] *adj* mountainous; 干し草の山 [hoshikusa no yama] *n* haystack; 一番近い山小屋はどこですか? [ichiban chikai yama-goya wa doko desu ka?] Where is the nearest mountain hut?

山積み [yamazumi] *n* pileup

やめる [yameru] *v* (よす) give up, (よす) quit

闇 [yami] *n* dark

ヤナギ [yanagi] *n* willow

屋根 [yane] *n* roof; 萱葺き屋根の [kayabuki yane no] *adj* thatched; 屋根裏 [yaneura] *n* attic

家主 [yanushi] *n* landlord; 女家主 [onna yanushi] *n* landlady

八百屋 [yaoya] *n* greengrocer

やり方 [yarikata] これのやり方をご存知ですか? [kore no yarikata o go-zonji desu ka?] Do you know how to do this?

やり直す [yarinaosu] *v* redo

やりすぎ [yarisugi] やりすぎの [yarisugi no] *adj* overdone

野菜 [yasai] *n* vegetable; 野菜は生鮮品ですか、それとも冷凍品ですか? [yasai wa seisen-hin desu ka, sore tomo reitou-hin desu ka?] Are the vegetables fresh or frozen?; 野菜も付いてきますか? [yasai mo tsuite kimasu ka?] Are the vegetables included?

優しい [yasashii] *adj* gentle

優しく [yasashiku] *adv* gently

野生 [yasei] 野生の [yasei no] *adj* wild; 野生生物 [yaseiseibutsu] *n* wildlife

野生生物 [yaseiseibutsu] *n* wildlife; 野生生物を見たいのですが [yasei-seibutsu o mitai no desu ga] We'd like to see wildlife

やせこけた [yasekoketa] *v* skinny

ヤシ [yashi] *n* palm *(tree)*

野心 [yashin] *n* ambition; 野心的な [yashinteki na] *adj* ambitious

安い [yasui] *adj* cheap, inexpensive; 一番安い方法がいいのですが [ichiban yasui houhou ga ii no desu ga] I'd like the cheapest option; もっと安いものが欲しいのです [motto yasui mono ga hoshii no desu] I want something cheaper; 安いフライトはありますか? [yasui furaito wa arimasu ka?] Are there any cheap flights?; 安い電車料金はありますか? [yasui densha-ryoukin wa arimasu ka?] Are there any cheap train fares?; 安めのものはありますか? [yasume no mono wa arimasu ka?] Do you have anything

cheaper?

休み [yasumi] *n* rest; 昼休み [hiruyasumi] *n* lunch hour

休む [yasumu] *v* rest

やすり [yasuri] *n* file *(tool)*; やすりをかける [yasuri-o kakeru] *v* file *(smoothing)*

屋台 [yatai] *n* stall

柔らかい [yawarakai] *adj* soft, tender

夜明け [yoake] *n* dawn

予備 [yobi] *adj* spare; 予備の寝室 [yobi no shinshitsu] *n* spare room; 予備の寝具はありますか? [yobi no shingu wa arimasu ka?] Is there any spare bedding?

呼び出す [yobidasu] ポケットベルで呼び出す [poketto beru de yobidasu] *v* page; ···さんをポケットベルで呼び出してもらえますか? [...san o pokettoberu de yobidashite moraemasu ka?] Could you page...?

呼び声 [yobigoe] *n* call

呼び鈴 [yobisuzu] 玄関の呼び鈴 [genkan no yobisuzu] *n* doorbell

呼び止める [yobitomeru] *v* hail

予防 [yobou] *n* prevention; 予防接種 [yobou sesshu] *n* vaccination; 予防接種をする [yobou sesshu-o suru] *v* vaccinate

呼ぶ [yobu] *v* call; 消防隊を呼んでください [shoubou-tai o yonde kudasai] Please call the fire department; 救急車を呼んでください [kyuukyuu-sha o yonde kudasai] Call an ambulance; 救急医を呼んでください [kyuukyuu-i o yonde kudasai] Please call the emergency doctor; 救助艇を呼んで! [kyuujotei o yonde!] Call out the lifeboat!; 警察を呼んでください [keisatsu o yonde kudasai] Call the police; 医者を呼んで! [isha o yonde!] Call a doctor!

余分 [yobun] 余分な [yobun na] *adj* surplus; 余分に [yobun ni] *adv* extra; 余分の [yobun no] *adj* extra, spare; 余分に袋をいただけますか? [yobun ni fukuro o itadakemasu ka?] May I have an extra bag, please?; 私は余分に請求されています [watashi wa yobun ni seikyuu sarete imasu] I've been overcharged; ・・・を余分につけてお願いします [... o yobun ni tsukete o-negai shimasu] I'd like it with extra..., please

よだれ掛け [yodarekake] n bib

ヨガ [yoga] n yoga

汚れ [yogore] n smudge; 汚れの跡 [yogore no ato] v mark; 汚れの跡をつける [yogore no ato-o tsukeru] n stain

汚れる [yogoreru] v be dirty

汚る [yogoru] 汚れた [yogoreta] adj dirty

予報 [yohou] 天気予報 [tenkiyohou] n forecast, weather forecast; 天気予報はどうですか? [tenki-yohou wa dou desu ka?] What's the weather forecast?

よい [yoi] 居心地のよい [igokochi no yoi] adj cozy; よいところをご存知ですか? [yoi tokoro o go-zonji desu ka?] Do you know a good place to go?

良い [yoi] adj good

余剰 [yojou] 余剰人員の解雇 [yojou jin'in no kaiko] n redundancy; 余剰人員として解雇された [yojou jin'in to shite kaiko sareta] adj laid off

余暇 [yoka] n leisure, spare time

予感 [yokan] n premonition

予見 [yoken] 予見する [yoken suru] v foresee

予期 [yoki] 予期しない [yoki shinai] adj unexpected

預金 [yokin] n deposit; 預金口座 [yokin kouza] n account (in bank); 共同預金口座 [kyoudou yokin kouza] n joint account; 当座預金 [touzayokin] n checking account

横丁 [yokochou] n side street

横切る [yokogiru] v cross; ・・・を横切って [...-o yokogitte] prep across

横向き [yokomuki] 横向きに [yokomuki ni] adv sideways

横すべり [yoko suberi] 横すべりする [yokosuberi suru] v skid; 車が横すべりしました [kuruma ga yokosuberi shimashita] The car skidded

よく [yoku] 最もよく [mottomo yoku] adv best; よく眠れましたか? [yoku nemuremashita

ka?] Did you sleep well?

抑圧 [yokuatsu] n inhibition

欲ばり [yokubari] 欲ばりの [yokubari no] adj greedy

浴場 [yokujou] 公衆浴場 [koushuu yokujou] n public swimming pool

抑制 [yokusei] 発汗抑制剤 [hakkan yokuseizai] n antiperspirant

浴槽 [yokusou] n bath, bathtub

読み上げる [yomiageru] v read out

読み書き [yomikaki] 読み書きのできない [yomikaki no dekinai] adj illiterate

読みやすい [yomiyasui] adj legible

読む [yomu] v read; 拾い読みする [hiroiyomi suru] v browse; それは読めません [sore wa yomemasen] I can't read it

夜中 [yonaka] 夜中の十二時に [yonaka no juuni-ji ni] at midnight

世慣れる [yonareru] 世慣れた [yonareta] adj streetwise

四番目 [yonbanme] 四番目の [yon banme no] adj fourth

4分の1 [yonbun no ichi] n quarter

余念 [yonen] ・・・に余念がない [... ni yonen ga nai] adj preoccupied

四輪駆動 [yonrinkudou] n four-wheel drive

ヨーグルト [yooguruto] n yogurt

ヨーロッパ [yooroppa] n Europe; ヨーロッパ人 [yooroppajin] n European (person); ヨーロッパの [yooroppa no] adj European; ヨーロッパ大陸式の簡単な朝食 [Yooroppa tairikushiki no kantan na choushoku] n continental breakfast

ヨーロッパヤマウズラ [yooroppayamauzura] n partridge

酔っぱらい [yopparai] n drunk

酔っぱらう [yopparau] 酔っぱらって [yopparatte] adj plastered; 酔っぱらった [yopparatta] adj drunk

より [yori] より早く [yori hayaku] adv sooner

より少ない [yori sukunai] adj fewer

よりよい [yoriyoi] adj better

よりよく [yoriyoku] adv better

Y

喜び [yorokobi] n joy; 沸き立つ喜び
[wakitatsu yorokobi] n overbrimming
excitement; 大喜び [ooyorokobi] n delight;
大喜びの [ooyorokobi no] adj delighted
喜ぶ [yorokobu] v be happy
よろめく [yoromeku] v stagger
世論 [yoron] n public opinion; 世論調査
[yoronchousa] n opinion poll, poll
よろよろ [yoroyoro] よろよろする [yoroyoro
suru] adj shaky
夜 [yoru] n night; 明日の夜 [asu no yoru]
tomorrow night; 夜に [yoru ni] at night
ヨルダン [yorudan] n Jordan
ヨルダン人 [yorudanjin] n Jordanian
(person)
ヨルダンの [yorudan no] adj Jordanian
予算 [yosan] n budget
よそ [yoso] どこかよそで [dokoka yoso de] adv
elsewhere
予測 [yosoku] 予測できない [yosoku dekinai]
adj unpredictable
予想 [yosou] 予想する [yosou suru] v predict;
予想できる [yosou dekiru] adj predictable
予定 [yotei] n schedule; ・・・する予定で [...
suru yotei de] adj due; 私たちは予定どおりで
す [watashi-tachi wa yotei doori desu] We're
on schedule; 私たちは予定より少し遅れてい
ます [watashi-tachi wa yotei yori sukoshi
okurete imasu] We're slightly behind
schedule
ヨット [yotto] n sailboat, yacht
洋 [you] インド洋 [indoyou] n Indian Ocean
よう [you] ように思われる [youni omowareru] v
seem
酔う [you] 船に酔った [fune ni yotta] adj
seasick; 飛行機に酔った [hikouki ni yotta]
adj airsick; 酔った [yotta] adj drunk
幼稚園 [youchien] n kindergarten
洋服だんす [youfukudansu] n wardrobe
溶岩 [yougan] n lava
容疑 [yougi] 容疑者 [yougisha] n suspect
用語 [yougo] n term (description)
養護 [yougo] 児童養護 [jidou yougo] n

childcare
用具 [yougu] n gear (equipment); 洗面用具バ
ッグ [senmen yougu baggu] n toiletries
bag; 用具一式 [yougu isshiki] n kit
用品 [youhin] 園芸用品店 [engei youhinten] n
garden center; スタイリング用品を売ってい
ますか? [sutairingu youhin o utte imasu ka?]
Do you sell styling products?
用意 [youi] 用意のできた [youi no dekita] adj
ready; 用意ができた [youi ga dekita] adj
prepared; 用意はできましたか? [youi wa
dekimashita ka?] Are you ready?; 用意でき
ていません [youi dekite imasen] I'm not
ready; 用意できました [youi dekimashita]
I'm ready; ・・・を使わずにこれを用意していた
だけますか? [... o tsukawazu ni kore o youi
shite itadakemasu ka?] Could you prepare
this one without...?
容易 [youi] 容易に [youi ni] adv easily
養育 [youiku] 養育する [youiku suru] v foster
要員 [youin] 作業要員 [sagyou youin] n
workforce
要因 [youin] 複雑な要因 [fukuzatsu na youin]
n complication
幼児 [youji] よちよち歩きの幼児 [yochiyochi
aruki no youji] n toddler; 幼児用の便器
[youjiyou no benki] n potty; 幼児用の便器は
ありますか? [youji-you no benki wa arimasu
ka?] Do you have a potty?
用心 [youjin] n precaution
陽気 [youki] 陽気な [youki na] adj cheerful,
hilarious, jolly, merry
容器 [youki] n container
陽気な [youki na] adj cheerful
ようこそ! [youkoso] excl welcome!
要求 [youkyuu] n demand, requirement; 要
求の厳しい [youkyuu no kibishii] adj
demanding; 要求する [youkyuu suru] v call
for
要求する [youkyuu suru] v demand
容者 [you mono] 被収容者 [hishuuyousha] n
inmate
羊毛 [youmou] n wool

用務員 [youmuin] *n* janitor

容認 [younin] 容認できない [younin dekinai] *adj* unacceptable

妖精 [yousei] *n* fairy

容積 [youseki] *n* volume

容赦 [yousha] 容赦する [yousha suru] *v* spare

用紙 [youshi] *n* blank printed form; アンケート用紙 [ankeeto youshi] *n* questionnaire; メモ用紙 [memoyoushi] *n* notepaper; 注文用紙 [chuumon youshi] *n* order form

養子 [youshi] 養子になった [youshi ni natta] *adj* adopted; 養子にする [youshi ni suru] *v* adopt; 養子縁組 [youshiengumi] *n* adoption

様式 [youshiki] *n* style; ロマネスク様式の [Romanesuku youshiki no] *adj* Romanesque; 建築様式 [kenchikuyoushiki] *n* architecture

要素 [youso] *n* element; 構成要素 [kousei youso] *n* component

要点 [youten] *n* point

腰痛 [youtsuu] *n* back pain, backache

要約 [youyaku] *n* summary; 要約する [youyaku suru] *v* sum up, summarize

溶剤 [youzai] *n* solvent

弱火 [yowabi] 弱火でとろとろ煮る [yowabi de torotoro niru] *v* simmer

弱い [yowai] *adj* weak; 弱いこと [yowai koto] *n* weakness

弱い者いじめをする者 [yowai mono ijime wo suru mono] *n* bully

予約 [yoyaku] *n* appointment, reservation; 予約する [yoyaku suru] *v* reserve; 予約オフィス [yoyaku ofisu] *n* ticket office; 事前予約 [jizen yoyaku] *n* advance reservation; 予約してあります [yoyaku shite arimasu] I have a reservation; 予約をキャンセルしたいのですが [yoyaku o kyanseru shitai no desu ga] I want to cancel my reservation; 予約を取りたいのですが [yoyaku o toritai no desu ga] I'd like to make an appointment; 七時半に二人分の予約をお願いします [shichi-ji-han ni futari-bun no yoyaku o o-negai shimasu] I'd like to make a reservation for seven-thirty for two people; お医者さんの予約を取れますか？ [o-isha-san no yoyaku o toremasu ka?] Can I have an appointment with the doctor?; 私は手紙で予約を確認しました [watashi wa tegami de yoyaku o kakunin shimashita] I confirmed my reservation by letter; 私は座席予約をしてあります [watashi wa zaseki-yoyaku o shite arimasu] I have a seat reservation; 私のためにホテルの部屋を予約してもらえますか？ [watashi no tame ni hoteru no heya o yoyaku shite moraemasu ka?] Could you make a hotel reservation for me?

予約する [yoyaku suru] どこでコートを予約できますか？ [doko de kooto o yoyaku dekimasu ka?] Where can I reserve a court?

余裕 [yoyuu] …する余裕がある [... suru yoyuu ga aru] *v* afford

指 [yubi] 人差し指 [hitosashi yubi] *n* index finger; 手の指 [te no yubi] *n* finger; 足の指 [ashi no yubi] *n* toe

指輪 [yubiwa] *n* ring; 結婚指輪 [kekkon yubiwa] *n* wedding ring; 婚約指輪 [konyaku yubiwa] *n* engagement ring

油断 [yudan] 油断のならない [yudan no naranai] *adj* tricky

ユダヤ人 [yudayajin] *n* Jew

ユダヤ人の [yudayajin no] *adj* Jewish

ユダヤ教 [yudayakyou] ユダヤ教の掟に従って料理された清浄な [Yudaya kyou no okite ni shitagatte ryouri sareta seijou na] *adj* kosher

ゆでる [yuderu] ゆで卵 [yudetamago] *n* hard-boiled egg

故… [yue...] *adj* late *(dead)*

遺言 [yuigon] *n* will *(document)*

唯一 [yuiitsu] 唯一の [yuiitsu no] *adj* only

床 [yuka] *n* floor

愉快 [yukai] 愉快な [yukai na] *adj* entertaining

輸血 [yuketsu] *n* blood transfusion, transfusion

Y

雪 [yuki] n snow; ひとひらの雪 [hitohira no yuki] n snowflake ▷ v 雪が降る [yuki ga furu] v snow; 雪はどんなですか? [yuki wa donna desu ka?] What is the snow like?; 雪の状態はどんなですか? [yuki no joutai wa donna desu ka?] What are the snow conditions?; 雪が降っています [yuki ga futte imasu] It's snowing; 雪が降ると思いますか? [yuki ga furu to omoimasu ka?] Do you think it's going to snow?

雪だるま [yukidaruma] n snowman

雪つぶて [yukitsubute] n snowball

ゆっくり [yukkuri] もっとゆっくり話していただけますか? [motto yukkuri hanashite itadakemasu ka?] Could you speak more slowly, please?

行方 [yukue] 私の息子が行方不明です [watashi no musuko ga yukue-fumei desu] My son is missing; 私の娘が行方不明です [watashi no musume ga yukue-fumei desu] My daughter is missing

油膜 [yumaku] n oil slick

夢 [yume] n dream; 夢を見る [yume wo miru] v dream

弓 [yumi] n bow (weapon)

優美 [yumi] 優美な [yuubi na] adj delicate, graceful

輸入 [yunyuu] n import; 輸入する [yunyuu suru] v import

揺れ [yure] n swing

揺れる [yureru] v rock, swing ▷ vi shake

ユリ [yuri] n lily

揺りかご [yurikago] n cradle

ユーロ [yuro] n euro; 二十五ユーロのテレホンカードが欲しいのですが [nijuugo yuuro no terehon-kaado ga hoshii no desu ga] I'd like a twenty-five-euro phone card

揺る [yuru] 揺り木馬 [yurimokuba] n rocking horse

緩い [yurui] adj loose, slack

緩める [yurumeru] ねじを緩める [neji-o yurumeru] v unscrew

許し [yurushi] n pardon

許す [yurusu] v allow, forgive; 入場を許す [nyuujou-o yurusu] v admit (allow in)

揺さぶる [yusa buru] 揺さぶられた [yusaburareta] adj shaken

油井 [yusei] n oil well

輸出 [yushutsu] n export; 輸出する [yushutsu suru] v export

輸送 [yusou] n transit, transportation; 輸送する [yusou suru] v transport; 貨物輸送 [kamotsu yusou] n freight

輸送車 [yusousha] 護衛されている輸送車隊 [goei sareteiru yusoushatai] n convoy; 大型輸送車 [ougata yusousha] n semi (truck)

ゆすぶる [yusuburu] v sway

湯たんぽ [yutanpo] n hot-water bottle

ゆったり [yuttari] ゆったりとした [yuttarito shita] adj easygoing

URL [yuuaarueru] n URL [yuuaarueru]

郵便 [yuubin] n mail; 郵便料金 [yuubin ryoukin] n postage; 郵便為替 [yuubin kawase] n postal money order; 郵便番号 [yuubin bangou] n zip code; 郵便配達人 [yuubin haitatsunin] n mail deliverer; 郵便局 [yuubinkyoku] n post office; 郵便受 [yuubinju] n mailbox; 女性郵便配達人 [josei yuubin haitatsunin] n female mail deliverer; 普通郵便でどのくらいの日数がかかりますか? [futsuu-yuubin de dono kurai no nissuu ga kakarimasu ka?] How long will it take by regular mail?; 書留郵便でどのくらいの日数がかかりますか? [kakitome-yuubin de dono kurai no nissuu ga kakarimasu ka?] How long will it take by certified mail?; 私あての郵便物がありますか? [watashi ate no yuubinbutsu ga arimasu ka?] Is there any mail for me?; 優先郵便でどのくらいの日数がかかりますか? [yuusen-yuubin de dono kurai no nissuu ga kakarimasu ka?] How long will it take by priority mail?

郵便物 [yuubinbutsu] n mail; 私あての郵便物をこの住所に回送してください [watashi ate no yuubinbutsu o kono juusho ni kaisou shite kudasai] Please forward my mail to this address

郵便受 [yuubinju] n mailbox

郵便局 [yuubinkyoku] n post office; 郵便局は
いつ開きますか? [yuubinkyoku wa itsu
hirakimasu ka?] When does the post office
open?

有望な [yuubou na] 将来有望な [shourai
yuubou na] adj promising

有毒 [yuudoku] 有毒な [yuudoku na] adj toxic

有毒な [yuudoku na] adj poisonous

誘導 [yuudou] 誘導ループはありますか?
[yuudou-ruupu wa arimasu ka?] Is there an
induction loop?

遊園地 [yuuenchi] n amusement park

裕福 [yuufuku] 裕福な [yuufuku na] adj
well-off

優雅 [yuuga] 優雅な [yuuga na] adj elegant

有害 [yuugai] 有害な [yuugai na] adj harmful

夕暮れ [yuugure] n dusk

遊歩道 [yuuhodou] 海岸の遊歩道 [kaigan no
yuuhodou] n promenade; 近くにおもしろい
遊歩道はありますか? [chikaku ni omoshiroi
yuuhodou wa arimasu ka?] Are there any
interesting places to walk nearby?

友情 [yuujou] n friendship

優柔 [yuujuu] 優柔不断な [yuujuu fudan na]
adj indecisive

誘拐 [yuukai] 誘拐する [yuukai suru] v
abduct, kidnap

勇敢 [yuukan] n bravery; 勇敢な [yuukan na]
adj brave

勇気 [yuuki] n courage; ···の勇気をくじく [...
no yuuki-o kujiku] v discourage; 勇気のある
[yuuki no aru] adj courageous

有機体 [yuukitai] n organism; 有機体の
[yuukitai no] adj organic

勇気づける [yuukizukeru] v encourage

有名 [yuumei] n fame; 有名人 [yuumeijin] n
celebrity; 有名な [yuumei na] adj famous,
well-known

有名な [yuumei na] adj renowned

ユーモア [yuumoa] n humor; ユーモアのある
[yuumoa no aru] adj humorous; ユーモアの

センス [yuumoa no sensu] n sense of
humor

有能 [yuunou] 有能な [yuunou na] adj
competent

遊覧 [yuuran] その川の遊覧ツアーはあります
か? [sono kawa no yuuran-tsuaa wa
arimasu ka?] Are there any boat trips on
the river?

幽霊 [yuurei] n ghost; 幽霊が出没する [yuurei
ga shutsubotsu suru] adj haunted

有利 [yuuri] n advantage

有料 [yuuryou] n toll; この高速道路は有料で
すか? [kono kousoku-douro wa yuuryou
desu ka?] Is there a toll on this highway?

優先 [yuusen] n priority; 優先権 [yuusenken]
n right of way; 優先郵便でどのくらいの日数
がかかりますか? [yuusen-yuubin de dono
kurai no nissuu ga kakarimasu ka?] How
long will it take by priority mail?

優先権 [yuusenken] あなたには優先権があり
ませんでした [anata ni wa yuusen-ken ga
arimasen deshita] It wasn't your right of
way

有史前 [yuushimae] 有史前の [yuushi mae
no] adj prehistoric

夕食 [yuushoku] n supper

優勝 [yuushou] 優勝者 [yuushousha] n
champion

郵送 [yuusou] 郵送する [yuusou suru] v mail

ユースホステル [yuusuhosuteru] n youth
hostel; 近くにユースホステルはありますか?
[chikaku ni yuusu-hosuteru wa arimasu ka?]
Is there a youth hostel nearby?

ユースクラブ [yuusukurabu] n youth club

Uターン [yuutaan] n U-turn

ユーティリティールーム [yuutiritii ruumu] n
utility room

憂鬱 [yuuutsu] n depression; 憂鬱な [yuuutsu
na] adj depressing, gloomy

誘惑 [yuuwaku] n temptation; 誘惑する
[yuuwaku suru] adj tempt; 誘惑する
[yuuwaku suru] adj tempting

有用 [yuuyou] 有用性 [yuuyousei] n

Y

availability

v convict

有罪 [yuuzai] *n* guilt; **有罪の** [yuuzai no] *adj* guilty; **有罪と決定する** [yuuzai to kettei suru]

譲る [yuzuru] *v* give way

Z

座 [za] 牡牛座 [oushiza] *n* Taurus

剤 [zai] しみ抜き剤 [shiminuki zai] *n* stain remover; 殺菌剤 [sakkinzai] *n* antiseptic; 抗ヒスタミン剤 [kouhisutaminzai] *n* antihistamine; 抗鬱剤 [kouutsuzai] *n* antidepressant; 解毒剤 [gedokuzai] *n* antidote; 発汗抑制剤 [hakkan yokuseizai] *n* antiperspirant; 精神安定剤 [seishin anteizai] *n* tranquilizer; 錠剤 [jouzai] *n* pill; 鎮静剤 [chinseizai] *n* sedative; 除草剤 [josouzai] *n* weedkiller; 強壮剤 [kyou-souzai] *n* tonic

財宝 [zaihou] *n* treasure

在庫 [zaiko] 在庫を置く [zaiko-o oku] *v* stock; 在庫品 [zaikohin] *n* stock

材木 [zaimoku] *n* lumber, wood *(material)*

財務 [zaimu] *n* finance; 財務の [zaimu no] *adj* financial

材料 [zairyou] *n* ingredient, material; 材料は何ですか? [zairyou wa nan desu ka?] What is the material?

財政 [zaisei] 財政の [zaisei no] *adj* fiscal

雑貨 [zakka] 食料雑貨類 [shokuryou zakkarui] *n* groceries; 食料雑貨店 [shokuryou zakkaten] *n* grocery store; 食料雑貨商 [shokuryou zakkashou] *n* grocer

ザクロ [zakuro] *n* pomegranate

ザンビア [zanbia] *n* Zambia; ザンビア人 [Zanbia jin] *n* Zambian *(person)*; ザンビアの [Zanbia no] *adj* Zambian

残高 [zandaka] 銀行の残高 [ginkou no zandaka] *n* bank balance

残骸 [zangai] *n* wreckage

残酷 [zankoku] *n* cruelty; 残酷な [zankoku na] *adj* cruel

残忍 [zannin] 残忍な [zannin na] *adj* brutal

暫定 [zantei] 暫定的な [zanteiteki na] *adj* provisional

ザリガニ [zarigani] *n* crayfish

座席 [zaseki] *n* seat *(furniture)*; 今夜の座席を2つ予約したいのですが [kon'ya no zaseki o futatsu yoyaku shitai no desu ga] We'd like to reserve two seats for tonight; 一緒の座席を取れますか? [issho no zaseki o toremasu ka?] Can we have seats together?; 私は座席予約をしてあります [watashi wa zaseki-yoyaku o shite arimasu] I have a seat reservation

挫折 [zasetsu] 挫折した [zasetsu shita] *adj* frustrated

雑誌 [zasshi] *n* magazine *(periodical)*; どこで雑誌を買えますか? [doko de zasshi o kaemasu ka?] Where can I buy a magazine?

雑種 [zasshu] 雑種の犬 [zasshu no inu] *n* mongrel

雑草 [zassou] *n* weed

雑多 [zatta] 雑多な [zatta na] *adj* miscellaneous

税 [zei] *n* tax; 付加価値税 [fukakachizei] *n* value-added tax, VAT; 所得税 [shotokuzei] *n* income tax; 自動車の道路利用税 [jidousha no douro riyou zei] *n* highway tax

税関 [zeikan] 税関係官 [zeikan kakarikan] *n* customs officer

税金 [zeikin] *n* tax

贅沢 [zeitaku] *n* luxury; 贅沢な [zeitaku na] *adj* luxurious

全部 [zenbu] *pron* all

前景 [zenkei] *n* foreground

前方 [zenpou] 前方へ [zenpou-e] *adv* forward

全力 [zenryoku] 全力で走る [zenryoku de hashiru] *v* sprint

全粒小麦 [zenryuukomugi] 全粒小麦の [zenryuu komugi no] *adj* whole wheat

全身 [zenshin] 全身麻酔 [zenshin masui] *n* general anesthetic

前進 [zenshin] *n* advance; 前進する [zenshin suru] *v* advance

喘息 [zensoku] *n* asthma; 私は喘息があります [watashi ha zensoku gaarimasu] I suffer from asthma

全体 [zentai] *n* whole; 全体の [zentai no] *adj* whole; 全体的に [zentaiteki ni] *adv* overall

前夜 [zenya] *n* eve

ゼラニウム [zeraniumu] *n* geranium

ゼリー [zerii] *n* Jell-O®

絶望 [zetsubou] *n* despair

絶縁材 [zetsuenzai] *n* insulation

絶滅 [zetsumetsu] 絶滅した [zetsumetsu shita] *adj* extinct

絶対 [zettai] 絶対禁酒の [zettai kinshu no] *adj* teetotal

俗語 [zokugo] *n* slang

続篇 [zokuhen] *n* sequel

続人 [zoku nin] 女相続人 [onna souzokunin] *n* heiress

ぞくぞく [zokuzoku] ぞくぞくさせる [zokuzoku saseru] *adj* thrilling; ぞくぞくした [zokuzoku shita] *adj* thrilled; ぞくぞくする感じ [zokuzoku suru kanji] *n* thrill

ぞっと [zotto] ぞっとさせる [zotto saseru] *adj* horrifying; ぞっとするような [zotto suru you na] *adj* appalling

ぞっとする [zotto suru] *v* gruesome, hideous

像 [zou] *n* statue

ゾウ [zou] *n* elephant

増築 [zouchiku] *n* extension

象牙 [zouge] *n* ivory

増加 [zouka] *n* increase

臓器 [zouki] *n* organ *(body part)*

造船 [zousen] *n* shipbuilding; 造船所 [zousenjo] *n* shipyard

贈収賄 [zoushuuwai] *n* bribery

図 [zu] *n* diagram, drawing

ズボン [zubon] *n* pants, trousers; 半ズボン [hanzubon] *n* shorts

ズボン吊り [zubontsuri] *n* suspenders

ずぶぬれ [zubunure] ずぶぬれの [zubunure no] *adj* soaked, soggy

ずぶとい [zubutoi] ずぶとさ [zubutosa] *n* nerve *(boldness)*

頭蓋 [zugai] 頭蓋骨 [zugaikotsu] *n* skull

図表 [zuhyou] *n* chart

髄膜 [zuimaku] 髄膜炎 [zuimakuen] *n* meningitis

ズッキーニ [zukkiini] *n* zucchini

ずるい [zurui] *adj* sly

ずさんな [zusanna] *adj* sloppy

ずたずた [zutazuta] ずたずたに引き裂く [zutazuta ni hikisaku] *v* tear up

頭痛 [zutsuu] *n* headache; 頭痛に効くものが欲しいのですが [zutsuu ni kiku mono ga hoshii no desu ga] I'd like something for a headache

ズーム [zuumu] ズームレンズ [zuumurenzu] *n* zoom lens

English-Japanese
Dictionary

A

a [ə, STRONG eɪ] *art* 一つの [hitotsu no]

abandon [əbændən] *v* 見捨てる [misuteru]

abbey [æbi] *n* 僧院 [souin]

abbreviation [əbriːvieɪʃᵃn] *n* 略語 [ryakugo]

abdomen [æbdoʊmən] *n* 腹 [hara]

abduct [æbdʌkt] *v* 誘拐する [yuukai suru]

ability [əbɪlɪti] *n* 能力 [nouryoku]

able [eɪbᵃl] *adj* ・・・ができる [... ga dekiru]

abnormal [æbnɔrmᵃl] *adj* 異常な [ijou na]

abolish [əbɒlɪʃ] *v* 廃止する [haishi suru]

abolition [æbəlɪʃᵃn] *n* 廃止 [haishi]

abortion [əbɔrʃᵃn] *n* 妊娠中絶 [ninshinchu-uzetsu]

about [əbaʊt] *adv* およそ [oyoso] ▷ *prep* ・・・について [...nitsuite]

above [əbʌv] *prep* ・・・の上に [... no ue ni]

abroad [əbrɒd] *adv* 海外に [kaigai ni]

abscess [æbsɛs] *n* 膿瘍 [nouyou]; **I have an abscess** 私は膿瘍があります [watashi wa nouyou ga arimasu]

absence [æbsᵃns] *n* 不在 [fuzai]

absent [æbsᵃnt] *adj* 不在の [fuzai no]

absentminded [æbsᵃntmaɪndɪd] *adj* ぼんやりした [bonyari shita]

absolutely [æbsəlutli] *adv* 全く [mattaku]

abstract [æbstrækt] *adj* 抽象的な [chuushouteki na]

absurd [æbsɜrd, -zɜrd] *adj* ばかげた [bakageta]

Abu Dhabi [ˈæbuː ˈdɑːbɪ] *n* アブダビ [abudabi]

abuse *n* [əbyus] 虐待 [gyakutai] ▷ *v* [əbyuz] 濫用する [ran'you suru], 虐待する [gyakutai suru]; **child abuse** *n* 児童虐待 [jidou gyakutai]

abusive [əbyusɪv] *adj* 口汚い [kuchi kitanai]

academic [ækədɛmɪk] *adj* 大学の [daigaku no]; **academic year** *n* 学年 [gakunen]

academy [əkædəmi] *n* 学士院 [gakushiin]

accelerate [æksɛləreɪt] *v* 加速する [kasoku suru]

acceleration [æksɛləreɪʃᵃn] *n* 加速 [kasoku]

accelerator [æksɛləreɪtər] *n* アクセル [akuseru]

accept [æksɛpt] *v* 受け入れる [ukeireru]

acceptable [æksɛptəbᵃl] *adj* 無難な [bunan na]

access [æksɛs] *n* 接近 [sekkin] ▷ *v* アクセスする [akusesu suru]

accessible [æksɛsɪbᵃl] *adj* 近づきやすい [chikadukiyasui]

accessory [æksɛsəri] *n* 付属物 [fuzokubut-su]

accident [æksɪdənt] *n* 事故 [jiko], 傷害 [shougai]; **accident insurance** *n* 事故保険 [jiko hoken]; **I'd like to arrange personal accident insurance** 個人傷害保険をかけたいのですが [kojin-shougai-hoken o kaketai no desu ga]; **I've had an accident** 私は事故にあいました [watashi wa jiko ni aimashita]; **There's been an accident!** 事故がありました! [jiko ga arimashita!]; **What do I do if I have an accident?** 事故にあったらどうすればいいのですか? [jiko ni attara dou sureba ii no desu ka?]

accidental [æksɪdɛntᵃl] *adj* 偶然の [guuzen no]

accidentally [æksɪdɛntli] *adv* ばったり [battari], 偶然に [guuzen ni]

accommodate [əkɒmədeɪt] *v* 宿を提供する [yado-o teikyou suru]

accommodations [əkɒmədeɪʃᵃnz] *n* 住む場

所 [sumu basho]

accompany [əkʌmpəni] v 同行する [doukou suru]

accomplice [əkɒmplɪs] n 共犯者 [kyouhansha]

according [əkɔrdɪŋ] prep **according to** prep ･･･に従って [... ni shitagatte]

accordingly [əkɔrdɪŋli] adv それに応じて [sore ni oujite]

accordion [əkɔrdiən] n アコーディオン [akoodeion]

account [əkaunt] n 口座 [kouza], (in bank) 預金口座 [yokin kouza], (report) 説明 [setsumei]; **account number** n 口座番号 [kouzabangou]; **bank account** n 銀行口座 [ginkoukouza]; **checking account** n 当座預金 [touzayokin]; **joint account** n 共同預金口座 [kyoudou yokin kouza]

accountable [əkauntəb*l] adj 説明する責任がある [setsumei suru sekinin ga aru]

accountancy [əkauntənsi] n 会計 [kaikei]

accountant [əkauntənt] n 会計士 [kaikeishi]

account for [əkaunt fər] v ･･･の説明がつく [... no setsumei ga tsuku]

accuracy [ækyərəsi] n 正確さ [seikakusa]

accurate [ækyərɪt] adj 正確 [seikaku], 正確な [seikaku na]

accurately [ækyərɪtli] adv 正確に [seikaku ni]

accusation [ækyuzeɪʃn] n 非難 [hinan]

accuse [əkyuz] v 訴える [uttaeru]

accused [əkyuzd] n 被告人 [hikokunin]

ace [eɪs] n エース [eesu]

ache [eɪk] n 痛み [itami] ▷ v 痛む [itamu]

achieve [ətʃiv] v 達成する [tassei suru]

achievement [ətʃivmənt] n 達成 [tassei]

acid [æsɪd] n 酸 [san]; **acid rain** n 酸性雨 [sanseiu]

acknowledgment [æknɒlɪdʒmənt] n 承認 [shounin]

acne [ækni] n にきび [nikibi]

acorn [eɪkɔrn] n どんぐり [donguri]

acoustic [əkustɪk] adj 聴覚の [choukaku no]

acre [eɪkər] n エーカー [eekaa]

acrobat [ækrəbæt] n 軽業師 [karuwazashi]

acronym [ækrənɪm] n 頭字語 [toujigo]

across [əkrɒs] prep ･･･を横切って [...-o yokogitte]; **across the street** adv 向かい側に [mukaigawa ni]

act [ækt] n 行為 [koui] ▷ v 行動する [koudou suru]

acting [æktɪŋ] adj 臨時代理の [rinji dairi no] ▷ n 演技 [engi]

action [ækʃn] n 活動 [katsudou]

active [æktɪv] adj 活動的な [katsudouteki na]; **active vacation** n アクティブホリデー [akutibu horidee]

activity [æktɪvɪti] n 活動 [katsudou]

actor [æktər] n 俳優 [haiyuu], 男優 [danyuu]

actress [æktrɪs] n 女優 [joyuu]

actual [æktʃuəl] adj 実際の [jissai no]

actually [æktʃuəli] adv 実際に [jissai ni]

acupuncture [ækyupʌŋktʃər] n 鍼 [hari]

ad [æd] abbr 広告 [koukoku] ▷ n 広告 [koukoku]; **classified ads** npl 分類広告 [bunruikoukoku]

AD [eɪ di] abbr 西暦 [seireki]

adapt [ədæpt] v 適合させる [tekigou saseru]

adapter [ədæptər] n ソケットアダプタ [soketto adaputa]

add [æd] v 足す [tasu]

addict [ædɪkt] n 中毒者 [chuudokusha]; **drug addict** n 麻薬常用者 [mayaku jouyousha]

addicted [ədɪktɪd] adj 常習的な [joushuuteki na]

addition [ədɪʃn] n 追加 [tsuika]

additional [ədɪʃən*l] adj 追加の [tsuika no]

additive [ædɪtɪv] n 添加剤 [tenkazai]

address [ædrɛs] n アドレス [adoresu], (location) 住所 [juusho], (speech) 演説 [enzetsu]; **address book** n 住所録 [juushoroku]; **home address** n 自宅住所 [jitaku juusho]; **web address** n ウェブアドレス [uebuadoresu]; **Could you write down the address, please?** その住所を紙に書いてもらえますか? [sono juusho o kami ni kaite

moraemasu ka?]; **My e-mail address is...**
私のEメールアドレスは・・・です [watashi no
ii-meeru-adoresu wa... desu]; **Please
forward my mail to this address** 私あての
郵便物をこの住所に回送してください
[watashi ate no yuubinbutsu o kono juusho
ni kaisou shite kudasai]; **The website
address is...** ウェブサイトアドレスは・・・です
[webu-saito-adoresu wa... desu]; **What's
your e-mail address?** あなたのEメールアド
レスは何ですか [anata no ii-meeru-adoresu wa nan desu ka?]

add up v ・・・を合計する [...-o goukei suru]

adequate [ǽdɪkwɪt] *adj* 結構 [kekkou]

adherent [ædhíərənt] *n* 教徒 [kyouto]

adjacent [ədʒéɪsᵊnt] *adj* 近接した [kinsetsu
shita]

adjective [ǽdʒɪktɪv] *n* 形容詞 [keiyoushi]

adjust [ədʒʌ́st] *v* 順応する [junnou suru]

adjustable [ədʒʌ́stəbᵊl] *adj* 調整できる
[chousei dekiru]

adjustment [ədʒʌ́stmənt] *n* 調整 [chousei]

administration [ædmɪ̀nɪstréɪʃᵊn] *n* 管理
[kanri]

administrative [ædmɪ́nɪstreɪtɪv] *adj* 管理上
の [kanrijou no]

admiration [ædmɪréɪʃᵊn] *n* 称賛 [shousan]

admire [ədmáɪər] *v* 感心する [kanshin suru]

admission [ædmɪ́ʃᵊn] *n* 入場 [nyuujou];
admission charge *n* 入場料 [nyuujouryou];
admission fee *n* 入場料 [nyuujouryou]

admit [ædmɪ́t] *v* (allow in) 入場を許す
[nyuujou-o yurusu], (confess) 認める
[mitomeru]

admittance [ædmɪ́tᵊns] *n* 入場許可 [nyuujou
kyoka]

adolescence [ædᵊlésᵊns] *n* 思春期
[shishunki]

adolescent [ædᵊlésᵊnt] *n* 若者 [wakamono]

adopt [ədɒ́pt] *v* 養子にする [youshi ni suru]

adopted [ədɒ́ptɪd] *adj* 養子になった [youshi
ni natta]

adoption [ədɒ́pʃᵊn] *n* 養子縁組
[youshiengumi]

adore [ədɔ́r] *v* あこがれる [akogareru]

Adriatic [eɪdriǽtɪk] *adj* アドリア海の
[adoriakai no]

Adriatic Sea *n* アドリア海 [adoriakai]

adult [ədʌ́lt] *n* 大人 [otona]; **adult education**
n 生涯教育 [shougai kyouiku]; **adult learner**
n 成人学生 [seijin gakusei]

advance [ædvǽns] *n* 前進 [zenshin] ▷ *v* 前進
する [zenshin suru]; **advance reservation** *n*
事前予約 [jizen yoyaku]

advanced [ædvǽnst] *adj* 進歩した [shinpo
shita]

advantage [ædvɒ́ntɪdʒ, -væn-] *n* 有利 [yuuri]

advent [ǽdvɛnt] *n* 出現 [shutsugen]

adventure [ædvɛ́ntʃər] *n* 冒険 [bouken]

adventurous [ædvɛ́ntʃərəs] *adj* 冒険好きな
[bouken zuki na]

adverb [ǽdvɜrb] *n* 副詞 [fukushi]

adversary [ǽdvərsɛri] *n* 敵対者 [tekitaisha]

advertise [ǽdvərtaɪz] *v* 広告する [koukoku
suru]

advertisement [ædvərtáɪzmənt] *n* 広告
[koukoku]

advertising [ǽdvərtaɪzɪŋ] *n* 広告すること
[koukoku suru koto]

advice [ædváɪs] *n* 助言 [jogen]

advisable [ædváɪzəbᵊl] *adj* 賢明な [kenmei
na]

advise [ædváɪz] *v* 助言する [jogen suru]

aerobics [ɛəroʊbɪks] *npl* エアロビクス
[earobikusu]

aerosol [ɛ́ərəsɔl] *n* エアゾール [eazooru]

affair [əfɛ́ər] *n* 事柄 [kotogara]

affect [əfɛ́kt] *v* 影響を与える [eikyou-o ataeru]

affectionate [əfɛ́kʃənət] *adj* 愛情のこもった
[aijou no komotta]

afford [əfɔ́rd] *v* ・・・する余裕がある [... suru
yoyuu ga aru]

affordable [əfɔ́rdəbᵊl] *adj* 手ごろな [tegoro
na]

Afghan [ǽfgæn] *adj* アフガニスタンの
[afuganisutan no] ▷ *n* アフガニスタン人

[afuganisutanjin]

Afghanistan [æfgǽnɪstæn] *n* アフガニスタ
ン [afuganisutan]

afraid [əfréɪd] *adj* ···が怖い [... ga kowai]

Africa [ǽfrɪkə] *n* アフリカ [afurika]; **North
Africa** *n* 北アフリカ [kitaafurika]; **South
Africa** *n* 南アフリカ [minami afurika]

African [ǽfrɪkən] *adj* アフリカの [afurika no]
▷ *n* アフリカ人 [afurikajin]; **Central African
Republic** *n* 中央アフリカ共和国 [Chuuou
Afurika Kyouwakoku]; **North African** *n* 北ア
フリカ人 [Kita Afurika jin], 北アフリカの [Kita
Afurika no]; **South African** *n* 南アフリカ人
[minami afurikajin], 南アフリカの [minami
afurika no]

Afrikaans [æfrɪkɑ́ns] *n* アフリカーンス語
[afurikaansugo]

Afrikaner [æfrɪkɑ́nər] *n* アフリカーナー
[afurikaanaa]

after [ǽftər] *conj* ···した後に [... shita nochi
ni] ▷ *prep* ···の後に [... no nochi ni]

afternoon [æftərnún] *n* 午後 [gogo]; **in the
afternoon** 午後に [gogo ni]; **tomorrow
afternoon** 明日の午後 [asu no gogo]

aftershave [ǽftərʃeɪv] *n* アフターシェーブロ
ーション [afutaasheeburooshon]

afterwards [ǽftərwərdz] *adv* 後で [ato de]

again [əgɛ́n, əgéɪn] *adv* 再び [futatabi]

against [əgɛ́nst, əgéɪnst] *prep* ···にもたれて
[... ni motarete]

age [eɪdʒ] *n* 年齢 [nenrei]; **age limit** *n* 年齢制
限 [nenreiseigen]; **Middle Ages** *npl* 中世
[chuusei]

aged [eɪdʒd, eɪdʒɪd] *adj* 年老いた [toshi oita]

agency [éɪdʒənsi] *n* 代理店 [dairiten]; **travel
agency** *n* 旅行代理店 [ryokoudairiten]

agenda [ədʒɛ́ndə] *n* 議事日程 [giji nittei]

agent [éɪdʒənt] *n* 代理人 [dairinin]; **real
estate agent** *n* 不動産屋 [fudousanya];
travel agent *n* 旅行業者 [ryokougyousha]

aggressive [əgrɛ́sɪv] *adj* 攻撃的な
[kougekiteki na]

ago [əgóʊ] *adv* **a month ago** 一か月前

[ikkagetsu mae]; **a week ago** 一週間前
[isshuukan mae]

agony [ǽgəni] *n* 苦悶 [kumon]

agree [əgríː] *v* 賛成する [sansei suru]

agreed [əgríːd] *adj* 合意された [goui sareta]

agreement [əgríːmənt] *n* 合意 [goui], 同意
[doui]

agricultural [ægrɪkʌ́ltʃərəl] *adj* 農業の
[nougyou no]

agriculture [ǽgrɪkʌltʃər] *n* 農業 [nougyou]

ahead [əhɛ́d] *adv* 前に [mae ni]

aid [eɪd] *n* 援助 [enjo]; **first aid** *n* 救急処置
[kyuukyuu shochi]; **first-aid kit** *n* 救急処置キ
ット [kyuukyuu shochi kitto]; **hearing aid** *n*
補聴器 [hochouki]

aide [eɪd] *n* **teacher's aide** *n* 教室助手
[kyoushitsu joshu]

AIDS [eɪdz] *n* エイズ [eizu]

aim [eɪm] *n* 目的 [mokuteki] ▷ *v* ねらう [nerau]

air [ɛər] *n* 空気 [kuuki]; **air-traffic controller**
n 航空管制官 [koukuu kanseikan]; **Air Force**
n 空軍 [kuugun]; **Could you check the air,
please?** 空気圧を点検してもらえますか?
[kuukiatsu o tenken shite moraemasu ka?]

air bag *n* エアバッグ [eabaggu]

air-conditioned [ɛərkəndɪ́nd] *adj* 空調され
た [kuuchou sareta]

air conditioning *n* 空調 [kuuchou]

aircraft [ɛ́ərkræft] *n* 航空機 [koukuuki]

airline [ɛ́ərlaɪn] *n* 航空会社 [koukuu gaisha]

airmail [ɛ́ərmeɪl] *n* 航空便 [koukuubin]

airport [ɛ́ərpɔrt] *n* 空港 [kuukou]; **airport bus**
n 空港バス [kuukou basu]; **How do I get to
the airport?** 空港へはどう行けばいいのです
か? [kuukou e wa dou ikeba ii no desu ka?];
How much is the taxi to the airport? 空港
までのタクシーはいくらですか? [kuukou
made no takushii wa ikura desu ka?]; **Is
there a bus to the airport?** 空港へ行くバス
はありますか? [kuukou e iku basu wa
arimasu ka?]

airsick [ɛ́ərsɪk] *adj* 飛行機に酔った [hikouki
ni yotta]

airspace [ˈɛərspeɪs] *n* 領空 [ryoukuu]

airtight [ˈɛərtaɪt] *adj* 気密の [kimitsu no]

aisle [aɪl] *n* 通路 [tsuuro]; **I'd like an aisle seat** 通路側の席をお願いします [tsuuro-gawa no seki o o-negai shimasu]

alarm [əˈlɑrm] *n* 恐怖 [kyoufu], 警報 [keihou], 報知器 [houchiki]; **alarm clock** *n* 目覚まし時計 [mezamashi tokei]; **false alarm** *n* 間違い警報 [machigai keihou]; **fire alarm** *n* 火災報知器 [kasai houchiki]

alarming [əˈlɑrmɪŋ] *adj* 警戒心をいだかせる [keikaishin-o idakaseru]

Albania [ælˈbeɪniə] *n* アルバニア [arubania]

Albanian [ælˈbeɪniən] *adj* アルバニアの [arubania no] ▷ *n (language)* アルバニア語 [arubaniago], *(person)* アルバニア人 [arubaniajin]

album [ˈælbəm] *n* アルバム [arubamu]; **photo album** *n* アルバム [arubamu]

alcohol [ˈælkəhɔl] *n* アルコール [arukooru]; **Does that contain alcohol?** それにはアルコールが入っていますか? [sore ni wa arukooru ga haitte imasu ka?]; **I don't drink alcohol** 私はアルコールを飲みません [watashi wa arukooru o nomimasen]

alcohol-free *adj* アルコールを含まない [arukooru wo fukumanai]

alcoholic [ˌælkəˈhɔlɪk] *adj* アルコールの [arukooru no] ▷ *n* アルコール中毒者 [arukooru chuudokusha]

alert [əˈlɜrt] *adj* 油断なく警戒して [yudan naku keikai shite] ▷ *v* 警報を出す [keihou-o dasu]

Algeria [ælˈdʒɪəriə] *n* アルジェリア [arujeria]

Algerian [ælˈdʒɪəriən] *adj* アルジェリアの [arujieria no] ▷ *n* アルジェリア人 [arujieriajin]

alias [ˈeɪliəs] *adv* 別名 [betsumei] ▷ *prep* ・・・の別名で知られる [... no betsumei de shirareru]

alibi [ˈælɪbaɪ] *n* アリバイ [aribai]

alien [ˈeɪliən] *n* 外国人 [gaikokujin]

alive [əˈlaɪv] *adj* 生きている [ikite iru]

all [ɔl] *adj* できるかぎりの [dekiru kagiri no] ▷ *pron* 全部 [zenbu]

Allah [ˈælə, ˈælɑ] *n* アッラー [arraa]

allegation [ˌælɪˈgeɪʃən] *n* 申し立て [moushi-tate]

alleged [əˈlɛdʒd] *adj* 申し立てられた [moushitaterareta]

allergic [əˈlɜrdʒɪk] *adj* アレルギーの [arerugii no]

allergy [ˈælərdʒi] *n* アレルギー [arerugii]; **peanut allergy** *n* ピーナッツアレルギー [piinattsu arerugii]

alley [ˈæli] *n* 路地 [roji]

alliance [əˈlaɪəns] *n* 提携 [teikei]

alligator [ˈælɪgeɪtər] *n* ワニ [wani]

allow [əˈlaʊ] *v* 許す [yurusu]

all right *adv* 申し分なく [moushibun naku]

ally *n* 同盟国 [doumeikoku]

almond [ˈɑmənd, ˈæm-, ˈælm-] *n* アーモンド [aamondo]

almost [ˈɔlmoʊst] *adv* ほとんど [hotondo]

alone [əˈloʊn] *adj* ただ一人の [tada hitori no]

along [əˈlɔŋ] *prep* ・・・に沿って [... ni sotte]

aloud [əˈlaʊd] *adv* 声を出して [koe wo dashite]

alphabet [ˈælfəbɛt, -bɪt] *n* アルファベット [arufabetto]

Alps [ælps] *npl* アルプス山脈 [arupusu sanmyaku]

already [ɔlˈrɛdi] *adv* すでに [sude ni]

also [ˈɔlsoʊ] *adv* ・・・も [...mo]

altar [ˈɔltər] *n* 祭壇 [saidan]

alter [ˈɔltər] *v* 変更する [henkou suru]

alternate *adj* 交互の [kougo no]

alternative [ɔlˈtɜrnətɪv] *adj* 代わりの [kawari no] ▷ *n* 選択肢 [sentakushi]

although [ɔlˈðoʊ] *conj* ・・・とはいえ [...towaie]

altitude [ˈæltɪtud] *n* 高度 [koudo] *(海抜)*

altogether [ˌɔltəˈgɛðər] *adv* 全く [mattaku]

aluminum [əˈlumɪnəm] *n* アルミニウム [aruminiumu]

always [ˈɔlweɪz] *adv* 常に [tsune ni]

a.m. [ˈeɪ ˈɛm] *abbr* 午前の [gozen no]

amateur [ˈæmətʃɜr, -tʃʊər] *n* アマチュア [amachua]

amaze [əmeɪz] v 驚かせる [odoroka seru]

amazed [əmeɪzd] adj 驚いて [odoroi te]

amazing [əmeɪzɪŋ] adj 驚くべき [odor-okubeki]

ambassador [æmbæsədər] n 大使 [taishi]

amber [æmbər] n 琥珀色 [kohaku iro]

ambition [æmbɪʃᵊn] n 野心 [yashin]

ambitious [æmbɪʃəs] adj 野心的な [yashinteki na]

ambulance [æmbyələns] n 救急車 [kyuukyuu-usha]; Call an ambulance 救急車を呼んでください [kyuukyuu-sha o yonde kudasai]

ambush [æmbʊʃ] n 待ち伏せ [machifuse]

amenities [əmɪnɪtɪz] npl アメニティー [ameniteii]

America [əmerɪkə] n アメリカ [amerika]; Central America n 中央アメリカ [Chuuou Amerika]; North America n 北アメリカ [kitaamerika]; South America n 南アメリカ [minamiamerika]

American [əmerɪkən] adj アメリカの [amerika no] ▷ n アメリカ人 [amerikajin]; modified American plan n 二食付き [nishokutsuki]; North American n 北アメリカ人 [Kita Amerika jin], 北アメリカの [Kita Amerika no]; South American n 南アメリカ人 [Minami Amerika jin], 南アメリカの [Minami Amerika no]

ammunition [æmyʊnɪʃᵊn] n 弾薬 [dan-yaku]

among [əmʌŋ] prep …の中で [… no naka de]

amount [əmaʊnt] n 量 [ryou]

ampere [æmpər] n アンペア [anpea]

amplifier [æmplɪfaɪər] n アンプ [anpu]

amuse [əmyuz] v 楽しませる [tanoshimaseru]

an [ən, STRONG æn] art 一つの [hitotsu no]

analysis [ənælɪsɪs] n 分析 [bunseki]

analyze [ænəlaɪz] v 分析する [bunseki suru]

ancestor [ænsɛstər] n 先祖 [senzo]

anchor [æŋkər] n 錨 [ikari]

anchovy [æntʃoʊvi] n アンチョビー [anchobii]

ancient [eɪnʃənt] adj 大昔の [oumukashi no]

and [ənd, STRONG ænd] conj …と… [...to...]

Andes [ændiz] npl アンデス山脈 [andesu sanmyaku]

Andorra [ændɔrə] n アンドラ [andora]

anemic [ənimɪk] adj 貧血の [hinketsu no]

anesthetic [ænɪsθɛtɪk] n 麻酔薬 [masuiyaku]; general anesthetic n 全身麻酔 [zenshin masui]; local anesthetic n 局所麻酔薬 [kyokusho masuiyaku]

angel [eɪndʒᵊl] n 天使 [tenshi]

anger [æŋgər] n 怒り [ikari]

angina [ændʒaɪnə] n 狭心症 [kyoushinshou]

angle [æŋgᵊl] n 角 [kado] (数学); right angle n 直角 [chokkaku]

Angola [æŋgoʊlə] n アンゴラ [angora]

Angolan [æŋgoʊlᵊn] adj アンゴラの [angora no] ▷ n アンゴラ人 [angorajin]

angry [æŋgri] adj 怒った [okotta]

animal [ænɪmᵊl] n 動物 [doubutsu]

aniseed [ænɪsid] n アニシード [anishiido]

ankle [æŋkᵊl] n くるぶし [kurubushi]

anniversary [ænɪvɜrsəri] n 記念日 [kinenbi]; wedding anniversary n 結婚記念日 [kekkon kinenbi]

announce [ənaʊns] v 発表する [happyou suru]

announcement [ənaʊnsmənt] n 発表 [happyou]

annoy [ənɔɪ] v うるさがらせる [urusagaraseru]

annoyance [ənɔɪəns] n 面倒 [mendou]

annoying [ənɔɪɪŋ] adj うるさい [urusai]

annual [ænyuəl] adj 年一回の [nen'ikkai no], 年次 [nenji]

annually [ænyuəli] adv 年一回 [nen'ikkai]

anonymous [ənɒnɪməs] adj 匿名の [tokumei no]

anorexia [ænərɛksiə] n 拒食症 [kyo-oshokushou]

anorexic [ænərɛksɪk] adj 拒食症的な [kyoshokushouteki na]

another [ənʌðər] adj もう一つの [mou hitotsu no], 別な [betsu na]

answer [ænsər] *n* 答え [kotae] ▸ *v* 答える [kotaeru]

answering machine [ænsərɪŋ məʃin] *n* 留守番電話 [rusubandenwa]

ant [ænt] *n* アリ [ari]

antagonize [æntægənaɪz] *v* 敵にまわす [teki ni mawasu]

Antarctic [æntɑrktɪk] *adj* 南極大陸 [Nankyoku tairiku] ▸ *n* 南極 [nankyoku]

antelope [æntˈloup] *n* レイヨウ [reiyou]

antenna [æntɛnə] *n* アンテナ [antena]

anthem [ænθəm] *n* 国歌 [kokka]

anthropology [ænθrəpɒlədʒi] *n* 人類学 [jinruigaku]

antibiotic [æntibaɪɒtɪk, -taɪ-] *n* 抗生物質 [kousei busshitsu]

antibody [æntibɒdi, æntaɪ-] *n* 抗体 [koutai]

antidepressant [æntidiprɛsənt, æntaɪ-] *n* 抗鬱剤 [kouutsuzai]

antidote [æntidoʊt] *n* 解毒剤 [gedokuzai]

antifreeze [æntifriz, æntaɪ-] *n* 不凍液 [futoueki]

antihistamine [æntihɪstəmɪn, æntaɪ-] *n* 抗ヒスタミン剤 [kouhisutaminzai]

antiperspirant [æntipɜrspirənt, æntaɪ-] *n* 発汗抑制剤 [hakkan yokuseizai]

antique [æntik] *n* 骨董品 [kottouhin]; **antique store** *n* 骨董屋 [kottou ya]

antiseptic [æntəsɛptɪk] *n* 殺菌剤 [sakkinzai]

antivirus [æntivaɪrəs] *n* アンチウイルス [anchiuirusu]

anxiety [æŋzaɪɪti] *n* 心配 [shinpai]

any [ɛni] *adj* どれでも [dore de mo] ▸ *pron* どれでも [dore de mo]

anybody [ɛnibɒdi, -bʌdi] *pron* 誰でも [dare demo]

anyhow [ɛnihaʊ] *adv* とにかく [tonikaku]

anyone [ɛniwʌn] *pron* 誰でも [dare demo]

anything [ɛniθɪŋ] *pron* 何でも [nandemo]

anyway [ɛniweɪ] *adv* とにかく [tonikaku]

anywhere [ɛniwɛər] *adv* どこでも [dokodemo]

apart [əpɑrt] *adv* 別個に [bekko ni]

apart from *prep* ・・・は別として [... wa betsu to shite]

apartment [əpɑrtmənt] *n* アパート [apaato], アパートメント [apaatomento], フラット [furatto]; **studio apartment** *n* ワンルームのアパート [wanruumu no apaato]; **studio apartment** *n* スタジオフラット [sutajiofuratto]; **We're looking for an apartment** 私たちはアパートメントを探しています [watashi-tachi wa apaatomento o sagashite imasu]; **We've reserved an apartment in the name of...** ・・・の名前でアパートメントを予約してあります [... no namae de apaatomento o yoyaku shite arimasu]

aperitif [æpɛrɪtif] *n* アペリチフ [aperichifu]; **We'd like an aperitif** アペリチフをいただきます [aperichifu o itadakimasu]

aperture [æpərtʃər] *n* 開口部 [kaikoubu]

apologize [əpɒlədʒaɪz] *v* 謝る [ayamaru]

apology [əpɒlədʒi] *n* 詫び [wabi]

apostrophe [əpɒstrəfi] *n* アポストロフィ [aposutorofi]

appalling [əpɔlɪŋ] *adj* ぞっとするような [zotto suru you na]

apparatus [æpərætəs, -reɪ-] *n* 器具 [kigu]

apparent [əpærənt] *adj* 明らかな [akiraka na]

apparently [əpærəntli] *adv* 明らかに [akiraka ni]

appeal [əpil] *n* 懇願 [kongan] ▸ *v* 懇願する [kongan suru]

appealing [əpilɪŋ] *adj* 魅力的な [miryokuteki na]

appear [əpɪər] *v* 現れる [arawareru]

appearance [əpɪərəns] *n* 出現 [shutsugen]

appendicitis [əpɛndɪsaɪtɪs] *n* 虫垂炎 [chuusuien]

appetite [æpɪtaɪt] *n* 食欲 [shokuyoku]

appetizer [æpɪtaɪzər] *n* **I'd like pasta as an appetizer** スターターにパスタをいただきます [sutaataa ni pasuta o itadakimasu]

applaud [əplɔd] *v* 拍手を送る [hakushu-o okuru]

applause [əplɔz] *n* 拍手 [hakushu]

apple [æpᵊl] n リンゴ [ringo]; **apple pie** n アップルパイ [appurupai]

appliance [əplaɪəns] n 器具 [kigu]

applicant [æplɪkənt] n 応募者 [oubosha]

application [æplɪkeɪʃn] n 申し込み [moushikomi]; **application form** n 申込書 [moushikomisho]

apply [əplaɪ] v 申し込む [moushikomu]

appoint [əpɔɪnt] v 任命する [ninmei suru]

appointment [əpɔɪntmənt] n 予約 [yoyaku]; **Can I have an appointment with the doctor?** お医者さんの予約を取れますか? [o-isha-san no yoyaku o toremasu ka?]; **I'd like to make an appointment** 予約を取りたいのですが [yoyaku o toritai no desu ga]

appreciate [əpriʃieɪt] v 高く評価する [takaku hyouka suru]

apprehensive [æprɪhɛnsɪv] adj 心配して [shinpai shite]

apprentice [əprɛntɪs] n 見習い [minarai]

approach [əproʊtʃ] v 近づく [chikaduku]

appropriate [əproʊpriɪt] adj いい [ii], 適切な [tekisetsu na]

approval [əpruvᵊl] n 承認 [shounin]

approve [əpruv] v 承認する [shounin suru]

approximate adj 近似の [kinji no]

approximately [əprɒksɪmətli] adv およそ [oyoso]

apricot [eɪprɪkɒt] n アプリコット [apurikotto]

April [eɪprɪl] n 四月 [shigatsu]; **April Fools' Day** n エープリルフールの日 [eepuriru fuuru no nichi]

apron [eɪprən] n エプロン [epuron]

aquarium [əkwɛəriəm] n 水槽 [suisou]

Aquarius [əkwɛəriəs] n 水瓶座 [mizugameza]

Arab [ærəb] adj アラビアの [arabia no] ▷ n アラビア人 [arabiajin]; **United Arab Emirates** npl アラブ首長国連邦 [arabu shuchou-kokurenpou]

Arabic [ærəbɪk] adj アラビア語の [arabiago no] ▷ n アラビア語 [arabiago]

arbitration [ɑrbɪtreɪʃn] n 仲裁 [chuusai]

arch [ɑrtʃ] n アーチ [aachi]

archaeologist [ɑrkiɒlədʒɪst] n 考古学者 [koukogakusha]

archaeology [ɑrkiɒlədʒi] n 考古学 [koukogaku]

archbishop [ɑrtʃbɪʃəp] n 大主教 [dai shukyou]

architect [ɑrkɪtɛkt] n 建築家 [kenchikuka]

architecture [ɑrkɪtɛktʃər] n 建築 [kenchiku], 建築様式 [kenchikuyoushiki]

archive [ɑrkaɪv] n 文書館 [bunshokan]

Arctic [ɑrktɪk] n 北極 [hokkyoku]; **Arctic Circle** n 北極圏 [hokkyokuken]; **Arctic Ocean** n 北極海 [Hokkyokukai]

area [ɛəriə] n エリア [eria], 地域 [chiiki]; **area code** n 局番 [kyokuban]; **pedestrian area** n 歩行者天国 [hokoushatengoku]; **service area** n サービスエリア [saabisu eria]; **I'd like a seat in the smoking area** 喫煙エリアの席が欲しいのですが [kitsuen-eria no seki ga hoshii no desu ga]; **Is there a non-smoking area?** 禁煙エリアはありますか? [kin'en-eria wa arimasu ka?]

Argentina [ɑrdʒəntinə] n アルゼンチン [aruzenchin]

Argentine [ɑrdʒəntin, -taɪn] adj アルゼンチンの [aruzenchin no] ▷ n (person) アルゼンチン人 [aruzenchinjin]

argue [ɑrgyu] v 立証する [risshou suru]

argument [ɑrgyəmənt] n 口論 [kouron]

Aries [ɛəriz] n 牡羊座 [ohitsujiza]

arm [ɑrm] n 腕 [ude]; **I can't move my arm** 私は腕を動かせません [watashi wa ude o ugokasemasen]

armchair [ɑrmtʃɛər] n 肘掛け椅子 [hijikakeke isu]

armed [ɑrmd] adj 武装した [busou shita]

Armenia [ɑrminiə] n アルメニア [arumenia]

Armenian [ɑrminiən] adj アルメニアの [arumenia no] ▷ n (language) アルメニア語 [arumeniago], (person) アルメニア人 [arumeniajin]

armor [ɑrmər] n 甲冑 [kouchuu]

armpit [ˈɑrmpɪt] *n* 腋の下 [waki no shita]

army [ˈɑrmi] *n* 軍隊 [guntai]

aroma [əˈroumə] *n* 芳香 [houkou]

aromatherapy [əˌrouməˈθɛrəpi] *n* アロマセラピー [aromaserapii]

around [əˈraund] *adv* 周りに [mawari ni] ▷ *prep* あちこち [achikochi]

arrange [əˈreɪndʒ] *v* 手配する [tehai suru]

arrangement [əˈreɪndʒmənt] *n* 手配 [tehai]

arrears [əˈrɪərz] *npl* 未払金 [miharaikin]

arrest [əˈrɛst] *n* 逮捕 [taiho] ▷ *v* 逮捕する [taiho suru]

arrival [əˈraɪvl] *n* 到着 [touchaku]

arrive [əˈraɪv] *v* 着く [tsuku]

arrogant [ˈærəgənt] *adj* 横柄な [ouhei na]

arrow [ˈæroʊ] *n* 矢 [ya]

arson [ˈɑrsn] *n* 放火 [houka]

art [ɑrt] *n* 芸術 [geijutsu], 美術 [bijutsu]; **art gallery** *n* 美術館 [bijutsukan]; **art museum** *n* 画廊 [garou]; **art school** *n* 美術学校 [bijutsugakkou]; **work of art** *n* 美術品 [bijutsuhin]

artery [ˈɑrtəri] *n* 動脈 [doumyaku]

arthritis [ɑrˈθraɪtɪs] *n* 関節炎 [kansetsuen]; **I suffer from arthritis** 私は関節炎をわずらっています [watashi wa kansetsuen o wazuratte imasu]

artichoke [ˈɑrtɪtʃoʊk] *n* アーティチョーク [aatichooku]

article [ˈɑrtɪkl] *n* 記事 [kiji]

artificial [ˌɑrtɪˈfɪʃl] *adj* 人工の [jinkou no]

artist [ˈɑrtɪst] *n* 芸術家 [geijutsuka]

artistic [ɑrˈtɪstɪk] *adj* 芸術的な [geijutsuteki na]

as [əz, STRONG æz] *adv* ···と同じくらい [... to onaji kurai] ▷ *conj* ···している時 [... shite iru toki] ▷ *prep* ···として [...toshite]

ASAP [eɪ ɛs eɪ pi] *abbr* できるだけ早く [dekiru dake hayaku]

ascent [əˈsɛnt] *n* **When is the last ascent?** 最後に昇るのはいつですか? [saigo ni noboru no wa itsu desu ka?]

ash [æʃ] *n* はい [hai]

ashamed [əˈʃeɪmd] *adj* 恥じて [hajite]

ashore [əˈʃɔr] *adv* **Can we go ashore now?** もう下船できますか? [mou gesen dekimasu ka?]

ashtray [ˈæʃtreɪ] *n* 灰皿 [haizara]; **May I have an ashtray?** 灰皿をいただけますか? [haizara o itadakemasu ka?]

Asia [ˈeɪʒə] *n* アジア [ajia]

Asian [ˈeɪʒn] *adj* アジアの [ajia no] ▷ *n* アジア人 [ajiajin]

Asiatic [ˌeɪʒiˈætɪk] *adj* アジアの [ajia no]

ask [ɑsk, æsk] *v* 尋ねる [tazuneru]

ask for *v* ···を求める [...-o motomeru]

asleep [əˈslip] *adj* 眠って [nemutte]

asparagus [əˈspærəgəs] *n* アスパラガス [asuparagasu]

aspect [ˈæspɛkt] *n* 局面 [kyokumen]

aspirin [ˈæspərɪn, -prɪn] *n* アスピリン [asupirin]; **I can't take aspirin** 私はアスピリンを飲めません [watashi wa asupirin o nomemasen]; **I'd like some aspirin** アスピリンが欲しいのですが [asupirin ga hoshii no desu ga]

assembly [əˈsɛmbli] *n* 集会 [shuukai]

assertion [əˈsɜrʃn] *n* 断言 [dangen]

asset [ˈæsɛt] *n* 強み [tsuyomi]

assignment [əˈsaɪnmənt] *n* 割り当て [wariate]

assistance [əˈsɪstəns] *n* 援助 [enjo]

assistant [əˈsɪstənt] *n* 助手 [joshu]; **assistant professor** *n* 講師 [koushi]; **personal assistant** *n* 個人秘書 [kojin hisho]; **sales assistant** *n* 販売スタッフ [hanbai sutaffu]

associate *adj* [əˈsoʊʃɪt, -sɪt] 準··· [jun...] ▷ *n* [əˈsoʊʃɪt, -sɪt] 提携者 [teikeisha]

association [əˌsoʊʃiˈeɪʃn, -siˈeɪ-] *n* 協会 [kyoukai]

assortment [əˈsɔrtmənt] *n* 各種取り合わせ [kakushu toriawase]

assume [əˈsum] *v* 想定する [soutei suru]

assure [əˈʃʊər] *v* 確約する [kakuyaku suru]

asthma [ˈæzmə] *n* 喘息 [zensoku]

astonish [əˈstɒnɪʃ] *v* 驚かす [odorokasu]

astonished [əstɒnɪʃt] *adj* 驚いた [odoroita]

astonishing [əstɒnɪʃɪŋ] *adj* 驚くばかりの [odoroku bakarino]

astrology [əstrɒlədʒi] *n* 占星術 [senseijutsu]

astronaut [æstrənɔt] *n* 宇宙飛行士 [uchuuhikoushi]

astronomy [əstrɒnəmi] *n* 天文学 [tenmongaku]

asylum [əsaɪləm] *n* 亡命 [boumei]; **asylum seeker** *n* 亡命者 [boumeisha]

at [ət, STRONG æt] *prep* ···に [···ni]; **at least** *adv* 少なくとも [sukunakutomo]; **Do we stop at...?** ···に停車しますか? [... ni teisha shimasu ka?]

atheist [eɪθiːɪst] *n* 無神論者 [mushinronsha]

athlete [æθliːt] *n* 運動選手 [undousenshu]

athletic [æθlɛtɪk] *adj* 運動選手らしい [undou senshu rashii]

Atlantic [ətlæntɪk] *n* 大西洋 [taiseiyou]

atlas [ætləs] *n* 地図帳 [chizuchou]

ATM [eɪ tiː ɛm] *n* 支払機 [shiharaiki], 現金自動支払い機 [genkin jidoushiharaiki]; **Can I use my card with this ATM?** この現金自動支払い機で私のカードを使えますか? [kono genkin-jidou-shiharaiki de watashi no kaado o tsukaemasu ka?]; **Is there an ATM here?** ここに現金自動支払い機がありますか? [koko ni genkin-jidou-shiharaiki ga arimasu ka?]; **The ATM swallowed my card** 現金自動支払い機が私のカードを吸い込んでしまいました [genkin-jidou-shiharaiki ga watashi no kaado o suikonde shimaimashita]; **Where is the nearest ATM?** 一番近い現金自動支払い機はどこですか? [ichiban chikai genkin-jidou-shiharaiki wa doko desu ka?]

atmosphere [ætməsfɪər] *n* 大気 [taiki]

atom [ætəm] *n* 原子 [genshi]; **atom bomb** *n* 原子爆弾 [genshibakudan]

atomic [ətɒmɪk] *adj* 原子力の [genshiryoku no]

attach [ətætʃ] *v* 取り付ける [toritsukeru]

attached [ətætʃt] *adj* 決まった相手がいる [kimatta aite ga iru]

attachment [ətætʃmənt] *n* 愛着 [aichaku]

attack [ətæk] *n* 攻撃 [kougeki] ▷ *v* 攻撃する [kougeki suru]; **heart attack** *n* 心臓発作 [shinzouhossa]; **terrorist attack** *n* テロリストによる攻撃 [terorisuto niyoru kougeki]

attempt [ətɛmpt] *n* 試み [kokoromi] ▷ *v* 試みる [kokoromiru]

attend [ətɛnd] *v* 出席する [shusseki suru]

attendance [ətɛndəns] *n* 出席 [shusseki]

attendant [ətɛndənt] *n* **flight attendant** *n* スチュワーデス [suchuwaadesu], 客室乗務員 [kyakushitsu joumuin]

attention [ətɛnʃən] *n* 注意 [chuui]

attic [ætɪk] *n* 屋根裏 [yaneura]

attitude [ætɪtud] *n* 態度 [taido]

attorney [ətɜrni] *n* 弁護士 [bengoshi]

attract [ətrækt] *v* ひきつける [hikitsukeru]

attraction [ətrækʃən] *n* 魅力 [miryoku]

attractive [ətræktɪv] *adj* 魅力的な [miryokuteki na]

auburn [ɔbərn] *adj* 赤褐色の [akakasshoku no]

auction [ɔkʃən] *n* 競売 [kyoubai]

audience [ɔdiəns] *n* 聴衆 [choushuu]

audit [ɔdɪt] *n* 監査 [kansa] ▷ *v* 監査する [kansa suru]

audition [ɔdɪʃən] *n* オーディション [oodishon]

auditor [ɔdɪtər] *n* 会計監査人 [kaikei kansanin]

August [ɔgəst] *n* 八月 [hachigatsu]

aunt [ænt, ɑnt] *n* おば [oba] (伯母・叔母)

auntie [ænti, ɑnti] *n* おばちゃん [obachan]

au pair [oʊ pɛər] *n* オーペア [oopea]

austerity [ɔstɛrɪti] *n* 厳格さ [genkakusa]

Australasia [ɔːstrəleɪziə] *n* オーストラレーシア [oosutorareeshia]

Australia [ɒstreɪliə] *n* オーストラリア [oosutoraria]

Australian [ɒstreɪlyən] *adj* オーストラリアの [oosutoraria no] ▷ *n* オーストラリア人 [oosutorariajin]

Austria [ɒstriə] *n* オーストリア [oosutoria]

Austrian [ɒstriən] *adj* オーストリアの

[oosutoria no] ▷ *n* オーストリア人 [oosutoria-jin]

authentic [ɔθɛ̃ntɪk] *adj* 本物の [honmono no]

author [ɔθər] *n* 著者 [chosha]

authorize [ɔθəraɪz] *v* 権限を与える [kengen-o ataeru]

auto [ɔtoʊ] *n* **auto mechanic** *n* 自動車整備士 [jidousha seibishi]; **auto racing** *n* モーターレース [mootaareesu]

autobiography [ɔtəbaɪɒɡrəfi] *n* 自叙伝 [jijoden]

autograph [ɔtəɡræf] *n* サイン [sain]

automatic [ɔtəmætɪk] *adj* 自動的な [jidouteki na], 児童 [jidou]

automatically [ɔtəmætɪkli] *adv* 自動的に [jidouteki ni]

autonomous [ɔtɒnəməs] *adj* 自治権のある [jichiken no aru]

autonomy [ɔtɒnəmi] *n* 自治国家 [jichi kokka]

autumn [ɔtəm] *n* 秋 [aki]

availability [əveɪləbɪlɪti] *n* 有用性 [yuuyousei]

available [əveɪləbᵊl] *adj* 利用できる [riyou dekiru]

avalanche [ævəlæntʃ] *n* なだれ [nadare]; **Is there a danger of avalanches?** なだれの危険はありますか? [nadare no kiken wa arimasu ka?]

avenue [ævɪnyu, -nu] *n* 大通り [oudouri]

average [ævərɪdʒ, ævrɪdʒ] *adj* 平均の [heikin no] ▷ *n* 平均 [heikin]

avocado [ævəkɑdoʊ] *n* アボカド [abokado]

avoid [əvɔɪd] *v* 避ける [sakeru]; **avoid work** *v* 仕事をサボる [shigoto-o saboru]

awake [əweɪk] *adj* 眠らずに [nemurazu ni] ▷ *v* 目が覚める [me ga sameru]

award [əwɔrd] *n* 賞 [shou]; **awards ceremony** 授賞式 [jushoushiki]

aware [əwɛər] *adj* 気がついて [ki ga tsuite]

away [əweɪ] *adv* 離れて [hanarete]; **away game** *n* アウェーの試合 [auee no shiai]

awful [ɔfəl] *adj* ひどい [hidoi]; **What awful weather!** なんてひどい天気でしょう! [nante hidoi tenki deshou!]

awfully [ɔfli] *adv* ひどく [hidoku]

awkward [ɔkwərd] *adj* 不器用な [bukiyou na]

ax [æks] *n* 斧 [ono]

axle [æksᵊl] *n* 車軸 [shajiku]

Azerbaijan [ɑzərbaɪdʒɑn] *n* アゼルバイジャン [azerubaijan]

Azerbaijani [ɑzərbaɪdʒɑni] *adj* アゼルバイジャンの [azerubaijan no] ▷ *n* アゼルバイジャン人 [azerubaijanjin]

B

B&B [bi ən bi] *n* ベッド＆ブレックファースト [beddo burekkufaasuto]

BA [bi eɪ] *abbr* 文学士 [bungakushi]

baby [beɪbi] *n* ベビー [bebii], 赤ちゃん [akachan], 赤ん坊 [akanbou]; **baby bottle** *n* 哺乳瓶 [honyuubin]; **baby carriage** *n* 乳母車 [ubaguruma]; **baby wipe** *n* 赤ちゃん用ウェットティシュー [akachanyouuettotishuu]; **Are there facilities for parents with babies?** 赤ちゃんがいる両親のための設備はありますか? [akachan ga iru ryoushin no tame no setsubi wa arimasu ka?]

baby-seat *n* ベビーシート [bebiishiito]

babysit [beɪbɪsɪt] *v* ベビーシッターをする [bebiishittaa wo suru]

baby-sitter [beɪbɪsɪtər] *n* 子守 [komori]

babysitter [beɪbɪsɪtər] *n* ベビーシッター [bebiishittaa]

babysitting [beɪbɪsɪtɪŋ] *n* 子守り [komori]

bachelor [bætʃələr] *n* 独身の男性 [dokushin no dansei]; **bachelor party** *n* スタッグパーティー [sutaggupaateii]

back [bæk] *adj* 後ろの [ushiro no] ▷ *adv* 後ろに [ushiro ni] ▷ *n* 背中 [senaka] ▷ *v* 後退させる [koutai saseru]; **back pain** *n* 腰痛 [youtsuu]; **call back** *v* 電話をかけなおす [denwa-o kakenaosu]; **I have a bad back** 私は背中が痛みます [watashi wa senaka ga itamimasu]; **I've hurt my back** 私は背中を痛めました [watashi wa senaka o itamemashita]

backache [bækeɪk] *n* 腰痛 [youtsuu]

backbone [bækboun] *n* 背骨 [sebone]

backfire [bækfaɪər] *v* 裏目に出る [urame ni deru]

background [bækgraʊnd] *n* 背景 [haikei]

backing [bækɪŋ] *n* 支援 [shien]

back out *v* 約束を取り消す [yakusoku-o torikesu]

backpack [bækpæk] *n* リュックサック [ryukkusakku], バックパック [bakkupakku]

backpacker [bækpækər] *n* バックパッカー [bakkupakkaa]

backpacking [bækpækɪŋ] *n* バックパッキング [bakkupakkingu]

backside [bæksaɪd] *n* 臀部 [denbu]

backslash [bæklæʃ] *n* バックスラッシュ [bakkusurasshu]

backstroke [bækstroʊk] *n* 背泳 [haiei]

back up *v* 支援する [shien suru]

backup [bækʌp] *n* バックアップ [bakkuappu]

backwards [bækwərdz] *adv* 後方に [kouhou ni]

bacon [beɪkən] *n* ベーコン [beekon]

bacteria [bæktɪəriə] *npl* バクテリア [bakuteria]

bad [bæd] *adj* 悪い [warui]; **It's a bad line** 回線が悪いです [kaisen ga warui desu]

badger [bædʒər] *n* アナグマ [anaguma]

badly [bædli] *adv* 悪く [waruku]

badminton [bædmɪntən] *n* バドミントン [badominton]

bad-tempered [bædtɛmpərd] *adj* 機嫌の悪い [kigen no warui]

baffled [bæfəld] *adj* 困惑した [konwaku shita]

bag [bæg] *n* 袋 [fukuro], かばん [kaban]; **cosmetics bag** *n* 洗面用具入れ [senmen yougu ire]; **overnight bag** *n* 一泊旅行用かばん [ippaku ryokou you kaban]; **plastic bag** *n* ビニール袋 [biniiru bukuro]; **polyethylene bag** *n* ポリエチレンの袋 [poriechiren no fukuro]; **shopping bag** *n* 買物袋

[kaimonobukuro]; **sleeping bag** n 寝袋 [neb-ukuro]; **tea bag** n ティーバッグ [tiibaggu]; **toiletries bag** n 洗面用具バッグ [senmen yougu baggu]; **I don't need a bag, thanks** 袋は要りません [fukuro wa irimasen]; **May I have a bag, please?** 袋をいただけますか? [fukuro o itadakemasu ka?]

baggage [bǽgɪdʒ] n 手荷物 [tenimotsu]; **baggage allowance** n 無料手荷物許容量 [muryou tenimotsu kyoouryou]; **baggage cart** n 手荷物カート [tenimotsu kaato]; **baggage claim** n 手荷物受取所 [tenimotsu uketorisho]; **carry-on baggage** n 手荷物 [tenimotsu]; **excess baggage** n 超過手荷物 [choukatenimotsu]; **Are there any baggage carts?** 手荷物カートはありますか? [tenimotsu-kaato wa arimasu ka?]; **What is the baggage allowance?** 無料手荷物許容量はどう規定されていますか? [muryou-tenimotsu-kyoouryou wa dou kitei sarete imasu ka?]

baggy [bǽgi] adj だぶだぶの [dabudabu no]

bagpipes [bǽgpaɪps] npl バグパイプ [bagupaipu]

Bahamas [bəhɑ́məz] npl バハマ [bahama]

Bahrain [bɑreɪn] n バーレーン [baareen]

bail [beɪl] n 保釈金 [hoshakukin]

bake [beɪk] v 焼く [yaku]

baked [beɪkt] adj 焼いた [yaita]; **baked potato** n ジャケットポテト [jaketto poteto], ベークドポテト [beekudopoteto]

baker [beɪkər] n パン屋の主人 [pan ya no shujin]

bakery [beɪkəri, beɪkri] n パン屋 [pan-ya]

baking [beɪkɪŋ] n ベーキング [beekingu]; **baking powder** n ベーキングパウダー [beekingupaudaa]

balance [bǽləns] n バランス [baransu]; **balance sheet** n 貸借対照表 [taishakutaishouhyou]; **bank balance** n 銀行の残高 [ginkou no zandaka]

balanced [bǽlənst] adj バランスのとれた [baransu no toreta]

balcony [bǽlkəni] n バルコニー [barukonii]; **Do you have a room with a balcony?** バルコニー付きの部屋はありますか? [barukonii-tsuki no heya wa arimasu ka?]

bald [bɔld] adj 頭のはげた [atama no hageta]

Balkan [bɔlkən] adj バルカン諸国の [Barukan shokoku no]

ball [bɔl] n (dance) 舞踏会 [butoukai], (toy) ボール [booru]

ballerina [bælərinə] n バレリーナ [bareriina]

ballet [bæleɪ] n バレエ [baree]; **ballet dancer** n バレエダンサー [bareedansaa]; **ballet shoes** npl バレエシューズ [baree shuuzu]; **Where can I buy tickets for the ballet?** どこでそのバレエのチケットを買えますか? [doko de sono baree no chiketto o kaemasu ka?]

balloon [bəlun] n 風船 [fuusen]

ballpoint [bɔlpɔɪnt] n **ballpoint pen** n バイロウ® [bairou]

balm [bɑm] n **lip balm** n おべっか [obekka]

bamboo [bæmbu] n 竹 [take]

ban [bæn] n 禁止 [kinshi] ▷ v 禁止する [kinshi suru]

banana [bənǽnə] n バナナ [banana]

band [bænd] n (musical group) バンド [bando] (strip) 帯状のひも [obijou no himo]; **brass band** n ブラスバンド [burasubando]; **rubber band** n 輪ゴム [wagomu]

bandage [bǽndɪdʒ] n 包帯 [houtai], (for wound) 絆創膏 [iedomo chimakemu] ▷ v 包帯をする [houtai-o suru]; **I'd like a bandage** 包帯をしてください [houtai o shite kudasai]; **I'd like a fresh bandage** 新しい包帯をしてください [atarashii houtai o shite kudasai]

Band-Aid® [bǽndeɪd] n エラストプラスト® [erasutopurasuto]

bang [bæŋ] n 砲声 [housei] ▷ v パンと打つ [ban to utsu]

Bangladesh [bɑŋglədɛʃ] n バングラデシュ [banguradeshu]

Bangladeshi [bæŋglədɛʃi] adj バングラデシ

ュの [Banguradeshu no] ▷ n バングラデシュ人 [banguradeshujin]

bangs [bæŋz] n (hair) 切下げ前髪 [kirisagemaegami]

banister [bænɪstər] n 手すり [tesuri]

banjo [bændʒoʊ] n バンジョー [banjoo]

bank [bæŋk] n (finance) 銀行 [ginkou], (ridge) 土手 [dote]; **bank account** n 銀行口座 [ginkoukouza]; **bank balance** n 銀行の残高 [ginkou no zandaka]; **bank charges** npl 銀行の手数料 [ginkou no tesuuryou]; **bank statement** n 銀行の明細書 [ginkou no meisaisho]; **merchant bank** n マーチャントバンク [maachantobanku]; **How far away is the bank?** 銀行までどのくらいの距離ですか? [ginkou made dono kurai no kyori desu ka?]; **I'd like to transfer some money from my bank in...** ···にある取引銀行から送金したいのですが [... ni aru torihiki-ginkou kara soukin shitai no desu ga]; **Is the bank open today?** その銀行は今日開いていますか? [sono ginkou wa kyou hiraite imasu ka?]; **Is there a bank here?** ここに銀行はありますか? [koko ni ginkou wa arimasu ka?]; **When does the bank close?** その銀行はいつ閉まりますか? [sono ginkou wa itsu shimarimasu ka?]

banker [bæŋkər] n 銀行家 [ginkouka]

bankrupt [bæŋkrʌpt] adj 破産した [hasan shita]

banned [bænd] adj 禁止された [kinshi sareta]

baptism [bæptɪzəm] n 洗礼 [senrei]

Baptist [bæptɪst] n バプテスト [baputesuto]

bar [bɑr] n (alcohol) バー [baa] (酒場), (strip) 棒 [bou]; **snack bar** n 軽食堂 [keishokudou]; **Where is the bar?** バーはどこですか? [baa wa doko desu ka?]; **Where is there a nice bar?** どこかに感じの良いバーはありますか? [doko-ka ni kanji no yoi baa wa arimasu ka?]

Barbados [bɑrbeɪdoʊs] n バルバドス [barubadosu]

barbaric [bɑrbærɪk] adj 野蛮な [yaban na]

barbecue [bɑrbɪkyu] n バーベキュー [baabekyuu]; **Where is the barbecue area?** バーベキュー場はどこですか? [baabekyuu-jou wa doko desu ka?]

barber [bɑrbər] n 床屋 [tokoya]

bare [bɛər] adj むき出しの [mukidashi no] ▷ v むき出しにする [mukidashi ni suru]

barefoot [bɛərfʊt] adj 裸足の [hadashi no] ▷ adv 裸足で [hadashi de]

barely [bɛərli] adv かろうじて [karoujite]

bargain [bɑrgɪn] n 売買契約 [baibai keiyaku]

barge [bɑrdʒ] n バージ [baaji]

bark [bɑrk] v 吠える [hoeru]

barley [bɑrli] n 大麦 [oumugi]

barn [bɑrn] n 納屋 [naya]

barrel [bærəl] n 樽 [taru]

barrier [bæriər] n 柵 [saku]; **ticket barrier** n 改札口 [kaisatsuguchi]

bartender [bɑrtɛndər] n バーテンダー [baatendaa]

base [beɪs] n 土台 [dodai]

baseball [beɪsbɔl] n 野球 [yakyuu]; **baseball cap** n 野球帽 [yakyuubou]

baseboard [beɪsbɔrd] n 幅木 [habaki]

based [beɪst] adj ···に基づく [... ni motozuku]

basement [beɪsmənt] n 地階 [chikai]

bash [bæʃ] n 強打 [kyouda] ▷ v 強打する [kyouda suru]

basic [beɪsɪk] adj 基本的な [kihonteki na]

basically [beɪsɪkli] adv 基本的に [kihonteki ni]

basics [beɪsɪks] npl 基本 [kihon]

basil [beɪzəl] n バジル [bajiru]

basin [beɪsən] n 洗面器 [senmenki]

basis [beɪsɪs] n 基礎 [kiso]

basket [bæskɪt, bæs-] n かご [kago]; **wastepaper basket** n くずかご [kuzukago]

basketball [bæskɪtbɔl, bæs-] n バスケットボール [basukettobooru]

Basque [bæsk] adj バスク地方の [Basuku chihou no] ▷ n (language) バスク語 [basuku go], (person) バスク人 [basukujin]

bass [beɪs] *n* バス [basu] *(声楽)*; **bass drum** *n* バスドラム [basudoramu]; **double bass** *n* コントラバス [kontorabasu]

bassoon [bəsuːn] *n* ファゴット [fagotto]

bat [bæt] *n (mammal)* コウモリ [koumori] *(動物)*, *(with ball)* バット [batto]

bath [bæθ] *n* **bubble bath** *n* 泡風呂 [awaburo]

bathe [beɪð] *v* **bathing suit** *n* 水着 [mizugi]

bathrobe [bæθroʊb] *n* ドレッシングガウン [doresshingugaun], バスローブ [basuroobu]

bathroom [bæθrum] *n* トイレ [toire], バスルーム [basuruumu]: **Are there support railings in the bathroom?** バスルームに介助の手すりはありますか? [basu-ruumu ni kaijo no tesuri wa arimasu ka?]; **Does the room have a private bathroom?** その部屋に専用のバスルームはありますか? [sono heya ni senyou no basu-ruumu wa arimasu ka?]; **The bathroom is flooded** バスルームが水浸しになっています [basu-ruumu ga mizu-bitashi ni natte imasu]

bathtub [bæθtʌb] *n* 浴槽 [yokusou]

batter [bætər] *n* (料理用の)ころも [(ryouriyou no) koromo]

battery [bætəri] *n* バッテリー [batterii], 電池 [denchi]: **Do you have any batteries?** バッテリーはありますか? [batterii wa arimasu ka?]; **Do you have batteries for this camera?** このカメラ用のバッテリーはありますか? [kono kamera-you no batterii wa arimasu ka?]; **I need a new battery** 私は新しいバッテリーが必要です [watashi wa atarashii batterii ga hitsuyou desu]; **The battery is dead** バッテリーが上がってしまいました [batterii ga agatte shimaimashita]

battle [bætᵊl] *n* 戦闘 [sentou]

battleship [bætᵊlʃɪp] *n* 戦艦 [senkan]

bay [beɪ] *n* 湾 [wan]; **bay leaf** *n* ローリエ [roorie]

BC [bi si] *abbr* 紀元前 [kigenzen]

be [bi, STRONG bi] *v* いる [iru]

beach [biːtʃ] *n* ビーチ [biichi], 浜辺 [hamabe];

Are there any good beaches near here? この近くにいいビーチはありますか? [kono chikaku ni ii biichi wa arimasu ka?]; **How far away is the beach?** ビーチまでどのくらいの距離ですか? [biichi made dono kurai no kyori desu ka?]; **I'm going to the beach** 私はビーチに行きます [watashi wa biichi ni ikimasu]; **Is there a bus to the beach?** ビーチへ行くバスはありますか? [biichi e iku basu wa arimasu ka?]

bead [bid] *n* ビーズ [biizu]

beak [bik] *n* くちばし [kuchibashi]

beam [bim] *n* 笑顔 [egao]

bean [bin] *n* 豆 [mame]; **bean sprouts** *npl* 豆もやし [mame moyashi]; **coffee bean** *n* コーヒー豆 [koohiimame]; **fava bean** *n* ソラマメ [soramame]; **green beans** *npl* サヤインゲン [saya ingen]; **scarlet runner bean** *n* ベニバナインゲン [benibanaingen]

bear [bɛər] *n* クマ [kuma] *(動物)* ▷ *v* 支える [sasaeru] *(支持)*; **polar bear** *n* 北極グマ [hokkyokuguma]; **teddy bear** *n* テディーベア [tedeiibea]

beard [bɪərd] *n* あごひげ [agohige]

bearded [bɪərdɪd] *adj* あごひげを生やした [agohige-o hayashita]

bear up *v* がんばる [ganbaru]

beat [bit] *n* 打つこと [utsu koto] ▷ *v (outdo)* ···に勝つ [... ni katsu], *(strike)* 続けざまに打つ [tsuzukezama ni utsu]

beautiful [byutɪfəl] *adj* 美しい [utsukushii]

beautifully [byutɪfli] *adv* 美しく [utsukushiku]

beauty [byuti] *n* 美しさ [utsukushisa]; **beauty parlor** *n* 美容院 [biyouin]

beaver [bivər] *n* ビーバー [biibaa]

be careful *v* 気をつける [ki wo tsukeru]

because [bɪkɔz, bɪkʌz] *conj* ···だから [... dakara]

become [bɪkʌm] *v* ···になる [... ni naru]

bed [bɛd] *n* ベッド [beddo]; **bed and breakfast** *n* ベッド＆ブレックファースト [beddo burekkufaasuto]; **bunk beds** *npl* 二段ベッド [nidanbeddo]; **double bed** *n* ダブル

ベッド [daburubeddo]; **king-size bed** n キングサイズのベッド [kingu saizu no beddo]; **single bed** n シングルベッド [shingurubeddo]; **sofa bed** n ソファーベッド [sofaabeddo]; **twin beds** npl ツインベッド [tsuinbeddo]; **The bed is uncomfortable** ベッドの寝心地がよくありません [beddo no ne-gokochi ga yoku arimasen]

bedding [bɛdɪŋ] n 寝具 [shingu]; **Is there any spare bedding?** 予備の寝具はありますか? [yobi no shingu wa arimasu ka?]

bedroom [bɛdrum] n 寝室 [shinshitsu]

bedside [bɛdsaɪd] n ベッドサイド [beddosaido]

bedspread [bɛdsprɛd] n ベッドカバー [beddokabaa]

bedtime [bɛdtaɪm] n 就寝時刻 [shuushin jikoku]

bee [bi] n ハチ [hachi] (昆虫)

beech [bitʃ] n **beech (tree)** n ブナ [buna]

beef [bif] n ビーフ [biifu], 牛肉 [gyuuniku]

beefburger [bifbɜrgər] n ビーフバーガー [biifu baagaa]

beeper [bipər] n ポケットベル [poketto beru]

beer [bɪər] n ビール [biiru]; **another beer** ビールをもう一杯 [biiru o mou ippai]; **A draft beer, please** 生ビールをください [nama-biiru o kudasai]

beet [bit] n ビートルート [biitoruuto]

beetle [bitᵊl] n カブトムシ [kabutomushi]

before [bɪfɔr] adv 以前に [izen ni] ▷conj ・・・する前に [... suru mae ni] ▷prep ・・・の前に [... no mae ni]

beforehand [bɪfɔrhænd] adv あらかじめ [arakajime], 慈善 [jizen]

beg [bɛg] v 物乞いをする [monogoi-o suru]

beggar [bɛgər] n 乞食 [kojiki]

begin [bɪgɪn] v 始める [hajimeru]

beginner [bɪgɪnər] n 初心者 [shoshinsha]

beginning [bɪgɪnɪŋ] n 始め [hajime]

behave [bɪheɪv] v 振舞う [furumau]

behavior [bɪheɪvyər] n 態度 [taido]

behind [bɪhaɪnd] adv 後ろに [ushiro ni] ▷n 臀部 [denbu] ▷prep ・・・の後ろに [... no ushiro ni]; **lag behind** v 遅れる [okureru]

beige [beɪʒ] adj ベージュ [beeju], ベージュの [beeju no]

Beijing [beɪdʒɪŋ] n 北京 [pekin]

Belarus [bɛlərʊs] n ベラルーシ [beraruushi]

Belarussian [bɛlarʃən] adj ベラルーシの [Beraruushi no] ▷n (language) ベラルーシ語 [beraruushi go], (person) ベラルーシ人 [beraruushijin]

Belgian [bɛldʒən] adj ベルギーの [berugii no] ▷n ベルギー人 [berugiijin]

Belgium [bɛldʒəm] n ベルギー [berugii]

belief [bɪlif] n 信頼 [shinrai]

believe [bɪliv] v 判断する [handan suru] ▷vi 信仰する [shinkou suru] ▷vt 信じる [shinjiru]

bell [bɛl] n 鐘 [kane]

belly [bɛli] n 腹部 [fukubu]; **belly button** n おへそ [oheso]

belong [bɪlɔŋ] v 所属する [shozoku suru]; **belong to** v ・・・のものである [... no mono de aru]

belongings [bɪlɔŋɪŋz] npl 所持品 [shojihin]

beloved [bɪlʌvɪd] n いとしい人 [itoshii hito]

below [bɪloʊ] adv 下に [shita ni] ▷prep ・・・より下に [... yori shitani]

belt [bɛlt] n ベルト [beruto]; **conveyor belt** n コンベヤベルト [konbeyaberuto]; **money belt** n マネーベルト [maneeberuto]; **safety belt** n 安全ベルト [anzenberuto]

bench [bɛntʃ] n ベンチ [benchi]

bend [bɛnd] n 曲がり [magari] ▷v 曲げる [mageru]; **bend down** v かがむ [kagamu]; **bend over** v かがむ [kagamu]

beneath [bɪniθ] prep ・・・の下に [...no shita ni]

benefit [bɛnɪfɪt] n 利益 [rieki] (もうけ) ▷v 利益を得る [rieki wo eru]

bent [bɛnt] adj (not straight) 曲がった [magatta]

beret [bəreɪ] n ベレー帽 [bereebou]

berry [bɛri] n ベリー [berii]

berth [bɜrθ] n 寝台 [shindai]; **sleeping berth**

n 寝台車コンパートメントの寝台 [shindaisha konpaatomento no shindai]

beside [bɪsaɪd] *prep* ···のそばに [... no soba ni]

besides [bɪsaɪdz] *adv* その上 [sono ue]

best [bɛst] *adj* 最もよい [mottomo yoi] ▷ *adv* 最もよく [mottomo yoku]; **best man** *n* 新郎の付添い役 [shinrou no tsukisoiyaku]; **best-if-used-by date** *n* 賞味期限 [shoumikigen]

bestseller [bɛstsɛlər] *n* ベストセラー [besutoseraa]

bet [bɛt] *n* 賭け [kake] ▷ *v* 賭ける [kakeru]

betray [bɪtreɪ] *v* 裏切る [uragiru]

better [bɛtər] *adj* よりよい [yoriyoi] ▷ *adv* よりよく [yoriyoku]

betting [bɛtɪŋ] *n* 賭け事 [kakegoto]; **betting shop** *n* 賭け屋 [kakeya]

between [bɪtwiːn] *prep* ···の間に [... no aida ni]

bewildered [bɪwɪldərd] *adj* 困惑した [konwaku shita]

beyond [bɪyɒnd] *prep* ···の向こうに [... no mukou ni]

biased [baɪəst] *adj* 偏った [katayotta]

bib [bɪb] *n* よだれ掛け [yodarekake]

Bible [baɪbəl] *n* 聖書 [seisho]

bicarbonate [baɪkɑrbəneɪt] *n* **bicarbonate of soda** *n* 重炭酸ソーダ [juutansansooda]

bicycle [baɪsɪkəl] *n* 自転車 [jitensha], *(bike)* 自転車 [jitensha]; **bicycle lane** *n* サイクルレーン [saikurureen]; **bicycle path** *n* サイクルパス [saikuru pasu]; **bicycle pump** *n* 自転車ポンプ [jitensha ponpu]; **tandem bicycle** *n* タンデム自転車 [tandemu jitensha]; **the bicycle path to...?** ···へ行く自転車道はどこですか? [... e iku jitensha-dou wa doko desu ka?]

bid [bɪd] *n* 入札 [nyuusatsu] ▷ *v (at auction)* 入札する [nyuusatsu suru]

bifocals [baɪfoukəlz] *npl* 遠近両用メガネ [enkin ryouyou megane]

big [bɪg] *adj* 大きい [ookii]; **The house is** quite big 家はかなり大きいです [ie wa kanari ookii desu]

bigger [bɪgər] *adj* より大きい [yori ookii]

bike [baɪk] *n* 自転車 [jitensha]; **mountain bike** *n* マウンテンバイク [mauntenbaiku]; **Can I keep my bike here?** ここに自転車を置いておけますか? [koko ni jitensha o oite okemasu ka?]; **Does the bike have brakes?** 自転車はブレーキ付きですか? [jitensha wa bureeki tsuki desu ka?]; **Does the bike have gears?** 自転車はギア付きですか? [jitensha wa gia tsuki desu ka?]; **Where can I rent a bike?** どこで自転車をレンタルできますか? [doko de jitensha o rentaru dekimasu ka?]; **Where is the nearest bike repair shop?** 一番近い自転車修理店はどこですか? [ichiban chikai jitensha shuuri-ten wa doko desu ka?]

bikini [bɪkini] *n* ビキニ [bikini]

bilingual [baɪlɪŋgwəl] *adj* バイリンガルの [bairingaru no]

bill [bɪl] *n* 紙幣 [shihei], 勘定 [kanjou], *(account)* 請求書 [seikyuusho], *(banknote)* 紙幣 [shihei], *(legislation)* 法案 [houan]; **phone bill** *n* 電話の請求書 [denwa no seikyuusho]; **Do you have change for this bill?** この紙幣でお釣りがありますか? [kono shihei de o-tsuri ga arimasu ka?]; **May I have an itemized bill?** 請求書の明細をもらえますか? [seikyuusho no meisai o moraemasu ka?]; **Please prepare the bill** 請求書を用意してください [seikyuusho o youi shite kudasai]; **Put it on my bill** それを私の勘定につけておいてください [sore o watashi no kanjou ni tsukete oite kudasai]; **The bill is wrong** 請求書が間違っています [seikyuusho ga machigatte imasu]

billiards [bɪliərdz] *npl* ビリヤード [biriyaado]

billion [bɪlyən] *n* 10億 [juuoku]

binding [baɪndɪŋ] *n* **Could you adjust my bindings, please?** ビンディングを調節していただけますか? [bindingu o chousetsu shite itadakemasu ka?]; **Could you tighten my**

bindings, please? ビンディングを締めていた
だけますか? [bindingu o shimete
itadakemasu ka?]

bindings npl ビンディング [bindeingu]

bingo [bɪŋgou] n ビンゴ [bingo]

binoculars [bɪnɒkyələrz] npl 双眼鏡
[sougankyou]

biochemistry [baɪoukɛmɪstri] n 生化学
[seikagaku]

biodegradable [baɪoudɪgreɪdəbəl] adj 生物
分解性の [seibutsu bunkaisei no]

biography [baɪɒgrəfi] n 伝記 [denki]

biological [baɪəlɒdʒɪkəl] adj 生物学の
[seibutsugaku no]

biology [baɪɒlədʒi] n 生物学 [seibutsugaku]

biometric [baɪoumɛtrɪk] adj 生物測定の
[seibutsu sokutei no]

birch [bɜrtʃ] n 樺 [kaba]

bird [bɜrd] n 鳥 [tori]; **bird flu** n 鳥インフルエ
ンザ [tori infuruenza]; **bird of prey** n 猛禽
[moukin]

birdie [bɜrdi] n バドミントンのシャトル
[badominton no shatoru]

birdwatching [bɜrdwɒtʃɪŋ] n バードウォッチ
ング [baadowotchingu]

birth [bɜrθ] n 誕生 [tanjou]; **birth certificate**
n 出生証明書 [shusshou (shussei)
shoumeisho]; **birth control** n 避妊 [hinin];
place of birth n 出生地 [shusseichi]

birthday [bɜrθdeɪ, -dɪ] n 誕生日 [tanjoubi];
Happy birthday! お誕生日おめでとう!
[o-tanjoubi omedetou!]

birthplace [bɜrθpleɪs] n 出身 [shusshin], 出
生地 [shusseichi]

bishop [bɪʃəp] n 主教 [shukyou]

bit [bɪt] n 小片 [shouhen]

bitch [bɪtʃ] n (female dog) 雌犬 [mesuinu]

bite [baɪt] n かむこと [kamu koto] (歯) ▷ v か
む [kamu] (歯)

bitter [bɪtər] adj にがい [nigai]

black [blæk] adj 黒い [kuroi]; **black ice** n 路
面の薄い透明な氷 [romen no usui toumei na
kouri]

blackberry [blækbɛri] n ブラックベリー
[burakkuberii]

BlackBerry® [blækbɛri] n ブラックベリー®
[burakkuberii]

blackbird [blækbɜrd] n クロウタドリ
[kuroutadori]

blackboard [blækbɔrd] n 黒板 [kokuban]

blackmail [blækmeɪl] n 恐喝 [kyoukatsu] ▷ v
恐喝する [kyoukatsu suru]

blackout [blækaut] n 灯火管制 [toukakansei]

blacktop [blæktɒp] n タールマカダム
[taarumakadamu]

bladder [blædər] n 膀胱 [boukou]; **gall
bladder** n 胆嚢 [tannou]

blade [bleɪd] n 刃 [ha]; **razor blade** n 安全か
みそりの刃 [anzen kamisori no ha];
shoulder blade n 肩甲骨 [kenkoukotsu]

blame [bleɪm] n 非難 [hinan] ▷ v 責める
[semeru]

blank [blæŋk] adj 白紙の [hakushi no] ▷ n 空
欄 [kuuran]; **blank check** n 白地小切手
[shiraji kogitte]

blanket [blæŋkɪt] n 毛布 [moufu]; **electric
blanket** n 電気毛布 [denkimoufu]; **Please
bring me an extra blanket** 追加の毛布を持
ってきてください [tsuika no moufu o motte
kite kudasai]; **We need more blankets** 毛布
がもっと必要です [moufu ga motto hitsuyou
desu]

blast [blæst] n 爆発 [bakuhatsu]

blatant [bleɪtənt] adj 露骨な [rokotsu na]

blaze [bleɪz] n 火炎 [kaen]

blazer [bleɪzər] n ブレザー [burezaa]

bleach [blitʃ] n 漂白剤 [hyouhakuzai]

bleached [bli:tʃt] adj 漂白した [hyouhaku
shita]

bleak [blik] adj 荒涼とした [kouryou to shita]

bleed [blid] v 出血する [shukketsu suru]

blender [blɛndər] n ブレンダー [burendaa], ミ
キサー [mikisaa]

bless [blɛs] v 祝福する [shukufuku suru]

blind [blaɪnd] adj 目の見えない [me no
mienai] ▷ n ブラインド [buraindo]; **Venetian**

blind n ベネチアンブラインド [benechian-buraindo]

blindfold [bl**aɪ**ndfould] n 目隠し布 [mekakushi nuno] ▷ v 目隠しする [mekakushi suru]

blink [bl**ɪ**ŋk] v まばたきする [mabataki suru]

bliss [bl**ɪ**s] n 至福 [shifuku]

blister [bl**ɪ**stər] n 水ぶくれ [mizubukure]

blizzard [bl**ɪ**zərd] n ブリザード [burizaado]

block [bl**ɒ**k] n (buildings) ブロック [burokku], (obstruction) 閉塞物 [heisokubutsu], (solid piece) 塊 [katamari] ▷ v ふさぐ [fusagu]

blockage [bl**ɒ**kɪdʒ] n 封鎖 [fuusa]

blocked [bl**ɒ**kt] adj 封鎖された [fuusa sareta]

blog [bl**ɒ**g] n ブログ [burogu] ▷ v ブログを書く [burogu-o kaku]

blonde [bl**ɒ**nd] adj ブロンドの [burondo no]

blood [bl**ʌ**d] n 血 [chi], 血液 [ketsueki]; **blood type** n 血液型 [ketsuekigata]; **blood poisoning** n 敗血症 [haiketsushou]; **blood pressure** n 血圧 [ketsuatsu]; **blood sports** n 血を見るスポーツ [chi-o miru supootsu]; **blood test** n 血液検査 [ketsuekikensa]; **blood transfusion** n 輸血 [yuketsu]; **My blood type is O positive** 私の血液型はO型Rhプラスです [watashi no ketsueki-gata wa oo-gata aaru-eichi-purasu desu]; **This stain is blood** このしみは血です [kono shimi wa chi desu]

bloody [bl**ʌ**di] adj 血まみれの [chi mamire no]

blossom [bl**ɒ**səm] n 花 [hana] ▷ v 花が咲く [hana ga saku]

blouse [bl**aʊ**s] n ブラウス [burausu]

blow [bl**oʊ**] n 強打 [kyouda] ▷ v 吹く [fuku]

blow-dry n ブロードライ [buroodorai]

blow up v 爆破する [bakuha suru]

blue [bl**u**] adj 青い [aoi]

blueberry [bl**u**bɛri] n ブルーベリー [buruuberii]

blues [bl**u**z] npl ブルース [buruusu]

bluff [bl**ʌ**f] n 虚勢 [kyosei] ▷ v 虚勢を張る [kyosei-o haru]

blunder [bl**ʌ**ndər] n 大失敗 [daishippai]

blunt [bl**ʌ**nt] adj 鈍い [nibui]

blush [bl**ʌ**ʃ] v 赤面する [sekimen suru]

board [b**ɔ**rd] n (meeting) 役員会 [yakuinkai], (wood) 板 [ita]; **board game** n ボードゲーム [boodo geemu]; **boarding pass** n 搭乗券 [toujouken]; **boarding school** n 寄宿学校 [kishuku gakkou]; **bulletin board** n 掲示板 [keijiban]; **diving board** n 飛込台 [tobikomidai]; **ironing board** n アイロン台 [airondai]

boarder [b**ɔ**rdər] n 寄宿生 [kishukusei]

boarding [b**ɔ**rdɪn] n 乗車 [jousha]

boast [b**oʊ**st] v 自慢する [jiman suru]

boat [b**oʊ**t] n ボート [booto], 舟 [fune]; **fishing boat** n 漁船 [gyosen]

body [b**ɒ**di] n 体 [karada]

bodybuilding [b**ɒ**dibɪldɪn] n ボディービル [bodiibiru]

bodyguard [b**ɒ**digɑrd] n ボディーガード [bodiigaado]

bog [b**ɒ**g] n 沼 [numa]

boil [b**ɔ**ɪl] vi 沸騰する [futtou suru] ▷ vt 沸かす [wakasu]

boiled [b**ɔ**ɪl] adj 沸騰した [futtou shita]; **hard-boiled egg** n ゆで卵 [yudetamago]

boiler [b**ɔ**ɪlər] n ボイラー [boiraa]

boiling [b**ɔ**ɪlɪn] adj 沸き立つ [wakitatsu]

boil over v 噴きこぼれる [fukikoboreru]

Bolivia [bəl**ɪ**viə] n ボリビア [boribia]

Bolivian [bəl**ɪ**viən] adj ボリビアの [Boribia no] ▷ n ボリビア人 [boribiajin]

bolt [b**oʊ**lt] n かんぬき [kannuki]

bomb [b**ɒ**m] n 爆弾 [bakudan] ▷ v 爆撃する [bakugeki suru]; **atom bomb** n 原子爆弾 [genshibakudan]

bombing [b**ɒ**mɪn] n 爆撃 [bakugeki]

bond [b**ɒ**nd] n 縛るもの [shibaru mono]

bone [b**oʊ**n] n 骨 [hone]; **bone dry** adj ひからびた [hikarabita]

bonfire [b**ɒ**nfaɪər] n 大かがり火 [oukagaribi]

bonus [b**oʊ**nəs] n ボーナス [boonasu]

book [b**ʊ**k] n チョウ [chou], 本 [hon] (書物);

address book n 住所録 [juushoroku]

bookcase [bʊkkeɪs] n 本箱 [honbako]

booklet [bʊklɪt] n 小冊子 [shousasshi]

bookmark [bʊkmɑrk] n しおり [shiori]

bookshelf [bʊkʃɛlf] n 本棚 [hondana]

bookstore [bʊkstɔr] n 書店 [shoten]

boost [bust] v 高める [takameru]

boot [but] n ブーツ [buutsu]; **rubber boots** npl ウェリントンブーツ [uerintonbuutsu]

booth [buθ] n **phone booth** n 電話ボックス [denwa bokkusu], 公衆電話ボックス [koushuu denwa bokkusu]

border [bɔrdər] n 境界 [kyoukai]

bore [bɔr] v 穴をあける [ana-o akeru]

bored [bɔrd] adj 退屈した [taikutsu shita]

boredom [bɔrdəm] n 退屈 [taikutsu]

boring [bɔrɪŋ] adj 退屈な [taikutsu na], 面白くない [omoshirokunai]; **boring task** n つまらない仕事 [tsumaranai shigoto]

born [bɔrn] adj 生まれながらの [umare nagara no]

borrow [bɒroʊ] v 借りる [kariru]

Bosnia [bæzniə] n ボスニア [bosunia]; **Bosnia and Herzegovina** n ボスニア・ヘルツェゴビナ [bosunia herutsuegobina]

Bosnian [bæzniən] adj ボスニアの [Bosunia no] ▷ n (person) ボスニア人 [bosuniajin]

boss [bɔs] n ボス [bosu]

boss around v こき使う [kokitsukau]

bossy [bɔsi] adj 威張った [ibatta]

both [boʊθ] adj 両方の [ryouhou no] ▷ pron 両方 [ryouhou]

bother [bɒðər] v 悩ます [nayamasu]

Botswana [botswɒnə] n ボツワナ [botsuwana]

bottle [bɒtl] n ボトル [botoru]; **baby bottle** n 哺乳瓶 [honyuubin]; **hot-water bottle** n 湯たんぽ [yutanpo]; **a bottle of mineral water** ミネラルウォーターのボトル1本 [mineraru-uootaa no botoru 1 hon]; **a bottle of red wine** 赤ワインのボトルを1本 [aka-wain no botoru o ippon]; **Please bring another bottle** ボトルをもう1本持ってきてください [botoru o mou ippon motte kite kudasai]

bottle-opener [bɒtl oʊpənər] n 栓抜き [sennuki]

bottom [bɒtəm] adj 底の [soko no] ▷ n 底 [soko]

bought [bɔt] adj 既製の [kisei no]

bouillon [bulyɒn] n **bouillon cube** n 固形スープの素 [kokei suupu no moto]

bounce [baʊns] v 弾む [hazumu]

bouncer [baʊnsər] n 用心棒 [youjinbou] (バーなどの)

boundary [baʊndəri] n 境界 [kyoukai]

bouquet [boʊkeɪ, bu-] n ブーケ [buuke]

bow [baʊ] n (weapon) 弓 [yumi] ▷ v お辞儀をする [ojigi-o suru]

bowels [baʊəlz] npl 腸 [chou]

bowl [boʊl] n ボウル [bouru]

bowling [boʊlɪŋ] n テンピンボウリング [tenpinbouringu], ボウリング [bouringu]; **bowling alley** n ボウリング場 [bouringu jou]

bow tie [boʊ taɪ] n **bow tie** n 蝶ネクタイ [chounekutai]

box [bɒks] n ボックス [bokkusu], 箱 [hako]; **box lunch** n 弁当 [bentou]; **box office** n 切符売場 [kippu uriba]; **fuse box** n ヒューズボックス [hyuuzobokkusu]

boxer [bɒksər] n ボクサー [bokusaa]; **boxer shorts** npl ボクサーショーツ [bokusaa shootsu]

boxing [bɒksɪŋ] n ボクシング [bokushingu]

boy [bɔɪ] n 少年 [shounen]

boyfriend [bɔɪfrɛnd] n ボーイフレンド [booifurendo]; **I have a boyfriend** 私にはボーイフレンドがいます [watashi ni wa booifurendo ga imasu]

bra [brɑ] n ブラジャー [burajaa]

brace [breɪs] n 突っ張り [tsuppari]

bracelet [breɪslɪt] n ブレスレット [buresuret-to]

braid [breɪd] n おさげ [osage]

brain [breɪn] n 脳 [nou]

brainy [breɪni] adj 頭のいい [atama no ii]

brake [breɪk] n ブレーキ [bureeki] ▷ v ブレー

キをかける [bureeki-o kakeru]; **brake light** *n* ブレーキランプ [bureeki ranpu]; **emergency brake** *n* ハンドブレーキ [handobureeki]; **Does the bike have coaster brakes?** 自転車はコースターブレーキ付きですか? [jitensha wa koosutaa-bureeki tsuki desu ka?]; **The brakes don't work** ブレーキがききません [bureeki ga kikimasen]

bran [bræn] *n* ふすま [fusuma] (小麦外皮)

branch [bræntʃ] *n* 枝 [eda]

brand [brænd] *n* ブランド [burando], ⋯製 […sei]; **brand name** *n* ブランド名 [burando mei]

brand-new *adj* 新品の [shinpin no]

brandy [brændi] *n* ブランデー [burandee]; **I'll have a brandy** ブランデーをください [burandee o kudasai]

brass [bræs] *n* ブラス [burasu], 真鍮 [shinchuu]; **brass band** *n* ブラスバンド [burasubando]

brat [bræt] *n* 悪がき [warugaki]

brave [breɪv] *adj* 勇敢な [yuukan na]

bravery [breɪvəri] *n* 勇敢 [yuukan]

Brazil [brəzɪl] *n* ブラジル [burajiru]

Brazilian [brəzɪliən] *adj* ブラジルの [burajiru no] ▷ *n* ブラジル人 [burajirujin]

bread [brɛd] *n* パン [pan]; **brown bread** *n* 黒パン [kuropan]; **Please bring more bread** パンをもっと持ってきてください [pan o motto motte kite kudasai]; **Would you like some bread?** パンはいかがですか? [pan wa ikaga desu ka?]

breadbox [brɛdbɒks] *n* パンケース [pan keesu]

breadcrumbs [brɛdcrʌmz] *npl* パン粉 [panko]

break [breɪk] *n* 破壊 [hakai] ▷ *v* 割る [waru]

break down *v* 故障する [koshou suru]

breakdown [breɪkdaʊn] *n* 故障 [koshou]; **nervous breakdown** *n* 神経衰弱 [shinkeisuijaku]; **Call the breakdown service, please** 故障時緊急修理サービスを呼んでください [koshou-ji kinkyuu-shuuri-saabisu o yonde kudasai]

breakfast [brɛkfəst] *n* 朝食 [choushoku]; **bed and breakfast** *n* ベッド＆ブレックファースト [beddo burekkufaasuto]; **continental breakfast** *n* ヨーロッパ大陸式の簡単な朝食 [Yorooppa tairikushiki no kantan na choushoku]; **Can I have breakfast in my room?** 自分の部屋で朝食を取ることができますか? [jibun no heya de choushoku o toru koto ga dekimasu ka?]; **Is breakfast included?** 朝食は含まれていますか? [choushoku wa fukumarete imasu ka?]; **with breakfast** 朝食付きで [choushoku-tsuki de]; **without breakfast** 朝食なしで [choushoku nashi de]; **What time is breakfast?** 朝食は何時ですか? [choushoku wa nan-ji desu ka?]; **What would you like for breakfast?** 朝食には何を召し上がりますか? [choushoku ni wa nani o meshiagarimasu ka?]

break in *v* 押し入る [oshiiru]

break-in *n* 押し入ること [oshiiru koto]

break up *v* ばらばらにする [barabara ni suru]

breast [brɛst] *n* 乳房 [chibusa]

breast-feed *v* 授乳する [junyuu suru]

breaststroke [brɛststroʊk, brɛsstroʊk] *n* 平泳ぎ [hiraoyogi]

breath [brɛθ] *n* 息 [iki]

Breathalyzer® [brɛθəlaɪzər] *n* ブレサライザー® [buresaraizaa]

breathe [briːð] *v* 息をする [iki-o suru]

breathe in *v* 息を吸い込む [iki-o suikomu]

breathe out *v* 息を吐き出す [iki-o hakidasu]

breathing [briːðɪŋ] *n* 呼吸 [kokyuu]

breed [briːd] *n* 品種 [hinshu] ▷ *v* 品種改良する [hinshu kairyou suru]

breeze [briːz] *n* そよ風 [soyokaze]

brewery [bruːəri] *n* 醸造所 [jouzoujo]

bribe [braɪb] *v* 賄賂を使う [wairo-o tsukau]

bribery [braɪbəri] *n* 贈収賄 [zoushuuwai]

brick [brɪk] *n* 煉瓦 [renga]

bricklayer [brɪkleɪər] *n* 煉瓦職人 [renga shokunin]

bride [braɪd] *n* 花嫁 [hanayome]

bridegroom [braɪdgrum] n 花婿 [hanamuko]

bridesmaid [braɪdzmeɪd] n 新婦の付添い役 [shinpu no tsukisoiyaku]

bridge [brɪdʒ] n 橋 [hashi]; **suspension bridge** n 吊橋 [tsuribashi]

brief [brif] adj 短い [mijikai]

briefcase [brifkeɪs] n かばん [kaban], ブリーフケース [buriifukeesu]; **Could you watch my briefcase for a minute, please?** ちょっと私のかばんを見張っていただけますか? [chotto watashi no kaban o mihatte itadakemasu ka?]; **Someone's stolen my briefcase** 誰かが私のかばんを盗みました [dare ka ga watashi no kaban o nusumimashita]

briefing [brifɪŋ] n ブリーフィング [buriifingu]

briefly [brifli] adv 簡単に [kantan ni]

briefs [bri:fs] npl ブリーフ [buriifu]

bright [braɪt] adj 明るい [akarui]

brilliant [brɪliənt] adj 光り輝く [hikari kagayaku]

bring [brɪŋ] v 持ってくる [motte kuru]

bring back v 戻す [modosu]

bring forward v 繰り上げる [kuriageru]

bring up v 育てる [sodateru]

Britain [brɪtᵊn] n 英国 [eikoku]

British [brɪtɪʃ] adj 英国の [eikoku no] ▷ n 英国人 [eikokujin]

broad [brɔd] adj 広い [hiroi]

broadband [brɔdbænd] n ブロードバンド [buroodobando]

broadcast [brɔdkæst] n 放送 [housou] ▷ v 放送する [housou suru]

broad-minded [brɔdmaɪndɪd] adj 心の広い [kokoro no hiroi]

broccoli [brɒkəli] n ブロッコリー [burokkorii]

brochure [broʊʃʊr] n ちらし [chirashi] (印刷物), パンフレット [panfuretto]

broiled [brɔɪld] adj 網焼きにする [amiyaki ni suru]

broiler [brɔɪlər] v グリルで焼く [guriru de yaku]

broke [broʊk] adj 破産した [hasan shita]

broken [broʊkən] adj 壊れた [kowareta]; **broken down** adj 故障した [koshou shita]

broker [broʊkər] n ブローカー [burookaa]

bronchitis [brɒŋkaɪtɪs] n 気管支炎 [kikanshien]

bronze [brɒnz] n ブロンズ [buronzu]

brooch [broʊtʃ] n ブローチ [buroochi]

broom [brum] n ほうき [houki]

broth [brɔθ] n 煮出し汁 [nidashijiru]

brother [brʌðər] n 兄弟 [kyoudai]

brother-in-law [brʌðərɪnlɔ] n 義兄弟 [gikyoudai]

brown [braʊn] adj 茶色 [chairo], 茶色の [chairo no]; **brown bread** n 黒パン [kuropan]; **brown rice** n 玄米 [genmai]

browse [braʊz] v 拾い読みする [hiroiyomi suru]

browser [braʊzər] n ブラウザ [burauza]

bruise [bruz] n 打撲傷 [dabokushou]

brush [brʌʃ] n ブラシ [burashi] ▷ v ブラシをかける [burashi wo kakeru]

brutal [brutᵊl] adj 残忍な [zannin na]

bubble [bʌbᵊl] n 泡 [awa]; **bubble bath** n 泡風呂 [awaburo]; **bubble gum** n 風船ガム [fuusengamu]

bucket [bʌkɪt] n バケツ [baketsu]

buckle [bʌkᵊl] n バックル [bakkuru]

Buddha [budə, budə] n 仏陀 [budda]

Buddhism [budɪzəm, bud-] n 仏教 [bukkyou]

Buddhist [budɪst, bud-] adj 仏教の [Bukkyou no] ▷ n 仏教徒 [Bukkyouto]

buddy [bʌdi] n 仲間 [nakama]

budget [bʌdʒɪt] n 予算 [yosan]

buffalo [bʌfəloʊ] n 水牛 [suigyuu]

bug [bʌg] n 虫 [mushi]; **There are bugs in my room** 私の部屋に虫がいます [watashi no heya ni mushi ga imasu]

buggy [bʌgi] n 乳母車 [ubaguruma]

build [bɪld] v 建てる [tateru]

building [bɪldɪŋ] n 建物 [tatemono]; **building contractor** n 建築業者 [kenchikugyousha]

bulb [bʌlb] n (electricity) 電球 [denkyuu], (plant) 球根 [kyuukon]

Bulgaria [bʌlgɛ́əriə] *n* ブルガリア [burugaria]

Bulgarian [bʌlgɛ́əriən] *adj* ブルガリアの [burugaria no] ▷ *n (language)* ブルガリア語 [burugaria go], *(person)* ブルガリア人 [burugariajin]

bulimia [bulíːmiə, -lɪm-] *n* 過食症 [kashokushou]

bull [bʊl] *n* 雄牛 [oushi]

bulldozer [bʊldóʊzər] *n* ブルドーザー [burudoozaa]

bullet [bʊ́lɪt] *n* 弾丸 [dangan]

bulletin [bʊ́lɪtɪn] *n* **bulletin board** *n* 掲示板 [keijiban]

bully [bʊ́li] *n* 弱い者いじめをする者 [yowai mono ijime wo suru mono] ▷ *v* いじめる [ijimeru]

bumblebee [bʌ́mb·lbi] *n* マルハナバチ [maruhanabachi]

bump [bʌmp] *n* 衝突 [shoutotsu]; **bump into** *v* ばったり出会う [battari deau]

bumper [bʌ́mpər] *n* バンパー [banpaa]

bumpy [bʌ́mpi] *adj* でこぼこのある [dekoboko no aru]

bun [bʌn] *n* パン [ban] *(食べ物)*

bunch [bʌntʃ] *n* 束 [taba] *(ひとまとめ)*

bungalow [bʌ́ŋgəloʊ] *n* バンガロー [bangaroo]

bungee jumping [bʌ́ndʒi dʒʌ́mpɪŋ] *n* バンジージャンプ [banjiijanpu]; **Where can I go bungee jumping?** どこに行けばバンジージャンプができますか? [doko ni ikeba banjii-janpu ga dekimasu ka?]

bunion [bʌ́nyən] *n* バニオン [banion]

bunk [bʌŋk] *n* 作り付け寝台 [tsukuri zuke shindai]; **bunk beds** *npl* 二段ベッド [nidanbeddo]

buoy [bʊi] *n* ブイ [bui]

bureau [byʊ́əroʊ] *n* 整理だんす [seiridansu]

bureaucracy [byʊrɒ́krəsi] *n* 官僚主義 [kanryoushugi]

burger [bɜ́rgər] *n* バーガー [baagaa]

burglar [bɜ́rglər] *n* 不法侵入者 [fuhou shinnyuusha]; **burglar alarm** *n* 盗難警報機 [tounankeihouki]

burglary [bɜ́rgləri] *n* 住居侵入罪 [juukyoshin-nyuuzai]

burgle [bɜ́rg·l] *v* 泥棒に入る [dorobou ni hairu]

Burma [bɜ́rmə] *n* ビルマ [biruma]

Burmese [bɜrmíz] *adj* ビルマの [biruma no] ▷ *n (language)* ビルマ語 [biruma go], *(person)* ビルマ人 [birumajin]

burn [bɜrn] *n* 火傷 [yakedo] ▷ *v* 燃やす [moyasu]

burn down *v* 焼け落ちる [yakeochiru]

burp [bɜrp] *n* げっぷ [geppu] *(口)* ▷ *v* げっぷをする [geppu wo suru]

burst [bɜrst] *v* 破裂する [haretsu suru]

bury [bɛ́ri] *v* 埋葬する [maisou suru]

bus [bʌs] *n* バス [basu] *(乗り物)*, *(vehicle)* 長距離バス [choukyori basu]; **airport bus** *n* 空港バス [kuukou basu]; **bus station** *n* バスターミナル [basutaaminaru]; **bus stop** *n* バス停 [basutei]; **bus ticket** *n* バスの切符 [basu no kippu]; **Does this bus go to...?** このバスは・・・へ行きますか? [kono basu wa... e ikimasu ka?]; **Excuse me, which bus goes to...?** すみません、・・・へ行くバスはどれですか? [sumimasen,... e iku basu wa dore desu ka?]; **How often are the buses to...?** ・・・へ行くバスはどのくらい出ていますか? [... e iku basu wa dono kurai dete imasu ka?]; **Is there a bus to the airport?** 空港へ行くバスはありますか? [kuukou e iku basu wa arimasu ka?]; **The bus has left without me** 長距離バスが私を乗せずに出発してしまいました [choukyori-basu ga watashi o nosezu ni shuppatsu shite shimaimashita]; **What time does the bus leave?** バスは何時に出ますか? [basu wa nan-ji ni demasu ka?]; **What time is the last bus?** 最終のバスは何時ですか? [saishuu no basu wa nan-ji desu ka?]; **When does the bus leave in the morning?** 長距離バスは朝何時に出ますか? [choukyori-basu wa asa nan-ji ni demasu ka?]; **When is the next bus to...?** ・・・へ行く

次のバスは何時ですか? [... e iku tsugi no basu wa nan-ji desu ka?]; **Where can I buy a bus card?** バスのカードはどこで買えますか? [basu no kaado wa doko de kaemasu ka?]; **Where can I get a bus to...?** ···へ行くバスにはどこで乗れますか? [... e iku basu ni wa doko de noremasu ka?]; **Where is the bus station?** バスターミナルはどこですか? [basu-taaminaru wa doko desu ka?]

bush [bʊʃ] *n (shrub)* 低木 [teiboku], *(thicket)* 茂み [shigemi]

business [bɪznɪs] *n* ビジネス [bijinesu]; **business class** *n* ビジネスクラス [bijinesu kurasu]; **business trip** *n* 出張 [shutchou]; **show business** *n* ショービジネス [shoobijinesu]

businessman [bɪznɪsmæn] *n* ビジネスマン [bijinesuman]; **I'm a businessman** 私はビジネスマンです [watashi wa bijinesu-man desu]

businesswoman [bɪznɪswʊmən] *n* ビジネスウーマン [bijinesuuman]

bust [bʌst] *n* バスト [basuto]

busy [bɪzi] *adj* 忙しい [isogashii]; **busy signal** *n* 話し中の信号音 [hanashichuu no shingouon], 話し中を示す信号 [hanashichuu-o shimesu shingou]; **Sorry, I'm busy** ごめんなさい、忙しいのです [gomen nasai, isogashii no desu]

butcher [bʊtʃər] *n* 肉屋 [nikuya]; **butcher shop** *n* 肉屋 [nikuya]

butt [bʌt] *n* お尻 [oshiri]

butter [bʌtər] *n* バター [bataa]; **peanut butter** *n* ピーナッツバター [piinattsubataa]

buttercup [bʌtərkʌp] *n* キンポウゲ [kinpouge]

butterfly [bʌtərflaɪ] *n* チョウ [chou]

buttocks [bʌteks] *npl* 臀部 [denbu]

button [bʌtᵊn] *n* ボタン [botan] *(服)*, バッジ [bajji]; **belly button** *n* おへそ [oheso]; **Which button do I press?** どのボタンを押すのですか? [dono botan o osu no desu ka?]

buy [baɪ] *v* 買う [kau]; **Where do I buy a ticket?** 切符はどこで買うのですか? [kippu wa doko de kau no desu ka?]

buyer [baɪr] *n* 買い手 [kaite]

buyout [baɪaʊt] *n* 買収 [baishuu]

by [baɪ] **Can I pay by credit card?** クレジットカードで支払えますか? [kurejitto-kaado de shiharaemasu ka?]; **Can we park by our site?** 私たちのキャンプサイトのそばに駐車できますか? [watashi-tachi no kyanpu-saito no soba ni chuusha dekimasu ka?]; **Could you take me by car?** 私を車で連れて行ってもらえますか? [watashi o kuruma de tsurete itte moraemasu ka?]; **How long will it take by air?** 航空便でどのくらいの日数がかかりますか? [koukuu-bin de dono kurai no nissuu ga kakarimasu ka?]; **Please come home by eleven p.m.** 午後11時までに帰宅してください [gogo juuichi-ji made ni kitaku shite kudasai]

bye [baɪ] *excl* さよなら! [sayonara], ではまた! [deha mata]

bye-bye [baɪbaɪ] *excl* バイバイ! [baibai]

bypass [baɪpæs] *n* バイパス [baipasu]

bystander [baɪstændər] *n* 傍観者 [boukansha]

C

cab [kæb] n タクシー [takushii]

cabbage [kæbɪdʒ] n キャベツ [kyabetsu]

cabin [kæbɪn] n キャビン [kyabin]; cabin crew n 乗務員 [joumuin]; Where is cabin number five? 5番のキャビンはどこですか? [go-ban no kyabin wa doko desu ka?]

cabinet [kæbɪnɪt] n キャビネット [kyabinetto]

cable [keɪbᵊl] n ケーブル [keeburu]; cable car n ケーブルカー [keeburukaa]; cable television n ケーブルテレビ [keeburu terebi]; jumper cables npl ブースターコード [buusutaakoodo]; Do you have jumper cables? ブースターケーブルはありますか? [buusutaa-keeburu wa arimasu ka?]

cactus [kæktəs] n サボテン [saboten]

cadet [kədɛt] n 生徒 [seito]

café [kæfeɪ] n カフェ [kafe]; Internet café n インターネットカフェ [intaanetto kafe]; Are there any Internet cafés here? ここにインターネットカフェはありますか? [koko ni intaanetto-kafe wa arimasu ka?]

cafeteria [kæfɪtɪəriə] n カフェテリア [kafeteria]

caffeine [kæfin] n カフェイン [kafein]

cage [keɪdʒ] n かご [kago]

cake [keɪk] n ケーキ [keeki]; layer cake n 菓子 [kashi]; sponge cake n スポンジケーキ [suponji keeki] (cake)

calcium [kælsiəm] n カルシウム [karushiumu]

calculate [kælkyəleɪt] v 計算する [keisan suru]

calculation [kælkyəleɪʃᵊn] n 計算 [keisan]

calculator [kælkyəleɪtər] n 計算機 [keisanki]; pocket calculator n 電卓 [dentaku]

calendar [kælɪndər] n カレンダー [karendaa]

calf [kæf] (pl calves) n 子牛 [koushi]

call [kɔl] n 呼び声 [yobigoe] ▷ v 呼ぶ [yobu]; call back v 電話をかけなおす [denwa-o kakenaosu]; call center n コールセンター [kooru sentaa]; roll call n 点呼 [tenko]; wake-up call n モーニングコール [mooningukooru]

call back v 電話しなおす [denwa shinaosu]

call for v 要求する [youkyuu suru]

call off v 取りやめる [toriyameru]

calm [kɑm] adj 落ち着いた [ochitsuita]

calm down v 落ち着く [ochitsuku] (気分)

calorie [kæləri] n カロリー [karorii]

Cambodia [kæmboʊdiə] n カンボジア [kanbojia]

Cambodian [kæmboʊdiən] adj カンボジアの [kanbojia no] ▷ n (person) カンボジア人 [kanbojiajin]

camcorder [kæmkɔrdər] n カムコーダー [kamukoodaa]

camel [kæmᵊl] n ラクダ [rakuda]

camera [kæmrə] n カメラ [kamera]; camera phone n カメラ付き携帯電話 [kamera tsuki keitai denwa]; digital camera n デジタルカメラ [dejitaru kamera]; video camera n ビデオカメラ [bideokamera]

cameraman [kæmrəmæn] (pl cameramen) n カメラマン [kameraman]

Cameroon [kæmərun] n カメルーン [kameruun]

camp [kæmp] n キャンプ [kyanpu] ▷ v キャンプする [kyanpu suru]; Can we camp here overnight? ここで一晩キャンプできますか? [koko de hitoban kyanpu dekimasu ka?]

campaign [kæmpeɪn] n 運動 [undou] (行動)

camper [kæmpər] n キャンピングカー

[kyanpingukaa], キャンプする人 [kyanpu suru
nin]; **How much is it for a camper with
four people?** 4人用のキャンピングカーでいく
らですか? [yonin-you no kyanpingukaa de
ikura desu ka?]

camping [kæmpɪŋ] n キャンプ生活 [kyanpu
seikatsu]

campsite [kæmpsaɪt] n キャンプ場
[kyanpujou]; **Is there a campsite here?** ここ
にキャンプ場はありますか? [koko ni
kyanpu-jou wa arimasu ka?]; **Is there a
restaurant on the campsite?** キャンプ場に
レストランはありますか? [kyanpu-jou ni
resutoran wa arimasu ka?]

campus [kæmpəs] n キャンパス [kyanpasu]

can [kən, STRONG kæn] v ･･･できる [...
dekiru]; **can opener** n 缶切り [kankiri];
garbage can n ごみ箱 [gomibako]; **trash
can** n くずかご [kuzukago]; **watering can** n
じょうろ [jouro]

Canada [kænədə] n カナダ [kanada]

Canadian [kəneɪdiən] adj カナダの [kanada
no] ▷ n カナダ人 [kanadajin]

canal [kənæl] n 運河 [unga]

Canaries [kənɛəriz] npl カナリア諸島
[kanaria shotou]

canary [kənɛəri] n カナリア [kanaria]

cancel [kænsᵊl] v 取り消す [torikesu]

cancellation [kænsəleɪʃᵊn] n キャンセル
[kyanseru]; **Are there any cancellations?**
キャンセルされたフライトはありますか?
[kyanseru sareta furaito wa arimasu ka?]

cancer [kænsər] n (illness) 癌 [gan]

Cancer [kænsər] n (horoscope) 蟹座 [kaniza]

candidate [kændɪdeɪt] n 候補者 [kouhosha]

candle [kændᵊl] n ろうそく [rousoku]

candlestick [kændᵊlstɪk] n ろうそく立て
[rousokutate]

candy [kændi] n キャンデー [kyandee];
cotton candy n 綿菓子 [watagashi]

cane [keɪn] n ステッキ [sutekki]

canister [kænɪstər] n キャニスター
[kyanisutaa]

cannabis [kænəbɪs] n 大麻 [taima]

canned [kænd] adj 缶詰にした [kanzume ni
shita], 缶詰めにした [kanzume ni shita]

canoe [kənu] n カヌー [kanuu]

canoeing [kənuɪŋ] n カヌー漕ぎ [kanuu kogi]

canola [kənoʊlə] n レイプする [reipu suru]

canteen [kæntin] n キャンティーン [kyantiin]

canter [kæntər] v 普通駆け足で行く [futsuu
kakeashi de iku]

canvas [kænvəs] n キャンバス [kyanbasu]

canvass [kænvəs] v 投票を頼んで回る
[touhyou-o tanonde mawaru]

cap [kæp] n 縁なし帽子 [fuchinashi boushi];
baseball cap n 野球帽 [yakyuubou]

capable [keɪpəbᵊl] adj ･･･ができる [... ga
dekiru]

capacity [kəpæsɪti] n 収容力 [shuuyouryoku]

capital [kæpɪtᵊl] n 首都 [shuto]

capitalism [kæpɪtᵊlɪzəm] n 資本主義
[shihonshugi]

Capricorn [kæprɪkɔrn] n 山羊座 [yagiza]

capsize [kæpsaɪz] v 転覆する [tenpuku suru]

capsule [kæpsᵊl] n カプセル [kapuseru]

captain [kæptɪn] n 船長 [senchou]

caption [kæpʃᵊn] n キャプション [kyapushon]

capture [kæptʃər] v 捕える [toraeru]

car [kɑr] n 車 [kuruma], 自動車 [jidousha],
(train) 客車 [kyakusha]; **cable car** n ケーブ
ルカー [keeburukaa]; **car rental** n レンタカー
[rentakaa]; **car wash** n 洗車機 [senshaki];
company car n 社用車 [shayousha]; **dining
car** n 食堂車 [shokudousha]; **patrol car** n パ
トロールカー [patorooarukaa]; **rental car** n レ
ンタカー [rentakaa]; **rented car** n レンタカー
[rentakaa]; **sleeping car** n 寝台車
[shindaisha]; **Could you take me by car?**
私を車で連れて行ってもらえますか? [watashi
o kuruma de tsurete itte moraemasu ka?];
Do I have to return the car here? 車はここ
に返さなければなりませんか? [kuruma wa
koko ni kaesanakereba narimasen ka?];
How much is it for a car with two people?
2人用の車両はいくらですか? [futari-you no

sharyou wa ikura desu ka?]; **I want to rent a car** 車を借りたいのですが [kuruma o karitai no desu ga]; **I've wrecked my car** 私は自分の車を衝突させました [watashi wa jibun no kuruma o shoutotsu sasemashita]; **Is there a dining car on the train?** 電車にはビュッフェ車がありますか? [densha ni wa byuffe-sha ga arimasu ka?]; **My car has been broken into** 私の車が壊されて侵入されました [watashi no kuruma ga kowasarete shinnyuu saremashita]; **When will the car be ready?** 車はいつ直りますか? [kuruma wa itsu naorimasu ka?]; **Where can I park the car?** どこに駐車できますか? [doko ni chuusha dekimasu ka?]

car ferry n カーフェリー [kaaferii]

carafe [kəræf] n カラフ [karafu]; **a carafe of the house wine** ハウスワインをカラフで1本 [hausu-wain o karafu de ippon]

caramel [kærəmɛl, -məl, kɑrməl] n キャラメル [kyarameru]

carat [kærət] n カラット [karatto]

carbohydrate [kɑrbouhaɪdreɪt] n 炭水化物 [tansuikabutsu]

carbon [kɑrbən] n 炭素 [tanso]; **carbon footprint** n カーボンフットプリント [kaabon futtopurinto]

carbonated [kɑrbəneɪtɪd] adj シュシュと泡立つ [shushu to awadatsu]

carburetor [kɑrbəreɪtər] n キャブレター [kyaburetaa]

card [kɑrd] n カード [kaado]; **credit card** n クレジットカード [kurejittokaado]; **debit card** n デビットカード [debitto kaado]; **greeting card** n グリーティングカード [guriitingukaado]; **ID card** abbr 身分証明書 [mibunshomeisho]; **membership card** n メンバーカード [menbaakaado]; **playing card** n トランプ [toranpu]; **report card** n 通知表 [tsuuchihyou]; **A memory card for this digital camera, please** このデジタルカメラ用のメモリカードをください [kono dejitaru-kamera-you no memori-kaado o

kudasai]; **Can I use my card to get cash?** 私のカードを使って現金を引き出せますか? [watashi no kaado o tsukatte genkin o hikidasemasu ka?]; **Can I use my card with this ATM?** この現金自動支払い機で私のカードを使えますか? [kono genkin-jidou-shiharaiki de watashi no kaado o tsukaemasu ka?]; **Do you sell phone cards?** テレホンカードを売っていますか? [terehon-kaado o utte imasu ka?]; **Do you take credit cards?** クレジットカードは使えますか? [kurejitto-kaado wa tsukaemasu ka?]; **Do you take debit cards?** デビットカードは使えますか? [debitto-kaado wa tsukaemasu ka?]; **I need to cancel my card** 私はカードをキャンセルしなければなりません [watashi wa kaado o kyanseru shinakereba narimasen]; **My card has been stolen** 私のカードが盗まれました [watashi no kaado ga nusuma remashita]; **Where can I buy a phone card?** どこでテレホンカードを買えますか? [doko de terehon-kaado o kaemasu ka?]; **Where can I mail these cards?** このカードをどこで投函できますか? [kono kaado o doko de toukan dekimasu ka?]

cardboard [kɑrdbɔrd] n ボール紙 [boorugami]

cardigan [kɑrdɪgən] n カーディガン [kaadigan]

cardphone [kɑrdfoun] n カード式公衆電話 [kaado shiki koushuu denwa]

care [kɛər] n 注意 [chuui] ▷ v 心配する [shinpai suru]; **intensive care unit** n 集中治療室 [shuuchuuchiryoushitsu, ICU aishiiyuu]; **take care of** v ···の世話をする [... no sewa-o suru]

career [kərɪər] n キャリア [kyaria]

careful [kɛərfəl] adj 注意深い [chuuibukai]

carefully [kɛərfəli] adv 注意深く [chuuibukaku]

careless [kɛərlɪs] adj 不注意な [fuchuui na]

caretaker [kɛərteɪkər] n 管理人 [kanrinin]

cargo [kɑrgou] n 貨物 [kamotsu]

Caribbean [kærəbiən, kərɪbiən] *adj* カリブ海
の [karibukai no] ▷ *n* カリブ人 [karibujin]

caring [kɛərɪŋ] *adj* 思いやりのある [omoiyari
no aru]

carnation [kɑrneɪʃn] *n* カーネーション
[kaaneeshon]

carnival [kɑrnɪvl] *n* カーニバル [kaanibaru]

carol [kærəl] *n* キャロル [kyaroru]

carpenter [kɑrpɪntər] *n* 建具屋 [tateguya], 大
工 [daiku]

carpentry [kɑrpɪntri] *n* 大工仕事
[daikushigoto]

carpet [kɑrpɪt] *n* カーペット [kaapetto];
wall-to-wall carpeting *n* ぴったり合うように
敷かれたカーペット [pittari au youni
shikareta kaapetto]

carriage [kærɪdʒ] *n* **baby carriage** *n* 乳母車
[ubaguruma]; **Where is carriage number
thirty?** 三十号車はどこですか? [sanjuu-gou-
sha wa doko desu ka?]

carrier [kæriər] *n* **baby carrier** *n* 持ち運び用
ベッド [mochihakobi you beddo]

carrot [kærət] *n* ニンジン [ninjin]

carry [kæri] *v* 運ぶ [hakobu]

carry on *v* 続ける [tsuzukeru]

carry out *v* 実行する [jikkou suru]

cart [kɑrt] *n* ワゴン [wagon], 荷馬車 [nibasha];
baggage cart *n* 手荷物カート [tenimotsu
kaato]; **shopping cart** *n* ショッピングカート
[shoppingukaato]

carton [kɑrtn] *n* ボール箱 [boorubako]

cartoon [kɑrtun] *n* 漫画 [manga]

cartridge [kɑrtrɪdʒ] *n* カートリッジ [kaatorijji],
弾薬 [dan-yaku]

carve [kɑrv] *v* 彫る [horu]

case [keɪs] *n* ケース [keesu], 場合 [baai];
pencil case *n* 筆箱 [fudebako]

cash [kæʃ] *n* 現金 [genkin]; **cash register** *n*
レジ [reji]; **Can I cash my traveler's checks
here?** ここで私のトラベラーズチェックを現金
化できますか? [koko de watashi no
toraberaazu-chekku o genkinka dekimasu
ka?]; **Do you offer a discount for cash?** 現

金で払うと割引がありますか? [genkin de
harau to waribki ga arimasu ka?]; **I don't
have any cash** 私は現金がありません
[watashi wa genkin ga arimasen]; **I want to
cash a check, please** 小切手を現金化してく
ださい [kogitte o genkinka shite kudasai]

cashew [kæʃu, kæʃu] *n* カシューナッツ
[kashuunattsu]

cashier [kæʃɪər] *n* 会計係 [kaikeigakari]

cashmere [kæʒmɪər] *n* カシミヤ [kashimiya]

casino [kəsinou] *n* カジノ [kajino]

casserole [kæsəroul] *n* キャセロール
[kyaserooru]

cassette [kəsɛt] *n* カセット [kasetto]

cast [kæst] *n* キャスト [kyasuto]

castle [kæsl] *n* 城 [shiro]

casual [kæʒuəl] *adj* 不断 [fudan], 偶然の
[guuzen no]

casually [kæʒuəli] *adv* 偶然に [guuzen ni]

casualty [kæʒuəlti] *n* 死傷者 [shishousha]

cat [kæt] *n* 猫 [neko]

catalog [kætlɔg] *n* カタログ [katarogu]; **I'd
like a catalog** カタログが欲しいのですが
[katarogu ga hoshii no desu ga]

cataract [kætərækt] *n* (*eye*) 白内障
[hakunaishou], (*waterfall*) 大きな滝 [ouki na
taki]

catarrh [kətɑr] *n* カタル [kataru]

catastrophe [kətæstrəfi] *n* 大災害 [daisaigai]

catch [kætʃ] *v* つかまえる [tsukamaeru]

catching [kætʃɪŋ] *adj* 伝染性の [densensei
no]

catch up *v* 追いつく [oitsuku]

category [kætɪgori] *n* 部門 [bumon]

catering [keɪtərɪŋ] *n* ケータリング
[keetaringu]

caterpillar [kætərpɪlər] *n* イモムシ
[imomushi]

cathedral [kəθidrəl] *n* 大聖堂 [daiseidou];
When is the cathedral open? その大聖堂
はいつ開きますか? [sono daiseidou wa itsu
hirakimasu ka?]

Catholic [kæθlɪk] *adj* カトリックの [katorikku

no] ▷ n カトリック教徒 [katorikkukyouto];
Roman Catholic n ローマカトリック教会の
[Rooma Katorikku kyoukai no], ローマカトリ
ック教徒 [Rooma Katorikku kyouto]

cattle [kæt·l] npl 畜牛 [chikugyuu]

Caucasus [kɔkəsəs] n カフカス山脈
[Kafukasu sanmyaku]

cauliflower [kɔliflauər] n カリフラワー
[karifurawaa]

cause [kɔz] n 素 [moto], (ideals) 大義 [taigi],
(reason) 理由 [riyuu] ▷ v 引き起こす
[hikiokosu]

caution [kɔʃ·n] n 注意 [chuui]

cautious [kɔʃəs] adj 慎重な [shinchou na]

cautiously [kɔʃəsli] adv 慎重に [shinchou ni]

cave [keɪv] n ほら穴 [horaana]

cayenne pepper [kaɪɛn pɛpər] n トウガラシ
[tougarashi]

CCTV [si si ti vi] abbr 閉回路テレビ [heikairo
terebi]

CD [si di] n CD [siidii]; **CD burner** n CDバーナ
ー [shiidii baanaa]; **CD player** n CDプレーヤ
ー [shiidii pureiyaa]; **Can I make CDs at this
computer?** このコンピューターでCDを作成で
きますか? [kono konpyuutaa de shii-dii o
sakusei dekimasu ka?]; **When will the CD
be ready?** CDはいつできますか? [shii-dii wa
itsu dekimasu ka?]

CD-ROM [si di rɒm] n CD-ROM [siidii romu]

cease-fire [sisfaɪər] n 停戦 [teisen]

ceiling [silɪŋ] n 天井 [tenjou]

celebrate [sɛlɪbreɪt] v 祝う [iwau]

celebration [sɛlɪbreɪʃ·n] n 祝い [iwai]

celebrity [sɪlɛbrɪti] n 有名人 [yuumeijin]

celery [sɛləri] n セロリ [serori]

celiac [siliæk] adj 腹腔の [fukkou no]

cell [sɛl] n 細胞 [saibou]; **cell phone** n 携帯
電話 [keitai denwa]; **cell phone number** n
携帯電話番号 [keitai denwa bangou]

cellar [sɛlər] n 地下室 [chikashitsu]

cello [tʃɛlou] n チェロ [chero]

cellular [sɛlyələr] n **My cellular number is...**
私の携帯電話番号は・・・です [watashi no

keitai-denwa-bangou wa... desu]

cement [sɪmɛnt] n セメント [semento]

cemetery [sɛmətɛri] n 墓地 [bochi]

census [sɛnsəs] n 国勢調査 [kokuzeichousa]

cent [sɛnt] n セント [sento]

centenary [sɛntʃnɛri] n 100周年記念祭
[hyakushuunen kinensai]

center [sɛntər] n 中心 [chuushin], センター
[sentaa]; **call center** n コールセンター
[kooru sentaa]; **leisure center** n レジャーセ
ンター [rejaasentaa]; **shopping center** n シ
ョッピングセンター [shoppingu sentaa];
visitor center n ビジターセンター
[bijitaasentaa]; **How do I get to the center
of...?** ・・・の中心部へはどう行けばいいのです
か? [... no chuushinbu e wa dou ikeba ii no
desu ka?]

centimeter [sɛntɪmitər] n センチメートル
[senchimeetoru]

central [sɛntrəl] adj 中央の [chuuou no];
central heating n セントラルヒーティング
[sentoraruhiitingu]; **Central America** n 中央
アメリカ [Chuuou Amerika]

century [sɛntʃəri] n 世紀 [seiki]

CEO [si i ou] abbr 最高経営責任者 [saikou
keiei sekininsha]

ceramic [sɪræmɪk] adj セラミックの
[seramikku no]

cereal crops n 穀草 [koku kusa], 穀類 [koku-
rui]

ceremony [sɛrɪmouni] n 儀式 [gishiki];
master of ceremonies n 司会者 [shikaisha]

certain [sɜrt·n] adj 確信している [kakushin
shite iru]

certainly [sɜrt·nli] adv 確かに [tashika ni]

certainty [sɜrt·nti] n 確実なこと [kakujitsu na
koto]

certificate [sərtɪfɪkɪt] n 証明書 [shoumeisho],
証書 [shousho]; **birth certificate** n 出生証明
書 [shusshou (shussei) shoumeisho]; **gift
certificate** n 商品券 [shouhinken]; **marriage
certificate** n 結婚証明書 [kekkonshou-
meisho]; **medical certificate** n 診断書

[shindansho]; **I need a 'fit to fly' certificate** 私は「飛行機搭乗の適性」証明書が必要です [watashi wa "hikouki-toujou no tekisei" shoumei-sho ga hitsuyou desu]

certified [sɜrtɪfaɪd] *adj* **How long will it take by certified mail?** 書留郵便でどのくらいの日数がかかりますか? [kakitome-yuubin de dono kurai no nissuu ga kakarimasu ka?]

certify [sɜrtɪfaɪ] *v* **certified mail** *n* 簡易書留 [kan-i kakitome]

Chad [tʃæd] *n* チャド [chado]

chain [tʃeɪn] *n* 鎖 [kusari]

chair [tʃeər] *n* チェア [chea], *(furniture)* 椅子 [isu]; **easy chair** *n* 安楽椅子 [anraku isu]; **rocking chair** *n* ロッキングチェア [rokkinguchea]; **Do you have a high chair?** 子供用の椅子はありますか? [kodomo-you no isu wa arimasu ka?]

chairlift [tʃeərlɪft] *n* チェアリフト [chearifuto]; **When does the first chairlift go?** 最初のチェアリフトはいつ出ますか? [saisho no chea-rifuto wa itsu demasu ka?]

chairman [tʃeərmən] *(pl chairmen)* *n* 議長 [gichou]

chalk [tʃɔk] *n* チョーク [chooku] (白墨)

challenge [tʃælɪndʒ] *n* 挑戦 [chousen] ▷ *v* 挑戦する [chousen suru]

challenging [tʃælɪndʒɪŋ] *adj* 挑戦的な [chousenteki na]

champagne [ʃæmpeɪn] *n* シャンパン [shanpan]

champion [tʃæmpiən] *n* 優勝者 [yuushou-sha]

championship [tʃæmpiənʃɪp] *n* 選手権 [senshuken]

chance [tʃæns] *n* 見込み [mikomi]

change [tʃeɪndʒ] *n* 変化 [henka], 小銭 [kozeni] ▷ *vi* 変わる [kawaru] ▷ *vt* 変える [kaeru]; **changing room** *n* 更衣室 [kouishitsu], 試着室 [shichakushitsu]; **Could you give me some change, please?** 小銭をいくらかいただけますか? [kozeni o ikura ka itadakemasu ka?]; **Do you have any**

small change? 小銭がありますか? [kozeni ga arimasu ka?]; **Sorry, I don't have any change** すみません、小銭がありません [sumimasen, kozeni ga arimasen]

changeable [tʃeɪndʒəbʰl] *adj* 変わりやすい [kawariyasui]

channel [tʃænʰl] *n* チャンネル [channeru]

chaos [keɪɒs] *n* 大混乱 [daikonran]

chaotic [keɪɒtɪk] *adj* 大混乱した [daikonran shita]

chapel [tʃæpʰl] *n* 礼拝堂 [reihaidou]

chapter [tʃæptər] *n* 章 [shou]

character [kærɪktər] *n* 特質 [tokushitsu]

characteristic [kærɪktərɪstɪk] *n* 特徴 [tokuchou]

charcoal [tʃɑrkoʊl] *n* 木炭 [mokutan]

charge [tʃɑrdʒ] *n* チャージ [chaaji], *(accusation)* 告訴 [kokuso], *(electricity)* 充電 [juuden], *(price)* 料金 [ryoukin] ▷ *v* *(accuse)* 告訴する [kokuso suru], *(electricity)* 充電する [juuden suru], *(price)* 請求する [seikyuu suru]; **admission charge** *n* 入場料 [nyuujouryou]; **cover charge** *n* カバーチャージ [kabaa chaaji]; **service charge** *n* サービス料 [saabisuryou]; **Is there a charge for the service?** サービスに料金がかかりますか? [saabisu ni ryoukin ga kakarimasu ka?]; **Is there a mileage charge?** 走行距離に対して料金がかかりますか? [soukou-kyori ni taishite ryoukin ga kakarimasu ka?]; **Is there a service charge to pay?** 予約料金がかかりますか? [yoyaku-ryoukin ga kakarimasu ka?]; **It isn't charging** 充電されません [juuden saremasen]; **Where can I charge my cell phone?** どこで携帯電話を充電できますか? [doko de keitai-denwa o juuden dekimasu ka?]; **Why are you charging me so much?** なぜそんなにたくさん請求するのですか? [naze sonna ni takusan seikyuu suru no desu ka?]

charger [tʃɑrdʒər] *n* 充電器 [juudenki]

charity [tʃærɪti] *n* 慈善団体 [jizen dantai];

charity store n チャリティーショップ [charitii shoppu]

charm [tʃɑrm] n 魅力 [miryoku]

chart [tʃɑrt] n 図表 [zuhyou]; **pie chart** n 円グラフ [engurafu]

charter [tʃɑrtər] n チャーター [chaataa]

chase [tʃeɪs] n 追跡 [tsuiseki] ▷ v 追跡する [tsuiseki suru]

chat [tʃæt] n おしゃべり [o-shaberi] ▷ v おしゃべりする [o-shaberi suru]

chatroom [tʃætrum] n チャットルーム [chatto ruumu]

chauffeur [ʃoufər, ʃoufɜr] n おかかえ運転手 [okakae untenshu]

chauvinist [ʃouvɪnɪst] n 熱狂的愛国主義者 [nekkyoutekiaikokushugisha]

cheap [tʃip] adj 安い [yasui]; **I'd like the cheapest option** 一番安い方法がいいのですが [ichiban yasui houhou ga ii no desu ga]

cheat [tʃit] n 詐欺師 [sagishi] ▷ v だます [damasu]

Chechnya [tʃɛtʃniə] n チェチェン共和国 [Chechen kyouwakoku]

check [tʃɛk] n チェック [chekku], 照合 [shougou], 小切手 [kogitte] ▷ v 調べる [shiraberu], 照合の印をつける [shougou no in-o tsukeru]; **blank check** n 白地小切手 [shiraji kogitte]; **check mark** n 照合の印 [shougou no in]; **traveler's check** n 旅行者用小切手 [ryokousha you kogitte]; **Can I cash a check?** 小切手を現金化できますか? [kogitte o genkinka dekimasu ka?]; **Can I pay by check?** 小切手で支払えますか? [kogitte de shiharaemasu ka?]; **I want to cash these traveler's checks** このトラベラーズチェックを現金化したいのですが [kono toraberaazu-chekku o genkinka shitai no desu ga]; **Someone's stolen my traveler's checks** 誰かが私のトラベラーズチェックを盗みました [dare ka ga watashi no toraberaazu-chekku o nusumimashita]

checkbook [tʃɛkbʊk] n 小切手帳 [kogittechou]

checked [tʃɛkt] adj チェックの [chekku no]

checkers [tʃɛkərz] npl チェッカー [chekkaa]

check in v チェックインする [chekkuin suru]; **Where do I check in for the flight to...?** ···行きのフライトはどこでチェックインするのですか? [... iki no furaito wa doko de chekku-in suru no desu ka?]

check-in [tʃɛkɪn] n チェックイン [chekkuin]

checking account [tʃɛkɪŋ əkaʊnt] n **checking account** n 当座預金 [touzayokin]

check off v チェックする [chekku suru]

check out v チェックアウトする [chekkuauto suru]

checkout [tʃɛkaʊt] n チェックアウト [chekkuauto]

checkup [tʃɛkʌp] n 検査 [kensa]

cheek [tʃik] n ほお [hoo]

cheekbone [tʃikboun] n ほお骨 [hoobone]

cheer [tʃɪər] n 喝采 [kassai] ▷ v 声援する [seien suru]

cheerful [tʃɪərfəl] adj 陽気な [youki na]

cheers [tʃɪərz] excl 乾杯! [kanpai]

cheese [tʃiz] n チーズ [chiizu]; **cottage cheese** n カッテージチーズ [katteeji chiizu]; **What kind of cheese?** どんなチーズですか? [donna cheezu desu ka?]

chef [ʃɛf] n シェフ [shiefu]; **What is the chef's specialty?** シェフの得意料理は何ですか? [shefu no tokui-ryouri wa nan desu ka?]

chemical [kɛmɪkəl] n 化学薬品 [kagakuyakuhin]

chemistry [kɛmɪstri] n 化学 [kagaku]

cherry [tʃɛri] n サクランボ [sakuranbo]

chess [tʃɛs] n チェス [chesu]

chest [tʃɛst] n (body part) 胸 [mune], (storage) 収納箱 [shuunoubako]; **I have a pain in my chest** 私は胸に痛みがあります [watashi wa mune ni itami ga arimasu]

chestnut [tʃɛsnʌt, -nət] n クリ [kuri]

chew [tʃu] v 噛む [kamu]; **chewing gum** n チューインガム [chuuingamu]

chick [tʃɪk] n ひよこ [hiyoko]

chicken [tʃɪkɪn] n 鶏 [niwatori]

chickenpox [tʃɪkɪnpɒks] n 水疱瘡 [mizubousou]

chickpea [tʃɪkpi] n ヒヨコマメ [hiyokomame]

chief [tʃif] adj 主要な [shuyou na] ▷ n ···長 [···chou] (統率)

child, children [tʃaɪld, tʃɪldrən] n 子供 [kodomo]; **child abuse** n 児童虐待 [jidou gyakutai]; **Do you have a children's menu?** 子供用のメニューはありますか? [kodomo-you no menyuu wa arimasu ka?]; **I have no children** 私には子供がいません [watashi ni wa kodomo ga imasen]; **I have three children** 私には子供が三人います [watashi ni wa kodomo ga sannin imasu]; **I need someone to watch the children tonight** 私は今晩子供たちの面倒を見てくれる人が必要です [watashi wa konban kodomo-tachi no mendou o mite kureru hito ga hitsuyou desu]; **I'd like a child seat for a two-year-old child** 2歳の子供用のチャイルドシートが欲しいのですが [ni-sai no kodomo-you no chairudo-shiito ga hoshii no desu ga]; **I'm looking for a present for a child** 私は子供へのプレゼントを探しています [watashi wa kodomo e no purezento o sagashite imasu]; **Is it safe for children?** それは子供にも安全ですか? [sore wa kodomo ni mo anzen desu ka?]; **My child is ill** 私の子供が病気です [watashi no kodomo ga byouki desu]; **My child is missing** 私の子供が行方不明です [watashi no kodomo ga yukue-fumei desu]; **My children are in the car** 子供たちが車の中にいます [kodomo-tachi ga kuruma no naka ni imasu]; **The child is on this passport** 子供はこのパスポートに載っています [kodomo wa kono pasupooto ni notte imasu]; **What is there for children to do?** 子供ができることは何がありますか? [kodomo ga dekiru koto wa nani ga arimasu ka?]

childcare [tʃaɪldkɛər] n 児童養護 [jidou yougo]

childhood [tʃaɪldhʊd] n 子供時代 [kodomo jidai]

childish [tʃaɪldɪʃ] adj 子供じみた [kodomo-jimita]

Chile [tʃɪli] n チリ [chiri]

Chilean [tʃɪliən] adj チリの [chiri no] ▷ n チリ人 [chirijin]

chill [tʃɪl] v 冷やす [hiyasu]

chilly [tʃɪli] adj 寒い [samui]

chimney [tʃɪmni] n 煙突 [entotsu]

chimpanzee [tʃɪmpænzi] n チンパンジー [chinpanjii]

chin [tʃɪn] n あご [ago]

china [tʃaɪnə] n 磁器 [jiki]

China [tʃaɪnə] n 中国 [chuugoku]

Chinese [tʃaɪniz] adj 中国の [chuugoku no] ▷ n (language) 中国語 [chuugokugo], (person) 中国人 [chuugokujin]

chip [tʃɪp] n (electronic) チップ [chippu] (電子), (small piece) かけら [kakera]; **potato chips** npl ポテトチップス [potetochippusu]; **silicon chip** n マイクロチップ [maikuro-chippu]

chip in v 合同する [goudou suru]

chips npl チップス [chippusu]

chisel [tʃɪzˌl] n 鑿 [saku]

chives [tʃaɪvz] npl チャイブ [chaibu]

chlorine [klɔrin] n 塩素 [enso]

chocolate [tʃɒkəlɪt, tʃɒklɪt] n チョコレート [chokoreeto]; **dark chocolate** n ブラックチョコレート [burakku chokoreeto]; **milk chocolate** n ミルクチョコレート [miruku-chokoreeto]

choice [tʃɔɪs] n 選択 [sentaku]

choir [kwaɪər] n 聖歌隊 [seikatai]

choke [tʃoʊk] v 息が詰まる [iki ga tsumaru]

cholesterol [kəlɛstərol] n コレステロール [koresuterooru]

choose [tʃuz] v 選ぶ [erabu]

chop [tʃɒp] n たたき切ること [tatakikiru koto] ▷ v たたき切る [tatakikiru]; **pork chop** n ポークチョップ [pookuchoppu]

chopsticks [tʃɒpstɪks] npl 箸 [hashi]

chosen [tʃoʊzˌn] adj 選ばれた [erabareta]

Christ [kraɪst] n キリスト [kirisuto]

Christian [krɪstʃən] *adj* キリスト教の
[kirisutokyou no] ▷ *n* キリスト教徒
[kirisutokyouto]

Christianity [krɪstʃiænɪti] *n* キリスト教
[kirisutokyou]

Christmas [krɪsməs] *n* クリスマス
[kurisumasu]; **Christmas card** *n* クリスマス
カード [kurisumasu kaado]; **Christmas Eve**
n クリスマスイブ [kurisumasu ibu];
Christmas tree *n* クリスマスツリー
[kurisumasu tsurii]; **Merry Christmas!** メリー
クリスマス! [merii kurisumasu!]

chrome [kroʊm] *n* クロム [kuromu]

chronic [krɒnɪk] *adj* 慢性の [mansei no]

chrysanthemum [krɪsænθəməm] *n* キク
[kiku]

chubby [tʃʌbi] *adj* 丸々太った [marumaru
futotta]

chunk [tʃʌŋk] *n* 厚く切ったもの [atsuku kitta
mono]

church [tʃɜrtʃ] *n* 教会 [kyoukai]; **Can we visit
the church?** 私たちがその教会を訪れること
はできますか? [watashi-tachi ga sono
kyoukai o otozureru koto wa dekimasu ka?]

cigar [sɪgɑr] *n* 葉巻き [hamaki]

cigarette [sɪgərɛt] *n* タバコ [tabako], 紙巻き
タバコ [kamimakitabako]; **cigarette lighter**
n シガレットライター [shigaretto raitaa]

cinnamon [sɪnəmən] *n* シナモン [shinamon]

circle [sɜrk°l] *n* 円 [en] (丸); **Arctic Circle** *n*
北極圏 [hokkyokuken]

circuit [sɜrkɪt] *n* 一周 [isshuu]

circular [sɜrkyələr] *adj* 円形の [enkei no]

circulation [sɜrkyəleɪʃ°n] *n* 循環 [junkan]

circumstances [sɜrkəmstæns] *npl* 事情
[jijou]

circus [sɜrkəs] *n* サーカス [saakasu]

citizen [sɪtɪz°n] *n* 市民 [shimin]; **senior
citizen** *n* 老齢年金受給者 [rourei nenkin
jukyuusha], 高齢者 [koureisha]

citizenship [sɪtɪz°nʃɪp] *n* 市民権 [shiminken]

city [sɪti] *n* 都市 [toshi]

civilian [sɪvɪlyən] *adj* 民間の [minkan no] ▷ *n*
民間人 [minkanjin]

civilization [sɪvɪlɪzeɪʃ°n] *n* 文明 [bunmei]

claim [kleɪm] *n* 主張 [shuchou] ▷ *v* 主張する
[shuchou suru]; **baggage claim** *n* 手荷物受
取所 [tenimotsu uketorisho]; **claim form** *n* ク
レームフォーム [kureemufoomu]

clap [klæp] *v* 拍手する [hakushu suru]

clarify [klærɪfaɪ] *v* 明らかにする [akiraka ni
suru]

clarinet [klærɪnɛt] *n* クラリネット [kurarinetto]

clash [klæʃ] *v* 衝突する [shoutotsu suru]

clasp [klæsp] *n* 留め金 [tomegane]

class [klæs] *n* 暮らす [kurasu], 分類 [bunrui];
business class *n* ビジネスクラス [bijinesu
kurasu]; **economy class** *n* エコノミークラス
[ekonomiikurasu]; **night class** *n* 夜間クラス
[yakan kurasu]; **second class** *n* 二等 [nitou]

classic [klæsɪk] *adj* 典型的な [tenkeiteki na]
▷ *n* 一流の芸術作品 [ichiryuu no
geijutsusakuhin]

classical [klæsɪk°l] *adj* 伝統的な [dentouteki
na]

classified [klæsɪfaɪd] *adj* **classified ads** *npl*
分類広告 [bunruikoukoku]

classmate [klæsmeɪt] *n* 同級生 [doukyuusei]

classroom [klæsrum] *n* 教室 [kyoushitsu]

clause [klɒz] *n* 条項 [joukou]

claustrophobic [klɒstrəfoʊbɪk] *adj* 閉所恐怖
症の [heisho kyoufushou no]

claw [klɒ] *n* かぎづめ [kagizume]

clay [kleɪ] *n* 粘土 [nendo]

clean [klin] *adj* きれい [kirei], 清潔な [seiketsu
na] ▷ *v* 掃除する [souji suru]; **The room isn't
clean** 部屋がきれいではありません [heya ga
kirei de wa arimasen]

cleaner [klinər] *n* 清掃人 [seisounin];
vacuum cleaner *n* フーバー® [fuubaa]

cleaning [klinɪŋ] *n* クリーニング [kuriiningu],
掃除 [souji]; **cleaning lady** *n* 掃除婦 [soujifu]

cleanser [klɛnzər] *n* クレンザー [kurenzaa]

clear [klɪər] *adj* 明白な [meihaku na]

clearance [klɪərəns] *n* 頭上スペース [zujou
supeesu]

clearly [klɪ̱ərli] *adv* はっきり [hakkiri]

clear up *v* 片付ける [katazukeru]

clementine [klɛ̱məntaɪn] *n* クレメンタイン [kurementain]

clever [klɛ̱vər] *adj* 賢い [kashikoi]

click [klɪ̱k] *n* カチッという音 [kachitto iu oto] ▷*v* カチッと鳴る [kachitto naru]

client [klaɪ̱ənt] *n* 依頼人 [irainin]

cliff [klɪ̱f] *n* 崖 [gake]

climate [klaɪ̱mɪt] *n* 気候 [kikou]; **climate change** *n* 気候変動 [kikou hendo]

climb [klaɪ̱m] *v* 登る [noboru]

climber [klaɪ̱mər] *n* クライマー [kuraimaa]

climbing [klaɪ̱mɪŋ] *n* クライミング [kuraimingu]

clinic [klɪ̱nɪk] *n* 診療所 [shinryoujo]

clip [klɪ̱p] *n* 刈り込み [karikomi]

clippers [klɪ̱pərz] *npl* はさみ [hasami]

clipping [klɪ̱pɪŋ] *n* 切り抜き [kirinuki]

cloakroom [klo̱ʊkrum] *n* クローク [kurooku]

clock [klɒ̱k] *n* 時計 [tokei]; **alarm clock** *n* 目覚まし時計 [mezamashi tokei]

clockwise [klɒ̱kwaɪz] *adv* 右回りに [migimawari ni]

clog [klɒ̱g] *n* 木靴 [kigutsu]

clone [klo̱ʊn] *n* クローン [kuroon] ▷*v* クローンを作る [kuroon-o tsukuru]

close [klo̱ʊz] *adj* 近い [chikai] ▷*adv* 近くに [chikaku ni] ▷*v* 閉める [shimeru]; **close by** *adj* すぐ近くの [sugu chikaku no]; **closing time** *n* 閉店時刻 [heiten jikoku]

closed [klo̱ʊzd] *adj* 閉まっている [shimatte iru]

closely [klo̱ʊsli] *adv* ぴったりと [pittarito]

closure [klo̱ʊʒər] *n* 閉鎖 [heisa]

cloth [klɒ̱θ] *n* 布地 [nunoji]

clothes [klo̱ʊz, klo̱ʊðz] *npl* 服 [fuku], 複層 [fukusou]; **Is there somewhere to dry clothes?** 服を干すところがありますか? [fuku o hosu tokoro ga arimasu ka?]; **My clothes are damp** 私の服が湿っています [watashi no fuku ga shimette imasu]

clothesline [klo̱ʊzlaɪn, klo̱ʊðz-] *n* 洗濯ロープ [sentaku roopu], 物干し綱 [monohoshi tsuna]

clothespin [klo̱ʊzpɪn, klo̱ʊðz-] *n* 洗濯ばさみ [sentakubasami]

clothing [klo̱ʊðɪŋ] *n* 衣類 [irui]

cloud [kla̱ʊd] *n* 雲 [kumo]

cloudy [kla̱ʊdi] *adj* 曇った [kumotta]

clove [klo̱ʊv] *n* クローブ [kuroobu]

clown [kla̱ʊn] *n* ピエロ [piero]

club [klʌ̱b] *n (group)* クラブ [kurabu] *(集団)*, *(weapon)* 棍棒 [konbou]; **golf club** *n (game)* ゴルフ用クラブ [gorufu you kurabu], *(society)* ゴルフクラブ [gorufukurabu]; **Do they rent out golf clubs?** ゴルフクラブを貸し出していますか? [gorufu-kurabu o kashidashite imasu ka?]; **Where is there a good club?** どこかによいクラブはありますか? [doko-ka ni yoi kurabu wa arimasu ka?]

clue [klu̱] *n* 手がかり [tegakari]

clumsy [klʌ̱mzi] *adj* 不器用な [bukiyou na]

clutch [klʌ̱tʃ] *n* クラッチ [kuratchi]

clutter [klʌ̱tər] *n* 散らかしたもの [chirakashita mono]

coach [ko̱ʊtʃ] *n (trainer)* コーチ [koochi]

coal [ko̱ʊl] *n* 石炭 [sekitan]

coarse [kɔ̱rs] *adj* きめの粗い [kime no komakai]

coast [ko̱ʊst] *n* 沿岸 [engan]; **coast guard** *n* 沿岸警備隊 [engankeibitai]

coat [ko̱ʊt] *n* コート [kooto] *(洋服)*; **coat hanger** *n* ハンガー [hangaa]; **fur coat** *n* 毛皮のコート [kegawa no kooto]

cobweb [kɒ̱bwɛb] *n* くもの巣 [kumo no su]

cocaine [ko̱ʊke̱ɪn] *n* コカイン [kokain]

cockerel [kɒ̱kərəl, kɒ̱krəl] *n* 若いおんどり [wakai ondori]

cockpit [kɒ̱kpɪt] *n* コックピット [kokkupitto]

cockroach [kɒ̱kroʊtʃ] *n* ゴキブリ [gokiburi]

cocktail [kɒ̱kteɪl] *n* カクテル [kakuteru]; **Do you sell cocktails?** カクテルはありますか? [kakuteru wa arimasu ka?]

cocoa [ko̱ʊkoʊ] *n* ココア [kokoa]

coconut [ko̱ʊkənʌt] *n* ココナツ [kokonatsu]

cod [kɒ̱d] *n* タラ [tara]

code [koud] *n* 暗号 [angou]; **area code** *n* 局番 [kyokuban]; **traffic code** *n* 交通規則集 [koutsuu kisokushuu]; **zip code** *n* 郵便番号 [yuubin bangou]

co-ed *adj* 男女 [danjo]

coffee [kɔfi] *n* コーヒー [koohii]; **black coffee** *n* ブラックコーヒー [burakku koohii]; **coffee bean** *n* コーヒー豆 [koohiimame]; **decaffeinated coffee** *n* カフェイン抜きのコーヒー [kafein nuki no koohii]; **Coffee with milk, please** ミルク入りコーヒーをください [miruku-iri koohii o kudasai]; **Could we have another cup of coffee, please?** コーヒーをもう一杯いただけますか? [koohii o mou ippai itadakemasu ka?]; **Do you have fresh coffee?** 挽きたてのコーヒーはありますか? [hikitate no koohii wa arimasu ka?]

coffeepot [kɔfipɒt] *n* コーヒーポット [koohiipotto]

coffin [kɔfin] *n* ひつぎ [hitsugi]

coin [kɔɪn] *n* コイン [koin], 硬貨 [kouka]; **I'd like some coins for the phone, please** 電話に使うコインをいくらかお願いします [dehwa ni tsukau koin o ikura ka o-negai shimasu]

coincide [kouɪnsaɪd] *v* 同時に起こる [douji ni okoru]

coincidence [kouɪnsɪdəns] *n* 偶然 [guuzen]

Coke® [kouk] *n* コカコーラ® [kokakoora]

colander [kɒləndə, kʌl-] *n* 水切り [mizukiri]

cold [kould] *adj* 寒い [samui], 冷たい [tsumetai] ▷ *n* 寒さ [samusa]; **cold sore** *n* 口辺ヘルペス [kouhenherupesu]; **I'm cold** 寒いです [samui desu]

coleslaw [koulslɔ] *n* コールスロー [koorusuroo]

collaborate [kəlæbəreɪt] *v* 共同して働く [kyoudou shite hataraku]

collapse [kəlæps] *v* 崩れる [kuzureru]

collar [kɒlər] *n* 襟 [eri]

collarbone [kɒlərboun] *n* 鎖骨 [sakotsu]

colleague [kɒlig] *n* 同僚 [douryou]

collect [kəlɛkt] *v* 集める [atsumeru]

collection [kəlɛkʃ·n] *n* コレクション [korekushon]

collective [kəlɛktɪv] *adj* 集団の [shuudan no] ▷ *n* 集団 [shuudan]

collector [kəlɛktər] *n* 収集家 [shuushuuka]; **ticket collector** *n* 改札係 [kaisatsugakari]

college [kɒlɪdʒ] *n* カレッジ [karejji]

collide [kəlaɪd] *v* 衝突する [shoutotsu suru]

collie [kɒli] *n* コリー [korii]

colliery [kɒljəri] *n* 炭鉱 [tankou]

collision [kəlɪʒ·n] *n* 衝突 [shoutotsu]

Colombia [kəlʌmbiə] *n* コロンビア [koronbia]

Colombian [kəlʌmbiən] *adj* コロンビアの [koronbia no] ▷ *n* コロンビア人 [koronbiajin]

colon [koulən] *n* コロン [koron]

colonel [kɜrn·l] *n* 大佐 [taisa]

color [kʌlər] *n* 色 [iro]; **Do you have this in another color?** これの別の色はありますか? [kore no betsu no iro wa arimasu ka?]; **I don't like the color** 色が好きではありません [iro ga suki de wa arimasen]

colorblind [kʌlərblaɪnd] *adj* 色盲の [shikimou no]

colorful [kʌlərfəl] *adj* 色彩に富んだ [shikisai ni tonda]

coloring [kʌlərɪŋ] *n* 着色 [chakushoku]

column [kɒləm] *n* 円柱 [enchuu]

coma [koumə] *n* 昏睡 [konsui]

comb [koum] *n* 櫛 [kushi] ▷ *v* 櫛でとかす [kushi de tokasu]

combination [kɒmbɪneɪʃ·n] *n* 組み合わせ [kumiawase]

combine [kəmbaɪn] *v* 結合する [ketsugou suru]

come [kʌm] *v* 来る [kuru]

come around *v* 意識を回復する [ishiki-o kaifuku suru]

come back *v* 戻ってくる [modotte kuru]

comedian [kəmidiən] *n* コメディアン [komedian], 喜劇俳優 [kigeki haiyuu]

come down *v* 降りてくる [orite kuru]

comedy [kɒmədi] *n* コメディー [komedii]

come from *v* …の出身である […… no

shusshin de aru]

come in v 入る [hairu]

come off v The handle has come off 取っ手が外れました [totte ga hazuremashita]

come out v 公になる [ooyake ni naru]

comet [kɒmɪt] n 彗星 [suisei]

come up v 上がる [agaru]

comfort [kʌmfərt] n 安楽 [anraku]

comfortable [kʌmftəbˈl, -fərtəbˈl] adj 快適な [kaiteki na]

comforter [kʌmfərtər] n キルトの掛け布団 [kiruto no kakebuton]

comic book 漫画本 [mangabon]

comic strip コマ割り漫画 [komawari manga]

comma [kɒmə] n コンマ [konma]

command [kəmænd] n 命令 [meirei]

commemoration [kəmɛməreɪʃ'n] n 記念 [kinen]

comment [kɒmɛnt] n 論評 [ronpyou] ▸ v 論評する [ronpyou suru]

commentary [kɒmənteri] n 実況解説 [jikkyou kaisetsu]

commentator [kɒmənteɪtər] n 解説者 [kaisetsusha]

commercial [kəmɜrʃ'l] n コマーシャル [komaasharu, CM shiiemu]; **commercial break** n コマーシャルの時間 [komaasharu no jikan]

commission [kəmɪʃ'n] n 制作依頼 [seisaku irai]

commit [kəmɪt] v (crime) 犯す [okasu]

committee [kəmɪti] n 委員会 [iinkai]

common [kɒmən] adj 普通の [futsuu no]; **common sense** n 常識 [joushiki]

communicate [kəmyunɪkeɪt] v 伝える [tsutaeru]

communication [kəmyunɪkeɪʃ'n] n コミュニケーション [komyunikeeshon]

communion [kəmyunyən] n 共有 [kyouyuu]

communism [kɒmyənɪzəm] n 共産主義 [kyousanshugi]

communist [kɒmyənɪst] adj 共産主義の [kyousanshugi no] ▸ n 共産主義者 [kyousanshugisha]

community [kəmyunɪti] n 地域社会 [chiiki shakai]

commute [kəmyut] v 通勤する [tsuukin suru]

commuter [kəmyutər] n 通勤者 [tsuukinsha]

compact [kəmpækt] adj ぎっしり詰まった [gisshiri tsumatta]; **compact disc** n コンパクトディスク [konpakuto disuku]

companion [kəmpænyən] n 仲間 [nakama]

company [kʌmpəni] n 会社 [kaisha], 弊社 [heisha]; **company car** n 社用車 [shayousha]; **I'd like some information about the company** 会社についての情報を教えていただきたいのですが [kaisha ni tsuite no jouhou o oshiete itadakitai no desu ga]

comparable [kɒmpərəbˈl] adj 匹敵する [hitteki suru]

comparatively [kəmpærətɪvli] adv 比較的 [hikakuteki]

compare [kəmpɛər] v 比較する [hikaku suru]

comparison [kəmpærɪsən] n 比較 [hikaku]

compartment [kəmpɑrtmənt] n コンパートメント [konpaatomento]

compass [kʌmpəs] n コンパス [konpasu]

compatible [kəmpætɪbˈl] adj 両立できる [ryouritsu dekiru]

compensate [kɒmpənseɪt] v 補償する [hoshou suru]

compensation [kɒmpənseɪʃ'n] n 賠償金 [baishoukin], 補償 [hoshou]

compete [kəmpit] v 競争する [kyousou suru]

competent [kɒmpɪtənt] adj 有能な [yuunou na]

competition [kɒmpɪtɪʃ'n] n 競争 [kyousou]

competitive [kəmpɛtɪtɪv] adj 競争的な [kyousouteki na]

competitor [kəmpɛtɪtər] n 競争者 [kyousousha]

complain [kəmpleɪn] v 不平を言う [fuhei wo iu]

complaint [kəmpleɪnt] n 不平 [fuhei], 苦情 [kujou]; **I'd like to make a complaint** 苦情があるのですが [kujou ga aru no desu ga];

Where can I make a complaint? 誰に苦情を言えばいいのですか？ [dare ni kujou o ieba ii no desu ka?]

complementary [kɒmplɪmɛntəri, -mɛntri] *adj* 補完的な [hokanteki na]

complete [kəmplit] *adj* 全くの [mattaku no]

completely [kəmplitli] *adv* 全く [mattaku]; **I want a completely new style** 全く新しいスタイルにしてください [mattaku atarashii sutairu ni shite kudasai]

complex *adj* [kɒmplɛks] 複合の [fukugou no] ▷ *n* [kɒmplɛks] 複合体 [fukugoutai], 団地 [danchi]

complexion [kəmplɛkʃn] *n* 顔色 [kaoiro]

complicated [kɒmplɪkeɪtɪd] *adj* 複雑な [fukuzatsu na]

complication [kɒmplɪkeɪʃn] *n* 複雑な要因 [fukuzatsu na youin]

compliment *n* [kɒmplɪmənt] ほめことば [homekotoba] ▷ *v* [kɒmplɪmɛnt] ほめる [homeru]

complimentary [kɒmplɪmɛntəri, -mɛntri] *adj* 称賛の [shousan no]

component [kəmpoʊnənt] *adj* 構成している [kousei shite iru] ▷ *n* 構成要素 [kousei youso]

composer [kəmpoʊzər] *n* 作曲家 [sakkyokuka]

composition [kɒmpəzɪʃn] *n* 構成 [kousei]

comprehension [kɒmprɪhɛnʃn] *n* 理解 [rikai]

comprehensive [kɒmprɪhɛnsɪv] *adj* 総合的な [sougouteki na]

compromise [kɒmprəmaɪz] *n* 妥協 [dakyou] ▷ *v* 妥協する [dakyou suru]

compulsory [kəmpʌlsəri] *adj* 強制的な [kyouseiteki na]

computer [kəmpyutər] *n* コンピューター [konpyuutaa]; **computer game** *n* コンピューターゲーム [konpyuutaa geemu]; **computer science** *n* コンピューター科学 [konpyuutaa kagaku]; **May I use your computer?** あなたのコンピューターをお借りできますか？ [anata no konpyuutaa o o-kari dekimasu ka?]; **My**

computer has frozen 私のコンピューターがフリーズしました [watashi no konpyuutaa ga furiizu shimashita]; **Where is the computer room?** コンピューター室はどこですか？ [konpyuutaa-shitsu wa doko desu ka?]

computing [kəmpyutɪŋ] *n* 計算 [keisan]

conceited [kənsitɪd] *adj* うぬぼれた [unuboreta]

concentrate [kɒnsntreɪt] *v* 集中する [shuuchuu suru]

concentration [kɒnsntreɪʃn] *n* 集中 [shuuchuu]

concern [kənsɜrn] *n* 関心 [kanshin], 心配 [shinpai]

concerned [kənsɜrnd] *adj* 関係している [kankei shiteiru]

concert [kɒnsərt] *n* コンサート [konsaato]; **Are there any good concerts?** 何かよいコンサートがありますか？ [nani ka yoi konsaato ga arimasu ka?]; **What's on tonight at the concert hall?** コンサートホールでは今晩何をやっていますか？ [konsaato-hooru de wa konban nani o yatte imasu ka?]; **Where can I buy tickets for the concert?** どこでそのコンサートのチケットを買えますか？ [doko de sono konsaato no chiketto o kaemasu ka?]

concerto [kəntʃɛərtoʊ] *n* コンチェルト [koncheruto]

concession [kənsɛʃn] *n* 譲歩 [jouho]

concise [kənsaɪs] *adj* 簡潔な [kanketsu na]

conclude [kənklud] *v* 結論を出す [ketsuron-o dasu]

conclusion [kənkluʒn] *n* 結論 [ketsuron]

concrete [kɒnkrit] *n* コンクリート [konkuriito]

concussion [kənkʌʃn] *n* 脳震盪 [noushintou]

condemn [kəndɛm] *v* 非難する [hinan suru]

condensation [kɒndɛnseɪʃn] *n* 結露 [ketsuro]

condition [kəndɪʃn] *n* 状態 [joutai], 具合 [guai]; **What are the snow conditions?** 雪の状態はどんなですか？ [yuki no joutai wa donna desu ka?]

conditional [kəndɪʃənl] *adj* 条件付きの

[joukentsuki no]

conditioner [kəndɪʃənər] *n* コンディショナー [kondeishonaa]; **Do you sell conditioner?** コンディショナーを売っていますか? [kondishonaa o utte imasu ka?]

condom [kɒndəm] *n* コンドーム [kondoomu]

conduct *v* 行う [okonau]

conductor [kəndʌktər] *n* 指揮者 [shikisha]; **bus conductor** *n* バスの車掌 [basu no shashou]

cone [koʊn] *n* 円錐形のもの [ensuikei no mono]

conference [kɒnfərəns, -frəns] *n* 会議 [kaigi]; **press conference** *n* 記者会見 [kishakaiken]

confess [kənfɛs] *v* 自白する [jihaku suru]

confession [kənfɛʃn] *n* 自白 [jihaku], 白状 [hakujou]

confetti [kənfɛti] *npl* 紙吹雪 [kamifubuki]

confidence [kɒnfɪdəns] *n* 革新 [kakushin], *(secret)* 秘密 [himitsu], *(self-assurance)* 自信 [jishin], *(trust)* 信頼 [shinrai]

confident [kɒnfɪdənt] *adj* 確信して [kakushin shite]

confidential [kɒnfɪdɛnʃl] *adj* 内密の [naimitsu no]

confirm [kənfɜrm] *v* 確認する [kakunin suru]

confirmation [kɒnfərmeɪʃn] *n* 確認 [kakunin]

confiscate [kɒnfɪskeɪt] *v* 没収する [bosshuu suru]

conflict *n* 衝突 [shoutotsu]

confuse [kənfyuz] *v* 困惑させる [konwaku saseru]

confused [kənfyuzd] *adj* 当惑した [touwaku shita]

confusing [kənfyuzɪŋ] *adj* 困惑させる [konwaku saseru]

confusion [kənfyuʒn] *n* 混乱状態 [konranjoutai], 混同 [kondou]

congestion [kəndʒɛstʃn] *n* 密集 [misshuu]

Congo [kɒŋoʊ] *n* コンゴ [kongo]

congratulate [kəngrætʃəleɪt] *v* 祝う [iwau]

congratulations [kəngrætʃəleɪʃnz] *npl* おめでとう [omedetou]

conifer [kɒnɪfər] *n* 針葉樹 [shin-youju]

conjugation [kɒndʒəgeɪʃn] *n* 語形変化 [gokei henka]

conjunction [kəndʒʌŋkʃn] *n* 結合 [ketsugou]

connection [kənɛkʃn] *n* 関係 [kankei]

conquer [kɒŋkər] *v* 征服する [seifuku suru]

conscience [kɒnʃns] *n* 良心 [ryoushin]

conscientious [kɒnʃiɛnʃəs] *adj* 念入りな [nen'iri na]

conscious [kɒnʃəs] *adj* 意識がある [ishiki ga aru]

consciousness [kɒnʃəsnɪs] *n* 意識 [ishiki]

consecutive [kənsɛkyətɪv] *adj* 連続的な [renzokuteki na]

consensus [kənsɛnsəs] *n* コンセンサス [konsensasu]

consequence [kɒnsɪkwɛns, -kwəns] *n* 結果 [kekka]

conservation [kɒnsərveɪʃn] *n* 保全 [hozen]

conservative [kənsɜrvətɪv] *adj* 保守的な [hoshuteki na]

conservatory [kənsɜrvətɔri] *n* コンサーバトリー [konsaabatorii]

consider [kənsɪdər] *v* みなす [minasu]

considerate [kənsɪdərɪt] *adj* 思いやりのある [omoiyari no aru]

consist [kənsɪst] *v* **consist of** *v* ⋯から成る [... kara naru]

consistent [kənsɪstənt] *adj* 一貫した [ikkan shita]

consonant [kɒnsənənt] *n* 子音 [shiin]

conspiracy [kənspɪrəsi] *n* 陰謀 [inbou]

constant [kɒnstənt] *adj* 絶えず続く [taezu tsuzuku]

constantly [kɒnstəntli] *adv* 絶えず [taezu]

constipated [kɒnstɪpeɪtɪd] *adj* 便秘した [benpi shita]

constipation [kɒnstɪpeɪʃn] *n* 便秘 [benpi]

constituency [kənstɪtʃuənsi] *n* 選挙区 [senkyoku]

constitution [kɒnstɪtuʃn] *n* 憲法 [kenpou]

construct [kənstrʌkt] *v* 建設する [kensetsu suru]

construction [kənstrʌkʃⁿn] *n* 建設 [kensetsu];
    construction site *n* 建設現場 [kensetsu
    genba]

constructive [kənstrʌktɪv] *adj* 建設的な
    [kensetsuteki na]

consul [kɒnsⁿl] *n* 領事 [ryouji]

consulate [kɒnsəlɪt] *n* 領事館 [ryoujikan]

consult [kənsʌlt] *v* 相談する [soudan suru]

consumer [kənsumər] *n* 消費者 [shouhisha]

contact [kɒntækt] *n* 連絡 [renraku]▷*v* 連絡を
    取る [renraku-o toru]; **contact lenses** *npl* コ
    ンタクトレンズ [kontakutorenzu]; **Where can
    I contact you?** どこであなたに連絡を取れま
    すか? [doko de anata ni renraku o toremasu
    ka?]; **Who do we contact if there are
    problems?** 問題があったときに誰に連絡すれ
    ばいいのですか? [mondai ga atta toki ni
    dare ni renraku sureba ii no desu ka?]

contagious [kənteɪdʒəs] *adj* 伝染性の
    [densensei no]

contain [kənteɪn] *v* 含む [fukumu]

container [kənteɪnər] *n* 容器 [youki]; **glass
    recycling container** *n* 空き瓶回収ボックス
    [akikan kaishuu bokkusu]

contemporary [kəntɛmpərɛri] *adj* 現代の
    [gendai no]

contempt [kəntɛmpt] *n* 軽蔑 [keibetsu]

content [kɒntɛnt] *n* 中身 [nakami]

contents ['kɒntɛntz] *npl* 目次 [mokuji]

contest *n* 競争 [kyousou]

contestant [kəntɛstənt] *n* 競争者
    [kyousousha]

context [kɒntɛkst] *n* 状況 [joukyou]

continent [kɒntɪnənt] *n* 大陸 [tairiku]

continual [kəntɪnyuəl] *adj* 継続的な
    [keizokuteki na]

continually [kəntɪnyuəli] *adv* 継続的に
    [keizokuteki ni]

continue [kəntɪnyu] *vi* 続く [tsuzuku]▷ *vt* 続
    ける [tsuzukeru]

continuous [kəntɪnyuəs] *adj* 連続的な
    [renzokuteki na]

contraception [kɒntrəsɛpⁿn] *n* 避妊 [hinin]; **I**

need contraception 私は避妊が必要です
    [watashi wa hinin ga hitsuyou desu]

contraceptive [kɒntrəsɛptɪv] *n* 避妊具
    [hiningu]

contract *n* 契約 [keiyaku]

contractor [kɒntræktər, kɒntræk-] *n* 契約人
    [keiyakunin]

contradict [kɒntrədɪkt] *v* 反駁する [hanbaku
    suru]

contradiction [kɒntrədɪkʃⁿn] *n* 反駁
    [hanbaku]

contrary [kɒntrɛri] *n* 正反対 [seihantai]

contrast *n* 相違 [soui]

contribute [kəntrɪbyut] *v* 寄付する [kifu suru]

contribution [kɒntrɪbyuʃⁿn] *n* 寄付 [kifu]

control [kəntroʊl] *n* 支配 [shihai]▷*v* 支配する
    [shihai suru]; **birth control** *n* 避妊 [hinin];
    passport control *n* パスポート審査窓口
    [pasupooto shinsa madoguchi]; **remote
    control** *n* リモコン [rimokon]

controller [kəntroʊlər] *n* **air-traffic
    controller** *n* 航空管制官 [koukuu kanseikan]

controls *npl* 制御装置 [seigyosouchi]

controversial [kɒntrəvɜrʃⁿl] *adj* 論争の
    [ronsou no]

convenient [kənvinyənt] *adj* 便利 [benri], 都
    合のよい [tsugou no yoi], 便利な [benri na]

convent [kɒnvɛnt, -vⁿnt] *n* 女子修道院
    [joshishuudouin]

conventional [kənvɛnʃənⁿl] *adj* 慣例にのっと
    った [kanrei ni nottotta]

conversation [kɒnvərseɪʃⁿn] *n* 会話 [kaiwa]

convert *v* 変える [kaeru]; **catalytic
    converter** *n* 触媒コンバーター [shokubai
    konbaataa]

convertible [kənvɜrtɪbⁿl] *adj* 変えられる
    [kaerareru]▷*n* コンバーティブル [kon-
    baateiburu]

convict *v* 有罪と決定する [yuuzai to kettei
    suru]

convince [kənvɪns] *v* 確信させる [kakushin
    saseru]

convincing [kənvɪnsɪn] *adj* 説得力のある

[settokuryoku no aru]

convoy [kɒnvɔɪ] n 護衛されている輸送車隊 [goei sareteiru yusoushatai]

cook [kʊk] n 料理人 [ryourinin] ▷ v 料理する [ryouri suru]

cookbook [kʊkbʊk] n 料理の本 [ryouri no hon]

cookery [kʊkəri] n 料理法 [ryourihou]

cookie [kʊki] n ビスケット [bisuketto]

cooking [kʊkɪŋ] n 料理 [ryouri], 調理 [chouri]

cool [kul] adj (cold) 涼しい [suzushii], (stylish) かっこいい [kakkoii]

coolant [kulənt] n 冷却水 [reikyakusui]

cooperation [koʊɒpəreɪʃn] n 協力 [kyouryoku]

cop [kɒp] n 警官 [keikan]

cope [koʊp] v うまく対処する [umaku taisho suru]

copper [kɒpər] n 銅 [dou]

copy [kɒpi] n (reproduction) 複製 [fukusei], (written text) 原稿 [genkou] ▷ v 複製する [fukusei suru]

copyright [kɒpiraɪt] n 版権 [hanken]

coral [kɒrəl] n 珊瑚 [sango]

cord [kɔrd] n electric cord n 電気コード [denki koodo]; spinal cord n 脊髄 [sekizui]

cordless [kɔrdlɪs] adj コードレスの [koodoresu no]

corduroy [kɔrdərɔɪ] n コーデュロイ [koodeyuroi]

core [kɔr] n 芯 [shin]

coriander [kɔriændər] n (seed) コリアンダー [koriandaa]

cork [kɔrk] n コルク [koruku]

corkscrew [kɔrkskru] n コルク栓抜き [koruku sennuki]

corn [kɔrn] n トウモロコシ [toumorokoshi]

corner [kɔrnər] n 角 [kado], 角 [kado] (場所); It's around the corner その角を曲がったところです [sono kado o magatta tokoro desu]; It's on the corner その角です [sono kado desu]

cornet [kɔrnɛt] n コルネット [korunetto]

cornflakes [kɔrnfleɪks] npl コーンフレーク [koonfureeku]

cornstarch [kɔrnstɑrtʃ] n コーンフラワー [koonfurawaa]

corporal [kɔrpərəl, -prəl] n 伍長 [gochou]

corpse [kɔrps] n 死体 [shitai]

correct [kərɛkt] adj 正しい [tadashii] ▷ v 訂正する [teisei suru]

correction [kərɛkʃn] n 訂正 [teisei]; corrections officer n 看守 [kanshu]

correctly [kərɛktli] adv 正しく [tadashiku]

correspondence [kɔrɪspɒndəns] n 文通 [buntsuu]

correspondent [kɔrɪspɒndənt] n 文通者 [buntsuusha]

corridor [kɔrɪdər, -dɔr] n 廊下 [rouka]

corrupt [kərʌpt] adj 腐敗した [fuhai shita]

corruption [kərʌpʃn] n 腐敗行為 [fuhaikoui]

cosmetic [kɒzmɛtɪk] adj cosmetics bag n 洗面用具入れ [senmen yougu ire]

cosmetics [kɒzˈmɛtɪkz] npl 化粧品 [keshouhin]

cost [kɒst] n コスト [kosuto], 費用 [hiyou] ▷ v かかる [kakaru] (費用); cost of living n 生活費 [seikatsuhi]

Costa Rica [koʊstə rikə] n コスタリカ [kosutarika]

costume [kɒstum] n 身なり [minari], (party) 仮装服 [kasoufuku]

cot [kɒt] n キャンプベッド [kyanpubeddo]

cottage [kɒtɪdʒ] n 田舎屋 [inakaya]; cottage cheese n カッテージチーズ [katteeji chiizu]

cotton [kɒtən] n 脱脂綿 [dasshimen], 綿 [men]; cotton candy n 綿菓子 [watagashi]; cotton swab n 綿棒 [menbou]

couch [kaʊtʃ] n カウチソファー [kauchisofaa], 背付きの長椅子 [setsuki no nagaisu]

cough [kɒf] n 咳 [seki] ▷ v 咳をする [seki-o suru]; cough syrup n 咳止め薬 [sekidome-gusuri]; I have a cough 私は咳がでます [watashi wa seki ga demasu]

council [kaʊnsl] n 審議会 [shingikai]; council member n 地方議会議員 [chihou gikai giin]

count [kaʊnt] v 数える [kazoeru]

counter [kaʊntər] n カウンター [kauntaa]

counterclockwise [kaʊntərklɒkwaɪz] adv 左回りに [hidari mawari ni]

count on v ···に頼る [... ni tayoru]

country [kʌntri] n 国 [kuni]; **developing country** n 発展途上国 [hattentojoukoku]; **Where can I buy a map of the country?** どこでその国の地図を買えますか? [doko de sono kuni no chizu o kaemasu ka?]

countryside [kʌntrisaɪd] n 田舎 [inaka]

couple [kʌp·l] n カップル [kappuru]

courage [kɜrɪdʒ] n 勇気 [yuuki]

courageous [kəreɪdʒəs] adj 勇気のある [yuuki no aru]

courier [kʊəriər, kɜr-] n 急使 [kyuushi]

course [kɔrs] n コース [koosu], 過程 [katei]; **golf course** n ゴルフ場 [gorufujou]; **main course** n メインコース [meinkoosu]; **refresher course** n 再教育コース [saikyouiku koosu]; **training course** n トレーニングコース [toreeningukoosu]; **Is there a public golf course near here?** この近くに公共のゴルフコースはありますか? [kono chikaku ni kookyou no gorufu-koosu wa arimasu ka?]

court [kɔrt] n 法廷 [houtei]; **tennis court** n テニスコート [tenisukooto]

courtyard [kɔrtyɑrd] n 中庭 [nakaniwa]

cousin [kʌz·n] n いとこ [itoko]

cover [kʌvər] n 覆い [oui] ▷ v 覆う [oou]; **cover charge** n カバーチャージ [kabaa chaaji]

coverage [kʌvərɪdʒ] n **How much extra is comprehensive insurance coverage?** 総合自動車保険に加入する追加料金はいくらですか? [sougou-jidousha-hoken ni kanyuu suru tsuika-ryoukin wa ikura desu ka?]

cow [kaʊ] n 雌牛 [meushi]

coward [kaʊərd] n 臆病者 [okubyoumono]

cowardly [kaʊərdli] adj 臆病な [okubyou na]

cowboy [kaʊbɔɪ] n カウボーイ [kaubooi]

cozy [koʊzi] adj 居心地のよい [igokochi no yoi]

crab [kræb] n カニ [kani]

crack [kræk] n (cocaine) クラック [kurakku], (fracture) 割れ目 [wareme] ▷ v 割れる [wareru]; **crack down on** v ···に断固たる措置を取る [... ni dankotaru sochi-o toru]

cracked [krækt] adj ひびの入った [hibi no haitta]

cracker [krækər] n クラッカー [kurakkaa]

cradle [kreɪd·l] n 揺りかご [yurikago]

craft [kræft] n 熟練職業 [jukuren shokugyou]

craftsman [kræftsmən] n 職人 [shokunin]

cram [kræm] v 詰め込む [tsumekomu], (study) ガリ勉する [gariben suru]

crammed [kræmd] adj 詰め込んだ [tsumekonda]

cranberry [krænbɛri] n クランベリー [kuranberii]

crane [kreɪn] n (bird) ツル [tsuru] (鳥), (for lifting) クレーン [kureen]

crash [kræʃ] vi 衝突する [shoutotsu suru]

crawl [krɔl] v 這う [hau]

crayfish [kreɪfɪʃ] n ザリガニ [zarigani]

crayon [kreɪɒn] n クレヨン [kureyon]

crazily [kreɪzɪli] adv 気違いのように [kichigai no youni]

crazy [kreɪzi] adj 無茶な [mucha na], (insane) 気の狂った [kino kurutta]

cream [krim] adj クリーム色の [kuriimuiro no] ▷ n クリーム [kuriimu]; **ice cream** n アイスクリーム [aisukuriimu]; **shaving cream** n シェービングクリーム [sheebingukuriimu]; **whipped cream** n ホイップクリーム [hoippukuriimu]

crease [kris] n 折り目 [orime]

creased [krist] adj 折り目をつけた [orime-o tsuketa]

create [krieɪt] v 創造する [souzou suru]

creation [krieɪʃ·n] n 創造 [souzou]

creative [krieɪtɪv] adj 創造的な [souzouteki na]

Creator n 造り主 [tsukurinushi]

credentials [krɪdɛnʃ·lz] npl 信用を保証するもの [shin'you-o hoshou suru mono]

credible [krɛdɪb*ᵊl*] *adj* 信用できる [shinyou dekiru]

credit [krɛdɪt] *n* 信用販売 [shinyou hanbai], クレジット [kurejitto]; **credit card** *n* クレジットカード [kurejittokaado]; **Can I pay by credit card?** クレジットカードで支払えますか? [kurejitto-kaado de shiharaemasu ka?]; **Do you take credit cards?** クレジットカードは使えますか? [kurejitto-kaado wa tsukaemasu ka?]

creepy [kripi] *adj* 薄気味悪い [usukimiwarui]

crematorium [krɛmətɔːriəm, krɛmə-] *n* 火葬場 [kasouba]

cress [krɛs] *n* コショウソウ [koshousou]

crew [kruː] *n* 乗組員 [norikumiin]; **crew cut** *n* クルーカット [kuruukatto]

crib [krɪb] *n* 小児用ベッド [shouni you beddo]

cricket [krɪkɪt] *n* (*game*) クリケット [kurikketto], (*insect*) コオロギ [koorogi]

crime [kraɪm] *n* 犯罪 [hanzai]

criminal [krɪmɪn*ᵊl*] *adj* 犯罪の [hanzai no] ▷ *n* 犯人 [hannin], 犯罪者 [hanzaisha]

crisis [kraɪsɪs] *n* 重大局面 [juudai kyokumen]

crisp [krɪsp] *adj* パリパリした [paripari shita]

crispy [krɪspi] *adj* パリパリする [paripari suru]

criterion, criteria [kraɪtɪəriən, kraɪtɪəriə] *n* 基準 [kijun]

critic [krɪtɪk] *n* 批評家 [hihyouka]

critical [krɪtɪk*ᵊl*] *adj* 重大な [juudai na]

criticism [krɪtɪsɪzəm] *n* 批判 [hihan]

criticize [krɪtɪsaɪz] *v* 批判する [hihan suru]

Croatia [krouˈeɪʃə] *n* クロアチア [kuroachia]

Croatian [krouˈeɪʃən] *adj* クロアチアの [kuroachia no] ▷ *n* (*language*) クロアチア語 [kuroachiago], (*person*) クロアチア人 [kuroachiajin]

crochet [krouˈʃeɪ] *v* かぎ針編みをする [kagiamibari-o suru]

crocodile [krɒkədaɪl] *n* ワニ [wani]

crocus [kroukəs] *n* クロッカス [kurokkasu]

crook [krʊk] *n* 湾曲 [wankyoku]

crooked [krʊkɪd] *adj* (*dishonest*) 不正直な [fushoujiki na]

crop [krɒp] *n* 収穫 [shuukaku]

cross [krɔs] *adj* 不機嫌な [fukigen na] ▷ *n* 十字形 [juujigata] ▷ *v* 横切る [yokogiru]; **Red Cross** *n* 赤十字社 [Sekijuujisha]

cross-country [krɔskʌntri] *n* クロスカントリー [kurosukantorii]; **I want to rent cross-country skis** クロスカントリースキーの板を借りたいのですが [kurosukantorii-sukii no ita o karitai no desu ga]; **Is it possible to go cross-country skiing?** クロスカントリースキーに行くことは可能ですか? [kurosukantorii-sukii ni iku koto wa kanou desu ka?]

crossing [krɔsɪŋ] *n* 交差点 [kousaten]; **pedestrian crossing** *n* 横断歩道 [oudanhodou]; **pelican crossing** (*crosswalk*) *n* 押しボタン信号式横断歩道 [oshibotan shingoushiki oudanhodou]; **railroad crossing** *n* 踏切 [fumikiri]; **zebra crossing** (*crosswalk*) *n* 太い白線の縞模様で示した横断歩道 [futoi hakusen no shimamoyou de shimeshita oudanhodou]

cross out *v* 帳消しにする [choukeshi ni suru]

crossroads [krɔsroudz] *n* 交差路 [kousaro]

crosswalk [krɔswɔk] *n* 横断歩道 [oudanhodou]

crossword puzzle [krɔswɜrd pʌzᵊl] *n* クロスワードパズル [kurosuwaadopazuru]

crouch [kraʊtʃ] *v* うずくまる [uzukumaru]

crow [krou] *n* カラス [karasu]

crowd [kraʊd] *n* 群集 [gunshuu]

crowded [kraʊdɪd] *adj* 込み合った [komiatta]

crown [kraʊn] *n* 王冠 [oukan]

crucial [kruʃᵊl] *adj* 重大な [juudai na]

crucifix [krusɪfɪks] *n* 十字架 [juujika]

crude [krud] *adj* 粗雑な [sozatsu na]

cruel [kruəl] *adj* 残酷な [zankoku na]

cruelty [kruəlti] *n* 残酷 [zankoku]

cruise [kruz] *n* 巡航 [junkou]

crumb [krʌm] *n* パン粉 [panko]

crush [krʌʃ] *v* 押しつぶす [oshitsubusu]

crutch [krʌtʃ] *n* 松葉杖 [matsubadue]

cry [kraɪ] *n* 泣き叫ぶ声 [nakisakebu koe] ▷ *v* 泣く [naku]

crystal [krɪstᵊl] *n* 水晶 [suishou]

cub [kʌb] *n* 野獣の子 [yajuu no ko]

Cuba [kyubə] *n* キューバ [kyuuba]

Cuban [kyubən] *adj* キューバの [kyuuba no] ▷ *n* キューバ人 [kyuubajin]

cube [kyub] *n* 立方体 [rippoutai]; **bouillon cube** *n* 固形スープの素 [kokei suupu no moto]; **ice cube** *n* アイスキューブ [aisukyuubu]

cubic [kyubɪk] *adj* 立方の [rippou no]

cuckoo [kuku, kuku] *n* カッコウ [kakkou]

cucumber [kyukʌmbər] *n* キュウリ [kyuuri]

cuddle [kʌdᵊl] *n* 抱擁 [houyou] ▷ *v* 抱きしめる [dakishimeru]

cue [kyu] *n* キュー [kyuu]

cufflinks [kʌflɪŋks] *npl* カフスリンク [kafusurinku]

culprit [kʌlprɪt] *n* 犯罪者 [hanzaisha]

cultural [kʌltʃərəl] *adj* 文化の [bunka no]

culture [kʌltʃər] *n* 文化 [bunka]

cumin [kʌmɪn, kumɪn] *n* クミン [kumin]

cunning [kʌnɪŋ] *adj* 狡猾な [koukatsu na]

cup [kʌp] *n* カップ [kappu]; **World Cup** *n* ワールドカップ [waarudokappu]

cupboard [kʌbərd] *n* 戸棚 [todana], 食器棚 [shokkidana]

curb [kɜrb] *n* 拘束 [kousoku], 縁石 [fuchiishi]

cure [kyuər] *n* 治療 [chiryou] ▷ *v* 治す [naosu]

curfew [kɜrfyu] *n* 門限 [mongen], 夜間外出禁止令 [yakan gaishutsu kinshirei]; **Is there a curfew?** 門限はありますか? [mongen wa arimasu ka?]

curious [kyuəriəs] *adj* 知りたがる [shiritagaru]

curl [kɜrl] *n* 巻き毛 [makige]

curler [kɜrlər] *n* カーラー [kaaraa]

curly [kɜrli] *adj* 巻き毛の [makige no]

currant [kɜrənt] *n* 小粒の種なし干しブドウ [kotsubu no tanenashi hoshibudou]; **black currant** *n* クロスグリ [kurosuguri]; **red currant** *n* 赤スグリ [aka suguri]

currency [kɜrənsi] *n* 通貨 [tsuuka]; **currency exchange counter** *n* 外貨両替所 [gaika ryougaesho]

current [kɜrənt] *adj* 現在の [genzai no] ▷ *n* (electricity) 電流 [denryuu], (flow) 流れ [nagare]; **current affairs** *npl* 時事問題 [jiji mondai]

currently [kɜrəntli] *adv* 目下 [meshita] (今)

curriculum [kərɪkyələm] *n* カリキュラム [karikyuramu]

curry [kɜri] *n* カレー料理 [karee ryouri]; **curry powder** *n* カレー粉 [kareeko]

curse [kɜrs] *n* ののしり [nonoshiri]

cursor [kɜrsər] *n* カーソル [kaasoru]

curtain [kɜrtᵊn] *n* カーテン [kaaten]

cushion [kʊʃᵊn] *n* クッション [kusshon]

custard [kʌstərd] *n* **custard sauce** *n* カスタード [kasutaado]

custody [kʌstədi] *n* 保護 [hogo]

custom [kʌstəm] *n* 慣例 [kanrei], 風習 [fuushuu]

customer [kʌstəmər] *n* 顧客 [kokyaku], 客 [kyaku]

customized [kʌstəmaɪzd] *adj* カスタマイズされた [kasutamaizu sareta]

customs [kʌstəmz] *npl* 関税 [kanzei]; **customs officer** *n* 税関係官 [zeikan kakarikan]

cut [kʌt] *n* 切断 [setsudan] ▷ *v* 切る [kiru]; **crew cut** *n* クルーカット [kuruukatto]

cutback [kʌtbæk] *n* 縮小 [shukushou]

cut down *v* 伐り倒す [kiritaosu]

cute [kyut] *adj* かわいい [kawaii]

cutlet [kʌtlɪt] *n* 薄い肉片 [usui nikuhen]

cut off *v* 切り離す [kirihanasu]

cut up *v* 切り分ける [kiriwakeru]

CV [si vi] *abbr* 履歴書 [rirekisho]

cybercafé [saɪbərkæfeɪ] *n* サイバーカフェ [saibaakafe]

cybercrime [saɪbərkraɪm] *n* サイバー犯罪 [saibaa hanzai]

cycle [saɪkᵊl] *n* (recurring period) 周期 [shuuki] ▷ *v* 自転車に乗る [jitensha ni noru]

cycling [saɪklɪŋ] *n* サイクリング [saikuringu]; **Let's go cycling** サイクリングに行きましょう

[saikuringu ni ikimashou]; **We'd like to go cycling** 私たちはサイクリングに行きたいのですが [watashi-tachi wa saikuringu ni ikitai no desu ga]

cyclist [saɪklɪst] *n* サイクリスト [saikurisuto]

cyclone [saɪkloun] *n* サイクロン [saikuron]

cylinder [sɪlɪndər] *n* 円筒 [entou]; **portable gas cylinder** *n* キャンプ用ガス [kyanpu you gasu]

cymbals [sɪmbəlz] *npl* シンバル [shinbaru]

Cypriot [sɪpriət] *adj* キプロスの [kipurosu no] ▷ *n* (*person*) キプロス人 [kipurosujin]

Cyprus [saɪprəs] *n* キプロス [kipurosu]

cyst [sɪst] *n* 嚢胞 [nouhou]

cystitis [sɪstaɪtɪs] *n* 膀胱炎 [boukouen]

Czech [tʃɛk] *adj* チェコの [cheko no] ▷ *n* (*language*) チェコ語 [cheko go], (*person*) チェコ人 [chekojin]; **Czech Republic** *n* チェコ共和国 [Cheko kyouwakoku]

D

dad [dæd] *n* パパ [papa]

daddy [dædi] *n* パパ [papa]

daffodil [dæfədɪl] *n* ラッパズイセン [rappazuisen]

daily [deɪli] *adj* 毎日の [mainichi no] ▷ *adv* 毎日 [mainichi]

dairy [dɛəri] *n* 乳製品販売店 [nyuuseihin hanbaiten]; **dairy products** *npl* 乳製品 [nyuuseihin]

daisy [deɪzi] *n* ヒナギク [hinagiku]

dam [dæm] *n* ダム [damu]

damage [dæmɪdʒ] *n* 損傷 [sonshou], 破損 [hason] ▷ *v* 損傷する [sonshou suru]

damaged [dæmɪdʒd] *adj* **My luggage has been damaged** 私の手荷物が破損しています [watashi no tenimotsu ga hason shite imasu]; **My suitcase has arrived damaged** 着いた私のスーツケースが破損しています [tsuita watashi no suutsukeesu ga hason shite imasu]

damn [dæm] *adj* いまいましい [imaimashii]

damp [dæmp] *adj* 湿気のある [shikke no aru]

dance [dæns] *n* ダンス [dansu] ▷ *v* 踊る [odoru]; **Would you like to dance?** ダンスはいかがですか? [dansu wa ikaga desu ka?]

dancer [dænsər] *n* ダンサー [dansaa]

dancing [dænsɪŋ] *n* 踊ること [odoru koto]; **ballroom dancing** *n* 社交ダンス [shakou dansu]

dandelion [dændɪlaɪən] *n* タンポポ [tanpopo]

dandruff [dændrəf] *n* ふけ [fuke]

Dane [deɪn] *n* デンマーク人 [denmaakujin]

danger [deɪndʒər] *n* 危険 [kiken]; **Is there a danger of avalanches?** なだれの危険はありますか? [nadare no kiken wa arimasu ka?]

dangerous [deɪndʒərəs, deɪndʒrəs] *adj* 危険な [kiken na]

Danish [deɪnɪʃ] *adj* デンマークの [denmaaku no] ▷ *n (language)* デンマーク語 [denmaakugo]

dare [dɛər] *v* 思い切って・・・する [omoikitte... suru]

daring [dɛərɪŋ] *adj* 思い切った [omoikitta]

dark [dɑrk] *adj* 暗い [kurai] ▷ *n* 闇 [yami]; **dark chocolate** *n* ブラックチョコレート [burakku chokoreeto]; **It's dark** 暗いです [kurai desu]

darkness [dɑrknɪs] *n* 暗さ [kurasa]

darling [dɑrlɪŋ] *n* いとしい人 [itoshii hito]

dart [dɑrt] *n* ダーツ用の投げ矢 [daatsu you no nageya]

darts [dɑrts] *npl* ダーツ [daatsu]

dash [dæʃ] *v* 突進する [tosshin suru]

dashboard [dæʃbɔrd] *n* ダッシュボード [dasshuboodo]

data [deɪtə, dætə] *npl* データ [deeta]

database [deɪtəbeɪs, dætə-] *n* データベース [deetabeesu]

date [deɪt] *n* 日付 [hiduke]; **best-if-used-by date** *n* 賞味期限 [shoumikigen]; **expiration date** *n* 使用期限 [shiyou kigen]; **sell-by date** *n* 販売期限 [hanbai kigen]

datebook [deɪtbuk] *n (appointments)* 日記 [nikki]

daughter [dɔtər] *n* 娘 [musume]; **My daughter is lost** 娘の姿が見当たりません [musume no sugata ga miatarimasen]; **My daughter is missing** 私の娘が行方不明です [watashi no musume ga yukue-fumei desu]

daughter-in-law *(pl* **daughters-in-law)** *n* 息子の妻 [musuko no tsuma]

dawn [dɔn] *n* 夜明け [yoake]

day [deɪ] *n* 一日 [tsuitachi], 日 [nichi]; **Valentine's Day** *n* 聖バレンタインの祭日 [sei barentain no saijitsu]; **Do you run day trips to...?** ···に行く日帰りツアーを実施していますか? [... ni iku higaeri-tsuaa o jisshi shite imasu ka?]; **I want to rent a car for five days** 車を5日間借りたいのですが [kuruma o itsuka-kan karitai no desu ga]; **Is the museum open every day?** その博物館は毎日開いていますか? [sono hakubutsukan wa mainichi hiraite imasu ka?]; **What a beautiful day!** なんてすばらしい日でしょう! [nante subarashii hi deshou!]; **What day is it today?** 今日は何曜日ですか? [kyou wa nani-youbi desu ka?]; **What's the dish of the day?** 今日のおすすめ料理は何ですか? [kyou no osusume ryouri wa nan desu ka?]

daytime [deɪtaɪm] *n* 昼間 [hiruma]

dead [dɛd] *adj* 死んだ [shinda]; **dead end** *n* 行き止まり [ikidomari]

deadline [dɛdlaɪn] *n* 締切り期限 [shimekiri kigen]

deaf [dɛf] *adj* 耳の聞こえない [mimi no kikoenai]

deafening [dɛfənɪŋ] *adj* 耳を聾するような [mimi-o rousuru you na]

deal [diːl] *n* 取引 [torihiki]

dealer [diːlər] *n* ディーラー [diiraa]; **drug dealer** *n* 麻薬ディーラー [mayaku diiraa]; **fish dealer** *n* 魚屋 [sakanaya]

deal with *v* 扱う [atsukau]

dear [dɪər] *adj (loved)* 親愛な [shin'ai na]

death [dɛθ] *n* 死 [shi]

debate [dɪbeɪt] *n* 討論 [touron] ▷ *v* 討論する [touron suru]

debit [dɛbɪt] *n* デビット [debitto], 借方 [karikata] ▷ *v* 借方に記入する [karikata ni kinyuu suru]; **debit card** *n* デビットカード [debitto kaado]; **direct debit** *n* 口座引き落とし [kouza hikiotoshi]; **Do you take debit cards?** デビットカードは使えますか? [debitto-kaado wa tsukaemasu ka?]

debt [dɛt] *n* 借金 [shakkin]

decade [dɛkeɪd] *n* 十年間 [juunenkan]

decaffeinated [dikæfɪneɪtɪd, -kæfiə-] *adj* カフェイン抜きの [kafein nuki no]; **decaffeinated coffee** *n* カフェイン抜きのコーヒー [kafein nuki no koohii]

decay [dɪkeɪ] *n* 腐敗 [fuhai] ▷ *v* 衰える [otoroeru]

deceive [dɪsiːv] *v* だます [damasu]

December [dɪsɛmbər] *n* 十二月 [juunigatsu]; **on Friday, December thirty-first** 十二月三十一日の金曜日に [juuni-gatsu sanjuuichi-nichi no kinyoubi ni]

decide [dɪsaɪd] *v* 決定する [kettei suru]

decimal [dɛsɪm·l] *adj* 十進法の [jusshinhou no]

decision [dɪsɪʒ·n] *n* 決定 [kettei]

decisive [dɪsaɪsɪv] *adj* 決定的な [ketteiteki na]

deck [dɛk] *n* デッキ [dekki]; **Can we go out on deck?** デッキに出られますか? [dekki ni deraremasu ka?]; **How do I get to the car deck?** カーデッキへはどう行けばいいのですか? [kaa-dekki e wa dou ikeba ii no desu ka?]

deck chair *n* デッキチェア [dekkichea]

declare [dɪklɛər] *v* 断言する [dangen suru]

decorate [dɛkəreɪt] *v* 装飾する [soushoku suru]

decrease *n* [dɪkriːs] 減少 [genshou] ▷ *v* [dɪkriːs] 減少する [genshou suru]

dedicated [dɛdɪkeɪtɪd] *adj* 専用の [sen'you no]

dedication [dɛdɪkeɪʃ·n] *n* 献身 [kenshin]

deduct [dɪdʌkt] *v* 差し引く [sashihiku]

deep [diːp] *adj* 深い [fukai]

deep-fry *v* 油で揚げる [abura de ageru]

deeply [diːpli] *adv* 深く [fukaku]

deer [dɪər] *n* シカ [shika]

defeat [dɪfiːt] *n* 負け [make] ▷ *v* 負かす [makasu]

defect *n* 欠陥 [kekkan]

defend [dɪfɛnd] *v* 防御する [bougyo suru]

defendant [dɪfɛndənt] *n* 被告人 [hikokunin]

defender [dɪfɛndər] *n* 防御者 [bougyosha]

defense [dɪfɛns] *n* 防御 [bougyo]

deficit [dɛfəsɪt] *n* 欠損 [kesson]

define [dɪfaɪn] *v* 定義する [teigi suru]

definite [dɛfɪnɪt] *adj* 明確な [meikaku na]

definitely [dɛfɪnɪtli] *adv* 明確に [meikaku ni]

definition [dɛfɪnɪʃən] *n* 定義 [teigi]

degree [dɪgriː] *n* 程度 [teido]; **degree centigrade** *n* 摂氏温度 [sesshi ondo]; **degree Celsius** *n* 摂氏温度 [sesshi ondo]; **degree Fahrenheit** *n* 華氏温度 [kashi ondo]

dehydrated [dihaɪdreɪtɪd] *adj* 乾燥の [kansou no]

de-icer [deɪt] *n* 除氷装置 [johyou souchi]

delay [dɪleɪ] *n* 遅れ [okure] ▷ *v* 遅れる [okureru]

delayed [dɪleɪd] *adj* 遅れた [okureta]

delegate *n* [dɛlɪgɪt] 代表 [daihyou] ▷ *v* [dɛlɪgeɪt] 代表として派遣する [daihyou toshite haken suru]

delete [dɪliːt] *v* 削除する [sakujo suru]

deliberate *adj* 故意の [koi no]

deliberately [dɪlɪbərtli] *adv* 故意に [koi ni]

delicate [dɛlɪkɪt] *adj* 優美な [yuubi na]

delicatessen [dɛlɪkətɛsən] *n* デリカテッセン [derikatessen]

delicious [dɪlɪʃəs] *adj* 美味しい [oishii]

delight [dɪlaɪt] *n* 大喜び [ooyorokobi]

delighted [dɪlaɪtɪd] *adj* 大喜びの [ooyorokobi no]

delightful [dɪlaɪtfəl] *adj* 楽しい [tanoshii]

deliver [dɪlɪvər] *v* 配達する [haitatsu suru]

delivery [dɪlɪvəri] *n* 配達 [haitatsu]

demand [dɪmænd] *n* 要求 [youkyuu] ▷ *v* 要求する [youkyuu suru]

demanding [dɪmændɪŋ] *adj* 要求の厳しい [youkyuu no kibishii]

demo [dɛmoʊ] *n* デモ [demo]

democracy [dɪmɒkrəsi] *n* 民主主義 [minshushugi]

democratic [dɛməkrætɪk] *adj* 民主主義の [minshu shugi no]

demolish [dɪmɒlɪʃ] *v* 取り壊す [torikowasu]

demonstrate [dɛmənstreɪt] *v* 立証する [risshou suru]

demonstration [dɛmənstreɪʃən] *n* デモ [demo]

demonstrator [dɛmənstreɪtər] *n* デモンストレーター [demonsutoreeetaa]

denim [dɛnɪm] *n* デニム [denimu]

Denmark [dɛnmɑrk] *n* デンマーク [denmaaku]

dense [dɛns] *adj* 密集した [misshuu shita]

density [dɛnsɪti] *n* 密集 [misshuu]

dent [dɛnt] *n* へこみ [hekomi] ▷ *v* へこむ [hekomu]

dental [dɛntəl] *adj* 歯の [ha no]; **dental floss** *n* デンタルフロス [dentaru furosu]

dentist [dɛntɪst] *n* 歯科医 [shikai], 歯医者 [haisha]; **I need a dentist** 私は歯医者さんに診てもらわなければなりません [watashi wa haisha-san ni mite morawanakereba narimasen]

dentistry [dɛntɪstri] *n* 歯科 [shika]

dentures [dɛntʃərz] *npl* 入れ歯 [ireba]; **Can you repair my dentures?** 私の入れ歯を修理してもらえますか? [watashi no ireba o shuuri shite moraemasu ka?]

deny [dɪnaɪ] *v* 否定する [hitei suru]

deodorant [dioʊdərənt] *n* デオドラント [deodoranto]

depart [dɪpɑrt] *v* 出発する [shuppatsu suru]

department [dɪpɑrtmənt] *n* 部門 [bumon]; **department store** *n* デパート [depaato]; **lost-and-found department** *n* 遺失物取扱所 [ishitsubutsu toriatsukaijo]

departure [dɪpɑrtʃər] *n* 出発 [shuppatsu]; **departure lounge** *n* 出発ラウンジ [shuppatsu raunji]

depend [dɪpɛnd] *v* あてにする [ate ni suru]

deport [dɪpɔrt] *v* 国外退去させる [kokugai taikyo saseru]

deposit [dɪpɒzɪt] *n* 保証金 [hoshoukin], 預金 [yokin]; **Can I have my deposit back, please?** 保証金を返していただけますか? [hoshoukin o kaeshite itadakemasu ka?];

How much is the deposit? 保証金はいくらですか? [hoshoukin wa ikura desu ka?]

depravity [dɪprǽvɪti] n 堕落 [daraku]

depressed [dɪprɛ́st] adj 意気消沈した [ikishouchin shita]

depressing [dɪprɛ́sɪŋ] adj 憂鬱な [yuuutsu na]

depression [dɪprɛ́ʃn] n 憂鬱 [yuuutsu]

depth [dɛpθ] n 深さ [fukasa]

descend [dɪsɛ́nd] v 降りる [oriru]

describe [dɪskráɪb] v 記述する [kijutsu suru]

description [dɪskrɪ́pʃn] n 記述 [kijutsu]

desert n 砂漠 [sabaku]; **desert island** n 無人島 [mujintou]

deserve [dɪzɜ́rv] v ···に値する [···ni atai suru]

design [dɪzáɪn] n デザイン [dezain]▷v デザインする [dezain suru]

designer [dɪzáɪnər] n デザイナー [dezainaa]; **interior designer** n インテリアデザイナー [interiadezainaa]

desire [dɪzáɪər] n 希望 [kibou]▷v 希望する [kibou suru]

desk [dɛsk] n 机 [tsukue]; **information desk** n 照会デスク [shoukai desuku]; **May I use your desk?** あなたの机をお借りできますか? [anata no tsukue o o-kari dekimasu ka?]

despair [dɪspɛ́ər] n 絶望 [zetsubou]

desperate [dɛ́spərɪt] adj 必死の [hisshi no]

desperately [dɛ́spərtli] adv 必死で [hisshi de]

despise [dɪspáɪz] v 軽蔑する [keibetsu suru]

dessert [dɪzɜ́rt] n デザート [dezaato], プディング [pudingu], 甘いもの [amai mono]; **dessert spoon** n デザートスプーン [dezaato supuun]; **The dessert menu, please** デザートのメニューをください [dezaato no menyuu o kudasai]; **We'd like dessert** 私たちはデザートをいただきます [watashi-tachi wa dezaato o itadakimasu]

destination [dɛstɪnéɪʃn] n 目的地 [mokutekichi]

destiny [dɛ́stɪni] n 運命 [unmei]

destroy [dɪstrɔ́ɪ] v 破壊する [hakai suru]

destruction [dɪstrʌ́kʃn] n 破壊 [hakai]

detail [díteɪl] n 細部 [saibu]

detailed [díteɪld] adj 詳細な [shousai na]

detainment n 被収 [hi shuu]

detective [dɪtɛ́ktɪv] n 刑事 [keiji]

detention [dɪtɛ́nʃn] n 拘留 [kouryuu]

detergent [dɪtɜ́rdʒənt] n 洗剤 [senzai]; **laundry detergent** n 粉末洗剤 [funmatsusenzai], 粉石鹸 [kona sekken]

deteriorate [dɪtɪ́əriəreɪt] v 悪化する [akka suru]

determined [dɪtɜ́rmɪnd] adj 断固とした [danko to shita]

detour [dítuər] n 回り道 [mawarimichi], *(road)* 迂回路 [ukairo]; **Is there a detour?** 迂回路はありますか? [ukairo wa arimasu ka?]

devaluation [dívælyueɪʃn] n 平価切下げ [heikakirisage]

devastated [dɛ́vəsteɪtɪd] adj 打ちのめされた [uchinomesareta]

devastating [dɛ́vəsteɪtɪŋ] adj さんざんな [sanzan na]

develop [dɪvɛ́ləp] vi 発展する [hatten suru]▷vt 発展させる [hatten saseru]; **developing country** n 発展途上国 [hattentojoukoku]

development [dɪvɛ́ləpmənt] n 発展 [hatten]

device [dɪváɪs] n 気 [ki], 装置 [souchi]

devil [dɛ́vl] n 悪魔 [akuma]

devise [dɪváɪz] v 考案する [kouan suru]

devoted [dɪvóʊtɪd] adj 献身的な [kenshinteki na]

diabetes [daɪəbítɪs, -tiz] n 糖尿病 [tounyoubyou]

diabetic [daɪəbɛ́tɪk] adj 糖尿病の [tounyoubyou no]▷n 糖尿病患者 [tounyoubyoukanja]

diagnosis [daɪəgnóʊsɪs] n 診断 [shindan]

diagonal [daɪǽgənl, -ægnl] adj 対角の [taikaku no]

diagram [daɪəgrǽm] n 図 [zu]

dial [daɪəl] v ダイヤルする [daiyaru suru]; **dial tone** n 発信音 [hasshin-on]

dialect [daɪəlɛkt] n 方言 [hougen]

dialogue [daɪəlɔg] n 対話 [taiwa]

diameter [daɪæmɪtər] n 直径 [chokkei]

diamond [daɪmənd, daɪə-] n ダイヤモンド [daiyamondo]

diaper [daɪpər, daɪə-] n おむつ [omutsu]

diarrhea [daɪəriə] n 下痢 [geri]; **I have diarrhea** 私は下痢しています [watashi wa geri shite imasu]

dice [daɪs] npl さいころ [saikoro]

dictation [dɪkteɪʃᵊn] n 口述 [koujutsu]

dictator [dɪkteɪtər] n 独裁者 [dokusaisha]

dictionary [dɪkʃənɛri] n 次点 [jiten], 辞書 [jisho]

die [daɪ] v 死ぬ [shinu]

diesel [dizᵊl] n ディーゼルエンジン [diizeruenjin]

diet [daɪɪt] n ダイエット [daietto], 日常の食べ物 [nitchijou no tabemono] ▷ v ダイエットする [daietto suru]; **I'm on a diet** 私はダイエットしています [watashi wa daietto shite imasu]

difference [dɪfərəns, dɪfrəns] n 違い [chigai]

different [dɪfərənt, dɪfrənt] adj 違う [chigau]

difficult [dɪfɪkʌlt, -kəlt] adj 困難な [konnan na]

difficulty [dɪfɪkʌlti, -kəlti] n 困難 [konnan]

dig [dɪg] v 掘る [horu]

digest v 消化する [shouka suru]

digestion [daɪdʒɛstʃən] n 消化 [shouka]

digger [dɪgər] n 掘削機 [kussakuki]

digital [dɪdʒɪtᵊl] adj デジタルの [dejitaru no]; **digital camera** n デジタルカメラ [dejitaru kamera]; **digital radio** n デジタルラジオ [dejitaru rajio]; **digital television** n デジタルテレビ [dejitaru terebi]; **digital watch** n デジタル時計 [dejitaru tokei]

dignity [dɪgnɪti] n 威厳 [igen]

dilemma [dɪlɛmə] n ジレンマ [jirenma]

dilute [daɪlut] v 希釈する [kishaku suru]

diluted [daɪlutɪd] adj 希釈した [kishaku shita]

dim [dɪm] adj 薄暗い [usugurai]

dimension [dɪmɛnʃᵊn, daɪ-] n 寸法 [sunpou]

diminish [dɪmɪnɪʃ] v 減らす [herasu]

din [dɪn] n やかましい音 [yakamashii oto]

diner [daɪnər] n 食事する人 [shokuji suru hito]

dinghy [dɪŋgi] n ディンギー [deingii]

dining n ダイニング [dainingu]

dining car [daɪnɪn kar] n ビュッフェ車 [byuffesha]; **Is there a dining car on the train?** 電車にはビュッフェ車がありますか? [densha ni wa byuffe-sha ga arimasu ka?]; **Where is the dining car?** ビュッフェ車はどこですか? [byuffe-sha wa doko desu ka?]

dinner [dɪnər] n ディナー [deinaa]; **dinner jacket** n ディナージャケット [dinaa jaketto]; **dinner party** n ディナーパーティー [dinaa paatii]; **dinnertime** n ディナーの時刻 [dinaa no jikoku]

dinosaur [daɪnəsɔr] n 恐竜 [kyouryuu]

dip [dɪp] n (food/sauce) ディップソース [dippu sousu] ▷ v ちょっと浸す [chotto hitasu]

diploma [dɪploumə] n 免状 [menjou]

diplomat [dɪpləmæt] n 外交官 [gaikoukan]

diplomatic [dɪpləmætɪk] adj 外交上の [gaikoujou no]

dipstick [dɪpstɪk] n ディップスティック [dippu sutikku]

direct [dɪrɛkt, daɪ-] adj 率直な [sotchoku na] ▷ v 監督する [kantoku suru]; **direct debit** n 口座引き落とし [kouza hikiotoshi]

direction [dɪrɛkʃᵊn, daɪ-] n 方向 [houkou]

directions [dɪrɛkʃᵊnz] npl 指示 [shiji]

directly [dɪrɛktli, daɪ-] adv 直接に [chokusetsu ni]

director [dɪrɛktər, daɪ-] n 管理者 [kanrisha]; **funeral director** n 葬儀屋 [sougiya]

directory [dɪrɛktəri, daɪ-] n 住所氏名録 [juusho shimei roku]; **directory assistance** npl 番号案内サービス [bangou annai saabisu]; **telephone directory** n 電話帳 [denwachou]

dirt [dɜrt] n 汚物 [obutsu]

dirty [dɜrti] adj 汚れた [yogoreta]

disability [dɪsəbɪlɪti] n 身体障害 [shintaishougai]

disabled [dɪseɪbᵊld] *adj* 体の不自由な [karada no fujiyuu na] ▷ *npl* 身体障害者 [shintaishougaisha]; **Are there any restrooms for the disabled?** 身体障害者用のトイレはありますか? [shintai-shougaisha-you no toire wa arimasu ka?]; **Do you provide access for the disabled?** 身体障害者のためのスロープなどがありますか? [shintai-shougaisha no tame no suroopu nado ga arimasu ka?]; **Is there a discount for disabled people?** 身体障害者用の割引がありますか? [shintai-shougaisha-you no waribiki ga arimasu ka?]; **What facilities do you have for disabled people?** 身体障害者用のどんな設備をそなえていますか? [shintai-shougaisha-you no donna setsubi o sonaete imasu ka?]

disadvantage [dɪsədvæntɪdʒ] *n* 不利 [furi]

disagree [dɪsəgriː] *v* 意見が異なる [iken ga kotonaru]

disagreement [dɪsəgriːmənt] *n* 不和 [fuwa], 意見の相違 [iken no soui]

disappear [dɪsəpɪər] *v* 見えなくなる [mienaku naru]

disappearance [dɪsəpɪərəns] *n* 見えなくなること [mienaku naru koto]

disappoint [dɪsəpɔɪnt] *v* 失望させる [shitsubou saseru]

disappointed [dɪsəpɔɪntɪd] *adj* 失望した [shitsubou shita]

disappointing [dɪsəpɔɪntɪŋ] *adj* がっかりさせる [gakkari saseru]

disappointment [dɪsəpɔɪntmənt] *n* 失望 [shitsubou]

disaster [dɪzæstər] *n* 災害 [saigai]

disastrous [dɪzæstrəs] *adj* 大災害の [daisaigai no]

disc [dɪsk] *n* ディスク [disuku]; **compact disc** *n* コンパクトディスク [konpakuto disuku]; **disc jockey** *n* ディスクジョッキー [disukujokkii]; **slipped disc** *n* 椎間板ヘルニア [tsuikanban herunia]

discharge *v* **When will I be discharged?** 私、はいつ退院できますか? [watashi wa itsu taiin dekimasu ka?]

discipline [dɪsɪplɪn] *n* 規律 [kiritsu]

disclose [dɪsklouz] *v* 明らかにする [akiraka ni suru]

disco [dɪskou] *n* ディスコ [disuko]

disconnect [dɪskənekt] *v* 接続を断つ [setsuzoku-o tatsu]

discount [dɪskaunt] *n* 割引 [waribiki]; **student discount** *n* 学生割引 [gakusei waribiki]; **Are there any discounts for children?** 子供割引はありますか? [kodomo-waribiki wa arimasu ka?]; **Are there any discounts for groups?** 団体割引はありますか? [dantai-waribiki wa arimasu ka?]; **Are there any discounts for senior citizens?** 高齢者割引はありますか? [koureisha-waribiki wa arimasu ka?]; **Do you offer a discount for cash?** 現金で払うと割引がありますか? [genkin de harau to waribki ga arimasu ka?]; **Is there a discount for disabled people?** 身体障害者用の割引がありますか? [shintai-shougaisha-you no waribiki ga arimasu ka?]; **Is there a discount with this pass?** このパスで割引がありますか? [kono pasu de waribiki ga arimasu ka?]

discourage [dɪskɜrɪdʒ] *v* ・・・の勇気をくじく [... no yuuki-o kujiku]

discover [dɪskʌvər] *v* 発見する [hakken suru]

discovery [dɪskʌvəri] *n* 発見 [hakken]

discretion [dɪskrɛʃᵊn] *n* 分別 [bunbetsu]

discrimination [dɪskrɪmɪneɪʃᵊn] *n* 差別 [sabetsu]

discuss [dɪskʌs] *v* ・・・を話し合う [...-o hanashiau]

discussion [dɪskʌʃᵊn] *n* 討議 [tougi]

disease [dɪziːz] *n* 病気 [byouki]; **Alzheimer's disease** *n* アルツハイマー病 [arutsuhaimaa byou]

disembarking *n* 下船 [gesen]

disgrace [dɪsgreɪs] *n* 不名誉 [fumeiyo]

disgraceful [dɪsgreɪsfᵊl] *adj* 不名誉な

[fumeiyo na]

disguise [dɪsgaɪz] v 変装する [hensou suru]

disgusted [dɪsgʌstɪd] adj むかつく [mukatsuku] (腹が立つ)

disgusting [dɪsgʌstɪŋ] adj いやな [iya na], むかむかする [mukamuka suru] (腹が立つ)

dish [dɪʃ] n 皿 [sara]; **dish towel** n 布巾 [fukin]; **satellite dish** n 衛星放送用パラボラアンテナ [eisei housou you parabora antena]; **soap dish** n 石鹸入れ [sekken ire]; **wash the dishes** v 洗って片付ける [aratte katazukeru]; **washing the dishes** n 食器洗い [shokkiarai]

dishcloth [dɪʃklɔθ] n 布巾 [fukin]

dishonest [dɪsɒnɪst] adj 不正直な [fushoujiki na]

dishwasher [dɪʃwɒʃər] n 食器洗い機 [shokkiaraiki]

disinfectant [dɪsɪnfɛktənt] n 消毒剤 [shoudokuzai]

disk [dɪsk] n ディスク [disuku]; **disk drive** n ディスクドライブ [disukudoraibu]

diskette [dɪskɛt] n ディスケット [deisuketto]

dislike [dɪslaɪk] v 嫌う [kirau]

dismal [dɪzmᵊl] adj 陰気な [inki na]

dismiss [dɪsmɪs] v 解雇する [kaiko suru]

dismissal [dɪsmɪsᵊl] n 解雇 [kaiko]

disobedient [dɪsəbidiənt] adj 不従順な [fujuujun na]

disobey [dɪsəbeɪ] v ···に従わない [... ni shitagawanai]

dispenser [dɪspɛnsər] n 調剤師 [chouzaishi]

display [dɪspleɪ] n 展示 [tenji] ▷ v 展示する [tenji suru]

disposable [dɪspoʊzəbᵊl] adj 使い捨ての [tsukaisute no]

disqualify [dɪskwɒlɪfaɪ] v ···の資格を取り上げる [... no shikaku-o toriageru]

disrupt [dɪsrʌpt] v 混乱させる [konran saseru]

dissatisfaction [dɪssætɪsfækʃᵊn] n 不満 [fuman]

dissatisfied [dɪssætɪsfaɪd] adj 不満な [fuman na]

dissolution [dɪsəluʃᵊn] n 分解 [bunkai]

dissolve [dɪzɒlv] v 溶かす [tokasu]

distance [dɪstəns] n 距離 [kyori]

distant [dɪstənt] adj 離れた [hanareta]

distasteful [dɪsteɪstfʊl] adj 嫌い [kirai]

distillery [dɪstɪləri] n 蒸留所 [jouryuujo]

distinction [dɪstɪŋkʃᵊn] n 区別 [kubetsu]

distinctive [dɪstɪŋktɪv] adj 特徴的な [tokuchouteki na]

distinguish [dɪstɪŋgwɪʃ] v 区別する [kubetsu suru]

distract [dɪstrækt] v 注意をそらす [chuui-o sorasu]

distribute [dɪstrɪbyut] v 配る [kubaru]

distributor [dɪstrɪbyətər] n 卸売業者 [oroshiuri gyousha]

district [dɪstrɪkt] n 地区 [chiku]

disturb [dɪstɜrb] v 邪魔をする [jama-o suru]

ditch [dɪtʃ] n 溝 [mizo]

dive [daɪv] n 飛び込み [tobikomi] ▷ v 飛び込む [tobikomu]

diver [daɪvər] n 潜水夫 [sensuifu]

divide [dɪvaɪd] v 分ける [wakeru]

diving [daɪvɪŋ] n ダイビング [daibingu], 飛び込み [tobikomi]; **diving board** n 飛込台 [tobikomidai]; **scuba diving** n スキューバダイビング [sukyuubadaibingu]

division [dɪvɪʒᵊn] n 分裂 [bunretsu], 分割 [bunkatsu]

divorce [dɪvɔrs] n 離婚 [rikon]

divorced [dɪvɔrst] adj 離婚した [rikonshita]

dizzy [dɪzi] adj めまいがする [memai ga suru]

DJ [di dʒeɪ] abbr ディスクジョッキー [disukujokkii]

DNA [di ɛn eɪ] n DNA [dii enu ee]

do [də, STRONG du] v ···をする [...-o suru]

dock [dɒk] n ドック [dokku]

doctor [dɒktər] n 医 [i], 医者 [isha]; **family doctor** abbr 一般医 [ippan'i]; **Call a doctor!** 医者を呼んで! [isha o yonde!]; **I need a doctor** 私はお医者さんに診てもらわなければなりません [watashi wa o-isha-san ni mite morawanakereba narimasen]; **Is there a doctor who speaks English?** 英語を話せるお医者さんはいらっしゃいますか? [eigo o hanaseru o-isha-san wa irasshaimasu ka?]; **Please call the emergency doctor** 救急医を呼んでください [kyuukyuu-i o yonde kudasai]

document n 文書 [bunsho], 書類 [shorui]; **Here are my vehicle documents** 私の車両書類です [watashi no sharyou-shorui desu]; **I want to copy this document** この書類のコピーを取りたいのですが [kono shorui no kopii o toritai no desu ga]

documentary [dɒkyəmɛntəri, -tri] n ドキュメンタリー [dokyumentarii]

documentation [dɒkyəmɛnteɪʃn] n ドキュメンテーション [dokyumenteeshon]

documents [dɒkyəmɛntz] npl ドキュメント [dokyumento]

dodge [dɒdʒ] v さっと身をかわして避ける [satto mi-o kawashite sakeru]

dog [dɒg] n 犬 [inu]; **hot dog** n ホットドッグ [hottodokku]; **Seeing Eye® dog** n 盲導犬 [moudouken]

do-it-yourself [duɪtyɔrsɛlf] abbr 日曜大工 [nichiyoudaiku]

doll [dɒl] n 人形 [ningyou]

dollar [dɒlər] n ドル [doru]; **Do you take dollars?** ドルを使えますか? [doru o tsukaemasu ka?]

dolphin [dɒlfɪn] n イルカ [iruka]

domestic [dəmɛstɪk] adj 国内の [kokunai no]

Dominican Republic n ドミニカ共和国 [Dominika kyouwakoku]

domino [dɒmɪnoʊ] n ドミノ [domino]

dominoes [dɒmənoʊz] npl ドミノ [domino]

donate [doʊneɪt] v 寄付する [kifu suru]

done [dʌn] adj 終了した [shuuryou shita]

donkey [dɒŋki] n ロバ [roba]

donor [doʊnər] n ドナー [donaa]

door [dɔr] n ドア [doa]; **door handle** n ドアハンドル [doahandoru]; **Keep the door locked** ドアをロックしておいてください [doa o rokku

shite oite kudasai]; **The door handle has come off** ドアの取っ手が外れました [doa no totte ga hazuremashita]; **The door won't close** ドアが閉まりません [doa ga shimarimasen]; **The door won't lock** ドアに鍵がかかりません [doa ni kagi ga kakarimasen]; **The door won't open** ドアが開きません [doa ga akimasen]

doorbell [dɔrbɛl] n 玄関の呼び鈴 [genkan no yobisuzu]

doorman [dɔrmæn, -mən] n ドアマン [doaman]

door phone n インターホン [intaahon]

doorstep [dɔrstɛp] n 戸口の上がり段 [toguchi no agaridan]

dorm [dɔrm] n **Do you have any single sex dorms?** 男女別々の部屋はありますか? [danjo betsubetsu no heya wa arimasu ka?]

dormitory [dɔrmɪtɔri] n (large bedroom) 共同寝室 [kyoudoushinshitsu]

dose [doʊs] n 服用量 [fukuyouryou]

dot [dɒt] n 点 [ten] (符号)

double [dʌbl] adj 2倍の [nibai no] ▷ v 2倍にする [nibai ni suru]; **double bass** n コントラバス [kontorabasu]; **double bed** n ダブルベッド [daburubeddo]; **double room** n ダブルルーム [dabururuumu]

double-room n ダブルルーム [dabururuumu]

doubt [daʊt] n 疑い [utagai] ▷ v 疑う [utagau]

doubtful [daʊtfəl] adj 疑わしい [utagawashii]

dough [doʊ] n パン生地 [pankiji]

doughnut [doʊnʌt, -nət] n ドーナツ [doonatsu]

do up v 包む [tsutsumu]

dove [dʌv] n ハト [hato]

do without v ···なしで済ます [... nashide sumasu]

down [daʊn] adv 下へ [shita e]

download [daʊnloʊd] n ダウンロード [daunroodo] ▷ v ダウンロードする [daunroodo suru]; **Can I download photos to here?** ここに写真をダウンロードできますか? [koko ni shashin o daunroodo dekimasu ka?]

downpour [daʊnpɔr] *n* 土砂降り [doshaburi]

downstairs [daʊnstɛərz] *adj* 階下の [kaika no] ▷ *adv* 階下へ [kaika-e]

downtown [daʊntaʊn] *adv* 繁華街へ [hankagai-e]; **downtown area** *n* 街の中心部 [machi no chuushinbu], 町の中心部 [machi no chuushinbu]

doze [doʊz] *v* うたた寝する [utatane suru]

dozen [dʌʌn] *n* 12個 [juuniko]

doze off *v* まどろむ [madoromu]

drab [dræb] *adj* さえない [saenai]

draft [dræft] *n* 下書き [shitagaki], 隙間風 [sukimakaze]

drag [dræg] *v* 引っ張る [hipparu]

dragon [drægən] *n* 竜 [ryuu]

dragonfly [drægənflaɪ] *n* トンボ [tonbo]

drain [dreɪn] *n* 排水管 [haisuikan], 排水口 [haisuikou] ▷ *v* 排水する [haisui suru]; **The drain is blocked** 排水管が詰まっています [haisuikan ga tsumatte imasu]

drainboard [dreɪnbɔrd] *n* 水切り板 [mizukiriban]

drainpipe [dreɪnpaɪp] *n* 排水管 [haisuikan]

drama [drɑmə, dræmə] *n* 劇 [geki]

dramatic [drəmætɪk] *adj* 演劇の [engeki no]

drastic [dræstɪk] *adj* 思い切った [omoikitta]; **I don't want anything drastic** 思い切ったスタイルにしたくありません [omoikitta sutairu ni shitaku arimasen]

draw [drɔ] *n* くじ [kuji] (抽選) ▷ *v* (*sketch*) 描く [egaku]

drawback [drɔbæk] *n* 欠点 [ketten]

drawer [drɔr] *n* 引き出し [hikidashi]; **The drawer is jammed** 引き出しが動きません [hikidashi ga ugokimasen]

drawers [drɔrz] *n* **chest of drawers** *n* 整理だんす [seiridansu]

drawing [drɔɪŋ] *n* 図 [zu]

dreadful [drɛdfəl] *adj* 恐ろしい [osoroshii]

dream [drim] *n* 夢 [yume] ▷ *v* 夢を見る [yume wo miru]

drench [drɛntʃ] *v* びしょぬれにする [bishonure ni suru]

dress [drɛs] *n* ワンピース [wanpiisu] ▷ *v* 服を着る [fuku wo kiru]; **wedding dress** *n* ウェディングドレス [uedeingudoresu]; **May I try on this dress?** このワンピースを試着していいですか? [kono wanpiisu o shichaku shite ii desu ka?]

dressed [drɛst] *adj* 服を着た [fuku-o kita]

dressing [drɛsɪŋ] *n* **salad dressing** *n* サラダドレッシング [saradadoresshingu]

dressing table *n* **dressing table** *n* 鏡台 [kyoudai]

dress up *v* 盛装する [seisou suru]

dried [draɪd] *adj* 乾燥させた [kansou saseta]

drift [drɪft] *n* 押し流されるもの [oshinagasareru mono] ▷ *v* 漂流する [hyouryuu suru]

drill [drɪl] *n* ドリル [doriru] ▷ *v* 穴をあける [ana-o akeru]; **pneumatic drill** *n* 空気ドリル [kuukidoriru]

drink [drɪŋk] *n* 飲み物 [nomimono] ▷ *v* 飲む [nomu]; **binge drinking** *n* 飲み騒ぐこと [nomisawagu koto]; **drinking water** *n* 飲料水 [inryousui]; **soft drink** *n* ソフトドリンク [sofutodorinku]; **Can I get you a drink?** お飲み物を持ってきましょうか? [o-nomimono o motte kimashou ka?]; **The drinks are on me** 飲み物は私のおごりです [nomimono wa watashi no ogori desu]; **What is your favorite drink?** お好きな飲み物は何ですか? [o-suki na nomimono wa nan desu ka?]; **Would you like a drink?** お飲み物はいかがですか? [o-nomimono wa ikaga desu ka?]

drinking [drɪŋkɪŋ] *n* 飲酒 [inshu]

drip [drɪp] *v* したたる [shitataru]

drive [draɪv] *n* ドライブ [doraibu] ▷ *v* 運転する [unten suru]; **driving instructor** *n* 自動車教習指導員 [jidousha kyoushuu shidouin]; **drunk driving** *n* 飲酒運転 [inshu unten]; **four-wheel drive** *n* 四輪駆動 [yonrinkudou]; **left-hand drive** *n* 左側通行 [hidarigawa tsuukou]; **right-hand drive** *n* 右ハンドル [migi handoru]

driver [draɪvər] *n* 運転手 [untenshu]; **driver's license** *n* 運転免許証 [untenmenkyoshou];

driver's test *n* 運転免許試験 [untenmenky-oshiken]; **racecar driver** *n* レーシングドライバー [reeshingudoraibaa]; **student driver** *n* 仮免許運転者 [karimenkyo untensha]; **truck driver** *n* トラック運転手 [torakku untenshu]

driveway [draɪvweɪ] *n* 車道 [shadou]

driving [draɪvɪŋ] *n* 運転 [unten]

driving lesson *n* 自動車教習 [jidoushaky-oushuu]

drizzle [drɪzᵊl] *n* 霧雨 [kirisame]

drop [drɒp] *n* しずく [shizuku], したたり [shitatari] ▷ *v* 落ちる [ochiru]

drought [draʊt] *n* 日照り [hideri]

drown [draʊn] *v* 溺死する [dekishi suru]

drowsy [draʊzi] *adj* 眠い [nemui]

drug [drʌg] *n* 薬 [kusuri]; **drug addict** *n* 麻薬常用者 [mayaku jouyousha]; **drug dealer** *n* 麻薬ディーラー [mayaku diiraa]; **drugs** *npl* 薬剤 [yakuzai]

drugstore [drʌgstɔr] *n* **Where is the nearest drugstore?** 一番近い薬局はどこですか? [ichiban chikai yakkyoku wa doko desu ka?]

drum [drʌm] *n* ドラム [doramu]

drummer [drʌmər] *n* ドラマー [doramaa]

drunk [drʌŋk] *adj* 酔った [yotta] ▷ *n* 酔っぱらい [yopparai]; **drunk driving** *n* 飲酒運転 [inshu unten]

dry [draɪ] *adj* 乾燥した [kansou shita], ドライ [dorai] ▷ *v* 乾燥させる [kansou saseru]; **bone dry** *adj* ひからびた [hikarabita]; **A dry sherry, please** ドライシェリーをください [dorai-sherii o kudasai]

dry-cleaner's [draɪklinərz] *n* ドライクリーニング屋 [doraikuriininguya]

dry-cleaning [draɪklinɪŋ] *n* ドライクリーニング [doraikuriiningu]

dryer [draɪər] *n* 乾燥機 [kansouki]; **spin dryer** *n* 脱水機 [dassuiki]; **(clothes) dryer** *n* 回転式乾燥機 [kaitenshiki kansouki]

dubious [dubiəs] *adj* 怪しげな [ayashige na]

duck [dʌk] *n* アヒル [ahiru]

due [du] *adj* ···する予定で [... suru yotei de]

duffel bag [dʌfᵊl bæg] *n* 大型の旅行かばん [ougata no ryokou kaban]

dummy [dʌmi] *n* マネキン [manekin]

dump [dʌmp] *n* ごみ捨て場 [gomi suteba] ▷ *v* 投げ捨てる [nagesuteru]

dumpling [dʌmplɪŋ] *n* ダンプリング [danpuringu]

dune [dun] *n* **sand dune** *n* 砂丘 [sakyuu]

dungarees [dʌŋgəriz] *npl* ダンガリーのオーバーオール [dangari no oobaaooru]

dungeon [dʌndʒᵊn] *n* 地下牢 [chikarou]

duplex [duplɛks] *n* 二戸建て住宅 [nikodate juutaku]

durable [dʊərəbᵊl] *adj* 丈夫な [joubu na]

duration [dʊəreɪʃᵊn] *n* 持続期間 [jizoku kikan]

during [dʊərɪŋ] *prep* **during the summer** 夏の間 [natsu no aida]

dusk [dʌsk] *n* 夕暮れ [yuugure]

dust [dʌst] *n* ほこり [hokori] (ごみ) ▷ *v* ほこりを払う [hokori-o harau]

dustpan [dʌstpæn] *n* ちり取り [chiritori]

dusty [dʌsti] *adj* ほこりっぽい [hokorippoi]

Dutch [dʌtʃ] *adj* オランダの [oranda no] ▷ *n* オランダ人 [orandajin]

Dutchman [dʌtʃmən] (*pl* **Dutchmen**) *n* オランダ人男性 [orandajin dansei]

Dutchwoman [di:aʃər] (*pl* **Dutchwomen**) *n* オランダ人女性 [orandajin josei]

duty [duti] *n* 任務 [ninmu]

duty-free *adj* 免税の [menzei no]; **duty-free goods** *n* 免税品 [menzeihin]

DVD [di vi di] *n* DVD [dii bui dii]; **DVD burner** *n* DVDバーナー [dlibuidii baanaa]; **DVD player** *n* DVDプレーヤー [diibuidii pureiyaa]

dwarf [dwɔrf] *n* 小人 [kobito]

dwelling [dwɛlɪŋ] *n* **government-subsidized dwelling** *n* 公営住宅 [koueijuutaku]

dye [daɪ] *n* 染料 [senryou] ▷ *v* 染める [someru]

dynamic [daɪnæmɪk] *adj* 活動的な [katsudouteki na]

dyslexia [dɪslɛksiə] *n* 失読症 [shitsudokushou]

dyslexic [dɪslɛksɪk] *adj* 失読症の [shitsudokushou no] ▷ *n* 失読症の人 [shitsudokushou no hito]

E

eagle [igᵊl] n ワシ [washi]

ear [ɪər] n 耳 [mimi]

earache [ɪəreɪk] n 耳の痛み [mimi no itami]

eardrum [ɪərdrʌm] n 鼓膜 [komaku]

earlier [ɜrliər] adv 前に [mae ni]

early [ɜrli] adj 早い [hayai] ▷ adv 早く [hayaku]; **We arrived early / late** 私たちは早く／遅く着きました [watashi-tachi wa hayaku / osoku tsukimashita]

earn [ɜrn] v 稼ぐ [kasegu]

earnings [ɜrnɪŋz] npl 所得 [shotoku]

earphones [ɪərfoʊnz] npl イヤホン [iyahon]

earplugs [ɪərplʌgz] npl 耳栓 [mimisen]

earring [ɪərɪŋ] n イヤリング [iyaringu]

earth [ɜrθ] n 地球 [chikyuu]

earthquake [ɜrθkweɪk] n 地震 [jishin]

easily [izɪli] adv 容易に [youi ni]

east [ist] adj 東の [higashi no] ▷ adv 東へ [higashi e] ▷ n 東 [higashi]; **Far East** n 極東 [kyokutou]; **Middle East** n 中東 [chuutou]

eastbound [istbaʊnd] adj 東行きの [higashi yuki no]

Easter [istər] n 復活祭 [fukkatsusai]; **Easter egg** n 復活祭の卵 [Fukkatsusai no tamago]

eastern [istərn] adj 東の [higashi no]

easy [izi] adj 簡単な [kantan na]; **easy chair** n 安楽椅子 [anraku isu]

easygoing [izigoʊɪŋ] adj ゆったりとした [yuttarito shita]

eat [it] v 食べる [taberu]

e-book [ibʊk] n 電子書籍 [denshi shoseki]

eccentric [ɪksɛntrɪk] adj 風変わりな [fuugawari na]

echo [ɛkoʊ] n 反響 [hankyou]

ecofriendly [ikoʊfrɛndli] adj 環境にやさしい [kankyou ni yasashii]

ecological [ɛkəlɒdʒɪkᵊl, ik-] adj 生態学の [seitaigaku no]

ecology [ɪkɒlədʒi] n 生態学 [seitaigaku]

e-commerce [ikɒmɜrs] n Eコマース [iikomaasu]

economic [ɛkənɒmɪk, ik-] adj 経済の [keizai no]

economical [ɛkənɒmɪkᵊl, ik-] adj 経済的な [keizaiteki na]

economics [ɛkənɒmɪks, ik-] npl 経済学 [keizaigaku]

economist [ɪkɒnəmɪst] n 経済学者 [keizaigakusha]

economize [ɪkɒnəmaɪz] v 節約する [setsuyaku suru]

economy [ɪkɒnəmi] n 経済 [keizai]; **economy class** n エコノミークラス [ekonomiikurasu]

ecstasy [ɛkstəsi] n エクスタシー [ekusutashii]

Ecuador [ɛkwədɔr] n エクアドル [ekuadoru]

eczema [ɛksəmə, ɛgzə-, ɪgzi-] n 湿疹 [shisshin]

edge [ɛdʒ] n 端 [hashi]

edgy [ɛdʒi] adj いらいらした [irairashita]

edible [ɛdɪbᵊl] adj 食べられる [tabereraru]

edition [ɪdɪʃᵊn] n 版 [han]

editor [ɛdɪtər] n 編集者 [henshuusha]

educated [ɛdʒʊkeɪtɪd] adj 教育のある [kyouiku no aru]

education [ɛdʒʊkeɪʃᵊn] n 教育 [kyouiku]; **adult education** n 生涯教育 [shougai kyouiku]; **higher education** n 高等教育 [koutoukyouiku], (lower-level) 継続教育 [keizoku kyouiku]

educational [ɛdʒʊkeɪʃᵊnᵊl] adj 教育の [kyouiku no]

eel [il] *n* ウナギ [unagi]

effect [ɪfɛkt] *n* 影響 [eikyou]; **side effect** *n* 副作用 [fukusayou]

effective [ɪfɛktɪv] *adj* 効果的な [koukateki na]

effectively [ɪfɛktɪvli] *adv* 効果的に [koukateki ni]

efficient [ɪfɪʃnt] *adj* 効率的な [kouritsuteki na]

efficiently [ɪfɪʃntli] *adv* 効率的に [kouritsuteki ni]

effort [ɛfərt] *n* 努力 [doryoku]

egg [ɛg] *n* 卵 [tamago]; **egg white** *n* 卵の白身 [tamago no shiromi]; **egg yolk** *n* 卵の黄身 [tamago no kimi]; **Easter egg** *n* 復活祭の卵 [Fukkatsusai no tamago]; **hard-boiled egg** *n* ゆで卵 [yudetamago]; **scrambled eggs** *npl* 炒り卵 [iritamago]; **Could you prepare a meal without eggs?** 卵を使わずに食事を用意していただけますか? [tamago o tsukawazu ni shokuji o youi shite itadakemasu ka?]; **I can't eat raw eggs** 私は生卵を食べられません [watashi wa nama-tamago o taberaremasen]

eggcup [ɛgcʌp] *n* エッグカップ [eggukappu]

eggplant [ɛgplænt] *n* ナス [nasu]

Egypt [idʒɪpt] *n* エジプト [ejiputo]

Egyptian [idʒɪpʃn] *adj* エジプトの [ejiputo no] ▷ *n* エジプト人 [ejiputojin]

eight [eɪt] *number* 八 [hachi]

eighteen [eɪtin] *number* 十八 [juuhachi]

eighteenth [eɪtinθ] *adj* 十八番目の [juuhachi banme no]

eighth [eɪtθ] *adj* 八番目の [hachi banme no] ▷ *n* 八番目 [hachibanme]

eighty [eɪti] *number* 八十 [hachijuu]

Eire [ɛərə] *n* アイルランド [airurando]

either [iðər, aɪðər] *pron* **I don't like it either** それも好きではありません [sore mo suki de wa arimasen]

elbow [ɛlbou] *n* ひじ [hiji]

elder [ɛldər] *adj* 年上の [toshiue no]

elderly [ɛldərli] *adj* 年配の [nenpai no]

eldest [ɛldɪst] *adj* 最年長の [sainenchou no]

elect [ɪlɛkt] *v* 選挙する [senkyo suru]

election [ɪlɛkʃn] *n* 選挙 [senkyo]; **general election** *n* 総選挙 [sousenkyo]

electorate [ɪlɛktərət] *n* 選挙人 [senkyonin]

electric [ɪlɛktrɪk] *adj* 電気の [denki no]; **electric blanket** *n* 電気毛布 [denkimoufu]; **electric cord** *n* 電気コード [denki koodo]; **electric shock** *n* 感電 [kanden]

electrical [ɪlɛktrɪkl] *adj* 電気に関する [denki ni kansuru]

electrician [ɪlɛktrɪʃn, ilɛk-] *n* 電気技師 [denki gishi]

electricity [ɪlɛktrɪsɪti, ilɛk-] *n* 電気 [denki]; **Do we have to pay extra for electricity?** 電気代は別に払わなければなりませんか? [denki-dai wa betsu ni harawanakereba narimasen ka?]; **Is the cost of electricity included?** 電気代は含まれていますか? [denki-dai wa fukumarete imasu ka?]; **There's no electricity** 電気がきていません [denki ga kite imasen]; **Where's the electricity meter?** 電気のメーターはどこですか? [denki no meetaa wa doko desu ka?]

electronic [ɪlɛktrɒnɪk, i-] *adj* 電子 [denshi], 電子の [denshi no]

electronics [ɪlɛktrɒnɪks, i-] *npl* 電子工学 [denshikougaku]

elegant [ɛlɪgənt] *adj* 優雅な [yuuga na]

element [ɛlɪmənt] *n* 要素 [youso]

elementary [ɛlɪmɛntəri, -tri] *adj* **elementary school** *n* 小学校 [shougakkou]

elephant [ɛlɪfənt] *n* ゾウ [zou]

elevator [ɛlɪveɪtər] *n (up/down)* エレベーター [erebeetaa]; **Is there an elevator in the building?** 建物内にエレベーターはありますか? [tatemono-nai ni erebeetaa wa arimasu ka?]; **Where is the elevator?** エレベーターはどこですか? [erebeetaa wa doko desu ka?]

eleven [ɪlɛvn] *number* 十一 [juuichi]

eleventh [ɪlɛvnθ] *adj* 十一番目の [juuichi banme no]

eliminate [ɪlɪmɪneɪt] *v* 除去する [jokyo suru]

elm [ɛlm] *n* ニレ [nire]

elsewhere [ɛlswɛər] *adv* どこかよそで [dokoka yoso de]

e-mail [imeɪl] *n* 電子メール [denshi meeru] ▷ *v* 電子メールを送る [denshi meeru-o okuru]; **e-mail address** *npl* 電子メールアドレス [denshi meeru adoresu]

embankment [ɪmbæŋkmənt] *n* 堤防 [teibou]

embarassed *adj* 恥ずかしい [hazukashii]

embarrassed [ɪmbærəst] *adj* 当惑した [touwaku shita]

embarrassing [ɪmbærəsɪŋ] *adj* 当惑させるような [touwaku saseru you na]

embarrassment [ɪmbærəsmənt] *n* 困惑 [konwaku]

embassy [ɛmbəsi] *n* 大使館 [taishikan]; **I need to call my embassy** 私は大使館に電話をしなければなりません [watashi wa taishikan ni denwa o shinakereba narimasen]

embroider [ɪmbrɔɪdər] *v* 刺繍する [shishuu suru]

embroidery [ɪmbrɔɪdəri] *n* 刺繍 [shishuu]

emergency [ɪmɜrdʒənsi] *n* 緊急事態 [kinkyuujitai]; **emergency brake** *n* ハンドブレーキ [handobureeki]; **emergency exit** *n* 非常口 [hijouguchi]; **emergency landing** *n* 緊急着陸 [kinkyuu chakuriku]; **emergency room** *n* 救急病棟 [kyuukyuubyoutou]; **It's an emergency!** 緊急事態です! [kinkyuu-jitai desu!]

emigrate [ɛmɪgreɪt] *v* 移住する [ijuu suru]

emotion [ɪmoʊʃⁿ] *n* 感情 [kanjou]

emotional [ɪmoʊʃənⁿl] *adj* 感情の [kanjou no]

emperor, empress [ɛmpərər, ɛmprɪs] *n* 皇帝 [koutei]

emphasize [ɛmfəsaɪz] *v* 強調する [kyouchou suru]

empire [ɛmpaɪər] *n* 帝国 [teikoku]

employ [ɪmplɔɪ] *v* 雇用する [koyou suru]

employee [ɪmplɔɪi] *n* 従業員 [juugyouin]

employer [ɪmplɔɪər] *n* 雇用主 [koyounushi]

employment [ɪmplɔɪmənt] *n* 雇用 [koyou]; **employment office** *n* 公共職業安定所 [koukyoushokugyou anteisho]

empty [ɛmpti] *adj* 空の [kara no] ▷ *v* 空にする [kara ni suru]

enamel [ɪnæmⁿl] *n* エナメル [enameru]

encourage [ɪnkɜrɪdʒ] *v* 勇気づける [yuukidukeru]

encouragement [ɪnkɜrɪdʒmənt] *n* 奨励 [shourei], 励み [hagemi]

encouraging [ɪnkɜrɪdʒɪŋ] *adj* 励みになる [hagemi ni naru]

encyclopedia [ɪnsaɪkləpidiə] *n* 百科事典 [hyakka jiten]

end [ɛnd] *n* 終わり [owari] ▷ *v* 終わる [owaru]; **dead end** *n* 行き止まり [ikidomari]; **at the end of June** 六月の終わりに [roku-gatsu no owari ni]

endanger [ɪndeɪndʒər] *v* 危険にさらす [kiken ni sarasu]

ending [ɛndɪŋ] *n* 結末 [ketsumatsu]

endless [ɛndlɪs] *adj* 終わりのない [owari no nai]

enemy [ɛnəmi] *n* 敵 [teki]

energetic [ɛnərdʒɛtɪk] *adj* 精力的な [seiryokuteki na]

energy [ɛnərdʒi] *n* エネルギー [enerugii], 元気 [genki]

enfant *n* 小児 [shouni]

engaged [ɪngeɪdʒd] *adj* 婚約している [konyaku shiteiru]

engagement [ɪngeɪdʒmənt] *n* 約束 [yakusoku]; **engagement ring** *n* 婚約指輪 [konyaku yubiwa]

engine [ɛndʒɪn] *n* エンジン [enjin]; **search engine** *n* 検索エンジン [kensaku enjin]; **The engine is overheating** エンジンがオーバーヒートしています [enjin ga oobaahiito shite imasu]

engineer [ɛndʒɪnɪər] *n* 技師 [gishi]

engineering [ɛndʒɪnɪərɪŋ] *n* 工学 [kougaku]

England [ɪŋglənd] *n* イングランド [ingurando]

English [ɪŋglɪʃ] *adj* イングランドの

[inngurando no] ▷ *n* 英語 [eigo]; **Do you speak English?** あなたは英語を話しますか? [anata wa eigo o hanashimasu ka?]; **Does anyone speak English?** 誰か英語を話せる人はいますか? [dare ka eigo o hanaseru hito wa imasu ka?]; **I don't speak English** 私は英語を話せません [watashi wa eigo o hanasemasen]; **I speak very little English** 私は英語をほとんど話せません [watashi wa eigo o hotondo hanasemasen]

Englishman [ɪŋglɪʃmən] (*pl* **Englishmen**) *n* イングランド人男性 [ingurandojin dansei]

Englishwoman [ɪŋglɪʃwumən] (*pl* **Englishwomen**) *n* イングランド人女性 [ingurandojin josei]

engrave [ɪngreɪv] *v* 彫る [horu]

enjoy [ɪndʒɔɪ] *v* 楽しむ [tanoshimu]

enjoyable [ɪndʒɔɪəbəl] *adj* 楽しい [tanoshii]

enlargement [ɪnlɑrdʒmənt] *n* 拡大 [kakudai]

enormous [ɪnɔrməs] *adj* 巨大な [kyodai na]

enough [ɪnʌf] *adj* 十分 [juubun], 十分な [juubun na]

ensure [ɪnʃuər] *v* 保証する [hoshou suru]

enter [ɛntər] *v* 入る [hairu]

enterprise [ɛntərpraɪz] *n* 事業 [jigyou]

entertain [ɛntərteɪn] *v* 楽しませる [tanoshimaseru]

entertainer [ɛntərteɪnər] *n* エンターテイナー [entaateinaa]

entertaining [ɛntərteɪnɪŋ] *adj* 愉快な [yukai na]

entertainment [ɛntərteɪnmənt] *n* **What entertainment is there?** どんな娯楽がありますか? [donna goraku ga arimasu ka?]

enthusiasm [ɪnθuziæzəm] *n* 熱意 [netsui]

enthusiastic [ɪnθuziæstɪk] *adj* 熱心な [nesshin na]

entirely [ɪntaɪərli] *adv* 全く [mattaku]

entrance [ɛntrəns] *n* 入口 [iriguchi]; **Where's the wheelchair-accessible entrance?** 車椅子で利用できる入口はどこですか? [kuruma-isu de riyou dekiru iriguchi wa doko desu ka?]

entry [ɛntri] *n* 入口 [iriguchi]

envelope [ɛnvəloup, ɒn-] *n* 封筒 [fuutou]

envious [ɛnviəs] *adj* うらやましそうな [urayamashisouna]

environment [ɪnvaɪrənmənt, -vaɪərn-] *n* 環境 [kankyou]

environmental [ɪnvaɪrənmɛntəl, -vaɪərn-] *adj* 環境の [kankyou no]; **environmentally friendly** *adj* 環境にやさしい [kankyou ni yasashii]

envy [ɛnvi] *n* ねたみ [netami] ▷ *v* うらやむ [urayamu]

epidemic [ɛpɪdɛmɪk] *n* 流行病 [ryuukou-byou]

epileptic [ɛpɪlɛptɪk] *n* 癲癇患者 [tenkan kanja]; **epileptic seizure** *n* 癲癇の発作 [tenkan no hossa]

episode [ɛpɪsoud] *n* エピソード [episoodo]

equal [ikwəl] *adj* 等しい [hitoshii] ▷ *v* ···に等しい [... ni hitoshii]

equality [ɪkwɒlɪti] *n* 平等 [byoudou]

equalize [ikwəlaɪz] *v* 等しくする [hitoshiku suru]

equation [ɪkweɪʒən] *n* 等しくすること [hitoshiku suru koto]

equator [ɪkweɪtər] *n* 赤道 [sekidou]

Equatorial Guinea *n* 赤道ギニア [Sekidou Ginia]

equipment [ɪkwɪpmənt] *n* 装置 [souchi]

equipped [ɪkwɪpt] *adj* 備えた [sonaeta]

equivalent [ɪkwɪvələnt] *n* 同等のもの [doutou no mono]

era [ɪərə] *n* 時代 [jidai]

erase [ɪreɪs] *v* 消す [kesu] (*消去*)

Eritrea [ɛrɪtreɪə] *n* エリトリア [eritoria]

erotic [ɪrɒtɪk] *adj* エロチックな [erochikku na]

error [ɛrər] *n* 間違い [machigai]

escalator [ɛskəleɪtər] *n* エスカレーター [esukareetaa]

escape [ɪskeɪp] *n* 逃亡 [toubou] ▷ *v* 逃げる [nigeru]; **fire escape** *n* 非常階段 [hijoukaidan]

escort *v* 護衛する [goei suru]

especially [ɪspɛʃli] *adv* 特に [toku ni]

espionage [ɛspiɑnɑʒ] *n* スパイ行為 [supai koui]

essay [ɛseɪ] *n* エッセイ [essei]

essential [ɪsɛnʃl̩] *adj* 最も重要な [mottomo juuyou na]

estate [ɪsteɪt] *n* 地所 [jisho]; **real estate agent** *n* 不動産屋 [fudousanya]

estimate *n* [ɛstɪmɪt] 見積もり [mitsumori] ▷ *v* [ɛstɪmeɪt] 見積もる [mitsumoru]

Estonia [ɛstoʊniə] *n* エストニア [esutonia]

Estonian [ɛstoʊniən] *adj* エストニアの [esutonia no] ▷ *n* (*language*) エストニア語 [esutoniago], (*person*) エストニア人 [esutoniajin]

etc. [ɛt sɛtərə, -sɛtrə] *abbr* ・・・など [... nado]

eternal [ɪtɜrn l̩] *adj* 永遠の [eien no]

eternity [ɪtɜrnɪti] *n* 永遠性 [eiensei]

ethical [ɛθɪkl̩] *adj* 倫理的な [rinriteki na]

Ethiopia [iθioʊpiə] *n* エチオピア [echiopia]

Ethiopian [iθioʊpiən] *adj* エチオピアの [echiopia no] ▷ *n* エチオピア人 [echiopiajin]

ethnic [ɛθnɪk] *adj* 民族の [minzoku no]

e-ticket [itɪkɪt] *n* Eチケット [iichiketto]

EU [i yu] *abbr* EU [iiyuu]

euro [yʊəroʊ] *n* ユーロ [yuro]

Europe [yʊərəp] *n* ヨーロッパ [yooroppa]

European [yʊərəpiən] *adj* ヨーロッパの [yooroppa no] ▷ *n* ヨーロッパ人 [yooroppajin]; **European Union** *n* 欧州連合 [OUshuu Rengou]

evacuate [ɪvækyueɪt] *v* 避難させる [hinan saseru]

eve [iv] *n* 前夜 [zenya]

even [ivn̩] *adj* 平らな [taira na] ▷ *adv* ・・・でさえ [... de sae]

evening [ivnɪŋ] *n* 晩 [ban]; **in the evening** 晩に [ban ni]; **The table is reserved for nine o'clock this evening** 今晩九時にテーブルを予約しました [konban ku-ji ni teeburu o yoyaku shimashita]; **What are you doing this evening?** 今晩のご予定は? [konban no go-yotei wa?]; **What is there to do in the evenings?** 晩にできることは何がありますか? [ban ni dekiru koto wa nani ga arimasu ka?]

event [ɪvɛnt] *n* イベント [ibento], 出来事 [dekigoto]; **Which sporting events can we go to?** 私たちはどのスポーツイベントに行けますか? [watashi-tachi wa dono supootsu-ibento ni ikemasu ka?]

eventful [ɪvɛntfəl] *adj* 出来事の多い [dekigoto no oui]

eventually [ɪvɛntʃuəli] *adv* ついに [tsuini]

ever [ɛvər] *adv* 今までに [ima made ni]

every [ɛvri] *pron* **The bus runs every twenty minutes** バスは二十分おきに出ています [basu wa nijup-pun oki ni dete imasu]

everywhere [ɛvriwɛər] *adv* どこでも [dokodemo]

evidence [ɛvɪdəns] *n* 証拠 [shouko]

evil [ivl̩] *adj* 悪い [warui]

evolution [ivəluʃ n̩, ɛv-] *n* 発展 [hatten]

ewe [yu] *n* 雌羊 [mehitsuji]

exact [ɪgzækt] *adj* 正確な [seikaku na]

exactly [ɪgzæktli] *adv* 正確に [seikaku ni]

exaggerate [ɪgzædʒəreɪt] *v* 大げさに言う [oogesa ni iu]

exaggeration [ɪgzædʒəreɪʃn̩] *n* 誇張 [kochou]

exam [ɪgzæm] *n* 試験 [shiken]; **exam proctor** *n* 試験監督者 [shiken kantokusha]

examination [ɪgzæmɪneɪʃn̩] *n* 試験 [shiken]

examine [ɪgzæmɪn] *v* 試験する [shiken suru]

examiner [ɪgzæmɪnər] *n* 試験官 [shikenkan]

example [ɪgzæmpl̩] *n* 例 [rei], 模範 [mohan]

excellent [ɛksələnt] *adj* すばらしい [subarashii]

exception [ɪksɛpʃn̩] *n* 例外 [reigai]

exceptional [ɪksɛpʃən l̩] *adj* 例外的な [reigaiteki na]

excess *n* 超過 [chouka]

excessive [ɪksɛsɪv] *adj* 度を超えた [do-o koeta]

exchange [ɪkstʃeɪndʒ] *n* 為替 [kawase] ▷ *v* 取り交わす [torikawasu]; **currency exchange**

counter n 外貨両替所 [gaika ryougaesho];
exchange rate n 為替レート [kawase reeto];
foreign-exchange rate n 為替レート
[kawase reeto]; **stock exchange** n 証券取引
所 [shouken torihikijo]; **What's the**
exchange rate? 為替レートはいくらですか?
[kawase-reeto wa ikura desu ka?]

excited [ɪksaɪtɪd] adj 興奮した [koufun shita]

exciting [ɪksaɪtɪŋ] adj 興奮させる [koufun
saseru]

exclude [ɪksklud] v 除外する [jogai suru]

exclusively [ɪksklusɪvli] adv もっぱら
[moppara]

excuse n [ɪkskyus] 弁解 [benkai] ▷ v
[ɪkskyuz] 弁解する [benkai suru]

execute [ɛksɪkyut] v 処刑する [shokei suru]

execution [ɛksɪkyuʃən] n 処刑 [shokei]

executive [ɪgzɛkyətɪv] n エグゼクティブ
[eguzekuteibu]

exercise [ɛksərsaɪz] n 運動 [undou] (身体)

exhaust [ɪgzɔst] n **The exhaust is broken**
エキゾーストが壊れています [ekizoosuto ga
kowarete imasu]

exhausted [ɪgzɔstɪd] adj 疲れきった
[tsukarekitta]

exhibition [ɛksɪbɪʃən] n 展示 [tenji]

ex-husband n 先夫 [senpu]

exile [ɛksaɪl, ɛgz-] n 追放 [tsuihou]

exist [ɪgzɪst] v 存在する [sonzai suru]

exit [ɛgzɪt, ɛksɪt] n 出口 [deguchi];
emergency exit n 非常口 [hijouguchi];
Where is the exit? 出口はどこですか?
[deguchi wa doko desu ka?]; **Which exit**
for...? ···へ行く出口はどれですか? [... e iku
deguchi wa dore desu ka?]

exotic [ɪgzɒtɪk] adj エキゾチックな
[ekizochikku na]

expect [ɪkspɛkt] v 期待する [kitai suru]

expedition [ɛkspɪdɪʃən] n 探検 [tanken]

expel [ɪkspɛl] v 追い出す [oidasu]

expenditure [ɪkspɛndɪtʃər] n 支出
[shishutsu]

expense [ɪkspɛns] n 費 [hi]

expenses [ɪkspɛnsɪz] npl 経費 [keihi]

expensive [ɪkspɛnsɪv] adj 高価な [kouka na]

experience [ɪkspɪəriəns] n 経験 [keiken];
work experience n 労働体験 [roudou
taiken]

experienced [ɪkspɪəriənst] adj 経験のある
[keiken no aru]

experiment n 実験 [jikken]

expert [ɛkspɜrt] n 専門家 [senmonka]

expiration [ɛkspɪreɪʃən] n **expiration date** n
使用期限 [shiyou kigen]

expire [ɪkspaɪər] v 期限が切れる [kigen ga
kireru]

explain [ɪkspleɪn] v 説明する [setsumei suru]

explanation [ɛkspləneɪʃən] n 説明 [setsumei]

explode [ɪksploʊd] v 爆発する [bakuhatsu
suru]

exploit v 利用する [riyou suru]

exploitation [ɛksplɔɪteɪʃən] n 搾取 [sakushu]

explore [ɪksplɔr] v 調査する [chousa suru]

explorer [ɪksplɔrər] n 探検家 [tankenka]

explosion [ɪksploʊʒən] n 爆発 [bakuhatsu]

explosive [ɪksploʊsɪv] n 爆発物 [bakuhat-
subutsu]

export n [ɛksport] 輸出 [yushutsu] ▷ v
[ɪksport] 輸出する [yushutsu suru]

express [ɪksprɛs] v 表現する [hyougen suru]

expression [ɪksprɛʃən] n 表現 [hyougen]

expressway [ɪksprɛsweɪ] n 高速道路
[kousokudouro]

extension [ɪkstɛnʃən] n 延長 [enchou], 増築
[zouchiku]; **extension cord** n 延長コード
[enchoukoodo]

extensive [ɪkstɛnsɪv] adj 広い [hiroi]

extensively [ɪkstɛnsɪvli] adv 広く [hiroku]

extent [ɪkstɛnt] n 広がり [hirogari]

exterior [ɪkstɪəriər] adj 外側の [sotogawa no]

external [ɪkstɜrnəl] adj 外部の [gaibu no]

extinct [ɪkstɪŋkt] adj 絶滅した [zetsumetsu
shita]

extinguisher [ɪkstɪŋgwɪʃər] n 消火器
[shoukaki]

extortionate [ɪkstɔrʃnɪt] adj 法外な [hougai

extra [ɛkstrə] *adj* 余分の [yobun no] ▷ *adv* 余分に [yobun ni]; **I'd like it with extra..., please** ···を余分につけてお願いします [... o yobun ni tsukete o-negai shimasu]; **May I have an extra bag, please?** 余分に袋をいただけますか? [yobun ni fukuro o itadakemasu ka?]

extraordinary [ɪkstrɔ̱rdₙnɛri] *adj* 異常な [ijou na]

extravagant [ɪkstrǽvəgənt] *adj* 金遣いが荒い [kanezukai ga arai]

extreme [ɪkstri̱m] *adj* 極度の [kyokudo no]

extremely [ɪkstri̱mli] *adv* 極度に [kyokudo ni], 大変 [taihen]

extremism [ɪkstri̱mɪzəm] *n* 過激主義 [kageki shugi]

extremist [ɪkstri̱mɪst] *n* 過激派 [kagekiha]

ex-wife *n* 先妻 [sensai]

eye [aɪ] *n* 目 [me]; **eye shadow** *n* アイシャドウ [aishadou]; **Seeing-Eye® dog** *n* 盲導犬 [moudouken]; **I have something in my eye** 私は目に何か入っています [watashi wa me ni nani ka haitte imasu]; **My eyes are sore** 私は目が痛みます [watashi wa me ga itamimasu]

eyebrow [aɪbraʊ] *n* 眉 [mayu]

eyedrops [aɪdrɒps] *npl* 目薬 [megusuri]

eyelash [aɪlæʃ] *n* まつげ [matsuge]

eyelid [aɪlɪd] *n* まぶた [mabuta]

eyeliner [aɪlaɪnər] *n* アイライナー [airainaa]

eyesight [aɪsaɪt] *n* 視力 [shiryoku]

F

fabric [fǽbrɪk] *n* 織物 [orimono]

fabulous [fǽbyələs] *adj* すばらしい [subarashii]

face [feɪs] *n* 顔 [kao] ▷ *v* ・・・に向かう [... ni mukau] (方角)

facial [féɪʃl] *adj* 顔の [kao no] ▷ *n* 美顔術 [biganjutsu]

facilities [fəsɪ́lɪtiz] *npl* 設備 [setsubi]; **Do you have facilities for children?** 子供用の設備はありますか? [kodomo-you no setsubi wa arimasu ka?]; **What facilities do you have for disabled people?** 身体障害者用のどんな設備をそなえていますか? [shintai-shou-gaisha-you no donna setsubi o sonaete imasu ka?]; **What facilities do you have here?** ここにはどんな設備がありますか? [koko ni wa donna setsubi ga arimasu ka?]

facility [fəsɪ́lɪti] *n* 施設 [shisetsu]

fact [fækt] *n* 事実 [jijitsu]

factory [fǽktəri, -tri] *n* 工場 [koujou]; **I work in a factory** 私は工場で働いています [watashi wa koujou de hataraite imasu]

fade [feɪd] *v* 褪せる [aseru]

fail [feɪl] *v* 失敗する [shippai suru]

failure [féɪlyər] *n* 失敗 [shippai]

faint [feɪnt] *adj* かすかな [kasuka na] ▷ *v* 気絶する [kizetsu suru]

fair [fɛər] *adj* (light color) 色白の [irojiro no], (reasonable) 公正な [kousei na] ▷ *n* 縁日 [ennichi]

fairground [fɛ́ərgraʊnd] *n* 屋外市を催す場所 [okugai ichi-o moyousu basho]

fairly [fɛ́ərli] *adv* 公正に [kousei ni]

fairness [fɛ́ərnɪs] *n* 公正 [kousei]

fairy [fɛ́əri] *n* 妖精 [yousei]; **fairy tale** *n* おとぎ話 [otogibanashi]

faith [feɪθ] *n* 信念 [shinnen]

faithful [féɪθfəl] *adj* 忠実な [chuujitsu na]

faithfully [féɪθfəli] *adv* 忠実に [chuujitsuni]

fake [feɪk] *adj* 模造の [mozou no] ▷ *n* 模造品 [mozouhin]

fall [fɔl] *n* 落下 [rakka] ▷ *v* 落ちる [ochiru]

fall down *v* 倒れる [taoreru]

fall for *v* ・・・が好きになる [... ga suki ni naru]

fall out *v* 不和になる [fuwa ni naru]

false [fɔls] *adj* 偽りの [itsuwari no]; **false alarm** *n* 間違い警報 [machigai keihou]

fame [feɪm] *n* 有名 [yuumei], 名声 [meisei]

familiar [fəmɪ́lyər] *adj* よく知られている [yoku shirarete iru]

family [fǽmɪli, fǽmli] *n* 家族 [kazoku]; **family name** *n* 姓 [sei]; **family room** *n* ラウンジ [raunji]; **I'm here with my family** 私は家族と来ています [watashi wa kazoku to kite imasu]

famine [fǽmɪn] *n* 飢饉 [kikin]

famous [féɪməs] *adj* 有名な [yuumei na]

fan [fæn] *n* 扇風機 [senpuuki]; **fan belt** *n* ファンベルト [fanberuto]; **Does the room have a fan?** その部屋に扇風機はありますか? [sono heya ni senpuuki wa arimasu ka?]

fanatic [fənǽtɪk] *n* 熱狂者 [nekkyousha]

fanny pack *n* **fanny pack** *n* ウエストバッグ [uesutobaggu]

fantastic [fæntǽstɪk] *adj* すばらしい [subarashii]

FAQ [fæk] *abbr* FAQ [efueekyuu]

far [fɑr] *adj* 遠い [toui] ▷ *adv* 遠くに [touku ni]; **Far East** *n* 極東 [kyokutou]; **Is it far away?** 遠いですか? [tooi desu ka?]

fare [fɛər] *n* 運賃 [unchin]

Far East *n* 東洋 [touyou]

far-eastern *adj* 東洋の [touyou no]

farewell [fɛərwɛl] *excl* さらば! [saraba]

farm [fɑrm] *n* 農場 [noujou]

farmer [fɑrmər] *n* 農場主 [noujoushu]

farmhouse [fɑrmhaus] *n* 農家 [nouka]

farming [fɑrmɪŋ] *n* 農業 [nougyou]

Faroe Islands *npl* フェロー諸島 [Feroo shotou]

fascinating [fæsɪneɪtɪŋ] *adj* 魅惑的な [miwakuteki na]

fashion [fæʃⁿ] *n* 流行 [ryuukou]

fashionable [fæʃənəbⁱl] *adj* 流行の [ryuukou no]

fast [fæst] *adj* 速い [hayai] ▷ *adv* 速く [hayaku]

fat [fæt] *adj* 太った [futotta] ▷ *n* 脂肪 [shibou]

fatal [feɪtⁱl] *adj* 致命的な [chimeiteki na]

fate [feɪt] *n* 運命 [unmei]

father [fɑðər] *n* 父 [chichi]

father-in-law (*pl* **fathers-in-law**) *n* 義父 [gifu]

fault [fɔlt] *n* 責任 [sekinin]; **It wasn't my fault** それは私の責任ではありません [sore wa watashi no sekinin de wa arimasen]

faulty [fɔlti] *adj* 欠陥のある [kekkan no aru]

fauna [fɔnə] *npl* 動物相 [doubutsusou]

favor [feɪvər] *n* 賛成 [sansei]

favorite [feɪvərɪt, feɪvrɪt] *adj* 大好きな [daisuki na] ▷ *n* お気に入り [o-kiniiri]

fax [fæks] *n* ファックス [fakkusu] ▷ *v* ファックスを送る [fakkusu-o okuru]; **Do you have a fax?** ファックスがありますか? [fakkusu ga arimasu ka?]; **How much does it cost to send a fax?** ファックスを送るのはいくらですか? [fakkusu o okuru no wa ikura desu ka?]; **I want to send a fax** 私はファックスを送りたいのですが [watashi wa fakkusu o okuritai no desu ga]; **Is there a fax machine I can use?** 私が使えるファックス機はありますか? [watashi ga tsukaeru fakkusuki wa arimasu ka?]; **Please resend your fax** あなたのファックスを再送信してください [anata no fakkusu o sai-soushin shite kudasai];

There's a problem with your fax あなたのファックスに問題があります [anata no fakkusu ni mondai ga arimasu]; **What is the fax number?** ファックス番号は何番ですか? [fakkusu-bangou wa nan-ban desu ka?]

fear [fɪər] *n* 恐怖 [kyoufu] ▷ *v* 恐れる [osoreru]

feasible [fizəbⁱl] *adj* 実行可能な [jikkoukanou na]

feather [fɛðər] *n* 羽 [hane]

feature [fitʃər] *n* 顔立ち [kaodachi]

February [fɛbyuɛri, fɛbru-] *n* 二月 [nigatsu]

fed up *adj* うんざりして [unzari shite]

fee [fi] *n* 料金 [ryoukin], 量 [ryou]; **admission fee** 入場料 [nyuujouryou]; **tuition fees** *npl* 授業料 [jugyouryou]

feed [fid] *v* 食物を与える [tabemono o ataeru]

feedback [fidbæk] *n* 意見 [iken]

feel [fil] *v* 感じる [kanjiru]

feeling [filɪŋ] *n* 気持ち [kimochi], 勘定 [kanjou]

feet [fit] *npl* 足 [ashi]; **My feet are a size seven** 私の足は六号です [watashi no ashi wa roku-gou desu]; **My feet are sore** 私は足が痛みます [watashi wa ashi ga itamimasu]

felt [fɛlt] *n* フェルト [feruto]

female [fimeɪl] *adj* 女性の [josei no] ▷ *n* 女性 [josei]

feminine [fɛmɪnɪn] *adj* 女らしい [onnarashii]

feminist [fɛmɪnɪst] *n* フェミニスト [feminisuto]

fence [fɛns] *n* 柵 [saku]

fender [fɛndər] *n* 泥よけ [doroyoke]

fennel [fɛnⁱl] *n* フェンネル [fenneru]

fern [fɜrn] *n* シダ [shida]

ferret [fɛrɪt] *n* ケナガイタチ [kenagaitachi]

ferry [fɛri] *n* フェリー [ferii]; **Is there a ferry to...?** ···行きのフェリーはありますか? [... iki no ferii wa arimasu ka?]; **Where do we catch the ferry to...?** ···行きのフェリーはどこで乗るのですか? [... iki no ferii wa doko de noru no desu ka?]

fertile [fɜrtⁱl] *adj* 繁殖力のある [hanshokuryoku no aru]

fertility [fɜrtⁱlɪti] *n* 繁殖力 [hanshokuryoku]

fertilizer [fɜrt·laɪzər] *n* 肥料 [hiryou]

festival [fɛstɪv·l] *n* フェスティバル [fesutibaru]

fetch [fɛtʃ] *v* 行って連れて来る [itte tsurete kuru]

fetus [fitəs] *n* 胎児 [taiji]

fever [fivər] *n* 熱 [netsu]; **hay fever** *n* 花粉症 [kafunshou]; **He has a fever** 彼は熱があります [kare wa netsu ga arimasu]

few [fyu] *adj* 少しの [sukoshi no]

fewer [fyuər] *adj* より少ない [yori sukunai]

fiancé [fiɑnseɪ] *n* 婚約中の男性 [kon'yakuchuu no dansei]

fiancée [fiɑnseɪ] *n* 婚約中の女性 [kon'yakuchuu no josei]

fiber [faɪbər] *n* 繊維 [sen-i]

fiberglass [faɪbərglæs] *n* ガラス繊維 [garasu sen'i]

fiction [fɪkʃ·n] *n* フィクション [fikushon]; **science fiction** *n* サイエンスフィクション [saiensu fikushon]

field [fild] *n* 野原 [nohara]; **playing field** *n* グラウンド [guraundo]

fierce [fiərs] *adj* 凶暴な [kyoubou na]

fifteen [fɪftin] *number* 十五 [juugo]

fifteenth [fɪftinθ] *adj* 十五番目の [juugo banme no]

fifth [fɪfθ] *adj* 五番目の [go banme no]

fifty [fɪfti] *number* 五十 [gojuu]

fifty-fifty [fɪfti fɪfti] *adj* 五分五分の [gobugobu no] ▷ *adv* 五分五分で [gobugobu de]

fig [fɪg] *n* イチジク [ichijiku]

fight [faɪt] *n* 戦い [tatakai] ▷ *v* 戦う [tatakau]

fighting [faɪtɪŋ] *n* 戦い [tatakai]

figure [fɪgyər] *n* 数字 [suuji]

figure out *v* 計算して出す [keisan shite dasu]

Fiji [fidʒi] *n* フィジー [fijii]

file [faɪl] *n* (*folder*) ファイル [fairu], (*tool*) やすり [yasuri] ▷ *v* (*folder*) ファイルする [fairu suru], (*smoothing*) やすりをかける [yasuri-o kakeru]

Filipino, Filipina [fɪlɪpinou, fɪlɪpinə] *adj* フィリピンの [firipin no] ▷ *n* フィリピン人 [firipinjin]

fill [fɪl] *v* いっぱいにする [ippai ni suru]

fillet [fɪleɪ] *n* ヒレ肉 [hireniku] ▷ *v* ···からヒレ肉を取る [... kara hireniku-o toru]

filling [fɪlɪŋ] *n* **A filling has fallen out** 詰め物がとれてしまいました [tsumemono ga torete shimaimashita]; **Can you do a temporary filling?** 仮の詰め物をしてもらえますか? [kari no tsumemono o shite moraemasu ka?]

fill out *v* 記入する [kinyuu suru]

fill up *v* 記入する [kinyuu suru]

film [fɪlm] *n* フィルム [firumu]; **A color film, please** カラーフィルムをください [karaa-firumu o kudasai]; **Could you develop this film, please?** このフィルムを現像していただけますか? [kono firumu o genzou shite itadakemasu ka?]; **The film has jammed** フィルムが動かなくなってしまいました [firumu ga ugokanaku natte shimaimashita]

filter [fɪltər] *n* 濾過器 [rokaki] ▷ *v* 濾過する [roka suru]

filthy [fɪlθi] *adj* 不潔な [fuketsu na]

final [faɪn·l] *adj* 最終の [saishuu no] ▷ *n* 決勝 [kesshou]

finalize [faɪn·laɪz] *v* 決定的にする [ketteiteki ni suru]

finally [faɪn·li] *adv* ついに [tsuini]

finance [faɪnæns, fɪnæns] *n* 財務 [zaimu] ▷ *v* 資金を調達する [shikin-o choutatsu suru]

financial [faɪnænʃ·l, fɪn-] *adj* 財務の [zaimu no]; **financial year** *n* 会計年度 [kaikeinendo]

find [faɪnd] *v* 見つける [mitsukeru]

find out *v* 発見する [hakken suru]

fine [faɪn] *adj* 見事な [migoto na] ▷ *adv* 見事に [migoto ni] ▷ *n* 罰金 [bakkin]; **How much is the fine?** 罰金はいくらですか? [bakkin wa ikura desu ka?]; **Where do I pay the fine?** どこで罰金を払うのですか? [doko de bakkin o harau no desu ka?]

finger [fɪŋgər] *n* 手の指 [te no yubi]; **index finger** *n* 人差し指 [hitosashi yubi]

fingernail [fɪŋgərneɪl] *n* 指の爪 [yubi no tsume]

fingerprint [fɪŋgərprɪnt] *n* 指紋 [shimon]

finish [fɪnɪʃ] n 終わり [owari] ▷ v 終える [oeru];
When does it finish? いつ終わりますか？
[itsu owarimasu ka?]; **When will you have
finished?** 何時に終わりますか？ [nan-ji ni
owarimasu ka?]

finished [fɪnɪʃt] adj 終えた [oeta]

Finland [fɪnlænd] n フィンランド [finrando]

Finn [fɪn] n フィンランド人 [finrandojin]

Finnish [fɪnɪʃ] adj フィンランドの [finrando
no] ▷ n フィンランド人 [finrandojin]

fir [fɜr] n fir (tree) n モミ [momi]

fire [faɪər] n 火 [hi] ▷ v 首にする [kubi ni suru];
fire alarm n 火災報知器 [kasai houchiki];
fire department n 消防隊 [shouboutai]; **fire
escape** n 非常階段 [hijoukaidan]; **fire
extinguisher** n 消火器 [shoukaki]; **Fire!** 火
事だ! [kaji da!]

fireman [faɪərmən] n 消防士 [shouboushi]

fireplace [faɪərpleɪs] n 暖炉 [danro]

firewall [faɪərwɔl] n 防火壁 [boukaheki]

fireworks [faɪərwɜrks] npl 花火 [hanabi]

firm [fɜrm] adj 堅い [katai] ▷ n 会社 [kaisha]

first [fɜrst] adj 最初の [saisho no], 第一
[daiichi] ▷ adv 最初に [saisho ni] ▷ n 最初のも
の [saisho no mono]; **first aid** n 救急処置
[kyuukyuu shochi]; **first floor** n 一階 [ikkai];
first name n ファーストネーム [faasu-
toneemu]; **When does the first chairlift
go?** 最初のチェアリフトはいつ出ますか？
[saisho no chea-rifuto wa itsu demasu ka?]

first-class adj 第一級の [daiikkyuu no]

firstly [fɜrstli] adv まず第一に [mazu daiichi
ni]

fiscal [fɪskəl] adj 財政の [zaisei no]; **fiscal
year** n 会計年度 [kaikeinendo]

fish [fɪʃ] n 魚 [sakana] ▷ v 魚を捕る [sakana-o
toru]; **fish dealer** n 魚屋 [sakanaya];
freshwater fish n 淡水魚 [tansuigyo]; **Could
you prepare a meal without fish?** 魚を使
わずに食事を用意していただけますか？
[sakana o tsukawazu ni shokuji o youi shite
itadakemasu ka?]; **I don't eat fish** 私は魚を
食べません [watashi wa sakana o

tabemasen]; **I'll have the fish** 私はこの魚を
いただきます [watashi wa kono sakana o
itadakimasu]; **Is the fish fresh or frozen?**
魚は生鮮品ですか、それとも冷凍品ですか？
[sakana wa seisen-hin desu ka, sore tomo
reitou-hin desu ka?]; **Is this cooked in fish
stock?** これは魚のストックで料理してありま
すか？ [kore wa sakana no sutokku de ryouri
shite arimasu ka?]; **What fish dishes do
you have?** どんな魚料理がありますか？
[donna sakana-ryouri ga arimasu ka?]

fisherman [fɪʃərmən] n 漁師 [ryoushi], 魚を釣
る人 [sakana wo tsuru hito]

fishing [fɪʃɪŋ] n 漁業 [gyogyou], 魚釣り
[sakana tsuri], 釣り [tsuri]; **fishing boat** n 漁
船 [gyosen]; **fishing rod** n 釣竿 [tsurizao];
fishing tackle n 釣具 [tsurigu]

fist [fɪst] n 握りこぶし [nigiri kobushi]

fit [fɪt] adj 適した [tekishita] ▷ n 発作 [hossa]
▷ v 適する [teki suru]; **epileptic fit** n 癲癇の
発作 [tenkan no hossa]; **fitted sheet** n マット
レスにぴったり合うシーツ [mattoresu ni
pittari au shiitsu]

fit in v 組み込む [kumikomu]

fitness [fɪtnɪs] n フィットネス [fittonesu];
fitness program n フィットネス運動
[fittonesu undou]

five [faɪv] number 五 [go]

fix [fɪks] v 固定する [kotei suru], 直す [naosu]

fixed [fɪkst] adj 固定した [kotei shita]

flabby [flæbi] adj たるんだ [tarunda]

flag [flæg] n 旗 [hata]

flame [fleɪm] n 炎 [hono-o]

flamingo [fləmɪŋgoʊ] n フラミンゴ
[furamingo]

flammable [flæməbəl] adj 可燃性の
[kanensei no]

flan [flæn, flɑn] n フラン [furan] (食べ物)

flap [flæp] v パタパタ動かす [patapata
ugokasu]

flash [flæʃ] n フラッシュ [furasshu], 閃光
[senkou] ▷ v パッと発火する [patsu to hakka
suru]; **The flash isn't working** フラッシュが

働きません [furasshu ga hatarakimasen]

flashlight [flǽʃlaɪt] *n* 懐中電灯 [kaichuuden-tou]

flat [flæt] *adj* 平らな [taira na]

flat-screen *adj* フラットスクリーンの [furatto sukuriin no]

flatter [flǽtər] *v* おだてる [odateru]

flattered [flǽtərd] *adj* おだてられた [odaterareta]

flatware [flǽtwɛər] *n* 食卓用ナイフ・フォーク・スプーン類 [shokutaku yoo naifu. fouku. supuun rui]

flavor [fleɪvər] *n* フレーバー [fureebaa], 味 [aji]; **What flavors do you have?** どんなフレーバーがありますか? [donna fureebaa ga arimasu ka?]

flavoring [fleɪvərɪŋ] *n* 調味料 [choumiryou]

flaw [flɔ] *n* きず [kizu] (損傷)

flea [fli] *n* 蚤 [nomi]; **flea market** *n* ノミの市 [nomi no ichi]

flee [fli] *v* 逃げる [nigeru]

fleece [flis] *n* フリース [furiisu]

fleet [flit] *n* 艦隊 [kantai]

flexible [flɛ́ksɪbᵊl] *adj* 曲げやすい [mageyasui]

flexitime [flɛ́ksitaɪm] *n* フレックスタイム [furekkusutaimu]

flight [flaɪt] *n* フライト [furaito], 瓶 [bin], 飛行 [hikou]; **charter flight** *n* チャーター便 [chaataa bin]; **flight attendant** *n* スチュワーデス [suchuwaadesu], 客室乗務員 [kyakushitsu joumuin]; **scheduled flight** *n* 定期便 [teikibin]; **Are there any cheap flights?** 安いフライトはありますか? [yasui furaito wa arimasu ka?]; **I'd like to cancel my flight** フライトをキャンセルしたいのですが [furaito o kyanseru shitai no desu ga]; **I'd like to change my flight** フライトを変更したいのですが [furaito o henkou shitai no desu ga]; **I'd rather have an earlier flight** もっと早いフライトがいいのですが [motto hayai furaito ga ii no desu ga]; **I've missed my flight** 私はフライトに乗り遅れました [watashi wa furaito ni noriokuremashita]; **The flight has been delayed** フライトは遅れています [furaito wa okurete imasu]; **Where do I check in for the flight to...?** ・・・行きのフライトはどこでチェックインするのですか? [... iki no furaito wa doko de chekku-in suru no desu ka?]; **Where is the luggage for the flight from...?** ・・・からのフライトの手荷物はどこですか? [... kara no furaito no tenimotsu wa doko desu ka?]; **Which gate for the flight to...?** ・・・行きフライトの搭乗ゲートはどれですか? [... iki furaito no toujou-geeto wa dore desu ka?]

fling [flɪŋ] *v* 投げ飛ばす [nagetobasu]

flip-flops *npl* ビーチサンダル [biichi sandaru]

flippers [flɪpərz] *npl* ひれ足 [hireashi]

flirt [flɜrt] *n* 浮気者 [uwakimono] ▷ *v* 恋をもてあそぶ [koi wo moteasobu]

float [floʊt] *v* 浮く [uku]

flock [flɒk] *n* 群れ [mure]

flood [flʌd] *n* 洪水 [kouzui] ▷ *vi* 氾濫する [hanran suru] ▷ *vt* 氾濫させる [hanran saseru]

flooding [flʌdɪŋ] *n* 氾濫 [hanran]

floodlight [flʌdlaɪt] *n* 投光照明 [toukou shoumei]

floor [flɔr] *n* 床 [yuka]; **first floor** *n* 一階 [ikkai]

flop [flɒp] *n* 失敗 [shippai]

floppy [flɒpi] *adj* **floppy disk** *n* フロッピーディスク [furoppii disuku]

flora [flɔrə] *npl* 植物相 [shokubutsusou]

florist [flɔrɪst] *n* 花屋 [hanaya]

flour [flaʊər] *n* 小麦粉 [komugiko]

flow [floʊ] *v* 流れる [nagareru]

flower [flaʊər] *n* 花 [hana] ▷ *v* 花が咲く [hana ga saku]

flowerpot [flaʊərpɒt] *n* ハチ [hachi]

flu [flu] *n* インフルエンザ [infuruenza]; **bird flu** *n* 鳥インフルエンザ [tori infuruenza]; **I had the flu recently** 私は最近インフルエンザにかかりました [watashi wa saikin infuruenza ni kakarimashita]; **I have the flu** 私はインフ

ルエンザにかかりました [watashi wa infuruenza ni kakarimashita]

fluent [fluənt] *adj* 流暢な [ryuuchou na]

fluorescent [flʊrɛsənt] *adj* 蛍光性の [keikousei no]

flush [flʌʃ] *n* 赤面 [sekimen] ▷ *v* 赤面する [sekimen suru]

flute [flut] *n* フルート [furuuto]

fly [flaɪ] *n* ハエ [hae] ▷ *v* 飛ぶ [tobu]

fly away *v* 飛び去る [tobisaru]

foal [foʊl] *n* 馬の子 [uma no ko]

foam [foʊm] *n* **shaving foam** *n* シェービングフォーム [shieebingufoomu]

focus [foʊkəs] *n* 焦点 [shouten] ▷ *v* 焦点を合わせる [shouten-o awaseru]

fog [fɒg] *n* 霧 [kiri]; **fog light** *n* フォグランプ [foguranpu]

foggy [fɒgi] *adj* 霧の立ちこめた [kiri no tachikometa]

foil [fɔɪl] *n* ホイル [hoiru]

fold [foʊld] *n* 囲い [kakoi] ▷ *v* 折りたたむ [oritatamu]

folder [foʊldər] *n* ホルダー [horudaa]

folding [foʊldɪŋ] *adj* 折りたたみの [oritatami no]

folklore [foʊklɔr] *n* 民間伝承 [minkanden-shou]

follow [fɒloʊ] *v* ・・・について行く [... ni tsuite iku], ・・・を追う [...-o ou]

following [fɒloʊɪŋ] *adj* 以下の [ika no] *(次の)*

fondness [fɒndnɪs] *n* 好き [suki]

food [fud] *n* 食べ物 [tabemono]; **food poisoning** *n* 食中毒 [shokuchuudoku]; **food processor** *n* フードプロセッサー [fuudopurosessaa]; **whole foods** *npl* 自然食品 [shizen shokuhin]; **Do you have food?** 食べ物はありますか? [tabemono wa arimasu ka?]; **The food is too hot** 食べ物が熱すぎます [tabemono ga atsu-sugimasu]; **The food is very greasy** 食べ物がとても脂っこいです [tabemono ga totemo aburakkoi desu]

fool [ful] *n* ばか者 [bakamono] ▷ *v* だます [damasu]

foolish [fulɪʃ] *adj* ばかな [baka na]

foot, feet [fʊt, fit] *n* 足 [ashi]; **My feet are a size seven** 私の足は六号です [watashi no ashi wa roku-gou desu]

football [futbɔl] *n* アメリカンフットボール [Amerikan futtobooru]

footpath [futpæθ] *n* 歩行者用の小道 [hokoushayou no komichi]

footprint [futprɪnt] *n* フットプリント [futtopurinto], 足跡 [ashiato]

footstep [futstɛp] *n* 足取り [ashidori]

for [fər, STRONG fɔr] *prep* **Can I have a tape for this video camera, please?** このビデオカメラ用のテープをいただけますか? [kono bideo-kamera-you no teepu o itadakemasu ka?]; **Could you give me change for...?** ・・・の小銭をいただけますか? [... no kozeni o itadakemasu ka?]; **Could you watch my briefcase for a minute, please?** ちょっと私のかばんを見張っていただけますか? [chotto watashi no kaban o mihatte itadakemasu ka?]; **I want an injection for the pain** 私は痛み止めの注射が欲しいのです [watashi wa itami-dome no chuusha ga hoshi no desu]; **I want to rent a car for the weekend** 車を週末借りたいのですが [kuruma o shuumatsu karitai no desu ga]; **I work for...** 私は・・・に勤めています [watashi wa... ni tsutomete imasu]; **I'd like to exchange a hundred... for...** 百・・・を・・・に両替したいのですが [hyaku... o... ni ryougae shitai no desu ga]; **I'd like to reserve a table for four people for tonight at eight o'clock** 今晩八時に四人用のテーブルを予約したいのですが [konban hachi-ji ni yonin-you no teeburu o yoyaku shitai no desu ga]; **I'd like two tickets for tonight** 今夜の切符を2枚ください [kon'ya no kippu o nimai kudasai]; **Is it safe for children?** それは子供にも安全ですか? [sore wa kodomo ni mo anzen desu ka?]; **We're here for a wedding** 私たちは結婚式で来ています [watashi-tachi wa kekkon-shiki de kite imasu]

F

forbid [fərbɪd, for-] v 禁じる [kinjiru]

forbidden [fərbɪdn, for-] adj 禁じられた [kinjirareta]

force [fors] n 力 [chikara] ▷ v 強いる [shiiru]; **Air Force** n 空軍 [kuugun]

forecast [forkæst] n 天気予報 [tenkiyohou]; **What's the weather forecast?** 天気予報はどうですか? [tenki-yohou wa dou desu ka?]

foreground [forgraʊnd] n 前景 [zenkei]

forehead [forhɛd, forɪd] n 額 [hitai] (顔)

foreign [forɪn] adj 外国の [gaikoku no]

foreigner [forɪnər] n 外国人 [gaikokujin]

foresee [forsi] v 予見する [yoken suru]

forest [forɪst] n 森 [mori]

forever [forɛvər, fər-] adv 永久に [eikyuu ni]

for example abbr たとえば [tatoeba]

forge [fordʒ] v 鍛造する [tanzou suru]

forgery [fordʒəri] n 偽造 [gizou]

forget [fərgɛt] v 忘れる [wasureru]

forgive [fərgɪv] v 許す [yurusu]

forgotten [fərgɒtn] adj 忘れられた [wasurerareta]

fork [fork] n フォーク [fooku]; **Could I have a clean fork, please?** 新しいフォークをいただけますか? [atarashii fooku o itadakemasu ka?]

form [form] n 形 [katachi]; **application form** n 申込書 [moushikomisho]; **order form** n 注文用紙 [chuumon youshi]

formal [form-l] adj 正式の [seishiki no]; **formal attire** n イブニングドレス [ibuningu doresu]

formality [formælɪti] n 儀礼的行為 [gireiteki koui]

format [formæt] n 図書形態 [tosho keitai] ▷ v 形式を定める [keishiki-o sadameru]

former [formər] adj 以前の [izen no]

formerly [formərli] adv 以前は [izen wa]

formula [formyələ] n 公式 [koushiki]、ベビーミルク [bebii miruku]

fort [fort] n 砦 [toride]

fortunate [fortʃənɪt] adj 幸運な [kouun na]

fortunately [fortʃənɪtli] adv 幸運にも [kouun nimo]

fortune [fortʃən] n 大金 [taikin]

forty [forti] number 四十 [shijuu]

forward [forwərd] adv 前方へ [zenpou-e] ▷ v 転送する [tensou suru]; **forward slash** n フォワードスラッシュ [fowaadosurasshu]; **lean forward** v 前かがみになる [maekagami ni naru]

foster [fostər] v 養育する [youiku suru]; **foster child** n 里子 [satogo]

foul [faʊl] adj いやな [iya na] ▷ n ファウル [fauru]

foundations [faʊndeɪʃnz] npl 基礎 [kiso]

fountain [faʊntɪn] n 噴水 [funsui]; **fountain pen** n 万年筆 [mannenhitsu]

four [for] number 四 [shi]

fourteen [fortin] number 十四 [juuyon]

fourteenth [fortinθ] adj 十四番目の [juuyon banme no]

fourth [forθ] adj 四番目の [yon banme no]

fox [fɒks] n キツネ [kitsune]

fracture [fræktʃər] n 骨折 [kossetsu]

fragile [frædʒ-l] adj 壊れやすい [koware-yasui]

frail [freɪl] adj かよわい [kayowai]

frame [freɪm] n 骨組み [honegumi]; **picture frame** n 額縁 [gakubuchi]

France [fræns] n フランス [furansu]

frankly [fræŋkli] adv 率直に [sotchoku ni]

frantic [fræntɪk] adj 半狂乱の [hankyouran no]

fraud [frɔd] n 詐欺 [sagi]

freckles [frɛkəlz] npl そばかす [sobakasu]

free [fri] adj フリー [furii]、(no cost) 無料の [muryou no]、(no restraint) 自由な [jiyuu na] ▷ v …を自由にする […o jiyuu ni suru]; **free kick** n フリーキック [furiikikku]

freedom [fridəm] n 自由 [jiyuu]

freelance [frilæns] adj 自由契約の [jiyuu keiyaku no] ▷ adv 自由契約で [jiyuu keiyaku de]

freeway [friweɪ] n **How do I get to the freeway?** 高速道路へはどう行くのですか?

[kousoku-douro e wa dou iku no desu ka?];
Is there a toll on this freeway? この高速道
路は有料ですか? [kono kousoku-douro wa
yuuryou desu ka?]
freeze [friz] v 凍る [kouru]
freezer [frizər] n 冷凍庫 [reitouko]
freezing [frizɪŋ] adj 凍るような [kouru you na]
freight [freɪt] n 貨物輸送 [kamotsu yusou]
French [frɛntʃ] adj フランスの [furansuno] ▷ n
フランス人 [furansujin]; **french fries** npl フラ
イドポテト [furaidopoteto]; **French horn** n フ
レンチホルン [furenchihorun]
Frenchman [frɛntʃmən] (pl **Frenchmen**) n
フランス人 [furansujin]
Frenchwoman [frɛntʃwʊmən] (pl
Frenchwomen) n フランス人 [furansujin]
frequency [frikwənsi] n 頻発 [hinpatsu]
frequent [frikwənt] adj たびたびの [tabitabi
no]
fresh [frɛʃ] adj 新鮮な [shinsen na]
freshen up v 洗面する [senmen suru]
fret [frɛt] v 気をもむ [ki-o momu]
Friday [fraɪdeɪ, -di] n 金曜日 [kin-youbi];
Good Friday n 聖金曜日 [seikinyoubi]; **on
Friday** 金曜日に [kinyoubi ni]; **on Friday,
December thirty-first** 十二月三十一日の金
曜日に [juuni-gatsu sanjuuichi-nichi no
kinyoubi ni]
fridge [frɪdʒ] n 冷蔵庫 [reizouko]
fried [fraɪd] adj フライ [furai], 油で揚げた
[abura de ageta]
friend [frɛnd] n 友だち [tomodachi]; **I'm here
with my friends** 私は友だちと来ています
[watashi wa tomo-dachi to kite imasu]
friendly [frɛndli] adj 親しい [shitashii]
friendship [frɛndʃɪp] n 友情 [yuujou]
fright [fraɪt] n 恐怖 [kyoufu]
frighten [fraɪtən] v 怖がらせる [kowagar-
aseru]
frightened [fraɪtənd] adj おびえた [obieta]
frightening [fraɪtnɪŋ] adj ぎょっとさせる
[gyotto saseru]
frog [frɒg] n カエル [kaeru]

from [frəm, STRONG fræm] **a month from
now** 一か月後に [ikkagetsu go ni]; **How far
are we from the beach?** ビーチまでどのくら
いありますか? [biichi made dono kurai
arimasu ka?]; **I'm from...** ･･･です [...desu];
Where are you from? ご出身はどちらです
か? [go-shusshin wa dochira desu ka?]
front [frʌnt] adj 前の [mae no] ▷ n 前 [mae]
frontier [frʌntɪər, frɒn-] n 国境 [kokkyou]
frost [frɒst] n 霜 [shimo]
frosting [frɒstɪŋ] n 降霜 [kousou]
frosty [frɒsti] adj 霜の降りる [shimo no oriru]
frown [fraʊn] v まゆをひそめる [mayu wo
hisomeru]
frozen [froʊzən] adj 凍った [koutta]
fruit [frut] n フルーツ [furuutsu], 果物
[kudamono]; **fruit and vegetable store** n 八
百屋 [yaoya]; **fruit juice** n フルーツジュース
[furuutsujuusu]; **fruit salad** n フルーツサラダ
[furuutsusarada]; **passion fruit** n パッション
フルーツ [passhonfuruutsu]
frustrated [frʌstreɪtɪd] adj 挫折した [zasetsu
shita]
fry [fraɪ] v 油で揚げる [abura de ageru];
frying pan n フライパン [furaipan]; **French
fries** npl フライドポテト [furaidopoteto]
fuel [fyuəl] n 燃料 [nenryou]
fulfill [fʊlfɪl] v 果たす [hatasu]
full [fʊl] adj いっぱい [ippai], 満ちた [michita];
full moon n 満月 [mangetsu]
full-time [fʊltaɪm] adj フルタイムの
[furutaimu no] ▷ adv フルタイムで [furutaimu
de]
fully [fʊli] adv 十分に [juubun ni]
fumes [fyumz] npl 煙霧 [enmu]; **exhaust
fumes** npl 排気ガス [haikigasu]
fun [fʌn] adj 楽しい [tanoshii] ▷ n 楽しみ
[tanoshimi], 遊び [asobi]
funds [fʌndz] npl 資金 [shikin]
funeral [fyunərəl] n 葬式 [soushiki]; **funeral
director** n 葬儀屋 [sougiya]; **funeral home**
n 葬儀場 [sougiba]
funnel [fʌnəl] n じょうご [jougo]

funny [fʌni] *adj* 面白い [omoshiroi]

fur [fɜr] *n* 毛皮 [kegawa]; **fur coat** *n* 毛皮のコート [kegawa no kooto]

furious [fyuəriəs] *adj* 怒り狂った [ikarikurutta]

furnished [fɜrnɪʃt] *adj* 家具付きの [kagu tsuki no]

furniture [fɜrnɪtʃər] *n* 家具 [kagu]

further [fɜrðər] *adj* それ以上の [sore ijou no] ▷ *adv* さらに [sara ni]

fuse [fyuz] *n* ヒューズ [hyuuzu]; **fuse box** *n* ヒューズボックス [hyuuzubokkusu]; **A fuse has blown** ヒューズがとびました [hyuuzu ga tobimashita]; **Can you fix a fuse?** ヒューズを直してもらえますか? [hyuuzu o naoshite moraemasu ka?]

fusebox [fyuzbɒks] *n* **Where's the fusebox?** ヒューズボックスはどこですか? [hyuuzubokkusu wa doko desu ka?]

fuss [fʌs] *n* 大騒ぎ [ousawagi]

fussy [fʌsi] *adj* 騒ぎたてる [sawagitateru]

future [fyutʃər] *adj* 未来の [mirai no] ▷ *n* 未来 [mirai]

G

Gabon [gəboʊn] *n* ガボン [gabon]

gain [geɪn] *n* 利得 [ritoku] ▷ *v* 得る [eru]

gale [geɪl] *n* 強風 [kyoufuu]

gallery [gæləri] *n* art gallery *n* 美術館 [bijutsukan]

gallop [gæləp] *n* ギャロップ [gyaroppu] ▷ *v* ギャロップで走る [gyaroppu de hashiru]

gallstone [gɔlstoʊn] *n* 胆石 [tanseki]

Gambia [gæmiə] *n* ガンビア [ganbia]

gamble [gæmbəl] *v* 賭け事をする [kakegoto-o suru]

gambler [gæmblər] *n* ギャンブラー [gyanburaa]

gambling [gæmblɪŋ] *n* ギャンブル [gyanburu]

game [geɪm] *n* ゲーム [geemu]; away game *n* アウェーの試合 [auee no shiai]; board game *n* ボードゲーム [boodo geemu]; game arcade *n* ゲームセンター [geemu sentaa]; game console *n* ゲームコンソール [geemu konsooru]; home game *n* ホームの試合 [hoomu no shiai]; Can I play video games? ビデオゲームができますか? [bideo-geemu ga dekimasu ka?]

gang [gæŋ] *n* ギャング [gyangu]

gangster [gæŋstər] *n* ギャングの一員 [gyangu no ichiin]

gap [gæp] *n* 隙間 [sukima]

garage [gərɑʒ] *n* ガレージ [gareeji]

garbage [gɑrbɪdʒ] *n* ごみ [gomi]; garbage can *n* ごみ箱 [gomibako]; garbage collector *n* ごみ収集人 [gomishuushuunin]

garden [gɑrdən] *n* 庭 [niwa], 庭園 [teien]; garden center *n* 園芸用品店 [engei youhinten]; Can we visit the gardens? 私たちがその庭園を訪れることはできますか? [watashi-tachi ga sono teien o otozureru koto wa dekimasu ka?]

gardener [gɑrdənər] *n* 庭師 [niwashi]

gardening [gɑrdənɪŋ] *n* 庭仕事 [niwa shigoto]

garlic [gɑrlɪk] *n* ガーリック [gaarikku], ニンニク [ninniku]; Is there any garlic in it? それにはガーリックが入っていますか? [sore ni wa gaarikku ga haitte imasu ka?]

garment [gɑrmənt] *n* 衣服 [ifuku]

garters [gɑrtərz] *npl* 靴下留め [kutsushita-dome]

gas [gæs] *n* ガス [gasu]; gas stove *n* ガスレンジ [gasurenji]; gas tank *n* ガソリンタンク [gasorintanku]; natural gas *n* 天然ガス [tennengasu]; portable gas cylinder *n* キャンプ用ガス [kyanpu you gasu]; I can smell gas ガスのにおいがします [gasu no nioi ga shimasu]; Where's the gas meter? ガスのメーターはどこですか? [gasu no meetaa wa doko desu ka?]

gasket [gæskɪt] *n* ガスケット [gasuketto]

gasoline [gæsəlin] *n* ガソリン [gasorin]; unleaded gasoline *n* 無鉛ガソリン [muen gasorin]

gas station *n* ガソリンスタンド [gasorinsutando]

gate [geɪt] *n* ゲート [geeto], 門 [mon]; Please go to gate... ···ゲートに行ってください [... geeto ni itte kudasai]; Which gate for the flight to...? ···行きフライトの搭乗ゲートはどれですか? [... iki furaito no toujou-geeto wa dore desu ka?]

gather [gæðər] *v* 集める [atsumeru]

gaudy [gɔdi] *adj* 派手な [hade na]

gauge [geɪdʒ] *n* 計器 [keiki] ▷ *v* 測る [hakaru]

gaze [geɪz] *v* 見つめる [mitsumeru]

gear [gɪər] *n* (equipment) 用具 [yougu], (mechanism) ギア [gia]; **Does the bike have gears?** 自転車はギア付きですか? [jitensha wa gia tsuki desu ka?]; **The gears don't work** ギアがききません [gia ga kikimasen]

gearshift [gɪərʃɪft] *n* ギアシフト [giashifuto], ギアレバー [giarebaa]

gel [dʒɛl] *n* ジェル [jeru]; **hair gel** *n* ヘアジェル [heajieru]

gem [dʒɛm] *n* 宝石 [houseki]

Gemini [dʒɛmɪnɪ] *n* 双子座 [futagoza]

gender [dʒɛndər] *n* 性 [sei]

gene [dʒin] *n* 遺伝子 [idenshi]

general [dʒɛnrəl] *adj* 一般の [ippan no] ▷ *n* 将軍 [shougun]; **general anesthetic** *n* 全身麻酔 [zenshin masui]; **general election** *n* 総選挙 [sousenkyo]; **general knowledge** *n* 一般知識 [ippan chishiki]

generalize [dʒɛnrəlaɪz] *v* 法則化する [housokuka suru]

generally [dʒɛnrəli] *adv* 一般に [ippan ni]

generation [dʒɛnəreɪʃn] *n* 世代 [sedai]

generator [dʒɛnəreɪtər] *n* 発電機 [hatsudenki]

generosity [dʒɛnərɒsɪti] *n* 寛大 [kandai]

generous [dʒɛnərəs] *adj* 気前のよい [kimae no yoi]

genetic [dʒɪnɛtɪk] *adj* 遺伝子の [idenshi no]

genetics [dʒɪnɛtɪks] *n* 遺伝学 [idengaku]

genius [dʒinyəs] *n* 天才 [tensai]

gentle [dʒɛntl] *adj* 優しい [yasashii]

gentleman [dʒɛntlmən] *n* 紳士 [shinshi]

gently [dʒɛntli] *adv* 優しく [yasashiku]

genuine [dʒɛnyuɪn] *adj* 本物の [honmono no]

geography [dʒiɒgrəfi] *n* 地理学 [chirigaku]

geology [dʒiɒlədʒi] *n* 地質学 [chishitsugaku]

Georgia [dʒɔrdʒə] *n* (country) グルジア [gurujia], (US state) ジョージア [joojia]

Georgian [dʒɔrdʒᵊn] *adj* (re Georgia) グルジアの [Gurujia no] ▷ *n* (inhabitant of Georgia) グルジア人 [gurujiajin]

geranium [dʒɪreɪniəm] *n* ゼラニウム [zeraniumu]

gerbil [dʒɜrbɪl] *n* アレチネズミ [arechinezumi]

geriatric [dʒɛriætrɪk] *adj* 老人病学の [roujinbyougaku no] ▷ *n* 老人病患者 [roujinbyou kanja]

germ [dʒɜrm] *n* 細菌 [saikin]

German [dʒɜrmən] *adj* ドイツの [doitsu no] ▷ *n* (language) ドイツ語 [doitsugo], (person) ドイツ人 [doitsujin]; **German measles** *n* 風疹 [fuushin]

Germany [dʒɜrməni] *n* ドイツ [doitsu]

gesture [dʒɛstʃər] *n* 身振り [miburi]

get [gɛt] *v* 得る [eru]

get away *v* 逃げる [nigeru]

get back *v* 戻る [modoru]

get in *v* 乗る [noru]

get into *v* ···に到着する [... ni touchaku suru]

get off *v* 降りる [oriru]

get on *v* 乗る [noru]; **Can you help me get on, please?** 私が乗るのを手伝っていただけますか? [watashi ga noru nowo tetsudatte itadakemasuka?]

get out *v* 逃げる [nigeru]

get over *v* 立ち直る [tachinaoru]

get through *v* **I can't get through** つながりません [tsunagarimasen]

getting up *v* 起きている [okite iru]

get together *v* 集まる [atsumaru]

get up *v* 起きる [okiru]

Ghana [gɑnə] *n* ガーナ [gaana]

Ghanaian [gɑneɪən] *adj* ガーナの [gaana no] ▷ *n* ガーナ人 [gaanajin]

ghost [goʊst] *n* 幽霊 [yuurei]

giant [dʒaɪənt] *adj* 巨大な [kyodai na] ▷ *n* 巨人 [kyojin]

gift [gɪft] *n* ギフト [gifuto], 贈り物 [okurimono]; **gift certificate** *n* 商品券 [shouhinken]; **gift shop** *n* ギフトショップ [gifuto shoppu]; **Could you gift-wrap it, please?** それをギフト用にラッピングしていただけますか? [sore o gifuto-you ni rappingu shite itadakemasu

ka?]; **Where can I buy gifts?** どこでギフトを
買えますか? [doko de gifuto o kaemasu ka?]

gifted [gɪftɪd] *adj* 生まれつき才能のある
[umaretsuki sainou no aru]

gigantic [dʒaɪgæntɪk] *adj* 巨大な [kyodai na]

giggle [gɪgᵊl] *v* くすくす笑う [kusukusu warau]

gin [dʒɪn] *n* ジン [jin]; **I'll have a gin and
tonic, please** ジントニックをお願いします
[jin-tonikku o o-negai shimasu]

ginger [dʒɪndʒər] *n* ショウガ [shouga]

giraffe [dʒɪræf] *n* キリン [kirin]

girl [gɜrl] *n* 除草 [josou], 少女 [shoujo]

girlfriend [gɜrlfrɛnd] *n* ガールフレンド
[gaarufurendo]; **I have a girlfriend** 私にはガ
ールフレンドがいます [watashi ni wa
gaarufurendo ga imasu]

give [gɪv] *v* 与える [ataeru]

give back *v* 返す [kaesu]

give in *v* 屈服する [kuppuku suru]

give out *v* 配布する [haifu suru]

give up *v* やめる [yameru] (よす)

glacier [gleɪʃər] *n* 氷河 [hyouga]

glad [glæd] *adj* 嬉しい [ureshii]

glamorous [glæmərəs] *adj* 魅力的な
[miryokuteki na]

glance [glæns] *n* ちらっと見ること [chiratto
miru koto] ▷ *v* ちらっと見る [chiratto miru]

gland [glænd] *n* 腺 [sen]

glare [glɛər] *v* にらみつける [niramitsukeru]

glass [glɑs, glæs] *n* ガラス [garasu]; **glass
recycling container** *n* 空き瓶回収ボックス
[akikan kaishuu bokkusu]; **magnifying
glass** *n* 拡大鏡 [kakudaikyou]; **stained
glass** *n* ステンドグラス [sutendogurasu]

glass/cup *n* コップ [koppu]

glasses [glæsɪz] *npl* 眼鏡 [megane]

glider [glaɪdər] *n* グライダー [guraidaa]

gliding [glaɪdɪŋ] *n* グライダー競技 [guraidaa
kyougi]

global [gloʊbᵊl] *adj* グローバル [guroobaru],
地球の [chikyuu no]; **global warming** *n* 地球
温暖化 [chikyuuondanka]

globalization [gloʊbəlɪzeɪʃᵊn] *n* グローバル

化 [guroobaruka]

globe [gloʊb] *n* 地球儀 [chikyuugi]

gloomy [glumi] *adj* 憂鬱な [yuuutsu na]

glorious [glɔriəs] *adj* すばらしい [subarashii]

glory [glɔri] *n* 栄誉 [eiyo]

glove [glʌv] *n* グローブ [guroobu], 手袋
[tebukuro]; **glove compartment** *n* グローブ
ボックス [guroobubokkusu]; **oven glove** *n* オ
ーブンミット [oobunmitto]; **rubber gloves**
npl ゴム手袋 [gomu tebukuro]

glucose [glukous] *n* グルコース [gurukoosu]

glue [glu] *n* 接着剤 [setchakuzai] ▷ *v* 接着剤で
つける [setchakuzai de tsukeru]

gluten [glutᵊn] *n* グルテン [guruten]; **Could
you prepare a meal without gluten?** グル
テンを使わずに食事を用意していただけます
か? [guruten o tsukawazu ni shokuji o youi
shite itadakemasu ka?]; **Do you have
gluten-free dishes?** グルテンを使っていな
い料理はありますか? [guruten o tsukatte inai
ryouri wa arimasu ka?]

GM [dʒi ɛm] *abbr* (= *genetically modified*) 遺
伝子組み換えの [idenshi kumikae no]

go [goʊ] *v* 行く [iku]; **Excuse me, which bus
goes to...?** すみません、···へ行くバスはどれ
ですか? [sumimasen,... e iku basu wa dore
desu ka?]; **Is it time to go?** もう行く時間で
すか? [mou iku jikan desu ka?]

go ahead *v* 先へ進む [saki-e susumu]

goal [goʊl] *n* ゴール [gouru]

goalkeeper [goʊlkipər] *n* ゴールキーパー
[gourukiipaa]

go around *v* 皆に行き渡る [mina ni iki
wataru]

goat [goʊt] *n* ヤギ [yagi]

go away *v* 立ち去る [tachisaru]

go back *v* 戻る [modoru]

go by *v* 通過する [tsuuka suru]

god [gɒd] *n* 神 [kami]

godchild [gɒdtʃaɪld] (*pl* **godchildren**) *n* 教
子 [kyouko] (男女)

goddaughter [gɒddɔtər] *n* 教女 [kyoujo]

godfather [gɒdfɑðər] *n* (*baptism*) 教父

[kyoufu] (名づけ親), *(criminal leader)* ゴッドファーザー [goddofaazaa]

godmother [gɒdmʌðər] *n* 教母 [kyoubo]

go down *v* 下がる [sagaru]

godson [gɒdsʌn] *n* 教子 [kyouko] (男子)

goggles [gɒglz] *npl* ゴーグル [gouguru]; **I want to rent goggles** ゴーグルを借りたいのですが [googuru o karitai no desu ga]

go in *v* 入る [hairu]

gold [gould] *n* 金 [kin] (金 [kin]属)

golden [gouldⁿn] *adj* 金製の [kinsei no]

goldfish [gouldfɪʃ] *n* 金魚 [kingyo]

gold-plated [gouldpleɪtɪd] *adj* 金めっきの [kinmekki no]

golf [gɒlf] *n* ゴルフ [gorufu]; **golf club** *n (game)* ゴルフ用クラブ [gorufu you kurabu], *(society)* ゴルフクラブ [gorufukurabu]; **golf course** *n* ゴルフ場 [gorufujou]; **Do they rent out golf clubs?** ゴルフクラブを貸し出していますか? [gorufu-kurabu o kashidashite imasu ka?]; **Is there a public golf course near here?** この近くに公共のゴルフコースはありますか? [kono chikaku ni kookyou no gorufu-koosu wa arimasu ka?]; **Where can I play golf?** どこでゴルフができますか? [doko de gorufu ga dekimasu ka?]

gone [gɔn] *adj* いなくなって [inaku natte]

good [gʊd] *adj* 良い [yoi]

goodbye [gʊdbaɪ] *excl* さようなら! [sayounara]

good-looking [gʊdlʊkɪŋ] *adj* 美貌の [bibou no]

good-natured [gʊdneɪtʃərd] *adj* 気だてのよい [kidate no yoi]

goods [gʊdz] *npl* 商品 [shouhin]

go off *v* 止まる [tomaru]

Google® [gugⁿl] *v* グーグル®で調べる [Guuguru® de shiraberu]

go on *v* 続ける [tsuzukeru]

goose [gus] *n* ガチョウ [gachou]; **goose bumps** *npl* 鳥肌 [torihada]

gooseberry [gusbɛri] *n* グーズベリー [guuzuberii]

go out *v* 外出する [gaishutsu suru]

go past *v* ···を過ぎる [...-o sugiru]

gorgeous [gɔrdʒəs] *adj* 華麗な [karei na]

gorilla [gərɪlə] *n* ゴリラ [gorira]

gospel [gɒspⁿl] *n* 福音 [fukuin]

gossip [gɒsɪp] *n* うわさ話 [uwasabanashi] ▷ *v* うわさ話をする [uwasabanashi-o suru]

go through *v* 経験する [keiken suru]

go up *v* 上がる [agaru]

government [gʌvərnmənt] *n* 政府 [seifu]; **government-subsidized dwelling** *n* 公営住宅 [koueijuutaku]

GPS [dʒi pi ɛs] *abbr* グローバルポジショニングシステム [guroobarupojishoningushisutemu]

grab [græb] *v* ひっつかむ [hittsukamu]

graceful [greɪsfəl] *adj* 優美な [yuubi na]

grade [greɪd] *n* 等級 [toukyuu] ▷ *v (grade)* 採点する [saiten suru]

gradual [grædʒuəl] *adj* 徐々の [jojo no]

gradually [grædʒuəli] *adv* 徐々に [jojo ni]

graduate *n* 大学の卒業生 [daigaku no sotsugyousei]; **graduate student** *n* 大学院生 [daigakuinsei]

graduation [grædʒueɪʃⁿn] *n* 大学卒業 [daigaku sotsugyou]

graffiti [grəfiti] *npl* 落書き [rakugaki]

grain [greɪn] *n* 穀粒 [kokutsubu]

gram [græm] *n* グラム [guramu]

grammar [græmər] *n* 文法 [bunpou]

grammatical [grəmætɪkⁿl] *adj* 文法の [bunpou no]

grand [grænd] *adj* 壮大な [sodai na]

grandchild [græntʃaɪld] *n* 孫 [mago]

grandchildren [grændtʃɪldrən] *npl* 孫 [mago]

granddad [grændæd] *n* おじいちゃん [ojiichan]

granddaughter [grændotər] *n* 孫娘 [magomusume]

grandfather [grænfaðər] *n* 祖父 [sofu]

grandma [grænmɑ] *n* おばあちゃん [obaachan]

grandmother [grænmʌðər] *n* 祖母 [sobo]

grandpa [grǽnpɑ] *n* おじいちゃん [ojiichan]

grandparents [grǽnpɛərənts] *npl* 祖父母 [sofubo]

grandson [grǽnsʌn] *n* 孫息子 [magomusuko]

granite [grǽnɪt] *n* みかげ石 [mikageishi]

granny [grǽni] *n* おばあちゃん [obaachan]

grant [grǽnt] *n* 助成金 [joseikin]

grape [greɪp] *n* ブドウ [budou]

grapefruit [greɪpfrut] *n* グレープフルーツ [gureepufuruutsu]

graph [grǽf] *n* グラフ [gurafu]

graphics [grǽfɪks] *npl* 画像 [gazou]

grasp [grǽsp] *v* しっかりつかむ [shikkari tsukamu]

grass [grǽs] *n* 草 [kusa]

grasshopper [grǽshɑpər] *n* イナゴ [inago]

grate [greɪt] *v* すりおろす [suriorosu]

grateful [greɪtfəl] *adj* 感謝している [kansha shite iru]

gratitude [grǽtɪtud] *n* 感謝 [kansha]

grave [greɪv] *n* 墓 [haka]

gravel [grǽvˑl] *n* 砂利 [jari]

gravestone [greɪvstoun] *n* 墓石 [hakaishi]

graveyard [greɪvyɑrd] *n* 墓地 [bochi]

gravy [greɪvi] *n* グレービーソース [gureebiisoosu]

gray [greɪ] *adj* 灰色の [hai iro no]

gray-haired [greɪ(h)ɛərd] *adj* 白髪のある [shiraga no aru]

grease [gris] *n* 獣脂 [juushi]

greasy [grisi, -zi] *adj* 脂を含んだ [abura-o fukunda]

great [greɪt] *adj* 大きな [ooki na]

Great Britain [greɪt brɪtˑn] *n* グレートブリテン [gureetoburiten]

great-grandfather *n* 曾祖父 [sousofu]

great-grandmother *n* 曾祖母 [sousobo]

Greece [gris] *n* ギリシャ [girisha]

greedy [gridi] *adj* 欲ばりの [yokubari no]

Greek [grik] *adj* ギリシャの [girisha no] ▷ *n* *(language)* ギリシャ語 [girishago], *(person)* ギリシャ人 [girishajin]

green [grin] *adj* *(color)* 緑色の [midori iro no], *(inexperienced)* 未熟な [mijuku na] *(経験不足)* ▷ *n* 緑色 [ryokushoku]; **green beans** *npl* サヤインゲン [saya ingen]; **green salad** *n* グリーンサラダ [guriin sarada]

greenhouse [grinhaus] *n* 温室 [onshitsu]

Greenland [grinlənd] *n* グリーンランド [guriinrando]

greet [grit] *v* ・・・に挨拶する [… ni aisatsu suru]

greeting [gritɳ] *n* グリーティン [guriitin], 挨拶 [aisatsu]; **greeting card** *n* グリーティングカード [guriitingukaado]

grid [grɪd] *n* グリッド [guriddo]

grief [grif] *n* 深い悲しみ [fukai kanashimi]

grill [grɪl] *n* グリル [guriru]

grim [grɪm] *adj* いやな [iya na]

grin [grɪn] *n* にこにこ笑い [nikoniko warai] ▷ *v* 歯を見せてにっこり笑う [ha-o misete nikkori warau]

grind [graɪnd] *v* 挽く [hiku]; **ground meat** *n* 挽肉 [hikiniku]

grip [grɪp] *v* しっかりつかむ [shikkari tsukamu]

gripe [graɪp] *n* *(complaint)* 不平 [fuhei]

gripping [grɪpɪŋ] *adj* 心を強くとらえる [kokoro wo tsuyoku toraeru]

grit [grɪt] *n* 粗い砂 [araisuna]

groan [groun] *v* うなる [unaru]

grocer [grousər] *n* 食料雑貨商 [shokuryou zakkashou]

groceries [grousˑriz] *npl* 食料雑貨類 [shokuryou zakkarui]

grocery [grousəri, grousri] *n* **grocery store** *n* 食料雑貨店 [shokuryou zakkaten]

groom [grum] *n* 馬の飼育係 [uma no shiikugakari]

grope [group] *v* 手探りする [tesaguri suru]

gross [grous] *adj* ひどい [hidoi]

grossly [grousli] *adv* ひどく [hidoku]

ground [graund] *n* 地面 [jimen] ▷ *v* 地面に置く [jimen ni oku]

group [grup] *n* タイ [tai], グループ [guruupu],

群れ [mure], 刃 [ha], 団体 [dantai]; **Are there any discounts for groups?** 団体割引はありますか? [dantai-waribiki wa arimasu ka?]

grouse [graʊs] n *(game bird)* ライチョウ [raichou]

grow [groʊ] vi 成長する [seichou suru] ▷ vt 育てる [sodateru]

growl [graʊl] v 怒ってうなる [ikatte unaru]

grown-up n 成人 [seijin]

growth [groʊθ] n 成長 [seichou]

grow up v 大人になる [otona ni naru]

grub [grʌb] n 地虫 [jimushi]

grudge [grʌdʒ] n 恨み [urami]

gruesome [grusəm] adj ぞっとする [zotto suru]

grumpy [grʌmpi] adj 気むずかしい [kimuzukashii]

guarantee [gærənti] n 保証 [hoshou] ▷ v 保証する [hoshou suru]

guard [gɑrd] n 見張り [mihari], 警備 [keibi] ▷ v 見張る [miharu]; **coast guard** n 沿岸警備隊 [engankeibitai]; **security guard** n 警備員 [keibiin]

Guatemala [gwɑtəmglə] n グアテマラ [guatemara]

guess [gɛs] n 推測 [suisoku] ▷ v 推測する [suisoku suru]

guest [gɛst] n 客 [kyaku]

guesthouse [gɛsthaʊs] n ゲストハウス [gesutohausu]

guide [gaɪd] n ガイド [gaido]; **guided tour** n ガイドツアー [gaidotsuaa]; **tour guide** n ツアーガイド [tsuaagaido]; **Do you have a guide book in...?** ···語のガイドブックはありますか? [... go no gaidobukku wa arimasu ka?];

Do you have a guide book in English? 英語のガイドブックはありますか? [eigo no gaidobukku wa arimasu ka?]; **Do you have a guide to local trails?** 地元のウォーキングのガイドはいますか? [jimoto no wookingu no gaido wa imasu ka?]; **Is there a guide who speaks English?** 英語を話すガイドはいますか? [eigo o hanasu gaido wa imasu ka?]

guidebook [gaɪdbʊk] n ガイドブック [gaidobukku]

guilt [gɪlt] n 有罪 [yuuzai]

guilty [gɪlti] adj 有罪の [yuuzai no]

Guinea [gɪni] n ギニア [ginia]; **guinea pig** n *(for experiment)* 実験台 [jikkendai], *(rodent)* モルモット (動物) [morumotto]

guitar [gɪtɑr] n ギター [gitaa]

gum [gʌm] n ガム [gamu], 粘性ゴム [nenseigomu]; **chewing gum** n チューインガム [chuuingamu]

gums n 歯ぐき [haguki]

gun [gʌn] n 銃 [juu]; **machine gun** n マシンガン [mashingan]

gust [gʌst] n 突風 [toppuu]

gut [gʌt] n 腸 [chou]

guy [gaɪ] n 男 [otoko]

Guyana [gaɪænə] n ガイアナ [gaiana]

gym [dʒɪm] n ジム [jimu]; **gym shoes** npl トレーニングシューズ [toreeningushuuzu]; **Where's the gym?** ジムはどこですか? [jimu wa doko desu ka?]

gymnast [dʒɪmnæst] n 体操家 [taisouka]

gymnastics [dʒɪmnæstɪks] npl 体操 [taisou]

gynecologist [gaɪnɪkɒlədʒɪst] n 婦人科医 [fujinkai]

gypsy [dʒɪpsi] n ジプシー [jipushii]

H

habit [hǽbɪt] *n* 癖 [kuse]

hack [hæk] *v* たたき切る [tatakikiru]

hacker [hǽkər] *n* ハッカー [hakkaa]

haddock [hǽdək] *n* ハドック [hadokku]

haggle [hǽgl] *v* うるさく値切る [urusaku negiru]

hail [heɪl] *n* 雹 [hyou] ▷ *v* 呼び止める [yobitomeru]

hair [hɛər] *n* ヘア [hea], 髪 [kami]; **hair gel** *n* ヘアジェル [heajieru]; **hair spray** *n* ヘアスプレー [heasupuree]; **Can you straighten my hair?** 髪をまっすぐにしてもらえますか? [kami o massugu ni shite moraemasu ka?]; **Could you color my hair, please?** 髪を染めていただけますか? [kami o somete itadakemasu ka?]; **I have oily hair** 私の髪は脂性です [watashi no kami wa aburashou desu]; **I need a hair dryer** 私はヘアドライヤーが必要です [watashi wa hea-doraiyaa ga hitsuyou desu]; **What do you recommend for my hair?** 私の髪には何がいいと思いますか? [watashi no kami ni wa nani ga ii to omoimasu ka?]

hairbrush [hɛərbrʌʃ] *n* ヘアブラシ [heaburashi]

haircut [hɛərkʌt] *n* カット [katto], ヘアカット [heakatto]

hairdo [hɛərdu] *n* ヘアスタイル [heasutairu]

hairdresser [hɛərdrɛsər] *n* 美容師 [biyoushi]

hairdresser's [hɛərdrɛsərs] *n* 美容院 [biyouin]

hair dryer [hɛərdraɪr] *n* ヘアドライヤー [headoraiyaa]

hairstyle [hɛərstaɪl] *n* ヘアスタイル [heasutairu]

hairy [hɛəri] *adj* 毛深い [kebukai]

Haiti [heɪti] *n* ハイチ [haichi]

halal [həlɑl] *adj* ハラール [haraaru]

half [hæf] *adj* 半分の [hanbun no] ▷ *adv* 半分だけ [hanbun dake] ▷ *n* 半 [han], 半分 [hanbun]; **half hour** *n* 三十分 [sanjuppun]

half-price [hæf praɪs] *adj* 半額の [hangaku no] ▷ *adv* 半額で [hangaku de]

half-time *n* ハーフタイム [haafutaimu]

halfway [hæfweɪ] *adv* 中程で [nakahodo de]

hall [hɔl] *n* 入口の廊下 [iriguchi no rouka]; **town hall** *n* タウンホール [taunhooru]

hallway [hɔlweɪ] *n* 玄関 [genkan]

halt [hɔlt] *n* 停止 [teishi]

ham [hæm] *n* ハム [hamu]

hamburger [hǽmbɜrgər] *n* ハンバーガー [hanbaagaa]

hammer [hǽmər] *n* ハンマー [hanmaa]

hammock [hǽmək] *n* ハンモック [hanmokku]

hamster [hǽmstər] *n* ハムスター [hamusutaa]

hand [hænd] *n* 手 [te] ▷ *v* 手渡す [tewatasu]; **Where can I wash my hands?** どこで手を洗えばいいのですか? [doko de te o araeba ii no desu ka?]

handbag [hǽndbæg] *n* ハンドバッグ [handobaggu]

handball [hǽndbɔl] *n* ハンドボール [handobooru]

handbook [hǽndbʊk] *n* ハンドブック [handobukku]

handcuffs [hǽndkʌfs] *npl* 手錠 [tejou]

handicap [hǽndikæp] *n* **My handicap is...** 私のハンディーキャップは···です [watashi no handiikyappu wa... desu]; **What's your handicap?** あなたのハンディーキャップはどのくらいですか? [anata no handiikyappu wa dono kurai desu ka?]

handicapped [hændikæpt] *adj* 障害のある [shougai no aru]

handkerchief [hæŋkərtʃɪf] *n* ハンカチ [hankachi]

handle [hænd·l] *n* ハンドル [handoru] (取っ手) ▷ *v* 取り扱う [toriatsukau]

handlebars [hænd·lbɑrz] *npl* ハンドル [handoru] (自転車・バイク)

hand-made *adj* ハンドメイド [handomeido]

handmade [hændmeɪd] *adj* 手製の [tesei no]

hands-free [hændzfri] *adj* ハンズフリーの [hanzufurii no]; **hands-free kit** *n* ハンズフリーキット [hanzu furii kitto]

handsome [hænsəm] *adj* ハンサムな [hansamu na]

handwriting [hændraɪtɪŋ] *n* 手書き [tegaki]

hang [hæŋ] *vi* 掛かる [kaka ru] ▷ *vt* 掛ける [kakeru]

hanger [hæŋər] *n* ハンガー [hangaa]; **coat hanger** *n* ハンガー [hangaa]

hang-gliding *n* ハンググライディング [hanguguraideingu]; **I'd like to go hang-gliding** 私はハンググライディングをしたいのですが [watashi wa hanguguraidingu o shitai no desu ga]

hang on *v* そのまま待つ [sono mama matsu]

hangover [hæŋoʊvər] *n* 二日酔い [futsukayoi]

hang up *v* 電話を切る [denwa wo kiru]

hankie [hæŋki] *n* ハンカチ [hankachi]

happen [hæpən] *v* 起こる [okoru]

happily [hæpɪli] *adv* 幸福に [koufuku ni]

happiness [hæpɪnɪs] *n* 幸福 [koufuku]

happy [hæpi] *adj* うれしい [ureshii], 幸福な [koufuku na]

harassment [həræsmənt, hærəs-] *n* いやがらせ [iyagarase]

harbor [hɑrbər] *n* 港 [minato]

hard [hɑrd] *adj* (difficult) 困難な [konnan na], (firm, rigid) 堅い [katai] ▷ *adv* 懸命に [kenmei ni]; **hard disk** *n* ハードディスク

[haadodisuku]; **hard shoulder** *n* 路肩 [rokata]

hardboard [hɑrdbɔrd] *n* ハードボード [haadoboodo]

hard cider [-saɪdər] *n* りんご酒 [ringoshu]

hardly [hɑrdli] *adv* ほとんど・・・ない [hotondo... nai]

hardware [hɑrdwɛr] *n* ハードウェア [haadouea]; **hardware store** *n* 金物屋 [kanamonoya]

hare [hɛər] *n* 野ウサギ [nousagi]

harm [hɑrm] *v* 害する [gai suru]

harmful [hɑrmfəl] *adj* 有害な [yuugai na]

harmless [hɑrmlɪs] *adj* 無害な [mugai na]

harmonica [hɑrmɒnɪkə] *n* ハーモニカ [haamonika]

harp [hɑrp] *n* ハープ [haapu]

harsh [hɑrʃ] *adj* 厳しい [kibishii]

harvest [hɑrvɪst] *n* 収穫 [shuukaku] ▷ *v* 収穫する [shuukaku suru]

hastily [heɪstɪli] *adv* 急いで [isoide]

hat [hæt] *n* 帽子 [boushi]

hatchback [hætʃbæk] *n* ハッチバック [hatchibakku]

hate [heɪt] *v* 憎む [nikumu]

hatred [heɪtrɪd] *n* 憎しみ [nikushimi]

haunted [hɒntɪd] *adj* 幽霊が出没する [yuurei ga shutsubotsu suru]

have [həv, STRONG hæv] *v* 持っている [motte iru]

have to *v* ・・・しなければならない [... shinakereba naranai]

hawthorn [hɔθɔrn] *n* サンザシ [sanzashi]

hay [heɪ] *n* 干し草 [hoshikusa]; **hay fever** *n* 花粉症 [kafunshou]

haystack [heɪstæk] *n* 干し草の山 [hoshikusa no yama]

hazelnut [heɪz·lnʌt] *n* ヘーゼルナッツ [heezerunattsu]

head [hɛd] *n* (body part) 頭 [atama]; **head office** *n* 本社 [honsha]

headache [hɛdeɪk] *n* 頭痛 [zutsuu]; **I'd like something for a headache** 頭痛に効くもの

が欲しいのですが [zutsuu ni kiku mono ga hoshii no desu ga]

headband [hɛdbænd] *n* ヘアバンド [heabando]

headlight [hɛdlaɪt] *n* ヘッドライト [heddoraito], ヘッドランプ [heddoranpu]; **The headlights aren't working** ヘッドランプがつきません [heddoranpu ga tsukimasen]

headline [hɛdlaɪn] *n* 見出し [midashi]

headphones [hɛdfoʊnz] *npl* ヘッドホン [heddohon]; **Does it have headphones?** ヘッドホンはついていますか? [heddohon wa tsuite imasu ka?]

headquarters [hɛdkwɔrtərz] *npl* 本社 [honsha]

headscarf [hɛdskɑrf] (*pl* **headscarves**) *n* ヘッドスカーフ [heddosukaafu]

heal [hil] *v* 治る [naoru]

health [hɛlθ] *n* 健康 [kenkou]

healthy [hɛlθi] *adj* 健康な [kenkou na]

heap [hip] *n* 積み重なったもの [tsumikasan-atta mono]

hear [hɪər] *v* 聞く [kiku]

hearing [hɪərɪŋ] *n* 聴力 [chouryoku]; **hearing aid** *n* 補聴器 [hochouki]

heart [hɑrt] *n* 心 [kokoro], 心臓 [shinzou]; **heart attack** *n* 心臓発作 [shinzouhossa]; **I have a heart condition** 私は心臓病があります [watashi wa shinzou-byou ga arimasu]

heartbroken [hɑrtbroʊkən] *adj* 失恋した [shitsuren shita]

heartburn [hɑrtbɜrn] *n* 胸焼け [muneyake]

heat [hit] *n* 熱 [netsu] ▷ *v* 熱する [nessuru]

heater [hitər] *n* 暖房器具 [danbou kigu]

heather [hɛðər] *n* ヘザー [hezaa]

heating [hitɪŋ] *n* 暖房 [danbou]; **central heating** *n* セントラルヒーティング [sentoraruhiitingu]; **Does the room have heating?** その部屋に暖房はありますか? [sono heya ni danbou wa arimasu ka?]; **How does the heating work?** 暖房はどうやって使うのですか? [danbou wa dou-yatte tsukau no desu ka?]; **The heating doesn't work** 暖

房がつきません [danbou ga tsukimasen]

heat up *v* 加熱する [kanetsu suru]

heaven [hɛvən] *n* 天国 [tengoku]

heavily [hɛvɪli] *adv* 重く [omoku]

heavy [hɛvi] *adj* 重い [omoi]

hedge [hɛdʒ] *n* 垣根 [kakine]

hedgehog [hɛdʒhɔg] *n* ハリネズミ [harinezumi]

heel [hil] *n* かかと [kakato]; **high heels** *npl* ハイヒール [haihiiru]

height [haɪt] *n* 高さ [takasa]

heir [ɛər] *n* 相続人 [souzokunin]

heiress [ɛərɪs] *n* 女相続人 [onna souzokunin]

helicopter [hɛlikɒptər] *n* ヘリコプター [herikoputaa]

hell [hɛl] *n* 地獄 [jigoku]

hello [hɛloʊ] *excl* こんにちは! [konnichi ha]

helmet [hɛlmɪt] *n* ヘルメット [herumetto]; **May I have a helmet?** ヘルメットをください [herumetto o kudasai]

help [hɛlp] *n* 援助 [enjo] ▷ *v* 助ける [tasukeru]

help [hɛlp] *excl* 助けて! [tasukete]

helpful [hɛlpfʊl] *adj* 役に立つ [yaku ni tatsu]

helpline [hɛlplaɪn] *n* ヘルプライン [herupurain]

hemorrhoids [hɛmərɔɪdz] *npl* 痔 [di]

hen [hɛn] *n* めんどり [mendori]

hepatitis [hɛpətaɪtɪs] *n* 肝炎 [kanen]

her [hər, STRONG hɜr] *pron* **She's hurt her leg** 彼女は脚を痛めました [kanojo wa ashi o itamemashita]

herbs [ɜrbz] *npl* ハーブ [haabu]

here [hɪər] *adv* ここに [koko ni]

hereditary [hɪrɛdɪtɛri] *adj* 遺伝的な [identeki na]

heredity [hɪrɛdɪti] *n* 遺伝 [iden]

heritage [hɛrɪtɪdʒ] *n* 先祖伝来のもの [senzo denrai no mono]

hernia [hɜrniə] *n* ヘルニア [herunia]

hero [hɪəroʊ] *n* ヒーロー [hiiroo]

heroin [hɛroʊɪn] *n* ヘロイン [heroin]

heroine [hɛroʊɪn] *n* ヒロイン [hiroin]

heron [hɛrən] *n* サギ [sagi] (鳥)

herring [hɛrɪŋ] *n* ニシン [nishin]; **smoked herring** *n* キッパー [kippaa]

herself [hərsɛlf] *pron* **She's hurt herself** 彼女は怪我をしました [kanojo wa kega o shimashita]

hesitate [hɛzɪteɪt] *v* ためらう [tamerau]

heterosexual [hɛtərəʊsɛkʃuəl] *adj* 異性愛の [iseiai no]

hi [haɪ] *excl* やあ! [yaa]

hiccups [hɪkʌps] *npl* しゃっくり [shakkuri]

hidden [hɪd·n] *adj* 隠された [kakusareta]

hide [haɪd] *vi* 隠れる [kakureru] ▷ *vt* 隠す [kakusu]

hide-and-seek *n* 隠れん坊 [kakurenbou]

hideous [hɪdiəs] *adj* ぞっとする [zotto suru]

hi-fi [haɪ faɪ] *n* ハイファイ装置 [haifai souchi]

high [haɪ] *adj* 高い [takai] (高低) ▷ *adv* 高く [takaku]; **high heels** *npl* ハイヒール [haihiiru]; **high jump** *n* 走り高跳び [hashiri takatobi]

high chair *n* 小児用の食事椅子 [shouni you no shokuji isu]

high-heeled *adj* ハイヒールの [haihiiru no]

highlight [haɪlaɪt] *n* ハイライト [hairaito] (やま場) ▷ *v* 強調する [kyouchou suru]

highlighter [haɪlaɪtər] *n* ハイライト [hairaito] (化粧品)

high-rise *n* 高層建築 [kousou kenchiku]

high-tide *n* 満ち潮 [michishio]

highway [haɪweɪ] *n* 高速道路 [kousoku-douro]; **divided highway** *n* 中央分離帯付き道路 [chuuou bunritai tsuki douro]; **highway ramp** *n* 高速道路の進入退出路 [kousoku douro no shinnyuu taishutsuro]; **highway tax** *n* 自動車の道路利用税 [jidousha no douro riyou zei]

hijack [haɪdʒæk] *v* ハイジャックする [haijakku suru]

hijacker [haɪdʒækər] *n* ハイジャックの犯人 [haijakku no hannin]

hike [haɪk] *n* ハイキング [haikingu], *(long walk)* 徒歩旅行 [tohoryokou]

hiker [haɪkər] *n* ハイカー [haikaa]

hiking [haɪkɪŋ] *n* ハイキング [haikingu], ヒルウォーキング [hiruuookingu]; **I'd like to go hiking** ヒルウォーキングに行きたいのですが [hiru-wookingu ni ikitai no desu ga]

hilarious [hɪlɛəriəs] *adj* 陽気な [youki na]

hill [hɪl] *n* 丘 [oka]; **bunny hill** *n* 初心者用ゲレンデ [shoshinshayou gerende]

him [hɪm] *pron* **We have to get him to a hospital** 私たちは彼を病院に連れて行かなければなりません [watashi-tachi wa kare o byouin ni tsurete ikanakereba narimasen]

himself [hɪmsɛlf] *pron* **He's cut himself** 彼は怪我をしました [kare wa kega o shimashita]

Hindu [hɪndu] *adj* ヒンズー教の [Hinzuu kyou no] ▷ *n* ヒンズー教徒 [Hinzuu kyouto]

Hinduism [hɪnduɪzəm] *n* ヒンズー教 [hinzuukyou]

hinge [hɪndʒ] *n* ちょうつがい [choutsugai]

hint [hɪnt] *n* ヒント [hinto] ▷ *v* ほのめかす [honomekasu]

hip [hɪp] *n* 腰 [koshi]

hippie [hɪpi] *n* ヒッピー [hippii]

hippo [hɪpoʊ] *n* カバ [kaba] (植物)

hippopotamus [hɪpəpɒtəməs] *(pl* **hippopotami)** *n* カバ [kaba] (植物)

hire [haɪər] *n* (rental) 賃借り [chingari] ▷ *v* (people) 賃借りする [chingari suru]

his [hɪz] *pron* **He can't move his leg** 彼は脚を動かせません [kare wa ashi o ugokase-masen]

historian [hɪstɔriən] *n* 歴史家 [rekishika]

historical [hɪstɒrɪk·l] *adj* 歴史上の [rekishijou no]

history [hɪstəri, -tri] *n* 歴史 [rekishi]

hit [hɪt] *n* 衝突 [shoutotsu] ▷ *v* 打つ [utsu]

hitch [hɪtʃ] *n* 障害 [shougai]

hitchhike [hɪtʃhaɪk] *v* ヒッチハイクする [hitchihaiku suru]

hitchhiker [hɪtʃhaɪkər] *n* ヒッチハイクをする人 [hitchihaiku wo suru hito]

hitchhiking [hɪtʃhaɪkɪŋ] *n* ヒッチハイク

[hicchihaiku]

HIV-negative *adj* HIV陰性の [eichiaibui insei no]

HIV-positive *adj* HIV陽性の [eichiaibui yousei no]

hobby [hɒbi] *n* 趣味 [shumi]

hockey [hɒki] *n* アイスホッケー [aisuhokkee]; **field hockey** *n* ホッケー [hokkee]

hold [hould] *v* 手に持つ [te ni motsu]

hold on *v* しっかりつかまる [shikkari tsukamaru]

hold up *v* 持ちこたえる [mochikotaeru]

hold-up *n* 強盗 [goutou] (量・程度)

hole [houl] *n* 穴 [ana]; **I have a hole in my shoe** 靴に穴があきました [kutsu ni ana ga akimashita]

holiday [hɒlɪdeɪ] *n* **public holiday** *n* 祝祭日 [shukusaijitsu]

Holland [hɒlənd] *n* オランダ [oranda]

hollow [hɒlou] *adj* 空洞の [kuudou no]

holly [hɒli] *n* セイヨウヒイラギ [seiyouhiiragi]

holy [houli] *adj* 神聖な [shinsei na]

home [houm] *adj* ホーム [hoomu] ▷ *adv* 我が家へ [wagaya-e] ▷ *n* 自宅 [jitaku]; **home address** *n* 自宅住所 [jitaku juusho]; **home game** *n* ホームの試合 [hoomu no shiai]; **home page** *n* ホームページ [hoomupeeji]; **mobile home** *n* モビールハウス [mobiiru-hausu]; **nursing home** *n* 老人ホーム [roujin hoomu]

homeland [houmlænd] *n* 祖国 [sokoku]

homeless [houmlɪs] *adj* 住む家のない [sumu ie no nai]

homemade [hoummeɪd] *adj* 自家製の [jikasei no]

homeopathic [houmioupæθɪk] *adj* ホメオパシーの [homeopashii no]

homeopathy [houmippəθi] *n* ホメオパシー [homeopashii]

homesick [houmsɪk] *adj* ホームシックの [hoomushikku no]

homework [houmwɜrk] *n* 宿題 [shukudai]

Honduras [hɒndjʊərəs] *n* ホンジュラス [honjurasu]

honest [ɒnɪst] *adj* 正直な [shoujiki na]

honestly [ɒnɪstli] *adv* 正直に [shoujiki ni]

honesty [ɒnɪsti] *n* 正直 [shoujiki]

honey [hʌni] *n* 蜂蜜 [hachimitsu]

honeymoon [hʌnimun] *n* ハネムーン [hanemuun]; **We're on our honeymoon** 私たちはハネムーン中です [watashi-tachi wa hanemuun-chuu desu]

honeysuckle [hʌnisʌkᵊl] *n* スイカズラ [suikazura]

honor [ɒnər] *n* 道義心 [dougishin], 光栄 [kouei]

hood [hʊd] *n* フード [fuudo], *(car)* ボンネット [bonnetto]

hook [hʊk] *n* フック [fukku]

hooky [hʊki] *n* **play hooky** *v* サボる [saboru]

hooray [hʊreɪ] *excl* 万歳! [banzai]

hope [houp] *n* 希望 [kibou] ▷ *v* 望む [nozomu]

hopeful [houpfəl] *adj* 希望が持てる [kibou ga moteru]

hopefully [houpfəli] *adv* 希望を持って [kibou-o motte]

hopeless [houplɪs] *adj* 希望を失って [kibou-o ushinatte]

horizon [həraɪzᵊn] *n* 地平線 [chiheisen]

horizontal [hɒrɪzɒntᵊl] *adj* 水平な [suihei na]

hormone [hɔrmoun] *n* ホルモン [horumon]

horn [hɔrn] *n* 角 [kado] *(動物)*; **French horn** *n* フレンチホルン [furenchihorun]

horoscope [hɒrəskoup] *n* 星占い [hoshiuranai]

horrendous [hɒrɛndəs, hɒ-, hə-] *adj* 恐ろしい [osoroshii]

horrible [hɒrɪbᵊl, hɒr-] *adj* 実にひどい [jitsu ni hidoi]

horrifying [hɒrɪfaɪɪŋ, hɒr-] *adj* ぞっとさせる [zotto saseru]

horror [hɒrər, hɒr-] *adj* ホラー [horaa] ▷ *n* 恐怖 [kyoufu]; **horror movie** *n* ホラー映画 [horaa eiga]

horse [hɔrs] *n* 馬 [uma]; **horse racing** *n* 競馬 [keiba]; **rocking horse** *n* 揺り木馬

[yurimokuba]; **I'd like to see a horse race**
私は競馬を観戦したいのですが [watashi wa
keiba o kansen shitai no desu ga]
horseback [hɔrsbæk] *n* **Can we go
horseback riding?** 乗馬に行けますか?
[jouba ni ikemasu ka?]; **Let's go horseback
riding** 乗馬に行きましょう [jouba ni
ikimashou]
horseradish [hɔrsrædɪʃ] *n* セイヨウワサビ
[seiyouwasabi]
horseshoe [hɔrsʃu] *n* 蹄鉄 [teitetsu]
hose [houz] *n* ホース [hoosu]
hosepipe [houzpaɪp] *n* ホース [hoosu]
hospital [hɒspɪtl] *n* 病院 [byouin]; **maternity
hospital** *n* 産科病院 [sanka byouin]; **mental
hospital** *n* 精神病院 [seishinbyouin]; **How
do I get to the hospital?** その病院へはどう
行けばいいのですか? [sono byouin e wa
dou ikeba ii no desu ka?]; **I work in a
hospital** 私は病院で働いています [watashi
wa byouin de hataraite imasu]; **We have to
get him to a hospital** 私たちは彼を病院に
連れて行かなければなりません [watashi-
tachi wa kare o byouin ni tsurete
ikanakereba narimasen]; **Where is the
hospital?** 病院はどこですか? [byouin wa
doko desu ka?]; **Will he have to go to the
hospital?** 彼は病院に行かなければなりませ
んか? [kare wa byouin ni ikanakereba
narimasen ka?]
hospitality [hɒspɪtælɪti] *n* 歓待 [kantai]
hospitalization [hɒspɪtələzeɪʃn] *n* 入院
[nyuuin]
host [houst] *n* プレゼンター [purezentaa],
(entertains) ホスト [hosuto], *(multitude)* 多
数 [tasuu]
hostage [hɒstɪdʒ] *n* 人質 [hitojichi]
hostel [hɒstl] *n* ホステル [hosuteru]; **Is there
a youth hostel nearby?** 近くにユースホステ
ルはありますか? [chikaku ni yuusu-hosuteru
wa arimasu ka?]
hostile [hɒstl] *adj* 敵意のある [teki-i no aru]
hot [hɒt] *adj* 熱い [atsui]; 厚い [atsui]; **hot**

dog *n* ホットドッグ [hottodokku]
hotel [houtɛl] *n* ホテル [hoteru]; **Could you
make a hotel reservation for me?** 私のた
めにホテルの部屋を予約してもらえますか?
[watashi no tame ni hoteru no heya o
yoyaku shite moraemasu ka?]; **Could you
recommend a hotel?** いいホテルを教えても
らえますか? [ii hoteru o oshiete moraemasu
ka?]; **He runs the hotel** 彼がホテルの経営者
です [kare ga hoteru no keieisha desu]; **I'm
staying at a hotel** 私はホテルに滞在してい
ます [watashi wa hoteru ni taizai shite
imasu]; **Is your hotel accessible to
wheelchairs?** おたくのホテルは車椅子で利
用できますか? [otaku no hoteru wa
kuruma-isu de riyou dekimasu ka?]; **We're
looking for a hotel** 私たちはホテルを探して
います [watashi-tachi wa hoteru o sagashite
imasu]; **What's the best way to get to this
hotel?** このホテルへ行く一番よい方法は何で
すか? [kono hoteru e iku ichiban yoi houhou
wa nan desu ka?]
hour [auər] *n* 一時間 [ichijikan]; **half hour** *n*
三十分 [sanjuppun]; **lunch hour** *n* 昼休み
[hiruyasumi]; **office hours** *npl* 営業時間
[eigyoujikan]; **opening hours** *npl* 営業時間
[eigyoujikan]; **peak hours** *npl* ピーク時
[piikuji]; **rush hour** *n* ラッシュアワー
[rasshuawaa]; **visiting hours** *npl* 面会時間
[menkaijikan]
hourly [auərli] *adj* 一時間ごとの [ichijikan
goto no] ▷ *adv* 一時間ごとに [ichijikan goto ni]
house *n* 家 [ie], 土地付き一戸建て家屋 [tochi
tsuki ikkodate kaoku]; **Do we have to clean
the house before we leave?** 出る前に家を
掃除しなければなりませんか? [deru mae ni
ie o souji shinakereba narimasen ka?]
household [haushould] *n* 家族 [kazoku]
housewife [hauswaɪf] *n* 主婦 [shufu]
housework [hauswɜrk] *n* 家事 [kaji]
hovercraft [hʌvərkræft] *n* ホバークラフト
[hobaakurafuto]
how [hau] *adv* どのように [dono you ni]

howl [haʊl] v 遠吠えする [tooboe suru]

how/what adv どう [dou]

HQ [eɪtʃ kyu] abbr 本社 [honsha]

hubcap [hʌbkæp] n ハブキャップ [habukyappu]

hug [hʌg] n 抱きしめること [dakishimeru koto] ▷ v 抱きしめる [dakishimeru]

huge [hyudʒ] adj 巨大な [kyodai na]

hull [hʌl] n 船体 [sentai]

hum [hʌm] v ブンブンいう [bunbun iu]

human [hyumən] adj 人間の [ningen no]; human being n 人間 [ningen]; human rights npl 人権 [jinken]

humanitarian [hyumænɪtɛəriən] adj 人道主義の [jindou shugi no]

humble [hʌmbəl] adj 謙虚な [kenkyo na]

humid [hyumɪd] adj 湿気の多い [shikke no oui]

humidity [hyumɪdɪti] n 湿気 [shikke]

humming n ブンブン [bunbun]

humor [hyumər] n ユーモア [yuumoa]; sense of humor n ユーモアのセンス [yuumoa no sensu]

humorous [hyumərəs] adj ユーモアのある [yuumoa no aru]

hundred [hʌndrɪd] number 百 [hyaku]; I'd like five hundred... 五百・・・欲しいのですが [gohyaku... hoshii no desu ga]

Hungarian [hʌŋgɛəriən] adj ハンガリーの [hangarii no] ▷ n ハンガリー人 [hangariijin]

Hungary [hʌŋgəri] n ハンガリー [hangarii]

hunger [hʌŋgər] n 空腹 [kuufuku]

hungry [hʌŋgri] adj 腹の減った [hara no hetta]

hunt [hʌnt] v 狩りをする [kari-o suru]

hunter [hʌntər] n ハンター [hantaa]

hunting [hʌntɪŋ] n 狩り [kari]

hurdle [hɜrdəl] n ハードル [haadoru]

hurricane [hɜrɪkeɪn, hʌr-] n ハリケーン [harikeen]

hurry [hɜri, hʌr-] n 大急ぎ [ooisogi] ▷ v 急ぐ [isogu]

hurry up v 急ぐ [isogu]

hurt [hɜrt] adj 傷ついた [kizutsuita] ▷ v 傷つける [kizutsukeru]

husband [hʌzbənd] n 夫 [otto]; This is my husband 私の夫です [watashi no otto desu]

hut [hʌt] n 小屋 [koya]; Where is the nearest mountain hut? 一番近い山小屋はどこですか? [ichiban chikai yama-goya wa doko desu ka?]

hutch [hʌtʃ] n 食器棚 [shokkidana]

hyacinth [haɪəsɪnθ] n ヒヤシンス [hiyashinsu]

hydrogen [haɪdrədʒ-n] n 水素 [suiso]

hygiene [haɪdʒin] n 衛生 [eisei]

hymn [hɪm] n 賛美歌 [sanbika]

hypermarket [haɪpərmɑrkɪt] n 郊外の大型スーパー [kougai no ougata suupaa]

hyphen [haɪf-n] n ハイフン [haifun]

H

I

I [aɪ] *pron* **I don't like...** 私は···が好きではありません [watashi wa... ga suki de wa arimasen]; **I have an appointment with...** 私は···さまとお約束をしています [watashi wa... sama to o-yakusoku o shite imasu]; **I like...** 私は···が好きです [watashi wa... ga suki desu]; **I love...** 私は···が大好きです [watashi wa... ga daisuki desu]; **I'm HIV-positive** 私はHIVに感染しています [watashi wa eichi-ai-vui ni kansen shite imasu]

ice [aɪs] *n* 氷 [kouri]; **black ice** *n* 路面の薄い透明な氷 [romen no usui toumei na kouri]; **ice cube** *n* アイスキューブ [aisukyuubu]; **ice rink** *n* スケートリンク [sukeetorinku]; **With ice, please** 氷を入れてください [koori o irete kudsai]

iceberg [aɪsbɜrg] *n* 氷山 [hyouzan]

icebox [aɪsbɒks] *n* アイスボックス [aisu bokkusu]

ice cream *n* アイスクリーム [aisukuriimu]; **I'd like some ice cream** 私はアイスクリームをいただきます [watashi wa aisukuriimu o itadakimasu]

Iceland [aɪslənd] *n* アイスランド [aisurando]

Icelandic [aɪslændɪk] *adj* アイスランドの [aisurando no] ▷ *n* アイスランド人 [aisurandojin]

ice-skating *n* アイススケート [aisusukeeto]

icing [aɪsɪŋ] *n* アイシング [aishingu]

icon [aɪkɒn] *n* 聖像 [seizou]

icy [aɪsi] *adj* 凍結した [touketsu shita]

idea [aɪdiə] *n* 考え [kangae]

ideal [aɪdiəl] *adj* 理想的な [risouteki na]

ideally [aɪdiəli] *adv* 理想的に [risouteki ni]

identical [aɪdɛntɪkəl] *adj* 同一の [douitsu no]

identification [aɪdɛntɪfɪkeɪʃən] *n* 身分証明 [mibun shoumei]

identify [aɪdɛntɪfaɪ] *v* 識別する [shikibetsu suru]

identity [aɪdɛntɪti] *n* 身元 [mimoto]; **identity card** *n* 身分証明書 [mibunshomeisho]; **identity theft** *n* 個人情報泥棒 [kojin jouhou dorobou]

ideology [aɪdiplədʒi, ɪdi-] *n* イデオロギー [ideorogii]

idiot [ɪdiət] *n* ばか [baka]

idiotic [ɪdiɒtɪk] *adj* ばかな [baka na]

idle [aɪdəl] *adj* 何もしない [nanimo shinai]

idly *adv* ぶらぶら [burabura]

i.e. [aɪ i] *abbr* すなわち [sunawachi]

if [ɪf] *conj* **Do you mind if I smoke?** タバコを吸ってもいいですか? [tabako o sutte mo ii desu ka?]; **Please call us if you're going to be late** 遅くなるときは電話してください [osoku naru toki wa denwa shite kudasai]; **What do I do if I have car trouble?** 故障したらどうすればいいのですか? [koshou shitara dou sureba ii no desu ka?]

ignition [ɪgnɪʃən] *n* 点火装置 [tenkasouchi]

ignorance [ɪgnərəns] *n* 無知 [muchi]

ignorant [ɪgnərənt] *adj* 無知の [muchi no]

ignore [ɪgnɔr] *v* 無視する [mushi suru]

ill [ɪl] *adj* 病気の [byouki no]

illegal [ɪligəl] *adj* 不法な [fuhou na]

illegible [ɪlɛdʒɪbəl] *adj* 判読しにくい [handokushinikui]

illiterate [ɪlɪtərɪt] *adj* 読み書きのできない [yomikaki no dekinai]

illness [ɪlnɪs] *n* 病気 [byouki]

illusion [ɪluʒən] *n* 錯覚 [sakkaku]

illustration [ɪləstreɪʃən] *n* 挿絵 [sashie]

image [ɪmɪdʒ] *n* イメージ [imeeji]

imaginary [ɪmædʒɪnɛri] *adj* 想像の [souzou no]

imagination [ɪmædʒɪneɪʃən] *n* 想像 [souzou]

imagine [ɪmædʒɪn] *v* 想像する [souzou suru]

imitate [ɪmɪteɪt] *v* 模倣する [mohou suru]

imitation [ɪmɪteɪʃən] *n* 模造品 [mozouhin]

immature [ɪmətʃʊər, -tʊər] *adj* 未成熟の [miseijuku no]

immediate [ɪmidiɪt] *adj* 早速の [sassoku no]

immediately [ɪmidiɪtli] *adv* すぐ [sugu], 早速 [sassoku], 至急 [shikyuu]

immigrant [ɪmɪgrənt] *n* 移住者 [ijuusha]

immigration [ɪmɪgreɪʃən] *n* 移住 [ijuu]

immoral [ɪmɔrəl] *adj* 不道徳な [fudoutoku na]

impact *n* 影響 [eikyou]

impaired [ɪmpɛərd] *adj* **I'm visually impaired** 私は視覚障害があります [watashi wa shikaku-shougai ga arimasu]

impartial [ɪmpɑrʃəl] *adj* 偏らない [katayora-nai]

impatience [ɪmpeɪʃns] *n* 短気 [tanki]

impatient [ɪmpeɪʃənt] *adj* いらいらしている [iraira shiteiru]

impatiently [ɪmpeɪʃəntli] *adv* いらいらして [iraira shite]

impersonal [ɪmpɜrsənəl] *adj* 個人にかかわらない [kojin ni kakawaranai]

import *n* [ɪmpɔrt] 輸入 [yunyuu] ▷ *v* [ɪmpɔrt] 輸入する [yunyuu suru]

importance [ɪmpɔrtns] *n* 重要 [juuyou], 重要性 [juuyousei]

important [ɪmpɔrtnt] *adj* 重要な [juuyou na]

impossible [ɪmpɒsɪbəl] *adj* 不可能な [fukanou na]

impractical [ɪmpræktɪkəl] *adj* 実際的でない [jissaiteki denai]

impress [ɪmprɛs] *v* 強く印象づける [tsuyoku inshou zukeru]

impressed [ɪmprɛst] *adj* 感動した [kandou shita]

impression [ɪmprɛʃən] *n* 印象 [inshou]

impressive [ɪmprɛsɪv] *adj* 印象的な [inshouteki na]

improper [ɪmprɒpər] *adj* 不正 [fusei]

improve [ɪmpruv] *v* 改善する [kaizen suru]

improvement [ɪmpruvmənt] *n* 改善 [kaizen]

in *prep* **in summer** 夏に [natsu ni]; **in the evening** 晩に [ban ni]; **I live in...** 私は・・・に住んでいます [watashi wa... ni sunde imasu]; **I've been in an accident** 私は事故にあいました [watashi wa jiko ni aimashita]; **Is the museum open in the morning?** その博物館は午前中開いていますか? [sono hakubutsukan wa gozen-chuu hiraite imasu ka?]; **We'll be in bed when you get back** あなたが帰ってくるころには私たちは寝ています [anata ga kaette kuru koro ni wa watashi-tachi wa nete imasu]

inaccurate [ɪnækyərɪt] *adj* 不正確な [fuseikaku na]

inadequate [ɪnædɪkwɪt] *adj* 不十分な [fujuubun na]

inadvertently [ɪnədvɜrtntli] *adv* 不注意で [fuchuui de]

in-box [ɪnbɒks] *n* 書類受け [shoruiuke]

incentive [ɪnsɛntɪv] *n* 奨励 [shourei]

inch [ɪntʃ] *n* インチ [inchi]

incident [ɪnsɪdənt] *n* 出来事 [dekigoto]

include [ɪnklud] *v* 含む [fukumu]

included [ɪnkludɪd] *adj* 含まれた [fukumare-ta]

inclusive [ɪnklusɪv] *adj* 含めた [fukumeta]

income [ɪnkʌm] *n* 所得 [shotoku]; **income tax** *n* 所得税 [shotokuzei]

incompetent [ɪnkɒmpɪtənt] *adj* 無能な [munou na]

incomplete [ɪnkəmplit] *adj* 不完全な [fukanzen na]

inconsistent [ɪnkənsɪstənt] *adj* 一貫性のない [ikkansei no nai]

inconvenience [ɪnkənvinyəns] *n* 不便 [fuben]

inconvenient [ɪnkənvinyənt] *adj* 不便な [fuben na]

incorrect [ɪnkərɛkt] *adj* 不正確な [fuseikaku

na]

increase *n* [ɪnkris] 増加 [zouka] ▷ *v* [ɪnkris] 増す [masu]

increasingly [ɪnkrisɪŋli] *adv* ますます [masumasu]

incredible [ɪnkrɛdɪbl̩] *adj* 信じられない [shinjirarenai]

indecisive [ɪndɪsaɪsɪv] *adj* 優柔不断な [yuujuu fudan na]

indeed [ɪndid] *adv* 全く [mattaku]

independence [ɪndɪpɛndəns] *n* 独立 [dokuritsu]

independent [ɪndɪpɛndənt] *adj* 独立した [dokuritsu shita]

index [ɪndɛks] *n (list)* 索引 [sakuin], *(numerical scale)* 指数 [shisuu]; **index finger** *n* 人差し指 [hitosashi yubi]

India [ɪndiə] *n* インド [indo]

Indian [ɪndiən] *adj* インドの [indo no] ▷ *n* インド人 [indojin]; **Indian Ocean** *n* インド洋 [indoyou]

indicate [ɪndɪkeɪt] *v* 示す [shimesu]

indicator [ɪndɪkeɪtər] *n* 指標 [shihyou]

indigestion [ɪndɪdʒɛstʃn̩, -daɪ-] *n* 消化不良 [shoukafuryou]

indignation [ɪndɪgneɪʃn̩] *n* 憤慨 [fungai]

indirect [ɪndaɪrɛkt, -dɪr-] *adj* 間接的な [kansetsuteki na]

indispensable [ɪndɪspɛnsəbl̩] *adj* 不可欠な [fukaketsu na]

individual [ɪndɪvɪdʒuᵊl] *adj* 個々の [koko no] ▷ *n* 個人 [kojin]

Indonesia [ɪndəneʒə] *n* インドネシア [indoneshia]

Indonesian [ɪndəniʒən] *adj* インドネシアの [indoneshia no] ▷ *n (person)* インドネシア人 [indoneshiajin]

indoor [ɪndɔr] *adj* 屋内の [okunai no]

indoors [ɪndɔrz] *adv* インドア [indoa], 屋内で [okunai de]

industrial [ɪndʌstriəl] *adj* 産業の [sangyou no]; **industrial park** *n* 工業団地 [kougyoudanchi]

industry [ɪndəstri] *n* 業 [gyou], 産業 [sangyou]

inefficient [ɪnɪfɪʃᵊnt] *adj* 効率の悪い [kouritsu no warui]

inevitable [ɪnɛvɪtəbl̩] *adj* 避けられない [sakerarenai]

inexpensive [ɪnɪkspɛnsɪv] *adj* 安い [yasui]

inexperienced [ɪnɪkspɪəriənst] *adj* 経験のない [keiken no nai]

infantry [ɪnfəntri] *n* 歩兵 [hohei]

infection [ɪnfɛkʃᵊn] *n* 感染 [kansen]

infectious [ɪnfɛkʃəs] *adj* 感染性の [kansensei no]

inferior [ɪnfɪəriər] *adj* 劣った [ototta] ▷ *n* 目下の者 [meshita no mono]

infertile [ɪnfɜrtl̩] *adj* 繁殖力のない [hanshokuryoku no nai]

infinitive [ɪnfɪnɪtɪv] *n* 不定詞 [futeishi]

infirmary [ɪnfɜrməri] *n* 診療所 [shinryoujo]

inflamed [ɪnfleɪmd] *adj* 炎症を起こした [enshou-o okoshita]

inflammation [ɪnfləmeɪʃᵊn] *n* 炎症 [enshou]

inflatable [ɪnfleɪtəbl̩] *adj* 膨張性の [bouchou sei no]

inflation [ɪnfleɪʃᵊn] *n* インフレーション [infureeshon]

inflexible [ɪnflɛksɪbl̩] *adj* 頑固な [ganko na]

influence [ɪnfluəns] *n* 影響 [eikyou] ▷ *v* 影響を与える [eikyou-o ataeru]

influenza [ɪnfluɛnzə] *n* インフルエンザ [infuruenza]

inform [ɪnfɔrm] *v* 知らせる [shiraseru]

informal [ɪnfɔrml̩] *adj* 形式ばらない [keishikibaranai]

information [ɪnfərmeɪʃᵊn] *n* 案内 [annai], 情報 [jouhou], 知識 [chishiki]; **information desk** *n* 照会デスク [shoukai desuku]; **information booth** *n* 案内所 [annaijo]; **Here's some information about my company** 弊社についての情報です [heisha ni tsuite no jouhou desu]; **I'd like some information about...** ···に関する情報が欲しいのですが [... ni kansuru jouhou ga hoshii no desu ga]

informative [ɪnfɔrmətɪv] *adj* 知識を与える [chishiki-o ataeru]

infrastructure [ɪnfrəstrʌktʃər] *n* インフラストラクチャー [infurasutorakuchaa]

infuriating [ɪnfyuərieɪtɪŋ] *adj* 腹立たしい [haradata shii]

ingenious [ɪndʒinyəs] *adj* 独創的な [dokusouteki na]

ingredient [ɪngridiənt] *n* 材料 [zairyou]

inhabitant [ɪnhæbɪtənt] *n* 住人 [juunin]

inhaler [ɪnheɪlər] *n* 吸入器 [kyuunyuuki]

inherit [ɪnhɛrɪt] *v* 相続する [souzoku suru]

inheritance [ɪnhɛrɪtəns] *n* 相続 [souzoku]

inhibition [ɪnɪbɪʃən] *n* 抑圧 [yokuatsu]

initial [ɪnɪʃəl] *adj* 最初の [saisho no] ▷ *v* 頭文字で署名する [atamamoji de shomei suru]

initially [ɪnɪʃəli] *adv* 最初に [saisho ni]

initials [ɪnɪʃəlz] *npl* 頭文字 [kashiramoji]

initiative [ɪnɪʃətɪv, -ʃətɪv] *n* イニシアチブ [inishiachibu]

inject [ɪndʒɛkt] *v* 注射する [chuusha suru]

injection [ɪndʒɛkʃən] *n* 注射 [chuusha]; **I want an injection for the pain** 私は痛み止めの注射が欲しいのです [watashi wa itami-dome no chuusha ga hoshi no desu]; **Please give me an injection** 注射を打ってください [chuusha o utte kudasai]

injure [ɪndʒər] *v* 傷つける [kizutsukeru]

injured [ɪndʒərd] *adj* 傷ついた [kizutsuita]

injury [ɪndʒəri] *n* 怪我 [kega]; **injury time-out** *n* サッカー・ラグビーなどで怪我の手当てなどに要した分の延長時間 [sakkaa / ragubii nado de kega no teate nado ni youshita bun no enchou jikan]

injustice [ɪndʒʌstɪs] *n* 不公平 [fukouhei]

ink [ɪŋk] *n* インク [inku]

in-laws [ɪnlɔ] *npl* 姻戚 [inseki]

inmate [ɪnmeɪt] *n* 被収容者 [hishuuyousha]

inn [ɪn] *n* 宿屋 [yadoya]

inner [ɪnər] *adj* 内側の [uchigawa no]; **inner tube** *n* インナーチューブ [innaachuubu]

innocent [ɪnəsənt] *adj* 潔白な [keppaku na]

innovation [ɪnəveɪʃən] *n* 革新 [kakushin]

innovative [ɪnəvɛɪtɪv] *adj* 革新的な [kakushinteki na]

inquest [ɪnkwɛst] *n* 検死審問 [kenshi shinmon]

inquire [ɪnkwaɪər] *v* 問い合わせる [toiawaseru], 尋ねる [tazuneru]

inquiry [ɪnkwaɪəri, ɪŋkwɪri] *n* 問い合わせ [toiawase]

inquisitive [ɪnkwɪzɪtɪv] *adj* 詮索好きな [sensaku zuki na]

insane [ɪnseɪn] *adj* 正気でない [shouki de nai]

inscription [ɪnskrɪpʃən] *n* 銘 [mei]

insect [ɪnsɛkt] *n* 昆虫 [konchuu]; **insect repellent** *n* 虫よけ [mushiyoke]; **stick insect** *n* ナナフシ [nanafushi]

insensitive [ɪnsɛnsɪtɪv] *adj* 鈍感な [donkan na]

insensitivity [ɪnsɛnsɪtɪvɪti] *n* 不快感 [fukaikan]

inside [ɪnsaɪd] *adv* 内側に [uchigawa ni] ▷ *n* 内側 [uchigawa]; **It's inside** 内側です [uchigawa desu]

insincere [ɪnsɪnsɪər] *adj* 誠意のない [seii no nai]

insist [ɪnsɪst] *v* 強要する [kyouyou suru]

insomnia [ɪnsɒmniə] *n* 不眠症 [fuminshou]

inspect [ɪnspɛkt] *v* 検査する [kensa suru]

inspection [ɪnspɛkʃən] *n* 点検 [tenken]

inspector [ɪnspɛktər] *n* 検査官 [kensakan]; **ticket inspector** *n* 検札係 [kensatsugakari]

instability [ɪnstəbɪlɪti] *n* 不安定 [fuantei]

installment [ɪnstɔlmənt] *n* 分割払い [bunkatsu harai]

instance [ɪnstəns] *n* 事例 [jirei]

instant [ɪnstənt] *adj* 即座の [sokuza no]

instantly [ɪnstəntli] *adv* 即座に [sokuza ni]

instead [ɪnstɛd] *adv* その代わりに [sono kawari ni]

instinct [ɪnstɪŋkt] *n* 本能 [honnou]

institute [ɪnstɪtut] *n* 学会 [gakkai]

institution [ɪnstɪtuʃən] *n* 機関 [kikan] (組織)

instruct [ɪnstrʌkt] v 指示する [shiji suru]

instructions [ɪnstrʌkʃ⁻nz] npl 指示 [shiji]

instructor [ɪnstrʌktər] n 指導者 [shidousha]; **driving instructor** n 自動車教習指導員 [jidousha kyoushuu shidouin]

instrument [ɪnstrəmənt] n 器具 [kigu]; **musical instrument** n 楽器 [gakki]

insufficient [ɪnsəfɪʃ⁻nt] adj 不十分な [fujuubun na]

insulation [ɪnsəleɪʃ⁻n] n 絶縁材 [zetsuenzai]

insulin [ɪnsəlɪn] n インシュリン [inshurin]

insult n [ɪnsʌlt] 侮辱 [bujoku] ▷ v [ɪnsʌlt] 侮辱する [bujoku suru]

insurance [ɪnʃʊərəns] n 保険 [hoken]; **accident insurance** n 事故保険 [jiko hoken]; **car insurance** n 自動車保険 [jidousha hoken]; **insurance certificate** n 保険契約書 [hoken keiyakusho]; **insurance policy** n 保険証書 [hokenshousho]; **liability insurance** n 第三者賠償責任保険 [daisansha baishousekinin hoken]; **life insurance** n 生命保険 [seimeihoken]; **travel insurance** n 旅行保険 [ryokou hoken]; **Do you have insurance?** あなたは保険に入っていますか? [anata wa hoken ni haitte imasu ka?]; **Give me your insurance information, please** あなたの保険の詳細を教えてください [anata no hoken no shousai o oshiete kudasai]; **Here's my insurance information** 私の保険の詳細です [watashi no hoken no shousai desu]; **How much extra is comprehensive insurance coverage?** 総合自動車保険に加入する追加料金はいくらですか? [sougou-jidousha-hoken ni kanyuu suru tsuika-ryoukin wa ikura desu ka?]; **I don't have dental insurance** 私は歯科保険に入っていません [watashi wa shika-hoken ni haitte imasen]; **I don't have health insurance** 私は医療保険に入っていません [watashi wa iryou-hoken ni haitte imasen]; **I have insurance** 私は保険に入っています [watashi wa hoken ni haitte imasu]; **I'd like to arrange personal accident insurance** 個人傷害保険をかけたいのですが [kojin-shougai-hoken o kaketai no desu ga]; **Is comprehensive insurance coverage included in the price?** 料金には総合自動車保険が含まれていますか? [ryoukin ni wa sougou-jidousha-hoken ga fukumarete imasu ka?]; **May I see your insurance certificate, please?** あなたの保険証書を見せていただけますか? [anata no hoken-shousho o misete itadakemasu ka?]; **Will the insurance pay for it?** 保険でそれが補償されますか? [hoken de sore ga hoshou saremasu ka?]

insure [ɪnʃʊər] v 保険をかける [hoken-o kakeru]

insured [ɪnʃʊərd] adj 保険に入った [hoken ni haitta]

intact [ɪntækt] adj 損なわれていない [sokonawareteinai]

intellectual [ɪntɪlɛktʃuəl] adj 知的 [chiteki], 知的な [chiteki na] ▷ n 知識人 [chishikijin]

intelligence [ɪntɛlɪdʒ⁻ns] n 知能 [chinou]

intelligent [ɪntɛlɪdʒ⁻nt] adj 利口な [rikou na]

intend [ɪntɛnd] v **intend to** v …するつもりだ [...suru tsumori da]

intense [ɪntɛns] adj 強烈な [kyouretsu na]

intensive [ɪntɛnsɪv] adj 集中的な [shuuchuuteki na]; **intensive care unit** n 集中治療室 [shuuchuuchiryoushitsu, ICU aishiiyuu]

intention [ɪntɛnʃ⁻n] n 意図 [ito]

intentional [ɪntɛnʃən⁻l] adj 意図的な [itoteki na]

intercom [ɪntərkɒm] n インターコム [intaakomu]

interest [ɪntrɪst, -tərɪst] n (curiosity) 興味 [kyoumi], (income) 利息 [risoku] ▷ v 興味を起こさせる [kyoumi-o okosaseru]; **interest rate** n 利率 [riritsu]

interested [ɪntərɛstɪd, -trɪstɪd] adj 興味がある [kyoumi ga aru]

interesting [ɪntərɛstɪŋ, -trɪstɪŋ] adj 興味深い [kyoumibukai], 面白い [omoshiroi]

interior [ɪntɪəriər] n 内側 [uchigawa]; **interior designer** n インテリアデザイナー [interiadezainaa]

intermediate [ɪntərmiːdiɪt] adj 中間の [chuukan no]

internal [ɪntɜːrnˑl] adj 内部の [naibu no]

international [ɪntərnæʃənˑl] adj 国際的な [kokusaiteki na]

Internet [ɪntərnɛt] n インターネット [intaanetto]; **Internet café** n インターネットカフェ [intaanetto kafe]; **Internet user** n インターネット利用者 [intaanetto riyousha]; **Are there any Internet cafés here?** ここにインターネットカフェはありますか? [koko ni intaanetto-kafe wa arimasu ka?]; **Does the room have wireless internet access?** その部屋で無線インターネット接続を利用できますか? [sono heya de musen-intaanetto-setsuzoku o riyou dekimasu ka?]; **Is there an Internet connection in the room?** その部屋にインターネットの接続ポイントはありますか? [sono heya ni intaanetto no setsuzoku-pointo wa arimasu ka?]

interpret [ɪntɜːrprɪt] v 解釈する [kaishaku suru]

interpretation [ɪntɜːrprɪteɪʃˑn] n 通訳 [tsuuyaku]

interpreter [ɪntɜːrprɪtər] n 通訳者 [tsuuyakusha]

interrogate [ɪntɛrəgeɪt] v 質問する [shitsumon suru]

interrupt [ɪntərʌpt] v 中断する [chuudan suru]

interruption [ɪntərʌpʃˑn] n 中断 [chuudan]

intersection [ɪntərsɛkʃˑn] n 交差点 [kousaten]; **Turn right at the next intersection** 次の交差点で右に進んでください [tsugi no kousaten de migi ni susunde kudasai]

interval [ɪntərvˑl] n 間隔 [kankaku]

interview [ɪntərvyu] n 面会 [menkai], 面接 [mensetsu] ▷ v 面接する [mensetsu suru]

interviewer [ɪntərvyuər] n 面接者 [mensetsusha]

intimate adj 親しい [shitashii]

intimidate [ɪntɪmɪdeɪt] v おじけづかせる [ojikedukaseru]

into [ɪntu] **bump into** v ばったり出会う [battari deau]; **Could you make a hotel reservation for me?** 私のためにホテルの部屋を予約してもらえますか? [watashi no tame ni hoteru no heya o yoyaku shite moraemasu ka?]; **How much is the taxi fare into town?** 街までのタクシー料金はいくらですか? [machi made no takushii-ryoukin wa ikura desu ka?]

intolerant [ɪntɒlərənt] adj 耐えられない [taerarenai]

intranet [ɪntrənɛt] n イントラネット [intouranetto]

introduce [ɪntrədus] v 紹介する [shoukai suru]

introduction [ɪntrədʌkʃˑn] n 紹介 [shoukai]

intruder [ɪntrudər] n 侵入者 [shinnyuusha]

intuition [ɪntuɪʃˑn] n 直感 [chokkan]

invade [ɪnveɪd] v 侵略する [shinryaku suru]

invalid n 病人 [byounin]

invasion [ɪnveɪʒˑn] n 侵入 [shinnyuu]

invent [ɪnvɛnt] v 発明する [hatsumei suru]

invention [ɪnvɛnʃˑn] n 発明 [hatsumei]

inventor [ɪnvɛntər] n 発明者 [hatsumeisha]

inventory [ɪnvˑntori] n 目録 [mokuroku]

invest [ɪnvɛst] v 投資する [toushi suru]

investigation [ɪnvɛstɪgeɪʃˑn] n 調査 [chousa]

investment [ɪnvɛstmənt] n 投資 [toushi]

investor [ɪnvɛstər] n 投資者 [toushisha]

invisible [ɪnvɪzɪbˑl] adj 目に見えない [me ni mienai]

invitation [ɪnvɪteɪʃˑn] n 招待 [shoutai]

invite v 誘う [sasou]

invoice [ɪnvɔɪs] n インボイス [inboisu] ▷ v インボイスを送る [inboisu-o okuru]

involve [ɪnvɒlv] v 伴う [tomonau]

iPod® [aɪpɒd] n iPod® [ipod]

IQ [aɪ kyu] abbr 知能指数 [chinoushisuu, IQ aikyuu]

Iran [ɪræn] *n* イラン [iran]

Iranian [ɪreɪniən] *adj* イランの [iran no] ▷ *n (person)* イラン人 [iranjin]

Iraq [ɪræk] *n* イラク [iraku]

Iraqi [ɪræki, ɪrɒki] *adj* イラクの [iraku no] ▷ *n* イラク人 [irakujin]

Ireland [aɪərlənd] *n* アイルランド [airurando]; **Northern Ireland** *n* 北アイルランド [kita airurando]

iris [aɪrɪs] *n* アヤメ [ayame]

Irish [aɪrɪʃ] *adj* アイルランドの [airurando no] ▷ *n* アイルランド人 [airurandojin]

Irishman [aɪrɪʃmən] *n* アイルランド人 [airurandojin]

Irishwoman [aɪrɪʃwumən] *n* アイルランド人 [airurandojin]

iron [aɪərn] *n* 鉄 [tetsu] ▷ *v* アイロンをかける [airon-o kakeru]

ironic [aɪrɒnɪk] *adj* 皮肉な [hiniku na]

ironing [aɪərnɪŋ] *n* アイロンをかけるべきもの [airon-o kakerubeki mono]; **ironing board** *n* アイロン台 [airondai]

irony [aɪrəni, aɪər-] *n* 皮肉 [hiniku]

irregular [ɪrɛgyələr] *adj* ふぞろいの [fuzoroi no]

irrelevant [ɪrɛlɪvənt] *adj* 無関係な [mukankei na]

irresponsible [ɪrɪspɒnsɪbəl] *adj* いい加減な [iikagen na]

irritable [ɪrɪtəbəl] *adj* 怒りっぽい [okorippoi]

irritated *adj* いらいらした [irairashita]

irritating [ɪrɪteɪtɪŋ] *adj* いらいらさせる [iraira saseru]

...is *v* ・・・です […desu]

Islam [ɪslɒm] *n* イスラム教 [isuramukyou]

Islamic [ɪslæmɪk, -lɑ-] *adj* イスラム教の [isuramukyou no]

island [aɪlənd] *n* 島 [shima]; **desert island** *n* 無人島 [mujintou]

isolated [aɪsəleɪtɪd] *adj* 孤立した [koritsu shita]

ISP [aɪ ɛs pi] *abbr* インターネットサービスプロバイダ [intaanetto saabisu purobaida]

Israel [ɪzriəl] *n* イスラエル [isuraeru]

Israeli [ɪzreɪli] *adj* イスラエルの [isuraeru no] ▷ *n* イスラエル人 [isuraerujin]

issue [ɪʃu] *n* 論点 [ronten] ▷ *v* 公布する [koufu suru]

it [ɪt] **How long will it take to transfer?** 送金にかかる期間はどのくらいですか? [soukin ni kakaru kikan wa dono kurai desu ka?]; **I can't read it** それは読めません [sore wa yomemasen]; **Is it safe for children?** それは子供にも安全ですか? [sore wa kodomo ni mo anzen desu ka?]; **It hurts** 痛みます [itamimasu]; **It won't turn on** つきません [tsukimasen]; **It's...** ・・・です […desu]; **It's ten to two** 二時十分前です [ni-ji jup-pun mae desu]; **What is it?** それは何ですか? [sore wa nan desu ka?]

IT [aɪ ti] *abbr* 情報技術 [jouho gijutsu]

Italian [ɪtæliən] *adj* イタリアの [itaria no] ▷ *n (language)* イタリア語 [itariago], *(person)* イタリア人 [itariajin]

Italy [ɪtəli] *n* イタリア [itaria]

itch [ɪtʃ] *v* かゆい [kayui]

itchy [ɪtʃi] *adj* かゆい [kayui]

item [aɪtəm] *n* 項目 [koumoku]

itinerary [aɪtɪnəreri] *n* 旅程 [ryotei]

its [ɪts] *pron* **It isn't holding its charge** 電荷がもちません [denka ga mochimasen]

ivory [aɪvəri] *n* 象牙 [zouge]

ivy [aɪvi] *n* ツタ [tsuta]

J

jab [dʒæb] n げんこつ [genkotsu], 突き [tsuki]

jack [dʒæk] n ジャッキ [jakki]

jacket [dʒækɪt] n ジャケット [jaketto]; **dinner jacket** n ディナージャケット [dinaa jaketto]; **life jacket** n 救命胴衣 [kyuumeidoui]

jackpot [dʒækpɒt] n 多額の賞金 [tagaku no shoukin]

jail [dʒeɪl] n 刑務所 [keimusho] ▷ v 投獄する [tougoku suru]

jam [dʒæm] n ジャム [jamu]; **jam jar** n ジャムの瓶 [jamu no bin]; **traffic jam** n 交通渋滞 [koutsuujuutai]

Jamaican [dʒəmeɪkən] adj ジャマイカの [jamaika no] ▷ n ジャマイカ人 [jamaikajin]

jammed [dʒæmd] adj ぎっしり詰め込んだ [gisshiri tsumekonda]

janitor [dʒænɪtər] n 用務員 [youmuin]

January [dʒænyuɛri] n 一月 [ichigatsu]

Japan [dʒəpæn] n 日本 [nihon(nippon)]

Japanese [dʒæpəniz] adj 日本の [nihon(nippon) no] ▷ n (language) 日本語 [nihongo], (person) 日本人 [nihon(nippon)jin]

jar [dʒɑr] n 瓶 [bin]; **jam jar** n ジャムの瓶 [jamu no bin]

jaundice [dʒɔndɪs] n 黄疸 [oudan]

javelin [dʒævlɪn] n 投げ槍 [nageyari]

jaw [dʒɔ] n あご [ago]

jazz [dʒæz] n ジャズ [jazu]

jealous [dʒɛləs] adj 嫉妬深い [shittobukai]

jeans [dʒinz] npl ジーンズ [jiinzu]

Jell-O® [dʒɛlou] n ゼリー [zerii]

jellyfish [dʒɛlifɪʃ] n クラゲ [kurage]; **Are there jellyfish here?** ここにクラゲはいますか? [koko ni kurage wa imasu ka?]

jersey [dʒɜrzi] n ジャージー [jaajii]

Jesus [dʒizəs] n イエス [iesu]

jet [dʒɛt] n ジェット機 [jettoki]; **jumbo jet** n ジャンボジェット [janbojetto]

jetlag [dʒɛtlæg] n 時差ぼけ [jisaboke]

jetty [dʒɛti] n 突堤 [tottei]

Jew [dʒu] n ユダヤ人 [yudayajin]

jewel [dʒuəl] n 宝石 [houseki]

jeweler [dʒuələr] n 宝石商 [housekishou]

jewelry [dʒuəlri] n 宝石類 [housekirui]; **jewelry store** n 宝石商 [housekishou]

Jewish [dʒuɪʃ] adj ユダヤ人の [yudayajin no]

jigsaw [dʒɪgsɔ] n **jigsaw puzzle** n ジグソーパズル [jigusoo pazuru]

jingoist n 熱狂的愛国主義者 [nekkyoutekiaikokushugisha]

job [dʒɒb] n 職 [shoku]

jobless [dʒɒblɪs] adj 失業中の [shitsugyouchuu no]

jockey [dʒɒki] n 競馬騎手 [keiba kishu]

jog [dʒɒg] v ジョギングする [jogingu suru]; **jogging suit** n シェルスーツ [shierusuutsu]

jogging [dʒɒgɪŋ] n ジョギング [jogingu]

join [dʒɔɪn] v 加わる [kuwawaru]

joint [dʒɔɪnt] adj 共同の [kyoudou no] ▷ n (junction) 継ぎ目 [tsugime], (meat) 骨付き肉 [honetsuki niku]; **joint account** n 共同預金口座 [kyoudou yokin kouza]

joke [dʒouk] n 冗談 [joudan] ▷ v 冗談を言う [joudan wo iu]

jolly [dʒɒli] adj 陽気な [youki na]

Jordan [dʒɔrdn] n ヨルダン [yorudan]

Jordanian [dʒɔrdeɪniən] adj ヨルダンの [yorudan no] ▷ n ヨルダン人 [yorudanjin]

jot down [dʒɒt daun] v ちょっと書き留める [chotto kakitodomeru]

journalism [dʒɜrnəlɪzəm] n ジャーナリズム [jaanarizumu]

journalist [dʒɜrnəlɪst] *n* ジャーナリスト [jaanarisuto]

journey [dʒɜrni] *n* 旅行 [ryokou]

joy [dʒɔɪ] *n* 喜び [yorokobi]

joystick [dʒɔɪstɪk] *n* 操縦桿 [soujuukan]

judge [dʒʌdʒ] *n* 裁判官 [saibankan], 判事 [hanji] ▷ *v* 審査する [shinsa suru]

judo [dʒudoʊ] *n* 柔道 [juudou]

jug [dʒʌg] *n* ジャグ [jagu]

juggler [dʒʌglər] *n* 手品師 [tejinashi]

juice [dʒus] *n* ジュース [juusu]; **orange juice** *n* オレンジジュース [orenjijuusu]

July [dʒulaɪ] *n* 七月 [shichigatsu]

jump [dʒʌmp] *v* 跳びはねる [tobihaneru]; **high jump** *n* 走り高跳び [hashiri takatobi]; **long jump** *n* 幅跳び [habatobi]

jumper [dʒʌmpər] *n* **jumper cables** *npl* ブースターコード [buusutaakoodo]; **Do you have jumper cables?** ブースターケーブルはありま すか? [buusutaa-keeburu wa arimasu ka?]

June [dʒun] *n* 六月 [rokugatsu]; **all through June** 六月いっぱい [roku-gatsu ippai]; **at the beginning of June** 六月の初めに [roku-gatsu no hajime ni]; **at the end of June** 六月の終わりに [roku-gatsu no owari ni]; **It's Monday, June fifteenth** 六月十五日 の月曜日です [roku-gatsu juugo-nichi no getsuyoubi desu]

jungle [dʒʌŋgl] *n* ジャングル [janguru]

junior [dʒuniər] *adj* 下級の [kakyuu no]

junk [dʒʌŋk] *n* がらくた [garakuta], ジャンク [janku]; **junk mail** *n* ジャンクメール [janku meeru]

jury [dʒuəri] *n* 陪審 [baishin]

just [dʒʌst] *adv* たった今 [tatta ima]

justice [dʒʌstɪs] *n* 正義 [seigi]

justify [dʒʌstɪfaɪ] *v* 正当化する [seitouka suru]

K

kangaroo [kæŋgəru] *n* カンガルー [kangaruu]

karaoke [kæriouki] *n* カラオケ [karaoke]

karate [kərɑti] *n* 空手 [karate]

Kazakhstan [kæzəkstæn] *n* カザフスタン [kazafusutan]

kebab [kəbɑb] *n* カバブ [kababu]

keep [kip] *v* 持ち続ける [mochitsudukeru]

keep out *v* 中に入れない [naka ni irenai]

keep up *v* 維持する [iji suru]

kennel [kɛnəl] *n* 犬小屋 [inugoya]

Kenya [kɛnyə] *n* ケニア [kenia]

Kenyan [kɛnyən] *adj* ケニアの [kenia no] ▷ *n* ケニア人 [keniajin]

kerosene [kɛrəsin] *n* 灯油 [touyu]

ketchup [kɛtʃəp, kætʃ-] *n* ケチャップ [kechappu]

key [ki] *n* (*for lock*) 鍵 [kagi], (*music/computer*) キー [kii]; **car keys** *npl* 車の鍵 [kuruma no kagi]; **I left the keys in the car** 私は車に鍵を置き忘れました [watashi wa kuruma ni kagi o okiwasuremashita]; **I'm having trouble with the key** 鍵に問題があります [kagi ni mondai ga arimasu]; **I've forgotten the key** 私は鍵を置き忘れました [watashi wa kagi o okiwasuremashita]; **May I have a key?** 鍵をもらえますか？ [kagi o moraemasu ka?]; **the key for room number two hundred and two** 202号室の鍵 [nihyaku-ni-gou-shitsu no kagi]; **The key doesn't work** 鍵が開きません [kagi ga akimasen]; **We need a second key** 鍵がもう一つ必要です [kagi ga mou hitotsu hitsuyou desu]; **What's this key for?** この鍵は何のためですか？ [kono kagi wa nan no tame desu ka?]; **Where do we get the key...?** ···の鍵

はどこでもらえばいいのですか？ [... no kagi wa doko de moraeba ii no desu ka?]; **Where do we hand in the key when we're leaving?** 出るときに鍵はどこに渡せばいいのですか？ [deru toki ni kagi wa doko ni wataseba ii no desu ka?]; **Which is the key to the back door?** 裏口の鍵はどれですか？ [uraguchi no kagi wa dore desu ka?]; **Which is the key to this door?** このドアの鍵はどれですか？ [kono doa no kagi wa dore desu ka?]

keyboard [kibord] *n* キーボード [kiiboodo]

keyring [kirɪŋ] *n* キーリング [kiiringu]

kick [kɪk] *n* 蹴り [keri] ▷ *v* 蹴る [keru]

kick off *v* キックオフする [kikkuofu suru]

kickoff [kɪkɔf] *n* キックオフ [kikkuofu]

kid [kɪd] *n* 子供 [kodomo] ▷ *v* ヤギが子を産む [yagi ga ko wo umu]

kidnap [kɪdnæp] *v* 誘拐する [yuukai suru]

kidney [kɪdni] *n* 腎臓 [jinzou]

kill [kɪl] *v* 殺す [korosu]

killer [kɪlər] *n* 殺人者 [satsujinsha]

kilo [kilou] *n* キロ [kiro]

kilometer [kɪləmitər, kɪlɒmɪtər] *n* キロメートル [kiromeetoru]

kilt [kɪlt] *n* キルト [kiruto] (タータン)

kind [kaɪnd] *adj* 親切な [shinsetsu na] ▷ *n* 種類 [shurui]

kindergarten [kɪndərgɑrtən] *n* 幼稚園 [youchien]

kindly [kaɪndli] *adv* せっかく [sekkaku], 親切に [shinsetsu ni]

kindness [kaɪndnɪs] *n* 親切 [shinsetsu]

king [kɪŋ] *n* 王 [ou]

kingdom [kɪŋdəm] *n* 王国 [oukoku]

kingfisher [kɪŋfɪʃər] *n* カワセミ [kawasemi]

K

kiosk [kiɒsk] *n* キオスク [kiosuku]

kiss [kɪs] *n* キス [kisu] (口)▷*v* キスする [kisu suru]

kit [kɪt] *n* 用具一式 [yougu isshiki]; **hands-free kit** *n* ハンズフリーキット [hanzu furii kitto]; **repair kit** *n* 修理キット [shuuri kitto]

kitchen [kɪtʃ·n] *n* 台所 [daidokoro]; **built-in kitchen** *n* 造り付けのキッチン [tsukuritsuke no kicchin]; **with kitchen** *(lodging)* *n* 自炊 [jisui]

kite [kaɪt] *n* 凧 [tako]

kitten [kɪt·n] *n* 子猫 [koneko]

kiwi [kiwi] *n* キーウィ [kiiui]

km/h *abbr* 毎時・・・キロ [maiji... kiro]

knee [ni] *n* ひざ [hiza]

kneecap [nikæp] *n* ひざがしら [hizagashira]

kneel [nil] *v* ひざを曲げる [hiza-o mageru]

kneel down *v* ひざまずく [hizamazuku]

knife [naɪf] *n* ナイフ [naifu]

knit [nɪt] *v* 編む [amu]

knitting [nɪtɪŋ] *n* 編物 [amimono]; **knitting needle** *n* 編み棒 [amibou]

knob [nɒb] *n* ノブ [nobu]

knock [nɒk] *n* たたくこと [tataku koto]▷*v* たた く [tataku]

knock down *v* 打ち倒す [uchitaosu]

knock out *v* 打ち負かす [uchimakasu]

knock over *v* ひっくり返す [hikkurigaesu]

knot [nɒt] *n* 結び目 [musubime]

know [nou] *v* 知っている [shitte iru]

know-how [nouhau] *n* ノウハウ [nouhau]

know-it-all [nouɪtol] *n* 知ったかぶりをする人 [shitta kaburi wo suru hito]

knowledge [nɒlɪdʒ] *n* 知識 [chishiki]

knowledgeable [nɒlɪdʒəbʰl] *adj* ・・・に精通し ている [... ni seitsuu shiteiru]

known [noun] *adj* 知られている [shirarete iru]

Koran [kɔrɑn] *n* コーラン [kooran]

Korea [kəriə] *n* 朝鮮 [chosen]; **North Korea** *n* 北朝鮮 [kitachousen]; **South Korea** *n* 韓国 [kankoku]

Korean [kɔriən] *adj* 朝鮮の [chousen no]▷*n* *(language)* 朝鮮語 [chousengo], *(person)* 朝 鮮人 [chousenjin]

kosher [kouʃər] *adj* ユダヤ教の掟に従って料 理された清浄な [Yudaya kyou no okite ni shitagatte ryouri sareta seijou na]

Kosovo [kɔsəvou] *n* コソボ [kosobo]

Kuwait [kuweɪt] *n* クウェート [kuueeto]

Kuwaiti [kuweɪti] *adj* クウェートの [kuueeto no]▷*n* クウェート人 [kuueetojin]

Kyrgyzstan [kɪrgɪstæn] *n* キルギスタン [kirugisutan]

L

lab [læb] *n* ラボ [rabo]

label [leɪbᵊl] *n* ラベル [raberu]

labor [leɪbər] *n* 労働 [roudou]; **labor union** *n* 労働組合 [roudoukumiai]

laboratory [læbrətɔri] *n* 実験室 [jikkenshitsu]; **language laboratory** *n* 語学ラボ [gogaku rabo]

laborer [leɪbərər] *n* 労働者 [roudousha]

lace [leɪs] *n* レース [reesu] (布)

lack [læk] *n* 欠乏 [ketsubou]

lacquer [lækər] *n* ラッカー [rakkaa]

ladder [lædər] *n* はしご [hashigo]

ladies [leɪdiz] *n* **ladies' room** 女性用トイレ [joseiyou toire]; **Where is the ladies' room?** 女性用トイレはどこですか? [josei-you toire wa doko desu ka?]

ladle [leɪdᵊl] *n* お玉 [otama]

lady [leɪdi] *n* 婦人 [fujin]

ladybug [leɪdibʌg] *n* テントウムシ [tentoumushi]

lag [læg] *n* **I'm suffering from jet lag** 私は時差ぼけに悩んでいます [watashi wa jisaboke ni nayande imasu]

lager [lægər] *n* **lager beer** ラガー [ragaa]

lagoon [ləgun] *n* 潟湖 [sekiko]

laid-back [leɪdbæk] *adj* くつろいだ [kutsuroida]

lake [leɪk] *n* 湖 [mizu-umi]

lamb [læm] *n* 子羊 [kohitsuji]

lambaste [læmbeɪst] *v* けなす [kenasu]

lame [leɪm] *adj* びっこの [bikko no]

lamp [læmp] *n* ランプ [ranpu], 電灯 [dentou]; **bedside lamp** *n* ベッドサイドランプ [beddosaido ranpu]; **The lamp isn't working** ランプがつきません [ranpu ga tsuki-masen]

lamppost [læmppoust] *n* 街灯柱 [gaitouchuu]

lampshade [læmpʃeɪd] *n* ランプシェード [ranpusheedo]

land [lænd] *n* 陸 [riku], 土地 [tochi] ▷ *v* 着陸する [chakuriku suru]

landfill [lændfɪl] *n* ごみ捨て場 [gomi suteba]

landing [lændɪŋ] *n* 踊り場 [odoriba]

landlady [lændleɪdi] *n* 女家主 [onna yanushi]

landlord [lændlɔrd] *n* 家主 [yanushi]

landmark [lændmɑrk] *n* ランドマーク [randomaaku]

landowner [lændounər] *n* 地主 [jinushi]

landscape [lændskeɪp] *n* 風景 [fuukei]

landslide [lændslaɪd] *n* 地すべり [jisuberi]

lane [leɪn] *n* 小道 [komichi]; **bicycle lane** *n* サイクルレーン [saikurureen]; **four-lane highway** *n* 中央分離帯付き道路 [chuuou bunritai tsuki douro]

language [læŋgwɪdʒ] *n* 言語 [gengo]; **language laboratory** *n* 語学ラボ [gogaku rabo]; **language school** *n* 語学学校 [gogaku gakkou]; **native language** *n* 母国語 [bokokugo]; **sign language** *n* 手話 [shuwa]

lanky [læŋki] *adj* ひょろ長い [hyoro nagai]

Laos [loʊs] *n* ラオス [raosu]

lap [læp] *n* ひざ [hiza]

laptop [læptɒp] *n* ラップトップ [rapputoppu]; **Can I use my own laptop here?** ここで自分のラップトップを使えますか? [koko de jibun no rappu-toppu o tsukaemasu ka?]

large [lɑrdʒ] *adj* 大きい [ookii]

largely [lɑrdʒli] *adv* 主として [shutoshite]

laryngitis [lærɪndʒaɪtɪs] *n* 喉頭炎 [koutouen]

laser [leɪzər] *n* レーザー [reezaa]

last [læst] *adj* 最後の [saigo no] ▷ *adv* 最後に

[saigo ni] ▸ v 続く [tsuzuku]; **When does the last chairlift go?** 最後のチェアリフトはいつ出ますか? [saigo no chea-rifuto wa itsu demasu ka?]

lastly [læstli] adv 最後に [saigo ni]

late [leɪt] adj (dead) 故… [yue...], (delayed) 遅れた [okureta] ▸ adv 遅れて [okurete]; **Is the train running late?** 電車は遅れていますか? [densha wa okurete imasu ka?]; **Sorry we're late** 遅れてすみません [okurete sumimasen]; **The train is running ten minutes late** 電車は十分遅れています [densha wa jup-pun okurete imasu]

lately [leɪtli] adv 最近 [saikin]

later [leɪtər] adv あとで [ato de]; **I'll call back later** あとでかけなおします [ato de kakenaoshimasu]; **Shall I come back later?** あとで出直しましょうか? [ato de denaoshi-mashou ka?]; **Would you mind trying again later?** あとでもう一度かけてもらえますか? [ato de mou ichido kakete moraemasu ka?]

Latin [lætɪn, -t‑n] n ラテン語 [ratengo]

Latin America n ラテンアメリカ [ratenameri-ka]

Latin American [lætɪn əmɛrɪkən] adj ラテンアメリカの [ratenamerika no]

latitude [lætɪtud] n 緯度 [ido]

Latvia [lætviə] n ラトビア [ratobia]

Latvian [lætviən] adj ラトビアの [ratobia no] ▸ n (language) ラトビア語 [ratobia go], (person) ラトビア人 [ratobiajin]

laugh [læf] n 笑い [warai] ▸ v 笑う [warau]

laughter [læftər] n 笑い声 [waraigoe]

launch [lɔntʃ] v 進水させる [shinsui saseru]

Laundromat® [lɔndrəmæt] n ローンドレット® [roondoretto]

laundry [lɔndri] n 洗濯物 [sentakumono], 選択 [sentaku]; **laundry detergent** n 粉末洗剤 [funmatsusenzai], 粉石鹸 [kona sekken]

laundry detergent [lɔndri dɪtɜrdʒ‑nt] n **Do you have laundry detergent?** 粉末洗剤はありますか? [funmatsu-senzai wa arimasu

ka?]

lava [lɑvə, lævə] n 溶岩 [yougan]

lavender [lævɪndər] n ラベンダー [rabendaa]

law [lɔ] n 法律 [houritsu]; **law school** n ロースクール [roosukuuru]

lawn [lɔn] n 芝生 [shibafu]

lawnmower [lɔnmouər] n 芝刈り機 [shibakariki]

lawyer [lɔɪər, lɔyər] n 事務弁護士 [jimubengoshi], 弁護士 [bengoshi]

laxative [læksətɪv] n 緩下剤 [kangezai]

lay [leɪ] v 置く [oku]

layer [leɪər] n 層 [sou]; **ozone layer** n オゾン層 [ozonsou]

lay off v 一時解雇する [ichiji kaiko suru]; **laid off** adj 余剰人員として解雇された [yojou jin'in to shite kaiko sareta]

layoff [leɪɔf] n 余剰人員の解雇 [yojou jin'in no kaiko]

layout [leɪaʊt] n 配置 [haichi]

lazy [leɪzi] adj 怠惰な [taida na]

lead [lid] n (in play/film) 主役 [shuyaku], (metal) 鉛 [namari] ▸ v 導く [michibiku], …の先頭に立つ [... no sentou ni tatsu]

lead [lid] n (position) トップ記事 [toppu kiji]; **lead singer** n リードシンガー [riidoshingaa]

leader [lidər] n リーダー [riidaa]

lead-free [lɛd fri] adj 無鉛の [muen no]

leaf [lif] n 葉 [ha]; **bay leaf** n ローリエ [roorie]

league [lig] n 連盟 [renmei]

leak [lik] n 漏れ口 [moreguchi] ▸ v 漏れる [moreru]

lean [lin] v もたれる [motareru] (寄りかかる); **lean forward** v 前かがみになる [maekagami ni naru]

lean on v おどす [odosu]

lean out v …から身を乗り出す [... kara mi-o noridasu]

leap [lip] v 跳ねる [haneru]; **leap year** n うるう年 [uruudoshi]

learn [lɜrn] v 学ぶ [manabu]

learner [lɜrnər] n 学習者 [gakushuusha]; **adult learner** n 成人学生 [seijin gakusei]

lease [liis] n 賃貸借契約 [chintaishaku keiyaku] ▷ v 賃貸借する [chintaishaku suru]

least [liist] adj 最も少ない [mottomo sukunai]; **at least** adv 少なくとも [sukunakutomo]

leather [lɛðər] n 革 [kawa]

leave [liiv] n 許可 [kyoka] ▷ v 出発する [shuppatsu suru]; **maternity leave** n 出産休暇 [shussan kyuuka]; **paternity leave** n 父親の育児休暇 [chichioya no ikuji kyuuka]; **sick leave** n 病気休暇 [byoukikyuuka]

leave out v 省く [habuku]

leaves [liivz] npl 葉 [ha]

Lebanese [lɛbəniz] adj レバノンの [rebanon no] ▷ n レバノン人 [rebanonjin]

Lebanon [lɛbənən] n レバノン [rebanon]

lecture [lɛktʃər] n 講義 [kougi] ▷ v 講義をする [kougi-o suru]

leek [liik] n ネギ [negi]

left [lɛft] adj 左の [hidari no] ▷ adv 左に [hidari ni] ▷ n 左 [hidari]; **Take the second turn on your left** 2番目の角を左に曲がってください [ni-ban-me no kado o hidari ni magatte kudasai]; **Turn left** 左に曲がってください [hidari ni magatte kudasai]

left-hand [lɛfthænd] adj 左側の [hidarigawa no]; **left-hand drive** n 左側通行 [hidarigawa tsuukou]

left-handed [lɛfthændɪd] adj 左利きの [hidarikiki no]

leftovers [lɛftoʊvərz] npl 食べ残し [tabenokoshi]

left-wing [lɛftwɪŋ] adj 左派の [saha no]

leg [lɛg] n 脚 [ashi]; **I can't move my leg** 私は脚を動かせません [watashi wa ashi o ugokasemasen]; **I've got a cramp in my leg** 私は脚がつっています [watashi wa ashi ga tsutte imasu]; **My leg itches** 私は脚がかゆみます [watashi wa ashi ga kayumimasu]; **She's hurt her leg** 彼女は脚を痛めました [kanojo wa ashi o itamemashita]

legal [liigᵊl] adj 合法的な [gouhouteki na]

legend [lɛdʒᵊnd] n 伝説 [densetsu]

leggings [lɛgɪŋz] npl レギングス [regingusu]

legible [lɛdʒɪbᵊl] adj 読みやすい [yomiyasui]

legislation [lɛdʒɪsleɪʃᵊn] n 法律制定 [houritsu seitei]

legumes [lɛgjum] npl 豆類 [mamerui]

leisure [liiʒər, lɛʒ-] n 余暇 [yoka]; **leisure center** n レジャーセンター [rejaasentaa]

lemon [lɛmən] n レモン [remon]; **with lemon** レモン入りで [remon-iri de]

lemonade [lɛməneɪd] n レモネード [remoneedo]

lemon zest レモン ゼスト [remon zesuto]

lend [lɛnd] v 貸し付ける [kashitsukeru], 貸す [kasu]

length [lɛŋθ] n 長さ [nagasa]

lens [lɛnz] n レンズ [renzu]; **contact lenses** npl コンタクトレンズ [kontakutorenzu]; **zoom lens** n ズームレンズ [zuumurenzu]; **cleansing solution for contact lenses** コンタクトレンズの洗浄液 [kontakuto-renzu no senjou-eki]; **I wear contact lenses** 私はコンタクトレンズをはめています [watashi wa kontakuto-renzu o hamete imasu]

Lent [lɛnt] n 四旬節 [shijunsetsu]

lentils [lɛntɪlz, -təlz] npl ヒラマメ [hiramame]

Leo [liou] n 獅子座 [shishiza]

leopard [lɛpərd] n ヒョウ [hyou] (動物)

leotard [liətɑrd] n レオタード [reotaado]

less [lɛs] adv 少なく [sukunaku]

lesson [lɛsᵊn] n レッスン [ressun], 授業 [jugyou]; **driving lesson** n 自動車教習 [jidoushakyoushuu]; **Can we take lessons?** レッスンを受けられますか? [ressun o ukeraremasu ka?]; **Do you give lessons?** レッスンを実施していますか? [ressun o jisshi shite imasu ka?]; **Do you organise skiing lessons?** スキーのレッスンを企画していますか? [sukii no ressun o kikaku shite imasu ka?]; **Do you organise snowboarding lessons?** スノーボードのレッスンを企画していますか? [sunooboodo no ressun o kikaku shite imasu ka?]

let [lɛt] v ・・・させる [... saseru]

let down v がっかりさせる [gakkari saseru]

L

let in v 入れる [ireru]

letter [lɛtər] n (a, b, c) 文字 [moji], (message) 手紙 [tegami]; **I'd like to send this letter** この手紙を送りたいのですが [kono tegami o okuritai no desu ga]

lettuce [lɛtɪs] n レタス [retasu]

leukemia [lukimiə] n 白血病 [hakketsubyou]

level [lɛvəl] adj 水平の [suihei no] ▷ n 水平 [suihei]; **sea level** n 海水面 [kaisui men]

lever [livər, lɛv-] n レバー [rebaa] (操作ハンドル)

liability [laɪəbɪlɪti] n **liability insurance** n 第三者賠償責任保険 [daisansha baishouseki-nin hoken]

liar [laɪər] n 嘘つき [usotsuki]

liberal [lɪbərəl, lɪbrəl] adj リベラルな [riberaru na]

liberation [lɪbəreɪʃən] n 解放 [kaihou]

Liberia [laɪbiriə] n リベリア [riberia]

Liberian [laɪbiriən] adj リベリアの [riberia no] ▷ n リベリア人 [riberiajin]

Libra [librə] n 天秤座 [tenbinza]

librarian [laɪbrɛəriən] n 図書館員 [toshokan-in]

library [laɪbrɛri] n 図書館 [toshokan]

Libya [lɪbiə] n リビア [ribia]

Libyan [lɪbiən] adj リビアの [ribia no] ▷ n リビア人 [ribiajin]

lice [laɪs] npl シラミ [shirami]

license [laɪsᵊns] n 免許 [menkyo], 免許証 [menkyoshou]; **driver's license** n 運転免許証 [untenmenkyoshou]; **license plate** n ナンバープレート [nanbaapureeto]; **Here is my driver's license** 私の運転免許証です [watashi no unten-menkyoshou desu]; **I don't have my driver's licence on me** 私は運転免許証を携帯していません [watashi wa unten-menkyoshou o keitai shite imasen]; **My driver's license number is...** 私の運転免許証番号は・・・です [watashi no unten-menkyoshou bangou wa... desu]

lick [lɪk] v なめる [nameru] (舌)

lid [lɪd] n 蓋 [futa]

lie [laɪ] n 嘘 [uso] ▷ v 嘘をつく [uso-o tsuku]

Liechtenstein [lɪktənstaɪn] n リヒテンシュタイン [rihitenshutain]

lieutenant [lutɛnənt] n 中尉 [chuui]

life [laɪf] n 生命 [seimei]; **life insurance** n 生命保険 [seimeihoken]; **life jacket** n 救命胴衣 [kyuumeidoui]; **life preserver** n 救命ベルト [kyuumei beruto]

lifeboat [laɪfboʊt] n 救命ボート [kyuumei-booto]

lifeguard [laɪfgɑrd] n 水泳場の救助員 [suieijou no kyuujoin]

life-saving adj 救命の [kyuumei no]

lifestyle [laɪfstaɪl] n ライフスタイル [raifusutairu]

lift [lɪft] v 持ち上げる [mochiageru]; **ski lift** n スキー場のリフト [sukii jou no rifuto]

light [laɪt] adj (not dark) 明るい [akarui], (not heavy) 軽い [karui] ▷ n 明かり [akari], 光 [hikari], 光り [hikari] ▷ v ともす [tomosu]; **brake light** n ブレーキランプ [bureeki ranpu]; **hazard warning lights** npl 故障警告灯 [koshou keikokutou]; **light bulb** n 電球 [denkyuu]; **parking light** n 側灯 [sokutou]; **pilot light** n 口火 [kuchibi]; **traffic lights** npl 交通信号 [koutsuu shingou]; **May I take it over to the light?** 明るいところに持っていってもいいですか? [akarui tokoro ni motte itte mo ii desu ka?]; **May I turn off the light?** 明かりを消してもいいですか? [akari o keshite mo ii desu ka?]; **May I turn on the light?** 明かりをつけてもいいですか? [akari o tsukete mo ii desu ka?]; **The light doesn't work** 明かりがつきません [akari ga tsukimasen]

lighter [laɪtər] n ライター [raitaa]

lighthouse [laɪthaʊs] n 灯台 [toudai]

lighting [laɪtɪŋ] n 照明 [shoumei]

lightning [laɪtnɪŋ] n 雷 [kaminari]

like [laɪk, laɪk] v 好む [konomu]

like (something or someone) [laɪk -] v ・・・が気に入る [... ga ki ni iru]

likely [laɪkli] adj ・・・しそうな [... shisou na]

lilac [laɪlɑk, -læk, -lək] adj ライラック色の

[rairakku iro no] ▷ n ライラック [rairakku]

lily [lɪli] n ユリ [yuri]; **lily of the valley** n ドイツスズラン [doitsusuzuran]

lime [laɪm] n (compound) 石灰 [sekkai], (fruit) ライム [raimu]

limestone [laɪmstoʊn] n 石灰岩 [sekkaigan]

limit [lɪmɪt] n 限界 [genkai]; **age limit** n 年齢制限 [nenreiseigen]; **speed limit** n 制限速度 [seigensokudo]

limousine [lɪməzin] n リムジン [rimujin]

limp [lɪmp] v びっこをひく [bikko wo hiku]

line [laɪn] n 線 [sen], 列 [retsu]; **wait in line** v 列を作る [retsu wo tsukuru]; **I want to make an outside call. May I have a line?** 外線電話をかけたいので、つないでもらえますか? [gaisen-denwa o kaketai no de, tsunaide moraemasu ka?]; **It's a bad line** 回線が悪いです [kaisen ga warui desu]; **Which line should I take for...?** ・・・へ行くにはどの路線を使えばいいのですか? [... e iku ni wa dono rosen o tsukaeba ii no desu ka?]

linen [lɪnɪn] n 麻 [asa]; **bed linen** n ベッドリネン [beddorinen]

liner [laɪnər] n 定期船 [teikisen]

lingerie [lɒnʒəreɪ, læn-] n ランジェリー [ranjerii]; **Where is the lingerie department?** ランジェリー売り場はどこですか? [ranjerii-uriba wa doko desu ka?]

linguist [lɪŋgwɪst] n 言語学者 [gengogakusha]

linguistic [lɪŋgwɪstɪks] adj 言語の [gengo no]

lining [laɪnɪŋ] n 裏地 [uraji]

link [lɪŋk] v つなぐ [tsunagu]

linoleum [lɪnoʊliəm] n リノリウム [rinoriumu]

lion [laɪən] n ライオン [raion]

lioness [laɪənɪs] n 雌ライオン [mesuraion]

lip [lɪp] n 唇 [kuchibiru]; **lip balm** n おべっか [obekka]

lip-read [lɪprid] v 読唇術で解する [dokushinjutsu de kaisuru]

lipstick [lɪpstɪk] n 口紅 [kuchibeni]

liqueur [lɪkɜr, -kyuər] n リキュール [rikyuuru];

What liqueurs do you have? どんなリキュールがありますか? [donna rikyuuru ga arimasu ka?]

liquid [lɪkwɪd] n 液体 [ekitai]; **dishwashing liquid** n 食器洗い用液体洗剤 [shokkiarai you ekitai senzai]

liquor [lɪkər] n 酒 [sake]; **liquor license** n 酒類販売免許 [sakerui hanbai menkyo]

list [lɪst] n 一覧表 [ichiranhyou] ▷ v 一覧表を作る [ichiranhyou-o tsukuru]; **mailing list** n メーリングリスト [meeringurisuto]; **price list** n 価格表 [kakakuhyou]; **waiting list** n 順番待ち名簿 [junbanmachi meibo]; **wine list** n ワインリスト [wainrisuto]

listen [lɪsᵊn] v 聞く [kiku]; **listen to** v ・・・を聞く [...-o kiku]

listener [lɪsᵊnər, lɪsnər] n 聞き手 [kikite]

liter [litər] n リットル [rittoru]

literally [lɪtərəli] adv 文字どおりに [mojidouri ni]

literature [lɪtərətʃər, -tʃʊr] n 文学 [bungaku]

Lithuania [lɪθuˈeɪniə] n リトアニア [ritoania]

Lithuanian [lɪθyuˈeɪniən] adj リトアニアの [ritoania no] ▷ n (language) リトアニア語 [ritoania go], (person) リトアニア人 [ritoaniajin]

litter [lɪtər] n (offspring) 動物の一腹子 [doubutsu no ippukushi], (trash) ごみ [gomi]

little [lɪtᵊl] adj 小さい [chiisa na]

live¹ [lɪv] v 生きる [ikiru]; **I live in...** 私は・・・に住んでいます [watashi wa... ni sunde imasu]; **We live in...** 私たちは・・・に住んでいます [watashi-tachi wa... ni sunde imasu]; **Where do you live?** どちらにお住まいですか? [dochira ni o-sumai desu ka?]

live² [lɪv] adj 生きている [ikite iru]; **Where can we hear live music?** どこでライブミュージックを聴けますか? [doko de raibu-myuujikku o kikemasu ka?]

lively [laɪvli] adj 元気のよい [genki no yoi]

live on v ・・・にたよって暮らす [... ni tayotte kurasu]

liver [lɪvər] n 肝臓 [kanzou]

L

live together *v* 同棲する [dousei suru]

living [lɪvɪŋ] *n* 生活 [seikatsu]; **cost of living** *n* 生活費 [seikatsuhi]; **living room** *n* 居間 [ima]; **standard of living** *n* 生活水準 [seikatsusuijun]

living room *n* 居間 [ima]

living thing *n* 生き物 [ikimono]

lizard [lɪzərd] *n* トカゲ [tokage]

load [loud] *n* 荷 [ni] ▷ *v* 荷を積む [ni-o tsumu]

loaf, loaves [louf, louvz] *n* パンのひと塊 [pan no hitokatamari]

loan [loun] *n* 貸し付け [kashizuke]

loathe [louð] *v* ひどく嫌う [hidoku kirau]

lobby [lɒbi] *n* I'll meet you in the lobby ロビーでお会いしましょう [robii de o-ai shimashou]

lobster [lɒbstər] *n* ロブスター [robusutaa]

local [louk•l] *adj* 局部の [kyokubu no]; **local anesthetic** *n* 局所麻酔薬 [kyokusho masuiyaku]

locality [loukælɪti] *n* 地方 [chihou]

location [loukeɪʃn] *n* 場所 [basho]; **My location is....** 今いる場所は・・・です [ima iru basho wa... desu]

lock [lɒk] *n* ロック [rokku], *(door)* 錠 [jou], *(hair)* 髪のふさ [kami no fusa] ▷ *v* 鍵をかける [kagi-o kakeru]; **May I have a lock?** ロックをください [rokku o kudasai]; **The wheels lock** ホイールがロックします [hoiiru ga rokku shimasu]

locker [lɒkər] *n* ロッカー [rokkaa]; **luggage locker** *n* コインロッカー [koinrokkaa]; **Are there any luggage lockers?** コインロッカーはありますか? [koin-rokkaa wa arimasu ka?]; **Where are the clothes lockers?** 服のロッカーはどこですか? [fuku no rokkaa wa doko desu ka?]; **Which locker is mine?** どれが私のロッカーですか? [dore ga watashi no rokkaa desu ka?]

locket [lɒkɪt] *n* ロケット [roketto]

lock out *v* 締め出す [shimedasu]

locksmith [lɒksmɪθ] *n* 錠前屋 [joumaeya]

lodger [lɒdʒər] *n* 下宿人 [geshukunin]

log [lɒg] *n* 丸太 [maruta]

logical [lɒdʒɪk•l] *adj* 論理的な [ronriteki na]

log in *v* ログインする [roguin suru]

logo [lougou] *n* ロゴ [rogo]

log off *v* ログオフする [roguofu suru]

log on *v* ログオンする [roguon suru]; **How much does it cost to log on for an hour?** 1時間ログオンするのにいくらですか? [ichi-jikan roguon suru no ni ikura desu ka?]

log out *v* ログアウトする [roguauto suru]

lollipop [lɒlipɒp] *n* 棒付きキャンデー [boutsuki kyandee]

London [lʌndən] *n* ロンドン [rondon]

loneliness [lounlinɪs] *n* 孤独 [kodoku]

lonely [lounli] *adj* 孤独の [kodoku no]

loner [lounər] *n* 独身 [dokushin]

lonesome [lounsəm] *adj* 孤独の [kodoku no]

long [lɒŋ] *adj* 長い [nagai] ▷ *adv* 長く [nagaku] ▷ *v* 切望する [setsubou suru]; **long jump** *n* 幅跳び [habatobi]

longer [lɒŋgər] *adv* より長く [yori nagaku]

longitude [lɒndʒɪtud] *n* 経度 [keido]

look [lʊk] *n* 目つき [metsuki] ▷ *v* 見る [miru]; **look at** *v* ・・・をよく見る [...-o yoku miru]

look around *v* あたりを見回す [atari-o miwatasu]

look for *v* ・・・をさがす [...-o sagasu]

look up *v* 調べる [shiraberu]

loose [lus] *adj* 緩い [yurui]

lose [luz] *vi* 負ける [makeru] ▷ *vt* なくす [nakusu]

loser [luzər] *n* 敗者 [haisha]

loss [lɒs] *n* 喪失 [soushitsu]

lost [lɒst] *adj* 失った [utta]

lost-and-found *n* 遺失物 [ishitsubutsu]; **lost-and-found department** *n* 遺失物取扱所 [ishitsubutsu toriatsukaijo]

lotion [louʃn] *n* ローション [rooshon]; **aftersun lotion** *n* アフターサンローション [afutaasan rooshon]; **cleansing lotion** *n* クレンジングローション [kurenjingurooshon]; **suntan lotion** *n* サンタンローション [santanrooshon]

lottery [lɒtəri] *n* 宝くじ [takarakuji]

loud [laud] *adj* 大声の [ougoe no]

loudly [laudli] *adv* 大声で [ougoe de]

loudspeaker [laudspikər] *n* スピーカー [supiikaa]

lounge [laundʒ] *n* departure lounge *n* 出発ラウンジ [shuppatsu raunji]; **transit lounge** *n* 通過ラウンジ [tsuuka raunji]; **Could we have coffee in the lounge?** ラウンジでコーヒーをいただけますか? [raunji de koohii o itadakemasu ka?]; **Is there a television lounge?** テレビラウンジはありますか? [terebi-raunji wa arimasu ka?]

lousy [lauzi] *adj* だめな [damena], 卑劣な [hiretsu na]

love [lʌv] *n* 愛 [ai], 恋愛 [ren-ai] ▷ *v* 愛する [ai suru]; **I love you** 私はあなたを愛しています [watashi wa anata o aishite imasu]

lovely [lʌvli] *adj* 美しい [utsukushii]

lover [lʌvər] *n* 愛人 [aijin]

low [lou] *adj* 低い [hikui] ▷ *adv* 低く [hikuku]

low-alcohol [louælkəhɒl] *adj* 低アルコールの [tei arukooru no]

lower [louər] *adj* より低い [yori hikui] ▷ *v* 下げる [sageru]

low-fat [loufæt] *adj* 低脂肪の [teishibou no]

loyalty [lɔɪəlti] *n* 忠誠 [chuusei]

luck [lʌk] *n* 運 [un]

luckily [lʌkɪli] *adv* 運よく [un yoku]

lucky [lʌki] *adj* 運のよい [un no yoi]

lucrative [lukrətɪv] *adj* 儲かる [moukaru]

luggage [lʌgɪdʒ] *n* 手荷物 [tenimotsu]; **luggage locker** *n* コインロッカー [koinrokkaa]; **luggage rack** *n* 手荷物置き棚 [tenimotsu okidana]; **luggage storage** *n* 預けた手荷物 [azuketa tenimotsu]; **luggage storage office** *n* 手荷物一時預かり所 [tenimotsu ichiji azukarisho]; **Can I insure my luggage?** 手荷物に保険をかけられますか? [tenimotsu ni hoken o kakeraremasu ka?]; **My luggage has been damaged** 私の手荷物が破損しています [watashi no tenimotsu ga hason shite imasu]; **My**

luggage has been lost 私の手荷物が紛失しました [watashi no tenimotsu ga funshitsu shimashita]; **My luggage hasn't arrived** 私の手荷物が着いていません [watashi no tenimotsu ga tsuite imasen]; **Where do I check in my luggage?** 手荷物のチェックインはどこでするのですか? [tenimotsu no chekku-in wa doko de suru no desu ka?]; **Where is the luggage for the flight from...?** ・・・からのフライトの手荷物はどこですか? [... kara no furaito no tenimotsu wa doko desu ka?]

lukewarm [lukwɔrm] *adj* なまぬるい [namanurui]

lullaby [lʌləbaɪ] *n* 子守歌 [komoriuta]

lumber [lʌmbər] *n* 材木 [zaimoku]

lump [lʌmp] *n* 塊 [katamari]

lunatic [lunətɪk] *n* 愚人 [gujin], 気違い [kichigai]

lunch [lʌntʃ] *n* 昼食 [chuushoku]; **box lunch** *n* 弁当 [bentou]; **lunch hour** *n* 昼休み [hiruyasumi]; **Can we meet for lunch?** 昼食をご一緒できますか? [chuushoku o go-issho dekimasu ka?]; **I'm free for lunch** 昼食には時間があいています [chuushoku ni wa jikan ga aite imasu]; **The lunch was excellent** 昼食はすばらしかったです [chuushoku wa subarashikatta desu]; **When will lunch be ready?** 昼食はいつ用意できますか? [chuushoku wa itsu youi dekimasu ka?]; **Where do we stop for lunch?** 昼食にはどこで停まりますか? [chuushoku ni wa doko de tomarimasu ka?]

lunchtime [lʌntʃtaɪm] *n* ランチタイム [ranchitaimu]

lung [lʌŋ] *n* 肺 [hai]

lush [lʌʃ] *adj* 青々とした [aoao to shita]

lust [lʌst] *n* 性欲 [seiyoku]

Luxembourg [lʌksᵊmbɜrg] *n* ルクセンブルク [rukusenburuku]

luxurious [lʌgʒuəriəs] *adj* 贅沢な [zeitaku na]

luxury [lʌkʃəri, lʌgʒɜ-] *n* 贅沢 [zeitaku]

lyrics [lɪrɪks] *npl* 抒情詩 [jojoushi]

L

M

macaroni [mækərouni] *npl* マカロニ [makaroni]

machine [məʃin] *n* 機械 [kikai]; **answering machine** *n* 留守番電話 [rusubandenwa]; **machine gun** *n* マシンガン [mashingan]; **machine washable** *adj* 洗濯機で洗える [sentakuki de araeru]; **sewing machine** *n* ミシン [mishin]; **ticket machine** *n* 券売機 [kenbaiki]; **vending machine** *n* スロットマシン [surottomashin], 自動販売機 [jidouhanbaiki]; **washing machine** *n* 洗濯機 [sentakuki]

machinery [məʃinəri] *n* 機械類 [kikairui]

mackerel [mækərəl, mækrəl] *n* サバ [saba]

mad [mæd] *adj (angry)* 腹を立てた [hara-o tateta]

Madagascar [mædəgæskər] *n* マダガスカル [madagasukaru]

madam [mædəm] *n* 奥様 [okusama]

madness [mædnɪs] *n* 狂気 [kyouki]

magazine [mægəzin, -zin] *n (ammunition)* 弾薬 [dan-yaku], *(periodical)* 雑誌 [zasshi]; **Where can I buy a magazine?** どこで雑誌を買えますか? [doko de zasshi o kaemasu ka?]

maggot [mægət] *n* うじ [uji] (虫)

magic [mædʒɪk] *adj* 魔法の [mahou no] ▷ *n* 魔法 [mahou], 魔術 [majutsu]

magical [mædʒɪk·l] *adj* 魔術的な [majutsuteki na]

magician [mədʒɪʃ·n] *n* 魔術師 [majutsushi]

magistrate [mædʒɪstreɪt] *n* 治安判事 [chian hanji]

magnet [mægnɪt] *n* 磁石 [jishaku]

magnetic [mægnɛtɪk] *adj* 磁石の [jishaku no]

magnificent [mægnɪfɪsənt] *adj* 壮大な [sodai na]

magpie [mægpaɪ] *n* カササギ [kasasagi]

mahogany [məhɒgəni] *n* マホガニー [mahoganii]

maid [meɪd] *n* お手伝い [otetsudai] (使用人), 客室係のメイド [kyakushitsugakari no meido]

maiden [meɪd·n] *n* **maiden name** *n* 女性の結婚前の旧姓 [josei no kekkonmae no kyuusei]

mail [meɪl] *n* メール [meeru], 郵便 [yuubin], 郵便物 [yuubinbutsu], *(mail)* 郵便 [yuubin] ▷ *v* 郵送する [yuusou suru]; **certified mail** *n* 簡易書留 [kan-i kakitome]; **junk mail** *n* ジャンクメール [janku meeru]; **How long will it take by certified mail?** 書留郵便でどのくらいの日数がかかりますか? [kakitome-yuubin de dono kurai no nissuu ga kakarimasu ka?]; **Is there any mail for me?** 私あての郵便物がありますか? [watashi ate no yuubinbutsu ga arimasu ka?]; **Please forward my mail to this address** 私あての郵便物をこの住所に回送してください [watashi ate no yuubinbutsu o kono juusho ni kaisou shite kudasai]

mailbox [meɪlbɒks] *n* 郵便受 [yuubinju]

mailing list [meɪlɪŋ lɪst] *n* **mailing list** *n* メーリングリスト [meeringurisuto]

main [meɪn] *adj* 主な [omo na]; **main course** *n* メインコース [meinkoosu]; **main road** *n* 幹線道路 [kansendouro]

mainland [meɪnlænd] *n* 本土 [hondo]

mainly [meɪnli] *adv* 主に [omo ni]

maintain [meɪnteɪn] *v* 維持する [iji suru]

maintenance [meɪntɪnəns] *n* 維持 [iji]

majesty [mædʒɪsti] *n* 威厳 [igen]

major [meɪdʒər] *adj* 大きい方の [oukii hou no]

majority [mədʒɔːrɪti] n 大部分 [daibubun]

make [meɪk] v 作る [tsukuru]

makeover [meɪkouvər] n 改造 [kaizou]

maker [meɪkər] n 造り主 [tsukurinushi]

make up [meɪkʌp] v 埋め合わせる [umeawaseru]

makeup n メーキャップ [meekyappu]

malaria [məlɛərɪə] n マラリア [mararia]

Malawi [məlɑːwɪ] n マラウィ [maraui]

Malaysia [məleɪʒə] n マレーシア [mareeshia]

Malaysian [məleɪʒ-n] adj マレーシアの [Mareeshia no] ▷ n マレーシア人 [Mareeshia jin]

male [meɪl] adj 男性の [dansei no] ▷ n 男性 [dansei]

malicious [məlɪʃəs] adj 悪意のある [akui no aru]

malignant [məlɪgnənt] adj 悪意のある [akui no aru]

malnutrition [mælnutrɪʃ-n] n 栄養不良 [eiyou furyou]

Malta [mɔːltə] n マルタ [maruta]

Maltese [mɔːltiz] adj マルタの [maruta no] ▷ n (language) マルタ語 [Maruta go], (person) マルタ人 [marutajin]

mammal [mæm-l] n 哺乳動物 [honyuu doubutsu]

mammoth [mæməθ] adj 巨大な [kyodai na] ▷ n マンモス [manmosu]

man [mæn] (pl men) n 男 [otoko]; **best man** n 新郎の付添い役 [shinrou no tsukisoiyaku]; **men's room** n 男性用トイレ [dansei you toire]; **Where is the men's room?** 男性用トイレはどこですか? [dansei-you toire wa doko desu ka?]

manage [mænɪdʒ] v うまく···する [umaku... suru]

manageable [mænɪdʒəb-l] adj 御しやすい [o shiyasui]

management [mænɪdʒmənt] n 経営 [keiei], 経営陣 [keieijin]

manager [mænɪdʒər] n 経営者 [keieisha], 女性経営者 [josei keieisha]

mandarin [mændərɪn] n (fruit) マンダリンオレンジ [mandarin orenji], (official) 上級官吏 [joukyuu kanri]

mango [mæŋɡou] n マンゴー [mangou]

mania [meɪniə] n ···熱 [... netsu] (熱狂)

maniac [meɪniæk] n 狂人 [kyoujin]

manicure [mænɪkyuər] n マニキュア [manikyua]

manipulate [mənɪpyəleɪt] v 巧みに扱う [takumi ni atsukau]

mankind [mænkaɪnd] n 人類 [jinrui]

man-made adj 人造の [jinzou no]

manner [mænər] n 方法 [houhou]

manners [mænərz] npl 行儀 [gyougi]

manpower [mænpaʊər] n 労働力 [roudouryoku]

mansion [mænʃ-n] n 大邸宅 [daiteitaku]

mantel [mænt-l] n マントルピース [mantorupiisu]

manual [mænyuəl] n マニュアル [manyuaru]

manufacture [mænyəfæktʃər] v 製造する [seizou suru]

manufacturer [mænyəfæktʃərər] n 製造業者 [seizougyousha]

manure [mənuər] n 堆肥 [taihi]

manuscript [mænyəskrɪpt] n 原稿 [genkou]

many [mɛni] adj 多くの [ouku no]

Maori [maʊri] adj マオリの [Maori no] ▷ n (language) マオリ語 [Maori go], (person) マオリ族 [Maori zoku]

map [mæp] n マップ [mappu], 地図 [chizu]; **road map** n ロードマップ [roodomappu]; **street map** n 街路地図 [gairo chizu]; **Could you draw me a map with directions?** 道順を示す地図を書いてもらえますか? [michijun o shimesu chizu o kaite moraemasu ka?]; **Could you show me where it is on the map?** 地図でそれがどこにあるか教えてもらえますか? [chizu de sore ga doko ni aru ka oshiete moraemasu ka?]; **Do you have a map of...?** ···の地図はありますか? [... no chizu wa arimasu ka?]; **Do you have a map of the ski runs?** ゲレンデのマップはあります

か? [gerende no mappu wa arimasu ka?];
Do you have a map of the subway? 地下
鉄のマップはありますか? [chikatetsu no
mappu wa arimasu ka?]; **I need a road map
of...** 私は・・・の道路マップが必要です
[watashi wa... no douro-mappu ga hitsuyou
desu]; **Is there a cycle map of this area?**
この地域のサイクルマップはありますか?
[kono chiiki no saikuru-mappu wa arimasu
ka?]; **May I have a map?** マップをください
[mappu o kudasai]; **Where can I buy a map
of the area?** どこでその地域の地図を買えま
すか? [doko de sono chiiki no chizu o
kaemasu ka?]

maple [meɪpl] *n* カエデ [kaede]

marathon [mærəθɒn] *n* マラソン [marason]

marble [mɑrbl] *n* 大理石 [dairiseki]

march [mɑrtʃ] *n* 行進 [koushin] ▷ *v* 行進する
[koushin suru]

March [mɑrtʃ] *n* 三月 [sangatsu]

Mardi Gras [mɑrdi grɑ] *n* 告解火曜日 [Kokkai
Kayoubi]

mare [mɛər] *n* 雌馬 [meuma]

margarine [mɑrdʒərɪn] *n* マーガリン
[maagarin]

margin [mɑrdʒɪn] *n* へり [heri]

marigold [mærɪgould] *n* マリーゴールド
[mariigourudo]

marijuana [mærɪwɑnə] *n* マリファナ
[marifana]

marina [mərinə] *n* マリーナ [mariina]

marinade [mærɪneɪd] *n* マリネ [marine]

marinate [mærɪneɪt] *v* マリネにする [marine
ni suru]

marital [mærɪtl] *adj* **marital status** *n* 婚姻関
係の有無 [kon'in kankei no umu]

maritime [mærɪtaɪm] *adj* 海事の [kaiji no]

marjoram [mɑrdʒərəm] *n* マヨラナ
[mayorana]

mark [mɑrk] *n* **check mark** *n* 照合の印
[shougou no in]; **question mark** *n* 疑問符
[gimonfu]; **quotation marks** *npl* 引用符
[in-youfu]

market [mɑrkɪt] *n* マーケット [maaketto], 市場
[ichiba]; **market research** *n* 市場調査
[shijouchousa]; **stock market** *n* 株式市場
[kabushikishijou]; **When is the market?** マー
ケットが立つのはいつですか? [maaketto ga
tatsu no wa itsu desu ka?]

marketing [mɑrkɪtɪŋ] *n* マーケティング
[maaketeingu]

marketplace [mɑrkɪtpleɪs] *n* 市場 [ichiba]

marmalade [mɑrməleɪd] *n* マーマレード
[maamareedo]

maroon [mərun] *adj* 栗色の [kuri iro no]

marriage [mærɪdʒ] *n* 結婚 [kekkon];
marriage certificate *n* 結婚証明書
[kekkonshoumeisho]

married [mærid] *adj* 結婚している [kekkon
shite iru]

marrow [mærou] *n* 骨髄 [kotsuzui]

marry [mæri] *v* 結婚する [kekkon suru]

marsh [mɑrʃ] *n* 沼 [numa]

martyr [mɑrtər] *n* 殉教者 [junkyousha]

marvelous [mɑrvələs] *adj* すばらしい [subar-
ashii]

Marxism [mɑrksɪzəm] *n* マルクス主義
[marukusushugi]

marzipan [mɑrzipæn] *n* マジパン [majipan]

mascara [mæskærə] *n* マスカラ [masukara]

masculine [mæskyəlɪn] *adj* 男らしい
[otokorashii]

mask [mæsk] *n* マスク [masuku]

masked [mæskt] *adj* マスクをした [masuku-o
shita]

mass [mæs] *n (amount)* 大量 [tairyou],
(church) ミサ [misa]; **When is mass?** ミサは
いつですか? [misa wa itsu desu ka?]

massacre [mæsəkər] *n* 大虐殺
[daigyakusatsu]

massage [məsɑʒ] *n* マッサージ [massaaji]

massive [mæsɪv] *adj* どっしりした [dosshiri
shita]

mast [mæst] *n* マスト [masuto]

master [mæstər] *n* 長 [chou] *(統率)* ▷ *v* 支配
する [shihai suru]; **master of ceremonies** *n*

司会者 [shikaisha]

masterpiece [mǽstərpis] *n* 傑作 [kessaku]

mat [mǽt] *n* マット [matto]

match [mǽtʃ] *n (partnership)* 縁組み [engumi], *(sport)* 試合 [shiai] ▷ *v* マッチさせる [matchi saseru]

matching [mǽtʃɪn] *adj* 合った [atta]

material [mətɪ́əriəl] *n* 材料 [zairyou]; **What is the material?** 材料は何ですか? [zairyou wa nan desu ka?]

maternal [mətɜ́rnəl] *adj* 母性の [bosei no]

math [mǽθ] *npl* 数学 [suugaku]

mathematical [mæ̀θəmǽtɪkəl] *adj* 数学の [suugaku no]

mathematics [mæ̀θəmǽtɪks] *npl* 数学 [suugaku]

matter [mǽtər] *n* 物質 [busshitsu] ▷ *v* 重要である [juuyou de aru]

mattress [mǽtrɪs] *n* マットレス [mattoresu]; **floating pool mattress** *n* ライロー® [rairoo]

mature [mətjʊ́ər, -tʊ̀ər, -tʃʊ̀ər] *adj* 成熟した [seijuku shita]

Mauritania [mɔ̀rətéɪniə] *n* モーリタニア [mooritania]

Mauritius [mɔrɪ́ʃəs] *n* モーリシャス [moorishasu]

mauve [móʊv] *adj* 藤紫色の [fuji murasaki iro no]

maximum [mǽksɪməm] *adj* 最大の [saidai no] ▷ *n* 最大限 [saidaigen]

may [méɪ] *v* **May I call you tomorrow?** 明日電話してもいいですか? [asu denwa shite mo ii desu ka?]; **May I open the window?** 窓を開けてもいいですか? [mado o akete mo ii desu ka?]; **May I sit here?** ここに座ってもいいですか? [koko ni suwatte mo ii desu ka?]

May [méɪ] *n* 五月 [gogatsu]

maybe [méɪbi] *adv* もしかしたら [moshikashi-tara]

mayonnaise [méɪənéɪz] *n* マヨネーズ [mayoneezu]

mayor [méɪər, mɛ́ər] *n* 市長 [shichou]

maze [méɪz] *n* 迷路 [meiro]

me [mi, STRONG mí] *pron* **Could you show me where it is on the map?** 地図でそれがどこにあるか教えてもらえますか? [chizu de sore ga doko ni aru ka oshiete moraemasu ka?]; **Excuse me** すみません [sumimasen]; **Please let me off** 降ろしてください [oroshite kudasai]

meadow [mɛ́doʊ] *n* 牧草地 [bokusouchi]

meal [míl] *n* 食事 [shokuji]; **Could you prepare a meal without eggs?** 卵を使わずに食事を用意していただけますか? [tamago o tsukawazu ni shokuji o youi shite itadakemasu ka?]; **Could you prepare a meal without gluten?** グルテンを使わずに食事を用意していただけますか? [guruten o tsukawazu ni shokuji o youi shite itadakemasu ka?]; **Enjoy your meal!** お食事をお楽しみください! [o-shokuji o o-tanoshimi kudasai!]; **The meal was delicious** 食事はおいしかったです [shokuji wa oishikatta desu]

mealtime [mɪ́ltaɪm] *n* 食事時間 [shokuji jikan]

mean [mín] *v* 意味する [imi suru]

meaning [mínɪn] *n* 意味 [imi]

means [mínz] *npl* 手段 [shudan]

meantime [mɪ́ntaɪm] *adv* その間に [sono aida ni]

meanwhile [mɪ́nwaɪl] *adv* その間に [sono aida ni]

measles [mɪ́zəlz] *npl* はしか [hashika]; **German measles** *n* 風疹 [fuushin]; **I had measles recently** 私は最近はしかにかかりました [watashi wa saikin hashika ni kakarimashita]

measure [mɛ́ʒər] *v* 測定する [sokutei suru] ▷ *n* **tape measure** *n* 巻尺 [makijaku]

measurements [mɛ́ʒərməntz] *npl* サイズ [saizu]

meat [mít] *n* 肉 [niku]; **ground meat** *n* 挽肉 [hikiniku]; **red meat** *n* 赤身肉 [akaminiku]; **Do you eat meat?** あなたは肉を食べますか? [anata wa niku o tabemasu ka?]; **I don't eat meat** 私は肉を食べません [watashi wa

M

niku o tabemasen]; **I don't eat red meat** 私
は赤身肉を食べません [watashi wa
akaminiku o tabemasen]; **I don't like meat**
私は肉が好きではありません [watashi wa
niku ga suki de wa arimasen]; **The meat is
cold** 肉が冷たいです [niku ga tsumetai
desu]; **This meat is spoiled** この肉はいたん
でいます [kono niku wa itande imasu]

meatball [mitbol] n ミートボール [miitobooru]

Mecca [mɛkə] n メッカ [mekka]

mechanic [mɪkæŋɪk] n 修理工 [shuurikou],
機械工 [kikaikou]; **auto mechanic** n 自動車
整備士 [jidousha seibishi]; **Could you send
a mechanic?** 修理工を手配してもらえます
か? [shuuri-kou o tehai shite moraemasu
ka?]

mechanical [mɪkæŋɪkᵊl] adj 機械の [kikai
no]

mechanism [mɛkənɪzəm] n 機構 [kikou] (機
械)

medal [mɛdᵊl] n メダル [medaru]

medallion [mɪdælyən] n 大メダル [dai
medaru]

media [midiə] npl マスメディア [masumedia]

medical [mɛdɪkᵊl] adj 医学の [igaku no];
medical certificate n 診断書 [shindansho]

medication [mɛdɪkeɪʃən] n **I'm on this
medication** 私はこの薬を飲んでいます
[watashi wa kono kusuri o nonde imasu]

medicine [mɛdɪsɪn] n 薬 [kusuri], (science)
医学 [igaku]; **I'm already taking this
medicine** 私はすでにこの薬を飲んでいます
[watashi wa sudeni kono kusuri o nonde
imasu]

medieval [midiivᵊl, mɪdivᵊl] adj 中世の
[chuusei no]

meditation [mɛdɪteɪʃən] n 瞑想 [meisou]

Mediterranean [mɛdɪtəreɪniən] adj 地中海
の [chichuukai no] ▷ n 地中海 [chichuukai]

medium [midiəm] adj (between extremes) 中
くらいの [naka kurai no]

medium-sized [midiəmsaɪzd] adj 中サイズ
の [naka saizu no]

meet [mit] v 待ち合わせる [machiawaseru]
▷ vi 会う [au] ▷ vt ~に会う [~ ni au]

meeting [mitɪŋ] n 会議 [kaigi], ミーティング
[miitingu]; **I'd like to arrange a meeting
with...** ···さんとのミーティングを設定したい
のですが [... san to no miitingu o settei shitai
no desu ga]

mega [mɛgə] adj とても大きい [totemo ookii]

melody [mɛlədi] n メロディー [merodii]

melon [mɛlən] n メロン [meron]

melt [mɛlt] vi 溶ける [tokeru] ▷ vt 溶かす
[tokasu]

member [mɛmbər] n 会員 [kaiin], メンバー
[menbaa] (会員), 議員 [giin]; **Do I have to be
a member?** 会員でなければなりませんか?
[kaiin de nakereba narimasen ka?]

membership [mɛmbərʃɪp] n メンバー
[menbaa] (会員資格); **membership card** n
メンバーカード [menbaakaado]

memento [mɪmɛntoʊ] n 思い出の品 [omoide
no shina]

memo [mɛmoʊ] n メモ [memo]

memorial [mɪmɔriəl] n 記念碑 [kinenhi]

memorize [mɛməraɪz] v 記憶する [kioku
suru]

memory [mɛməri] n 記憶 [kioku]; **memory
card** n メモリカード [memorikaado]

meningitis [mɛnɪndʒaɪtɪs] n 髄膜炎
[zuimakuen]

menopause [mɛnəpɔz] n 閉経期 [heikeiki]

menstruation [mɛnstrueɪʃᵊn] n 月経 [gekkei]

mental [mɛntᵊl] adj 精神の [seishin no];
mental hospital n 精神病院 [seishinbyouin]

mentality [mɛntælɪti] n 精神構造 [seishin
kouzou]

mention [mɛnʃᵊn] v 話に出す [hanashi ni
dasu]

menu [mɛnyu] n メニュー [menyuu]; **set
menu** n 定食 [teishoku]; **Do you have a
children's menu?** 子供用のメニューはありま
すか? [kodomo-you no menyuu wa arimasu
ka?]; **Do you have a set-price menu?** セッ
トメニューはありますか? [setto-menyuu wa

arimasu ka?]; **How much is the set menu?**
セットメニューはいくらですか? [setto-meny-
uu wa ikura desu ka?]; **The dessert menu,**
please デザートのメニューをください
[dezaato no menyuu o kudasai]; **The menu,**
please メニューをください [menyuu o
kudasai]; **We'll take the set menu** セットメ
ニューをください [setto-menyuu o kudasai]

mercury [mɜrkyəri] n 水銀 [suigin]

mercy [mɜrsi] n 慈悲 [jihi]

mere [mɪər] adj ほんの [hon no]

merge [mɜrdʒ] v 合併する [gappei suru]

merger [mɜrdʒər] n 合併 [gappei]

meringue [məræŋ] n メレンゲ [merenge]

mermaid [mɜrmeɪd] n 人魚 [ningyo]

merry [mɛri] adj 陽気な [youki na]

merry-go-round n 回転木馬 [kaitenmokuba]

mess [mɛs] n 散乱 [sanran]

message [mɛsɪdʒ] n 伝言 [dengon];
Multimedia Messaging Service n マルチメ
ディアメッセージングサービス [maruchimedia
messeejingu saabisu]; **text message** n テキ
ストメッセージ [tekisutomesseeji]; **Are there**
any messages for me? 私あての伝言があり
ますか? [watashi ate no dengon ga arimasu
ka?]; **May I leave a message with his**
secretary? 彼の秘書に伝言を残すことはでき
ますか? [kare no hisho ni dengon o nokosu
koto wa dekimasu ka?]; **May I leave a**
message? 伝言をお願いできますか?
[dengon o o-negai dekimasu ka?]

mess around v 無為に過ごす [mui ni
sugosu]

messenger [mɛsɪndʒər] n 使者 [shisha]

mess up v 散らかす [chirakasu]

messy [mɛsi] adj 散らかった [chira katta]

metabolism [mɪtæbəlɪzəm] n 代謝 [taisha]

metal [mɛtl] n 金属 [kinzoku]

meteorite [mitiəraɪt] n 隕石 [inseki]

meter [mitər] n メーター [meetaa], メートル
[meetoru]; **parking meter** n パーキングメー
ター [paakingumeetaa]; **Do you have a**
meter? メーターはありますか? [meetaa wa

arimasu ka?]; **Do you have change for the**
parking meter? パーキングメーター用の小
銭をお持ちですか? [paakingu-meetaa-you
no kozeni o o-mochi desu ka?]; **It's more**
than on the meter それではメーター料金よ
り高いです [sore de wa meetaa-ryoukin yori
takai desu]; **Please use the meter** メーター
を使ってください [meetaa o tsukatte
kudasai]; **The meter is broken** メーターが壊
れています [meetaa ga kowarete imasu];
The parking meter is broken パーキングメ
ーターが壊れています [paakingu-meetaa ga
kowarete imasu]; **Where's the electricity**
meter? 電気のメーターはどこですか? [denki
no meetaa wa doko desu ka?]; **Where's the**
gas meter? ガスのメーターはどこですか?
[gasu no meetaa wa doko desu ka?]

method [mɛθəd] n 法 [hou], 方法 [houhou]

Methodist [mɛθədɪst] adj メソジスト派の
[Mesojisuto ha no]

metric [mɛtrɪk] adj メートル法の [meetoruhou
no]

Mexican [mɛksɪkən] adj メキシコの
[mekishiko no] ▷ n メキシコ人 [mekishikojin]

Mexico [mɛksikoʊ] n メキシコ [mekishiko]

microchip [maɪkroutʃɪp] n マイクロチップ
[maikurochippu]

microphone [maɪkrəfoʊn] n マイクロホン
[maikurohon]; **Does it have a microphone?**
マイクロホンはついていますか? [maikurohon
wa tsuite imasu ka?]

microscope [maɪkrəskoʊp] n 顕微鏡
[kenbikyou]

mid [mɪd] adj 中間の [chuukan no]

middle [mɪdl] n 中央 [chuuou]; **Middle Ages**
npl 中世 [chuusei]; **Middle East** n 中東
[chuutou]

middle-aged [mɪdleɪdʒd] adj 中年の
[chuunen no]

middle-class adj 中流階級の [chuuryuu
kaikyuu no]

midge [mɪdʒ] n 小虫 [shou mushi]

midnight [mɪdnaɪt] n 真夜中 [mayonaka]

M

midterm vacation n 学期中の中間休暇 [gakkichuu no chuukan kyuuka]

midwife [mɪdwaɪf] (pl **midwives**) n 助産婦 [josanpu]

migraine [maɪgreɪn] n 片頭痛 [henzutsuu]

migrant [maɪgrənt] adj 移動性の [idousei no] ▷n 移住者 [ijuusha]

migration [maɪgreɪʃn] n 移住 [ijuu]

mike [maɪk] n マイク [maiku]

mild [maɪld] adj マイルドな [mairudo na]

mile [maɪl] n マイル [mairu]

mileage [maɪlɪdʒ] n 総マイル数 [sou mairu suu]

military [mɪlɪtɛri] adj 軍の [gun no]

milk [mɪlk] n ミルク [miruku], 牛乳 [gyuunyuu] ▷v 乳を搾る [chichi-o shiboru]; **UHT milk** n 超高温殺菌牛乳 [choukouon sakkin gyuunyuu]; **milk chocolate** n ミルクチョコレート [mirukuchokoreeto]; **reduced-fat milk** n 半脱脂乳 [han dasshi nyuu]; **skim milk** n 脱脂乳 [dasshinyuu]; **Do you drink milk?** あなたは牛乳を飲みますか? [anata wa gyuunyuu o nomimasu ka?]; **Do you have real milk?** 本物の牛乳はありますか? [honmono no gyuunyuu wa arimasu ka?]; **Is it made with unpasteurised milk?** それは低温殺菌していない牛乳を使って作られていますか? [sore wa teion-sakkin shite inai gyuunyuu o tsukatte tsukurarete imasu ka?]; **with the milk on the side** ミルクは別にください [miruku wa betsu ni kudasai]

milkshake [mɪlkʃeɪk] n ミルクシェイク [mirukusheiku]

mill [mɪl] n 製粉所 [seifunjou]

millennium [mɪlɛniəm] n 千年間 [sen-nenkan]

millimeter [mɪlɪmitər] n ミリメートル [mirimeetoru]

million [mɪlyən] n 100万 [hyakuman]

millionaire [mɪlyənɛər] n 大金持ち [ooganemochi]

mimic [mɪmɪk] v 物まねをする [monomane-o suru]

mind [maɪnd] n 心 [kokoro] ▷v いやだと思う [iyadato omou]

mine [maɪn] n 鉱山 [kouzan]

miner [maɪnər] n 炭坑労働者 [tankou roudousha]

mineral [mɪnərəl] adj 鉱物の [koubutsu no] ▷n 鉱物 [koubutsu]; **mineral water** n ミネラルウォーター [mineraru uootaa]

miniature [mɪniətʃer, -tʃuər] adj ミニチュアの [minichua no] ▷n ミニチュア [minichua]

minibar [mɪnibar] n ミニバー [minibaa]

minibus [mɪnibʌs] n マイクロバス [maikurobasu]

minimal [mɪnɪməl] adj 最小限の [saishougen no]

minimize [mɪnɪmaɪz] v 最小限度にする [saishougendo ni suru]

minimum [mɪnɪməm] adj 最小の [saishou no] ▷n 最小限 [saishougen]

mining [maɪnɪŋ] n 鉱業 [kougyou]

miniskirt [mɪniskɜrt] n ミニスカート [minisukaato]

minister [mɪnɪstər] n (clergy) 聖職者 [seishokusha], (government) 大臣 [daijin]; **prime minister** n 首相 [shushou]

ministry [mɪnɪstri] n (government) 省 [shou], (religion) 聖職 [seishoku]

mink [mɪŋk] n ミンク [minku]

minor [maɪnər] adj 小さい方の [chiisai hou no] ▷n 未成年者 [miseinensha]

minority [mɪnɔrɪti, maɪ-] n 少数派 [shousuuha]

mint [mɪnt] n (coins) 貨幣鋳造所 [kahei chuuzoujo], (herb/sweet) ミント [minto]

minute [mɪnɪt] adj 微小な [bishou na] ▷n 分 [fun]; **Could you wait here for a few minutes?** ここで数分待ってもらえますか? [koko de suu-fun matte moraemasu ka?]; **We're ten minutes late** 私たちは十分遅れました [watashi-tachi wa jup-pun okuremashita]

miracle [mɪrəkl] n 奇跡 [kiseki]

mirror [mɪrər] n 鏡 [kagami]; **rear-view**

mirror *n* バックミラー [bakkumiraa];
side-view mirror *n* サイドミラー [saidomiraa]

misbehave [mɪsbɪheɪv] *v* 不正を働く [fusei-o hataraku]

miscarriage [mɪskærɪdʒ, -kær-] *n* 流産 [ryuuzan]

miscellaneous [mɪsəleɪnɪəs] *adj* 雑多な [zatta na]

mischief [mɪstʃɪf] *n* いたずら [itazura]

mischievous [mɪstʃɪvəs] *adj* 腕白な [wanpaku na], いたずら好きな [itazura zuki na]

miser [maɪzər] *n* どけち [dokechi]

miserable [mɪzərəbəl] *adj* 惨めな [mijime na]

misery [mɪzəri] *n* 惨めさ [mijimesa]

misfortune [mɪsfɔrtʃən] *n* 不運 [fuun]

mishap [mɪshæp] *n* 不幸な出来事 [fukou na dekigoto]

misjudge [mɪsdʒʌdʒ] *v* 判断を誤る [handan-o ayamaru]

misleading [mɪslidɪŋ] *adj* 誤解を招きやすい [gokai-o manekiyasui]

misplace [mɪspleɪs] *v* 置き忘れる [okiwasureru]

misprint [mɪsprɪnt] *n* 誤植 [goshoku]

miss [mɪs] *v* 見逃す [minogasu]

Miss [mɪs] *n* 独身女性の名字の前に付ける敬称 [dokushin josei no myouji no mae ni tsukeru keishou]

missile [mɪsəl] *n* ミサイル [misairu]

missing [mɪsɪŋ] *adj* 不明 [fumei], あるべき所にない [aru beki tokoro ni nai]; **My child is missing** 私の子供が行方不明です [watashi no kodomo ga yukue-fumei desu]

missionary [mɪʃənɛri] *n* 宣教師 [senkyoushi]

mist [mɪst] *n* もや [moya]

mistake [mɪsteɪk] *n* 間違い [machigai] ▷ *v* 間違える [machigaeru]

mistaken [mɪsteɪkən] *adj* 間違えた [machigaeta]

mistakenly [mɪsteɪkənli] *adv* 間違って [machigatte]

mistletoe [mɪsəltoʊ] *n* ヤドリギ [yadorigi]

mistress [mɪstrɪs] *n* 女性の愛人 [josei no aijin]

misty [mɪsti] *adj* もやの立ち込めた [moya no tachikometa]

misunderstand [mɪsʌndərstænd] *v* 誤解する [gokai suru]

misunderstanding [mɪsʌndərstændɪŋ] *n* 誤解 [gokai]; **There's been a misunderstanding** 誤解があります [gokai ga arimasu]

mitten [mɪtən] *n* ミトン [miton]

mix [mɪks] *n* 混合物 [kongoubutsu] ▷ *v* 混ぜる [mazeru]

mixed [mɪkst] *adj* 混合した [kongou shita]; **mixed salad** *n* ミックスサラダ [mikkususarada]

mixer [mɪksər] *n* ミキサー [mikisaa]

mixture [mɪkstʃər] *n* 混合 [kongou], 混合物 [kongoubutsu]

mix up *v* 混同する [kondou suru]

mix-up *n* 混同 [kondou]

moan [moʊn] *v* うめく [umeku]

moat [moʊt] *n* 濠 [hori]

mobile [moʊbəl] *n* 移動可能な [idoukanou na]; **mobile home** *n* モビールハウス [mobiiruhausu]

mock [mɒk] *adj* まがいの [magai no] ▷ *v* あざける [azakeru]

model [mɒdəl] *adj* 模範的な [mohanteki na] ▷ *n* 模型 [mokei] ▷ *v* 模型を作る [mokei-o tsukuru]

modem [moʊdəm, -dɛm] *n* モデム [modemu]

moderate *adj* 適度の [tekido no]

moderation [mɒdəreɪʃən] *n* 適度 [tekido]

modern [mɒdərn] *adj* 現代の [gendai no]; **modern conveniences** *npl* 最新設備 [saishin setsubi]; **modern languages** *npl* 現代語 [gendaigo]

modernize [mɒdərnaɪz] *v* 現代化する [gendaika suru]

modest [mɒdɪst] *adj* 謙虚な [kenkyo na]

modification [mɒdɪfɪkeɪʃən] *n* 変更 [henkou]

modify [mɒdɪfaɪ] *v* 変更する [henkou suru];

M

genetically modified *adj* 遺伝子組み換えの [idenshi kumikae no]

module [mɒdʒul] *n* モジュール [mojuuru]

moist [mɔɪst] *adj* 湿った [shimetta]

moisture [mɔɪstʃər] *n* 湿気 [shikke]

moisturizer [mɔɪstʃəraɪzər] *n* モイスチャライザー [moisucharaizaa]

molasses [məlæsɪz] *n* 糖蜜 [toumitsu]

mold [moʊld] *n* (*fungus*) カビ [kabi], (*shape*) 型 [kata]

Moldova [mɒldoʊvə] *n* モルドバ [moruduba]

Moldovan [mɒldoʊvən] *adj* モルドバの [Moruduba no] ▷ *n* モルドバ人 [Moruduba jin]

moldy [moʊldi] *adj* かびた [kabita]

mole [moʊl] *n* (*infiltrator*) スパイ [supai], (*mammal*) モグラ [mogura], (*skin*) ほくろ [hokuro]

molecule [mɒlɪkyul] *n* 分子 [bunshi]

mom [mɒm] *n* ママ [mama]

moment [moʊmənt] *n* 瞬間 [shunkan]

momentarily [moʊməntɛərɪli] *adv* ちょっとの間 [chotto no aida]

momentary [moʊməntɛri] *adj* 瞬間の [shunkan no]

momentous [moʊmɛntəs] *adj* きわめて重大な [kiwamete juudai na]

mommy [mɒmi] *n* (*mother*) ママ [mama]

Monaco [mɒnəkoʊ] *n* モナコ [monako]

monarch [mɒnərk, -ark] *n* 君主 [kunshu]

monarchy [mɒnərki] *n* 君主制 [kunshusei]

monastery [mɒnəstɛri] *n* 修道院 [shuudouin]; **Is the monastery open to the public?** その修道院は一般公開されていますか? [sono shuudouin wa ippan-koukai sarete imasu ka?]

Monday [mʌndeɪ, -di] *n* 月曜 [getsuyou], 月曜日 [getsuyoubi]; **It's Monday, June fifteenth** 六月十五日の月曜日です [roku-gatsu juugo-nichi no getsuyoubi desu]; **on Monday** 月曜日に [getsuyoubi ni]

monetary [mɒnɪtɛri] *adj* 通貨の [tsuuka no]

money [mʌni] *n* 金銭 [kinsen]; **money belt** *n* マネーベルト [maneeberuto]; **pocket money** *n* ポケットマネー [pokettomanee]

Mongolia [mɒngoʊliə] *n* モンゴル [mongoru]

Mongolian [mɒngoʊliən] *adj* モンゴルの [mongoru no] ▷ *n* (*language*) モンゴル語 [Mongoru go], (*person*) モンゴル人 [Mongoru jin]

mongrel [mʌŋgrəl, mɒn-] *n* 雑種の犬 [zasshu no inu]

monitor [mɒnɪtər] *n* モニター [monitaa]

monk [mʌŋk] *n* 修道士 [shuudoushi]

monkey [mʌŋki] *n* サル [saru]

monopoly [mənɒpəli] *n* 独占 [dokusen]

monotonous [mənɒt·nəs] *adj* 単調な [tanchou na]

monsoon [mɒnsun] *n* モンスーン [monsuun]

monster [mɒnstər] *n* 怪物 [kaibutsu]

month [mʌnθ] *n* 月 [tsuki] (暦); **a month ago** 一か月前 [ikkagetsu mae]; **a month from now** 一か月後に [ikkagetsu go ni]

monthly [mʌnθli] *adj* 毎月の [maitsuki no]

monument [mɒnyəmənt] *n* 記念碑 [kinenhi]

mood [mud] *n* 意気 [iki], 気分 [kibun]

moody [mudi] *adj* むっつりした [muttsuri shita]

moon [mun] *n* 月 [tsuki] (天体); **full moon** *n* 満月 [mangetsu]

moor [mʊər] *n* 荒野 [areno] ▷ *v* 停泊させる [teihaku saseru]

mop [mɒp] *n* モップ [moppu]

moped [moʊpɛd] *n* モペッド [mopeddo]

mop up *v* モップでぬぐい取る [moppu de nuguitoru]

moral [mɔrəl] *adj* 道徳の [doutoku no] ▷ *n* 教訓 [kyoukun]

morale [məræl] *n* 士気 [shiki]

morals [mɔrlz] *npl* 品行 [hinkou]

more [mɔr] *adj* さらに多い [sarani oui] ▷ *adv* さらに多く [sara ni ooku]

morgue [mɔrg] *n* 死体保管所 [shitaihokanjo]

morning [mɔrnɪŋ] *n* 麻 [asa], 午前 [gozen]; **morning sickness** *n* つわりの時期の朝の吐き気 [tsuwari no jiki no asa no hakike]; **in the morning** 午前中に [gozen-chuu ni]; **Is** the museum open in the morning? その博物館は午前中開いていますか? [sono hakubutsukan wa gozen-chuu hiraite imasu ka?]

Moroccan [mərɒkən] *adj* モロッコの [Morokko no] ▷ *n* モロッコ人 [Morokko jin]

Morocco [mərɒkou] *n* モロッコ [morokko]

morphine [mɔrfin] *n* モルヒネ [moruhine]

Morse [mɔrs] *n* **Morse code** *n* モールス信号 [moorusu shingou]

mortar [mɔrtər] *n* (*military*) 臼砲 [kyuuhou], (*plaster*) モルタル [morutaru]

mortgage [mɔrgɪdʒ] *n* 抵当 [teitou] ▷ *v* 抵当に入れる [teitou ni ireru]

mosaic [mouzeɪɪk] *n* モザイク [mozaiku]

Moslem [mɒzləm, muzlɪm] *adj* イスラム教の [isuramukyou no]

mosque [mɒsk] *n* モスク [mosuku]; **Where is there a mosque?** どこかにモスクはありますか? [doko-ka ni mosuku wa arimasu ka?]

mosquito [məskitou] *n* 蚊 [ka]

moss [mɒs] *n* コケ [koke]

most [moust] *adj* 最も多い [mottomo ooi] ▷ *adv* 一番 [ichiban], 最も多く [mottomo ouku]

mostly [moustli] *adv* たいてい [taitei]

motel [moutɛl] *n* モーテル [mooteru]

moth [mɔθ] *n* 蛾 [ga]

mother [mʌðər] *n* 母 [haha]; **surrogate mother** *n* 代理母 [dairibo]

mother-in-law (*pl* **mothers-in-law**) *n* 義母 [gibo]

motionless [mouʃənlɪs] *adj* 動かない [ugokanai]

motivated [moutɪveɪtɪd] *adj* 動機づけられた [douki zukerareta]

motivation [moutɪveɪʃən] *n* 動機づけ [douki zuke]

motive [moutɪv] *n* 動機 [douki]

motor [moutər] *n* モーター [mootaa]

motorboat [moutərbout] *n* モーターボート [mootaabooto]

motorcycle [moutərsaɪkᵊl] *n* オートバイ [ootobai]

motorcyclist [moutərsaɪklɪst] *n* オートバイ乗り [ootobainori]

motorist [moutərɪst] *n* ドライバー [doraibaa] (人)

mountain [maunt‧n] *n* 山 [yama]; **mountain bike** *n* マウンテンバイク [mauntenbaiku]; **Where is the nearest mountain rescue station?** 一番近い山岳救助隊はどこですか? [ichiban chikai sangaku-kyuujo-tai wa doko desu ka?]

mountaineer [maunt‧nɪər] *n* 登山者 [tozansha]

mountaineering [maunt‧nɪərɪŋ] *n* 登山 [tozan]

mountainous [maunt‧nəs] *adj* 山の多い [yama no oui]

mourning [mɔrnɪŋ] *n* 悲嘆 [hitan]

mouse [maus] *n* ハツカネズミ [hatsukan-ezumi]; **mouse pad** *n* マウスパッド [mausupaddo]

mousse [mus] *n* ムース [muusu]

mouth *n* 口 [kuchi]

mouthwash [mauθwɒʃ] *n* マウスウォッシュ [mausu uosshu]

move [muv] *n* 移動 [idou] ▷ *v* 移す [utsusu] ▷ *vi* 動く [ugoku] ▷ *vt* 動かす [ugokasu]; **moving van** *n* 引越しトラック [hikkoshi torakku]

move back *v* 後ろに下がる [ushiro ni sagaru]

moved *adj* 感動した [kandou shita]

move forward *v* 前へ進む [mae-e susumu]

move in *v* …に転居する [... ni tenkyo suru]

movement [muvmənt] *n* 動き [douki]

movie [muvi] *n* 映画 [eiga]; **horror movie** *n* ホラー映画 [horaa eiga]; **movie star** *n* 映画スター [eigasutaa]; **movie theater** *n* 映画館 [eigakan]; **Are there any movies in English?** 英語の映画はありますか? [eigo no eiga wa arimasu ka?]; **When does the movie start?** 映画はいつ始まりますか? [eiga wa itsu hajimarimasu ka?]; **Where can we go to see a movie?** どこに行けば映画を

M

見られますか? [doko ni ikeba eiga o mirraremasu ka?]; **Which film is playing at the movie theater?** その映画館でどの映画が上映されていますか? [sono eigakan de dono eiga ga jouei sarete imasu ka?]

moving [múːvɪŋ] *adj* 感動させる [kandou saseru]; 感動的な [kandouteki na]

mow [moʊ] *v* 刈る [karu]

mower [moʊər] *n* 草刈り機 [kusakariki]

Mozambique [moʊzəmbíːk] *n* モザンビーク [mozanbiiku]

mph [maɪlz pə aʊə] *abbr* 毎時・・・マイル [maiji… mairu]

Mr. [mɪstər] *n* 男性の名字の前に付ける敬称 [dansei no myouji no mae ni tsukeru keishou]

Mrs. [mɪsɪz] *n* 既婚女性の名字の前に付ける敬称 [kikonjosei no myouji no mae ni tsukeru keishou]

Ms. [mɪz] *n* 未婚・既婚にかかわらず、女性に対する敬称 [mikon / kikon ni kakawarazu, josei ni taisuru keishou]

MS [ɛm ɛs] *abbr* 多発性硬化症 [tahatsusei koukashou]

much [mʌtʃ] *adj* 多くの [ouku no] ▷ *adv* 大いに [ooi ni]

mud [mʌd] *n* 泥 [doro]

muddy [mʌdi] *adj* 泥だらけの [doro darake no]

muesli [myúːzli] *n* ミューズリー [myuuzurii]

mug [mʌg] *n* マグ [magu] ▷ *v* 襲って強奪する [osotte goudatsu suru]

mugger [mʌgər] *n* 強盗 [goutou] (人)

mugging [mʌgɪŋ] *n* 強奪 [goudatsu]

muggy [mʌgi] *adj* **It's muggy** 蒸し暑いです [mushiatsui desu]

mule [myuːl] *n* ラバ [raba]

multinational [mʌltinǽʃənəl] *adj* 多国籍の [takokuseki no] ▷ *n* 多国籍企業 [takokuseki kigyou]

multiple [mʌltɪpəl] *adj* **multiple sclerosis** *n* 多発性硬化症 [tahatsusei koukashou]

multiplication [mʌltɪplɪkéɪʃən] *n* 掛け算 [kakezan]

multiply [mʌltɪplaɪ] *v* 増す [masu]

mummy [mʌmi] *n* (body) ミイラ [miira]

mumps [mʌmps] *n* おたふく風邪 [otafuku-kaze]

murder [mɜrdər] *n* 殺人 [satsujin] ▷ *v* 殺害する [satsugai suru]

murderer [mɜrdərər] *n* 殺人者 [satsujinsha]

muscle [mʌsəl] *n* 筋肉 [kinniku]

muscular [mʌskyələr] *adj* 筋骨たくましい [kinkotsu takumashii]

museum [myuziəm] *n* 博物館 [hakubutsu-kan]; **art museum** *n* 画廊 [garou]; **Is the museum open every day?** その博物館は毎日開いていますか? [sono hakubutsukan wa mainichi hiraite imasu ka?]; **When is the museum open?** その博物館はいつ開きますか? [sono hakubutsukan wa itsu hirakimasu ka?]

mushroom [mʌʃrum] *n* マッシュルーム [masshuruumu]

music [myúːzɪk] *n* 音楽 [ongaku]; **folk music** *n* フォークミュージック [fooku myuujikku]

musical [myúːzɪkəl] *adj* 音楽の [ongaku no] ▷ *n* ミュージカル [myuujikaru]; **musical instrument** *n* 楽器 [gakki]

musician [myuzɪʃən] *n* 音楽家 [ongakuka]; **street musician** *n* 大道芸人 [daidougeinin]

Muslim [mʌzlɪm, mʊs-] *adj* イスラム教の [isuramukyou no] ▷ *n* イスラム教徒 [isuramukyouto]

mussel [mʌsəl] *n* ムール貝 [muurugai]

must [məst, STRONG mʌst] *v* ・・・しなければならない [… shinakereba naranai]

mustache [mʌstæʃ] *n* 口ひげ [kuchi hige]

mustard [mʌstərd] *n* マスタード [masutaado]

mute [myuːt] *adj* 口のきけない [kuchi no kikenai]

mutter [mʌtər] *v* ブツブツ言う [butsubutsu iu]

mutton [mʌtn̩] *n* マトン [maton]

mutual [myúːtʃuəl] *adj* 相互の [sougo no]

my [maɪ] *pron* **Here is my insurance information** 私の保険の詳細です [watashi no hoken no shousai desu]

Myanmar [maɪænmɑr] *n* ミャンマー
[myanmaa]

myself [maɪsɛlf] *pron* **I've locked myself
out of my room** 部屋に鍵を置いたままドア
を閉めてしまいました [heya ni kagi o oita
mama doa o shimete shimaimashita]

mysterious [mɪstɪəriəs] *adj* 謎めいた
[nazomeita]

mystery [mɪstəri, mɪstri] *n* 謎 [nazo]

myth [mɪθ] *n* 神話 [shinwa]

mythology [mɪθɒlədʒi] *n* 神話体系 [shinwa
taikei]

N

nag [næg] v がみがみ小言を言う [gamigami kogoto-o iu]

nail [neɪl] n 釘 [kugi]; **nail polish** n マニキュア液 [manikyua eki]; **nail scissors** npl 爪切りばさみ [tsume kiri basami]; **nail-polish remover** n 除光液 [jokoueki]

nail brush n 爪ブラシ [tsumeburashi]

nail file [neɪlfeɪl] n 爪やすり [tsumeyasuri]

naive [nɑɪv] adj うぶな [ubuna]

naked [neɪkɪd] adj 裸の [hadaka no]

name [neɪm] n 名前 [namae]; **brand name** n ブランド名 [burando mei]; **family name** n 姓 [sei]; **first name** n ファーストネーム [faasutoneemu], 洗礼名 [senreimei]; **maiden name** n 女性の結婚前の旧姓 [josei no kekkonmae no kyuusei]; **I reserved a room in the name of...** ･･･の名前で部屋を予約しました [... no namae de heya o yoyaku shimashita]; **My name is...** 私の名前は･･･です [watashi no namae wa... desu]; **What's your name?** あなたのお名前は? [anata no o-namae wa?]

nanny [næni] n 乳母 [uba], チャイルドマインダー [chairudomaindaa]

nap [næp] n うたたね [utatane]

napkin [næpkɪn] n ナプキン [napukin]; **sanitary napkin** n 生理用ナプキン [seiriyou napukin]

narcotic [nɑrkɒtɪk] n 麻薬 [mayaku]

narrow [næroʊ] adj 狭い [semai]

narrow-minded [næroʊmɑɪndɪd] adj 了見の狭い [ryouken no semai]

nasty [næsti] adj 嫌な [iya na]

nation [neɪʃn] n 国民 [kokumin], 国家 [kokka]; **United Nations** n 国際連合 [kokusairengou]

national [næʃənl] adj 国民の [kokumin no]; **national anthem** n 国歌 [kokka]; **national park** n 国立公園 [kokuritsu kouen]

nationalism [næʃənlɪzəm] n 国家主義 [kokkashugi]

nationalist [næʃənlɪst] n 国家主義者 [kokkashugisha]

nationality [næʃənælɪti] n 国籍 [kokuseki]

nationalize [næʃənlɑɪz] v 国営にする [kokuei ni suru]

native [neɪtɪv] adj 出生地の [shusseichi no]; **native language** n 母国語 [bokokugo]; **native speaker** n 母国語とする人 [bokokugo to suru hito]

NATO [neɪtoʊ] abbr 北大西洋条約機構 [kitataiseiyou jouyaku kikou]

natural [nætʃərəl, nætʃrəl] adj 当然の [touzen no]; **natural gas** n 天然ガス [tennengasu]; **natural resources** npl 天然資源 [tennenshigen]

naturalist [nætʃərəlɪst, nætʃrəl-] n 自然誌研究者 [shizenshi kenkyuusha]

naturally [nætʃərəli, nætʃrəli] adv 当然 [touzen]

nature [neɪtʃər] n 自然 [shizen]

nausea [nɔziə, -ʒə, -siə, -ʃə] n 吐き気 [hakike]

naval [neɪvl] adj 海軍の [kaigun no]

navel [neɪvl] n へそ [heso]

navigation [nævɪgeɪʃn] n **satellite navigation** n 衛星ナビゲーション [eisei nabigeeshon]

navy [neɪvi] n 海軍 [kaigun]

navy-blue adj 濃紺の [noukon no]

NB [ɛn bi] abbr 注意せよ [chuui seyo]

near [nɪər] adj 近い [chikai] ▷ adv 近くに

[chikaku ni]; **Are there any good beaches near here?** この近くにいいビーチはありますか? [kono chikaku ni ii biichi wa arimasu ka?] [kono chikaku ni ii biichi wa arimasu ka?]; **How do I get to the nearest subway station?** 一番近い地下鉄の駅へはどう行けばいいのですか? [ichiban chikai chikatetsu no eki e wa dou ikeba ii no desu ka?]; **Where is the nearest bus stop?** 一番近いバス停はどこですか? [ichiban chikai basu-tei wa doko desu ka?]

nearby [nɪərbaɪ] *adj* 近くの [chikaku no] ▷ *adv* 近くに [chikaku ni]; **Is there a bank nearby?** 近くに銀行はありますか? [chikaku ni ginkou wa arimasu ka?]

nearly [nɪərli] *adv* ほとんど [hotondo]

nearsighted [nɪərsaɪtɪd] *adj* 近視の [kinshi no]

neat [nit] *adj* きちんとした [kichin to shita]

neatly [nitli] *adv* きちんと [kichin to]

necessarily [nɛsɪsɛərɪli] *adv* 必ず [kanarazu]

necessary [nɛsɪsɛri] *adj* 必要な [hitsuyou na]

necessity [nɪsɛsɪti] *n* 必要性 [hitsuyousei]

neck [nɛk] *n* 首 [kubi] *(体)*

necklace [nɛklɪs] *n* ネックレス [nekkuresu]

nectarine [nɛktərin] *n* ネクタリン [nekutarin]

need [nid] *n* 必要 [hitsuyou] ▷ *v* 必要とする [hitsuyou to suru]; **Do you need anything?** 何か必要ですか? [nani ka hitsuyou desu ka?]; **I need assistance** 私は介助が必要です [watashi wa kaijo ga hitsuyou desu]; **I need contraception** 私は避妊が必要です [watashi wa hinin ga hitsuyou desu]

needle [nidᵊl] *n* 縫い針 [nuihari], 鍼 [hari]; **knitting needle** *n* 編み棒 [amibou]

negative [nɛgətɪv] *adj* 否定の [hitei no] ▷ *n* 否定の答え [hitei no kotae]

neglect [nɪglɛkt] *n* 怠慢 [taiman] ▷ *v* おろそかにする [orosoka ni suru]

neglected [nɪglɛktɪd] *adj* おろそかにされた [orosoka ni sareta]

negligee [nɛglɪʒeɪ] *n* 化粧着 [keshougi]

negotiate [nɪgouʃieɪt] *v* 交渉する [koushou suru]

negotiations [nɪgouʃieɪʃɪnz] *npl* 交渉 [koushou]

negotiator [nɪgouʃieɪtər] *n* 交渉者 [koushousha]

neighbor [neɪbər] *n* 近所の人 [kinjo no hito]

neighborhood [neɪbərhʊd] *n* 近所 [kinjo]

neither [niðər, naɪ-] *adv* ···もまた···でない [···momata···denai]

neon [nɪɒn] *n* ネオン [neon]

Nepal [nɪpɔl] *n* ネパール [nepaaru]

nephew [nɛfyu] *n* 甥 [oi]

nerve [nɜrv] *n (boldness)* ずぶとさ [zubutosa], *(to/from brain)* 神経 [shinkei]

nerve-racking [nɜrvrækɪŋ] *adj* 神経を悩ます [shinkei-o nayamasu]

nervous [nɜrvəs] *adj* 神経質な [shinkeishitsu na]; **nervous breakdown** *n* 神経衰弱 [shinkeisuijaku]

nest [nɛst] *n* 巣 [su]

net [nɛt] *n* 網 [ami]

Net [nɛt] *n* 正味 [shoumi]

netball [nɛtbɔl] *n* ネットボール [nettobooru]

Netherlands [nɛðərləndz] *npl* オランダ [oranda]

nettle [nɛtᵊl] *n* イラクサ [irakusa]

network [nɛtwɜrk] *n* ネットワーク [nettowaaku]; **I can't get a network** ネットワークにつながりません [nettowaaku ni tsunagarimasen]

neurotic [nʊərɒtɪk] *adj* 神経過敏な [shinkeikabin na]

neutral [nutrəl] *adj* 中立の [chuuritsu no] ▷ *n* 中立国 [chuuritsukoku]

never [nɛvər] *adv* ···したことがない [···shita koto ga nai]

new [nu] *adj* 新しい [atarashii]; **New Year** *n* 新年 [shinnen]; **New Zealand** *n* ニュージーランド [nyuujiirando]; **New Zealander** *n* ニュージーランド人 [nyuujiirandojin]

newborn [nubɔrn] *adj* 生まれたばかりの [umareta bakari no]

N

newcomer [nuːkʌmər] *n* 最近来た人 [saikin kita hito]

news [nuːz] *npl* ニュース [nyuusu]; **When is the news?** ニュースはいつですか? [nyuusu wa itsu desu ka?]

newscaster [nuːzkæstər] *n* ニュースキャスター [nyuusukyasutaa]

newsdealer [nuːzdiːlər] *n* 新聞販売店 [shinbunhanbaiten]

newspaper [nuːzpeɪpər, nuːs-] *n* 新聞 [shinbun]; **Do you have newspapers?** 新聞はありますか? [shinbun wa arimasu ka?]; **I'd like a newspaper** 新聞をください [shinbun o kudasai]; **Where can I buy a newspaper?** どこで新聞を買えますか? [doko de shinbun o kaemasu ka?]; **Where is the nearest place to buy newspapers?** 新聞を売っている一番近い店はどこですか? [shinbun o utte iru ichiban chikai mise wa doko desu ka?]

newt [nuːt] *n* イモリ [imori]

next [nɛkst] *adj* つぎ [tsugi], 次の [tsugi no] ▷ *adv* 次に [tsugi ni]; **What is the next stop?** 次の駅はどこですか? [tsugi no eki wa doko desu ka?]; **When is the next bus to...?** ・・・へ行く次のバスは何時ですか? [... e iku tsugi no basu wa nan-ji desu ka?]

next-of-kin [nɛkstəvkɪn] *n* 近親者 [kinshinsha]

Nicaragua [nɪkərɑgwə] *n* ニカラグア [nikaragua]

Nicaraguan [nɪkərɑgwən] *adj* ニカラグアの [Nikaragua no] ▷ *n* ニカラグア人 [Nikaragua jin]

nice [naɪs] *adj* すてきな [sutekina]

nickname [nɪkneɪm] *n* ニックネーム [nikkuneemu]

nicknamed *adj* ・・・とあだ名をつけられた [... to adana-o tsukerareta]

nicotine [nɪkɪtin] *n* ニコチン [nikochin]

niece [nis] *n* 姪 [mei]

Niger [naɪdʒər] *n* ニジェール [nijieeru]

Nigeria [naɪdʒɪriə] *n* ナイジェリア [naijeria]

Nigerian [naɪdʒɪəriən] *adj* ナイジェリアの [naijeria no] ▷ *n* ナイジェリア人 [naijeriajin]

night [naɪt] *n* 夜 [yoru]; **night class** *n* 夜間クラス [yakan kurasu]; **night school** *n* 夜間学校 [yakangakkou]; **at night** 夜に [yoru ni]; **last night** 昨夜 [sakuya]; **tomorrow night** 明日の夜 [asu no yoru]

nightclothes [naɪtkləʊz, -kloʊðz] *n* ねまき [nemaki]

nightclub [naɪtklʌb] *n* ナイトクラブ [naitokurabu]

nightgown [naɪtgaʊn] *n* ネグリジェ [negurije]

nightlife [naɪtlaɪf] *n* 歓楽街での夜の楽しみ [kanrakugai deno yoru no tanoshimi]

nightmare [naɪtmɛər] *n* 悪夢 [akumu]

night shift [naɪtʃɪft] *n* 夜勤 [yakin]

nightstand [naɪtstænd] *n* ベッドサイドテーブル [beddosaido teeburu]

nine [naɪn] *number* 九 [kyuu]

nineteen [naɪntin] *number* 十九 [juukyuu]

nineteenth [naɪntinθ] *adj* 十九番目の [juukyuu banme no]

ninety [naɪnti] *number* 九十 [kyuujuu]

ninth [naɪnθ] *adj* 九番目の [kyuu banme no] ▷ *n* 九番目 [kyuubanme]

nitrogen [naɪtrədʒən] *n* 窒素 [chisso]

no [noʊ] *adv* ひとつの・・・もない [hitotsuno... monai]

no [noʊ] *excl* なんてことを! [nantekoto wo]

nobody [noʊbɒdi, -bʌdi] *pron* **We'd like to see nobody but ourselves all day!** 一日中自分たちだけになれる静かなところがいいのですが [ichinichi-juu jibun-tachi dake ni nareru shizuka na tokoro ga ii no desu ga]

nod [nɒd] *v* うなずく [unazuku]

noise [nɔɪz] *n* 騒音 [souon]

noisy [nɔɪzi] *adj* やかましい [yakamashii]

nominate [nɒmɪneɪt] *v* 指名する [shimei suru]

nomination [nɒmɪneɪʃn] *n* 指名 [shimei]

nonsense [nɒnsɛns, -səns] *n* ナンセンス [nansensu]

nonsmoker [nɒnsmoʊkər] *n* 非喫煙者 [hikitsuensha]

nonsmoking [nɒnsmoʊkɪŋ] *adj* 禁煙の [kin'en no]

non-stop *adv* 直行で [chokkou de]

noodles [nuːdˀlz] *npl* ヌードル [nuudoru]

noon [nuːn] *n* 正午 [shougo], 真昼 [mahiru]; **at noon** 正午に [shougo ni]; **It's twelve noon** 正午です [shougo desu]

normal [nɔrmˀl] *adj* 普通の [futsuu no]

normally [nɔrməli] *adv* 普通に [futsuu ni]

north [nɔrθ] *adj* 北の [kita no] ▷ *adv* 北に [kita ni] ▷ *n* 北 [kita]; **North Africa** *n* 北アフリカ [kitaafurika]; **North African** *n* 北アフリカ人 [Kita Afurika jin], 北アフリカの [Kita Afurika no]; **North America** *n* 北アメリカ [kitaamerika]; **North American** *n* 北アメリカ人 [Kita Amerika jin], 北アメリカの [Kita Amerika no]; **North Korea** *n* 北朝鮮 [kitachousen]; **North Pole** *n* 北極 [hokkyoku]; **North Sea** *n* 北海 [hokkai]

northbound [nɔrθbaʊnd] *adj* 北行きの [kitayuki no]

northeast [nɔrθist] *n* 北東 [hokutou]

northern [nɔrðern] *adj* 北の [kita no]; **Northern Ireland** *n* 北アイルランド [kita airurando]

northwest [nɔrθwɛst] *n* 北西 [hokusei]

Norway [nɔrweɪ] *n* ノルウェー [noruuee]

Norwegian [nɔrwidʒˀn] *adj* ノルウェーの [noruuee no] ▷ *n* (language) ノルウェー語 [noruueego], (person) ノルウェー人 [noruueejin]

nose [noʊz] *n* 鼻 [hana]

nosebleed [noʊzblid] *n* 鼻血 [hanaji]

nostril [nɒstrɪl] *n* 鼻の穴 [hana no ana]

nosy [noʊzi] *adj* 詮索好きな [sensaku zuki na]

not [nɒt] *adv* ・・・でない […denai]

note [noʊt] *n* (message) メモ [memo], (music) 音符 [onpu]; **make a note of** *v* 書き留める [kakitomeru]; **sick note** *n* 病欠届け [byouketsu todoke]

notebook [noʊtbʊk] *n* ノート [nooto]

notepad [noʊtpæd] *n* メモパッド [memo-paddo], メモ帳 [memochou]

notepaper [noʊtpeɪpər] *n* メモ用紙 [memoyoushi]

nothing [nʌθɪŋ] *n* 零 [rei]

notice [noʊtɪs] *n* 刑事 [keiji], (note) 注意 [chuui], (termination) 通告 [tsuukoku] (解雇) ▷ *v* 気づく [kizuku]

noticeable [noʊtɪsəbˀl] *adj* 目立つ [medatsu]

notify [noʊtɪfaɪ] *v* 通知する [tsuuchi suru]

noun [naʊn] *n* 名詞 [meishi]

novel [nɒvˀl] *n* 小説 [shousetsu]

novelist [nɒvəlɪst] *n* 小説家 [shousetsuka]

November [noʊvɛmbər] *n* 十一月 [juuichigatsu]

now [naʊ] *adv* 今 [ima]; **Do I pay now or later?** 払うのは今ですか、それとも後ですか? [harau no wa ima desu ka, sore tomo ato desu ka?]

nowadays [naʊədeɪz] *adv* このごろは [konogoro ha]

nowhere [noʊwɛər] *adv* どこにも・・・ない [dokonimo... nai]

nuclear [nukliər] *adj* 原子力の [genshiryoku no]

nude [nud] *adj* 裸の [hadaka no] ▷ *n* 裸体 [ratai]

nudist [nudɪst] *n* 裸体主義者 [rataishugisha]

nuisance [nusˀns] *n* 厄介なもの [yakkai na mono]

numb [nʌm] *adj* 感覚のない [kankaku no nai]

number [nʌmbər] *n* 数 [kazu]; **account number** *n* 口座番号 [kouzabangou]; **cell phone number** *n* 携帯電話番号 [keitai denwa bangou]; **phone number** *n* 電話番号 [denwabangou]; **reference number** *n* 参照番号 [sanshou bangou]; **room number** *n* 客室番号 [kyakushitsu bangou]; **wrong number** *n* 間違い電話 [machigai denwa]

numerous [numərəs] *adj* 多数の [tasuu no]

nun [nʌn] *n* 尼僧 [nisou]

nurse [nɜrs] *n* 看護師 [kangoshi]; **I'd like to speak to a nurse** 看護師さんと話をしたいのですが [kangoshi-san to hanashi o shitai no desu ga]

ナッツを使わずに食事を用意していただけま
すか? [nattsu o tsukawazu ni shokuji o youi
shite itadakemasu ka?]

nursery [nɜrsəri] *n* 子供部屋 [kodomobeya];
nursery rhyme *n* 伝承童謡 [denshou
douyou]; **nursery school** *n* 保育園 [hoikuen]

nursing home *n* nursing home *n* 老人ホー
ム [roujin hoomu]

nut [nʌt] *n (device)* ナット [natto], *(food)* ナッ
ツ [nattsu]; **nut allergy** *n* ナッツアレルギー
[nattsuarerugii]; **nut case** *n* 気違い [kichigai];
Could you prepare a meal without nuts?

nutmeg [nʌtmɛg] *n* ナツメグ [natsumegu]

nutrient [nutriənt] *n* 栄養分 [eiyoubun]

nutrition [nutrɑʃn] *n* 栄養 [eiyou], 栄養物摂取
[eiyoubutsu sesshu]

nutritious [nutrɪʃəs] *adj* 滋養のある [jiyou no
aru]

nylon [naɪlɒn] *n* ナイロン [nairon]

O

oak [oʊk] n オーク [ooku]

oar [ɔr] n オール [ooru]

oasis [oʊeɪsɪs] (pl oases) n オアシス [oashisu]

oath [oʊθ] n 誓い [chikai]

oatmeal [oʊtmil] n オートミール [ootomiiru], ポリッジ [porijji]

oats [oʊts] npl オート麦 [ooto mugi]

obedient [oʊbidiənt] adj 従順 [juujun], 従順な [juujun na]

obese [oʊbis] adj 肥満した [himan shita]

obey [oʊbeɪ] v 従う [shitagau]

obituary [oʊbɪtʃuɛri] n 死亡記事 [shiboukiji]

object n 物 [mono]

objection [əbdʒɛkʃ⁀n] n 異議 [igi], 反対 [hantai]

objective [əbdʒɛktɪv] n 目的 [mokuteki]

oblong [ɒblɒŋ] adj 長方形の [chouhoukei no]

obnoxious [əbnɒkʃəs] adj 不快な [fukai na]

oboe [oʊboʊ] n オーボエ [ooboe]

obscene [əbsin] adj 猥褻な [waisetu]

observant [əbzɜrvənt] adj 観察力の鋭い [kansatsuryoku no surudoi]

observatory [əbzɜrvətɔri] n 観測所 [kansokujo]

observe [əbzɜrv] v 観察する [kansatsu suru]

observer [əbzɜrvər] n 観察者 [kansatsusha]

obsessed [əbsɛst] adj 執着した [shuuchaku shita]

obsession [əbsɛʃ⁀n] n 執着 [shuuchaku]

obsolete [ɒbsəlit] adj すたれた [sutareta]

obstacle [ɒbstək⁀l] n 障害物 [shougaibutsu]

obstinate [ɒbstɪnɪt] adj 頑固な [ganko na]

obstruct [əbstrʌkt] v ふさぐ [fusagu] (じゃま)

obtain [əbteɪn] v 手に入れる [te ni ireru]

obvious [ɒbviəs] adj 明らかな [akiraka na]

obviously [ɒbviəsli] adv 明らかに [akiraka ni]

occasion [əkeɪʒ⁀n] n 場合 [baai]

occasional [əkeɪʒənⁱl] adj 時折の [tokiori no]

occasionally [əkeɪʒənⁱli] adv 時折 [tokiori]

occupation [ɒkyəpeɪʃ⁀n] n (invasion) 占領 [senryou], (work) 職業 [shokugyou]

occupy [ɒkyəpaɪ] v 占める [shimeru]

occur [əkɜr] v 起こる [okoru]

occurrence [əkɜrəns] n 出来事 [dekigoto]

ocean [oʊʃⁿ] n 海洋 [kaiyou]; Arctic Ocean n 北極海 [Hokkyokukai]; Indian Ocean n インド洋 [indoyou]

Oceania [oʊʃiˈæniə] n オセアニア [oseania]

o'clock [əklɒk] adv at three o'clock 三時に [san-ji ni]; I'd like to reserve a table for four people for tonight at eight o'clock 今晩八時に四人用のテーブルを予約したいのですが [konban hachi-ji ni yonin-you no teeburu o yoyaku shitai no desu ga]; It's one o'clock 一時です [ichi-ji desu]; It's six o'clock 六時です [roku-ji desu]

October [ɒktoʊbər] n 十月 [juugatsu]; It's Sunday, October third 十月三日の日曜日です [juu-gatsu mik-ka no nichiyoubi desu]

octopus [ɒktəpəs] n タコ [tako] (動物)

odd [ɒd] adj 変な [hen na]

odometer [oʊdɒmɪtər] n 走行マイル計 [soukou mairu kei]

odor [oʊdər] n におい [nioi]

of [əv, STRONG ʌv] prep Could I have a map of the subway, please? 地下鉄のマップをいただけますか? [chikatetsu no mappu o itadakemasu ka?]; How do I get to the center of...? ···の中心部へはどう行けばいのですか? [... no chuushinbu e wa dou ikeba ii no desu ka?]; **It's very kind of you to invite us** 私たちを招待してくださってありがとうございます [watashi-tachi o shoutai shite kudasatte arigatou gozaimasu]; **What kind of cheese?** どんなチーズですか? [donna cheezu desu ka?]

off *adv* 離れて [hanarete]; **off season** *n* シーズンオフ [shiizun'ofu]; **time off** *n* 欠勤時間 [kekkin jikan]

offend [əfɛnd] *v* 不快感を与える [fukaikan-o ataeru]

offense [əfɛns] *n* 違反 [ihan]

offensive [əfɛnsɪv] *adj* 嫌な [iya na]

offer [ɔfər] *n* 提供 [teikyou] ▷ *v* 提供する [teikyou suru]; **special offer** *n* 特別売り出し [tokubetsu uridashi]

office [ɔfɪs] *n* オフィス [ofisu]; **box office** *n* 切符売場 [kippu uriba]; **county clerk's office** *n* レジスターオフィス [rejisutaaofisu]; **doctor's office** *(doctor's) n* 診療所 [shinryoujo]; **employment office** *n* 公共職業安定所 [koukyoushokugyou anteisho]; **head office** *n* 本社 [honsha]; **information office** *n* 案内所 [annaijo]; **luggage storage office** *n* 手荷物一時預かり所 [tenimotsu ichiji azukarisho]; **office hours** *npl* 営業時間 [eigyoujikan]; **office supply store** *n* 文房具店 [bunbouguten]; **post office** *n* 郵便局 [yuubinkyoku]; **ticket office** *n* 予約オフィス [yoyaku ofisu], 切符売場 [kippu uriba]; **tourist office** *n* ツーリストオフィス [tsuurisutoofisu]; **How do I get to your office?** 貴社のオフィスへ伺うにはどう行けばいいでしょうか? [kisha no ofisu e ukagau ni wa dou ikeba ii deshou ka?]; **I work in an office** 私はオフィスで働いています [watashi wa ofisu de hataraite imasu]

officer [ɔfɪsər] *n* 士官 [shikan]; **corrections officer** *n* 看守 [kanshu]; **customs officer** *n* 税関係官 [zeikan kakarikan]; **parking enforcement officer** *n* 交通監視員 [koutsuu kanshiin]; **police officer** *n* 警察官 [keisatsukan]

official [əfɪʃl] *adj* 職務上の [shokumujou no]

off-peak *adv* ピーク時でなく [piikuji denaku]

off-season *adj* シーズンオフの [shiizun'ofu no] ▷ *adv* シーズンオフに [shiizun'ofu ni]

offside [ɔfsaɪd] *adj* オフサイドの [ofusaido no]

often [ɔfn] *adv* しばしば [shibashiba]

oil [ɔɪl] *n* 油 [abura] ▷ *v* 油を差す [abura-o sasu] *(注油)*; **olive oil** *n* オリーブ油 [oriibuyu]; **This stain is oil** このしみは油です [kono shimi wa abura desu]

oil refinery *n* oil refinery 石油精製所 [sekiyu seiseijo]

oil rig *n* oil rig 石油掘削装置 [sekiyu kussakusouchi]

oil slick *n* oil slick 油膜 [yumaku]

oil well *n* oil well 油井 [yusei]

ointment [ɔɪntmənt] *n* 軟膏 [nankou]

OK [ou keɪ] *excl* オーケー! [ookee]

okay [oukeɪ] *adj* オーケー [ookee]

okay [oukeɪ] *excl* オーケー! [ookee]

old [ould] *adj* 年取った [toshitotta]

old-fashioned [ouldfæʃn] *adj* 時代遅れの [jidaiokure no]

olive [ɒlɪv] *n* オリーブ [oriibu]; **olive oil** *n* オリーブ油 [oriibuyu]; **olive tree** *n* オリーブ [oriibu]

Oman [oumɑn] *n* オマーン [omaan]

omelette [ɒmlɪt] *n* オムレツ [omuretsu]

on *adv* 物の上に載って [mono no ueni notte]; **on time** *adj* 遅れずに [okurezu ni]

once [wʌns] *adv* 一度 [ichido], 一回 [ikkai]

one [wʌn] *number* 一 [ichi]

one-off *n* 一回限りのこと [ikkai kagiri no koto]

oneself [wʌnsɛlf] *n* 地震 [jishin]

one-way *adj* **one-way ticket** *n* 片道切符 [katamichi kippu]; **a one-way ticket to...** ···行き片道 [... iki katamichi]; **How much is a one-way ticket?** 片道切符はいくらですか? [katamichi-kippu wa ikura desu ka?]

onion [ʌnyən] *n* タマネギ [tamanegi]

online [ɒnlaɪn] *adj* オンラインの [onrain no] ▷ *adv* オンラインで [onrain de]

only [oʊnli] *adj* 唯一の [yuiitsu no] ▷ *adv* 単に [tan ni]

open [oʊpən] *adj* 開いた [aita] ▷ *v* 開ける [akeru]; **opening hours** *npl* 営業時間 [eigyoujikan]

opener [oʊpənər] *n* **can opener** *n* 缶切り [kankiri]

opera [ɒpərə, ɒprə] *n* オペラ [opera]; **soap opera** *n* ソープオペラ [soopuopera]; **What's on tonight at the opera house?** そのオペラ 劇場で今晩何が上演されますか? [sono opera-gekijou de konban nani ga jouen saremasu ka?]

operate [ɒpəreɪt] *v* (*to function*) 操作する [sousa suru], (*to perform surgery*) 手術する [shujutsu suru]

operating room [ɒpəreɪtɪŋ rum] *n* 手術室 [shujutsushitsu]

operation [ɒpəreɪʃⁿn] *n* (*surgery*) 手術 [shujutsu], (*undertaking*) 作業 [sagyou]

operator [ɒpəreɪtər] *n* オペレーター [opereetaa]

opinion [əpɪnyən] *n* 意見 [iken]; **opinion poll** *n* 世論調査 [yoronchousa]; **public opinion** *n* 世論 [yoron]

opponent [əpoʊnənt] *n* 敵対者 [tekitaisha]

opportunity [ɒpərtunɪti] *n* 機会 [kikai]

oppose [əpoʊz] *v* 反対する [hantai suru]

opposed [əpoʊzd] *adj* 反対した [hantai shita]

opposing [əpoʊzɪŋ] *adj* 反対する [hantai suru]

opposite [ɒpəzɪt] *adj* 向かい側の [mukaigawa no]

opposition [ɒpəzɪʃⁿn] *n* 反対 [hantai]

optician [ɒptɪʃⁿn] *n* 眼鏡士 [meganeshi]

optimism [ɒptɪmɪzəm] *n* 楽観主義 [rakkanshugi]

optimist [ɒptɪmɪst] *n* 楽観主義者 [rakkan shugisha]

optimistic [ɒptɪmɪstɪk] *adj* 楽観的な [rakkanteki na]

option [ɒpʃⁿn] *n* 選択 [sentaku]

optional [ɒpʃənᵊl] *adj* 自由選択の [jiyuusentakuno]

opt out *v* ・・・から脱退する [... kara dattai suru]

or [ər, STRONG ɔr] *conj* **Do I pay now or later?** 払うのは今ですか、それとも後ですか? [harau no wa ima desu ka, sore tomo ato desu ka?]

oral [ɔrəl] *adj* 口頭の [koutou no] ▷ *n* 口頭試験 [koutou shiken]

orange [ɔrɪndʒ] *adj* オレンジ色の [orenjiiro no] ▷ *n* オレンジ [orenji]; **orange juice** *n* オレ ンジジュース [orenjijuusu]

orchard [ɔrtʃərd] *n* 果樹園 [kajuen]

orchestra [ɔrkɪstrə] *n* オーケストラ [ookesutora]

orchid [ɔrkɪd] *n* ラン [ran]

ordeal [ɔrdil] *n* 苦しい体験 [kurushii taiken]

order [ɔrdər] *n* 注文 [chuumon], 命令 [meirei] ▷ *v* 命令する [meirei suru]; **order form** *n* 注 文用紙 [chuumon youshi]; **postal money order** *n* 郵便為替 [yuubin kawase]; **standing order** *n* 自動振替 [jidoufurikae]; **I'd like to order something local** 何か郷土料 理を注文したいのですが [nani ka kyoudo-ryouri o chuumon shitai no desu ga]; **May I order now, please?** 注文していいです か? [chuumon shite ii desu ka?]; **This isn't what I ordered** これは私が注文したものと違 います [kore wa watashi ga chuumon shita mono to chigaimasu]

ordinary [ɔrdⁿnɛri] *adj* 普通の [futsuu no]

oregano [ərɛgənoʊ] *n* オレガノ [oregano]

organ [ɔrgən] *n* (*body part*) 臓器 [zouki], (*music*) オルガン [orugan]

organic [ɔrgænɪk] *adj* 有機体の [yuukikai no]

organism [ɔrgənɪzəm] *n* 有機体 [yuukikai]

organization [ɔrgənɪzeɪʃⁿn] *n* 組織 [soshiki] (団体)

organize [ɔrgənaɪz] *v* 組織する [soshiki suru]

organizer [ɔrgənaɪzər] *n* **personal organizer** *n* システム手帳 [shisutemu techou]

orgasm [ɔrgæzəm] *n* オーガズム [oogazumu]

origin [ɔrɪdʒɪn] *n* 起源 [kigen]

original [ərɪdʒɪnᵊl] *adj* 最初の [saisho no]

originally [ərɪdʒɪnᵊli] *adv* 初めは [hajime wa]

ornament [ɔrnəmənt] *n* 装飾品 [soush-okuhin]

orphan [ɔrfən] *n* 孤児 [koji]

ostrich [ɔstrɪtʃ] *n* ダチョウ [dachou]

other [ʌðər] *adj* ほかの [hoka no]; **other than that** *adv* そのほかに [sono hoka ni]; **Do you have any others?** ほかの部屋はありますか? [hoka no heya wa arimasu ka?]

otherwise [ʌðərwaɪz] *adv* 代わりに [kawari ni], 別なふうに [betsu na fuuni]

otter [ɒtər] *n* カワウソ [kawauso]

ounce [aʊns] *n* オンス [onsu]

ourselves [aʊərsɛlvz] *pron* **We'd like to see nobody but ourselves all day!** 一日中自分たちだけになれる静かなところがいいのですが [ichinichi-juu jibun-tachi dake ni nareru shizuka na tokoro ga ii no desu ga]

out [aʊt] *adj* 外の [hoka no] ▷ *adv* 外に [hoka ni]

outage [aʊtɪdʒ] *n* **power outage** *n* 停電 [teiden]

outbreak [aʊtbreɪk] *n* 勃発 [boppatsu]

outcome [aʊtkʌm] *n* 結果 [kekka]

outdoor [aʊtdɔr] *adj* 屋外の [okugai no]

outdoors [aʊtdɔrz] *adv* アウトドア [autodoa], 屋外で [okugai de]

outfit [aʊtfɪt] *n* 衣装一式 [ishou isshiki]

outgoing [aʊtgoʊɪŋ] *adj* 出て行く [deteiku]

outing [aʊtɪŋ] *n* 遠足 [ensoku]

outline [aʊtlaɪn] *n* 概要 [gaiyou]

outlook [aʊtluk] *n* 見通し [mitoushi]

out-of-date *adj* 時代遅れの [jidaiokure no]

outrageous [aʊtreɪdʒəs] *adj* とんでもない [tonde mo nai]

outset [aʊtsɛt] *n* 最初 [saisho]

outside [aʊtsaɪd] *adj* 外側の [sotogawa no] ▷ *adv* 外側に [sotogawa ni] ▷ *n* 外側 [sotogawa]

outskirts [aʊtskɜrts] *npl* 郊外 [kougai]

outspoken [aʊtspoʊkən] *adj* 遠慮のない [enryo no nai]

outstanding [aʊtstændɪŋ] *adj* 傑出した [kesshutsu shita]

oval [oʊvᵊl] *adj* 卵形の [tamagogata no]

ovary [oʊvəri] *n* 卵巣 [ransou]

oven [ʌvᵊn] *n* オーブン [oobun]; **microwave oven** *n* 電子レンジ [denshi renji]; **oven mitt** *n* オーブンミット [oobunmitto]

ovenproof [ʌvᵊnpruf] *adj* オーブン耐熱性の [oobun tainetsusei no]

over [oʊvər] *adj* 終わって [owatte]

overall *adv* 全体的に [zentaiteki ni]

overalls [oʊvərɔl] *npl* オーバーオール [oobaaooru]

overbrimming excitement *n* 沸き立つ喜び [wakitatsu yorokobi]

overcast [oʊvərkæst] *adj* 曇った [kumotta]

overcharge [oʊvərtʃɑrdʒ] *v* 過大請求する [kadai seikyuu suru]

overcoat [oʊvərkoʊt] *n* オーバー [oobaa]

overcome [oʊvərkʌm] *v* 克服する [kokufuku suru]

overdone [oʊvərdʌn] *adj* やりすぎの [yarisugi no]

overdose [oʊvərdoʊs] *n* 過量服用 [karyou fukuyou]

overdraft [oʊvərdræft] *n* 当座借越し [touzakarikoshi]

overdrawn [oʊvərdrɔn] *adj* 当座借越しをした [touza karikoshi-o shita]

overdue [oʊvərdu] *adj* 遅れた [okureta]

overestimate *v* 過大評価する [kadai hyouka suru]

overhead *n* 諸経費 [shokeihi]

overlook [oʊvərlʊk] *v* 見落とす [miotosu]

overnight [oʊvərnaɪt] *adj* 一晩 [hitoban]; **Can I park here overnight?** ここに一晩駐車できますか? [koko ni hitoban chuusha dekimasu ka?]; **Can we camp here overnight?** ここで一晩キャンプできますか? [koko de hitoban kyanpu dekimasu ka?]; **Do I have to stay overnight** 私は一晩入院しなければなりませんか? [watashi wa hitoban nyuuin shinakereba narimasen ka?]

overrule [ouvərrul] *v* くつがえす [kutsugaesu]

overseas [ouvərsiz] *adv* 海外に [kaigai ni]

oversight [ouvərsaɪt] *n (mistake)* 見落とし [miotoshi], *(supervision)* 監督 [kantoku]

oversleep [ouvərslip] *v* 寝過ごす [nesugosu]

overtime [ouvərtaɪm] *n* 超過勤務 [chouka kinmu]

overturn *v* ひっくり返す [hikkurigaesu]

overweight [ouvərweɪt] *adj* 太りすぎの [futori sugi no]

owe [ou] *v* 借りがある [kari ga aru]

owl [aul] *n* フクロウ [fukurou]

own [oun] *adj* 自分自身の [jubunjishin no] ▷ *v*

所有する [shoyuu suru]

owner [ounər] *n* オーナー [oonaa], 所有者 [shoyuusha]; **pub owner** *n* パブの主人 [pabu no shujin]; **store owner** *n* 店主 [tenshu]; **Could I speak to the owner, please?** オーナーと話させていただけますか? [oonaa to hanasasete itadakemasu ka?]

own up *v* すっかり白状する [sukkari hakujou suru]

oxygen [ɒksɪdʒən] *n* 酸素 [sanso]

oyster [ɔɪstər] *n* 牡蠣 [kaki]

ozone [ouzoun] *n* オゾン [ozon]; **ozone layer** *n* オゾン層 [ozonsou]

O

P

PA [pi eɪ] *abbr* 個人秘書 [kojin hisho]

pace [peɪs] *n* 歩調 [hochou]

pacemaker [peɪsmeɪkər] *n* ペースメーカー [peesumeekaa]

Pacific [pəsɪfɪk] *n* 太平洋 [taiheiyou]

pack [pæk] *v* 荷造りをする [nizukuri wo suru]; **fanny pack** *n* ウエストバッグ [uesutobaggu]; **I need to pack now** これから荷物を詰めなければなりません [kore kara nimotsu o tsumenakereba narimasen]

package [pækɪdʒ] *n* 小包 [kozutsumi]; **vacation package** *n* パック旅行 [pakku ryokou]; **How much will it cost to send this package?** この小包を送るのにいくらかかりますか? [kono kozutsumi o okuru no ni ikura kakarimasu ka?]; **I'd like to send this package** この小包を送りたいのですが [kono kozutsumi o okuritai no desu ga]

packaging [pækɪdʒɪŋ] *n* パッケージ [pakkeeji]

packed [pækt] *adj* 荷造りが済んで [nizukuri ga sunde]

packet [pækɪt] *n* 小さな包み [chiisana tsutsumi]

pad [pæd] *n* パッド [paddo]; **mouse pad** *n* マウスパッド [mausupaddo]

paddle [pæd⁴l] *n* パドル [padoru] ▷ *v* パドルで漕ぐ [padoru de kogu]

padlock [pædlɒk] *n* 南京錠 [nankinjou]

page [peɪdʒ] *n* ページ [peeji] ▷ *v* ポケットベルで呼び出す [poketto beru de yobidasu]; **home page** *n* ホームページ [hoomupeeji]; **Yellow Pages®** *npl* イエローページ® [ieroopeeji]

pager [peɪdʒər] *n* ポケットベル [poketto beru]

paid [peɪd] *adj* 支払い済みの [shiharaizumi no]

pail [peɪl] *n* バケツ [baketsu]

pain [peɪn] *n* 痛み [itami]; **back pain** *n* 腰痛 [youtsuu]; **Can you give me something for the pain?** 痛み止めに何かもらえますか? [itami-dome ni nani ka moraemasu ka?]; **I have a pain here** 私はここが痛みます [watashi wa koko ga itamimasu]; **I have a pain in my chest** 私は胸に痛みがあります [watashi wa mune ni itami ga arimasu]; **I want an injection for the pain** 私は痛み止めの注射が欲しいのです [watashi wa itami-dome no chuusha ga hoshi no desu]

painful [peɪnfəl] *adj* 痛い [itai]

painkiller [peɪnkɪlər] *n* 痛み止め [itamidome]

paint [peɪnt] *n* ペンキ [penki] ▷ *v* 絵を描く [e-o egaku], 塗る [nuru]

paintbrush [peɪntbrʌʃ] *n* 絵筆 [efude]

painter [peɪntər] *n* 画家 [gaka], *(in house)* 室内装飾家 [shitsunai soushokuka]

painting [peɪntɪŋ] *n* 絵画 [kaiga]

pair [pɛər] *n* ひと組 [hitokumi]

pajamas [pədʒɑməz] *npl* パジャマ [pajama]

Pakistan [pækɪstæn] *n* パキスタン [pakisutan]

Pakistani [pækɪstæni, pɑkɪstɑni] *adj* パキスタンの [pakisutan no] ▷ *n* パキスタン人 [pakisutanjin]

pal [pæl] *n* 友だち [tomodachi]; **pen pal** *n* ペンパル [penparu]

palace [pælɪs] *n* 宮殿 [kyuuden]; **Is the palace open to the public?** その宮殿は一般公開されていますか? [sono kyuuden wa ippan-koukai sarete imasu ka?]; **When is the palace open?** その宮殿はいつ開きますか? [sono kyuuden wa itsu hirakimasu ka?]

pale [peɪl] *adj* 薄い [usui] (住居)

Palestine [pǽləstaɪn] *n* パレスチナ [paresuchina]

Palestinian [pæ̀lɪstɪ́nɪən] *adj* パレスチナの [paresuchina no] ▷ *n* パレスチナ人 [paresuchinajin]

palm [pɑm] *n (part of hand)* 手のひら [tenohira], *(tree)* ヤシ [yashi]

pamphlet [pǽmflɪt] *n* パンフレット [panfuretto]

pan [pæn] *n* 平なべ [taira nabe]; **frying pan** *n* フライパン [furaipan]

Panama [pǽnəmɑ] *n* パナマ [panama]

pancake [pǽnkeɪk] *n* パンケーキ [pankeeki]

panda [pǽndə] *n* パンダ [panda]

panic [pǽnɪk] *n* パニック [panikku] ▷ *v* うろたえる [urotaeru]

panther [pǽnθər] *n* ヒョウ [hyou] *(動物)*

pantomime [pǽntəmaɪm] *n* パントマイム [pantomaimu]

pantry [pǽntri] *n* 食料置場 [shokuryou okiba]

pants [pænts] *n* ズボン [zubon]; **May I try on these pants?** このズボンを試着していいですか? [kono zubon o shichaku shite ii desu ka?]

paper [peɪpər] *n* 紙 [kami]; **paper route** *n* 新聞配達 [shinbun haitatsu]; **scrap paper** *n* くず紙 [kuzugami]; **toilet paper** *n* トイレットペーパー [toirettopeepaa]; **tracing paper** *n* トレース紙 [toreesushi]; **wrapping paper** *n* 包装紙 [housoushi]; **writing paper** *n* 便箋 [binsen]

paperback [peɪpərbæk] *n* ペーパーバック [peepaabakku]

paperclip [peɪpərklɪp] *n* ペーパークリップ [peepaakurippu]

paperweight [peɪpərweɪt] *n* ペーパーウェイト [peepaaueito]

paperwork [peɪpərwɜrk] *n* 机上事務 [kijou jimu]

paprika [pəpríkə, pǽprɪkə] *n* パプリカ [papurika]

parachute [pǽrəʃut] *n* パラシュート [parashu-uto]

parade [pəreɪd] *n* パレード [pareedo]

paradise [pǽrədaɪs] *n* 楽園 [rakuen]

paraffin [pǽrəfɪn] *n* パラフィン [parafin]

paragraph [pǽrəgræf] *n* 段落 [danraku]

Paraguay [pǽrəgwaɪ] *n* パラグアイ [paraguai]

Paraguayan [pæ̀rəgwaɪən] *adj* パラグアイの [Paraguai no] ▷ *n* パラグアイ人 [Paraguai jin]

parakeet [pǽrəkit] *n* セキセイインコ [sekiseiinko]

parallel [pǽrəlɛl] *adj* 平行の [heikou no]

paralyzed [pǽrəlaɪzd] *adj* 麻痺した [mahi shita]

paramedic [pæ̀rəmɛ́dɪk] *n* 救急救命士 [kyuukyuu kyuumeishi]

pardon [pɑrd-n] *n* 許し [yurushi]

parent [pɛ́ərənt, pær-] *n* 親 [oya]; **single parent** *n* 片親で子育てをする人 [kataoya de kosodate-o suru hito]

parentheses [pɛ̀ərəntθ̄ez] *npl (round)* 括弧 [kakko]

parents [pɛ́ərənts] *npl* 両親 [ryoushin]

parish [pǽrɪʃ] *n* 教会区 [kyoukaiku]

park [pɑrk] *n* 公園 [kouen] ▷ *v* 駐車する [chuusha suru]; **amusement park** *n* 遊園地 [yuuenchi]; **industrial park** *n* 工業団地 [kougyoudanchi]; **national park** *n* 国立公園 [kokuritsu kouen]; **parking light** *n* 側灯 [sokutou]; **theme park** *n* テーマパーク [teemapaaku]; **trailer park** *n* トレーラーハウスキャンプ場 [toreeraa hausu kyanpu jou]

parka [pɑrkə] *n* アノラック [anorakku]

parking [pɑrkɪŋ] *n* 駐車 [chuusha]; **parking enforcement officer** *n* 交通監視員 [koutsuu kanshiin]; **parking meter** *n* パーキングメーター [paakingumeetaa]; **parking ticket** *n* 駐車違反切符 [chuushaihan kippu]

parking lot *n* 駐車場 [chuushajou]; **Is there a parking lot near here?** この近くに駐車場はありますか? [kono chikaku ni chuusha-jou wa arimasu ka?]

parliament [pɑrləmənt] *n* 議会 [gikai]

P

parlor [pɑrlər] *n* **beauty parlor** *n* 美容院 [biyouin]

parole [pəroul] *n* 仮釈放 [kari shakuhou]

parrot [pærət] *n* オウム [oumu]

parsley [pɑrsli] *n* パセリ [paseri]

parsnip [pɑrsnɪp] *n* パースニップ [paasunippu]

part [pɑrt] *n* 部分 [bubun]; **spare part** *n* スペアパーツ [supeapaatsu]

partial [pɑrʃl] *adj* 部分的な [bubunteki na]

participate [pɑrtɪsɪpeɪt] *v* 参加する [sanka suru]

participation [pɑrtɪsɪpeɪʃn] *n* 参加 [sanka]

particular [pərtɪkyələr] *adj* 特別の [tokubetsu no]

particularly [pərtɪkyəlɜrli] *adv* 特に [toku ni]

parting [pɑrtɪŋ] *n* 別れ [wakare]

partition [pɑrtɪʃn] *n* 閉所 [heisho]

partly [pɑrtli] *adv* 部分的に [bubunteki ni]

partner [pɑrtnər] *n* パートナー [paatonaa], 相手 [aite]; **I have a partner** 私にはパートナーがいます [watashi ni wa paatonaa ga imasu]; **This is my partner** 私のパートナーです [watashi no paatonaa desu]

partridge [pɑrtrɪdʒ] *n* ヨーロッパヤマウズラ [yooroppayamauzura]

parts *n* パーツ [paatsu]

part-time *adj* パートタイムの [paatotaimu no] ▷ *adv* パートタイムで [paatotaimu de]

part with *v* ・・・を手放す [...-o tebanasu]

party [pɑrti] *n* (*group*) 一行 [ikkou] (*集まり*), (*social gathering*) パーティー [paateii]; **bachelor party** *n* スタッグパーティー [sutaggupaateii]; **bachelorette party** *n* ヘンパーティー [henpaatii]; **dinner party** *n* ディナーパーティー [dinaa paatii]; **search party** *n* 捜索隊 [sousakutai]

pass [pæs] *n* (*in mountains*) 峠 [touge], (*meets standard*) 合格 [goukaku], (*permit*) 許可証 [kyokashou] ▷ *v* (*an exam*) 合格する [goukaku suru], (*on road*) 追い越す [oikosu] ▷ *vi* 過ぎる [sugiru] ▷ *vt* 通過する [tsuuka suru]; **boarding pass** *n* 搭乗券 [toujouken];

ski pass *n* スキー場のパス [sukii jou no pasu]

passage [pæsɪdʒ] *n* (*musical*) 楽節 [gakusetsu], (*route*) 通路 [tsuuro]

passenger [pæsɪndʒər] *n* 乗客 [joukyaku]

passion [pæʃn] *n* 熱情 [netsujou]; **passion fruit** *n* パッションフルーツ [passhonfuruutsu]

passive [pæsɪv] *adj* 受身の [ukemi no]

pass out *v* 意識を失う [ishiki-o ushinau]

Passover [pæsouvər] *n* 過越しの祭 [Sugikoshi no matsuri]

passport [pæsport] *n* パスポート [pasupooto]; **passport control** *n* パスポート審査窓口 [pasupooto shinsa madoguchi]; **Here is my passport** 私のパスポートです [watashi wa pasupooto desu]; **I've forgotten my passport** 私はパスポートを置き忘れました [watashi wa pasupooto o okiwasuremashita]; **I've lost my passport** 私はパスポートをなくしました [watashi wa pasupooto o nakushimashita]; **My passport has been stolen** 私のパスポートが盗まれました [watashi no pasupooto ga nusumaremashita]; **Please give me my passport back** 私のパスポートを返してください [watashi no pasupooto o kaeshite kudasai]; **The children are on this passport** 子供たちはこのパスポートに載っています [kodomo-tachi wa kono pasupooto ni notte imasu]

password [pæswɜrd] *n* パスワード [pasuwaado]

past [pæst] *adj* 過ぎ去った [sugisatta] ▷ *n* 過去 [kako]

pasta [pɑstə] *n* パスタ [pasuta]; **I'd like pasta as an appetizer** スターターにパスタをいただきます [sutaataa ni pasuta o itadakimasu]

paste [peɪst] *n* ペースト [peesuto]

pasteurized [pæstʃəraɪzd] *adj* 低温殺菌した [teion sakkin shita]

pastime [pæstaɪm] *n* 娯楽 [goraku]

pastor [pæstər] *n* 教区牧師 [kyouku bokushi]

pastry [peɪstri] *n* 生地 [kiji] (*料理*); **puff pastry** *n* パフペースト [pafupeesuto];

shortcrust pastry n ショートクラスト [shootokurasuto]

patch [pætʃ] n つぎ [tsugi] (布きれ)

patched [pætʃt] adj つぎを当てた [tsugi-o ateta]

path [pæθ] n パス [pasu], 小道 [komichi]; **bicycle path** n サイクルパス [saikuru pasu]

pathetic [pəθɛtɪk] adj 哀れっぽい [awareppoi]

patience [peɪʃns] n 忍耐 [nintai]

patient [peɪʃnt] adj 忍耐強い [nintaizuyoi] ▷ n 患者 [kanja]

patio [pætioʊ] n パティオ [pateio]

patriotic [peɪtriɒtɪk] adj 愛国的な [aikokuteki na]

patrol [pətroʊl] n パトロール [patorooru]; **patrol car** n パトロールカー [patoroorukaa]

pattern [pætərn] n 模様 [moyou]

pause [pɔz] n 小休止 [shoukyuushi]

pavilion [pəvɪljən] n 別館 [bekkan]

paw [pɔ] n 動物の足 [doubutsu no ashi]

pawnbroker [pɔnbroʊkər] n 質屋 [shichiya]

pay [peɪ] n 給料 [kyuuryou] ▷ v 支払う [shiharau]; **sick pay** n 病気休暇中の手当て [byouki kyuukachuu no teate]

payable [peɪəbl] adj 支払うべき [shiharaubeki]

pay back v 払い戻す [haraimodosu]

payment [peɪmənt] n 支払い [shiharai]

payphone [peɪfoʊn] n 公衆電話 [koushuudenwa]

PC [pi si] n PC [piishii]

PDF [pi di ɛf] n PDF [piidiiefu]

pea [pi] n **snow peas** npl サヤエンドウ [sayaendou]

peace [pis] n 平穏 [heion]

peaceful [pisfəl] adj 平和な [heiwa na]

peach [pitʃ] n モモ [momo]

peacock [pikɒk] n クジャク [kujaku]

peak [pik] n 尖端 [sentan]; **peak hours** npl ピーク時 [piikuji]; **peak season** n 最盛期 [saiseiki]

peanut [pinʌt, -nət] n ピーナッツ [piinattsu];

peanut allergy n ピーナッツアレルギー [piinattsu arerugii]; **peanut butter** n ピーナッツバター [piinattsubataa]; **Does that contain peanuts?** それにはピーナッツが入っていますか？ [sore ni wa piinattsu ga haitte imasu ka?]; **I'm allergic to peanuts** 私はピーナッツのアレルギーがあります [watashi wa piinattsu no arerugii ga arimasu]

pear [pɛər] n なし [nashi], 西洋ナシ [seiyounashi]

pearl [pɜrl] n 真珠 [shinju]

peas [piz] npl エンドウ [endou]

peat [pit] n 泥炭 [deitan]

pebble [pɛbl] n 小石 [koishi]

peculiar [pɪkyulyər] adj 変な [hen na]

pedal [pɛdl] n ペダル [pedaru]

pedestrian [pɪdɛstriən] n 歩行者 [hokousha]; **pedestrian area** n 指定地区 [shitei chiku], 歩行者天国 [hokoushatengoku]

pedestrianized [pɪdɛstriənaɪzd] adj 歩行者専用になった [hokousha sen'you ni natta]

pediatrician [pidiətrɪʃn] n 小児科医 [shounikai]

pedigree [pɛdɪgri] adj 血統の明らかな [kettou no akiraka na]

pedophile [pidəfaɪl] n 小児性愛者 [shouniseiaimono]

peel [pil] n 皮 [kawa] (果物・野菜) ▷ v 皮をむく [kawa-o muku]

peg [pɛg] n ペグ [pegu]

Pekinese [pikɪniz] n ペキニーズ [pekiniizu]

pelican [pɛlɪkən] n ペリカン [perikan]

pellet [pɛlɪt] n 小球 [shoukyuu]

pelvis [pɛlvɪs] n 骨盤 [kotsuban]

pen [pɛn] n ペン [pen]; **ballpoint pen** n バイロウ® [bairou], ボールペン [boorupen]; **felt-tip pen** n フェルトペン [ferutopen]; **fountain pen** n 万年筆 [mannenhitsu]; **pen pal** n ペンパル [penparu]; **Do you have a pen I could borrow?** ペンをお借りできますか？ [pen o o-kari dekimasu ka?]

penalize [pinəlaɪz] v 罰する [bassuru]

penalty [pɛnəlti] n 刑罰 [keibatsu]

P

pencil [pɛns‑l] *n* 鉛筆 [enpitsu]; **pencil case** *n* 筆箱 [fudebako]; **pencil sharpener** *n* 鉛筆削り [enpitsukezuri]

pendant [pɛndənt] *n* ペンダント [pendanto]

penguin [pɛŋgwɪn] *n* ペンギン [pengin]

penicillin [pɛnɪsɪlɪn] *n* ペニシリン [penishirin]

peninsula [pənɪnsələ, -nɪnsyə-] *n* 半島 [hantou]

penknife [pɛnnaɪf] *n* ペンナイフ [pennaifu]

penny [pɛni] *n* ペニー [penii]

pension [pɛnʃ‑n] *n* 年金 [nenkin]

pentathlon [pɛntæθlon] *n* 五種競技 [goshu kyougi]

penultimate [pɪnʌltɪmɪt] *adj* 終わりから2番目の [owari kara banme no]

people [pip‑l] (*pl* **persons**) *npl* 人々 [hitobito]

pepper [pɛpər] *n* コショウ [koshou]

peppermill [pɛpərmɪl] *n* コショウひき [koshou hiki]

peppermint [pɛpərmɪnt] *n* ペパーミント [pepaaminto]

per [pər, STRONG pɜr] *prep* **percent** *n* 百につき [hyaku ni tsuki]; **How much is it per hour?** 1時間あたりいくらですか? [ichi-jikan atari ikura desu ka?]; **How much is it per night?** 一泊いくらですか? [ippaku ikura desu ka?], それは一泊いくらですか? [sore wa ippaku ikura desu ka?]; **How much is it per person?** それは一人あたりいくらですか? [sore wa hitori atari ikura desu ka?]

percentage [pərsɛntɪdʒ] *n* パーセンテージ [paasenteeji]

percussion [pərkʌʃ‑n] *n* 衝突 [shoutotsu]

perfect *adj* 完璧な [kanpeki na], 完全 [kanzen]

perfection [pərfɛkʃ‑n] *n* 完璧 [kanpeki]

perfectly [pɜrfɪktli] *adv* 完璧に [kanpeki ni]

perform [pərfɔrm] *v* 行う [okonau]

performance [pərfɔrməns] *n* 上演 [jouen], 遂行 [suikou], 公園 [kouen]

performer [pərfɔrmər] *n* 芸人 [geinin]

perfume [pɜrfyum, pərfyum] *n* 香水 [kousui]

perhaps [pərhæps, præps] *adv* ことによると [koto ni yoru to]

period [pɪəriəd] *n* 期間 [kikan], (*punctuation*) 終止符 [shuushifu]; **trial period** *n* 試用期間 [shiyou kikan]

perjury [pɜrdʒəri] *n* 偽証 [gishou]

perm [pɜrm] *n* パーマ [paama]

permanent [pɜrmənənt] *adj* 永久の [eikyuu no]

permanently [pɜrmənəntli] *adv* 永久に [eikyuu ni]

permission [pərmɪʃ‑n] *n* 許可 [kyoka]

permit *n* 許可証 [kyokashou]; **work permit** *n* 労働許可証 [roudou kyokashou]

persecute [pɜrsɪkyut] *v* 迫害する [hakugai suru]

persevere [pɜrsɪvɪər] *v* 辛抱する [shinbou suru]

Persian [pɜrʒ‑n] *adj* ペルシャの [Perusha no]

persistent [pərsɪstənt] *adj* 持続性の [jizokusei no]

person [pɜrs‑n] *n* 人 [hito]; **How much is it per person?** それは一人あたりいくらですか? [sore wa hitori atari ikura desu ka?]

personal [pɜrsən‑l] *adj* 個人的な [kojinteki na]; **personal assistant** *n* 個人秘書 [kojin hisho]; **personal organizer** *n* システム手帳 [shisutemu techou]; **personal stereo** *n* パーソナルステレオ [paasonarusutereo]

personality [pɜrsənælɪti] *n* 個性 [kosei]

personally [pɜrsənəli] *adv* 直接自分で [chokusetsu jibun de]

personnel [pɜrsənɛl] *n* 人員 [jin-in]

perspective [pərspɛktɪv] *n* 観点 [kanten]

perspiration [pɜrspɪreɪʃ‑n] *n* 汗 [ase]

persuade [pərsweɪd] *v* 説得する [settoku suru]

persuasive [pərsweɪsɪv] *adj* 説得力のある [settokuryoku no aru]

Peru [pəru] *n* ペルー [peruu]

Peruvian [pəruviən] *adj* ペルーの [peruu no] ▷ *n* ペルー人 [peruujin]

pessimism [pɛsɪmɪzəm] *n* 悲観 [hikan]

pessimist [pɛsɪmɪst] *n* 悲観主義者 [hikanshugisha]

pessimistic [pɛsɪmɪstɪk] *adj* 悲観的な [hikanteki na]

pest [pɛst] *n* 害虫 [gaichuu]

pester [pɛstər] *v* 悩ませる [nayamaseru]

pesticide [pɛstɪsaɪd] *n* 農薬 [nouyaku]

pet [pɛt] *n* ペット [petto]

petition [pətɪʃn] *n* 嘆願書 [tangansho]

petrified [pɛtrɪfaɪd] *adj* すくむ [sukumu]

pewter [pyutər] *n* 白目 [shirome]

pharmacist [fɑrməsɪst] *n* 薬剤師 [yakuzaishi]

pharmacy [fɑrməsi] *n* 薬局 [yakkyoku]; **Which pharmacy provides emergency service?** どの薬局が夜間休日サービスを実施していますか? [dono yakkyoku ga yakan-kyuujitsu-saabisu o jisshi shite imasu ka?]

PhD [pi ertʃ di] *n* 博士号 [hakasegou]

pheasant [fɛzənt] *n* キジ [kiji]

philosophy [frɪlɒsəfi] *n* 哲学 [tetsugaku]

phobia [foubiə] *n* 恐怖症 [kyoufushou]

phone [foun] *n* 電話 [denwa] ▷ *v* 電話をかける [denwa o kakeru]; **camera phone** *n* カメラ付き携帯電話 [kamera tsuki keitai denwa]; **cell phone** *n* 携帯電話 [keitai denwa]; **cell phone number** *n* 携帯電話番号 [keitai denwa bangou]; **entry phone** *n* インターホン [intaahon]; **phone bill** *n* 電話の請求書 [denwa no seikyuusho]; **phone booth** *n* 電話ボックス [denwa bokkusu], 公衆電話ボックス [koushuu denwa bokkusu]; **phone number** *n* 電話番号 [denwabangou]; **smart phone** *n* スマートフォン [sumaatofon]; **Can I call from here?** ここから電話をかけられますか? [koko kara denwa o kakeraremasu ka?]; **Do you sell international phone cards?** 国際電話用のテレホンカードを売っていますか? [kokusai-denwa-you no terehon-kaado o utte imasu ka?]; **I have to make a phone call** 私は電話をかけなければなりません [watashi wa denwa o kakenakereba narimasen]; **I want to make a phone call** 電話をかけたいのですが [denwa o kaketai no desu ga]; **I'd like some coins for the phone, please** 電話に使うコインをいくらかお願いします [denwa ni tsukau koin o ikura ka o-negai shimasu]; **I'd like to phone my embassy** 私は大使館に電話したいのですが [watashi wa taishikan ni denwa shitai no desu ga]; **I'm having trouble with the phone** 電話に問題があります [denwa ni mondai ga arimasu]; **May I have your phone number?** 電話番号を教えてもらえますか? [denwa-bangou o oshiete moraemasu ka?]; **May I phone home?** 家に電話していいですか? [ie ni denwa shite ii desu ka?]; **May I use your phone, please?** 電話をお借りできますか? [denwa o o-kari dekimasu ka?]; **May I use your phone?** 電話をお借りできますか? [denwa o o-kari dekimasu ka?]; **Where can I charge my cell phone?** どこで携帯電話を充電できますか? [doko de keitai-denwa o juuden dekimasu ka?]; **Where can I make a phone call?** どこで電話をかけられますか? [doko de denwa o kakeraremasu ka?]

phonebook [founbuk] *n* 電話帳 [denwachou]

phone call [founkɔl] *n* 電話をかけること [denwa-o kakeru koto]

phone card [founkɑrd] *n* テレホンカード [terehon kaado]

photo [foutou] *n* 写真 [shashin]; **photo album** *n* アルバム [arubamu]; **Can I download photos to here?** ここに写真をダウンロードできますか? [koko ni shashin o daunroodo dekimasu ka?]; **Could you put these photos on CD, please?** この写真をCDに焼き付けていただけますか? [kono shashin no shii-dii ni yakitsukete itadakemasu ka?]; **How much do the photos cost?** 写真代はいくらですか? [shashin-dai wa ikura desu ka?]; **I'd like the photos glossy** 写真は光沢仕上げにしてください [shashin wa koutaku-shiage ni shite kudasai]; **I'd like the**

P

photos matt 写真はマット仕上げにしてくだ
さい [shashin wa matto-shiage ni shite
kudasai]; **When will the photos be ready?**
写真はいつできますか? [shashin wa itsu
dekimasu ka?]

photocopier [foutəkɒpiər] *n* コピー機
[kopiiki]

photocopy [foutəkɒpi] *n* コピー [kopii] (複写)
▷ *v* コピーする [kopii suru]; **I'd like a**
photocopy of this, please このコピーをお
願いします [kono kopii o o-negai shimasu];
Where can I get some photocopying
done? どこでコピーを取ってもらえますか?
[doko de kopii o totte moraemasu ka?]

photograph [foutəgræf] *n* 写真 [shashin] ▷ *v*
撮影する [satsuei suru]

photographer [fətɒgrəfər] *n* 写真家
[shashinka]

photography [fətɒgrəfi] *n* 写真撮影
[shashinsatsuei]

phrase [freɪz] *n* 慣用句 [kan'youku]

phrasebook [freɪzbʊk] *n* 外国語慣用句集
[gaikokugo kan'youku shuu]

physical [fɪzɪkᵊl] *adj* 身体の [shintai no] ▷ *n* 身
体検査 [shintai kensa], 健康診断 [kenk-
oushindan]

physicist [fɪzɪsɪst] *n* 物理学者
[butsurigakusha]

physics [fɪzɪks] *npl* 物理学 [butsurigaku]

physiotherapist [fɪziouθɛrəpɪst] *n* 理学療法
士 [rigaku ryouhoushi]

physiotherapy [fɪziouθɛrəpi] *n* 理学療法
[rigaku ryouhou]

pianist [piænɪst, piənɪst] *n* ピアニスト
[pianisuto]

piano [piænou, pyænou] *n* ピアノ [piano]

pick [pɪk] *n* 選択 [sentaku] ▷ *v* 選ぶ [erabu]

pick on *v* いじめる [ijimeru]

pick out *v* 選ぶ [erabu]

pickpocket [pɪkpɒkɪt] *n* スリ [suri]

pick up *v* 持ち上げる [mochiageru]

picnic [pɪknɪk] *n* ピクニック [pikunikku]

picture [pɪktʃər] *n* 絵 [e]; **picture frame** *n* 額

縁 [gakubuchi]

picturesque [pɪktʃərɛsk] *adj* 絵のように美し
い [e no youni utsukushii]

pie [paɪ] *n* パイ [pai]; **apple pie** *n* アップルパ
イ [appurupai]; **pie chart** *n* 円グラフ
[engurafu]

piece [pis] *n* 一つ [hitotsu]

pier [pɪər] *n* 埠頭 [futou]

pierce [pɪərs] *v* 穴をあける [ana-o akeru]

pierced [pɪərst] *adj* 穴をあけた [ana-o aketa]

piercing [pɪərsɪŋ] *n* ピアス [piasu]

pig [pɪg] *n* 豚 [buta]; **guinea pig** *n (for*
experiment) 実験台 [jikkendai], *(rodent)* モ
ルモット *(動物)* [morumotto]

pigeon [pɪdʒɪn] *n* 鳩 [hato]

piggy bank [pɪgibæŋk] *n* 貯金箱
[chokinbako]

pigtail [pɪgteɪl] *n* おさげ [osage]

pile [paɪl] *n* 積み重ね [tsumikasane]

pileup [paɪlʌp] *n* 山積み [yamadumi]

pile up *v* かさむ [kasamu]

pilgrim [pɪlgrɪm] *n* 巡礼者 [junreisha]

pilgrimage [pɪlgrɪmɪdʒ] *n* 巡礼 [junrei], 巡礼
の旅 [junrei no tabi]

pill [pɪl] *n* 丸薬 [ganyaku], ピル [piru], 錠剤
[jouzai]; **sleeping pill** *n* 睡眠薬 [suimin-
yaku]; **I'm not on the pill** 私はピルを飲んで
いません [watashi wa piru o nonde imasen];
I'm on the pill 私はピルを飲んでいます
[watashi wa piru o nonde imasu]

pillar [pɪlər] *n* 柱 [hashira]

pillow [pɪlou] *n* 枕 [makura]; **Please bring**
me an extra pillow 追加の枕を持ってきてく
ださい [tsuika no makura o motte kite
kudasai]

pillowcase [pɪloukeɪs] *n* 枕カバー
[makurakabaa]

pilot [paɪlət] *n* パイロット [pairotto], 非公認
[hikounin]; **pilot light** *n* 口火 [kuchibi]

pimple [pɪmpᵊl] *n* 吹き出物 [fukidemono]

pin [pɪn] *n* ピン [pin], バッジ [bajji]; **bobby pin**
n ヘアピン [heapin]; **rolling pin** *n* 麺棒
[menbou]; **safety pin** *n* 安全ピン [anzenpin];

I need a safety pin 私は安全ピンが必要です [watashi wa anzen-pin ga hitsuyou desu]

PIN [pɪn] *abbr (= personal identification number)* 暗証番号 [anshobango]

pinafore [pɪnəfɔr] *n* エプロン [epuron]

pinch [pɪntʃ] *v* つねる [tsuneru]

pine [paɪn] *n* マツ [matsu]

pineapple [paɪnæpᵊl] *n* パイナップル [painappuru]

pink [pɪŋk] *adj* ピンク色の [pinkuiro no]

pint [paɪnt] *n* パイント [painto]

pipe [paɪp] *n* パイプ [paipu]; **exhaust pipe** *n* エキゾーストパイプ [ekizoosutopaipu]

pipeline [paɪplaɪn] *n* パイプライン [paipurain]

pirate [paɪrɪt] *n* 海賊 [kaizoku]

Pisces [paɪsiz] *n* 魚座 [uoza]

pistol [pɪstᵊl] *n* ピストル [pisutoru]

piston [pɪstᵊn] *n* ピストン [pisuton]

pitch [pɪtʃ] *n (sound)* 調子 [choushi], *(sport)* ピッチ [pitchi] (競技場) ▷ *v* 投げる [nageru]

pity [pɪti] *n* 哀れみ [awaremi] ▷ *v* 哀れむ [awaremu]

pixel [pɪksᵊl] *n* 画素 [gaso]

pizza [pitsə] *n* ピザ [piza]

place [pleɪs] *n* ところ [tokoro], 場 [ba], 場所 [basho] ▷ *v* 置く [oku]; **place of birth** *n* 出生地 [shusseichi]; **Do you know a good place to go?** よいところをご存知ですか? [yoi tokoro o go-zonji desu ka?]; **Where is the best place to dive?** ダイビングに最適の場所はどこですか? [daibingu ni saiteki no basho wa doko desu ka?]

placement [pleɪsmənt] *n* 配置 [haichi]

plain [pleɪn] *adj* 平坦な [heitan na] ▷ *n* 平原 [heigen]

plan [plæn] *n* 計画 [keikaku] ▷ *v* 計画する [keikaku suru]; **modified American plan** *n* 二食付き [nishokutsuki]; **street plan** *n* 街路計画 [gairo keikaku]

plane [pleɪn] *n (airplane)* 飛行機 [hikouki] *(aeroplane)*, *(surface)* 平面 [heimen], *(tool)* かんな [kanna] *(道具)*; **My plane leaves at...** 私の飛行機は···に出発します [watashi no

hikouki wa... ni shuppatsu shimasu]

planet [plænɪt] *n* 惑星 [wakusei]

planning [plænɪŋ] *n* 計画 [keikaku]

plant [plænt] *n (site/equipment)* 製造工場 [seizou koujou], *(vegetable organism)* 植物 [shokubutsu] ▷ *v* 植える [ueru]; **potted plant** *n* 鉢植え植物 [hachiue shokubutsu]; **We'd like to see local plants and trees** 土地の植物と樹木を見たいのですが [tochi no shokubutsu to jumoku o mitai no desu ga]

planter [plæntər] *n* 植木鉢 [uekibachi]

plaque [plæk] *n* 記念銘板 [kinen meiban]

plaster [plæstər] *n (for wall)* 漆喰 [shikkui]

plastered [plæstərd] *adj* 酔っぱらって [yopparatte]

plastic [plæstɪk] *adj* プラスチックの [purasuchikku no] ▷ *n* プラスチック [purasuchikku]; **plastic bag** *n* ビニール袋 [biniiru bukuro]; **plastic surgery** *n* 形成外科 [keisei geka]

plate [pleɪt] *n* 平皿 [taira sara]; **license plate** *n* ナンバープレート [nanbaapureeto]

platform [plætfɔrm] *n* 演壇 [endan]

platinum [plætɪnəm, plætnəm] *n* プラチナ [purachina]

play [pleɪ] *n* 遊ぶ [asobu], 劇 [geki] ▷ *v (in sports)* 競技を行う [kyougi-o okonau] *(in sport)*, *(music)* 演奏する [ensou suru]; **play hooky** *v* サボる [saboru]; **playing card** *n* トランプ [toranpu]; **playing field** *n* グラウンド [guraundo]; **Where can we go to see a play?** どこに行けば観劇ができますか? [doko ni ikeba kangeki ga dekimasu ka?]

playboy [pleɪbɔɪ] *n* 浮気者 [uwakimono]

player [pleɪər] *n (instrumentalist)* 演奏者 [ensousha], *(of a sport)* 選手 [senshu]; **CD player** *n* CDプレーヤー [shiidii pureiyaa]; **MP3 player** *n* MP3プレーヤー [emu pi surii pyreeyaa]; **MP4 player** *n* MP4プレーヤー [emu pi foa pyreeyaa]

playground [pleɪgraʊnd] *n* プレーパーク [pureepaaku], 遊び場 [asobiba]; **Is there a playground near here?** この近くにプレーパ

P

ークはありますか? [kono chikaku ni puree-paaku wa arimasu ka?]

playgroup [pleɪɡrup] *n* プレイグループ [pureiguruupu]

PlayStation® [pleɪsteɪʃn] *n* プレイステーション® [pureisuteeshon]

playtime [pleɪtaɪm] *n* 遊び時間 [asobi jikan]

playwright [pleɪraɪt] *n* 脚本家 [kyakuhonka]

pleasant [plɛzənt] *adj* 楽しい [tanoshii]

please [pliz] *adv* I'd like to check in, please チェックインをお願いします [chekku-in o o-negai shimasu]; **Please order me a taxi** タクシーを呼んでください [takushii o yonde kudasai]

please [pliz] *excl* お願い! [onegai]

pleased [plizd] *adj* 嬉しい [ureshii]

pleasure [plɛʒər] *n* 楽しみ [tanoshimi]

plenty [plɛnti] *n* たっぷり [tappuri]

pliers [plaɪərz] *npl* プライヤー [puraiyaa]

plot [plɒt] *n (piece of land)* 小区画 [shou kukaku] ▷ *v (secret plan)* たくらむ [takura-mu]

plow [plaʊ] *n* 鋤 [suki] ▷ *v* 耕す [tagayasu]

plug [plʌɡ] *n* プラグ [puragu], 栓 [sen]; **spark plug** *n* スパークプラグ [supaakupuragu]

plug in *v* プラグで接続する [puragu de setsuzoku suru]

plum [plʌm] *n* プラム [puramu]

plumber [plʌmər] *n* 配管工 [haikankou]

plumbing [plʌmɪŋ] *n* 配管 [haikan]

plump [plʌmp] *adj* 丸々太った [marumaru futotta]

plunge [plʌndʒ] *v* 突っ込む [tsukkomu]

plural [plʊərəl] *n* 複数 [fukusuu]

plus-size *adj* 特大の [tokudai no]

plywood [plaɪwʊd] *n* ベニヤ板 [beniyaita]

p.m. [pi ɛm] *abbr* 午後の [gogo no]

pneumonia [nʊmoʊnyə, -moʊniə] *n* 肺炎 [haien]

poached [poʊtʃt] *adj (caught illegally)* 密漁した [mitsuryou shita], *(simmered gently)* ポーチした [poochi shita]

pocket [pɒkɪt] *n* ポケット [poketto]; **pocket**

calculator *n* 電卓 [dentaku]; **pocket money** *n* ポケットマネー [pokettomanee]

podcast [pɒdkæst] *n* ポッドキャスト [poddokyasuto]

podiatrist [pədaɪətrɪst] *n* 足治療医 [ashichiryoui]

poem [poʊəm] *n* 詩 [shi]

poet [poʊɪt] *n* 詩人 [shijin]

poetry [poʊɪtri] *n* 詩歌 [shiika]

point [pɔɪnt] *n* 要点 [youten] ▷ *v* 指し示す [sashishimesu]; **exclamation point** *n* 感嘆符 [kantanfu]

pointless [pɔɪntlɪs] *adj* 無意味な [muimi na]

point out *v* 指摘する [shiteki suru]

poison [pɔɪzən] *n* 毒 [doku] ▷ *v* 毒を盛る [doku-o moru]

poisoning *n* 中毒 [chuudoku]

poisonous [pɔɪzənəs] *adj* 有毒な [yuudoku na]

poke [poʊk] *v* つつく [tsutsuku]

poker [poʊkər] *n* ポーカー [pookaa]

Poland [poʊlənd] *n* ポーランド [poorando]

polar [poʊlər] *adj* 極地の [kyokuchi no]; **polar bear** *n* 北極グマ [hokkyokuguma]

pole [poʊl] *n* 棒 [bou]; **North Pole** *n* 北極 [hokkyoku]; **pole vault** *n* 棒高跳び [bou taka tobi]; **South Pole** *n* 南極 [nankyoku]; **tent pole** *n* テントポール [tentopooru]

Pole [poʊl] *n* ポーランド人 [poorandojin]

police [pəlis] *n* 警察 [keisatsu]; **police officer** *n* 警察官 [keisatsukan]; **police station** *n* 警察署 [keisatsusho]; **Call the police** 警察を呼んでください [keisatsu o yonde kudasai]; **I need a police report for my insurance** 私は保険請求に警察の証明書が必要です [watashi wa hoken-seikyuu ni keisatsu no shoumeisho ga hitsuyou desu]; **We'll have to report it to the police** 私たちはそれを警察に届け出なければなりません [watashi-tachi wa sore o keisatsu ni todokedenakereba narimasen]; **Where's the police station?** 警察署はどこですか? [keisatsusho wa doko desu ka?]

policeman [pəli̇smən] (*pl* **policemen**) *n* 警官 [keikan]

policewoman [pəli̇swumən] (*pl* **police-women**) *n* 婦人警官 [fujinkeikan]

policy [pɒli̇si] *n* **insurance policy** *n* 保険証書 [hokenshousho]

polio [pouliou] *n* ポリオ [porio]

polish [pɒli̇ʃ] *n* つや出し剤 [tsuyadashi zai] ▷*v* つやを出す [tsuya-o dasu]; **nail polish** *n* マニキュア液 [manikyua eki]; **shoe polish** *n* 靴墨 [kutsuzumi]

Polish [pouli̇ʃ] *adj* ポーランドの [poorando no] ▷*n* ポーランド人 [poorandojin]

polite [pəlai̇t] *adj* 丁寧な [teinei na]

politely [pəlai̇tli] *adv* 丁寧に [teinei ni]

politeness [pəlai̇tnɪs] *n* 丁寧 [teinei]

political [pəli̇tɪkᵊl] *adj* 政治の [seiji no]

politician [pɒli̇tɪʃᵊn] *n* 政治家 [seijika]

politics [pɒli̇tɪks] *npl* 政治 [seiji]

poll [poul] *n* 世論調査 [yoronchousa]; **opinion poll** *n* 世論調査 [yoronchousa]

pollen [pɒlən] *n* 花粉 [kafun]

pollute [pəlu̇t] *v* 汚染する [osen suru]

polluted [pəlu̇tɪd] *adj* 汚染された [osen sareta]

pollution [pəlu̇ʃᵊn] *n* 汚染 [osen]

Polynesia [pɒləni̇ʒə] *n* ポリネシア [porineshia]

Polynesian [pɒləni̇ʒən] *adj* ポリネシアの [Porineshia no] ▷*n* (*language*) ポリネシア語 [Porineshia go], (*person*) ポリネシア人 [Porineshia jin]

pomegranate [pɒmɪgrænɪt] *n* ザクロ [zakuro]

pond [pɒnd] *n* 池 [ike]

pony [pouni] *n* ポニー [ponii]

ponytail [pouniteɪl] *n* ポニーテール [poniiteeru]

poodle [pud·ᵊl] *n* プードル [puudoru]

pool [pul] *n* (*resources*) 共同資金 [kyoudou shikin], (*water*) プール [puuru] (水泳); **public swimming pool** *npl* 公衆浴場 [koushuu yokujou]; **swimming pool** *n* スイミ

ングプール [suimingupuuru]; **wading pool** *n* 子供用プール [kodomoyou puuru]; **Is it an outdoor pool?** それは屋外プールですか? [sore wa okugai-puuru desu ka?]; **Is the pool heated?** プールは温水ですか? [puuru wa onsui desu ka?]; **Is there a children's pool?** 子供用のプールはありますか? [kodomo-you no puuru wa arimasu ka?]; **Is there a shallow pool for the children?** 子供用の浅いプールはありますか? [kodomo-you no asai puuru wa arimasu ka?]; **Is there a swimming pool?** スイミングプールはありますか? [suimingu-puuru wa arimasu ka?]

poor [puər] *adj* 貧しい [mazushii]

popcorn [pɒpkɔrn] *n* ポップコーン [poppukoon]

pope [poup] *n* ローマ法王 [Rooma Houou]

poplar [pɒplər] *n* ポプラ [popura]

poppy [pɒpi] *n* ケシ [keshi]

Popsicle® [pɒpsɪkᵊl] *n* アイスキャンディー [aisu kyandii]

popular [pɒpyələr] *adj* 人気のある [ninki no aru]

popularity [pɒpyəlærɪti] *n* 人気 [ninki] (評判)

population [pɒpyəleɪʃᵊn] *n* 人口 [jinkou]

pop-up book *n* 開くと絵が飛び出す本 [hiraku to e ga tobidasu hon]

porch [pɔrtʃ] *n* ポーチ [poochi]

pork [pɔrk] *n* ポーク [pooku], 豚肉 [butaniku]; **pork chop** *n* ポークチョップ [pookuchoppu]; **I don't eat pork** 私は豚肉を食べません [watashi wa butaniku o tabemasen]

porn [pɔrn] *n* ポルノ [poruno]

pornographic [pɔrnəgræfɪk] *adj* ポルノの [poruno no]

pornography [pɔrnɒgrəfi] *n* ポルノ [poruno]

port [pɔrt] *n* (*ships*) 港 [minato], (*wine*) ポートワイン [pootowain]

portable [pɔrtəbᵊl] *adj* 持ち運びできる [mochihakobi dekiru]

porter [pɔrtər] *n* ポーター [pootaa]

portfolio [pɔrtfouliou] *n* 紙ばさみ [kamibasami]

P

portion [pɔrʃ·n] *n* 部分 [bubun]

portrait [pɔrtrɪt, -trɛɪt] *n* 肖像画 [shouzouga]

Portugal [pɔrtʃəg·l] *n* ポルトガル [porutogaru]

Portuguese [pɔrtʃugiz] *adj* ポルトガルの [porutogaru no] ▷ *n (language)* ポルトガル語 [porutogarugo], *(person)* ポルトガル人 [porutogarujin]

position [pəzɪʃ·n] *n* 位置 [ichi]

positive [pɒzɪtɪv] *adj* 確信している [kakushin shite iru]

possess [pəzɛs] *v* 所有する [shoyuu suru]

possession [pəzɛʃ·n] *n* 所有 [shoyuu]

possibility [pɒsɪbɪlɪti] *n* 可能性 [kanousei]

possible [pɒsɪb·l] *adj* 可能な [kanou na]

possibly [pɒsɪbli] *adv* ことによると [koto ni yoru to]

post [poust] *n (stake)* 柱 [hashira]; **post office** *n* 郵便局 [yuubinkyoku]

postage [poustɪdʒ] *n* 郵便料金 [yuubin ryoukin]

postal [poust·l] *adj* **postal worker** *n* 郵便配達人 [yuubin haitatsunin]

postcard [poustkɑrd] *n* はがき [hagaki], 郵便はがき [yuubin hagaki]; **Do you have any postcards?** 郵便はがきはありますか? [yuubin-hagaki wa arimasu ka?]; **I'm looking for postcards** 私は郵便はがきを探しています [watashi wa yuubin-hagaki o sagashite imasu]; **May I have stamps for four postcards to...** ···あての郵便はがき四枚分の切手をもらえますか? [... ate no yuubin-hagaki yonmai-bun no kitte o moraemasu ka?]; **Where can I buy some postcards?** どこで郵便はがきを買えますか? [doko de yuubin-hagaki o o kaemasu ka?]

poster [poustər] *n* ポスター [posutaa]

postmark [poustmɑrk] *n* 消印 [keshiin]

postpone [poustpoun, pouspoun] *v* 延期する [enki suru]

pot [pɒt] *n* ポット [potto], 深鍋 [shin nabe]; **potted plant** *n* 鉢植え植物 [hachiue shokubutsu]

potato [pəteɪtou] *(pl potatoes) n* ジャガイモ [jagaimo], ポテト [poteto]; **baked potato** *n* ジャケットポテト [jaketto poteto], ベークドポテト [beekudopoteto]; **mashed potatoes** *npl* マッシュポテト [masshu poteto]; **potato chips** *npl* ポテトチップス [potetochippusu]; **potato peeler** *n* 皮むき器 [kawamukiki]

potential [pətɛnʃ·l] *adj* 可能性のある [kanousei no aru] ▷ *n* 可能性 [kanousei]

pothole [pɒthoul] *n* ポットホール [pottohooru]

pottery [pɒtəri] *n* 陶器 [touki]

potty [pɒti] *n* 幼児用の便器 [youjiyou no benki]; **Do you have a potty?** 幼児用の便器はありますか? [youji-you no benki wa arimasu ka?]

pouch [pautʃ] *n* 入れ [ire]

pound [paund] *n* ポンド [pondo]; **pound sterling** *n* 英貨ポンド [Eika pondo]

pour [pɔr] *v* 流す [nagasu]

poverty [pɒvərti] *n* 貧困 [hinkon]

powder [paudər] *n* パウダー [paudaa], 粉 [kona], 粉末 [funmatsu]; **baking powder** *n* ベーキングパウダー [beekingupaudaa]; **talcum powder** *n* タルカムパウダー [tarukamupaudaa]

power [pauər] *n* 能力 [nouryoku]; **power outage** *n* 停電 [teiden]; **solar power** *n* 太陽エネルギー [taiyou enerugii]

powerful [pauərfəl] *adj* 強力な [kyouryoku na]

practical [præktɪk·l] *adj* 実際的な [jissaiteki na]

practically [præktɪkli] *adv* 実際に [jissai ni]

practice [præktɪs] *n* 練習 [renshuu] ▷ *v* 練習する [renshuu suru]

praise [preɪz] *v* ほめる [homeru]

prank [præŋk] *n* 戯れ [tawamure]

pray [preɪ] *v* 祈る [inoru]

prayer [prɛər] *n* 祈り [inori]

precaution [prɪkɔʃ·n] *n* 用心 [youjin]

preceding [prɪsidɪŋ] *adj* 前の [mae no]

precious [prɛʃəs] *adj* 貴重な [kichou na]

precise [prɪsaɪs] *adj* 正確な [seikaku na]

precisely [prɪsaɪsli] *adv* 正確に [seikaku ni]

predecessor [prɛdɪsɛsər] n 前任者 [zenninsha]

predict [prɪdɪkt] v 予想する [yosou suru]

predictable [prɪdɪktəbl] adj 予想できる [yosou dekiru]

prefect [prifɛkt] n 監督生 [kantokusei]

prefer [prɪfɜr] v ･･･の方を好む [...no hou wo konomu]

preferably [prɛfərəbli, prɛfrə-, prɪfɜrə-] adv 好んで [kononde]

preference [prɛfərəns] n 好み [konomi]

pregnancy [prɛgnənsi] n 妊娠 [ninshin]

pregnant [prɛgnənt] adj 妊娠した [ninshin shita]

prehistoric [prihɪstɔrɪk] adj 有史前の [yuushi mae no]

prejudice [prɛdʒədɪs] n 偏見 [henken]

prejudiced [prɛdʒədɪst] adj 偏見をもった [henken-o motta]

premature [primətʃuər] adj 時期尚早の [jikishousou no]

premiere [prɪmɪər, prɪmyɛər] n 初演 [shoen]

premises [prɛmɪsɪz] npl 土地建物 [tochi tatemono]

premonition [primənɪʃn, prɛm-] n 予感 [yokan]

prenatal [prineɪtl] adj 出産前の [shussan-mae no]

preoccupied [priɒkyəpaɪd] adj ･･･に余念がない [... ni yonen ga nai]

prepaid [pripeɪd] adj プリペイドの [puripeido no]

preparation [prɛpəreɪʃn] n 準備 [junbi]

prepare [prɪpɛər] v 準備する [junbi suru]

prepared [prɪpɛərd] adj 用意ができた [youi ga dekita]

Presbyterian [prɛzbɪtɪəriən] adj 長老派の [chourouha no] ▷ n 長老派の人 [chourouha no hito]

prescribe [prɪskraɪb] v 処方する [shohou suru]

prescription [prɪskrɪpʃn] n 処方箋 [shohousen]; **Where can I have this prescription filled?** どこでこの処方箋の薬を出してもらえますか? [doko de kono shohousen no kusuri o dashite moraemasu ka?]

presence [prɛzns] n 存在 [sonzai]

present [prɛznt] adj 居る [iru] ▷ n (gift) プレゼント [purezento], (time being) 現在 [genzai] ▷ v 紹介する [shoukai suru]; **I'm looking for a present for my husband** 私は夫へのプレゼントを探しています [watashi wa otto e no purezento o sagashite imasu]

presentation [prizɛnteɪʃn] n 紹介 [shoukai]

preservative [prɪzɜrvətɪv] n 保存料 [hozonryou]

preserve [prɪzɜrv] n (land) 保護区 [hogoku]

preserver [prɪzɜrvər] n **life preserver** n 救命ベルト [kyuumei beruto]

president [prɛzɪdənt] n 大統領 [daitouryou], (business) 社長 [shachou]

press [prɛs] n プレス機 [puresuki] ▷ v 押す [osu]; **press conference** n 記者会見 [kishakaiken]

pressure [prɛʃər] n 圧力 [atsuryoku] ▷ v 圧力を加える [atsuryoku o kuwaeru]; **blood pressure** n 血圧 [ketsuatsu]

prestige [prɛstiʒ, -stidʒ] n 名声 [meisei]

prestigious [prɛstɪdʒəs, -stidʒəs] adj 名声のある [meisei no aru]

presumably [prɪzuməbli] adv 思うに [omou ni]

presume [prɪzum] v 推定する [suitei suru]

pretend [prɪtɛnd] v ふりをする [furi wo suru]

pretext [pritɛkst] n 口実 [koujitsu]

prettily [prɪtɪli] adv きれいに [kirei ni]

pretty [prɪti] adj きれいな [kirei na] ▷ adv かなり [kanari]

prevent [prɪvɛnt] v 防ぐ [fusegu]

prevention [prɪvɛnʃn] n 予防 [yobou]

previous [priviəs] adj 以前の [izen no]

previously [priviəsli] adv 以前に [izen ni]

prey [preɪ] n 餌食 [ejiki]

price [praɪs] n 価格 [kakaku]; **price list** n 価格表 [kakakuhyou]; **retail price** n 小売価格

[kourikakaku]; **selling price** *n* 販売価格 [hanbai kakaku]

pricey [praɪsi] *adj (expensive)* 高価な [kouka na]

prick [prɪk] *v* チクリと刺す [chikuri to sasu], 突き刺さる [tsukisasaru]

pride [praɪd] *n* 誇り [hokori]

priest [prist] *n* 司祭 [shisai]

primarily [praɪmɛrɪli] *adv* 主として [shutoshite]

primary [praɪmɛri, -məri] *adj* 第一の [daiichi no]

primitive [prɪmɪtɪv] *adj* 初期の [shoki no]

primrose [prɪmrouz] *n* サクラソウ [sakurasou]

prince [prɪns] *n* 王子 [ouji]

princess [prɪnsɪs, -sɛs] *n* 王女 [oujo]

principal [prɪnsɪp·l] *adj* 主な [omo na] ▸ *n* 校長 [kouchou], *(principal)* 長 [chou] *(統率)*; **assistant principal** *n* 課長補佐 [kachouho-sa]

principle [prɪnsɪp·l] *n* 主義 [shugi]

print [prɪnt] *n* 印刷物 [insatsubutsu] ▸ *v* 印刷する [insatsu suru]

printer [prɪntər] *n (machine)* 印刷機 [insatsuki], *(person)* 印刷業者 [insatsu gyousha]

printing [prɪntɪŋ] *n* **How much is printing?** 印刷はいくらですか? [insatsu wa ikura desu ka?]

printout [prɪntaut] *n* ハードコピー [haadokopii]

priority [praɪɔrɪti] *n* 優先 [yuusen]; **How long will it take by priority mail?** 優先郵便でどのくらいの日数がかかりますか? [yuusen-yuubin de dono kurai no nissuu ga kakarimasu ka?]

prison [prɪz·n] *n* 刑務所 [keimusho]

prisoner [prɪzənər] *n* 囚人 [shuujin]

privacy [praɪvəsi] *n* プライバシー [puraibashii]

private [praɪvɪt] *adj* 個人的な [kojinteki na]; **private property** *n* 個人の所有物 [kojin no

shoyuubutsu]; **private school** *n* パブリックスクール [paburikkusukuuru]

privatize [praɪvətaɪz] *v* 民営化する [min'eika suru]

privilege [prɪvɪlɪdʒ, prɪvlɪdʒ] *n* 特権 [tokken]

prize [praɪz] *n* 賞 [shou]

prizewinner [praɪzwɪnər] *n* 受賞者 [jushousha]

probability [prɒbəbɪlɪti] *n* 見込み [mikomi]

probable [prɒbəb·l] *adj* ありそうな [arisou na]

probably [prɒbəbli] *adv* 多分 [tabun]

problem [prɒbləm] *n* 問題 [mondai]; **There's a problem with the room** 部屋に問題があります [heya ni mondai ga arimasu]; **Who do we contact if there are problems?** 問題があったときに誰に連絡すればいいのですか? [mondai ga atta toki ni dare ni renraku sureba ii no desu ka?]

proceedings [prəsidɪŋz] *npl* 進行 [shinkou]

proceeds [prousidz] *npl* 収益 [shoueki]

process [prɒsɛs] *n* 過程 [katei]

procession [prəsɛʃ·n] *n* 行進 [koushin]

produce *v* 生産する [seisan suru]

producer [prədusər] *n* プロデューサー [purodyuusaa]

product [prɒdʌkt] *n* 製品 [seihin], 品 [hin]

production [prədʌkʃ·n] *n* 聖像 [seizou], 生産 [seisan]

productivity [prɒdʌktɪvɪti] *n* 生産性 [seisansei]

profession [prəfɛʃ·n] *n* 職業 [shokugyou]

professional [prəfɛʃən·l] *adj* 職業的な [shokugyouteki na] ▸ *n* 専門家 [senmonka]

professionally [prəfɛʃənəli] *adv* 職業的に [shokugyouteki ni]

professor [prəfɛsər] *n* 教授 [kyouju]

profit [prɒfɪt] *n* 収益 [shoueki]

profitable [prɒfɪtəb·l] *adj* 収益の多い [shuueki no oui]

program [prougræm, -grəm] *n* プログラム [puroguramu], 番組 [bangumi] ▸ *v* プログラムを作成する [puroguramu-o sakusei suru]; **Can I use messenger programs?** メッセン

ジャープログラムを使えますか? [messenjaa-
proguramu o tsukaemasu ka?]

programmer [proʊgræmər] *n* プログラマー
[puroguramaa]

programming [proʊgræmɪŋ] *n* プログラム作
成 [puroguramu sakusei]

progress *n* 進歩 [shinpo]

prohibit [proʊhɪbɪt] *v* 禁止する [kinshi suru]

prohibited [proʊhɪbɪtɪd] *adj* 禁止された
[kinshi sareta]

project *n* 企画 [kikaku]

projector [prədʒɛktər] *n* プロジェクター
[purojekutaa]; **overhead projector** *n* オーバ
ーヘッドプロジェクター [oobaaheddopuro-
jekutaa]

promenade [prɒməneɪd, -nɑd] *n* 海岸の遊歩
道 [kaigan no yuuhodou]

promise [prɒmɪs] *n* 約束 [yakusoku] ▷ *v* 約束
する [yakusoku suru]

promising [prɒmɪsɪŋ] *adj* 将来有望な
[shourai yuubou na]

promote [prəmoʊt] *v* 促進する [sokushin
suru]

promotion [prəmoʊʃⁿn] *n* 促進 [sokushin]

prompt [prɒmpt] *adj* 即座の [sokuza no]

promptly [prɒmptli] *adv* 即座に [sokuza ni]

pronoun [proʊnaʊn] *n* 代名詞 [daimeishi]

pronounce [prənaʊns] *v* 発音する [hatsuon
suru]

pronunciation [prənʌnsieɪʃⁿn] *n* 発音
[hatsuon]

proof [pruf] *n* (*evidence*) 証拠 [shouko], (*for
checking*) 校正刷り [kouseizuri]

propaganda [prɒpəgændə] *n* プロパガンダ
[puropaganda]

proper [prɒpər] *adj* 適切な [tekisetsu na]

properly [prɒpərli] *adv* 適切に [tekisetsu ni]

property [prɒpərti] *n* 所有物 [shoyuubutsu];
private property *n* 個人の所有物 [kojin no
shoyuubutsu]

proportion [prəpɔrʃⁿn] *n* 比率 [hiritsu]

proportional [prəpɔrʃənⁿl] *adj* 比例した [hirei
shita]

proposal [prəpoʊzⁿl] *n* 提案 [teian]

propose [prəpoʊz] *v* 提案する [teian suru]

prosecute [prɒsɪkyut] *v* 起訴する [kiso suru]

prospect [prɒspɛkt] *n* 見通し [mitoushi]

prospectus [prəspɛktəs] *n* 案内書
[annaisho]

prosperity [prɒspɛrɪti] *n* 繁栄 [han-ei]

prostitute [prɒstɪtut] *n* 売春婦 [baishunfu]

prostitution [prɒstɪtuʃⁿn] *n* 売春 [baishun]

protect [prətɛkt] *v* 保護する [hogo suru]

protection [prətɛkʃⁿn] *n* 保護 [hogo]

protein [proʊtin] *n* 蛋白質 [tanpakushitsu]

protest *n* 抗議 [kougi] ▷ *vb* [prətɛst]
抗議する [kougi suru]

Protestant [prɒtɪstənt] *adj* プロテスタントの
[purotesutanto no] ▷ *n* プロテスタント
[purotesutanto]

proud [praʊd] *adj* 誇りに思う [hokori ni omou]

prove [pruv] *v* 立証する [risshou suru]

proverb [prɒvɜrb] *n* ことわざ [kotowaza]

provide [prəvaɪd] *v* 供給する [kyoukyuu
suru]; **provide for** *v* 準備する [junbi suru]

provisional [prəvɪʒənⁿl] *adj* 暫定的な
[zanteiteki na]

proximity [prɒksɪmɪti] *n* 近接 [kinsetsu]

prune [prun] *n* プルーン [puruun]

pry [praɪ] *v* 詮索する [sensaku suru]

pseudonym [sudənɪm] *n* ペンネーム
[penneemu]

psychiatric [saɪkiætrɪk] *adj* 精神科の
[seishinka no]

psychiatrist [sɪkaɪətrɪst] *n* 精神科医
[seishinka-i]

psychological [saɪkəlɒdʒɪkⁿl] *adj* 心理的な
[shinriteki na]

psychologist [saɪkɒləldʒɪst] *n* 心理学者
[shinrigakusha]

psychology [saɪkɒlədʒi] *n* 心理学
[shinrigaku]

psychotherapy [saɪkoʊθɛrəpi] *n* 心理療法
[shinri ryouhou]

pub [pʌb] *n* パブ [pabu]; **pub owner** *n* パブの
主人 [pabu no shujin]

public [pʌblɪk] *adj* 公衆の [koushuu no] ▷ *n* 公衆 [koushuu]; **public holiday** *n* 祝祭日 [shukusaijitsu]; **public opinion** *n* 世論 [yoron]; **public relations** *npl* 広報 [kouhou]; **public swimming pool** *npl* 公衆浴場 [koushuu yokujou]; **public transportation** *n* 公共交通機関 [koukyou koutsuu kikan]

publication [pʌblɪkeɪʃən] *n* 出版 [shuppan]

publicity [pʌblɪsɪtɪ] *n* 宣伝 [senden]

publish [pʌblɪʃ] *v* 出版する [shuppan suru]

publisher [pʌblɪʃər] *n* 出版業者 [shuppan gyousha]

puddle [pʌdᵊl] *n* 水たまり [mizutamari]

Puerto Rico [pwɛrtou riːkou] *n* プエルトリコ [puerutoriko]

pull [pʊl] *v* 引く [hiku]

pull down *v* 取り壊す [torikowasu]

pull out *vt* 車線から出る [shasen kara deru]

pullover [pʊlouvər] *n* プルオーバー [puruoobaa]

pull up *v* 止める [tomeru]

pulse [pʌls] *n* 脈拍 [myakuhaku], 同時 [douji]

pump [pʌmp] *n* ポンプ [ponpu] ▷ *v* ポンプで注入する [ponpu de chuunyuu suru]; **bicycle pump** *n* 自転車ポンプ [jitensha ponpu]; **Pump number three, please** 3番のポンプをお願いします [san-ban no ponpu o o-negai shimasu]

pumpkin [pʌmpkɪn] *n* カボチャ [kabocha]

pump up *v* ポンプで膨らませる [ponpu de fukuramaseru]

punch [pʌntʃ] *n* (blow) パンチ [panchi] (殴打), (hot drink) パンチ [panchi] (飲み物) ▷ *v* げんこつをくらわす [genkotsu-o kurawasu]

punctual [pʌŋktʃuəl] *adj* 時間厳守の [jikangenshu no]

punctuation [pʌŋktʃueɪʃᵊn] *n* 句読 [kutou]

puncture [pʌŋktʃər] *n* 刺し穴 [sashiana]

punish [pʌnɪʃ] *v* 罰する [bassuru]

punishment [pʌnɪʃmənt] *n* 罰 [batsu], 処罰 [shobatsu]; **capital punishment** *n* 死刑 [shikei]; **corporal punishment** *n* 体刑 [taikei]

punk [pʌŋk] *n* チンピラ [chinpira]

pupil [pyuːpɪl] *n* (eye) 瞳孔 [doukou], (learner) 生徒 [seito]

puppet [pʌpɪt] *n* あやつり人形 [ayatsuri ningyou]

puppy [pʌpi] *n* 子犬 [koinu]

purchase [pɜrtʃɪs] *v* 購入する [kounyuu suru]

pure [pyuər] *adj* 純粋な [junsui na]

purple [pɜrpᵊl] *adj* 紫色の [murasakiiro no]

purpose [pɜrpəs] *n* 目的 [mokuteki]

purr [pɜr] *v* ゴロゴロとのどを鳴らす [gorogoro to nodo-o narasu]

purse [pɜrs] *n* **coin purse** *n* 財布 [saifu]

pursue [pərsuː] *v* 追跡する [tsuiseki suru], ···を追う […-o ou]

pursuit [pərsuːt] *n* 追跡 [tsuiseki]

pus [pʌs] *n* 膿 [umi]

push [pʊʃ] *v* 押す [osu]

push-up *n* 腕立て伏せ [udetatefuse]

put [pʊt] *v* 置く [oku]

put away *v* 取っておく [totteoku]

put back *v* もとへ返す [moto-e kaesu]

put forward *v* 提唱する [teishou suru]

put in *v* 投入する [tounyuu suru]

put off *v* 延期する [enki suru]

put up *v* 建てる [tateru]

puzzle [pʌzᵊl] *n* 難問 [nanmon]; **jigsaw puzzle** *n* ジグソーパズル [jigusoo pazuru]

puzzled [pʌzᵊld] *adj* 困った [komatta]

puzzling [pʌzᵊlɪŋ] *adj* 困らせる [komaraseru]

pyramid [pɪrəmɪd] *n* ピラミッド [piramiddo]

Q

Qatar [kɑtɑr] n カタール [kataaru]

quail [kweɪl] n ウズラ [uzura]

quaint [kweɪnt] adj 古風で趣のある [kofuu de omomuki no aru]

Quaker [kweɪkər] n クエーカー [kueekaa]

qualification [kwɒlɪfɪkeɪʃⁿn] n 資格 [shikaku]

qualified [kwɒlɪfaɪd] adj 資格のある [shikaku no aru]

qualify [kwɒlɪfaɪ] v 資格を取る [shikaku wo toru]

quality [kwɒlɪti] n 質 [shitsu]

quantify [kwɒntɪfaɪ] v 量を決める [ryou-o kimeru]

quantity [kwɒntɪti] n 量 [ryou]

quarantine [kwɒrəntin] n 検疫期間 [ken'eki kikan]

quarrel [kwɒrəl] n 口論 [kouron], (argument) 喧嘩 [kenka] ▷ v 口論する [kouron suru], (to argue) 喧嘩する [kenka suru]

quarry [kwɒri] n 採石場 [saisekijou]

quarter [kwɔrtər] n 4分の1 [yonbun no ichi]; quarter final n 準々決勝 [junjunkesshou]

quartet [kwɔrtɛt] n 四重奏 [shijuusou]

quay [ki] n 埠頭 [futou]

queen [kwin] n 女王 [joou]

query [kwɪəri] n 疑問 [gimon] ▷ v 尋ねる [tazuneru]

question [kwɛstʃⁿn] n 質問 [shitsumon] ▷ v 質問する [shitsumon suru]; question mark n 疑問符 [gimonfu]

questionnaire [kwɛstʃənɛər] n アンケート用紙 [ankeeto youshi]

quick [kwɪk] adj 素早い [subayai]

quickly [kwɪkli] adv 素早く [subayaku]

quiet [kwaɪɪt] adj 静かな [shizuka na]; I'd like a quiet room 静かな部屋がいいのですが [shizuka na heya ga ii no desu ga]; Is there a quiet beach near here? この近くに静かなビーチはありますか? [kono chikaku ni shizuka na biichi wa arimasu ka?]

quietly [kwaɪɪtli] adv 静かに [shizuka ni]

quilt [kwɪlt] n キルト [kiruto] (ベッドの上掛け)

quit [kwɪt] v やめる [yameru] (よす)

quite [kwaɪt] adv かなり [kanari]; It's quite a long way かなり遠いです [kanari tooi desu]

quiz [kwɪz] (pl quizzes) n クイズ [kuizu]

quota [kwoʊtə] n 割当て [wariate]

quotation [kwoʊteɪʃⁿn] n 引用文 [in-youbun]; quotation marks npl 引用符 [in-youfu]

quote [kwoʊt] n 引用文 [in-youbun] ▷ v 引用する [inyou suru]

Q

R

rabbi [ræbaɪ] *n* ラビ [rabi]

rabbit [ræbɪt] *n* ウサギ [usagi]

rabies [reɪbiz] *n* 狂犬病 [kyoukenbyou]

race [reɪs] *n* (*contest*) レース [reesu] (*競争*), (*origin*) 人種 [...jinshu...] ▷ *v* 競争する [kyousou suru]

racecar [reɪskɑr] *n* レーシングカー [reeshingukaa]

racehorse [reɪshɔrs] *n* 競走馬 [kyousouba]

racer [reɪsər] *n* レーサー [reesaa]

racetrack [reɪstræk] *n* レーストラック [reesutorakku], 競馬場 [keibajou]

racial [reɪʃəl] *adj* 人種の [jinshu no]

racing [reɪsɪn] *n* **auto racing** *n* モーターレース [mootaareesu]; **horse racing** *n* 競馬 [keiba]

racism [reɪsɪzəm] *n* 人種差別 [jinshusabetsu]

racist [reɪsɪst] *adj* 人種差別主義者の [jinshu sabetsu shugisha no] ▷ *n* 人種差別主義者 [jinshusabetsushugisha]

rack [ræk] *n* ・・・掛け [...kake] (*帽子や洋服*); **luggage rack** *n* 手荷物置き棚 [tenimotsu okidana]

racket [rækɪt] *n* ラケット [raketto], 騒ぎ [sawagi]; **tennis racket** *n* テニスラケット [tenisuraketto]; **Where can I rent a racket?** どこでラケットを借りられますか? [doko de raketto o kariraremasu ka?]

racoon [rækun] *n* アライグマ [araiguma]

radar [reɪdɑr] *n* レーダー [reedaa]

radiation [reɪdieɪʃn] *n* 放射 [housha]

radiator [reɪdieɪtər] *n* ラジエーター [rajieetaa]; **There's a leak in the radiator** ラジエーターに漏れがあります [rajieetaa ni more ga arimasu]

radio [reɪdioʊ] *n* ラジオ [rajio]; **digital radio** *n* デジタルラジオ [dejitaru rajio]; **radio station** *n* ラジオ局 [rajio kyoku]; **May I turn off the radio?** ラジオを消してもいいですか? [rajio o keshite mo ii desu ka?]; **May I turn on the radio?** ラジオをつけてもいいですか? [rajio o tsukete mo ii desu ka?]

radioactive [reɪdioʊæktɪv] *adj* 放射性のある [houshasei no aru]

radio-controlled *adj* 無線制御の [musen seigyo no]

radish [rædɪʃ] *n* ラディッシュ [radisshu]

raffle [ræfl] *n* 富くじ [tomikuji]

raft [ræft] *n* いかだ [ikada]

rag [ræg] *n* ぼろきれ [borokire]

rage [reɪdʒ] *n* 激怒 [gekido]; **road rage** *n* ドライバーが路上で激怒すること [doraibaa ga rojou de gekido suru koto]

raid [reɪd] *n* 襲撃 [shuugeki] ▷ *v* 襲撃する [shuugeki suru]

rail [reɪl] *n* 手すり [tesuri]

railcard [reɪlkɑrd] *n* 鉄道割引証 [tetsudou waribikishou]

railings [reɪlɪnz] *npl* 手すり [tesuri]

railroad [reɪlroʊd] *n* 鉄道 [tetsudou]; **railroad crossing** *n* 踏切 [fumikiri]

rain [reɪn] *n* 雨 [ame] ▷ *v* 雨が降る [ame ga furu]; **acid rain** *n* 酸性雨 [sanseiu]; **Do you think it's going to rain?** 雨が降ると思いますか? [ame ga furu to omoimasu ka?]; **It's raining** 雨が降っています [ame ga futte imasu]

rainbow [reɪnboʊ] *n* 虹 [niji]

raincoat [reɪnkoʊt] *n* レインコート [reinkooto], カグール [kaguuru]

rainforest [reɪnfɔrɪst] *n* 熱帯雨林 [nettai urin]

rainy [reɪni] *adj* 雨の [ame no]

raise [reɪz] *v* 上げる [ageru]

raisin [reɪzⁿn] *n* レーズン [reezun]; **golden raisin** *n* スルタナ [surutana]

rake [reɪk] *n* 熊手 [kumade]

rally [ræli] *n* 大集会 [daishuukai]

ram [ræm] *n* 去勢していない雄羊 [kyosei shite inai ohitsuji] ▷ *v* 打ち固める [uchikatameru]

Ramadan [ræmədɑn] *n* ラマダーン [ramadaan]

ramp [ræmp] *n* 傾斜面 [keishamen]; **highway ramp** *n* 高速道路の進入退出路 [kousoku douro no shinnyuu taishutsuro]

random [rændəm] *adj* 手当たり次第の [teatari shidai no], 広い [hiroi]

range [reɪndʒ] *n* (limits) 範囲 [han-i], (mountains) 山脈 [sanmyaku] ▷ *v* 変化する [henka suru]

rank [ræŋk] *n* (line) 列 [retsu], (status) 階級 [kaikyuu], 地位 [chii] ▷ *v* ランク付けする [ranku zuke suru]

ransom [rænsəm] *n* 身代金 [minoshirokin]

rape [reɪp] *n* (plant) セイヨウアブラナ [seiyouaburana], (sexual attack) レイプ [reipu], 犯す [okasu]; **I've been raped** 私はレイプされました [watashi wa reipu saremashita]

rapids [ræpɪdz] *npl* 早瀬 [hayase]

rapist [reɪpɪst] *n* 強姦者 [goukansha]

rare [rɛər] *adj* (uncommon) 珍しい [mezurashii], (undercooked) 生焼けの [namayake no]

rarely [rɛərli] *adv* めったに・・・しない [mettani… shinai]

rash [ræʃ] *n* 発疹 [hasshin]; **I have a rash** 私は発疹がでました [watashi wa hasshin ga demashita]

raspberry [ræzbɛri] *n* ラズベリー [razuberii]

rat [ræt] *n* ドブネズミ [dobunezumi]

rate [reɪt] *n* レート [reeto], 割合 [wariai] ▷ *v* 評価する [hyouka suru]; **foreign-exchange rate** *n* 為替レート [kawase reeto]; **interest rate** *n* 利率 [riritsu]; **What is the rate for... to...?** ・・・を・・・に替える為替レートはいくらですか? [... o... ni kaeru kawase-reeto wa ikura desu ka?]; **What's the exchange rate?** 為替レートはいくらですか? [kawase-reeto wa ikura desu ka?]

rather [ræðər] *adv* かなり [kanari], 無思慮 [mu shiryo]

ratio [reɪʃou, -ʃiou] *n* 比率 [hiritsu]

rational [ræʃənⁿl] *adj* 理にかなった [ri ni kanatta]

rattle [rætⁿl] *n* ガラガラいう音 [garagara iu oto]

rattlesnake [rætⁿlsneɪk] *n* ガラガラヘビ [garagarahebi]

rave [reɪv] *n* べたぼめ [betabome] ▷ *v* わめく [wameku]

raven [reɪvⁿn] *n* カラス [karasu]

ravenous [rævənəs] *adj* 飢えた [ueta]

ravine [rəvin] *n* 峡谷 [kyoukoku]

raw [rɔ] *adj* 生の [nama no]

razor [reɪzər] *n* かみそり [kamisori]; **razor blade** *n* 安全かみそりの刃 [anzen kamisori no ha]

re- *pref* 再 [sai]

reach [riːtʃ] *v* 着く [tsuku]

react [riækt] *v* 反応する [hannou suru]

reaction [riækʃⁿn] *n* 反応 [hannou]

reactor [riæktər] *n* 原子炉 [genshiro]

read [riːd] *v* 読む [yomu]

reader [riːdər] *n* 読者 [dokusha]

readily [rɛdɪli] *adv* すぐに [sugu ni]

reading [riːdɪŋ] *n* 読書 [dokusho]

read out *v* 読み上げる [yomiageru]

ready [rɛdi] *adj* 用意のできた [youi no dekita], 容易 [youi]

ready-to-serve *adj* 調理済みの [chouri zumi no]

real [riːl] *adj* 実在の [jitsuzai no]

realistic [riəlɪstɪk] *adj* 現実的な [genjitsuteki na]

reality [riælɪti] *n* 現実 [genjitsu]; **reality TV** *n* リアリティーテレビ番組 [riaritii terebi

R

bangumi]; **virtual reality** n バーチャルリアリティー [baacharuriariteii]

realize [ríəlaɪz] v 十分に理解する [juubun ni rikai suru]

really [ríəli] adv 本当に [hontou ni]

rear [ɹɪəɹ] adj 後ろの [ushiro no] ▷ n 後ろ [ushiro]; **rearview mirror** n バックミラー [bakkumiraa]

reason [ríz·n] n 理由 [riyuu], 原因 [gen'in]

reasonable [rízənəb·l] adj 理にかなった [ri ni kanatta]

reasonably [rízənəbli] adv 理にかなって [ri ni kanatte]

reassure [riəʃʊəɹ] v 安心させる [anshin saseru]

reassuring [riəʃʊərɪŋ] adj 安心させる [anshin saseru]

rebate [ríbeɪt] n リベート [ribeeto]

rebellious [rɪbɛlyəs] adj 謀反の [muhon no]

rebuild [ribíld] v 再建する [saiken suru]

receipt [rɪsít] n 受領証 [juryoushou]

receipts [rɪsít] npl (money) 収入 [shuunyuu]

receive [rɪsív] v 受け取る [uketoru]

receiver [rɪsívəɹ] n (electronic) 受信機 [jushinki], (person) 受取人 [uketorinin]

recent [rís·nt] adj 最近の [saikin no]

recently [rís·ntli] adv 最近 [saikin]; **I had the flu recently** 私は最近インフルエンザにかかりました [watashi wa saikin infuruenza ni kakarimashita]

reception [rɪsɛpʃ·n] n 受付 [uketsuke]

receptionist [rɪsɛpʃənɪst] n 受付係 [uketsukegakari]

recession [rɪsɛʃ·n] n 景気後退 [keikikoutai]

recharge [ritʃɑrdʒ] v 再充電する [saijuuden suru]

recipe [rɛsɪpi] n 調理法 [chourihou]

recipient [rɪsɪpiənt] n 受取人 [uketorinin]

reclining [rɪklaɪnɪŋ] adj リクライニング式の [rikurainingu shiki no], 肘掛け [hijikake]

recognizable [rɛkəgnaɪzəb·l] adj 認識できる [ninshiki dekiru]

recognize [rɛkəgnaɪz] v 分かる [wakaru]

recollection [rɛkəlɛkʃ·n] n 思い出 [omoide]

recommend [rɛkəmɛnd] v 勧める [susumeru]

recommendation [rɛkəmɛndeɪʃ·n] n 勧め [susume]

reconsider [rikənsídəɹ] v 考え直す [kangaenaosu]

record n [rɛkərd] n 記録 [kiroku] ▷ v [rɪkɔrd] 記録する [kiroku suru]

recorder [rɪkɔrdəɹ] n (music) リコーダー [rikoodaa], (scribe) 記録係 [kirokugakari]

recording [rɪkɔrdɪŋ] n 録音 [rokuon]

recover [rɪkʌvəɹ] v 回復する [kaifuku suru]

recovery [rɪkʌvəri] n 回復 [kaifuku]

recruitment [rɪkrútmənt] n 新人補充 [shinjin hojuu]

rectangle [rɛktæŋɡ·l] n 長方形 [chouhoukei]

rectangular [rɛktæŋɡələɹ] adj 長方形の [chouhoukei no]

rectify [rɛktɪfaɪ] v 修正する [shuusei suru]

recurring [rɪkɜrɪŋ] adj 繰り返し発生する [kurikaeshi hassei suru]

recycle [risaɪk·l] v 再生利用する [saisei riyou suru]

recycling [risaɪk·lɪŋ] n リサイクル [risaikuru]

red [rɛd] adj 赤い [akai]; **red currant** n 赤スグリ [aka suguri]; **red meat** n 赤身肉 [akaminiku]; **red wine** n 赤ワイン [akawain]; **Red Cross** n 赤十字社 [Sekijuujisha]; **Red Sea** n 紅海 [koukai]

redecorate [ridɛkəreɪt] v 改装する [kaisou suru]

red-haired [rɛdhɛərd] adj 赤毛の [akage no]

redhead [rɛdhɛd] n 赤毛 [akage]

redheaded [rɛdhɛdɪd] adj ショウガ色の [shouga iro no]

redo [ridú] v やり直す [yarinaosu]

red pepper n トウガラシ [tougarashi]

reduce [rɪdús] v 減らす [herasu]

reduction [rɪdʌkʃ·n] n 減少 [genshou]

reed [rid] n アシ [ashi] (植物)

reel [ril] n リール [riiru]

refer [rɪfɜr] v 口に出す [kuchi ni dasu]

referee [rɛfəri] n レフェリー [referii]

reference [rɛfərəns, rɛfrəns] n 参考 [sankou]; reference number n 参照番号 [sanshou bangou]

refill n [rifɪl] 補給 [hokyuu] ▷ v [rifɪl] 補充する [hojuu suru]

refinery [rɪfaɪnəri] n 精製所 [seiseijo]; oil refinery n 石油精製所 [sekiyu seiseijo]

reflect [rɪflɛkt] v 反射する [hansha suru]

reflection [rɪflɛkʃᵊn] n 反射 [hansha]

reflex [riflɛks] n 反射作用 [hansha sayou]

refreshing [rɪfrɛʃɪŋ] adj さわやかな [sawayaka na]

refreshments [rɪfrɛʃmənts] npl 軽食 [keishoku]

refrigerator [rɪfrɪdʒəreɪtər] n 冷蔵庫 [reizouko]

refuel [rifyuəl] v 燃料を補給する [nenryou wo hokyuu suru]

refuge [rɛfyudʒ] n 避難所 [hinanjo]

refugee [rɛfyudʒi] n 避難者 [hinansha]

refund n [rifʌnd] 払い戻し [haraimodoshi], 返金 [henkin] ▷ v [rɪfʌnd] 払い戻す [haraimodosu]; Can I have a refund? 払い戻してもらえますか? [haraimodoshite moraemasu ka?]

refusal [rɪfyuzᵊl] n 拒否 [kyohi]

refuse n [rɛfyus] ごみ [gomi] ▷ v [rɪfyuz] 拒否する [kyohi suru]

regain [rɪgeɪn] v 回復する [kaifuku suru]

regard [rɪgɑrd] n 敬意 [keii] ▷ v みなす [minasu]

regiment [rɛdʒɪmənt] n 連隊 [rentai]

region [ridʒᵊn] n 地域 [chiiki]

regional [ridʒənᵊl] adj 地域の [chiiki no]

register [rɛdʒɪstər] n 登録簿 [tourokubo] ▷ v 登録する [touroku suru]; cash register n レジ [reji]; Where do I register? どこで登録するのですか? [doko de touroku suru no desu ka?]

registered [rɛdʒɪstərd] adj 登録した [touroku shita]

registration [rɛdʒɪstreɪʃᵊn] n 登録 [touroku]

regret [rɪgrɛt] n 後悔 [koukai] ▷ v 後悔する [koukai suru]

regular [rɛgyələr] adj 定期的な [teikiteki na]

regularly [rɛgyələrli] adv 定期的に [teikiteki ni]

regulation [rɛgyəleɪʃᵊn] n 規制 [kisei]

rehearsal [rɪhɜrsᵊl] n リハーサル [rihaasaru]

rehearse [rɪhɜrs] v リハーサルをする [rihaasaru-o suru]

reimburse [riɪmbɜrs] v 弁済する [bensai suru]

reindeer [reɪndɪər] n トナカイ [tonakai]

reins [reɪnz] npl 手綱 [tazuna]

reject v 拒否する [kyohi suru]

relapse [rɪlæps] n 逆戻り [gyakumodori]

related [rɪleɪtɪd] adj 親類の [shinrui no]

relation [rɪleɪʃᵊn] n 関係 [kankei]; public relations npl 広報 [kouhou]

relationship [rɪleɪʃᵊnʃɪp] n 関係 [kankei]

relative [rɛlətɪv] n 親戚 [shinseki]

relatively [rɛlətɪvli] adv 比較的 [hikakuteki]

relax [rɪlæks] v くつろぐ [kutsurogu]

relaxation [rilækseɪʃᵊn] n くつろぎ [kutsurogi]

relaxed [rɪlækst] adj くつろいだ [kutsuroida]

relaxing [rɪlæksɪŋ] adj くつろがせる [kutsurogaseru]

relay n relay race n 交替班 [koutai han]

release [rɪlis] n 解放 [kaihou] ▷ v 解放する [kaihou suru]

relegate [rɛlɪgeɪt] v 左遷する [sasen suru]

relevant [rɛləvᵊnt] adj 関連する [kanren suru]

reliable [rɪlaɪəbᵊl] adj 信頼できる [shinrai dekiru]

relief [rɪlif] n 安心 [anshin]

relieve [rɪliv] v 安心させる [anshin saseru]

relieved [rɪlivd] adj 安心した [anshin shita]

religion [rɪlɪdʒᵊn] n 宗教 [shuukyou]

religious [rɪlɪdʒəs] adj 宗教の [shuukyou no]

reluctant [rɪlʌktənt] adj いやいやながらの [iyaiya nagara no]

reluctantly [rɪlʌktəntli] adv いやいや [iyaiya]

rely [rɪlaɪ] v rely on v あてにする [ate ni suru]

remain [rɪmeɪn] v •••のままである […no mama de aru]

remaining [rɪˈmeɪnɪŋ] *adj* 残りの [nokori no]

remains [rɪˈmeɪnz] *npl* 遺物 [ibutsu], 使い残り [tsukainokori]

remake *n* リメイク [rimeiku]

remark [rɪˈmɑrk] *n* 意見 [iken]

remarkable [rɪˈmɑrkəbəl] *adj* 著しい [ichijirushii]

remarkably [rɪˈmɑrkəbli] *adv* 著しく [ichijirushiku]

remarry [riˈmæri] *v* 再婚する [saikon suru]

remedy [ˈrɛmədi] *n* 治療 [chiryou]

remember [rɪˈmɛmbər] *v* 思い出す [omoidasu]

remind [rɪˈmaɪnd] *v* 思い出させる [omoidasaseru]

reminder [rɪˈmaɪndər] *n* 思い出させるもの [omoidasaseru mono]

remittance [rɪˈmɪtˈns] *n* 送金 [soukin]

remorse [rɪˈmɔrs] *n* 良心の呵責 [ryoushin no kashaku]

remote [rɪˈmoʊt] *adj* 遠く離れた [touku hanareta]; **remote control** *n* リモコン [rimokon]

remotely [rɪˈmoʊtli] *adv* 遠く離れて [touku hanarete]

removable [rɪˈmuˈvəbˈl] *adj* 取り外せる [torihazuseru]

removal [rɪˈmuˈvˈl] *n* 移動 [idou]

remove [rɪˈmuv] *v* 移す [utsusu]

remover [rɪˈmuvər] *n* **nail-polish remover** *n* 除光液 [jokoueki]

rendezvous [ˈrɒndeɪvu] *n* 会う約束 [au yakusoku]

renew [rɪˈnu] *v* 再開する [saikai suru]

renewable [rɪˈnuˈəbˈl] *adj* 再び始められる [futatabi hajimerareru]

renovate [ˈrɛnəveɪt] *v* 修繕する [shuuzen suru]

renowned [rɪˈnaʊnd] *adj* 有名な [yuumei na]

rent [rɛnt] *n* 賃貸料 [chintairyou] ▷ *v* 賃貸する [chintai suru]; **rented car** *n* レンタカー [rentakaa]

rental [ˈrɛntˈl] *n* レンタル [rentaru]; **car rental** *n* レンタカー [rentakaa]; **rental car** *n* レンタカー [rentakaa]

reorganize [riˈɔrgənaɪz] *v* 再編成する [saihensei suru]

repair [rɪˈpɛər] *n* 修理 [shuuri] ▷ *v* 修理する [shuurisuru]; **repair kit** *n* 修理キット [shuuri kitto]; **Can you repair it?** 修理してもらえますか? [shuuri shite moraemasu ka?], それを修理できますか? [sore o shuuri dekimasu ka?]; **Can you repair my watch?** 私の時計を修理できますか? [watashi no tokei o shuuri dekimasu ka?]; **Can you repair this?** これを修理できますか? [kore o shuuri dekimasu ka?]; **Could you give me a ride to the repair shop?** 自動車修理工場まで私を乗せていってもらえますか? [jidousha-shuuri-koujou made watashi o nosete itte moraemasu ka?]; **Could you tow me to a repair shop?** 自動車修理工場までけん引してもらえますか? [jidousha-shuuri-koujou made ken'in shite moraemasu ka?]; **Do you have a repair kit?** 修理キットはありますか? [shuuri-kitto wa arimasu ka?]; **How long will it take to repair?** 修理にどのくらいの時間がかかりますか? [shuuri ni dono kurai no jikan ga kakarimasu ka?]; **How much will the repairs cost?** 修理代はいくらかかりますか? [shuuri-dai wa ikura kakarimasu ka?]; **Is there a repair shop near here?** この近くに自動車修理工場はありますか? [kono chikaku ni jidousha-shuuri-koujou wa arimasu ka?]; **May I have a repair kit?** 修理キットをください [shuuri-kitto o kudasai]; **Where can I get this repaired?** どこでこれを修理してもらえますか? [doko de kore o shuuri shite moraemasu ka?]; **Where is the nearest bike repair shop?** 一番近い自転車修理店はどこですか? [ichiban chikai jitensha shuuri-ten wa doko desu ka?]

reparation [ˌrɛpəreɪʃˈn] *n* 賠償 [baishou]

repay [rɪˈpeɪ] *v* 返済する [hensai suru]

repayment [rɪˈpeɪmənt] *n* 返済 [hensai]

repeat [rɪˈpit] *n* 繰り返し [kurikaeshi] ▷ *v* 繰り返

す [kurikaesu]

repeatedly [rɪpítɪdli] *adv* 繰り返して [kurikaeshite]

repellent [rɪpɛ́lənt] *adj* 嫌な [iya na]; **insect repellent** *n* 虫よけ [mushiyoke]

reperatory theater *n* レパートリー劇団 [repaatorii gekidan]

repercussions [ripərkʌ́ʃ⁻nz] *npl* 反動 [handou]

repetitive [rɪpɛ́tɪtɪv] *adj* 反復性の [hanpuku sei no]

replace [rɪpléɪs] *v* 取って代わる [tottekawaru]

replacement [rɪpléɪsmənt] *n* 置き換え [okikae]

replay *n* [rípleɪ] 再生 [saisei] ▷ *v* [rípleɪ] 再生 する [saisei suru]

replica [rɛ́plɪkə] *n* レプリカ [repurika]

reply [rɪpláɪ] *n* 返事 [henji] ▷ *v* 返事をする [henji-o suru]

report [rɪpɔ́rt] *n* 報告 [houkoku] ▷ *v* 報告する [houkoku suru]; **report card** *n* 通知表 [tsuuchihyou]

reporter [rɪpɔ́rtər] *n* 取材記者 [shuzai kisha]

represent [rɛprɪzɛ́nt] *v* 代表する [daihyou suru]

representative [rɛprɪzɛ́ntətɪv] *adj* 代表する [daihyou suru]

reproduction [riprədʌ́kʃ⁻n] *n* 繁殖 [hanshoku]

reptile [rɛ́ptaɪl, -tɪl] *n* 爬虫類 [hachuurui]

republic [rɪpʌ́blɪk] *n* 共和政体 [kyouwa seitai]

repulsive [rɪpʌ́lsɪv] *adj* むかつくような [mukatsuku you na] (腹が立つ)

reputable [rɛ́pyətəb⁻l] *adj* 信頼できる [shinrai dekiru]

reputation [rɛpyətéɪʃ⁻n] *n* 評判 [hyouban]

request [rɪkwɛ́st] *n* 頼み [tanomi] ▷ *v* 頼む [tanomu]

require [rɪkwáɪər] *v* 必要とする [hitsuyou to suru]

requirement [rɪkwáɪərmənt] *n* 要求 [youkyuu]

rescue [rɛ́skyu] *n* 救助 [kyuujo] ▷ *v* 救う

[sukuu]; **Where is the nearest mountain rescue station?** 一番近い山岳救助隊はどこ ですか? [ichiban chikai sangaku-kyuujo-tai wa doko desu ka?]

research [rɪsɜ́rtʃ, rísɜrtʃ] *n* 調査 [chousa]; **market research** *n* 市場調査 [shijouchousa]

researcher [rɪsɜ́rtʃər, rísɜrtʃər] *n* 研究者 [kenkyuusha]

resemblance [rɪzɛ́mbləns] *n* 類似 [ruiji]

resemble [rɪzɛ́mb⁻l] *v* 似ている [niteiru]

resent [rɪzɛ́nt] *v* 憤慨する [fungai suru]

resentful [rɪzɛ́ntfəl] *adj* 憤慨した [fungai shita]

reservation [rɛzərvéɪʃ⁻n] *n* 予約 [yoyaku], 懸 念 [kenen]; **advance reservation** *n* 事前予 約 [jizen yoyaku]; **Can I change my reservation?** 私の予約を変更できますか? [watashi no yoyaku o henkou dekimasu ka?]; **I have a reservation** 予約してあります [yoyaku shite arimasu]; **I have a seat reservation** 私は座席予約をしてあります [watashi wa zaseki-yoyaku o shite arimasu]; **I want to cancel my reservation** 予約をキ ャンセルしたいのですが [yoyaku o kyanseru shitai no desu ga]; **I'd like to make a reservation for seven-thirty for two people** 七時半に二人分の予約をお願いしま す [shichi-ji-han ni futari-bun no yoyaku o o-negai shimasu]

reserve [rɪzɜ́rv] *n* (*retention*) 蓄え [takuwae] ▷ *v* 予約する [yoyaku suru], 取っておく [totteoku]

reserved [rɪzɜ́rvd] *adj* 控えめの [hikaeme no]

reservoir [rɛ́zərvwɑr] *n* 貯水池 [chosuichi]

residence [rɛ́zɪdəns] *n* 住居 [juukyo], 住宅 [juutaku]

resident [rɛ́zɪdənt] *n* 居住者 [kyojuusha]

residential [rɛzɪdɛ́nʃ⁻l] *adj* 住宅地の [juutakuchi no]

resign [rɪzáɪn] *v* 辞職する [jishoku suru]

resin [rɛ́zɪn] *n* 樹脂 [jushi]

resist [rɪzɪ́st] *v* 抵抗する [teikou suru]

resistance [rɪzɪ́stəns] *n* 抵抗 [teikou]

R

resolution [rɛzəluʃⁿn] *n* 決意 [ketsui]

resort [rɪzɔrt] *n* 行楽地 [kourakuchi]; **resort to** *v* 頼る [tayoru]

resource [risɔrs] *n* 資源 [shigen]; **natural resources** *npl* 天然資源 [tennenshigen]

respect [rɪspɛkt] *n* 尊重 [sonchou] ▷ *v* 尊重する [sonchou suru]

respectable [rɪspɛktəbl] *adj* 尊敬すべき [sonkeisubeki]

respectively [rɪspɛktɪvli] *adv* それぞれ [sorezore]

respond [rɪspɒnd] *v* 返答する [hentou suru]

response [rɪspɒns] *n* 返答 [hentou]

responsibility [rɪspɒnsɪbɪlɪti] *n* 責任 [sekinin]

responsible [rɪspɒnsɪbl] *adj* 責任がある [sekinin ga aru]

rest [rɛst] *n* 休み [yasumi] ▷ *v* 休む [yasumu]; **rest area** *n* 待避場所 [taihi basho]

restaurant [rɛstərənt, -tərɑnt, -trɑnt] *n* レストラン [resutoran]; **Are there any vegetarian restaurants here?** ここにベジタリアン用のレストランはありますか? [koko ni bejitarian-you no resutoran wa arimasu ka?]

restful [rɛstfəl] *adj* 落ち着いた [ochitsuita]

restless [rɛstlɪs] *adj* 落ち着かない [ochitsukanai]

restore [rɪstɔr] *v* 修復する [shuufuku suru]

restrict [rɪstrɪkt] *v* 制限する [seigen suru]

restroom [rɛstrum, -rum] *n* **Are there any restrooms for the disabled?** 身体障害者用のトイレはありますか? [shintai-shougaisha-you no toire wa arimasu ka?]; **Can I use the restroom?** トイレをお借りできますか? [toire o o-kari dekimasu ka?]; **Is there a restroom on the bus?** 車内にトイレはありますか? [shanai ni toire wa arimasu ka?]; **Where are the restrooms?** トイレはどこですか? [toire wa doko desu ka?]

restructure [ristrʌktʃər] *v* 再編成する [saihensei suru]

result [rɪzʌlt] *n* 結果 [kekka] ▷ *v* 結果として生じる [kekka toshite shoujiru]

resume [rɪzum] *v* 再開する [saikai suru]

résumé [rɛzəmeɪ] *n* 履歴書 [rirekisho]

retail [riteɪl] *n* 小売り [kouri] ▷ *v* 小売りする [kouri suru]; **retail price** *n* 小売価格 [kourikakaku]

retailer [riteɪlər] *n* 小売業者 [kourigyousha]

retake *v* 再受験する [saijuken suru]

retire [rɪtaɪər] *v* 退職する [taishoku suru]

retired [rɪtaɪərd] *adj* 退職した [taishoku shita]

retirement [rɪtaɪərmənt] *n* 退職 [taishoku]

retrace [rɪtreɪs] *v* たどりなおす [tadorinaosu]

return [rɪtɜrn] *n* (*coming back*) 帰ること [kaeru koto], (*yield*) 収益 [shoueki] ▷ *vi* 戻る [modoru] ▷ *vt* 戻す [modosu]; **tax return** *n* 所得申告 [shotoku shinkoku]

reunion [riyuniən] *n* 再会 [saikai]

reuse *v* 再使用する [saishiyou suru]

reveal [rɪvil] *v* 明らかにする [akiraka ni suru]

revenge [rɪvɛndʒ] *n* 復讐 [fukushuu]

revenue [rɛvənyu] *n* 収入 [shuunyuu]

reverse [rɪvɜrs] *n* 逆 [gyaku] ▷ *v* 逆にする [gyaku ni suru]

review [rɪvyu] *n* 批評 [hihyou]

revise [rɪvaɪz] *v* 修正する [shuusei suru]

revision [rɪvɪʒⁿ] *n* 修正 [shuusei]

revive [rɪvaɪv] *v* 復活する [fukkatsu suru]

revolting [rɪvoʊltɪŋ] *adj* 実に嫌な [jitsu ni iya na]

revolution [rɛvəluʃⁿn] *n* 革命 [kakumei]

revolutionary [rɛvəluʃənɛri] *adj* 革命的な [kakumeiteki na]

revolver [rɪvɒlvər] *n* リボルバー [riborubaa]

reward [rɪwɔrd] *n* 報酬 [houshuu]

rewarding [rɪwɔrdɪŋ] *adj* 報いのある [mukui no aru]

rewind [riwaɪnd] *v* 巻き戻す [makimodosu]

rheumatism [rumətɪzəm] *n* リウマチ [riumachi]

rhubarb [rubɑrb] *n* ルバーブ [rubaabu]

rhyme [raɪm] *n* **nursery rhyme** *n* 伝承童謡 [denshou douyou]

rhythm [rɪðəm] *n* リズム [rizumu]

rib [rɪb] *n* 肋骨 [rokkotsu]

ribbon [ɑbən] *n* リボン [ribon]

rice [raɪs] *n* 米 [kome]; **brown rice** *n* 玄米 [genmai]

rice wine *n* 酒 [sake]

rich [ɑtʃ] *adj* 金持ちの [kanemochi no]

ride [raɪd] *n* 乗ること [noru koto], *(free ride)* 人を車に乗せてあげること [hito-o kuruma ni nosete ageru koto] ▷ *v* 乗る [noru]

rider [raɪdər] *n* 乗り手 [norite]

ridiculous [rɪdɪkyələs] *adj* ばかげた [bakageta]

riding [raɪdɪŋ] *n* 乗馬 [jouba]; **horseback riding** *n* 乗馬 [jouba]; **Can we go horseback riding?** 乗馬に行けますか? [jouba ni ikemasu ka?]

rifle [raɪfl] *n* ライフル銃 [raifuru juu]

rig [rɪg] *n* 掘削装置 [kussaku souchi]; **oil rig** *n* 石油掘削装置 [sekiyu kussakusouchi]

right [raɪt] *adj (correct)* 正しい [tadashii], *(not left)* 右の [migi no] ▷ *n* 権利 [kenri]; **civil rights** *npl* 公民権 [kouminken]; **human rights** *npl* 人権 [jinken]; **right angle** *n* 直角 [chokkaku]; **right of way** *n* 優先権 [yuusenken]

right-hand *adj* 右側の [migigawa no]; **right-hand drive** *n* 右ハンドル [migi handoru]

right-handed [raɪthændɪd] *adj* 右利きの [migikiki no]

rightly [raɪtli] *adv* 正しく [tadashiku]

right-wing *adj* 右派の [uha no]

rim [rɪm] *n* 縁 [en]

ring [rɪŋ] *n* 指輪 [yubiwa], 輪 [wa], 鳴らすこと [narasu koto]; **ring road** 環状道路 [kanjoudouro] ▷ *v* 鳴らす [narasu]; **engagement ring** *n* 婚約指輪 [konyaku yubiwa]; **ring binder** *n* リングバインダー [ringubaindaa]; **wedding ring** *n* 結婚指輪 [kekkon yubiwa]

ringtone [rɪŋtoʊn] *n* 着信メロディ [chakushin merodi]

rink [rɪŋk] *n* スケートリンク [sukeetorinku]; **ice rink** *n* スケートリンク [sukeetorinku]; **skating**

rink *n* スケートリンク [sukeetorinku]

rinse [rɪns] *n* すすぎ [susugi] ▷ *v* すすぐ [susugu]

riot [raɪət] *n* 暴動 [boudou] ▷ *v* 暴動を起こす [boudou-o okosu]

rip [rɪp] *v* 引き裂く [hikisaku]

ripe [raɪp] *adj* 熟した [juku shita]

rip off *v* 法外な値をふっかける [hougai na ne-o fukkakeru]

rip-off [rɪpɔf] *n* 暴利 [bouri]

rip up *v* 破棄する [haki suru]

rise [raɪz] *n* 上昇 [joushou] ▷ *v* 立ち上がる [tachiagaru]

risk [rɪsk] *n* 危険 [kiken] ▷ *v* 危険にさらす [kiken ni sarasu]

risky [rɪski] *adj* 危険な [kiken na]

ritual [rɪtʃuəl] *adj* 儀式の [gishiki no] ▷ *n* 儀式 [gishiki]

rival [raɪvl] *adj* 競争する [kyousou suru] ▷ *n* 競争相手 [kyousouaite]

rivalry [raɪvəlri] *n* 競争 [kyousou]

river [rɪvər] *n* 川 [kawa]; **Can you swim in the river?** その川で泳げますか? [sono kawa de oyogemasu ka?]

road [roʊd] *n* 未知 [michi], 道路 [douro]; **main road** *n* 幹線道路 [kansendouro]; **road map** *n* ロードマップ [roodomappu]; **road rage** *n* ドライバーが路上で激怒すること [doraibaa ga rojou de gekido suru koto]; **road sign** *n* 道路標識 [dourohyoushiki]; **road work** *n* 道路工事 [dourokouji]; **Are the roads icy?** 道路は凍結していますか? [douro wa touketsu shite imasu ka?]; **Do you have a road map of this area?** この地域の道路マップはありますか? [kono chiiki no douro-mappu wa arimasu ka?]; **I need a road map of...** 私は・・・の道路マップが必要です [watashi wa... no douro-mappu ga hitsuyou desu]

roadblock [roʊdblɒk] *n* 道路封鎖 [douro fuusa]

roast [roʊst] *adj* 焼いた [yaita]

rob [rɒb] *v* 奪う [ubau]

robber [rɒbər] *n* 強盗 [goutou] *(人)*

R

robbery [rɒbəri] n 強盗 [goutou] (行為)

robin [rɒbɪn] n コマドリ [komadori]

robot [roʊbɒt, -bɒt] n ロボット [robotto]

rock [rɒk] n 岩 [iwa] ▷ v 揺れる [yureru]; **rock climbing** n ロッククライミング [rokkukuraimingu]

rocket [rɒkɪt] n ロケット [roketto]

rod [rɒd] n 棒 [bou]

rodent [roʊdənt] n 齧歯動物 [gesshi doubutsu]

role [roʊl] n 役割 [yakuwari]

roll [roʊl] n ロールパン [roorupan], 転がり [korogari] ▷ v 転がる [korogaru]; **roll call** n 点呼 [tenko]

roller [roʊlər] n ローラー [rooraa]

rollercoaster [roʊlərkoʊstər] n ローラーコースター [rooraakoosutaa]

rollerskates [roʊlərskeɪts] npl ローラースケート靴 [rooraa sukeeto kutsu]

rollerskating [roʊlərskeɪtɪŋ] n ローラースケート [rooraasukeeto]

Roman [roʊmən] adj ローマの [rooma no]; **Roman Catholic** n ローマカトリック教会の [Rooma Katorikku kyoukai no], ローマカトリック教徒 [Rooma Katorikku kyouto]

romance [roʊmæns, rəʊmæns] n 恋愛 [ren-ai]

Romanesque [roʊmənɛsk] adj ロマネスク様式の [Romanesuku youshiki no]

Romania [roʊmeɪniə] n ルーマニア [ruumania]

Romanian [roʊmeɪniən] adj ルーマニアの [ruumania no] ▷ n (language) ルーマニア語 [ruumaniago], (person) ルーマニア人 [ruumaniajin]

romantic [roʊmæntɪk] adj ロマンチックな [romanchikku na]

roof [ruf] n 屋根 [yane]

roof rack n ルーフラック [ruufurakku]

room [rum] n 部屋 [heya]; **changing room** n 更衣室 [kouishitsu], 試着室 [shichakushitsu]; **dining room** n ダイニングルーム [dainingu ruumu]; **double room** n ダブルルーム [daburuuruumu]; **living room** n 居間 [ima]; **men's room** n 男性用トイレ [dansei you toire]; **room number** n 客室番号 [kyakushitsu bangou]; **room service** n ルームサービス [ruumusaabisu]; **single room** n シングルルーム [shingururuumu]; **spare room** n 予備の寝室 [yobi no shinshitsu]; **twin room** n ツインルーム [tsuinruumu]; **twin-bedded room** n ツインベッドルーム [tsuinbeddoruumu]; **utility room** n ユーティリティールーム [yuutiritii ruumu]; **waiting room** n 待合室 [machiaishitsu]; **Can I switch rooms?** 部屋を替えることができますか? [heya o kaeru koto ga dekimasu ka?]; **Can you clean the room, please?** 部屋を掃除してもらえますか? [heya o souji shite moraemasu ka?]; **Do you have a room for tonight?** 今晩部屋はありますか? [konban heya wa arimasu ka?]; **Does the room have air conditioning?** その部屋にエアコンはありますか? [sono heya ni eakon wa arimasu ka?]; **How much is the room?** その部屋はいくらですか? [sono heya wa ikura desu ka?]; **I need a room with wheelchair access** 私は車椅子で入れる部屋が必要です [watashi wa kuruma-isu de haireru heya ga hitsuyou desu]; **I reserved a room in the name of...** ・・・の名前で部屋を予約しました [... no namae de heya o yoyaku shimashita]; **I'd like a no smoking room** 禁煙の部屋がいいのですが [kin'en no heya ga ii no desu ga]; **I'd like a room with a view of the sea** 海が見える部屋がいいのですが [umi ga mieru heya ga ii no desu ga]; **I'd like to rent a room** 部屋を借りたいのですが [heya o karitai no desu ga]; **May I see the room?** その部屋を見せてもらえますか? [sono heya wo misete moraemasu ka?]; **Please charge it to my room** それを私の部屋の勘定につけておいてください [sore o watashi no heya no kanjou ni tsukete oite kudasai]; **The room is dirty** 部屋が汚れています [heya ga yogorete imasu]; **The room is too cold** 部屋が寒すぎ

ます [heya ga samu-sugimasu]; **There's a problem with the room** 部屋に問題があります [heya ni mondai ga arimasu]

roommate [rʌmmeɪt] *n* ルームメート [ruumumeeto], 同室者 [doushitsusha]

rooster [rustər] *n* おんどり [ondori]

root [rut] *n* 根 [kon]; **Could you color my roots, please?** 根元を染めていただけますか? [nemoto o somete itadakemasu ka?]

rope [roup] *n* ロープ [roopu]

rope in *v* 人を誘い込む [hito-o sasoi komu]

rose [rouz] *n* バラ [bara] (植物)

rosé [rouzeɪ] *n* ロゼワイン [rozewain]; **Can you recommed a good rosé wine?** よいロゼワインを教えてもらえますか? [yoi roze-wain o oshiete moraemasu ka?]

rosemary [rouzmɛəri] *n* ローズマリー [roozumarii]

rot [rɒt] *v* 腐る [kusaru]

rotary [routəri] *n* 環状交差路 [kanjou kousaro]

rotten [rɒtⁿn] *adj* 腐った [kusatta]

rouge [ruʒ] *n* ほお紅 [hoobeni]

rough [rʌf] *adj* 粗い [arai]

roughly [rʌflij] *adv* およそ [oyoso]

roulette [rulɛt] *n* ルーレット [ruuretto]

round [raʊnd] *adj* 丸い [marui] ▷ *n* (circle) 円 [en] (丸), (series) 連続 [renzoku]; **one-day round-trip ticket** *n* 日帰り往復割引切符 [higaeri oufuku waribiki kippu]; **round trip** *n* 往復 [oufuku]; **round-trip ticket** *n* 往復切符 [oufuku kippu]

round-trip *adj* **two round-trip tickets to...** ···行き往復切符2枚 [... iki oufuku-kippu nimai]

round up *v* かき集める [kakiatsumeru]

route [rut, raʊt] *n* ルート [ruuto], 路線 [rosen]; **paper route** *n* 新聞配達 [shinbun haitatsu]

routine [rutin] *n* 決まりきった仕事 [kimarikitta shigoto] ▷ *n, adj* 定期 [teiki]

row [rou] *n* (in boat) 漕ぐ [kogu]; **Where can we go rowing?** どこに行けばボートをこげますか? [doko ni ikeba booto o kogemasu

ka?]

rowboat [roubout] *n* 漕ぎ舟 [kogibune]

row house *n* テラス [terasu], テラスハウス [terasuhausu]; **Can I eat on the terrace?** テラスで食べられますか? [terasu de taberaremasu ka?]

rowing [rouɪŋ] *n* ボートを漕ぐこと [booto-o kogu koto]

royal [rɔɪəl] *adj* 王室の [oushitsu no]

rub [rʌb] *v* こする [kosuru]

rubber [rʌbər] *n* ゴム [gomu]; **rubber band** *n* 輪ゴム [wagomu], 弾性ゴム [dansei gomu]; **rubber boots** *npl* ウェリントンブーツ [uerintonbuutsu]; **rubber gloves** *npl* ゴム手袋 [gomu tebukuro]

rude [rud] *adj* 失礼な [shitsurei na]

rug [rʌg] *n* ラグ [ragu]

rugby [rʌgbi] *n* ラグビー [ragubii]

ruin [ruɪn] *n* 荒廃 [kouhai] ▷ *v* 荒廃させる [kouhai saseru], 台無しにする [dainashi ni suru]; **ruined** *adj* 台無しにされた [dainashi ni sareta]

rule [rul] *n* 規則 [kisoku]

rule out *v* 可能性を排除する [kanousei-o haijo suru]

ruler [rulər] *n* (commander) 支配者 [shihaisha], (measure) 定規 [jougi]

rum [rʌm] *n* ラム [ramu] (酒)

rumor [rumər] *n* うわさ [uwasa]

run [rʌn] *n* 走ること [hashiru koto] ▷ *vi* 走る [hashiru] ▷ *vt* を走る [-o hashiru]

run away *v* 逃げ出す [nigedasu]

runner [rʌnər] *n* ランナー [rannaa]; **scarlet runner bean** *n* ベニバナインゲン [benibanaingen]

runner-up *n* 次点者 [jitensha]

running [rʌnɪŋ] *n* ランニング [ranningu]

run out of *v* ···を使い果たす [...-o tsukaihatasu]

run over *v* 轢く [hiku]

runway [rʌnweɪ] *n* 滑走路 [kassouro]

rural [ruərəl] *adj* 田舎の [inaka no]

rush [rʌʃ] *n* 突進 [tosshin] ▷ *v* 急ぐ [isogu];

R

rush hour n ラッシュアワー [rasshuawaa]

Russia [rʌʃə] n ロシア [roshia]

Russian [rʌʃ°n] adj ロシアの [roshia no] ▷ n (language) ロシア語 [roshiago], (person) ロシア人 [roshiajin]

rust [rʌst] n さび [sabi] (腐食)

rusty [rʌsti] adj さびた [sabita]

rutabaga [rutəbeɪgə] n スウェーデンカブ [suueedenkabu]

ruthless [ruθlɪs] adj 無慈悲な [mujihi na]

rye [raɪ] n ライ麦 [raimugi]

S

Sabbath [sæbəθ] *n* 安息日 [ansokubi]

sabotage [sæbətɑʒ] *n* 悪意の破壊 [koi no hakai] ▷ *v* 故意に破壊する [koi ni hakai suru]

sachet [sæʃeɪ] *n* 小さな袋 [chiisana fukuro]

sack [sæk] *n* (container) 大袋 [oobukuro]

sacred [seɪkrɪd] *adj* 神聖な [shinsei na]

sacrifice [sækrɪfaɪs] *n* 犠牲 [gisei]

sad [sæd] *adj* 悲しい [kanashii]

saddle [sæd·l] *n* サドル [sadoru]

saddlebag [sæd·lbæg] *n* サドルバッグ [sadorubaggu]

sadly [sædli] *adv* 悲しんで [kanashinde]

safari [səfɑri] *n* サファリ [safari]

safe [seɪf] *adj* 安全な [anzen na] ▷ *n* 金庫 [kinko]; **I have some things in the safe** 金庫に入れたものがあります [kinko ni ireta mono ga arimasu]; **I'd like to put my jewelry in the safe** 私はジュエリーを金庫に入れたいのですが [watashi wa juerii o kinko ni iretai no desu ga]; **Put that in the safe, please** それを金庫に入れてください [sore o kinko ni irete kudasai]

safety [seɪfti] *n* 安全 [anzen]; **safety belt** *n* 安全ベルト [anzenberuto]; **safety pin** *n* 安全ピン [anzenpin]

saffron [sæfrən] *n* サフラン [safuran]

Sagittarius [sædʒɪtɛəriəs] *n* 射手座 [iteza]

Sahara [səhærə] *n* サハラ砂漠 [sahara sabaku]

sail [seɪl] *n* 帆 [ho] ▷ *v* 航海する [koukai suru]

sailboat [seɪlboʊt] *n* ヨット [yotto]

sailing [seɪlɪŋ] *n* 航海 [koukai]

sailor [seɪlər] *n* 船員 [sen'in]

saint [seɪnt] *n* 聖人 [seijin]

salad [sæləd] *n* サラダ [sarada]; **mixed salad** *n* ミックスサラダ [mikkususarada]; **salad dressing** *n* サラダドレッシング [saradadoresshingu]

salami [səlɑmi] *n* サラミ [sarami]

salary [sæləri] *n* 給料 [kyuuryou]

sale [seɪl] *n* 販売 [hanbai]; **sales assistant** *n* 販売スタッフ [hanbai sutaffu]; **sales rep** *n* 販売員 [hanbaiin]

saleslady [seɪlzleɪdi] *n* 女性店員 [josei ten'in]

salesman [seɪlzmən] *n* セールスマン [seerusuman]

salesperson [seɪlzpɜrsən] *n* 店員 [ten-in]

saliva [səlaɪvə] *n* 唾液 [daeki]

salmon [sæmən] *n* サケ [sake] *(魚)*

salt [sɔlt] *n* 塩 [shio]; **Pass the salt, please** 塩を取っていただけますか? [shio o totte itadakemasu ka?]

saltwater [sɔltwɔtər] *adj* 塩水の [shiomizu no]

salty [sɔlti] *adj* 塩気のある [shioke no aru]

salute [səlut] *v* 挨拶する [aisatsu suru]

same [seɪm] *adj* 同じ [onaji]; **I'll have the same** 私にも同じものをください [watashi ni mo onaji mono o kudasai]

sample [sæmp·l] *n* 見本 [mihon]

sand [sænd] *n* 砂 [suna]; **sand dune** *n* 砂丘 [sakyuu]

sandal [sænd·l] *n* サンダル [sandaru]

sandbox [sændbɒks] *n* 砂場 [sunaba]

sand castle *n* 砂のお城 [suna no oshiro]

sandpaper [sændpeɪpər] *n* サンドペーパー [sandopeepaa]

sandstone [sændstoʊn] *n* 砂岩 [sagan]

sandwich [sænwɪtʃ, sænd-] *n* サンドイッチ [sandoicchi]; **What kinds of sandwiches do you have?** どんなサンドイッチがありますか?

[donna sandoitchi ga arimasu ka?]

San Marino n サンマリノ [sanmarino]

sapphire [sǽfaɪər] n サファイア [safaia]

sarcastic [sɑrkǽstɪk] adj 皮肉な [hiniku na]

sardine [sɑrdín] n サーディン [saadein]

sassy [sǽsi] adj 生意気な [namaiki na]

satchel [sǽtʃəl] n 肩掛けかばん [katakake kaban]

satellite [sǽtˌlaɪt] n 人工衛星 [jinkou eisei]; **satellite dish** n 衛星放送用パラボラアンテナ [eisei housou you parabora antena]

satiated adj 満腹 [manpuku]

satisfaction [sæ̀tɪsfǽkʃ*n] n 満足 [manzoku]

satisfactory [sæ̀tɪsfǽktəri] adj 満足のいく [manzoku no iku]

satisfied [sǽtɪsfaɪd] adj 満足した [manzoku shita]

Saturday [sǽtərdeɪ, -di] n 土曜日 [doyoubi]; **every Saturday** 毎週土曜日に [maishuu doyoubi ni]; **last Saturday** 先週の土曜日に [senshuu no doyoubi ni]; **next Saturday** 来週の土曜日に [raishuu no doyoubi ni]; **on Saturday** 土曜日に [doyoubi ni]; **on Saturdays** 毎土曜日に [mai-doyoubi ni]; **this Saturday** 今週の土曜日に [konshuu no doyoubi ni]

sauce [sɔs] n ソース [soosu]; **soy sauce** n 醤油 [shouyu]; **tomato sauce** n トマトソース [tomatosoosu]

saucepan [sɔ́spæn] n ソースパン [soosupan]

saucer [sɔ́sər] n 受け皿 [ukezara]

Saudi [saudi] adj サウジアラビアの [saujiarabia no] ▷ n サウジアラビア人 [Saujiarabia jin]

Saudi Arabia [saudi ərerbiə] n サウジアラビア [saujiarabia]

Saudi Arabian [saudi ərerbiən] adj サウジアラビアの [saujiarabia no] ▷ n サウジアラビア人 [Saujiarabia jin]

sauna [sɔ́nə] n サウナ [sauna]

sausage [sɔ́sɪdʒ] n ソーセージ [sooseeji]

save [seɪv] v 救う [sukuu], (money) 取っておく [totteoku]

save up v 蓄える [takuwaeru]

savings [séɪvɪŋz] npl 貯金 [chokin]

savory [séɪvəri] adj 塩味の [shioaji no]

saw [sɔ] n のこぎり [nokogiri]

sawdust [sɔ́dʌst] n おがくず [ogakuzu]

saxophone [sǽksəfoʊn] n サクソフォーン [sakusofoon]

say [seɪ] v 言う [iu]

saying [séɪɪŋ] n ことわざ [kotowaza]

scaffolding [skǽfəldɪŋ] n 足場 [ashiba]

scale [skeɪl] n (measure) 尺度 [shakudo], (tiny piece) うろこ [uroko]

scales [skeɪlz] npl 天秤 [tenbin]

scallion [skǽlyən] n ネギ [negi]

scallop [skɒ́ləp, skǽl-] n ホタテガイ [hotategai]

scam [skæm] n 詐欺 [sagi]

scampi [skǽmpi] npl クルマエビ [kurumaebi]

scan [skæn] n 綿密な調査 [menmitsu na chousa] ▷ v 細かく調べる [komakaku shiraberu]

scandal [skǽnd*l] n スキャンダル [sukyandaru]

Scandinavia [skæ̀ndɪnéɪviə] n スカンジナビア [sukanjinabia]

Scandinavian [skæ̀ndɪnéɪviən] adj スカンジナビアの [Sukanjinabia no]

scanner [skǽnər] n スキャナー [sukyanaa]

scar [skɑr] n 傷痕 [kizuato]

scarce [skɛərs] adj 不足して [fusoku shite]

scarcely [skɛ́ərsli] adv ほとんど・・・ない [hotondo... nai]

scare [skɛər] n 恐怖 [kyoufu] ▷ v 怖がらせる [kowagaraseru]

scarecrow [skɛ́ərkroʊ] n かかし [kakashi]

scared [skɛərd] adj 怖がった [kowagatta]

scarf [skɑrf] (pl scarves) n スカーフ [sukaafu], マフラー [mafuraa]

scarlet [skɑ́rlɪt] adj 深紅色の [shinkoushoku no]

scary [skɛ́əri] adj 怖い [kowai]

scene [sin] n 場面 [bamen]

scenery [sínəri] n 風景 [fuukei]

scenic [sínɪk] adj scenic area n 景勝地 [keishouchi]

scent [sɛnt] n におい [nioi]

schedule [skɛdʒul, -uəl] n 予定 [yotei]; **We're on schedule** 私たちは予定どおりです [watashi-tachi wa yotei doori desu]; **We're slightly behind schedule** 私たちは予定より少し遅れています [watashi-tachi wa yotei yori sukoshi okurete imasu]

schizophrenic [skɪtsəfrɛnɪk] adj 統合失調症の [tougou shitchoushou no]

schmaltzy [ʃmɑltsi] adj いやにセンチメンタルな [iya ni senchimentaru na]

scholar [skɒlər] n 学者 [gakusha]

scholarship [skɒlərʃɪp] n 学問 [gakumon]

school [skul] n 学校 [gakkou]; **art school** n 美術学校 [bijutsugakkou]; **boarding school** n 寄宿学校 [kishuku gakkou]; **elementary school** n 小学校 [shougakkou]; **language school** n 語学学校 [gogaku gakkou]; **law school** n ロースクール [roosukuuru]; **middle school** n 中学校 [chuugakkou]; **night school** n 夜間学校 [yakangakkou]; **nursery school** n 保育園 [hoikuen]; **private school** n パブリックスクール [paburikkusukuuru]; **school uniform** n 学校の制服 [gakkou no seifuku]

schoolbag [skulbæg] n 通学かばん [tsuugaku kaban]

schoolbook [skulbʊk] n 教科書 [kyoukasho]

schoolboy [skulbɔɪ] n 男子生徒 [danshiseito]

schoolchildren [skult͡ʃɪldrən] n 学童 [gakudou]

schoolgirl [skulɡɜrl] n 女子生徒 [joshiseito]

schoolteacher [skultit͡ʃər] n 学校教師 [gakkou kyoushi]

science [saɪəns] n 科学 [kagaku]; **science fiction** n サイエンスフィクション [saiensu fikushon]

scientific [saɪəntɪfɪk] adj 科学の [kagaku no]

scientist [saɪəntɪst] n 科学者 [kagakusha]

sci-fi [saɪ faɪ] n サイエンスフィクション [saiensu fikushon]

scissors [sɪzərz] npl はさみ [hasami]; **nail scissors** npl 爪切りばさみ [tsume kiri basami]

sclerosis [sklərousɪs] n **multiple sclerosis** n 多発性硬化症 [tahatsusei koukashou]

scoff [skɒf] v あざける [azakeru]

scold [skould] v しかる [shikaru]

scooter [skutər] n 片足スケート [kataashi sukeeto]

score [skɔr] n (game/match) 得点 [tokuten], (of music) 楽譜 [gakufu nijuu] ▷ v 点を取る [ten-o toru]

Scorpio [skɔrpiou] n 蠍座 [sasoriza]

scorpion [skɔrpiən] n サソリ [sasori]

Scot [skɒt] n スコットランド人 [sukottorandojin]

Scotch [skɒtʃ] n **Scotch® tape** n セロテープ® [seroteepu]

Scotland [skɒtlənd] n スコットランド [sukottorando]

Scots [skɒts] adj スコットランドの [sukottorando no]

Scotsman [skɒtsmən] (pl **Scotsmen**) n スコットランド人男性 [Sukottorando jin dansei]

Scotswoman [skɒtswumən] (pl **Scotswomen**) n スコットランド人女性 [Sukottorando jin josei]

Scottish [skɒtɪʃ] adj スコットランドの [sukottorando no]

scout [skaut] n 偵察兵 [teisatsuhei]

scrap [skræp] n (dispute) けんか [kenka] (争い), (small piece) 小片 [shouhen] ▷ v 廃棄する [haiki suru]; **scrap paper** n くず紙 [kuzugami]

scrapbook [skræpbʊk] n スクラップブック [sukurappubukku]

scraps npl 使い残り [tsukainokori]

scratch [skrætʃ] n かき傷 [kakikizu] ▷ v 引っ掻く [hikkaku]

scream [skrim] n 金切り声 [kanakirigoe] ▷ v 金切り声を上げる [kanagiri koe-o ageru]

S

screen [skriːn] n スクリーン [sukuriin] ▷ v 仕切りをする [shikiri-o suru]; **plasma screen** n プラズマスクリーン [purazumasukuriin]

screensaver [skriːnseɪvər] n スクリーンセーバー [sukuriinseebaa]

screw [skruː] n ねじ [neji]; **The screw has come loose** ねじがゆるくなっています [neji ga yuruku natte imasu]

screwdriver [skruːdraɪvər] n ドライバー [doraibaa] (道具)

scribble [skrɪbᵊl] v 走り書きする [hashirigaki suru]

scrub [skrʌb] v ごしごし洗う [goshigoshi arau]

sculptor [skʌlptər] n 彫刻家 [choukokuka]

sculpture [skʌlptʃər] n 彫刻 [choukoku]

sea [siː] n 海 [umi]; **North Sea** n 北海 [hokkai]; **Red Sea** n 紅海 [koukai]; **sea level** n 海水面 [kaisui men]; **sea water** n 海水 [kaisui]; **Is the sea rough today?** 今日は海が荒れていますか? [kyou wa umi ga arete imasu ka?]

seafood [siːfud] n シーフード [shiifuudo]; **Do you like seafood?** シーフードはお好きですか? [shii-fuudo wa o-suki desu ka?]

seagull [siːgʌl] n カモメ [kamome]

seal [siːl] n (animal) アザラシ [azarashi], (mark) 封印 [fuuin] ▷ v 封をする [fuu-o suru]

seam [siːm] n 縫い目 [nuime]

seaman [siːmən] (pl **seamen**) n 船乗り [funanori]

search [sɜrtʃ] n 捜索 [sousaku] ▷ v 捜索する [sousaku suru]; **search engine** n 検索エンジン [kensaku enjin]; **search party** n 捜索隊 [sousakutai]

seashore [siːʃor] n 海岸 [kaigan]

seasick [siːsɪk] adj 船に酔った [fune ni yotta]

seaside [siːsaɪd] n 海岸 [kaigan]

season [siːzᵊn] n 季節 [kisetsu]; **off season** n シーズンオフ [shiizun'ofu]; **peak season** n 最盛期 [saiseiki]; **season ticket** n 定期券 [teikiken]

seasonal [siːzənᵊl] adj 季節の [kisetsu no]

seasoning [siːzənɪŋ] n 調味料 [choumiryou]

seat [siːt] n シート [shiito], (constituency) 議席 [giseki], (furniture) 座席 [zaseki]; **aisle seat** n 通路側の席 [tsuurogawa no seki]; **window seat** n 窓下の腰掛け [mado shita no koshikake]; **Can we have seats together?** 一緒の座席を取れますか? [issho no zaseki o toremasu ka?]; **Do you have a baby seat?** ベビーシートはありますか? [bebii-shiito wa arimasu ka?]; **I have a seat reservation** 私は座席予約をしてあります [watashi wa zaseki-yoyaku o shite arimasu]; **I'd like a child seat for a two-year-old child** 2歳の子供用のチャイルドシートが欲しいのですが [ni-sai no kodomo-you no chairudo-shiito ga hoshii no desu ga]; **The seat is too high** シートが高すぎます [shiito ga taka-sugimasu]; **The seat is too low** シートが低すぎます [shiito ga hiku-sugimasu]; **We'd like to reserve two seats for tonight** 今夜の座席を2つ予約したいのですが [kon'ya no zaseki o futatsu yoyaku shitai no desu ga]

seatbelt [siːtbɛlt] n シートベルト [shiitoberuto]

seaweed [siːwid] n 海藻 [kaisou]

second [sɛkənd] adj 二番目の [ni banme no] ▷ n 二番目 [nibanme]; **second class** n 二等 [nitou]

second-class adj 二等の [nitou no]

secondhand [sɛkəndhænd] adj 中古の [chuuko no]

secondly [sɛkəndli] adv 第二に [dai ni ni]

second-rate [sɛkəndreɪt] adj 二流の [niryuu no]

secret [siːkrɪt] adj 秘密の [himitsu no] ▷ n 気密 [kimitsu], 秘密 [himitsu]; **secret service** n 諜報機関 [chouhou kikan]

secretary [sɛkrɪtɛri] n 秘書 [hisho]

secretly [siːkrɪtli] adv 秘密に [himitsu ni]

sect [sɛkt] n 分派 [bunpa]

section [sɛkʃᵊn] n 部分 [bubun]

sector [sɛktər] n 部門 [bumon]

secure [sɪkyʊər] adj 安全な [anzen na]

security [sɪkyʊərɪti] n 防護 [bougo]; **security guard** n 警備員 [keibiin]; **social security** n

社会保障 [shakaihoshou]

sedan [sɪdæn] *n* セダン [sedan]

sedative [sɛdətɪv] *n* 鎮静剤 [chinseizai]

see [si] *v* 見る [miru]

seed [sid] *n* 種 [shu] (果実)、種 [shu] (植物)

seek [sik] *v* 捜す [sagasu]

seem [sim] *v* ように思われる [youni omowareru]

seesaw [siso] *n* シーソー [shiisoo]

see-through *adj* 透けて見える [sukete mieru]

seize [siz] *v* ぐいとつかむ [guito tsukamu]

seizure [siʒər] *n* 発作 [hossa]

seldom [sɛldəm] *adv* めったに・・・しない [mettani… shinai]

select [sɪlɛkt] *v* 選ぶ [erabu]

selection [sɪlɛkʃən] *n* 選択 [sentaku]

self-assured [sɛlfəʃuərd] *adj* 自信のある [jishin no aru]

self-centered [sɛlfsɛntərd] *adj* 自己本位の [jiko hon'i no]

self-conscious [sɛlfkɒnʃəs] *adj* 自意識の強い [jiishiki no tsuyoi]

self-contained [sɛlfkənteɪnd] *adj* 内蔵型の [naizougata no]

self-control [sɛlfkəntroʊl] *n* 自制 [jisei]

self-defense [sɛlfdɪfɛns] *n* 自衛 [jiei]

self-discipline *n* 自己訓練 [jiko kunren]

self-employed [sɛlfɪmplɔɪd] *adj* 自営業の [jieigyou no]

selfish [sɛlfɪʃ] *adj* 利己的な [rikoteki na]

self-service [sɛlfsɜrvɪs] *adj* セルフサービスの [serufusaabisu no]

sell [sɛl] *v* 売る [uru]; **sell-by date** *n* 販売期限 [hanbai kigen]; **selling price** *n* 販売価格 [hanbai kakaku]

sell off *v* 売り払う [uriharau]

sell out *v* 売り尽くす [uritsukusu]

semester [sɪmɛstər] *n* 二学期制度の一学期 [nigakki seido no ichigakki]

semi (truck) [sɛmi (trʌk), sɛmaɪ (trʌk)] *n* 大型輸送車 [ougata yusousha]

semicircle [sɛmisɜrkəl, sɛmaɪ-] *n* 半円 [han'en]

semicolon [sɛmikoʊlən] *n* セミコロン [semikoron]

semifinal [sɛmifaɪnəl, sɛmaɪ-] *n* 準決勝 [junkesshou]

send [sɛnd] *v* 送る [okuru]; **How much will it cost to send this package?** この小包を送るのにいくらかかりますか? [kono kozutsumi o okuru no ni ikura kakarimasu ka?]

send back *v* 送り返す [okurikaesu]

sender [sɛndər] *n* 送り主 [okurinushi]

send off *v* 追い払う [oiharau]

send out *v* 発送する [hassou suru]

Senegal [sɛnɪgɒl] *n* セネガル [senegaru]

Senegalese [sɛnɪɡəliz] *adj* セネガルの [Senegaru no] ▷ *n* セネガル人 [Senegaru jin]

senior [sinyər] *adj* 先輩の [senpai no] ▷ *n* 年金受給者 [nenkin jukyuusha]; **senior citizen** *n* 高齢者 [koureisha]

sensational [sɛnseɪʃənəl] *adj* 世間をあっといわせるような [seken-o atto iwaseru you na]

sense [sɛns] *n* 感覚 [kankaku]; **sense of humor** *n* ユーモアのセンス [yuumoa no sensu]

senseless [sɛnslɪs] *adj* 無意味な [muimi na]

sensible [sɛnsɪbəl] *adj* 分別のある [bunbetsu no aru]

sensitive [sɛnsɪtɪv] *adj* 傷つきやすい [kizutsukiyasui]

sensuous [sɛnʃuəs] *adj* 感覚に訴える [kankaku ni uttaeru]

sentence [sɛntəns] *n* (punishment) 刑罰 [keibatsu], (words) 文 [bun] (言葉) ▷ *v* 判決を下す [hanketsu-o kudasu]

sentimental [sɛntɪmɛntəl] *adj* 感傷的な [kanshouteki na]

separate *adj* [sɛpərɪt] 単独の [tandoku no] ▷ *v* [sɛpəreɪt] 分ける [wakeru]

separately [sɛpərɪtli] *adv* 別々に [betsubetsu ni]

separation [sɛpəreɪʃən] *n* 分離 [bunri]

September [sɛptɛmbər] *n* 九月 [kugatsu]

sequel [sikwəl] *n* 続篇 [zokuhen]

S

sequence [sikwəns] *n* 順序 [junjo]

Serbia [sɜrbiə] *n* セルビア [serubia]

Serbian [sɜrbiən] *adj* セルビアの [Serubia no] ▷ *n* (*language*) セルビア語 [Serubia go], (*person*) セルビア人 [Serubia jin]

sergeant [sɑrdʒənt] *n* 軍曹 [gunsou]

serial [siəriəl] *n* 連続もの [renzokumono]

series [siəriz] *n* ひと続き [hitotsuduki]

serious [siəriəs] *adj* 深刻な [shinkoku na], 十代 [juudai]

seriously [siəriəsli] *adv* 深刻に [shinkoku ni]

sermon [sɜrmən] *n* 説教 [sekkyou]

servant [sɜrvənt] *n* 使用人 [shiyounin]; **civil servant** *n* 公務員 [koumuin]

serve [sɜrv] *n* サーブ [saabu] ▷ *v* 仕える [tsukaeru]

server [sɜrvər] *n* (*computer*) サーバー [saabaa], (*person*) 給仕する人 [kyuuji suru hito]

service [sɜrvɪs] *n* サービス [saabisu] ▷ *v* サービスを提供する [saabisu-o teikyou suru]; **room service** *n* ルームサービス [ruumusaabisu]; **secret service** *n* 諜報機関 [chouhou kikan]; **service area** *n* サービスエリア [saabisu eria]; **service charge** *n* サービス料 [saabisuryou]; **service station** *n* ガソリンスタンド [gasorinsutando]; **social services** *npl* 政府の社会福祉事業 [seifu no shakai fukushi jigyou]; **Call the breakdown service, please** 故障時緊急修理サービスを呼んでください [koshou-ji kinkyuu-shuuri-saabisu o yonde kudasai]; **I want to complain about the service** 私はサービスについて苦情があります [watashi wa saabisu ni tsuite kujou ga arimasu]; **Is service included?** サービス料は入っていますか? [saabisu-ryou wa haitte imasu ka?]; **Is there a charge for the service?** サービスに料金がかかりますか? [saabisu ni ryoukin ga kakarimasu ka?]; **Is there child care service?** 託児サービスはありますか? [takuji saabisu wa arimasu ka?]; **Is there room service?** ルームサービスはありますか? [ruumu-saabisu wa arimasu ka?];

The service was terrible サービスがひどかったです [saabisu ga hidokatta desu]

serviceman [sɜrvɪsmən] (*pl* **servicemen**) *n* 軍人 [gunjin]

servicewoman [sɜrvɪswʊmən] (*pl* **servicewomen**) *n* 女性軍人 [josei gunjin]

session [sɛʃən] *n* 会期 [kaiki]

set [sɛt] *n* ひとそろい [hitosoroi] ▷ *v* 定める [sadameru]

setback [sɛtbæk] *n* 妨げ [samatage]

set menu *n* set menu 定食 [teishoku]

set off *v* 出発する [shuppatsu suru]

set out *v* 並べる [naraberu]

settle [sɛtˡ] *v* 解決する [kaiketsu suru]

settle down *v* 落ち着く [ochitsuku] (住居)

seven [sɛvˡn] *number* 七 [shichi]

seventeen [sɛvˡntin] *number* 十七 [juunana]

seventeenth [sɛvˡntinθ] *adj* 十七番目の [juushichi banme no]

seventh [sɛvˡnθ] *adj* 七番目の [shichi banme no] ▷ *n* 七番目 [shichi banme]

seventy [sɛvˡnti] *number* 七十 [shichijuu]

several [sɛvrəl] *adj* いくつかの [ikutsuka no]

sew [soʊ] *v* 縫う [nuu]

sewer [suər] *n* 下水 [gesui]

sewing [soʊɪŋ] *n* 裁縫 [saihou]; **sewing machine** *n* ミシン [mishin]

sew up *v* 縫い合わせる [nuiawaseru]

sex [sɛks] *n* 性別 [seibetsu]

sexism [sɛksɪzəm] *n* 性差別主義 [seisabetsu shugi]

sexist [sɛksɪst] *adj* 性差別主義の [seisabetsu shugi no]

sexual [sɛkʃuəl] *adj* 性的な [seiteki na]; **sexual intercourse** *n* 性交 [seikou]

sexuality [sɛkʃuælɪti] *n* 男女の別 [danjo no betsu]

sexy [sɛksi] *adj* セクシーな [sekushii na]

shabby [ʃæbi] *adj* みすぼらしい [misuborashii]

shade [ʃeɪd] *n* 陰 [in]

shadow [ʃædoʊ] *n* 影 [kage]; **eye shadow** *n* アイシャドウ [aishadou] shake [ʃeɪk] *vi* 揺れる [yureru] ▷ *vt* 振る [furu]

shaken [ʃeɪkən] *adj* 揺さぶられた [yusaburareta]

shaky [ʃeɪki] *adj* よろよろする [yoroyoro suru]

shallow [ʃæloʊ] *adj* 浅い [asai]

shambles [ʃæmbᵊlz] *npl* 乱雑な状態 [ranzatsu na joutai]

shame [ʃeɪm] *n* 恥ずかしい思い [hazukashii omoi]

shampoo [ʃæmpu] *n* シャンプー [shanpuu]; **Do you sell shampoo?** シャンプーを売っていますか? [shanpuu o utte imasu ka?]

shape [ʃeɪp] *n* 形 [katachi], 形態 [keitai]

share [ʃɛər] *n* 分け前 [wakemae] ▷ *v* 分ける [wakeru]

shareholder [ʃɛərhoʊldər] *n* 株主 [kabunushi]

share out *v* 分け合う [wakeau]

shark [ʃɑrk] *n* サメ [same]

sharp [ʃɑrp] *adj* 鋭い [surudoi]

shave [ʃeɪv] *v* 剃る [soru]; **shaving cream** *n* シェービングクリーム [sheebingukuriimu]; **shaving foam** *n* シェービングフォーム [shieebingufoomu]

shaver [ʃeɪvər] *n* シェーバー [shieebaa]

shawl [ʃɔl] *n* ショール [shooru]

shed [ʃɛd] *n* 小屋 [koya]

sheep [ʃip] *n* 羊 [hitsuji]

sheepdog [ʃipdɔg] *n* 牧羊犬 [bokuyouken]

sheepskin [ʃipskɪn] *n* 羊の毛皮 [hitsuji no kegawa]

sheer [ʃɪər] *adj* 全くの [mattaku no]

sheet [ʃit] *n* シーツ [shiitsu]; **balance sheet** *n* 貸借対照表 [taishakutaishouhyou]; **fitted sheet** *n* マットレスにぴったり合うシーツ [mattoresu ni pittari au shiitsu]; **My sheets are dirty** 私のシーツは汚れています [watashi no shiitsu wa yogorete imasu]; **The sheets are dirty** シーツが汚れています [shiitsu ga yogorete imasu]; **We need more sheets** シーツがもっと必要です [shiitsu ga motto hitsuyou desu]

shelf [ʃɛlf] (*pl* shelves) *n* 棚 [tana]

shell [ʃɛl] *n* 殻 [kara]

shellfish [ʃɛlfɪʃ] *n* 貝 [kai]; **I'm allergic to shellfish** 私は貝類のアレルギーがあります [watashi wa kairui no arerugii ga arimasu]

shelter [ʃɛltər] *n* 避難所 [hinanjo]

shepherd [ʃɛpərd] *n* 羊飼い [hitsujikai]

sherry [ʃɛri] *n* シェリー [shierii]

shield [ʃild] *n* 盾 [tate]

shift [ʃɪft] *n* 変化 [henka]

shifty [ʃɪfti] *adj* あてにならない [ate ni naranai]

Shiite [ʃiaɪt] *adj* シーア派の信徒の [Shiia ha no shinto no]

shin [ʃɪn] *n* むこうずね [mukouzune]

shine [ʃaɪn] *v* 光る [hikaru]

shiny [ʃaɪni] *adj* 光った [hikatta]

ship [ʃɪp] *n* 船 [fune]

shipbuilding [ʃɪpbɪldɪŋ] *n* 造船 [zousen]

shipment [ʃɪpmənt] *n* 積み荷 [tsumini]

shipwreck [ʃɪprɛk] *n* 難破 [nanpa]

shipwrecked [ʃɪprɛkt] *adj* 難破した [nanpa shita]

shipyard [ʃɪpjɑrd] *n* 造船所 [zousenjo]

shirt [ʃɜrt] *n* ワイシャツ [waishatsu]; **polo shirt** *n* ポロシャツ [poroshatsu]

shiver [ʃɪvər] *v* 震える [furueru]

shock [ʃɒk] *n* 衝撃 [shougeki] ▷ *v* 衝撃を与える [shougeki-o ataeru]; **electric shock** *n* 感電 [kanden]

shocking [ʃɒkɪŋ] *adj* ショッキングな [shokkingu na]

shoe [ʃu] *n* 靴 [kutsu]; **gym shoes** *npl* トレーニングシューズ [toreeningushuuzu]; **shoe polish** *n* 靴墨 [kutsuzumi]; **shoe store** *n* 靴屋 [kutsuya]; **Can you re-heel these shoes?** この靴のヒールを付け直すことができますか? [kono kutsu no hiiru o tsukenaosu koto ga dekimasu ka?]; **Can you repair these shoes?** この靴を修理できますか? [kono kutsu o shuuri dekimasu ka?]; **I have a hole in my shoe** 靴に穴があきました [kutsu ni ana ga akimashita]; **Which floor are shoes on?** 靴は何階にありますか?

S

[kutsu wa nan-kai ni arimasu ka?]

shoelace [ʃuleɪs] *n* 靴ひも [kutsuhimo]

shoot [ʃut] *v* 撃つ [utsu]

shooting [ʃutɪŋ] *n* 射撃 [shageki]

shop [ʃɒp] *n* **gift shop** *n* ギフトショップ [gifuto shoppu]; **Is there a repair shop near here?** この近くに自動車修理工場はありますか？ [kono chikaku ni jidousha-shuuri-koujou wa arimasu ka?]

shoplifting [ʃɒplɪftɪŋ] *n* 万引き [manbiki]

shopping [ʃɒpɪŋ] *n* 買物 [kaimono]; **shopping bag** *n* 買物袋 [kaimonobukuro]; **shopping cart** *n* ショッピングカート [shoppingukaato]; **shopping center** *n* ショッピングセンター [shoppingu sentaa]

shore [ʃɔr] *n* 岸 [kishi]

short [ʃɔrt] *adj* 短い [mijikai]; **short story** *n* 短篇小説 [tanpen shousetsu]

shortage [ʃɔrtɪdʒ] *n* 不足 [fusoku]

shortcoming [ʃɔrtkʌmɪŋ] *n* 欠点 [ketten]

shortcut [ʃɔrtkʌt] *n* 近道 [chikamichi]

shortfall [ʃɔrtfɔl] *n* 不足すること [fusoku suru koto]

shorthand [ʃɔrthænd] *n* 速記 [sokki]

short list [ʃɔrtlɪst] *n* 選抜候補者リスト [senbatsu kouhosha risuto]

shortly [ʃɔrtli] *adv* まもなく [mamonaku]

shorts [ʃɔrts] *npl* 半ズボン [hanzubon]

short-sleeved [ʃɔrtslivd] *adj* 半袖の [hansode no]

shot [ʃɒt] *n* 発砲 [happou]

shotgun [ʃɒtgʌn] *n* 散弾銃 [sandanjuu]

shoulder [ʃouldər] *n* 肩 [kata]; **hard shoulder** *n* 路肩 [rokata]; **shoulder blade** *n* 肩甲骨 [kenkoukotsu]; **I've hurt my shoulder** 私は肩を痛めました [watashi wa kata o itamemashita]

shout [ʃaut] *n* 叫び [sakebi] ▷ *v* 叫ぶ [sakebu]

shovel [ʃʌvl] *n* シャベル [shaberu]

show [ʃou] *n* ショー [shoo] ▷ *v* 見せる [miseru]; **show business** *n* ショービジネス [shoobijinesu]; **talk show** *n* トークショー [tookushoo]; **Where can we go to see a show?** どこに行けばショーを見られますか？ [doko ni ikeba shoo o miraremasu ka?]

shower [ʃauər] *n* シャワー [shawaa]; **shower cap** *n* シャワーキャップ [shawaakyappu]; **shower gel** *n* シャワージェル [shawaajieru]; **Are there showers?** シャワーはありますか？ [shawaa wa arimasu ka?]; **The shower doesn't work** シャワーが出ません [shawaa ga demasen]; **The shower is dirty** シャワーが汚れています [shawaa ga yogorete imasu]; **The showers are cold** シャワーが冷たいです [shawaa ga tsumetai desu]; **Where are the showers?** シャワーはどこですか？ [shawaa wa doko desu ka?]

showerproof [ʃauərpruf] *adj* ぬれても大丈夫な [nurete mo daijoubu na]

showing [ʃouɪŋ] *n* 展示 [tenji]

show off *v* 見せびらかす [misebirakasu]

show-off *n* 見せびらかし [misebirakashi]

show up *v* 現れる [arawareru]

shriek [ʃrik] *v* 金切り声を出す [kanakirigoe wo dasu]

shrimp [ʃrɪmp] *n* クルマエビ [kurumaebi]; 小エビ [koebi]

shrine [ʃraɪn] *n* 霊廟 [reibyou]

shrink [ʃrɪŋk] *v* 縮む [chijimu]

shrub [ʃrʌb] *n* 低木 [teiboku]

shrug [ʃrʌg] *v* 肩をすくめる [kata wo sukumeru]

shrunken [ʃrʌŋkən] *adj* 縮んだ [chijinda]

shudder [ʃʌdər] *v* 身震いする [miburui suru]

shuffle [ʃʌfl] *v* 足をひきずって歩く [ashi-o hikizutte aruku]

shut [ʃʌt] *v* 閉める [shimeru]

shut down *v* 閉鎖する [heisa suru]

shutters [ʃʌtərz] *n* シャッター [shattaa]

shuttle [ʃʌtl] *n* 定期往復便 [teiki oufuku bin]

shut up *v* 黙る [damaru]

shy [ʃaɪ] *adj* 内気な [uchiki na]

Siberia [saɪbɪriə] *n* シベリア [shiberia]

siblings [sɪblɪŋz] *npl* 兄弟姉妹 [kyoudaishi-mai]

sick [sɪk] *adj* 吐き気がする [hakike ga suru];

sick leave n 病気休暇 [byoukikyuuka]; **sick note** n 病欠届け [byouketsu todoke]; **sick pay** n 病気休暇中の手当て [byouki kyuukachuu no teate]

sickening [sɪkənɪn] adj 吐き気をもよおさせる [hakike-o moyousaseru]

sickness [sɪknɪs] n 病気 [byouki]; **morning sickness** n つわりの時期の朝の吐き気 [tsuwari no jiki no asa no hakike]; **travel sickness** n 乗物酔い [norimonoyoi]

side [saɪd] n 側 [gawa]; **side effect** n 副作用 [fukusayou]; **side street** n 横丁 [yokochou]; **side-view mirror** n サイドミラー [saidomiraa]

sidewalk [saɪdwɔk] n 歩道 [hodou]

sideways [saɪdweɪz] adv 横向きに [yokomuki ni]

sieve [sɪv] n ふるい [furui] (ざる)

sigh [saɪ] n ため息 [tameiki] ▷ v ため息をつく [tameiki wo tsuku]

sight [saɪt] n 視力 [shiryoku]

sightseeing [saɪtsiɪn] n 観光 [kankou], 見物 [kenbutsu]; **Are there any sightseeing tours of the town?** その街の観光ツアーはありますか？ [sono machi no kankou-tsuaa wa arimasu ka?]

sign [saɪn] n 兆候 [choukou] ▷ v 署名する [shomei suru]; **road sign** n 道路標識 [dourohyoushiki]; **sign language** n 手話 [shuwa]; **Where do I sign?** どこに署名するのですか？ [doko ni shomei suru no desu ka?]

signal [sɪgnəl] n 合図 [aizu] ▷ v 合図する [aizu suru]; **busy signal** n 話し中の信号音 [hanashichuu no shingouon], 話し中を示す信号 [hanashichuu-o shimesu shingou]

signature [sɪgnətʃər, -tʃʊər] n 署名 [shomei]

significance [sɪgnɪfɪkəns] n 重要性 [juuyousei]

significant [sɪgnɪfɪkənt] adj 重要な [juuyou na]

sign on v 失業登録をする [shitsugyou touroku-o suru]

signpost [saɪnpoust] n 道路標識 [dourohyoushiki]

Sikh [sik] adj シーク教の [Shiiku kyou no] ▷ n シーク教徒 [Shiiku kyouto]

silence [saɪləns] n 静けさ [shizukesa]

silencer [saɪlənsər] n 消音装置 [shouon souchi]

silent [saɪlənt] adj 寡黙な [kamoku na]

silk [sɪlk] n 絹 [kinu]

silly [sɪli] adj 愚かな [oroka na]

silver [sɪlvər] n 銀 [gin]

silverware [sɪlvərwɛər] n **My silverware is dirty** 私のナイフやフォークが汚れています [watashi no naifu ya fooku ga yogorete imasu]

similar [sɪmɪlər] adj 類似した [ruiji shita]

similarity [sɪmɪlærɪti] n 類似 [ruiji]

simmer [sɪmər] v 弱火でとろとろ煮る [yowabi de torotoro niru]

simple [sɪmpl] adj 簡単な [kantan na]

simplify [sɪmplɪfaɪ] v 簡単にする [kantan ni suru]

simply [sɪmpli] adv 簡単に [kantan ni]

simultaneous [saɪməlteɪniəs] adj 同時の [douji no]

simultaneously [saɪməlteɪniəsli] adv 同時に [douji ni]

sin [sɪn] n 罪 [tsumi] (宗教・道徳)

since [sɪns] adv その時以来 [sono toki irai]

sincere [sɪnsɪər] adj 心からの [kokoro kara no]

sincerely [sɪnsɪərli] adv 心から [kokoro kara]

sing [sɪn] v 歌う [utau]

singer [sɪnər] n 歌手 [kashu]; **lead singer** n リードシンガー [riidoshingaa]

singing [sɪnɪn] n 歌うこと [utau koto]

single [sɪngl] adj たった一つの [tatta hitotsu no] ▷ n シングル [shinguru]; **single bed** n シングルベッド [shingurubeddo]; **single parent** n 片親で子育てをする人 [kataoya de kosodate-o suru hito]; **single room** n シングルルーム [shingururuumu]; **I want to reserve a single room** シングルルームを予約したいのですが [shinguru-ruumu o yoyaku

S

shitai no desu ga]

singles [sɪŋɡ·lz] *npl* シングルス [shingurusu]

singular [sɪŋɡyələr] *n* 単数 [tansuu]

sinister [sɪnɪstər] *adj* 不吉な [fukitsu na]

sink [sɪŋk] *n* シンク [shinku], 洗面台 [senmendai] ▷ *v* 沈む [shizumu]; **The sink is dirty** 洗面台が汚れています [senmendai ga yogorete imasu]

sinus [saɪnəs] *n* 洞 [hora]

sir [sɜr] *n* あなた [anata]

siren [saɪrən] *n* サイレン [sairen]

sister [sɪstər] *n* 姉妹 [shimai]

sister-in-law (*pl* **sisters-in-law**) *n* 義理の姉妹 [giri no shimai]

sit [sɪt] *v* 座る [suwaru]

sitcom [sɪtkɒm] *n* シチュエーションコメディー [shichueeshonkomedii]

sit down *v* 着席する [chakuseki suru]

site [saɪt] *n* 敷地 [shikichi], 現場 [genba]; **construction site** *n* 建設現場 [kensetsu genba]

situated [sɪtʃueɪtɪd] *adj* 位置している [ichi shite iru]

situation [sɪtʃueɪʃ·n] *n* 事態 [jitai], 計器 [keiki], 状況 [joukyou]

six [sɪks] *number* 六 [roku]; **It's six o'clock** 六時です [roku-ji desu]

sixteen [sɪkstin] *number* 十六 [juuroku]

sixteenth [sɪkstinθ] *adj* 十六番目の [juuroku banme no]

sixth [sɪksθ] *adj* 六番目の [roku banme no]

sixty [sɪksti] *number* 六十 [rokujuu]

size [saɪz] *n* サイズ [saizu]; **Do you have this in a larger size?** これの大きなサイズはありますか? [kore no ooki-na saizu wa arimasu ka?]; **Do you have this in a smaller size?** これの小さなサイズはありますか? [kore no chiisa-na saizu wa arimasu ka?]; **I'm a size twelve** 私のサイズは十六号です [watashi no saizu wa jyuuroku-gou desu]

skate [skeɪt] *v* スケートをする [sukeeto wo suru]

skateboard [skeɪtbɔrd] *n* スケートボード [sukeetoboodo]; **I'd like to go skateboarding** 私はスケートボードをしたいのですが [watashi wa sukeetoboodo o shitai no desu ga]

skateboarding [skeɪtbɔrdɪŋ] *n* スケートボーディング [sukeetoboodeingu]

skates [skeɪtz] *npl* スケート靴 [sukeeto kutsu]; **Where can we rent skates?** どこでスケート靴を借りられますか? [doko de sukeeto-gutsu o kariraremasu ka?]

skating [skeɪtɪŋ] *n* スケート [sukeeto]; **skating rink** *n* スケートリンク [sukeetorinku]

skeleton [skɛlɪt·n] *n* 骨格 [kokkaku]

skeptical [skɛptɪk·l] *adj* 疑い深い [utagaibukai]

sketch [skɛtʃ] *n* スケッチ [suketchi] ▷ *v* スケッチを描く [suketchi-o egaku]

skewer [skyuər] *n* 焼き串 [yakigushi]

ski [ski] *n* スキー [sukii] ▷ *v* スキーをする [sukii wo suru]; **ski lift** *n* スキー場のリフト [sukii jou no rifuto]; **ski pass** *n* スキー場のパス [sukii jou no pasu]; **Can we rent skis here?** ここでスキー板を借りられますか? [koko de sukii-ita o kariraremasu ka?]; **How much is a ski pass?** スキーパスはいくらですか? [sukii-pasu wa ikura desu ka?]; **I want to rent cross-country skis** クロスカントリースキーの板を借りたいのですが [kurosukantorii-sukii no ita o karitai no desu ga]; **I want to rent downhill skis** ダウンヒルスキーの板を借りたいのですが [daunhiru-sukii no ita o karitai no desu ga]; **I want to rent skis** スキー板を借りたいのですが [sukii-ita o karitai no desu ga]; **I'd like a ski pass for a day** 1日スキーパスが欲しいのですが [ichinichi sukii-pasu ga hoshii no desu ga]; **Is there a ski school?** スキースクールはありますか? [sukii-sukuuru wa arimasu ka?]; **Where can I buy a ski pass?** どこでスキーパスを買えますか? [doko de sukii-pasu o kaemasu ka?]

skid [skɪd] *v* 横すべりする [yokosuberi suru]

skier [skiər] *n* スキーヤー [sukiiyaa]

skiing [skiːɪŋ] n スキー [sukii]; **Do you organise skiing lessons?** スキーのレッスンを企画していますか？ [sukii no ressun o kikaku shite imasu ka?]; **I'd like to go skiing** スキーに行きたいのですが [sukii ni ikitai no desu ga]; **Is it possible to go cross-country skiing?** クロスカントリースキーに行くことは可能ですか？ [kurosukantorii-sukii ni iku koto wa kanou desu ka?]; **Where can I rent skiing equipment?** どこでスキー用具を借りられますか？ [doko de sukii-yougu o kariraremasu ka?]

skill [skɪl] n 熟練 [jukuren]

skilled [skɪld] adj 熟練した [jukuren shita]

skillful [skɪlfəl] adj 熟練した [jukuren shita]

skimpy [skɪmpi] adj 不十分な [fujuubun na]

skin [skɪn] n 肌 [hada], 皮膚 [hifu]

skinhead [skɪnhɛd] n スキンヘッド [sukinheddo]

skinny [skɪni] adj やせこけた [yasekoketa]

skin-tight adj ぴったり体に合う [pittari karada ni au]

skip [skɪp] v 飛び跳ねる [tobihaneru]

skirt [skɜrt] n スカート [sukaato]

skull [skʌl] n 頭蓋骨 [zugaikotsu]

sky [skaɪ] n 空 [sora] (天)

skyscraper [skaɪskreɪpər] n 摩天楼 [matenrou]

slack [slæk] adj 緩い [yurui]

slam [slæm] v バタンと閉める [batan to shimeru]

slang [slæŋ] n 俗語 [zokugo]

slap [slæp] v ピシャリと打つ [pishari to utsu]

slash [slæʃ] n **forward slash** n フォワードスラッシュ [fowaadosurasshu]

slate [sleɪt] n スレート [sureeto]

slave [sleɪv] n 奴隷 [dorei]; **slave away** 奴隷のように働く [dorei no youni hataraku]

sled [slɛd] n そり [sori]

sledding [slɛdɪŋ] n スレッジング [surejjingu]

sledge [slɛdʒ] n **Where can we go sledding?** どこに行けばそりに乗れますか？ [doko ni ikeba sori ni noremasu ka?]

sleep [slip] n 眠り [nemuri] ▷ v 眠る [nemuru]; **sleep late** n 朝寝坊 [asanebou]; **sleeping bag** n 寝袋 [nebukuro]; **sleeping car** n 寝台車 [shindaisha]; **sleeping pill** n 睡眠薬 [suimin-yaku]

sleep around v 誰とでも寝る [dare todemo neru]

sleeper [slipər] n **Can I reserve a sleeper?** 寝台車を予約できますか？ [shindai-sha o yoyaku dekimasu ka?]; **I want to reserve a sleeper to...** ･･･行きの寝台車を予約したいのですが [... iki no shindai-sha o yoyaku shitai no desu ga]

sleep in v 寝過ごす [nesugosu]

sleep together v いっしょに寝る [issho ni neru]

sleepwalk [slipwɔk] v 夢遊病で歩く [muyuubyou de aruku]

sleepy [slipi] adj 眠い [nemui]

sleet [slit] n みぞれ [mizore] ▷ v みぞれが降る [mizore ga furu]

sleeve [sliv] n 袖 [sode]

sleeveless [slivlɪs] adj 袖なしの [sode nashi no]

sleight of hand [slaɪt əv hænd] n 手品 [tejina]

slender [slɛndər] adj ほっそりした [hossori shita]

slice [slaɪs] n 薄切り [usugiri] ▷ v 薄く切る [usuku kiru]

slick [slɪk] n **oil slick** n 油膜 [yumaku]

slide [slaɪd] n 滑ること [suberu koto] ▷ v 滑る [suberu]

slight [slaɪt] adj わずかな [wazuka na]

slightly [slaɪtli] adv わずかに [wazuka ni]

slim [slɪm] adj ほっそりした [hossori shita]

sling [slɪŋ] n 吊り包帯 [tsuri houtai]

slip [slɪp] n アンダースカート [andaasukaato]

slip [slɪp] n (mistake) 間違い [machigai], (paper) 伝票 [denpyou], (underwear) スリップ [surippu] (下着) ▷ v 滑る [suberu]; **slipped disc** n 椎間板ヘルニア [tsuikanban herunia]

slipper [slɪpər] n スリッパ [surippa]

S

slippery [slɪpəri] *adj* 滑りやすい [suberiya-sui]

slip up *v* 間違う [machigau]

slip-up *n* 間違い [machigai]

slope [sloup] *n* スロープ [suroopu], 坂 [saka]; **How difficult is this slope?** このスロープはどのくらい難しいですか? [kono suroopu wa dono kurai muzukashii desu ka?]; **Where are the beginners' slopes?** 初心者用のスロープはどこですか? [shoshinsha-you no suroopu wa doko desu ka?]

sloppy [slɒpi] *adj* ずさんな [zusanna]

slot [slɒt] *n* スロット [surotto]; **slot machine** *n* スロットマシン [surottomashin]

Slovak [slouvæk] *adj* スロバキアの [Surobakia no] ▷ *n (language)* スロバキア語 [Surobakia go], *(person)* スロバキア人 [Surobakia jin]

Slovakia [slouvækiə] *n* スロバキア [surobakia]

Slovenia [slouviniə] *n* スロベニア [surobenia]

Slovenian [slouviniən] *adj* スロベニアの [Surobenia no] ▷ *n (language)* スロベニア語 [Surobenia go], *(person)* スロベニア人 [Surobenia jin]

slow [slou] *adj* 遅い [osoi]; **The connection seems very slow** 接続がとても遅いようです [setsuzoku ga totemo osoi you desu]

slow down *v* もっとのんびりする [motto nonbiri suru]

slowly [slouli] *adv* 遅く [osoku]

slug [slʌg] *n* ナメクジ [namekuji]

slum [slʌm] *n* スラム街 [suramugai]

slush [slʌʃ] *n* ぬかるみ [nukarumi]

sly [slaɪ] *adj* ずるい [zurui]

smack [smæk] *v* ピシャリと打つ [pishari to utsu]

small [smɔl] *adj* 小い [chiisai], 小さい [chiisa na]

smart [smɑrt] *adj* スマートな [sumaato na]; **smart phone** *n* スマートフォン [sumaatofon]

smash [smæʃ] *v* 打ち砕く [uchikudaku]

smell [smɛl] *n* におい [nioi] ▷ *vi* においがする [nioi ga suru] ▷ *vt* においを嗅ぐ [nioi-o kagu]; **I can smell gas** ガスのにおいがします [gasu no nioi ga shimasu]; **My room smells like smoke** 私の部屋はタバコのにおいがします [watashi no heya wa tabako no nioi ga shimasu]; **There's a funny smell** 変なにおいがします [hen na nioi ga shimasu]

smelly [smɛli] *adj* いやなにおいのする [iya na nioino suru]

smile [smaɪl] *n* ほほ笑み [hohoemi] ▷ *v* ほほ笑む [hohoemu]

smiley [smaɪli] *n* スマイリー [sumairii]

smoke [smouk] *n* 煙 [kemuri] ▷ *v* 煙を出す [kemuri wo dasu]; **smoke detector** *n* 煙警報器 [kemuri keihouki]; **Where can I smoke?** どこで喫煙できますか? [doko de kitsuen dekimasu ka?]

smoked [smoukt] *adj* いぶした [ibushita]

smoker [smoukər] *n* 喫煙者 [kitsuensha]

smoking [smoukɪŋ] *n* 喫煙 [kitsuen]; **I'd like a seat in the smoking area** 喫煙エリアの席が欲しいのですが [kitsuen-eria no seki ga hoshii no desu ga]; **I'd like a smoking room** 喫煙できる部屋がいいのですが [kitsuen dekiru heya ga ii no desu ga]

smoky [smouki] *adj* **It's too smoky here** ここは煙たすぎます [koko wa kemuta-sugi-masu]

smooth [smuð] *adj* 滑らかな [nameraka na]

SMS [ɛs ɛm ɛs] *n* ショートメッセージサービス [shootomesseejisaabisu]

smudge [smʌdʒ] *n* 汚れ [yogore]

smug [smʌg] *adj* 一人よがりの [hitori yogari no]

smuggle [smʌgᵊl] *v* 密輸する [mitsuyu suru]

smuggler [smʌglər] *n* 密輸業者 [mitsuyu gyousha]

smuggling [smʌgᵊlɪŋ] *n* 密輸 [mitsuyu]

snack [snæk] *n* 軽食 [keishoku]; **snack bar** *n* 軽食堂 [keishokudou]

snack bar *n* ビュッフェ [byuffe]

snail [sneɪl] *n* カタツムリ [katatsumuri]

snake [sneɪk] *n* ヘビ [hebi]

snap [snæp] v ポキッっと折る [pokittto oru]

snapshot [snæpʃɒt] n スナップ写真 [sunappu shashin]

snarl [snɑrl] v 歯をむきだしてうなる [ha-o mukidashite unaru]

snatch [snætʃ] v ひったくる [hittakuru]

sneakers [snikərz] npl スニーカー [suniikaa]

sneeze [sniz] v くしゃみをする [kushami wo suru]

snicker [snɪkər] v にやにや笑う [niyaniya warau]

sniff [snɪf] v 鼻で吸う [hana de suu]

snob [snɒb] n 紳士気取りの俗物 [shinshi kidori no zokubutsu]

snooker [snʊkər] n スヌーカー [sunuukaa]

snooze [snuz] n 居眠り [inemuri] ▷ v 居眠りを する [inemuri-o suru]

snore [snɔr] v いびきをかく [ibiki wo kaku]

snoring [snɔrɪŋ] n いびき [ibiki]

snorkel [snɔrkəl] n シュノーケル [shunookeru]

snow [snoʊ] n 雪 [yuki] ▷ v 雪が降る [yuki ga furu]; **snow peas** npl サヤエンドウ [sayaendou]; **Do you think it's going to snow?** 雪が降ると思いますか? [yuki ga furu to omoimasu ka?]; **Is the road to... covered with snow?** ···へ行く道は積雪しています か? [... e iku michi wa sekisetsu shite imasu ka?]; **It's snowing** 雪が降っています [yuki ga futte imasu]; **The snow is very heavy** 大雪 です [ooyuki desu]; **What are the snow conditions?** 雪の状態はどんなですか? [yuki no joutai wa donna desu ka?]; **What is the snow like?** 雪はどんなですか? [yuki wa donna desu ka?]

snowball [snoʊbɔl] n 雪つぶて [yukitsubute]

snowboard [snoʊbord] n **I want to rent a snowboard** スノーボードを借りたいのですが [sunooboodo o karitai no desu ga]

snowflake [snoʊfleɪk] n ひとひらの雪 [hitohira no yuki]

snowman [snoʊmæn] n 雪だるま [yukidaruma]

snowplow [snoʊplaʊ] n 除雪車 [josetsusha]

snowstorm [snoʊstɔrm] n 吹雪 [fubuki]

so [soʊ] adv **Why are you charging me so much?** なぜそんなにたくさん請求するのです か? [naze sonna ni takusan seikyuu suru no desu ka?]

soak [soʊk] v 浸す [hitasu]

soaked [soʊkt] adj ずぶぬれの [zubunure no]

soap [soʊp] n 石鹸 [sekken]; **soap dish** n 石 鹸入れ [sekken ire]; **soap opera** n ソープオ ペラ [soopuopera]; **There's no soap** 石鹸が ありません [sekken ga arimasen]

sob [sɒb] v 泣きじゃくる [nakijakuru]

sober [soʊbər] adj しらふの [shirafu no]

soccer [sɒkər] n サッカー [sakkaa], フットボ ール [futtobooru]; **soccer game** n フットボール の試合 [futtobooru no shiai]; **soccer player** n フットボール選手 [futtobooru senshu]; **I'd like to see a soccer game** 私は サッカーの試合が観たいのですが [watashi wa sakkaa no shiai ga mitai no desu ga]; **Let's play soccer** サッカーをしましょう [sakkaa o shimashou]

sociable [soʊʃəbəl] adj 社交的な [shakouteki na]

social [soʊʃəl] adj 社会の [shakai no]; **social security** n 社会保障 [shakaihoshou]; **social services** npl 政府の社会福祉事業 [seifu no shakai fukushi jigyou]; **social worker** n ソー シャルワーカー [soosharuwaakaa]

socialism [soʊʃəlɪzəm] n 社会主義 [shakaishugi]

socialist [soʊʃəlɪst] adj 社会主義の [shakaishugi no] ▷ n 社会主義者 [shakaishugisha]

society [səsaɪɪti] n 社会 [shakai]

sociology [soʊsiɒlədʒi] n 社会学 [shakaigaku]

sock [sɒk] n ソックス [sokkusu]

socket [sɒkɪt] n コンセント [konsento]; **Where's the socket for my electric razor?** 電気カミソリのコンセントはどこですか? [denki-kamisori no konsento wa doko desu ka?]

S

sofa [soufə] n ソファー [sofaa]; **sofa bed** n ソファーベッド [sofaabeddo]

soft [sɔft] adj 柔らかい [yawarakai]; **soft drink** n ソフトドリンク [sofutodorinku]

softener [sɔfənər] n Do you have fabric softener? 柔軟剤はありますか？ [juunan-zai wa arimasu ka?]

software [sɔftwɛər] n ソフトウェア [sofutouea]

soggy [sɒgi] adj ずぶぬれの [zubunure no]

soil [sɔɪl] n 土 [tsuchi]

solar [soulər] adj 太陽の [taiyou no]; **solar power** n 太陽エネルギー [taiyou enerugii]; **solar system** n 太陽系 [taiyoukei]

soldier [souldʒər] n 兵 [hei], 兵士 [heishi]

sold out adj 売切れの [urikire no]

solid [sɒlɪd] adj 固体の [kotai no]

solo [soulou] n ソロ [soro]

soloist [soulouɪst] n ソリスト [sorisuto]

soluble [sɒlyəbəl] adj 溶ける [tokeru]

solution [səluʃən] n 解決 [kaiketsu]

solve [sɒlv] v 解決する [kaiketsu suru]

solvent [sɒlvənt] n 溶剤 [youzai]

Somali [soumɑli] adj ソマリアの [Somaria no] ▷ n (language) ソマリア語 [Somaria go], (person) ソマリア人 [Somaria jin]

Somalia [soumɑliə] n ソマリア [somaria]

some [səm, STRONG sʌm] Could you lend me some money? お金をいくらか貸していただけますか？ [o-kane o ikura ka kashite itadakemasu ka?]; Here's some information about my company 弊社についての情報です [heisha ni tsuite no jouhou desu]; I want to exchange some... for... ···を···に両替したいのですが [... o... ni ryougae shitai no desu ga]; I'd like some Tylenol® パラセタモールが欲しいのですが [parasetamooru ga hoshii no desu ga]; There are some people injured 怪我人がいます [keganin ga imasu]

something [sʌmθɪŋ] pron I'd like to order something local 何か郷土料理を注文したいのですが [nani ka kyoudo-ryouri o chuumon shitai no desu ga]; Would you like something to eat? 何か召し上がりますか？ [nani ka meshiagarimasu ka?]; Would you like to do something tomorrow? 明日何かなさりたいですか？ [asu nani ka nasaritai desu ka?]

somewhere [sʌmwɛər] adv Is there somewhere to eat on the boat? 船内で何か食べられるところはありますか？ [sennai de nani ka taberareru tokoro wa arimasu ka?]

son [sʌn] n 息子 [musuko]; My son is lost 息子の姿が見当たりません [musuko no sugata ga miatarimasen]; My son is missing 私の息子が行方不明です [watashi no musuko ga yukue-fumei desu]

song [sɔŋ] n 歌 [uta]

son-in-law (pl sons-in-law) n 娘の夫 [musume no otto]

soon [sun] adv まもなく [mamonaku], やがて [yagate]

sooner [sunər] adv より早く [yori hayaku]

soot [sut, sʊt] n すす [susu]

sophisticated [səfɪstɪkeɪtɪd] adj 洗練された [senren sareta]

soprano [səprænou, -prɑn-] n ソプラノ [sopurano]

sorbet [sɔrbɪt] n ソルベ [sorube]

sorcerer [sɔrsərər] n 魔法使い [mahoutsukai]

sore [sɔr] adj 痛い [itai] ▷ n さわると痛いところ [sawaru to itai tokoro]; **cold sore** n 口辺ヘルペス [kouhenherupesu]

sorry [sɒri] interj I'm sorry ごめんなさい [gomen nasai]; I'm sorry to bother you ご迷惑をかけてすみません [go-meiwaku o kakete sumimasen]; Sorry we're late 遅れてすみません [okurete sumimasen]; Sorry, I didn't catch that ごめんなさい、聞き取れませんでした [gomen nasai, kikitoremasen deshita]; Sorry, I'm not interested ごめんなさい、関心がありません [gomen nasai, kanshin ga arimasen]

sorry [sɒri] excl ごめんなさい！ [gomen nasai]

sort [sɔrt] *n* 種類 [shurui]

sort out *v* 解決する [kaiketsu suru]

SOS [ɛs ou ɛs] *n* 救難信号 [kyuunan shingou]

soul [soul] *n* 魂 [tamashii]

sound [saund] *adj* 健全な [kenzen na] ▷ *n* 音 [oto]

soundtrack [saundtræk] *n* サウンドトラック [saundotorakku]

soup [sup] *n* スープ [suupu]; **What is the soup of the day?** 今日のおすすめスープは何ですか? [kyou no osusume suupu wa nan desu ka?]

sour [sauər] *adj* 酸っぱい [suppai]

south [sauθ] *adj* 南の [minami no] ▷ *adv* 南に [minami ni] ▷ *n* 南 [minami]; **South Africa** *n* 南アフリカ [minami afurika]; **South African** *n* 南アフリカ人 [minami afurikajin], 南アフリカの [minami afurika no]; **South America** *n* 南アメリカ [minamiamerika]; **South American** *n* 南アメリカ人 [Minami Amerika jin], 南アメリカの [Minami Amerika no]; **South Korea** *n* 韓国 [kankoku]; **South Pole** *n* 南極 [nankyoku]

southbound [sauθbaund] *adj* 南行きの [minami yuki no]

southeast [sauθist] *n* 南東 [nantou]

southern [sʌðərn] *adj* 南の [minami no]

southwest [sauθwɛst] *n* 南西 [nansei]

souvenir [suvənɪər] *n* 記念品 [kinenhin]

souvenirs *n* おみやげ [omiyage]

soy [sɔɪ] *n* 大豆 [daizu]

spa [spa] *n* 鉱泉 [kousen]

space [speɪs] *n* スペース [supeesu], 空間 [kuukan]

spacecraft [speɪskræft] *n* 宇宙船 [uchuusen]

spade [speɪd] *n* 鋤 [suki]

spaghetti [spəgɛti] *n* スパゲッティ [supagetti]

Spain [speɪn] *n* スペイン [supein]

spam [spæm] *n* スパムメール [supa- mumeeru]

Spaniard [spænyərd] *n* スペイン人 [supeinjin]

spaniel [spænyəl] *n* スパニエル [supanieru]

Spanish [spænɪʃ] *adj* スペインの [supein no] ▷ *n* スペイン人 [supeinjin]

spank [spæŋk] *v* ひっぱたく [hippataku]

spare [spɛər] *adj* 予備 [yobi], 余分の [yobun no] ▷ *v* 容赦する [yousha suru]; **spare part** *n* スペアパーツ [supeapaatsu]; **spare room** *n* 予備の寝室 [yobi no shinshitsu]; **spare time** *n* 余暇 [yoka]; **spare tire** *n* スペアタイヤ [supeataiya]; **spare wheel** *n* スペアホイール [supeahoiiru]; **Is there any spare bedding?** 予備の寝具はありますか? [yobi no shingu wa arimasu ka?]

spark [spɑrk] *n* 火花 [hibana]; **spark plug** *n* スパークプラグ [supaakupuragu]

sparrow [spærou] *n* スズメ [suzume]

spasm [spæzəm] *n* 痙攣 [keirei]

spatula [spætʃələ] *n* へら [hera]

speak [spik] *v* 話す [hanasu]

speaker [spikər] *n* 話す人 [hanasu hito], 話し手 [hanashite]; **native speaker** *n* 母国語とする人 [bokokugo to suru hito]

speak up *v* 遠慮なく話す [enryo naku hanasu]

special [spɛʃl] *adj* 特別の [tokubetsu no]; **special offer** *n* 特別売り出し [tokubetsu uridashi]

specialist [spɛʃəlɪst] *n* 専門家 [senmonka], *(physician)* 顧問医 [komon-i]

specialize [spɛʃəlaɪz] *v* 専門にする [senmon ni suru]

specially [spɛʃəli] *adv* 特別に [tokubetsu ni]

specialty [spɛʃlti] *n* 専門 [senmon]

species [spiʃiz] *n* 種 [shu] *(生物)*

specific [spɪsɪfɪk] *adj* 特定の [tokutei no]

specifically [spɪsɪfɪkli] *adv* 特に [toku ni]

specify [spɛsɪfaɪ] *v* 明記する [meiki suru]

specs [spɛks] *npl* 眼鏡 [megane]

spectacles [spɛktəkəlz] *npl* 眼鏡 [megane]

spectacular [spɛktækyələr] *adj* 壮観な [soukan na]

spectator [spɛkteɪtər] *n* 観客 [kankyaku]

speculate [spɛkyəleɪt] *v* 推測する [suisoku suru]

S

speech [spitʃ] n 言葉 [kotoba]

speechless [spitʃlɪs] adj 口のきけない [kuchi no kikenai]

speed [spid] n スピード [supiido], 速さ [hayasa]; speed limit n 制限速度 [seigensokudo]

speedboat [spidboʊt] n 快速モーターボート [kaisoku mootaabooto]

speeding [spidɪŋ] n 高速進行 [kousoku shinkou]

speedometer [spidɒmɪtər] n 速度計 [sokudokei]

speed up v 速度を上げる [sokudo-o ageru]

spell [spɛl] n (magic) 呪文 [jumon], (time) 一時期 [ichijiki] ▷ v つづる [tsuduru]

spell checker n スペルチェッカー [superuchekkaa]

spelling [spɛlɪŋ] n つづり [tsuzuri]

spend [spɛnd] v 費やす [tsuiyasu]

sperm [spɜrm] n 精子 [seishi]

spice [spaɪs] n 香辛料 [koushinryou]

spicy [spaɪsi] adj 香辛料を入れた [koushinryou-o ireta]

spider [spaɪdər] n クモ [kumo] (動物)

spill [spɪl] v こぼす [kobosu] (漏らす)

spinach [spɪnɪtʃ] n ほうれん草 [hourensou]

spine [spaɪn] n 脊椎 [sekitsui]

spinster [spɪnstər] n 独身女性 [dokushinjosei]

spire [spaɪər] n 尖塔 [sentou]

spirit [spɪrɪt] n 精神 [seishin]

spirits [spɪrɪts] npl スピリッツ [supirittsu]

spiritual [spɪrɪtʃuəl] adj 精神的な [seishinteki na]

spit [spɪt] n つば [tsuba] (唾液) ▷ v つばを吐く [tsuba wo haku]

spite [spaɪt] n 意地悪 [ijiwaru] ▷ v 意地悪をする [ijiwaru-o suru]

spiteful [spaɪtfəl] adj 意地の悪い [iji no warui]

splash [splæʃ] v はねかける [hanekakeru]

splendid [splɛndɪd] adj すばらしい [subarashii]

splint [splɪnt] n 添え木 [soegi]

splinter [splɪntər] n 破片 [hahen]

split [splɪt] v 割る [waru]

split up v 分裂する [bunretsu suru]

spoilsport [spɔɪlspɔrt] n 人の興をそぐ人 [hito no kyou-o sogu hito]

spoke [spoʊk] n スポーク [supooku]

spokesman [spoʊksmən] (pl spokesmen) n スポークスマン [supookusuman]

spokesperson [spoʊkspɜrs·n] n スポークスパーソン [supookusupaason]

spokeswoman [spoʊkswʊmən] (pl spokeswomen) n スポークスウーマン [supookusuuuman]

sponge [spʌndʒ] n (for washing) スポンジ [suponji]

sponsor [spɒnsər] n 後援者 [kouensha] ▷ v 後援者となる [kouensha to naru]

sponsorship [spɒnsərʃɪp] n 後援 [kouen]

spontaneous [spɒnteɪniəs] adj 自発的な [jihatsuteki na]

spooky [spuki] adj 気味の悪い [kimi no warui]

spoon [spun] n スプーン [supuun]; Could I have a clean spoon, please? 新しいスプーンをいただけますか? [atarashii supuun o itadakemasu ka?]

spoonful [spunful] n ひとさじ [hitosaji]

sport [spɔrt] n スポーツ [supootsu]; winter sports npl ウィンタースポーツ [uintaasupootsu]; What sports facilities are there? どんなスポーツ施設がありますか? [donna supootsu-shisetsu ga arimasu ka?]; Which sporting events can we go to? 私たちはどのスポーツイベントに行けますか? [watashi-tachi wa dono supootsu-ibento ni ikemasu ka?]

sportsman [spɔrtsmən] (pl sportsmen) n スポーツマン [supootsuman]

sportswear [spɔrtswɛər] n スポーツウェア [supootsuuea]

sportswoman [spɔrtswʊmən] (pl sportswomen) n スポーツウーマン

[supootsuuuman]

sporty [spɔrti] *adj* スポーツ好きの
[supootsuzuki no]

spot [spɒt] *n (blemish)* しみ [shimi], *(place)*
地点 [chiten] ▷ *v* 見つける [mitsukeru]

spotless [spɒtlɪs] *adj* しみのない [shimi no
nai]

spotlight [spɒtlaɪt] *n* スポットライト
[supottoraito]

spouse [spaʊs] *n* 配偶者 [haiguusha]

sprain [spreɪn] *n* 捻挫 [nenza] ▷ *v* くじく
[kujiku]

spray [spreɪ] *n* 噴霧 [funmu] ▷ *v* 噴霧する
[funmu suru]; **hair spray** *n* ヘアスプレー
[heasupuree]

spread [sprɛd] *n* 広がること [hirogaru koto]
▷ *v* 広げる [hirogeru]

spread out *v* 広げる [hirogeru]

spreadsheet [sprɛdʃit] *n* スプレッドシート
[supureddoshiito]

spring [sprɪŋ] *n (coil)* ばね [bane], *(season)*
春 [haru]

spring-cleaning *n* 春季の大掃除 [shunki no
ousouji]

springtime [sprɪŋtaɪm] *n* 春季 [shunki]

sprinkler [sprɪŋklər] *n* スプリンクラー
[supurinkuraa]

sprint [sprɪnt] *n* 短距離競走 [tankyorikyou-
sou] ▷ *v* 全力で走る [zenryoku de hashiru]

sprinter [sprɪntər] *n* 短距離走者 [tankyori
sousha]

sprout [spraʊt] *n* bean sprouts *npl* 豆もやし
[mame moyashi]

sprouts [sprautz] *npl* 新芽 [shinme];
Brussels sprouts *npl* 芽キャベツ
[mekyabetsu]

spy [spaɪ] *n* スパイ [supai] ▷ *v* 見張る [miharu]

spying [spaɪɪŋ] *n* スパイ行為 [supai koui]

squabble [skwɒbl] *v* つまらないことで口論す
る [tsumaranai koto de kouron suru]

squander [skwɒndər] *v* 浪費する [rouhi suru]

square [skwɛər] *adj* 正方形の [seihoukei no]
▷ *n* 正方形 [seihoukei]

squash [skwɒʃ] *n* スカッシュ [sukasshu] ▷ *v* 押
しつぶす [oshitsubusu]

squeak [skwik] *v* きしる [kishiru]

squeeze [skwiz] *v* 強く押す [tsuyoku osu]

squeeze in *v* 割り込む [warikomu]

squid [skwɪd] *n* イカ [ika]

squint [skwɪnt] *v* 斜視である [shashi de aru]

squirrel [skwɜrəl] *n* リス [risu]

Sri Lanka [sri læŋkə] *n* スリランカ [suriranka]

stab [stæb] *v* 突き刺す [tsukisasu]

stability [stəbɪlɪti] *n* 安定 [antei]

stable [steɪbl] *adj* 安定した [antei shita] ▷ *n*
馬小屋 [umagoya]

stack [stæk] *n* 積み重ね [tsumikasane]

stadium [steɪdiəm] *(pl stadia)* *n* スタジアム
[sutajiamu]; **How do we get to the
stadium?** そのスタジアムにはどうやって行く
のですか? [sono sutajiamu ni wa dou-yatte
iku no desu ka?]

staff [stæf] *n (stick or rod)* 棒 [bou],
(workers) 職員 [shokuin]

staff room [stæfrum] *n* 職員室 [shokuins-
hitsu]

stage [steɪdʒ] *n* 段階 [dankai]

stage magician *n* 手品師 [tejinashi]

stagger [stægər] *v* よろめく [yoromeku]

stain [steɪn] *n* しみ [shimi], 汚れの跡 [yogore
no ato] ▷ *v* しみがつく [shimi ga tsuku], 汚れ
の跡をつける [yogore no ato-o tsukeru];
stain remover *n* しみ抜き剤 [shiminuki zai];
Can you remove this stain? このしみを落と
すことができますか? [kono shimi o otosu
koto ga dekimasu ka?]; **This stain is coffee**
このしみはコーヒーです [kono shimi wa
koohii desu]; **This stain is wine** このしみは
ワインです [kono shimi wa wain desu];

stained *adj* しみだらけの [shimidarake no]

staircase [stɛərkeɪs] *n* 階段 [kaidan]

stairs [steɪrz] *npl* 階段 [kaidan]

stale [steɪl] *adj* 古くなった [furuku natta]

stalemate [steɪlmeɪt] *n* ステイルメイト
[suteirumeito]

stall [stɔl] *n* 屋台 [yatai]

S

stamina [stæmɪnə] *n* スタミナ [sutamina]

stammer [stæmər] *v* どもる [domoru]

stamp [stæmp] *n* 切手 [kitte] ▷ *v* 踏みつける [fumitsukeru]; **Do you sell stamps?** 切手を売っていますか? [kitte o utte imasu ka?]; **May I have stamps for four postcards to...** ···あての郵便はがき四枚分の切手をもらえますか? [... ate no yuubin-hagaki yonmai-bun no kitte o moraemasu ka?]; **Where can I buy stamps?** どこで切手を買えますか? [doko de kitte o kaemasu ka?]; **Where is the nearest place to buy stamps?** 切手を売っている一番近い店はどこですか? [kitte o utte iru ichiban chikai mise wa doko desu ka?]

stand [stænd] *n* 具 [gu] ▷ *v* 立つ [tatsu]; **taxi stand** *n* タクシー乗り場 [takushii noriba]

standard [stændərd] *adj* 標準の [hyoujun no] ▷ *n* 標準 [hyoujun]; **standard of living** *n* 生活水準 [seikatsusuijun]

stand for *v* 表す [arawasu]

stand out *v* 突出する [tosshutsu suru]

standpoint [stændpɔɪnt] *n* 見地 [kenchi]

stands [stændz] *npl* スタンド [sutando]

stand up *v* 起立する [kiritsu suru]

staple [steɪpəl] *n* (*commodity*) 主要産物 [shuyou sanbutsu], (*wire*) ステープル [suteepuru] ▷ *v* ステープルで留める [suteepuru de todomeru]

stapler [steɪplər] *n* ステープラー [suteepuraa]

star [stɑr] *n* (*person*) スター [sutaa], (*sky*) 星 [hoshi] ▷ *v* 主演する [shuen suru]; **movie star** *n* 映画スター [eigasutaa]

starch [stɑrtʃ] *n* 澱粉 [denpun]

stare [stɛər] *v* じっと見つめる [jitto mitsumeru]

stark [stɑrk] *adj* がらんとした [garan to shita]

start [stɑrt] *n* 開始 [kaishi] ▷ *vi* 始まる [hajimaru] ▷ *vt* 始める [hajimeru]

starter [stɑrtər] *n* スターター [sutaataa]

startle [stɑrtəl] *v* びっくりさせる [bikkuri saseru]

start off *v* 旅立つ [tabidatsu]

starvation [stɑrveɪʃən] *n* 餓死 [gashi]

starve [stɑrv] *v* 餓死する [gashi suru]

state [steɪt] *n* 状態 [joutai] ▷ *v* 述べる [noberu]; **Gulf Coast states** *npl* メキシコ湾岸諸州 [Mekishiko wangan shoshuu]

statement [steɪtmənt] *n* 声明 [seimei]; **bank statement** *n* 銀行の明細書 [ginkou no meisaisho]

station [steɪʃən] *n* 駅 [eki]; **bus station** *n* バスターミナル [basutaaminaru]; **filling station** *n* ガソリンスタンド [gasorinsutando]; **police station** *n* 警察署 [keisatsusho]; **radio station** *n* ラジオ局 [rajio kyoku]; **service station** *n* ガソリンスタンド [gasorinsutando]; **station wagon** *n* エステートカー [esuteetokaa]; **subway station** *n* 地下鉄駅 [chikatetsu eki]; **train station** *n* 鉄道駅 [tetsudoueki]; **Where is the nearest subway station?** 一番近い地下鉄の駅はどこですか? [ichiban chikai chikatetsu no eki wa doko desu ka?]

stationery [steɪʃənɛri] *n* 文房具 [bunbougu]

statistics [stətɪstɪks] *npl* 統計 [toukei]

statue [stætʃu] *n* 像 [zou]

status [steɪtəs, stæt-] *n* 身分 [mibun], 地位 [chii]; **marital status** *n* 婚姻関係の有無 [kon'in kankei no umu]

status quo [steɪtəs kwoʊ, stæt-] *n* 現状 [genjou]

stay [steɪ] *n* 滞在 [taizai] ▷ *v* とどまる [todomaru]; **I'm staying at a hotel** 私はホテルに滞在しています [watashi wa hoteru ni taizai shite imasu]

stay in *v* 家にいる [ie ni iru]

steady [stɛdi] *adj* しっかりした [shikkari shita]

steak [steɪk] *n* ステーキ [suteeki]; **round steak** *n* ランプステーキ [ranpusuteeki]

steal [stil] *v* 盗む [nusumu]

steam [stim] *n* 蒸気 [jouki]

steel [stil] *n* 鋼鉄 [koutetsu]; **stainless steel** *n* ステンレススチール [sutenresusuchiiru]

steep [stip] *adj* 急な [kyuu na] (傾斜), 険しい [kewashii]; **Is it very steep?** それはとても険

しいですか? [sore wa totemo kewashii desu ka?]

steeple [stip·l] *n* 尖塔 [sentou]

steering [stiərɪŋ] *n* ステアリング [sutearingu]; **steering wheel** *n* ステアリングホイール [sutearinguhoiiru]

step [stɛp] *n* 歩み [ayumi]

stepbrother [stɛpbrʌðər] *n* 継兄弟 [mama kyoudai]

stepdaughter [stɛpdɔtər] *n* 継娘 [mama musume]

stepfather [stɛpfɑðər] *n* 継父 [mama chichi]

stepladder [stɛplædər] *n* 脚立 [kyatatsu]

stepmother [stɛpmʌðər] *n* 継母 [mama haha]

stepsister [stɛpsɪstər] *n* 継姉妹 [mama shimai]

stepson [stɛpsʌn] *n* 継子 [mamako]

stereo [stɛriou, stiər-] *n* ステレオ [sutereo], システムコンポ [shisutemukonpo]; **personal stereo** *n* パーソナルステレオ [paasonarusutereo]; **Is there a stereo in the car?** 車にカーステレオはついていますか? [kuruma ni kaa-stereo wa tsuite imasu ka?]

stereotype [stɛriətaɪp, stiər-] *n* ステレオタイプ [sutereotaipu]

sterile [stɛrəl] *adj* 滅菌した [mekkin shita]

sterilize [stɛrɪlaɪz] *v* 滅菌する [mekkin suru]

sterling [stɜrlɪŋ] *n* 英貨 [eika]

steroid [stɛrɔɪd, stɪr-] *n* ステロイド [suteroido]

stew [stu] *n* シチュー [shichuu]

steward [stuərd] *n* スチュワード [suchuwaado]

stewardship [stuərdʃɪp] *n* 護衛 [goei]

stick [stɪk] *n* 棒切れ [bou kire]; **stick insect** *n* ナナフシ [nanafushi]

sticker [stɪkər] *n* ステッカー [sutekkaa]

stick out *v* 突き出す [tsukidasu]

sticky [stɪki] *adj* べとべとした [betobeto shita]

stiff [stɪf] *adj* 堅い [katai]

stifling [staɪflɪŋ] *adj* むっとする [muttosuru] (息詰まる)

still [stɪl] *adj* 静かな [shizuka na] ▷ *adv* まだ

[mada]; **I'm still studying** 私はまだ学校に行っています [watashi wa mada gakkou ni itte imasu]; **The car is still under warranty** 車はまだ保証期間内です [kuruma wa mada hoshou-kikan nai desu]

sting [stɪŋ] *n* 刺し傷 [sashi kizu] ▷ *v* 刺す [sasu]

stingy [stɪndʒi] *adj* けちな [kechi na]

stink [stɪŋk] *n* 悪臭 [akushuu] ▷ *v* 悪臭を放つ [akushuu-o hanatsu]

stir [stɜr] *v* かき混ぜる [kakimazeru]

stitch [stɪtʃ] *n* ひと針 [hitohari] ▷ *v* 縫う [nuu]

stock [stɒk] *n* 在庫品 [zaikohin] ▷ *v* 在庫を置く [zaiko-o oku]; **stock exchange** *n* 証券取引所 [shouken torihikijo]; **stock market** *n* 株式市場 [kabushikishijou]

stockbroker [stɒkbroukər] *n* 株式仲買人 [kabushikinakagainin]

stockholder [stɒkhouldər] *n* 株主 [kabunushi]

stocking [stɒkɪŋ] *n* ストッキング [sutokkingu]

stock up *v* **stock up on** *v* 仕入れる [shiireru]

stomach [stʌmək] *n* 胃 [i], おなか [onaka]

stomachache [stʌməkeɪk] *n* 胃痛 [itsuu]

stone [stoun] *n* 石 [ishi]

stool [stul] *n* スツール [sutsuuru]

stop [stɒp] *n* 中止 [chuushi] ▷ *vi* 止まる [tomaru] ▷ *vt* 止める [tomeru]; **bus stop** *n* バス停 [basutei]

stopover [stɒpouvər] *n* 立ち寄ること [tachiyoru koto]

stopwatch [stɒpwɒtʃ] *n* ストップウォッチ [sutoppuuocchi]

storage [stɔrɪdʒ] *n* 保管 [hokan]

store [stɔr] *n* 店 [mise] ▷ *v* 蓄える [takuwaeru]; **antique store** *n* 骨董屋 [kottou ya]; **department store** *n* デパート [depaato]; **jewelry store** *n* 宝石商 [housekishou]; **liquor store** *n* 酒類販売免許 [sakerui hanbai menkyo]; **office supply store** *n* 文房具店 [bunbouguten]; **store owner** *n* 店主 [tenshu]; **store window** *n* ショーウィンドウ [shoouindou]; **What time do the stores**

S

close? お店は何時に閉まりますか? [o-mise wa nan-ji ni shimarimasu ka?]

storm [stɔrm] n 嵐 [arashi]; **Do you think there'll be a storm?** 嵐になると思いますか? [arashi ni naru to omoimasu ka?]

stormy [stɔrmi] adj 嵐の [arashi no]

story [stɔri] n 物語 [monogatari]; **short story** n 短篇小説 [tanpen shousetsu]

stove [stouv] n 料理用レンジ [ryouri you renji]; **gas stove** n ガスレンジ [gasurenji]

straight [streɪt] adj まっすぐな [massugu na]; **straight ahead** adv まっすぐに [massugu ni]; **straight up** adv まっすぐ上に [massugu ueni]

straighteners [streɪt&ənərz] npl ストレイトナー [sutoreitonaa]

straightforward [streɪtfɔrwərd] adj 率直な [sotchoku na]

strain [streɪn] n 極度の緊張 [kyokudo no kinchou]; ▷ v 緊張させる [kinchou saseru]

stranded [stræ̃ndɪd] adj 立ち往生した [tachioujou shita]

strange [streɪndʒ] adj 奇妙な [kimyou na]

stranger [streɪndʒər] n 知らない人 [shiranai hito]

strangle [stræŋgl] v 絞め殺す [shimekorosu]

strap [stræp] n 革ひも [kawa himo]

strategic [strətidʒɪk] adj 戦略的な [senryakuteki na]

strategy [strætədʒi] n 戦略 [senryaku]

straw [strɔ] n 麦わら [mugiwara]

strawberry [strɔbɛri] n イチゴ [ichigo]

stray [streɪ] n 迷い出た家畜 [mayoideta kachiku]

stream [strim] n 小川 [ogawa]

street [strit] n ストリート [sutoriito], 通り [touri]; **street map** n 街路地図 [gairo chizu]; **street plan** n 街路計画 [gairo keikaku]; **I want a street map of the city** その街のストリートマップが欲しいのですが [sono machi no sutoriito-mappu ga hoshii no desu ga]

streetcar [stritkɔr] n 路面電車 [romenden-sha]

streetlight [stritlaɪt] n 街灯 [gaitou]

streetwise [stritwaɪz] adj 世慣れた [yonareta]

strength [strɛŋkθ, strɛŋθ] n 強さ [tsuyosa], 力 [chikara]

strengthen [strɛŋθ·n] v 強くする [tsuyoku suru]

stress [strɛs] n ストレス [sutoresu]; ▷ v 強調する [kyouchou suru]

stressed [strɛst] adj ストレスがたまった [sutoresu ga tamatta]

stressful [strɛsfəl] adj ストレスの多い [sutoresu no oui]

stretch [strɛtʃ] v 伸びる [nobiru]

stretcher [strɛtʃər] n 担架 [tanka]

stretchy [strɛtʃi] adj 伸びる [nobiru]

strict [strɪkt] adj 厳しい [kibishii]

strictly [strɪktli] adv 厳しく [kibishiku]

strike [straɪk] n ストライキ [sutoraiki]; ▷ vi 襲う [osou], (suspend work) ストライキをする [sutoraiki wo suru]; ▷ vt 打つ [utsu]; **because there was a strike** ストライキがあったからです [sutoraiki ga atta kara desu]

striker [straɪkər] n ストライキ参加者 [sutoraiki sankasha]

striking [straɪkɪŋ] adj 目立つ [medatsu]

string [strɪŋ] n ひも [himo]

strip [strɪp] n ストリップ [sutorippu]; ▷ v はぐ [hagu]

stripe [straɪp] n 縞 [shima]

striped [straɪpt] adj 縞のある [shima no aru], 縞の入った [shima no haitta]

stripper [strɪpər] n ストリッパー [sutorippaa]

stroke [strouk] n なでること [naderu koto]; ▷ v なでる [naderu]

stroll [stroul] n ぶらぶら歩き [burabura aruki]

stroller [stroulər] n ベビーカー [bebiikaa], 乳母車 [ubaguruma]; **Do you rent out strollers?** ベビーカーのレンタルはありますか? [bebii-kaa no rentaru wa arimasu ka?]

strong [strɔŋ] adj 強い [tsuyoi], 丈夫な [joubu na]; **I need something stronger** 私はもっと強い薬が必要です [watashi wa motto tsuyoi kusuri ga hitsuyou desu]

strongly [strɔ́ŋli] *adv* 強く [tsuyoku]

structure [strʌ́ktʃər] *n* 構造 [kouzou]

struggle [strʌ́gəl] *n* 苦闘 [kutou] ▷ *v* 苦闘する [kutou suru]

stubborn [stʌ́bərn] *adj* 頑固な [ganko na]

stubborness *n* 意地 [iji]

stub out *v* 火をもみ消す [hi-o momikesu]

stuck [stʌ́k] *adj* 行きづまった [ikizumatta]

stuck-up *adj* 高慢ちきな [koumanchiki na]

stud [stʌ́d] *n* 鋲 [byou]

student [stúdənt] *n* 学生 [gakusei]; **graduate student** *n* 大学院生 [daigakuinsei]; **student discount** *n* 学生割引 [gakusei waribiki]; **student driver** *n* 仮免許運転者 [karimenkyo untensha]; **Are there any discounts for students?** 学生割引はありますか? [gakusei-waribiki wa arimasu ka?]; **I'm a student** 私は学生です [watashi wa gakusei desu]

studio [stúdioʊ] *n* スタジオ [sutajio]; **studio apartment** *n* スタジオフラット [sutajiofuratto], ワンルームのアパート [wanruumu no apaato]

study [stʌ́di] *v* 勉強する [benkyou suru]

stuff [stʌ́f] *n* もの [mono] (材料)

stuffy [stʌ́fi] *adj* 風通しの悪い [kazetoushi no warui]

stumble [stʌ́mbəl] *v* つまずく [tsumazuku]

stunned [stʌ́nd] *adj* どぎもを抜かれた [dogimo wo nukareta]

stunning [stʌ́nɪŋ] *adj* すばらしい [subarashii]

stunt [stʌ́nt] *n* 離れわざ [hanarewaza]

stuntman [stʌ́ntmæn] *n* スタントマン [sutantoman]

stupid [stúpɪd] *adj* 愚かな [oroka na]

stutter [stʌ́tər] *v* どもる [domoru]

style [staɪl] *n* スタイル [sutairu], 様式 [youshiki]; **I want a completely new style** 全く新しいスタイルにしてください [mattaku atarashii sutairu ni shite kudasai]

styling [staɪlɪŋ] *n* **Do you sell styling products?** スタイリング用品を売っています

か? [sutairingu youhin o utte imasu ka?]

stylist [staɪlɪst] *n* スタイリスト [sutairisuto]

subject *n* 主題 [shudai]

submarine [sʌ́bmərin] *n* 潜水艦 [sensuikan]

subscription [səbskrɪ́pʃn] *n* 定期購読 [teiki koudoku]

subsidiary [səbsɪ́diɛri] *n* 子会社 [kogaisha]

subsidize [sʌ́bsɪdaɪz] *v* 助成金を支給する [joseikin-o shikyuu suru]

subsidy [sʌ́bsɪdi] *n* 助成金 [joseikin]

substance [sʌ́bstəns] *n* 物質 [busshitsu], 実質 [jisshitsu]

substitute [sʌ́bstɪtut] *n* 代理 [dairi], 代用 [daiyou] ▷ *v* 代用する [daiyou suru]

substitute teacher *n* 臨時教員 [rinji kyouin]

subtitled [sʌ́btaɪtəld] *adj* 字幕を入れた [jimaku-o ireta]

subtitles [sʌ́btaɪtəlz] *npl* 字幕 [jimaku]

subtle [sʌ́təl] *adj* 微妙な [bimyou na]

subtract [səbtrǽkt] *v* 引く [hiku]

suburb [sʌ́bɜrb] *n* 郊外 [kougai]

suburban [səbɜ́rbən] *adj* 郊外の [kougai no]

subway [sʌ́bweɪ] *n* 地下鉄 [chikatetsu]; **subway station** *n* 地下鉄駅 [chikatetsu eki]; **Could I have a map of the subway, please?** 地下鉄のマップをいただけますか? [chikatetsu no mappu o itadakemasu ka?]; **Where is the nearest subway station?** 一番近い地下鉄の駅はどこですか? [ichiban chikai chikatetsu no eki wa doko desu ka?]

succeed [səksíd] *v* 成功する [seikou suru]

success [səksɛ́s] *n* 成功 [seikou]

successful [səksɛ́sfəl] *adj* 成功した [seikou shita]

successfully [səksɛ́sfəli] *adv* うまく [umaku]

successive [səksɛ́sɪv] *adj* 連続する [renzoku suru]

successor [səksɛ́sər] *n* 後継者 [koukeisha]

suck [sʌ́k] *v* 吸う [suu]

Sudan [sudǽn] *n* スーダン [suudan]

Sudanese [sudəníz] *adj* スーダンの [Suudan no] ▷ *n* スーダン人 [Suudan jin]

sudden [sʌ́dn] *adj* 突然の [totsuzen no]

S

suddenly [sʌd·nli] *adv* 突然に [totsuzen ni]

sue [su] *v* 訴える [uttaeru]

suede [sweɪd] *n* スエード [sueedo]

suffer [sʌfər] *v* 被る [koumuru]

suffocate [sʌfəkeɪt] *v* 窒息する [chissoku suru]

sugar [ʃugər] *n* 砂糖 [satou]; **confectioners' sugar** *n* 粉砂糖 [konazatou]; **no sugar** 砂糖なしで [satou nashi de]

sugar-free *adj* 砂糖を含まない [satou-o fukumanai]

suggest [səgdʒɛst] *v* 提案する [teian suru]

suggestion [səgdʒɛstʃ·n] *n* 提案 [teian]

suicide [suɪsaɪd] *n* 自殺 [jisatsu]; **suicide bomber** *n* 自爆者 [jibakusha]

suit [sut] *n* スーツ [suutsu] ▷ *v* 似合う [niau]; **bathing suit** *n* 水着 [mizugi]; **jogging suit** *n* シェルスーツ [shierusuutsu], トラックスーツ [torakkusuutsu]

suitable [sutəb·l] *adj* 適切な [tekisetsu na]

suitcase [sutkeɪs] *n* スーツケース [suutsukeesu]

suite [swit] *n* スイート [suiito]

sulk [sʌlk] *v* すねる [suneru]

sulky [sʌlki] *adj* すねた [suneta]

sum [sʌm] *n* 合計 [goukei]

summarize [sʌməraɪz] *v* 要約する [youyaku suru]

summary [sʌməri] *n* 要約 [youyaku]

summer [sʌmər] *n* 夏 [natsu]; **summer vacation** *npl* 夏の休暇 [natsu no kyuuka]; **after summer** 夏の後に [natsu no ato ni]; **during the summer** 夏の間 [natsu no aida]; **in summer** 夏に [natsu ni]

summertime [sʌmərtaɪm] *n* 夏季 [kaki]

summit [sʌmɪt] *n* 頂上 [choujou]

sum up *v* 要約する [youyaku suru]

sun [sʌn] *n* 太陽 [taiyou]

sunbathe [sʌnbeɪð] *v* 日光浴をする [nikkouyoku wo suru]

sunbed [sʌnbɛd] *n* 日光浴用ベッド [nikkouyoku you beddo]

sunblock [sʌnblɒk] *n* 日焼け止め [hiyakedome]

sunburn [sʌnbɜrn] *n* 日焼け [hiyake]

sunburned [sʌnbɜrnd] *adj* 日焼けした [hiyake shita]

Sunday [sʌndeɪ, -di] *n* 日曜日 [nichiyoubi]; **Is the museum open on Sundays?** その博物館は日曜日は開いていますか? [sono hakubutsukan wa nichiyoubi wa hiraite imasu ka?]; **on Sunday** 日曜日に [nichiyoubi ni]

sunflower [sʌnflaʊər] *n* ヒマワリ [himawari]

sunglasses [sʌnglæsɪz] *npl* サングラス [sangurasu]

sunlight [sʌnlaɪt] *n* 日光 [nikkou]

sunny [sʌni] *adj* 日当たりのよい [hiatari no yoi]

sunrise [sʌnraɪz] *n* 日の出 [hi no de]

sunroof [sʌnruf] *n* サンルーフ [sanruufu]

sunscreen [sʌnskrin] *n* サンスクリーン [sansukuriin]

sunset [sʌnsɛt] *n* 日没 [nichibotsu]

sunshine [sʌnʃaɪn] *n* 日光 [nikkou]

sunstroke [sʌnstroʊk] *n* 日射病 [nisshabyou]

suntan [sʌntæn] *n* 小麦色の日焼け [komugi iro no hiyake]; **suntan lotion** *n* サンタンローション [santanrooshon]; **suntan oil** *n* サンタンオイル [santan oiru]

super [supər] *adj* すばらしい [subarashii], スーパー [suupaa]

superb [supɜrb] *adj* すばらしい [subarashii]

superficial [supərfɪʃl] *adj* 表面的な [hyoumenteki na]

superior [supɪəriər] *adj* 優れた [sugureta] ▷ *n* 上役 [uwayaku]

supermarket [supərmɑrkɪt] *n* スーパーマーケット [suupaamaaketto]; **I need to find a supermarket** 私はスーパーマーケットをさがしています [watashi ha suupaamaaketto wosagashiteimasu]

supernatural [supərnætʃərəl, -nætʃrəl] *adj* 超自然の [choushizen no]

superstitious [supərstʃəs] *adj* 迷信的な [meishinteki na]

supervise [supərvaɪz] v 監督する [kantoku suru]

supervisor [supərvaɪzər] n 監督者 [kantokusha]

supper [sʌpər] n 夕食 [yuushoku]

supplement [sʌplɪmənt] n 補足 [hosoku], 補充 [hojuu]

supplier [səplaɪər] n 供給者 [kyoukyuusha]

supplies [səplaɪz] npl 食糧 [shokuryou]

supply [səplaɪ] n 供給 [kyoukyuu], 調達 [choutatsu] ▷ v 供給する [kyoukyuu suru]; office supply store n 文房具店 [bunbouguten]

support [səpɔrt] n 支え [sasae] ▷ v 支える [sasaeru] (支持)

supporter [səpɔrtər] n 支持者 [shijisha]

suppose [səpouz] v 想定する [soutei suru]

supposedly [səpouzɪdli] adv おそらく [osoraku]

supposing [səpouzɪŋ] conj もし・・・と仮定するならば [moshi... to katei surunaraba]

supposition [sʌpəzɪʃn] n 過程 [katei]

surcharge [sɜrtʃɑrdʒ] n 追加料金 [tsuikaryoukin]

sure [ʃuər] adj 確信している [kakushin shite iru]

surely [ʃuərli] adv 確かに [tashika ni]

surf [sɜrf] n 打ち寄せる波 [uchiyoseru nami] ▷ v サーフィンをする [saafin-o suru]

surface [sɜrfɪs] n 表面 [hyoumen], 面 [men]

surfboard [sɜrfbɔrd] n サーフボード [saafuboodo]

surfer [sɜrfər] n サーファー [saafaa]

surfing [sɜrfɪŋ] n サーフィン [saafin]

surge [sɜrdʒ] n 高まり [takamari]

surgeon [sɜrdʒən] n 外科医 [gekai]

surgery [sɜrdʒəri] n (operation) 手術 [shujutsu]; plastic surgery n 美容外科 [biyou geka], 形成外科 [keisei geka]

surplus [sɜrplʌs, -pləs] adj 余分な [yobun na] ▷ n 余り [amari]

surprise [sərpraɪz] n 驚き [odoroki] ▷ v びっくりさせる [bikkuri saseru]

surprised [sərpraɪzd] adj 驚いた [odoroita]

surprising [sərpraɪzɪŋ] adj 意外な [igai na]

surprisingly [sərpraɪzɪŋli] adv 驚くほど [odoroku hodo]

surrender [sərɛndər] v 降伏する [koufuku suru]

surround [səraund] v 囲む [kakomu]

surroundings [səraundɪŋz] npl 環境 [kankyou]

survey n 調査 [chousa]

surveyor [sərveɪər] n 鑑定士 [kanteishi]

survival [sərvaɪvl] n 生存 [seizon]

survive [sərvaɪv] v 生き残る [ikinokoru]

survivor [sərvaɪvər] n 生存者 [seizonsha]

suspect n [sʌspɛkt] 容疑者 [yougisha] ▷ v [səspɛkt] 疑いをかける [utagai-o kakeru]

suspend [səspɛnd] v つるす [tsurusu]

suspenders [səspɛndərz] npl ズボン吊り [zubontsuri]

suspense [səspɛns] n 不安 [fuan]

suspension [səspɛnʃn] n 一時停止 [ichiji teishi]; suspension bridge n 吊橋 [tsuribashi]

suspicious [səspɪʃəs] adj 疑わしい [utagawashii]

swallow [swɒlou] n 飲むこと [nomu koto] ▷ vi 飲み込む [nomikomu] ▷ vt を飲み込む [-o nomikomu]

swamp [swɒmp] n 沼地 [numachi]

swan [swɒn] n 白鳥 [hakuchou]

swat [swɒt] v ピシャリと打つ [pishari to utsu]

sway [sweɪ] v ゆすぶる [yusuburu]

Swaziland [swɑzilænd] n スワジランド [suwajirando]

swear [swɛər] v ののしる [nonoshiru]

swearword [swɛərwɜrd] n ののしり [nonoshiri]

sweat [swɛt] n 汗 [ase] ▷ v 汗をかく [ase wo kaku]

sweater [swɛtər] n セーター [seetaa]; polo-necked sweater n とっくり襟のセーター [tokkuri eri no seetaa]

sweatshirt [swɛtʃɜrt] n スエットシャツ

S

[suettoshatsu]

sweaty [swɛti] *adj* 汗だらけの [ase darake no]

Swede [swid] *n* スウェーデン人 [suueedenjin]

Sweden [swid•n] *n* スウェーデン [suueeden]

Swedish [swidɪʃ] *adj* スウェーデンの [suueeden no] ▸ *n* スウェーデン人 [suueedenjin]

sweep [swip] *v* 掃く [haku]

sweet [swit] *adj* (pleasing) 快い [kokoroyoi], (taste) 甘い [amai]

sweetener [swit•nər] *n* 甘味料 [kanmiryou]; **Do you have any artificial sweetener?** 甘味料はありますか? [kanmiryou wa arimasu ka?]

sweltering [swɛltərɪŋ] *adj* うだるように暑い [udaru youni atsui]

swerve [swɜrv] *v* 急にそれる [kyuu ni soreru]

swim [swɪm] *v* 泳ぐ [oyogu]

swimmer [swɪmər] *n* 泳ぐ人 [oyogu hito]

swimming [swɪmɪŋ] *n* 水泳 [suiei]; **swimming pool** *n* スイミングプール [suimingupuuru]; **swimming trunks** *npl* スイミングトランクス [suimingutorankusu]

swimsuit [swɪmsut] *n* 水着 [mizugi]

swing [swɪŋ] *n* 揺れ [yure] ▸ *v* 揺れる [yureru]

Swiss [swɪs] *adj* スイスの [suisu no] ▸ *n* スイス人 [suisujin]

switch [swɪtʃ] *n* スイッチ [suitchi] ▸ *v* 変える [kaeru]

switchboard [swɪtʃbord] *n* 電話交換台 [denwa koukandai]

Switzerland [swɪts•rlənd] *n* スイス [suisu]

swollen [swoul•n] *adj* 腫れた [hareta]

sword [sɔrd] *n* 剣 [tsurugi]

swordfish [sɔrdfɪʃ] *n* メカジキ [mekajiki]

syllable [sɪləb•l] *n* 音節 [onsetsu]

syllabus [sɪləbəs] *n* 摘要 [tekiyou]

symbol [sɪmb•l] *n* 象徴 [shouchou]

symmetrical [sɪmɛtrɪk•l] *adj* 左右対称の [sayuu taishou no]

sympathetic [sɪmpəθɛtɪk] *adj* 同情的な [doujouteki na]

sympathize [sɪmpəθaɪz] *v* 同情する [doujou suru]

sympathy [sɪmpəθi] *n* 同情 [doujou]

symphony [sɪmfəni] *n* 交響曲 [koukyoukyoku]

symptom [sɪmptəm] *n* 症状 [shoujou]

synagogue [sɪnəgog] *n* シナゴーグ [shinagoogu]; **Where is there a synagogue?** どこかにシナゴーグはありますか? [doko-ka ni shinagoogu wa arimasu ka?]

syndrome [sɪndroum] *n* **Down syndrome** *n* ダウン症候群 [Daun shoukougun]

Syria [sɪriə] *n* シリア [shiria]

Syrian [sɪriən] *adj* シリアの [shiria no] ▸ *n* シリア人 [shiriajin]

syringe [sɪrɪndʒ] *n* 注射器 [chuushaki]

syrup [sɪrəp, sɜr-] *n* シロップ [shiroppu]

system [sɪstəm] *n* 組織的な方法 [soshikiteki na houhou]; **immune system** *n* 免疫系 [men'ekikei]; **solar system** *n* 太陽系 [taiyoukei]; **systems analyst** *n* システムアナリスト [shisutemu anarisuto]

systematic [sɪstəmætɪk] *adj* 体系的な [taikeiteki na]

T

tabaconist *n* タバコ屋 [tabakoya]

table [teɪbᵊl] *n (chart)* 表 [omote] *(作表)*, *(furniture)* テーブル [teeburu]; **coffee table** *n* コーヒーテーブル [koohii teeburu]; **dressing table** *n* 鏡台 [kyoudai]; **table tennis** *n* 卓球 [takkyuu]; **table wine** *n* テーブルワイン [teeburuwain]; **A table for four people, please** 四人用のテーブルをお願いします [yonin-you no teeburu o o-negai shimasu]; **I'd like to reserve a table for three people for tonight** 今晩三人用のテーブルを予約したいのですが [konban sannin-you no teeburu o yoyaku shitai no desu ga]; **I'd like to reserve a table for two people for tomorrow night** 明日の晩二人用のテーブルを予約したいのですが [asu no ban futari-you no teeburu o yoyaku shitai no desu ga]; **The table is reserved for nine o'clock this evening** 今晩九時にテーブルを予約しました [konban ku-ji ni teeburu o yoyaku shimashita]

tablecloth [teɪbᵊlklɒθ] *n* テーブルクロス [teeburukurosu]

tablespoon [teɪbᵊlspun] *n* テーブルスプーン [teeburusupuun]

tableware [teɪbᵊlwɛər] *n* 食器 [shokki]

taboo [təbu] *adj* タブーとなっている [tabuu to natte iru] ▷ *n* タブー [tabuu]

tack [tæk] *n* 画鋲 [gabyou]

tackle [tækᵊl] *n* タックル [takkuru] ▷ *v* 取り組む [torikumu]; **fishing tackle** *n* 釣具 [tsurigu]

tact [tækt] *n* 機転 [kiten]

tactful [tæktfəl] *adj* 機転のきく [kiten no kiku]

tactics [tæktɪks] *npl* 戦術 [senjutsu]

tactless [tæktlɪs] *adj* 機転のきかない [kiten no kikanai]

tadpole [tædpoʊl] *n* オタマジャクシ [otamajakushi]

tag [tæg] *n* 付け札 [tsuke satsu]

Tahiti [təhiti] *n* タヒチ [tahichi]

tail [teɪl] *n* 尾 [o]

tailor [teɪlər] *n* テーラー [teeraa]

Taiwan [taɪwɒn] *n* 台湾 [taiwan]

Taiwanese [taɪwəniz] *adj* 台湾の [Taiwan no] ▷ *n* 台湾人 [Taiwan jin]

Tajikistan [tɑdʒɪkstɑn] *n* タジキスタン [tajikisutan]

take [teɪk] *v* 手に取る [te ni toru]; **take care of** *v* …の世話をする [... no sewa-o suru]

take after *v* …に似る [... ni niru]

take apart *v* 分解する [bunkai suru]

take away *v* 運び去る [hakobi saru]

take back *v* 取り消す [torikesu]

taken [teɪkən] *adj* **Is this seat taken?** この席には誰か座っていますか? [kono seki ni wa dare ka suwatte imasu ka?]

take off *v* 脱ぐ [nugu]

takeoff [teɪkɒf] *n* 離陸 [ririku]

takeout [teɪkoʊt] *n* テークアウト [teekuauto]

take over *v* 引き継ぐ [hikitsugu]

takeover [teɪkoʊvər] *n* 企業買収 [kigyou baishuu]

tale [teɪl] *n* 話 [hanashi], 物語 [monogatari]

talent [tælənt] *n* 才能 [sainou]

talented [tæləntɪd] *adj* 才能のある [sainou no aru]

talk [tɔk] *n* 話 [hanashi] ▷ *v* 話す [hanasu]; **talk show** *n* トークショー [tookushoo]; **talk to** *v* …に話しかける [... ni hanashikakeru]

talkative [tɔkətɪv] *adj* 話好きな [hanashi zuki na]

tall [tɔl] *adj* 高い [takai] *(高低)*

tame [teɪm] *adj* 飼いならされた [kainaras-areta]

tampon [tæmpɒn] *n* タンポン [tanpon]

tan [tæn] *n* 日焼け [hiyake]

tandem [tændəm] *n* tandem bicycle *n* タンデム自転車 [tandemu jitensha]

tangerine [tændʒərin] *n* タンジェリン [tanjierin]

tank [tæŋk] *n (combat vehicle)* 戦車 [sensha], *(large container)* タンク [tanku]; **gas tank** *n* ガソリンタンク [gasorintanku]; **septic tank** *n* 浄化槽 [joukasou]; **The gas tank is leaking** ガソリンタンクが漏れています [gasorin-tanku ga morete imasu]

tanker [tæŋkər] *n* タンカー [tankaa]

tanned [tænd] *adj* 日焼け色の [hiyake iro no]

tantrum [tæntrəm] *n* かんしゃく [kanshaku]

Tanzania [tænzəniə] *n* タンザニア [tanzania]

Tanzanian [tænzəniən] *adj* タンザニアの [Tanzania no] ▷ *n* タンザニア人 [Tanzania jin]

tap [tæp] *n* 軽くたたくこと [karuku tataku koto]

tap-dancing *n* タップダンス [tappudansu]

tape [teɪp] *n* テープ [teepu] ▷ *v* テープに記録する [teepu ni kiroku suru]; **Scotch® tape** *n* セロテープ® [seroteepu]; **tape measure** *n* 巻尺 [makijaku]; **tape recorder** *n* テープレコーダー [teepurekoodaa]; **Can I have a tape for this video camera, please?** このビデオカメラ用のテープをいただけますか？ [kono bideo-kamera-you no teepu o itadakemasu ka?]

target [tɑrgɪt] *n* 標的 [hyouteki]

tariff [tærɪf] *n* 関税率 [kanzeiritsu]

tarpaulin [tɑrpɔlɪn, tɑrpəlɪn] *n* タール塗り防水布 [taaru nuri bousuifu]

tarragon [tærəgɒn, -gən] *n* タラゴン [taragon]

tart [tɑrt] *n* タルト [taruto]

tartan [tɑrtn̩] *adj* タータンの [taatan no]

task [tæsk] *n* 任務 [ninmu]

Tasmania [tæzmeɪniə] *n* タスマニア [tasumania]

taste [teɪst] *n* 味 [aji] ▷ *v* 味をみる [aji-o miru];

It doesn't taste very good 味があまりよくありません [aji ga amari yoku arimasen]

tasteful [teɪstfəl] *adj* 趣味のよい [shumi no yoi]

tasteless [teɪstlɪs] *adj* 味のない [aji no nai]

tasty [teɪsti] *adj* 味のよい [aji no yoi]

tattoo [tætu] *n* 入れ墨 [irezumi]

Taurus [tɔrəs] *n* 牡牛座 [oushiza]

tax [tæks] *n* 税 [zei], 税金 [zeikin]; **highway tax** *n* 自動車の道路利用税 [jidousha no douro riyou zei]; **income tax** *n* 所得税 [shotokuzei]; **tax payer** *n* 納税者 [nouzeisha]; **tax return** *n* 所得申告 [shotoku shinkoku]; **value-added tax** *n* 付加価値税 [fukakachizei]; **Are taxes included?** 付加価値税は含まれていますか？ [fukakachi-zei wa fukumarete imasu ka?]

taxi [tæksi] *n* タクシー [takushii]; **private taxi** *n* 小型タクシー [kogata takushii]; **taxi driver** *n* タクシー運転手 [takushii untenshu]; **taxi stand** *n* タクシー乗り場 [takushii noriba]; **How much is the taxi fare into town?** 街までのタクシー料金はいくらですか？ [machi made no takushii-ryoukin wa ikura desu ka?]; **I left my bags in the taxi** 私はタクシーにかばんを置き忘れました [watashi wa takushii ni kaban o okiwasuremashita]; **I need a taxi** 私はタクシーが必要です [watashi wa takushii ga hitsuyou desu]; **Please order me a taxi for eight o'clock** 八時にタクシーを呼んでください [hachi-ji ni takushii o yonde kudasai]; **Where can I get a taxi?** どこでタクシーに乗れますか？ [doko de takushii ni noremasu ka?]; **Where is the taxi stand?** タクシー乗り場はどこですか？ [takushii-noriba wa doko desu ka?]

TB [ti bi] *n* 結核 [kekkaku]

tea [ti] *n* お茶 [o-cha]; **herbal tea** *n* ハーブティー [haabuteii]; **tea bag** *n* ティーバッグ [tiibaggu]

teach [titʃ] *v* 教える [oshieru]

teacher [titʃər] *n* 教師 [kyoushi]; **substitute teacher** *n* 臨時教員 [rinji kyouin]; **teacher's**

aide n 教室助手 [kyoushitsu joshu]; **I'm a teacher** 私は教師です [watashi wa kyoushi desu]

teaching [títʃɪŋ] n 教えること [oshieru koto]

teacup [tikʌp] n ティーカップ [tiikappu]

teakettle [tikɛt+l] n ケトル [ketoru]

team [tim] n チーム [chiimu]

teapot [tipɒt] n ティーポット [tiipotto]

tear[1] [tɪər] n (from eye) 涙 [namida], (split) 破れ目 [yabureme]

tear[2] [tɛər] v 破る [yaburu]; **tear up** v ずたずたに引き裂く [zutazuta ni hikisaku]

tear gas [tɪərgæs] n 催涙ガス [sairuigasu]

tease [tiz] v からかう [karakau]

teaspoon [tíspun] n ティースプーン [tiisupuun]

teatime [títaɪm] n ティータイム [tiitaimu]

technical [tɛknɪk+l] adj 専門的な [senmonteki na]

technician [tɛknɪ́ʃ+n] n 専門技術者 [senmon gijutsusha]

technique [tɛknik] n 専門技術 [senmon gijutsu]

technological [tɛknəlɒdʒɪk+l] adj 技術的な [gijutsuteki na]

technology [tɛknɒlədʒi] n 技術 [gijutsu]

techno (music) [tɛknou myuzɪk] n テクノポップ [tekunopoppu]

tee [ti] n ティー [tii] (ゴルフ)

teenager [tínerdʒər] n ティーンエージャー [tiineejaa]

teens [tinz] npl 十代 [juudai]

teethe [tið] v 歯が生える [ha ga haeru]

teetotal [títoʊt+l] adj 絶対禁酒の [zettai kinshu no]

telecommunications [tɛlɪkəmyunɪkeɪʃ+nz] npl 電気通信 [denkitsuushin]

telegram [tɛlɪgræm] n 電報 [denpou]; **Can I send a telegram from here?** ここから電報を送れますか? [koko kara denpou o okuremasu ka?]

telemarketing [tɛlɪmɑrkɪtɪŋ] npl 電話セールス [denwa seerusu]

telephone [tɛlɪfoʊn] n 電話 [denwa]; **telephone directory** n 電話帳 [denwachou]; **How much would it cost to telephone...?** ···に電話するのはいくらですか? [... ni denwa suru no wa ikura desu ka?]; **What's the telephone number?** 電話番号は何番ですか? [denwa-bangou wa nan-ban desu ka?]

telescope [tɛlɪskoʊp] n 望遠鏡 [bouenkyou]

television [tɛlɪvɪʒ+n, -vɪʒ-] n テレビ [terebi]; **cable television** n ケーブルテレビ [keeburu terebi]; **color television** n カラーテレビ [karaaterebi]; **digital television** n デジタルテレビ [dejitaru terebi]

tell [tɛl] v 告げる [tsugeru]

temp [tɛmp] n 臨時職員 [rinjishokuin]

temper [tɛmpər] n かんしゃく [kanshaku]

temperature [tɛmprətʃər, -tʃuər] n 温度 [ondo]

temple [tɛmp+l] n 寺院 [jiin]; **Is the temple open to the public?** その寺院は一般公開されていますか? [sono jiin wa ippan-koukai sarete imasu ka?]; **When is the temple open?** その寺院はいつ開きますか? [sono jiin wa itsu hirakimasu ka?]

temporary [tɛmpəreri] adj 一時の [ichiji no]

tempt [tɛmpt] v 誘惑する [yuuwaku suru]

temptation [tɛmpteɪʃ+n] n 誘惑 [yuuwaku]

tempting [tɛmptɪŋ] adj 誘惑する [yuuwaku suru]

ten [tɛn] number 十 [juu]; **It's ten o'clock** 十時です [juu-ji desu]

tenant [tɛnənt] n 賃借人 [chinshakunin]

tend [tɛnd] v 傾向がある [keikou ga aru]

tendency [tɛndənsi] n 傾向 [keikou]

tender [tɛndər] adj 柔らかい [yawarakai]

tendon [tɛndən] n 腱 [kou]

tennis [tɛnɪs] n テニス [tenisu]; **table tennis** n 卓球 [takkyuu]; **tennis player** n テニス選手 [tenisusenshu]; **tennis racket** n テニスラケット [tenisuraketto]; **How much does it cost to use a tennis court?** テニスコートを借りるのはいくらですか? [tenisu-kooto o

T

kariru no wa ikura desu ka?]; **Where can I play tennis?** どこでテニスができますか? [doko de tenisu ga dekimasu ka?]

tenor [tɛnər] n テノール [tenooru]

tense [tɛns] adj 緊張した [kinchou shita] ▷ n 時制 [jisei]

tension [tɛnʃ˄n] n 緊張 [kinchou]

tent [tɛnt] n テント [tento]; **tent peg** n テントペグ [tentopegu]; **tent pole** n テントポール [tentopooru]; **Can we pitch our tent here?** ここにテントを張ってもいいですか? [koko ni tento o hatte mo ii desu ka?]; **How much is it per night for a tent?** テント一つにつき一晩でいくらですか? [tento hitotsu ni tsuki hitoban de ikura desu ka?]; **How much is it per week for a tent?** テント一つにつき1週間でいくらですか? [tento hitotsu ni tsuki isshuukan de ikura desu ka?]; **We'd like a site for a tent** テント用のサイトが欲しいのですが [tento-you no saito ga hoshii no desu ga]

tenth [tɛnθ] adj 十番目の [juu banme no] ▷ n 十番目 [juu banme]

term [tɜrm] n 起源 [kigen], *(description)* 用語 [yougo], *(division of year)* 学期 [gakki]

terminal [tɜrmɪn˄l] adj 末期の [makki no] *(終わりの時期)* ▷ n ターミナル [taaminaru]

terminally [tɜrmɪn˄li] adv 末期的に [makkiteki ni]

terrible [tɛrɪb˄l] adj ひどい [hidoi]

terribly [tɛrɪbli] adv ひどく [hidoku]

terrier [tɛriər] n テリア [teria]

terrific [tərɪfɪk] adj すばらしい [subarashii], ものすごい [monosugoi]

terrified [tɛrɪfaɪd] adj 怖がった [kowagatta]

terrify [tɛrɪfaɪ] v 怖がらせる [kowagaraseru]

territory [tɛrətɔri] n 地域 [chiiki]

terrorism [tɛrərɪzəm] n テロリズム [terorizumu]

terrorist [tɛrərɪst] n テロリスト [terorisuto]; **terrorist attack** n テロリストによる攻撃 [terorisuto niyoru kougeki]

test [tɛst] n 試験 [shiken] ▷ v 試験する [shiken suru]; **driver's test** n 運転免許試験 [untenmenkyoshiken]; **Ministry of Transport test** *(vehicle safety)* n 車検 [shaken]; **smear test** n 塗沫検査 [tomatsu kensa]; **test tube** n 試験管 [shikenkan]

testicle [tɛstɪk˄l] n 精巣 [seisou]

tetanus [tɛt˄nəs] n 破傷風 [hashoufuu]; **I need a tetanus shot** 私は破傷風予防の注射が必要です [watashi wa hashoufuu yobou no chuusha ga hitsuyou desu]

text [tɛkst] n 本文 [honbun] ▷ v テキストメッセージを送る [tekisuto messeeji-o okuru]; **text message** n テキストメッセージ [tekisu-tomesseeji]

textbook [tɛkstbʊk] n 教科書 [kyoukasho]

textile [tɛkstaɪl] n 織物 [orimono]

Thai [taɪ] adj タイの [Tai no] ▷ n *(language)* タイ語 [taigo], *(person)* タイ人 [Tai jin]

Thailand [taɪlænd] n タイ [tai] (国)

than [ðən, STRONG ðæn] prep **It's more than on the meter** それではメーター料金より高いです [sore de wa meetaa-ryoukin yori takai desu]

thank [θæŋk] v 感謝する [kansha suru]

thanks [θæŋks] excl ありがとう! [arigatou]

that [ðæt] **Does that contain alcohol?** それにはアルコールが入っていますか? [sore ni wa arukooru ga haitte imasu ka?]; **How much does that cost?** あれはいくらですか? [are wa ikura desu ka?]; **Is there a route that avoids the traffic?** 混雑を避けられる道はありますか? [konzatsu o sakerareru michi wa arimasu ka?]; **Sorry, I didn't catch that** ごめんなさい、聞き取れませんでした [gomen nasai, kikitoremasen deshita]

thatched [θætʃt] adj 萱葺き屋根の [kayabuki yane no]

thaw [θɔ] v **It's thawing out** 雪解けしています [yukidoke shite imasu]

the [ðə, ði] def art **The lunch was excellent** 昼食はすばらしかったです [chuushoku wa subarashikatta desu]; **Where do I catch the bus to...?** ···へ行くバスにはどこで乗れます

か? [... e iku basu ni wa doko de noremasu ka?]; **Where is the nearest ATM?** 一番近い現金自動支払い機はどこですか? [ichiban chikai genkin-jidou-shiharaiki wa doko desu ka?]

theater [θiətər] *n* 劇場 [gekijou]; **movie theater** *n* 映画館 [eigakan]; **What's on at the theater?** その劇場で何が上演されていますか? [sono gekijou de nani ga jouen sarete imasu ka?]

theft [θɛft] *n* 盗み [nusumi]; **identity theft** *n* 個人情報泥棒 [kojin jouhou dorobou]

theme [θim] *n* テーマ [teema]; **theme park** *n* テーマパーク [teemapaaku]

then [ðɛn] *adv* その時 [sono toki]

theology [θiɒlədʒi] *n* 神学 [shingaku]

theory [θɪəri] *n* 理論 [riron]

therapy [θɛrəpi] *n* 療法 [ryouhou]

there [ðər, STRONG ðɛr, ðɛər] *adv* そこに [soko ni]

thermometer [θərmɒmɪtər] *n* 温度計 [ondokei]

Thermopane® [θɜrmoʊpeɪn] *n* 複層ガラス [fukusou garasu]

thermos [θɜrməs] *n* サーモス® [saamosu], 魔法瓶 [mahoubin]

thermostat [θɜrməstæt] *n* サーモスタット [saamosutatto]

these [ðiz] *pron* **Can you repair these shoes?** この靴を修理できますか? [kono kutsu o shuuri dekimasu ka?]

they [ðeɪ] *pron* **Do they rent out rackets?** ラケットを貸し出していますか? [raketto o kashidashite imasu ka?]

thick [θɪk] *adj* 厚い [atsui]

thickness [θɪknɪs] *n* 厚さ [atsusa]

thief [θif] *n* 泥棒 [dorobou]

thigh [θaɪ] *n* 腿 [momo]

thin [θɪn] *adj* 薄い [usui] (厚み)

thing [θɪŋ] *n* 物 [mono]

think [θɪŋk] *v* 考える [kangaeru]

third [θɜrd] *adj* 三番目の [san banme no] ▷ *n* 三番目 [san banme]; **Third World** *n* 第三世界 [dai san sekai]

thirdly [θɜrdli] *adv* 第三に [dai san ni]

thirst [θɜrst] *n* のどの渇き [nodo no kawaki]

thirsty [θɜrsti] *adj* のどが渇いた [nodo ga kawaita]

thirteen [θɜrtin] *number* 十三 [juusan]

thirteenth [θɜrtinθ] *adj* 十三番目の [juusan banme no]

thirty [θɜrti] *number* 三十 [sanjuu]

this [ðɪs] **I'll have this** 私はこれをいただきます [watashi wa kore o itadakimasu]; **This is...** ・・・です [...desu]; **This is your room** これがあなたの部屋です [kore ga anata no heya desu]; **What is in this?** これには何が入っていますか? [kore ni wa nani ga haitte imasu ka?]

thistle [θɪsəl] *n* アザミ [azami]

thorn [θɔrn] *n* とげ [toge]

thorough [θɜroʊ] *adj* 徹底的な [tetteiteki na]

thoroughly [θɜrouli] *adv* 徹底的に [tetteiteki ni]

thought [θɔt] *n* 思考 [shikou]

thoughtful [θɔtfəl] *adj* 思慮深い [shiryobukai]

thoughtless [θɔtlɪs] *adj* 無思慮な [mushiryo na]

thousand [θaʊzənd] *number* 千 [sen]

thousandth [θaʊzənθ] *adj* 千番目の [sen banme no] ▷ *n* 千番目 [sen banme]

thread [θrɛd] *n* 糸 [ito]

threat [θrɛt] *n* 脅し [odoshi]

threaten [θrɛtən] *v* 脅す [odosu]

threatening [θrɛtənɪŋ] *adj* 脅すような [odosu you na]

three [θri] *number* 三 [san]; **It's three o'clock** 三時です [san-ji desu]

three-dimensional [θridɪmɛnʃənəl] *adj* 立体的な [rittaiteki na]

thrifty [θrɪfti] *adj* 倹約な [kenyaku na]

thrill [θrɪl] *n* ぞくぞくする感じ [zokuzoku suru kanji]

thrilled [θrɪld] *adj* ぞくぞくした [zokuzoku shita]

T

thriller [θrɪlər] n スリラー [suriraa]

thrilling [θrɪlɪŋ] adj ぞくぞくさせる [zokuzoku saseru]

throat [θrout] n のど [nodo]

throb [θrɒb] v 動悸を打つ [douki-o utsu]

throne [θroun] n 王座 [ouza]

through [θru] all through June 六月いっぱい [roku-gatsu ippai]; I can't get through つながりません [tsunagarimasen]; Please let me through 通してください [tooshite kudasai]

throw [θrou] v 投げる [nageru]

throw away v 捨てる [suteru]

throw out v 拒否する [kyohi suru]

throw up v 吐く [haku]

thrush [θrʌʃ] n ツグミ [tsugumi]

thug [θʌg] n 凶悪犯 [kyouakuhan]

thumb [θʌm] n 親指 [oyayubi]

thumbtack [θʌmtæk] n 画鋲 [gabyou]

thump [θʌmp] v ゴツンと打つ [gotsun to utsu]

thunder [θʌndər] n 雷鳴 [raimei]

thunderstorm [θʌndərstɔrm] n 雷雨 [raiu]

thundery [θʌndəri] adj 雷鳴を伴った [raimei-o tomonatta]

Thursday [θɜrzdeɪ, -di] n 木曜日 [mokuyoubi]; on Thursday 木曜日に [mokuyoubi ni]

thyme [taɪm] n タイム [taimu]

Tibet [tɪbɛt] n チベット [chibetto]

Tibetan [tɪbɛtn] adj チベットの [Chibetto no] ▷ n (language) チベット語 [Chibetto go], (person) チベット人 [Chibetto jin]

ticket [tɪkɪt] n チケット [chiketto], 切符 [kippu], 券 [ken]; bus ticket n バスの切符 [basu no kippu]; one-day round-trip ticket n 日帰り往復割引切符 [higaeri oufuku waribiki kippu]; one-way ticket n 片道切符 [katamichi kippu]; parking ticket n 駐車違反切符 [chuushaihan kippu]; round-trip ticket n 往復切符 [oufuku kippu]; season ticket n 定期券 [teikiken]; stand-by ticket n キャンセル待ちの切符 [kyanserumachi no kippu]; ticket barrier n 改札口 [kaisatsuguchi]; ticket

collector n 改札係 [kaisatsugakari]; ticket inspector n 検札係 [kensatsugakari]; ticket machine n 券売機 [kenbaiki]; ticket office n 予約オフィス [yoyaku ofisu], 切符売場 [kippu uriba]; a child's ticket 子供のチケット [kodomo no chiketto]; Can I buy the tickets here? ここでそのチケットを買えますか? [koko de sono chiketto o kaemasu ka?]; Could you reserve the tickets for us? 私たちのためにそのチケットを予約してもらえますか? [watashi-tachi no tame ni sono chiketto o yoyaku shite moraemasu ka?]; Do I need to buy a ticket to park? 駐車チケットを買わなければなりませんか? [chuusha-chiketto o kawanakereba narimasen ka?]; Do you have multi-trip tickets? 複数回乗車できる切符はありますか? [fukusuukai jousha dekiru kippu wa arimasu ka?]; How much are the tickets? 切符はいくらですか? [kippu wa ikura desu ka?]; How much is a round-trip ticket? 往復切符はいくらですか? [oufuku-kippu wa ikura desu ka?]; I want to upgrade my ticket 切符をアップグレードしたいのですが [kippu o appugureedo shitai no desu ga]; I'd like two tickets for next Friday 来週の金曜の切符を2枚ください [raishuu no kinyou no kippu o nimai kudasai]; I'd like two tickets, please 切符を2枚ください [kippu o nimai kudasai]; I've lost my ticket 私はチケットをなくしました [watashi wa chiketto o nakushimashita]; two round-trip tickets to... ・・・行き往復切符2枚 [... iki oufuku-kippu nimai]; The ticket machine isn't working 自動券売機が故障しています [jidou-kenbaiki ga koshou shite imasu]; Two tickets for tonight, please 今晩のチケットを2枚お願いします [konban no chiketto o nimai o-negai shimasu]; Where can I buy tickets for the concert? どこでそのコンサートのチケットを買えますか? [doko de sono konsaato no chiketto o kaemasu ka?]; Where can I get tickets? 切符はどこで買えますか? [kippu wa doko de kaemasu ka?]; **Where is the ticket machine?** 自動券売機はどこですか? [jidou-kenbaiki wa doko desu ka?]

tickle [tɪkᵊl] v くすぐる [kusuguru]

ticklish [tɪklɪʃ] adj くすぐったがる [kusuguttagaru]

tide [taɪd] n 潮 [shio]; **When is high tide?** 満ち潮はいつですか? [michi-shio wa itsu desu ka?]

tidy [taɪdi] adj きちんとした [kichin to shita] ▷ v 片付ける [katazukeru]

tidy up v 整頓する [seiton suru]

tie [taɪ] n ネクタイ [nekutai] ▷ v 縛る [shibaru], (equal with) 引き分ける [hikiwakeru]; **bow tie** n 蝶ネクタイ [chounekutai]

tie up v 固く縛る [kataku shibaru]

tiger [taɪgər] n トラ [tora]

tight [taɪt] adj ぴんと張った [pin to hatta]

tighten [taɪtᵊn] v 締める [shimeru]

tightly [taɪtli] adj ぴったり [pittari] ▷ adv ぎっしり [gisshiri]

tights [taɪts] npl タイツ [taitsu]

tile [taɪl] n タイル [tairu]

tiled [taɪld] adj タイルを張った [tairu-o hatta]

till [tɪl] prep, conj **I want to stay from Monday till Wednesday** 月曜から水曜まで宿泊したいのですが [getsuyou kara suiyou made shukuhaku shitai no desu ga]

time [taɪm] n とき [toki], 時間 [jikan], 時刻 [jikoku]; **closing time** n 閉店時刻 [heiten jikoku]; **dinner time** n ディナーの時刻 [dinaa no jikoku]; **on time** adj 遅れずに [okurezu ni]; **spare time** n 余暇 [yoka]; **time off** n 欠勤時間 [kekkin jikan]; **time zone** n 標準時間帯 [hyoujun jikantai]; **I've had a great time** すばらしいときを過ごせました [subarashii toki o sugosemashita]; **Is it time to go?** もう行く時間ですか? [mou iku jikan desu ka?]; **Is the train on time?** 電車は時刻どおりですか? [densha wa jikoku doori desu ka?]; **What's the minimum amount of time?** 最低利用時間はどれだけですか? [saitei-riyou-jikan wa dore dake desu ka?]

timebomb [taɪmbɒm] n 時限爆弾 [jigenbakudan]

timer [taɪmər] n タイマー [taimaa]

timeshare [taɪmʃɛər] n 休暇施設の共同所有権 [kyuuka shisetsu no kyoudou shoyuuken]

timetable [taɪmteɪbᵊl] n 時刻表 [jikokuhyou]; **May I have a timetable, please?** 時刻表をいただけますか? [jikokuhyou o itadakemasu ka?]

tin [tɪn] n 錫 [suzu]

tinfoil [tɪnfɔɪl] n アルミ箔 [arumihaku]

tinsel [tɪnsᵊl] n 装飾用のぴかぴか光る金属片や糸 [soushoku you no pikapika hikaru kinzokuhen ya ito]

tinted [tɪntɪd] adj 薄く色を着けた [usuku iro-o tsuketa]

tiny [taɪni] adj 小さな [chiisa na]

tip [tɪp] n (end of object) 先端 [sentan], (reward) チップ [chippu] (心づけ), (suggestion) 助言 [jogen] ▷ v (incline) 傾ける [katamukeru], (reward) チップをやる [chippu-o yaru] (心づけ); **How much should I give as a tip?** チップはいくら渡せばよいですか? [chippu wa ikura wataseba yoi desu ka?]; **Is it usual to give a tip?** チップを渡すのは一般的なことですか? [chippu o watasu no wa ippan-teki na koto desu ka?]

tipsy [tɪpsi] adj ほろ酔いの [horo yoi no]

tiptoe [tɪptoʊ] n つまさき [tsumasaki]

tire [taɪər] n タイヤ [taiya]; **spare tire** n スペアタイヤ [supeataiya]; **I have a flat tire** タイヤがパンクしました [taiya ga panku shimashita]; **The tire has burst** タイヤが破裂しました [taiya ga haretsu shimashita]; **What should the tire pressure be?** 適正なタイヤ圧はどのくらいですか? [tekisei na taiya-atsu wa dono kurai desu ka?]

tired [taɪərd] adj 疲れた [tsukareta]

tiring [taɪərɪŋ] adj 疲れる [tsukareru]

tissue [tɪʃu] n 組織 [soshiki] (生物)

title [taɪtᵊl] n 題名 [daimei]

to [tə, tu] **I need to get to...** 私は・・・へ行かなければなりません [watashi wa... e ikanakereba narimasen]; **I'm allergic to peanuts** 私はピーナッツのアレルギーがあります [watashi wa piinattsu no arerugii ga arimasu]; **I'm going to...** 私は・・・へ行きます [watashi wa... e ikimasu]; **May I speak to Mr....?** ・・・さんをお願いできますか? [... san o o-negai dekimasu ka?]; **When is the first bus to...?** ・・・へ行く始発のバスは何時ですか? [... e iku shihatsu no basu wa nan-ji desu ka?]

toad [toud] n ヒキガエル [hikigaeru]

toadstool [toudstul] n 毒キノコ [doku kinoko]

toast [toust] n (grilled bread) トースト [toosuto], (tribute) 乾杯 [kanpai]; **zwieback toast** n ラスク [rasuku]

toaster [toustər] n トースター [toosutaa]

toboggan [təbɒgən] n トボガン [tobogan]

tobogganing [təbɒgənɪŋ] n トボガン [tobogan]

today [tədeɪ] adv 今日 [kyou]; **What day is it today?** 今日は何曜日ですか? [kyou wa nani-youbi desu ka?]; **What is today's date?** 今日は何日ですか? [kyou wa nan-nichi desu ka?]

toddler [tɒdlər] n よちよち歩きの幼児 [yochiyochi aruki no youji]

toe [tou] n 足の指 [ashi no yubi]

toffee [tɒfi] n トフィー [tofii]

together [təgɛðər] adv 一緒 [issho], 一緒に [issho ni], ご一緒 [go issho]; **All together, please** 全部一緒にお勘定をお願いします [zenbu issho ni o-kanjou o o-negai shimasu]

Togo [tougou] n トーゴ [toogo]

toilet [tɔɪlɪt] n 便器 [benki], トイレ [toire]; **toilet paper** n トイレットペーパー [toirettopeepaa]; **roll of toilet paper** n トイレットペーパーロール [toirettopeepaarooru]; **The toilet won't flush** トイレが流れません [toire ga nagaremasen]; **There's no toilet paper** トイレットペーパーがありません [toiretto-peepaa ga arimasen]

toiletries [tɔɪlətriz] npl 洗面化粧用品 [senmen keshou youhin]; **toiletries bag** n 洗面用具バッグ [senmen yougu baggu]

token [toukən] n しるし [shirushi] (現れ)

tolerant [tɒlərənt] adj 寛容な [kan'you na]

toll [toul] n 有料 [yuuryou], 鐘の音 [kane no oto]; **Is there a toll on this freeway?** この高速道路は有料ですか? [kono kousoku-douro wa yuuryou desu ka?]

tomato [təmeɪtou] (pl tomatoes) n トマト [tomato]; **tomato sauce** n トマトソース [tomatosoosu]

tomb [tum] n 墓 [haka]

tomboy [tɒmbɔɪ] n おてんば娘 [otemba musume]

tomorrow [təmɒrou] adv 明日 [asu]; **Is it open tomorrow?** それは明日開きますか? [sore wa asu hirakimasu ka?]; **tomorrow morning** 明日の朝 [asu no asa]

ton [tʌn] n トン [ton]

tone [toun] n **dial tone** n 発信音 [hasshin-on]

Tonga [tɒŋgə] n トンガ [tonga]

tongue [tʌŋ] n 舌 [shita]

tonic [tɒnɪk] n 強壮剤 [kyousouzai]

tonight [tənaɪt] adv 今夜 [konya]

tonsillitis [tɒnsɪlaɪtɪs] n 扁桃腺炎 [hentousen'en]

tonsils [tɒnsəlz] npl 扁桃 [hentou]

too [tu] adv また [mata] (おなじく)

tool [tul] n 道具 [dougu]

tooth [tuθ] (pl teeth) n 歯 [ha]; **wisdom tooth** n 親知らず [oyashirazu]; **I've broken a tooth** 私は歯を折りました [watashi wa ha o orimashita]; **This tooth hurts** この歯が痛みます [kono ha ga itamimasu]

toothache [tuθeɪk] n 歯痛 [shitsuu]

toothbrush [tuθbrʌʃ] n 歯ブラシ [haburashi]

toothpaste [tuθpeɪst] n 練り歯ミガキ [neri hamigaki]

toothpick [tuθpɪk] n つま楊枝 [tsuma youji]

top [tɒp] adj 一番上の [ichiban ue no] ▷ n 上 [ue]

topic [tɒpɪk] n 話題 [wadai]

topical [tɒpɪk·l] adj 時事的な [jijiteki na]

top-secret adj 最高機密の [saikou kimitsu

no]

top up *v* **Where can I buy a top-up card?** どこでトップアップカードを買えますか? [doko de toppu-appu-kaado o kaemasu ka?]

tornado [tɔrneɪdoʊ] *n* 竜巻 [tatsumaki]

tortoise [tɔrtəs] *n* カメ [kame] (動物)

torture [tɔrtʃər] *n* 拷問 [goumon] ▷ *v* 拷問にかける [goumon ni kakeru]

toss [tɔs] *v* 軽く投げる [karuku nageru]

total [toʊtʃl] *adj* 完全な [kanzen na] ▷ *n* 合計 [goukei]

totally [toʊtʃli] *adv* 完全に [kanzen ni]

touch [tʌtʃ] *v* 触れる [fureru]

touchdown [tʌtʃdaʊn] *n* 着地 [chakuchi]

touchline [tʌtʃlaɪn] *n* タッチライン [tacchirain]

touch pad [tʌtʃpæd] *n* タッチパッド [tacchipaddo]

touchy [tʌtʃi] *adj* 怒りっぽい [okorippoi]

toupee [tupeɪ] *n* かつら [katsura]

tour [tʊər] *n* ツアー [tsuaa], 旅行 [ryokou] ▷ *v* 旅行する [ryokou suru]; **guided tour** *n* ガイドツアー [gaidotsuaa]; **tour guide** *n* ツアーガイド [tsuaagaido]; **tour operator** *n* 旅行業者 [ryokougyousha]; **Are there any sightseeing tours of the town?** その街の観光ツアーはありますか? [sono machi no kankou-tsuaa wa arimasu ka?]; **How long does the tour take?** ツアーの所要時間はどのくらいですか? [tsuaa no shoyou-jikan wa dono kurai desu ka?]; **I enjoyed the tour** ツアーは楽しかったです [tsuaa ha tanoshi kattadesu]; **Is there a guided tour in English?** 英語のガイドツアーはありますか? [eigo no gaido-tsuaa wa arimasu ka?]; **What time does the guided tour begin?** ガイドツアーは何時に始まりますか? [gaido-tsuaa wa nan-ji ni hajimarimasu ka?]; **When is the bus tour of the town?** その街のバスツアーはいつですか? [sono machi no basu-tsuaa wa itsu desu ka?]

tourism [tʊərɪzəm] *n* 旅行業 [ryokou gyou]

tourist [tʊərɪst] *n* 旅行者 [ryokousha]; **tourist office** *n* ツーリストオフィス [tsuurisutoofisu]

tournament [tʊərnəmənt, tɜr-] *n* トーナメント [toonamento]

tow [toʊ] *n* **tow truck** *n* レッカー車 [rekkaasha]; **Could you send a tow truck?** レッカー車を手配してもらえますか? [rekkaa-sha o tehai shite moraemasu ka?]

tow away *v* レッカー移動する [rekkaa idou suru]

towel [taʊəl] *n* タオル [taoru]; **bath towel** *n* バスタオル [basutaoru]; **dish towel** *n* 布巾 [fukin]; **Could you lend me a towel?** タオルを貸していただけますか? [taoru o kashite itadakemasu ka?]; **Please bring me more towels** タオルをもっと持ってきてください [taoru o motto motte kite kudasai]

tower [taʊər] *n* 塔 [tou]; **electrical tower** *n* 鉄塔 [tettou]

town [taʊn] *n* 町 [machi]; **town hall** *n* タウンホール [taunhooru]; **town planning** *n* 都市計画 [toshikeikaku]

toxic [tɒksɪk] *adj* 有毒な [yuudoku na]

toy [tɔɪ] *n* おもちゃ [omocha]

trace [treɪs] *n* 跡 [ato]

tracing paper *n* トレース紙 [toreesushi]

track [træk] *n* 小道 [komichi]

track-and-field *npl* 陸上競技 [rikujou kyougi]

track down *v* 跡をたどって見つけ出す [ato-o tadotte mitsukedasu]

tractor [træktər] *n* トラクター [torakutaa]

trade [treɪd] *n* 商売 [shoubai] ▷ *v* 交換する [koukan suru]

trademark [treɪdmɑrk] *n* 商標 [shouhyou]

tradition [trədɪʃn] *n* 伝統 [dentou]

traditional [trədɪʃənl] *adj* 伝統的な [dentouteki na]

traffic [træfɪk] *n* 交通 [koutsuu]; **traffic code** *n* 交通規則集 [koutsuu kisokushuu]; **traffic jam** *n* 交通渋滞 [koutsuujuutai]; **traffic lights** *npl* 交通信号 [koutsu shingou]; **Is the traffic heavy on the freeway?** 高速道路は交通量が多いですか? [kousoku-douro wa koutsuu-ryou ga ooi desu ka?]

T

tragedy [trædʒɪdɪ] n 悲惨な出来事 [hisan na dekigoto]

tragic [trædʒɪk] adj 悲惨な [hisan na]

trail [treɪl] n trail riding n ポニートレッキング [poniitorekkingu]; **Do you have a guide to local trails?** 地元のウォーキングのガイドはいますか? [jimoto no wookingu no gaido wa imasu ka?]; **I'd like to go trail riding** 私はポニートレッキングに行きたいのですが [watashi wa ponii-torekkingu ni ikitai no desu ga]

trailer [treɪlər] n トレーラー [toreeraa], トレーラーハウス [toreeraahausu]; **trailer park** n トレーラーハウスキャンプ場 [toreeraa hausu kyanpu jou]; **Can we park our trailer here?** ここにトレーラーハウスを駐車してもいいですか? [koko ni toreeraa-hausu o chuusha shite mo ii desu ka?]; **We'd like a site for a trailer** トレーラーハウスのサイトが欲しいのですが [toreeraa-hausu no saito ga hoshii no desu ga]

train [treɪn] n 電車 [densha], 列車 [ressha]▷v 訓練する [kunren suru]; **train station** n 鉄道駅 [tetsudoueki]; **Does the train stop at...?** 電車は・・・に停まりますか? [densha wa... ni tomarimasu ka?]; **How frequent are the trains to...?** ・・・へ行く電車はどのくらいの間隔でありますか? [... e iku densha wa dono kurai no kankaku de arimasu ka?]; **I've missed my train** 私は電車に乗り遅れました [watashi wa densha ni noriokuremashita]; **Is the train wheelchair-accessible?** 電車は車椅子で乗れますか? [densha wa kuruma-isu de noremasu ka?]; **Is this the train for...?** これは・・・行きの電車ですか? [kore wa... iki no densha desu ka?]; **The next available train, please** 次に乗れる電車をお願いします [tsugi ni noreru densha o o-negai shimasu]; **What time does the train arrive in...?** 電車は・・・に何時に着きますか? [densha wa... ni nan-ji ni tsukimasu ka?]; **What time does the train leave?** 電車は何時に出ますか? [densha wa nan-ji ni demasu ka?]; **What times are the trains to...?** ・・・へ行く電車は何時にありますか? [... e iku densha wa nan-ji ni arimasu ka?]; **When is the first train to...?** ・・・へ行く始発の電車は何時ですか? [... e iku shihatsu no densha wa nan-ji desu ka?]; **When is the last train to...?** ・・・へ行く最終の電車は何時ですか? [... e iku saishuu no densha wa nan-ji desu ka?]; **When is the next train to...?** ・・・へ行く次の電車は何時ですか? [... e iku tsugi no densha wa nan-ji desu ka?]; **When is the train due?** 電車はいつ到着する予定ですか? [densha wa itsu touchaku suru yotei desu ka?]; **Where can I get a train to...?** ・・・へ行く電車にはどこで乗れますか? [... e iku densha ni wa doko de noremasu ka?]; **Which platform does the train leave from?** 電車は何番線から出ますか? [densha wa nan-ban-sen kara demasu ka?]

trained [treɪnd] adj 訓練された [kunren sareta]

trainee [treɪniː] n 訓練を受けている人 [kunren-o ukete iru hito]

trainer [treɪnər] n コーチ [koochi]

training [treɪnɪŋ] n トレーニング [toreeningu]; **training course** n トレーニングコース [toreeningukoosu]

tramp [træmp] n (beggar) 浮浪者 [furousha]

trampoline [træmpəlɪn] n トランポリン [toran-porin]

tranquilizer [træŋkwɪlaɪzər] n 精神安定剤 [seishin anteizai]

transaction [trænzækʃn] n 取引 [torihiki]

transcript [trænskrɪpt] n 写し [utsushi]

transfer n 乗り換え [norikae], 移転 [iten]; **You have to transfer at...** あなたは・・・で乗り換えなければなりません [anata wa... de norikaenakereba narimasen]

transform [trænsfɔrm] v 変容させる [hen'you saseru]

transfusion [trænsfyuːʒn] n 輸血 [yuketsu]; **blood transfusion** n 輸血 [yuketsu]

transistor [trænzɪstər] n トランジスター

[toranjisutaa]

transit [trænzɪt] *n* 輸送 [yusou]; **transit lounge** *n* 通過ラウンジ [tsuuka raunji]

transition [trænzɪʃᵊn] *n* 移行 [ikou]

translate [trænzleɪt] *v* 訳す [yakusu]

translation [trænzleɪʃᵊn] *n* 翻訳 [honyaku]

translator [trænzleɪtər] *n* 翻訳者 [hon'yakusha]

transmission [trænzmɪʃᵊn] *n* ギアボックス [giabokkusu]; **The transmission is broken** ギアボックスが壊れています [gia-bokkusu ga kowarete imasu]

transparent [trænspɛərənt, -pær-] *adj* 透明な [toumei na]

transplant *n* 移植 [ishoku]

transport *v* 輸送する [yusou suru]

transportation [trænspɔrteɪʃᵊn] *n* 輸送 [yusou]; **public transportation** *n* 公共交通機関 [koukyou koutsuu kikan]

transvestite [trænzvɛstaɪt] *n* 服装倒錯 [fukusou tousaku]

trap [træp] *n* わな [wana]

trash [træʃ] *n* くだらないこと [kudaranai koto], ごみ [gomi]; **Where do we leave the trash?** ごみはどこに出すのですか? [gomi wa doko ni dasu no desu ka?]

traumatic [trəmætɪk] *adj* 外傷性の [gaishou sei no]

travel [trævᵊl] *n* 旅行 [ryokou] ▷ *v* 移動する [idou suru]; **travel agency** *n* 旅行代理店 [ryokoudairiten]; **travel sickness** *n* 乗物酔い [norimonoyoi]; **I don't have travel insurance** 私は旅行保険に入っていません [watashi wa ryokou-hoken ni haitte imasen]; **I'm traveling alone** 私は一人で旅行しています [watashi wa hitori de ryokou shite imasu]

traveler [trævələr] *n* 旅行者 [ryokousha]; **traveler's check** *n* 旅行者用小切手 [ryokousha you kogitte]

traveling [trævəlɪŋ] *n* 旅行 [ryokou]

tray [treɪ] *n* 盆 [bon] (台所用品)

tread [trɛd] *v* **tread on** 踏む [fumu]

treasure [trɛʒər] *n* 財宝 [zaihou]

treasurer [trɛʒərər] *n* 会計係 [kaikeigakari]

treat [trit] *n* おごり [ogori], 歓待 [kantai] ▷ *v* 扱う [atsukau]

treatment [tritmənt] *n* 治療 [chiryou]

treaty [triti] *n* 条約 [jouyaku]

tree [tri] *n* 木 [ki]

trek [trɛk] *n* 苦難に満ちた旅 [kunan ni michita tabi] ▷ *v* 苦難に耐えつつ旅をする [kunan ni taetsutsu tabi-o suru]

trekking *n* トレッキング [torekkingu]

tremble [trɛmbᵊl] *v* 震える [furueru]

tremendous [trɪmɛndəs] *adj* 巨大な [kyodai na]

trench [trɛntʃ] *n* 深くて細長い溝 [fukakute hosonagai mizo]

trend [trɛnd] *n* 傾向 [keikou]

trendy [trɛndi] *adj* 今はやりの [ima hayari no]

trial [traɪəl] *n* 裁判 [saiban]; **trial period** *n* 試用期間 [shiyou kikan]

triangle [traɪæŋgᵊl] *n* 三角形 [sankakkei]

tribe [traɪb] *n* 部族 [buzoku]

tribunal [traɪbyunᵊl] *n* 裁定委員会 [saitei iinkai]

trick [trɪk] *n* 策略 [sakuryaku] ▷ *v* だます [damasu]

tricky [trɪki] *adj* 油断のならない [yudan no naranai]

tricycle [traɪsɪkᵊl] *n* 三輪車 [sanrinsha]

trifle [traɪfᵊl] *n* つまらないもの [tsumaranai mono]

trim [trɪm] *v* 整える [totonoeru]

Trinidad and Tobago *n* トリニダード・トバゴ [torinidaado tobago]

trip [trɪp] *n* 旅行 [ryokou] ▷ *v* つまずく [tsumazuku]; **business trip** *n* 出張 [shutchou]; **round trip** *n* 往復 [oufuku]; **Have a good trip!** よいご旅行を! [yoi go-ryokou o!]; **This is my first trip to...** ···への旅行はこれが初めてです [... e no ryokou wa kore ga hajimete desu]

triple [trɪpᵊl] *adj* 三重の [mie no] ▷ *v* 三倍にする [sanbai ni suru]

triplets [trɪplɪts] *npl* 三つ子 [mitsugo]

T

triumph [traɪʌmf] *n* 勝利 [shouri] ▷ *v* 勝利を収める [shouri-o osameru]

trivial [trɪviəl] *adj* 些細な [sasai na]

trombone [trɑmboʊn] *n* トロンボーン [toronboon]

troops [trups] *npl* 軍隊 [guntai]

trophy [troʊfi] *n* トロフィー [torofii]

tropical [trɑpɪkəl] *adj* 熱帯の [nettai no]

trot [trɑt] *v* 速足で駆ける [hayaashi de kakeru]

trouble [trʌbəl] *n* 迷惑 [meiwaku], 困難 [konnan]

troublemaker [trʌbəlmeɪkər] *n* もめごとを起こす人 [momegoto-o okosu hito]

trough [trɔf] *n* かいば桶 [kaibaoke]

trousers [traʊzərz] *npl* ズボン [zubon]

trout [traʊt] *n* マス [masu] (魚)

trowel [traʊəl] *n* 移植ごて [ishokugote]

truce [trus] *n* 休戦 [kyuusen]

truck [trʌk] *n* トラック [torakku], 無蓋貨車 [mugai kasha]; **tow truck** *n* レッカー車 [rekkaasha]; **truck driver** *n* トラック運転手 [torakku untenshu]

trucker [trʌkər] *n* トラック運転手 [torakku untenshu]

true [tru] *adj* 本当の [hontou no]

truly [truli] *adv* 偽りなく [itsuwari naku]

trumpet [trʌmpɪt] *n* トランペット [toranpetto]

trunk [trʌŋk] *n* 幹 [miki]; **swimming trunks** *npl* スイミングトランクス [suimingutorankusu]

trunks [trʌŋks] *npl* トランクス [torankusu]

trust [trʌst] *n* 信頼 [shinrai] ▷ *v* 信頼する [shinrai suru]

trusting [trʌstɪŋ] *adj* 信じている [shinjite iru]

truth [truθ] *n* 事実 [jijitsu]

truthful [truθfəl] *adj* 正直な [shoujiki na]

try [traɪ] *n* 努力 [doryoku] ▷ *v* 努める [tsutomeru]

try on *v* 試着する [shichaku suru]

try out *v* 試してみる [tameshite miru]

T-shirt [tiʃɜrt] *n* Tシャツ [tiishatsu]

tsunami [tsʊnɑmi] *n* 津波 [tsunami]

tube [tub] *n* チューブ [chuubu], 管 [kan]; **inner tube** *n* インナーチューブ [innaachuubu]; **test tube** *n* 試験管 [shikenkan]; **Do you have a new tube?** 新しいチューブはありますか? [atarashii chuubu wa arimasu ka?]

tuberculosis [tubɜrkyəloʊsɪs] *n* 結核 [kekkaku]

Tuesday [tuzdeɪ, -di] *n* 火曜日 [kayoubi]; **on Tuesday** 火曜日に [kayoubi ni]

tuft [tʌft] *n* ふさ [fusa]

tug-of-war *n* 綱引き [tsunahiki]

tuition [tuɪʃən] *n* 授業 [jugyou]; **tuition fees** *npl* 授業料 [jugyouryou]

tulip [tulɪp] *n* チューリップ [chuurippu]

tummy [tʌmi] *n* おなか [onaka]

tumor [tumər] *n* 腫瘍 [shuyou]

tuna [tunə] *n* マグロ [maguro]

tune [tun] *n* 曲 [kyoku]

Tunisia [tuniʒə] *n* チュニジア [chunijia]

Tunisian [tuniʒən] *adj* チュニジアの [Chunijia no] ▷ *n* チュニジア人 [Chunijia jin]

tunnel [tʌnəl] *n* トンネル [tonneru]

turbulence [tɜrbyələns] *n* 激動 [gekidou]

Turk [tɜrk] *n* トルコ人 [torukojin]

turkey [tɜrki] *n* 七面鳥 [shichimenchou]

Turkey [tɜrki] *n* トルコ [toruko]

Turkish [tɜrkɪʃ] *adj* トルコの [toruko no] ▷ *n* トルコ語 [torukogo]

turn [tɜrn] *n* 逸れること [soreru koto] ▷ *v* 向きを変える [muki wo kaeru]

turn around *v* 方向転換する [houkoutenkan suru]

turn back *v* 引き返す [hikikaesu]

turn down *v* 小さくする [chiisaku suru]

turnip [tɜrnɪp] *n* カブ [kabu] (食べ物)

turn off *v* わき道へ入る [wakimichi-e hairu], 切る [kiru]; **I can't turn the heat off** 暖房を切ることができません [danbou o kiru koto ga dekimasen]

turnoff [tɜrnɔf] *n* 分かれ道 [wakaremichi]

turn on *v* つける [tsukeru] (スイッチ); **How do you turn it on?** どうやってつけるのですか? [dou-yatte tsukeru no desu ka?]

turn out *v* 消す [kesu] *(切る)*

turnover [tɜrnoʊvər] *n* 総売上高 [souuriagedaka]

turn round *v* You have to turn round 反対に向きを変えなければなりません [hantai ni muki o kaenakereba narimasen]

turnstile [tɜrnstaɪl] *n* 回転式改札口 [kaitenshiki kaisatsuguchi]

turn up *v* 姿を現す [sugata-o arawasu]

turquoise [tɜrkwɔɪz] *adj* 青緑色の [aomidori iro no]

turtle [tɜrtⁱl] *n* カメ [kame] *(動物)*

tutor [tutər] *n* 個別指導教官 [kobetsu shidou kyoukan]

tutorial [tutɔriəl] *n* 個別指導 [kobetsu shidou]

tuxedo [tʌksidoʊ] *n* タキシード [takishiido]

TV [ti vi] *n* テレビ [terebi]; **plasma TV** *n* プラズマテレビ [purazumaterebi]; **reality TV** *n* リアリティーテレビ番組 [riaritii terebi bangumi]; **Does the room have a TV?** その部屋にテレビはありますか? [sono heya ni terebi wa arimasu ka?]; **Where is the TV set?** テレビはどこですか? [terebi wa doko desu ka?]

tweezers [twizərz] *npl* ピンセット [pinsetto]

twelfth [twɛlfθ] *adj* 十二番目の [juuni banme no]

twelve [twɛlv] *number* 十二 [juuni]

twentieth [twɛntiəθ] *adj* 二十番目の [nijuu banme no]

twenty [twɛnti] *number* 二十 [nijuu]

twice [twaɪs] *adv* 二度 [nido]

twin [twɪn] *n* 双子 [futago]; **twin beds** *npl* ツインベッド [tsuinbeddo]; **twin room** *n* ツインルーム [tsuinruumu]; **room with twin beds** *npl* ツインベッドルーム [tsuinbeddoruumu]

twinned [twɪnd] *adj* 対になった [tsui ni natta]

twist [twɪst] *v* ねじる [nejiru]

two [tu] *number* 二 [ni]; **I'd like two hundred....** 二百・・・欲しいのですが [nihyaku... hoshii no desu ga]

type [taɪp] *n* 種類 [shurui] ▷ *v* タイプする [taipu suru]

typewriter [taɪpraɪtər] *n* タイプライター [taipuraitaa]

typhoid [taɪfɔɪd] *n* 腸チフス [chouchifusu]

typical [tɪpɪkⁱl] *adj* 典型的な [tenkeiteki na]

typist [taɪpɪst] *n* タイピスト [taipisuto]

T

U

UFO [yu ɛf ou, yufou] *abbr* 未確認飛行物体 [mikakunin hikoubuttai]

Uganda [yugɑndə] *n* ウガンダ [uganda]

Ugandan [yugændən] *adj* ウガンダの [Uganda no] ▸ *n* ウガンダ人 [Uganda jin]

ugh *excl* ウッ [utsu]

ugly [ʌgli] *adj* 醜い [minikui]

UK [yu keɪ] *n* 英国 [eikoku]

Ukraine [yukreɪn] *n* ウクライナ [ukuraina]

Ukrainian [yukreɪniən] *adj* ウクライナの [Ukuraina no] ▸ *n (language)* ウクライナ語 [Ukuraina go], *(person)* ウクライナ人 [Ukuraina jin]

ulcer [ʌlsər] *n* 潰瘍 [kaiyou]

Ulster [ʌlstər] *n* アルスター [arusutaa]

ultimate [ʌltɪmɪt] *adj* 最終的な [saishuuteki na]

ultimately [ʌltɪmɪtli] *adv* 最終的に [saishuuteki ni]

ultimatum [ʌltɪmeɪtəm] *n* 最後通牒 [saigo tsuuchou]

ultrasound [ʌltrəsaund] *n* 超音波 [chouonpa]

umbrella [ʌmbrɛlə] *n* 傘 [kasa]

umpire [ʌmpaɪr] *n* アンパイア [anpaia]

UN [yu ɛn] *abbr* 国際連合 [kokusairengou]

unable [ʌneɪbᵊl] *adj* **unable to** *adj* …できない […dekinai]

unacceptable [ʌnəksɛptəbᵊl] *adj* 容認できない [younin dekinai]

unanimous [yunænɪməs] *adj* 満場一致の [manjouitchi no]

unattended [ʌnətɛndɪd] *adj* 番人のいない [bannin no inai]

unavoidable [ʌnəvɔɪdəbᵊl] *adj* 避けられない [sakerarenai]

unbearable [ʌnbɛərəbᵊl] *adj* 耐えられない [taerarenai]

unbeatable [ʌnbitəbᵊl] *adj* 太刀打ちできない [tachiuchi dekinai]

unbelievable [ʌnbɪlivəbᵊl] *adj* 信じられない [shinjirarenai]

unbreakable [ʌnbreɪkəbᵊl] *adj* 壊すことのできない [kowasu koto no dekinai]

uncertain [ʌnsɜrtᵊn] *adj* 不確実な [fukakujitsu na]

uncertainty [ʌnsɜrᵊnti] *n* 不確実 [fukakujitsu]

unchanged [ʌntʃeɪndʒd] *adj* 変わっていない [kawatteinai]

uncivilized [ʌnsɪvɪlaɪzd] *adj* 未開の [mikai no]

uncle [ʌŋkᵊl] *n* おじ [oji] (伯父・叔父)

unclear [ʌnklɪər] *adj* 不明瞭な [fumeiryou na]

uncomfortable [ʌnkʌmftəbᵊl, -kʌmfərtə-] *adj* 心地よくない [kokochi yokunai]

unconditional [ʌnkəndɪʃᵊnᵊl] *adj* 無条件の [mujouken no]

unconscious [ʌnkɒnʃəs] *adj* 意識を失った [ishiki wo ushinatta]

uncontrollable [ʌnkəntroulⱥbᵊl] *adj* 制御できない [seigyodekinai]

unconventional [ʌnkənvɛnʃənᵊl] *adj* 慣例に従わない [kanrei ni shitagawanai]

undecided [ʌndɪsaɪdɪd] *adj* 決心がついていない [kesshin ga tsuite inai]

undeniable [ʌndɪnaɪəbᵊl] *adj* 否定できない [hitei dekinai]

under [ʌndər] *prep* **The car is still under warranty** 車はまだ保証期間内です [kuruma wa mada hoshou-kikan nai desu]

underage [ʌndəreɪdʒ] *adj* 未成年の [miseinen no]

underestimate [ʌndərɛstɪmeɪt] *v* 過小評価する [kashouhyouka suru]

undergo [ʌndərgou] *v* 経験する [keiken suru]

undergraduate [ʌndərgrædʒuɪt] *n* 学部学生 [gakubu gakusei]

underground *adv* [ʌndərgraʊnd] 地下に [chika ni] ▷ *n* [ʌndərgraʊnd] **underground movement** 地下運動 [chika undou]

underline [ʌndərlaɪn] *v* 下線を引く [kasen-o hiku]

underneath [ʌndərniθ] *adv* 下に [shita ni]

underpaid [ʌndərpeɪd] *adj* 十分な額が払われていない [juubun na gaku ga harawarete inai]

underpants [ʌndərpænts] *npl* ショーツ [shootsu], パンティー [pantii]

underpass [ʌndərpæs] *n* アンダーパス [andaapasu], 地下道 [chikadou]

undershirt [ʌndərʃɜrt] *n* 肌着 [hadagi]

undershorts [ʌndərʃɔrts] *npl* パンツ [pantsu] (下着), パンツ [pantsu] (洋服)

understand [ʌndərstænd] *v* 理解する [rikai suru]

understandable [ʌndərstændəbəl] *adj* 理解できる [rikai dekiru]

understanding [ʌndərstændɪŋ] *adj* 話がわかる [hanashi ga wakaru]

underwater [ʌndərwɔtər] *adv* 水中に [suichuu ni]

underwear [ʌndərwɛər] *n* 下着 [shitagi]

undisputed [ʌndɪspyutɪd] *adj* 異議のない [igi no nai]

undo [ʌndu] *v* ほどく [hodoku]

undoubtedly [ʌndaʊtɪdli] *adv* 疑いなく [utagainaku]

undress [ʌndrɛs] *v* 服を脱ぐ [fuku wo nugu]

uneasiness *n* 不安 [fuan]

uneasy [ʌnizi] *adj* 不安な [fuan na]

unemployed [ʌnɪmplɔɪd] *adj* 失業している [shitsugyou shite iru]

unemployment [ʌnɪmplɔɪmənt] *n* 失業 [shitsugyou]

unexpected [ʌnɪkspɛktɪd] *adj* 予期しない [yoki shinai], 不意の [fui no]

unexpectedly [ʌnɪkspɛktɪdli] *adv* 思いがけなく [omoigakenaku], 不意に [fui ni]

unfair [ʌnfɛər] *adj* 不公平な [fukouhei na]

unfaithful [ʌnfeɪθfəl] *adj* 不貞な [futei na]

unfamiliar [ʌnfəmɪlyər] *adj* 不慣れの [funare no]

unfashionable [ʌnfæʃənəbəl] *adj* はやらない [hayaranai]

unfavorable [ʌnfeɪvərəbəl] *adj* 好ましくない [konomashikunai]

unfit [ʌnfɪt] *adj* 不向きな [fumuki na]

unforgettable [ʌnfərgɛtəbəl] *adj* 忘れられない [wasurerarenai]

unfortunately [ʌnfɔrtʃənɪtli] *adv* 運悪く [unwaruku]

unfriendly [ʌnfrɛndli] *adj* 不親切な [fushinsetsu na]

ungrateful [ʌngreɪtfəl] *adj* 感謝を表さない [kansha-o arawasanai]

unhappy [ʌnhæpi] *adj* 不幸な [fukou na]

unhealthy [ʌnhɛlθi] *adj* 不健康な [fukenkou na]

unhelpful [ʌnhɛlpfəl] *adj* 役に立たない [yaku ni tatanai]

unidentified [ʌnaɪdɛntɪfaɪd] *adj* 身元不詳の [mimoto fushou no]

uniform [yunɪform] *n* 制服 [seifuku]; **school uniform** *n* 学校の制服 [gakkou no seifuku]

unimportant [ʌnɪmpɔrtnt] *adj* 重要でない [juuyou de nai]

uninhabited [ʌnɪnhæbɪtɪd] *adj* 人の住んでいない [hito no sunde inai]

unintentional [ʌnɪntɛnʃənəl] *adj* 故意でない [koi de nai]

union [yunyən] *n* 結合 [ketsugou]; **European Union** *n* 欧州連合 [OUshuu Rengou]; **labor union** *n* 労働組合 [roudoukumiai]; **union member** *n* 労働組合主義者 [roudoukumiai shugisha]

unique [yunik] *adj* 独特の [dokutoku no]

unit [yunɪt] *n* 単一体 [tan'itsutai]

unite [yunaɪt] *v* 結合する [ketsugou suru]

U

United Kingdom [yunaɪtɪd kɪŋdəm] *n* 英国 [eikoku]

United States *n* 米国 [beikoku]

universe [yunɪvɜrs] *n* 宇宙 [uchuu]

university [yunɪvɜrsɪti] *n* 大学 [daigaku]

unknown [ʌnnoun] *adj* 未知の [michi no]

unleaded [ʌnlɛdɪd] *n* 無鉛ガソリン [muen gasorin]; **unleaded gasoline** *n* 無鉛ガソリン [muen gasorin]

unlikely [ʌnlaɪkli] *adj* ありそうもない [arisou mo nai]

unlisted [ʌnlɪstɪd] *adj* 目録に載っていない [mokuroku ni notte inai]

unload [ʌnloud] *v* 荷を降ろす [ni-o orosu]

unlock [ʌnlɒk] *v* 錠をあける [jou-o akeru]

unlucky [ʌnlʌki] *adj* 運の悪い [un no warui]

unmarried [ʌnmærid] *adj* 未婚の [mikon no]

unnatural [ʌnnætʃərəl] *adj* 不自然な [fushizen na]

unnecessary [ʌnnɛsəsɛri] *adj* 不必要な [fuhitsuyou na]

unofficial [ʌnəfɪʃəl] *adj* 非公認の [hikounin no]

unpack [ʌnpæk] *v* 荷を解く [ni-o toku]

unpaid [ʌnpeɪd] *adj* 無給の [mukyuu no]

unpleasant [ʌnplɛzənt] *adj* 不愉快な [fuyukai na]

unplug [ʌnplʌg] *v* プラグを抜いて電源を断つ [puragu-o nuite dengen-o tatsu]

unpopular [ʌnpɒpyulər] *adj* 人気のない [hitoke no nai]

unprecedented [ʌnprɛsɪdɛntɪd] *adj* 先例のない [senrei no nai]

unpredictable [ʌnprɪdɪktəbəl] *adj* 予測できない [yosoku dekinai]

unreal [ʌnril] *adj* 現実のものではない [genjitsu nomonodehanai]

unrealistic [ʌnriəlɪstɪk] *adj* 非現実的な [higenjitsuteki na]

unreasonable [ʌnrizənəbəl] *adj* 不当な [futou na]

unreliable [ʌnrɪlaɪəbəl] *adj* あてにならない [ate ni naranai]

unripe [ʌnraɪp] *adj* 未熟 [mijuku]

unroll [ʌnroul] *v* 広げる [hirogeru]

unsatisfactory [ʌnsætɪsfæktəri] *adj* 不満足な [fumanzoku na]

unscrew [ʌnskru] *v* ねじを緩める [neji-o yurumeru]

unshaven [ʌnʃeɪvən] *adj* ひげを剃っていない [hige-o sotte inai]

unskilled [ʌnskɪld] *adj* 熟練していない [jukuren shite inai]

unstable [ʌnsteɪbəl] *adj* 不安定な [fuantei na]

unsteady [ʌnstɛdi] *adj* 不安定な [fuantei na]

unstylish [ʌnstaɪlɪʃ] *adj* 趣味が悪い [shumi ga warui]

unsuccessful [ʌnsəksɛsfəl] *adj* 不成功に終わった [fuseikou ni owatta]

unsuitable [ʌnsutəbəl] *adj* 不適切な [futekisetsu na]

unsure [ʌnfuər] *adj* 確信のない [kakushin no nai]

untidy [ʌntaɪdi] *adj* だらしのない [darashi no nai]

untie [ʌntaɪ] *v* ほどく [hodoku]

unusual [ʌnyuʒuəl] *adj* 普通でない [futsuu de nai]

unwell [ʌnwɛl] *adj* 体調が悪い [taichou ga warui], 気分のすぐれない [kibun no sugurenai]

unwind [ʌnwaɪnd] *v* ほどく [hodoku]

unwise [ʌnwaɪz] *adj* 分別のない [funbetsu no nai]

unwrap [ʌnræp] *v* 包装を解く [housou-o toku]

unzip [ʌnzɪp] *v* ファスナーを開ける [fasunaa-o hirakeru]

up *adv* 上へ [ue-e]

upbringing [ʌpbrɪŋɪŋ] *n* しつけ [shitsuke]

update [ʌpdeɪt] *v* 更新する [koushin suru]

upgrade [ʌpgreɪd, -greɪd] *v* アップグレード [appugureedo]; **I want to upgrade my ticket** 切符をアップグレードしたいのですが [kippu o appugureedo shitai no desu ga]

uphill [ʌphɪl] *adv* 坂の上へ [saka no ue-e]

upper [ʌpər] *adj* 上の [ue no]

upset [ʌpsɛt] *adj* 狼狽した [roubai shita]

upside down [ʌpsaɪd daʊn] *adv* 逆さまに [sakasama ni]

upstairs [ʌpstɛərz] *adv* 上の階に [ueno kai ni]

uptight [ʌptaɪt] *adj* 緊張しきった [kinchou shikitta]

up-to-date *adj* 最新の [saishin no]

upward [ʌpwərd] *adv* 上へ向かって [ue he mukatte]

uranium [yureɪniəm] *n* ウラニウム [uraniumu]

urgency [ɜrdʒʌnsi] *n* 緊急 [kinkyuu]

urgent [ɜrdʒʌnt] *adj* 緊急の [kinkyuu no]

urine [yʊərɪn] *n* 尿 [nyou]

URL [yʊ ɑr ɛl] *n* URL [yuuaarueru]

Uruguay [yurəgwaɪ] *n* ウルグアイ [uruguai]

Uruguayan [yurəgwaɪən] *adj* ウルグアイの [Uruguai no] ▸ *n* ウルグアイ人 [Uruguai jin]

us [əs, STRONG ʌs] *pron* **Could you show us around the apartment?** アパートメントを案内していただけますか? [apaatomento o annai shite itadakemasu ka?]; **Please call us if you're going to be late** 遅くなるときは電話してください [osoku naru toki wa denwa shite kudasai]

US [yu ɛs] *n* 米国 [beikoku]

USA [yu ɛs eɪ] *n* 米国 [beikoku]

use [yuz] *n* 使用 [shiyou], 利用 [riyou] ▸ *v* 使用する [shiyou suru]

used [yust] *adj* 中古の [chuuko no]

useful [yusfəl] *adj* 役に立つ [yaku ni tatsu]

useless [yuslɪs] *adj* 役に立たない [yaku ni tatanai]

user [yuzər] *n* 使用者 [shiyousha]; **Internet user** *n* インターネット利用者 [intaanetto riyousha]

user-friendly *adj* 使いやすい [tsukaiyasui]

use up *v* 使い果たす [tsukaihatasu]

usual [yuʒuəl] *adj* 普通の [futsuu no]

usually [yuʒuəli] *adv* 普通は [futsuu wa]

U-turn [yutɜrn] *n* Uターン [yuutaan]

Uzbekistan [ʌzbɛkistɑn] *n* ウズベキスタン [uzubekisutan]

U

V

vacancy [veɪkənsi] n 欠員 [ketsuin], 空き室 [akishitsu]; **Do you have any vacancies?** 空き室はありますか? [akishitsu wa arimasu ka?]

vacant [veɪkənt] adj 空いている [aite iru]

vacate [veɪkeɪt] v 立ち退く [tachishirizoku]

vacation [veɪkeɪʃn] n 休暇 [kyuuka]; **activity vacation** n アクティブホリデー [akutibu horidee]; **summer vacation** npl 夏の休暇 [natsu no kyuuka]; **vacation home** n 別荘 [bessou]; **vacation job** n 休日の仕事 [kyuujitsu no shigoto]; **vacation package** n パック旅行 [pakku ryokou]; **Have a good vacation!** 楽しい休暇を! [tanoshii kyuuka o!]; **I'm here on vacation** 私は休暇で来ています [watashi wa kyuuka de kite imasu]

vaccinate [væksɪneɪt] v 予防接種をする [yobou sesshu-o suru]

vaccination [væksɪneɪʃn] n 予防接種 [yobou sesshu]; **I need a vaccination** 私は予防接種が必要です [watashi wa yobou-sesshu ga hitsuyou desu]

vacuum [vækyum, -yuəm] v 掃除機で掃除する [soujiki de souji suru], 電気掃除機で掃除する [denki soujiki de souji suru]; **vacuum cleaner** n フーバー® [fuubaa], 電気掃除機 [denki soujiki]

vague [veɪg] adj 曖昧な [aimai na]

vain [veɪn] adj うぬぼれの強い [unubore no tsuyoi]

valid [vælɪd] adj 正当な [seitou na]

valley [væli] n 谷間 [taniai]

valuable [vælyuəbl] adj 高価な [kouka na]

valuables [vælyuəblz] npl 貴重品 [kichouhin]; **I'd like to put my valuables in the safe** 私は貴重品を金庫に入れたいので

すが [watashi wa kichouhin o kinko ni iretai no desu ga]; **Where can I leave my valuables?** 貴重品はどこに置いておけますか? [kichouhin wa doko ni oite okemasu ka?]

value [vælyu] n 価値 [kachi]

vampire [væmpaɪər] n 吸血鬼 [kyuuketsuki]

van [væn] n バン [ban] (自動車); **moving van** n 引越しトラック [hikkoshi torakku]; **We'd like a site for a conversion van** キャンプ用バンのサイトが欲しいのですが [kyanpu-you ban no saito ga hoshii no desu ga]

vandal [vændl] n 破壊者 [hakaisha]

vandalism [vændlɪzəm] n 破壊行為 [hakai koui]

vandalize [vændlaɪz] v 故意に破壊する [koi ni hakai suru]

vanilla [vənɪlə] n バニラ [banira]

vanish [vænɪʃ] v 消える [kieru]

variable [vɛəriəbl] adj 変わりやすい [kawariyasui]

varied [vɛərid] adj さまざまな [samazama na]

variety [vəraɪɪti] n 多様性 [tayousei]

various [vɛəriəs] adj さまざまな [samazama na]

varnish [vɑrnɪʃ] n ニス [nisu] ▷ v ニスを塗る [nisu-o nuru]

vary [vɛəri] v 変わる [kawaru]

vase [veɪs, vɑz] n 花瓶 [kabin]

VAT [vi eɪ ti] abbr 付加価値税 [fukakachizei]

Vatican [vætɪkən] n バチカン [bachikan]

vault [vɔlt] n **pole vault** n 棒高跳び [bou taka tobi]

veal [vil] n 子牛の肉 [koushi no niku]

vegan [vigən] n ビーガン [biigan]; **Do you have any vegan dishes?** ビーガン料理はあ

りますか? [biigan-ryouri wa arimasu ka?]

vegetable [vɛdʒtəbᵊl, vɛdʒɪ-] *n* 野菜 [yasai];
Are the vegetables fresh or frozen? 野菜
は生鮮品ですか、それとも冷凍品ですか?
[yasai wa seisen-hin desu ka, sore tomo
reitou-hin desu ka?]; **Are the vegetables
included?** 野菜も付いてきますか? [yasai
mo tsuite kimasu ka?]

vegetarian [vɛdʒɪtɛəriən] *adj* ベジタリアンの
[bejitarian no] ▷ *n* ベジタリアン [bejitarian];
Do you have any vegetarian dishes? ベジ
タリアン料理はありますか? [bejitarian-ryouri
wa arimasu ka?]; **I'm a vegetarian** 私はベジ
タリアンです [watashi wa bejitarian desu]

vegetation [vɛdʒɪteɪʃᵊn] *n* 草木 [soumoku]

vehicle [viːɪkᵊl] *n* 乗り物 [norimono], 車両
[sharyou]

veil [veɪl] *n* ベール [beeru]

vein [veɪn] *n* 静脈 [joumyaku]

Velcro® [vɛlkroʊ] *n* ベルクロ® [berukuro]

velvet [vɛlvɪt] *n* ビロード [biroodo]

vendor [vɛndər] *n* 販売店 [hanbaiten], 売る人
[uru hito]

Venezuela [vɛnəzweɪlə] *n* ベネズエラ
[benezuera]

Venezuelan [vɛnəzweɪlən] *adj* ベネズエラの
[Benezuera no] ▷ *n* ベネズエラ人 [Benezuera
jin]

venison [vɛnɪsᵊn, -zᵊn] *n* 鹿肉 [shika niku]

venom [vɛnəm] *n* 悪意 [akui]

ventilation [vɛntᵊleɪʃᵊn] *n* 風通し [kazetooshi]

venue [vɛnyu] *n* 会場 [kaijou]

verb [vɜrb] *n* 動詞 [doushi]

verdict [vɜrdɪkt] *n* 評決 [hyouketsu]

versatile [vɜrsətᵊl] *adj* 多方面の [tahoumen
no]

version [vɜrʒᵊn] *n* 版 [han]

vertical [vɜrtɪkᵊl] *adj* 垂直の [suichoku no]

vertigo [vɜrtɪgoʊ] *n* めまい [memai]

very [vɛri] *adv* 非常に [hijou ni]

vest [vɛst] *n* ウエストコート [uesutokooto], 同
意 [doui]

vet [vɛt] *n* 獣医 [juui]

veteran [vɛtərən] *adj* 老練な [rouren na] ▷ *n*
老練な人 [rouren na hito]

veto [vitoʊ] *n* 拒否権 [kyohiken]

vice [vaɪs] *n* 悪徳 [akutoku]

vice versa [vaɪsə vɜrsə, vaɪs] *adv* 逆に
[gyaku ni]

vicinity [vɪsɪnɪti] *n* 近所 [kinjo]

vicious [vɪʃəs] *adj* ひどい [hidoi]

victim [vɪktəm] *n* 犠牲 [gisei]

victory [vɪktəri, vɪktri] *n* 勝利 [shouri]

video [vɪdioʊ] *n* ビデオ [bideo]; **video
camera** *n* ビデオカメラ [bideokamera]

videophone [vɪdioʊfoʊn] *n* テレビ電話
[terebi denwa]

Vietnam [vjɛtnɑm] *n* ベトナム [betonamu]

Vietnamese [vjɛtnəmiz] *adj* ベトナムの
[betonamu no] ▷ *n (language)* ベトナム語
[betonamugo], *(person)* ベトナム人
[betonamujin]

view [vyu] *n* 見解 [kenkai], 眺め [nagame];
We'd like to see spectacular views 壮観な
眺めを見たいのですが [soukan na nagame o
mitai no desu ga]

viewer [vyuər] *n* 見る人 [miru hito]

viewpoint [vyupɔɪnt] *n* 観点 [kanten]

vile [vaɪl] *adj* 堕落した [daraku shita]

villa [vɪlə] *n* ヴィラ [vira], 大邸宅 [daiteitaku],
別荘 [bessou]; **I'd like to rent a villa** ヴィラ
を借りたいのですが [vira o karitai no desu
ga]

village [vɪlɪdʒ] *n* 村 [mura]

villain [vɪlən] *n* 悪党 [akutou]

vinaigrette [vɪnɪgrɛt] *n* ビネグレットドレッシ
ング [binegurettodoresshingu]

vine [vaɪn] *n* つる植物 [tsuru shokubutsu]

vinegar [vɪnɪgər] *n* 酢 [su]

vineyard [vɪnyərd] *n* ブドウ園 [budouen]

vinyl [vaɪnɪl] *n* ビニール [biniiru]

viola [vioʊlə] *n* ビオラ [biora]

violence [vaɪələns] *n* 暴力 [bouryoku]

violent [vaɪələnt] *adj* 暴力的な [bouryokuteki
na]

violin [vaɪəlɪn] *n* バイオリン [baiorin]

V

violinist [vaɪəlɪnɪst] *n* バイオリン奏者 [baiorinsousha]

virgin [vɜrdʒɪn] *n* 処女 [shojo]

Virgo [vɜrgou] *n* 乙女座 [otomeza]

virtual [vɜrtʃuəl] *adj* 実質上の [jisshitsujou no]; **virtual reality** *n* バーチャルリアリティー [baacharuriariteii]

virus [vaɪrəs] *n* ウイルス [uirusu]

visa [vizə] *n* ビザ [biza]; **Here is my visa** 私 のビザです [watashi no biza desu]; **I have an entry visa** 入国ビザを持っています [nyuukoku-biza o motte imasu]

visibility [vɪzɪbɪlɪti] *n* 視界 [shikai]

visible [vɪzɪbᵊl] *adj* 目に見える [me ni mieru]

visit [vɪzɪt] *n* 訪問 [houmon] ▷ *v* 訪問する [houmon suru]; **visiting hours** *npl* 面会時間 [menkaijikan]

visitor [vɪzɪtər] *n* 訪問者 [houmonsha]; **visitor center** *n* ビジターセンター [bijitaasentaa]

visual [vɪʒuəl] *adj* 視覚の [shikaku no]

visualize [vɪʒuəlaɪz] *v* 思い描く [omoiegaku]

vital [vaɪtᵊl] *adj* きわめて重大な [kiwamete juudai na]

vitamin [vaɪtəmɪn] *n* ビタミン [bitamin]

vivid [vɪvɪd] *adj* 鮮やかな [azayaka na]

vocabulary [voukæbyəlɛri] *n* 語彙 [goi]

vocational [voukeɪʃənᵊl] *adj* 職業上の [shokugyou jou no]

vodka [vɒdkə] *n* ウオッカ [uokka]

voice [vɔɪs] *n* 声 [koe]

voicemail [vɔɪsmeɪl] *n* ボイスメール [boisumeeru]

void [vɔɪd] *adj* 無効の [mukou no] ▷ *n* 空虚な 感じ [kuukyo na kanji]

volcano [vɒlkeɪnoʊ] *(pl* **volcanoes)** *n* 噴火 口 [funkakou]

volleyball [vɒlibɔl] *n* バレーボール [bareebooru]

volt [voʊlt] *n* ボルト [boruto] *(電圧)*

voltage [voʊltɪdʒ] *n* 電圧 [den-atsu]; **What's the voltage?** 電圧は何ボルトですか? [denatsu wa nan-boruto desu ka?]

volume [vɒlyum] *n* ボリューム [boryuumu], 容 積 [youseki]; **Could you lower the volume, please?** ボリュームを下げてもらえますか? [boryuumu o sagete moraemasu ka?]; **May I turn up the volume?** ボリュームを上げても いいですか? [boryuumu o agete mo ii desu ka?]

voluntarily [vɒləntɛərɪli] *adv* 自発的に [jihatsuteki ni]

voluntary [vɒləntɛri] *adj* 自発的な [jihatsuteki na]

volunteer [vɒləntɪər] *n* 志願者 [shigansha] ▷ *v* 自発的に申し出る [jihatsuteki ni moushideru]

vomit [vɒmɪt] *v* 吐く [haku]

vote [voʊt] *n* 投票 [touhyou] ▷ *v* 投票する [touhyou suru]

voucher [vaʊtʃər] *n* 引換券 [hikikaeken]

vowel [vaʊəl] *n* 母音 [boin]

vulgar [vʌlgər] *adj* 低俗な [teizoku na]

vulnerable [vʌlnərəbᵊl] *adj* 傷つきやすい [kizutsukiyasui]

vulture [vʌltʃər] *n* ハゲワシ [hagewashi]

W

wafer [weɪfər] *n* ウエハース [uehaasu]

waffle [wɒfᵊl] *n* ワッフル [waffuru] ▷ *v* たわごとを並べる [tawagoto-o naraberu]

wage [weɪdʒ] *n* 賃金 [chingin]

wagon [wægən] *n* **station wagon** *n* エステートカー [esuteetokaa]

waist [weɪst] *n* ウエスト [uesuto]

wait [weɪt] *v* 待つ [matsu]; **wait for** 待つ [matsu]; **wait in line** *v* 列を作る [retsu wo tsukuru]; **waiting list** *n* 順番待ち名簿 [junbanmachi meibo]; **waiting room** *n* 待合室 [machiaishitsu]

waiter [weɪtər] *n* ウェイター [ueitaa]

waitress [weɪtrɪs] *n* ウェイトレス [ueitoresu]

wait up *v* 寝ないで待つ [nenaide matsu]

waive [weɪv] *v* 放棄する [houki suru]

wake up *v* 目が覚める [me ga sameru]; **wake-up call** *n* モーニングコール [mooningukooru]

Wales [weɪlz] *n* ウェールズ [ueeruzu]

walk [wɔk] *n* 散歩 [sanpo] ▷ *v* 歩く [aruku]

walker [wɔkər] *n* ジマー [jimaa]

walkie-talkie [wɔki tɔki] *n* トランシーバー [toranshiibaa]

walking [wɔkɪŋ] *n* ウォーキング [uookingu], 歩行 [hokou]

walkway [wɔkweɪ] *n* 歩行者用通路 [hokoushayou tsuuro]

wall [wɔl] *n* 壁 [kabe]; **wall-to-wall carpeting** *n* ぴったり合うように敷かれたカーペット [pittari au youni shikareta kaapetto]

wallet [wɒlɪt] *n* 財布 [saifu]; **I've lost my wallet** 私は財布をなくしました [watashi wa saifu o nakushimashita]; **My wallet has been stolen** 私の財布が盗まれました [watashi no saifu ga nusumaremashita]

wallpaper [wɔlpeɪpər] *n* 壁紙 [kabegami]

walnut [wɔlnʌt, -nət] *n* クルミ [kurumi]

walrus [wɔlrəs] *n* セイウチ [seiuchi]

waltz [wɔlts, wɒls] *n* ワルツ [warutsu] ▷ *v* ワルツを踊る [warutsu wo odoru]

wander [wɒndər] *v* 歩き回る [arukimawaru]

want [wɒnt] *v* 欲しい [hoshii]; **I want something cheaper** もっと安いものが欲しいのです [motto yasui mono ga hoshii no desu]

war [wɔr] *n* 戦争 [sensou]; **civil war** *n* 内戦 [naisen]

ward [wɔrd] *n* *(area)* 区 [ku], *(hospital room)* 病棟 [byoutou]; **Which ward is... in?** ⋯はどの病棟に入院していますか? [... wa dono byoutou ni nyuuin shite imasu ka?]

warden [wɔrdᵊn] *n* 管理者 [kanrisha]

wardrobe [wɔrdroʊb] *n* 洋服だんす [youfukudansu]

warehouse [wɛərhaʊs] *n* 倉庫 [souko]

warm [wɔrm] *adj* 暖かい [atatakai]

warm up *v* 暖まる [atatamaru]

warn [wɔrn] *v* 警告する [keikoku suru]

warning [wɔrnɪŋ] *n* 警告 [keikoku]; **hazard warning lights** *npl* 故障警告灯 [koshou keikokutou]; **The oil warning light won't go off** オイル警告灯が消えません [oiru keikoku-tou ga kiemasen]

warranty [wɔrənti] *n* 保証 [hoshou]; **It's still under warranty** まだ保証期間内です [mada hoshou-kikan nai desu]; **The car is still under warranty** 車はまだ保証期間内です [kuruma wa mada hoshou-kikan nai desu]

wart [wɔrt] *n* いぼ [ibo]

wash [wɒʃ] *v* 洗う [arau]; **car wash** *n* 洗車機 [senshaki]; **wash the dishes** *v* 洗って片付け

W

る [aratte katazukeru]; **washing the dishes**
n 食器洗い [shokkiarai]

washable [wɒʃəbᵊl] *adj* **machine washable**
adj 洗濯機で洗える [sentakuki de araeru]; **Is
it washable?** それは洗えますか? [sore wa
araemasu ka?]

washcloth [wɒʃklɔθ] *n* 浴用タオル [yokuyou
taoru], 洗面用タオル [senmen you taoru]

washing machine [wɒʃɪŋ məʃin] *n* 洗濯機
[sentakuki]

washroom [wɒʃrum] *n* トイレ [toire]

wasp [wɒsp] *n* スズメバチ [suzumebachi]

waste [weɪst] *n* 浪費 [rouhi] ▷ *v* 浪費する
[rouhi suru]

wastebasket [weɪstbæskɪt] *n* ごみ箱
[gomibako]

watch [wɒtʃ] *n* 腕時計 [udedokei] ▷ *v* じっと見
る [jitto miru]; **digital watch** *n* デジタル時計
[dejitaru tokei]

watchband [wɒtʃbænd] *n* 腕時計のバンド
[udedokei no bando]

watchman [wɒtʃmən] *n* 番人 [bannin]

water [wɒtər] *n* 水 [mizu] ▷ *v* 水をやる [mizu-o
yaru]; **drinking water** *n* 飲料水 [inryousui];
mineral water *n* ミネラルウォーター
[mineraru uootaa]; **sea water** *n* 海水 [kaisui];
sparkling water *n* たんさんすい [tansansui];
watering can *n* じょうろ [jouro]; **a glass of
water** コップ一杯の水 [koppu ippai no mizu];
Could you check the water, please? 冷却
水を点検してもらえますか? [reikyakusui o
tenken shite moraemasu ka?]; **Please bring
more water** 水をもっと持ってきてください
[mizu o motto motte kite kudasai]

watercolor [wɒtərkʌlər] *n* 水彩絵の具 [suisai
enogu]

watercress [wɒtərkrɛs] *n* クレソン [kureson]

waterfall [wɒtərfɔl] *n* 滝 [taki]

watermelon [wɒtərmɛlən] *n* スイカ [suika]

waterproof [wɒtərpruf] *adj* 防水の [bousui
no], ぬれても大丈夫な [nurete mo daijobu
na]

water skiing *n* 水上スキー [suijousukii]; **Is it

possible to go water skiing here?** ここで水
上スキーはできますか? [koko de suijou-sukii
wa dekimasu ka?]

wave [weɪv] *n* 波 [nami] ▷ *v* 手を振る [te wo
furu]

wavelength [weɪvlɛŋθ] *n* 波長 [hachou]

wavy [weɪvi] *adj* 波状の [hajou no]

wax [wæks] *n* 蝋 [rou]

way [weɪ] *n* 方法 [houhou]; **right of way** *n* 優
先権 [yuusenken]; **What's the best way to
get to the train station?** 鉄道駅へ行く一番
よい方法は何ですか? [tetsudou-eki e iku
ichiban yoi houhou wa nan desu ka?]

we [wɪ, STRONG wi] *pron* **We live in...** 私た
ちは・・・に住んでいます [watashi-tachi wa...
ni sunde imasu]

weak [wik] *adj* 弱い [yowai]

weakness [wiknɪs] *n* 弱いこと [yowai koto]

wealth [wɛlθ] *n* 富裕 [fuyuu]

wealthy [wɛlθi] *adj* 富裕な [fuyuu na]

weapon [wɛpən] *n* 武器 [buki]

wear [wɛər] *v* 身に着けている [mi ni tsukete
iru]

weasel [wizᵊl] *n* イタチ [itachi]

weather [wɛðər] *n* 天気 [tenki]; **weather
forecast** *n* 天気予報 [tenkiyohou]; **Is the
weather going to change?** 天気は変わりま
すか? [tenki wa kawarimasu ka?]; **What
awful weather!** なんてひどい天気でしょう!
[nante hidoi tenki deshou!]; **What will the
weather be like tomorrow?** 明日はどんな天
気でしょう? [asu wa donna tenki deshou?]

web [wɛb] *n* **spider web** *n* クモの巣 [kumo
no su]; **Web address** *n* ウェブアドレス
[uebuadoresu]; **Web browser** *n* ウェブブラウ
ザ [uebuburauza]

webcam [wɛbkæm] *n* ウェブカム [uebu
kamu]

Webmaster [wɛbmæstər] *n* ウェブマスター
[uebumasutaa]

Web site [wɛbsaɪt] *n* ウェブサイト [uebu
saito]

webzine [wɛbzin] *n* ウェブジン [uebujin]

wedding [wɛdɪŋ] *n* 結婚式 [kekkonshiki];
wedding anniversary *n* 結婚記念日
[kekkon kinenbi]; **wedding dress** *n* ウェディ
ングドレス [uedeingudoresu]; **wedding ring**
n 結婚指輪 [kekkon yubiwa]; **We're here for
a wedding** 私たちは結婚式で来ています
[watashi-tachi wa kekkon-shiki de kite
imasu]

Wednesday [wɛnzdeɪ, -dɪ] *n* 水曜日
[suiyoubi]; **Ash Wednesday** *n* 灰の水曜日
[hai no suiyoubi]; **on Wednesday** 水曜日に
[suiyoubi ni]

weed [wid] *n* 雑草 [zassou]

weedkiller [widkɪlər] *n* 除草剤 [josouzai]

week [wik] *n* 週 [shuu]; **two weeks** *n* 二週間
[nishuukan]; **a week ago** 一週間前
[isshuukan mae]; **How much is it for a
week?** 1週間でいくらですか? [isshuukan de
ikura desu ka?]; **last week** 先週 [senshuu];
next week 来週 [raishuu]

weekday [wikdeɪ] *n* 平日 [heijitsu]

weekend [wikɛnd] *n* 週末 [shuumatsu]; **I
want to rent a car for the weekend** 車を週
末借りたいのですが [kuruma o shuumatsu
karitai no desu ga]

weekly [wikli] *adv* **What are your weekly
rates?** 1週間の料金はいくらですか?
[isshuukan no ryoukin wa ikura desu ka?]

weep [wip] *v* 泣く [naku]

weigh [weɪ] *v* 重さが···ある [omosa ga…
aru]

weight [weɪt] *n* 重さ [omosa]

weightlifter [weɪtlɪftər] *n* 重量挙げ選手
[juuryouage senshu]

weightlifting [weɪtlɪftɪŋ] *n* 重量挙げ
[juuryouage]

weird [wɪərd] *adj* 変な [hen na]

welcome [wɛlkəm] *n* 歓迎 [kangei] ▷ *v* 歓迎す
る [kangei suru]

welcome [wɛlkəm] *excl* ようこそ! [youkoso]

welfare [wɛlfɛər] *n* 失業手当
[shitsugyouteate]

well [wɛl] *adj* 申し分ない [moushibun nai]

▷ *adv* 申し分なく [moushibun naku] ▷ *n* 井戸
[ido]; **oil well** *n* 油井 [yusei]; **well done!** *excl*
おみごと! [omigoto]

well-behaved [wɛlbɪheɪvd] *adj* 行儀のよい
[gyougi no yoi]

well-known [wɛlnoʊn] *adj* 有名な [yuumei
na], よく知られている [yoku shirarete iru]

well-off [wɛlɔf] *adj* 裕福な [yuufuku na]

well-paid [wɛlpeɪd] *adj* 給料のよい [kyuuryou
no yoi]

Welsh [wɛlʃ] *adj* ウェールズの [ueeruzu no]
▷ *n* ウェールズ語 [ueeruzugo]

west [wɛst] *adj* 西の [nishi no] ▷ *adv* 西に
[nishi ni] ▷ *n* 西 [nishi]; **West Indian** *n* 西イン
ド諸島の [nishiindoshotou no], 西インド諸島
の人 [nishiindoshotou no hito]; **West Indies**
npl 西インド諸島 [nishiindoshotou]

westbound [wɛstbaʊnd] *adj* 西行きの [nishi
yuki no]

western [wɛstərn] *adj* 西の [nishi no] ▷ *n* ウェ
スタン [uesutan]

wet [wɛt] *adj* 濡れた [nureta]

wetsuit [wɛtsut] *n* ウェットスーツ [uettosu-
utsu]

whack [wæk] *n* ゴツン [gotsun]

whale [weɪl] *n* クジラ [kujira]

what [wʌt, wɒt] *adv* 何 [nan], どうした [doushi-
ta]; **What do you do?** お仕事は何をなさって
いますか? [o-shigoto wa nani o nasatte
imasu ka?]; **What is it?** それは何ですか?
[sore wa nan desu ka?]; **What is the word
for...?** ···は何といいますか? [... wa nan to
iimasu ka?]; **What time is it, please?** 今何
時か教えていただけますか? [ima nan-ji ka
oshiete itadakemasu ka?]

wheat [wit] *n* 小麦 [komugi]; **wheat allergy** *n*
小麦アレルギー [komugi arerugii]

wheel [wil] *n* 車輪 [sharin]; **spare wheel** *n* ス
ペアホイール [supeahoiiru]; **steering wheel**
n ステアリングホイール [sutearinguhoiiru]

wheelbarrow [wilbæroʊ] *n* 手押し車
[teoshiguruma]

wheelchair [wiltʃɛər] *n* 車椅子 [kurumaisu];

W

Can you visit... in a wheelchair? 車椅子で・・・を訪れることができますか？ [kuruma-isu de... o otozureru koto ga dekimasu ka?]; **Do you have a wheelchair lift?** 車椅子用のエレベーターはありますか？ [kuruma-isu-you no erebeetaa wa arimasu ka?]; **Do you have wheelchairs?** おたくには車椅子がありますか？ [otaku ni wa kuruma-isu ga arimasu ka?]; **I need a room with wheelchair access** 私は車椅子で入れる部屋が必要です [watashi wa kuruma-isu de haireru heya ga hitsuyou desu]; **I use a wheelchair** 私は車椅子を使っています [watashi wa kuruma-isu o tsukatte imasu]; **Is there wheelchair-friendly transportation available to...?** ・・・へ行くのに車椅子で利用しやすい交通手段はありますか？ [... e iku no ni kuruma-isu de riyou shiyasui koutsuu-shudan wa arimasu ka?]; **Is your hotel accessible to wheelchairs?** おたくのホテルは車椅子で利用できますか？ [otaku no hoteru wa kuruma-isu de riyou dekimasu ka?]; **Where's the nearest repair shop for wheelchairs?** 一番近くの車椅子修理店はどこですか？ [ichiban chikaku no kuruma-isu shuuri-ten wa doko desu ka?]; **Where's the wheelchair-accessible entrance?** 車椅子で利用できる入口はどこですか？ [kuruma-isu de riyou dekiru iriguchi wa doko desu ka?]

when [wɛn] *adv* いつ [itsu]; **When does it begin?** いつ始まりますか？ [itsu hajimari-masu ka?]; **When does it finish?** いつ終わりますか？ [itsu owarimasu ka?]; **When is it due?** いつ到着する予定ですか？ [itsu touchaku suru yotei desu ka?]

where [wɛər] *adv* どこ [doko]; **Where are we?** ここはどこですか？ [koko wa doko desu ka?]; **Where can we meet?** どこでお会いできますか？ [doko de o-ai dekimasu ka?]; **Where can you go...?** どこに行けば・・・ができますか？ [doko ni ikeba... ga dekimasu ka?]; **Where do I pay?** どこで払うのですか？ [doko de harau no desu ka?]; **Where do I sign?** どこに署名するのですか？ [doko ni shomei suru no desu ka?]; **Where is...?** ・・・はどこですか？ [... wa doko desu ka?]

which [wɪtʃ] *pron* **Which is the key to this door?** このドアの鍵はどれですか？ [kono doa no kagi wa dore desu ka?]

while [waɪl] *n* 間 [aida]

whip [wɪp] *n* 鞭 [muchi]; **whipped cream** *n* ホイップクリーム [hoippukuriimu]

whisk [wɪsk] *n* 泡立て器 [awatateki]

whiskers [wɪskərz] *npl* ひげ [hige]

whiskey [wɪski] *n* ウイスキー [uisukii]; **malt whiskey** *n* モルトウイスキー [moruto uisukii]; **a whiskey and soda** ウイスキーのソーダ割り [uisukii no sooda wari]; **I'll have a whiskey** ウイスキーをください [uisukii o kudasai]

whisper [wɪspər] *v* ささやく [sasayaku]

whistle [wɪsəl] *n* 口笛 [kuchibue] ▷ *v* 口笛を吹く [kuchibue wo fuku]

white [waɪt] *adj* 白い [shiroi]; **egg white** *n* 卵の白身 [tamago no shiromi]

whiteboard [waɪtbord] *n* ホワイトボード [howaitoboodo]

whitewash [waɪtwɒʃ] *v* 漆喰を塗る [shikkui-o nuru]

whiting [waɪtɪŋ] *n* ホワイティング [howaitingu] (魚)

who [hu] *pron* どなた [donata], 誰 [dare]; **Who is it?** どなたですか？ [donata desu ka?]

whole [hoʊl] *adj* 全体の [zentai no] ▷ *n* 全体 [zentai]; **whole foods** *npl* 自然食品 [shizen shokuhin]

wholesale [hoʊlseɪl] *adj* 卸売りの [oroshiuri no] ▷ *n* 卸売り [oroshiuri]

whole wheat [hoʊlwit] *adj* 全粒小麦の [zenryuu komugi no]

whose [huz] *pron* **Whose round is it?** 誰の番ですか？ [dare no ban desu ka?]

wicked [wɪkɪd] *adj* 邪悪な [jaaku na]

wide [waɪd] *adj* 広い [hiroi] ▷ *adv* 広く [hiroku]

widespread [waɪdsprɛd] *adj* 広まった [hiromatta]

widow [wɪdoʊ] *n* 未亡人 [miboujin]

widower [wɪdoʊər] *n* 男やもめ [otokoyamome]

width [wɪdθ, wɪtθ] *n* 幅 [haba]

wife [waɪf] (*pl* **wives**) *n* 妻 [tsuma]; **This is my wife** 私の妻です [watashi no tsuma desu]

Wi-Fi [waɪfaɪ] *n* ワイファイ [waifai]

wig [wɪg] *n* かつら [katsura]

wild [waɪld] *adj* 野生の [yasei no]

wildlife [waɪldlaɪf] *n* 野生生物 [yaseiseibutsu]; **We'd like to see wildlife** 野生生物を見たいのですが [yasei-seibutsu o mitai no desu ga]

will [wɪl] *n* (document) 遺言 [yuigon], (motivation) 意志 [ishi]

willing [wɪlɪŋ] *adj* いとわない [itowanai]

willingly [wɪlɪŋli] *adv* 進んで [susunde]

willow [wɪloʊ] *n* ヤナギ [yanagi]

willpower [wɪlpaʊər] *n* 意志の力 [ishi no chikara]

wilt [wɪlt] *v* しおれる [shioreru]

win [wɪn] *v* 勝つ [katsu]

wind¹ [wɪnd] *n* 風 [kaze]

wind² [wɪnd] *v* (coil around) 巻く [maku]

windmill [wɪndmɪl] *n* 風車小屋 [fuushagoya]

window [wɪndoʊ] *n* 窓 [mado]; **store window** *n* ショーウィンドウ [shoouindou]; **window seat** *n* 窓下の腰掛け [mado shita no koshikake]; **I can't open the window** 窓を開けられません [mado o akeraremasen]; **I'd like a window seat** 窓側の席をお願いします [mado-gawa no seki o o-negai shimasu]; **May I close the window?** 窓を閉めてもいいですか? [mado o shimete mo ii desu ka?]; **May I open the window?** 窓を開けてもいいですか? [mado o akete mo ii desu ka?]

windowpane [wɪndoʊpeɪn] *n* 窓ガラス [madogarasu]

windowsill [wɪndoʊsɪl] *n* 窓の下枠 [mado no shitawaku]

windshield [wɪndʃild] *n* フロントガラス [furontogarasu]; **windshield wiper** *n* フロントガラスのワイパー [furonto garasu no waipaa]; **Could you add some windshield wiper fluid?** フロントガラスのウォッシャー液を補充してもらえますか? [furonto-garasu no wosshaa-eki o hojuu shite moraemasu ka?]; **Could you clean the windshield?** フロントガラスを拭いてもらえますか? [furonto-garasu o fuite moraemasu ka?]; **The windshield is broken** フロントガラスが割れています [furonto-garasu ga warete imasu]

windsurfing [wɪndsɜrfɪŋ] *n* ウインドサーフィン [uindosaafin]

windy [wɪndi] *adj* 風の強い [kaze no tsuyoi]

wine [waɪn] *n* ワイン [wain]; **house wine** *n* ハウスワイン [hausuwain]; **red wine** *n* 赤ワイン [akawain]; **table wine** *n* テーブルワイン [teeburuwain]; **wine list** *n* ワインリスト [wain-risuto]; **a bottle of white wine** 白ワインのボトルを1本 [shiro-wain no botoru o ippon]; **Can you recommend a good wine?** よいワインを教えてもらえますか? [yoi wain o oshiete moraemasu ka?]; **Is the wine chilled?** ワインは冷えていますか? [wain wa hiete imasu ka?]; **The wine list, please** ワインリストをください [wain-risuto o kudasai]; **This stain is wine** このしみはワインです [kono shimi wa wain desu]; **This wine isn't chilled** このワインは冷えていません [kono wain wa hiete imasen]

wineglass [waɪnglɑs] *n* ワイングラス [waingurasu]

wing [wɪŋ] *n* 翼 [tsubasa]

wink [wɪŋk] *v* ウインクする [uinku suru]

winner [wɪnər] *n* 勝者 [shousha]

winning [wɪnɪŋ] *adj* 勝利を得た [shouri-o eta]

winter [wɪntər] *n* 冬 [fuyu]; **winter sports** *npl* ウィンタースポーツ [uintaasupootsu]

wipe [waɪp] *v* 拭く [fuku]; **baby wipe** *n* 赤ちゃん用ウェットティシュー [akachanyouuetto-tishuu]

wipe up *v* 皿拭きをする [sarafuki-o suru]

W

wire [waɪər] n 針金 [harigane]; **barbed wire** n 有刺鉄線 [yuushitessen]

wireless [waɪərlɪs] adj 無線 [musen]

wisdom [wɪzdəm] n 賢明 [kenmei]; **wisdom tooth** n 親知らず [oyashirazu]

wise [waɪz] adj 賢い [kashikoi]

wish [wɪʃ] n 願い [negai] ▷ v 願う [negau]

wit [wɪt] n 機知 [kichi]

witch [wɪtʃ] n 魔女 [majo]

with [wɪð, wɪθ] prep **It's been a pleasure working with you** 一緒にお仕事できて楽しかったです [issho ni o-shigoto dekite tanoshikatta desu]; **May I leave a message with his secretary?** 彼の秘書に伝言を残すことはできますか? [kare no hisho ni dengon o nokosu koto wa dekimasu ka?]

withdraw [wɪðdrɔː, wɪθ-] v 抜き取る [nukitoru]

withdrawal [wɪðdrɔːəl, wɪθ-] n 引っ込めること [hikkomeru koto]

without [wɪðaʊt, wɪθ-] prep **I'd like it without..., please** ･･･なしでお願いします [... nashi de o-negai shimasu]

witness [wɪtnɪs] n 目撃者 [mokugekisha]; **Jehovah's Witness** n エホバの証人 [Ehoba no shounin]; **Can you be a witness for me?** 私の目撃者になってもらえますか? [watashi no mokugeki-sha ni natte moraemasu ka?]

witty [wɪti] adj 機知に富んだ [kichi ni tonda]

wolf [wʊlf] (pl wolves) n オオカミ [ookami]

woman, women [wʊmən, wɪmɪn] n 女性 [josei]

wonder [wʌndər] v 怪しむ [ayashimu]

wonderful [wʌndərfəl] adj すばらしい [subarashii]

wood [wʊd] n 材木 [zaimoku]

wooden [wʊdən] adj 木製の [mokusei no]

woods npl 森 [mori]

woodwind [wʊdwɪnd] n 木管楽器 [mokkangakki]

woodwork [wʊdwɜrk] n 木工部 [mokkoubu]

wool [wʊl] n 羊毛 [youmou]

woolen [wʊlən] adj 毛織りの [keori no]

woolens [wʊlənz] npl 毛織物衣類 [keorimono irui]

word [wɜrd] n 単語 [tango]; 言葉 [kotoba]

work [wɜrk] n 仕事 [shigoto], 労働 [roudou] ▷ v 働く [hataraku]; **road work** n 道路工事 [douroukouji]; **work experience** n 労働体験 [roudou taiken]; **work of art** n 美術品 [bijutsuhin]; **work permit** n 労働許可証 [roudou kyokashou]; **work station** n ワークステーション [waakusuteeshon]; **I hope we can work together again soon** また近いうちにお仕事でご一緒できることを願っています [mata chikai uchi ni o-shigoto de go-issho dekiru koto o negatte imasu]; **I'm here for work** 私は仕事で来ています [watashi wa shigoto de kite imasu]

worker [wɜrkər] n 働く人 [hatarakuhito]; **social worker** n ソーシャルワーカー [soosharuwaakaa]

workforce [wɜrkfɔrs] n 作業要員 [sagyou youin]

working-class adj 労働者階級の [roudoushakaikyuu no]

workman [wɜrkmən] (pl workmen) n 肉体労働者 [nikutairoudousha]

work out v 考え出す [kangaedasu]

workplace [wɜrkpleɪs] n 職場 [shokuba]

workshop [wɜrkʃɒp] n 仕事場 [shigotoba]

workspace [wɜrkspeɪs] n 作業スペース [sagyou supeesu]

workstation [wɜrksteɪʃən] n ワークステーション [waakusuteeshon]

world [wɜrld] n 世界 [sekai]; **Third World** n 第三世界 [dai san sekai]; **World Cup** n ワールドカップ [waarudokappu]

worm [wɜrm] n 虫 [mushi]

worn [wɔrn] adj 着古した [kifurushita]

worried [wɜrid] adj 心配している [shinpai shite iru]

worry [wɜri] v 心配する [shinpai suru]

worrying [wɜriɪŋ] adj 気がもめる [ki ga momeru]

worse [wɜrs] adj 一層悪い [issou warui] ▷ adv 一層悪く [issou waruku]

worsen [wɜrsən] v 悪化する [akka suru]

worship [wɜrʃɪp] v 礼拝する [reihai suru]

worst [wɜrst] adj 最悪の [saiaku no]

worth [wɜrθ] n 資産 [shisan]

worthless [wɜrθləs] adj 価値のない [kachi no nai]

would [wəd, STRONG wʊd] aux v **We'd like to go cycling** 私たちはサイクリングに行きたいのですが [watashi-tachi wa saikuringu ni ikitai no desu ga]

wound [waʊnd] n 傷 [kizu] ▷ v 傷つける [kizutsukeru]

wrap [ræp] v 包む [tsutsumu]; **wrapping paper** n 包装紙 [housoushi]

wrapping [ræpɪŋ] n ラッピング [rappingu], 包装 [housou]

wrap up v 包む [tsutsumu]

wreck [rɛk] n 衝突 [shoutotsu], 大破 [taiha] ▷ v 大破する [taiha suru] ▷ vt 衝突させる [shoutotsu saseru]; **I've wrecked my car** 私は自分の車を衝突させました [watashi wa jibun no kuruma o shoutotsu sasemashita]

wreckage [rɛkɪdʒ] n 残骸 [zangai]

wren [rɛn] n ミソサザイ [misosazai]

wrench [rɛntʃ] n ねじり [nejiri], スパナ [supana] ▷ v ねじる [nejiru]

wrestler [rɛslər] n レスラー [resuraa]

wrestling [rɛslɪŋ] n レスリング [resuringu]

wrinkle [rɪŋkᵊl] n しわ [shiwa]

wrinkled [rɪŋkəld] adj しわの寄った [shiwa no yotta]

wrist [rɪst] n 手首 [tekubi]

write [raɪt] v 書く [kaku]

write down v 書き留める [kakitomeru]

writer [raɪtər] n 作家 [sakka]

writing [raɪtɪŋ] n 書いたもの [kaita mono]; **writing paper** n 便箋 [binsen]

wrong [rɔŋ] adj 間違った [machigatta] ▷ adv 間違って [machigatte]; **wrong number** n 間違い電話 [machigai denwa]; **I think you've given me the wrong change** お釣りが間違っていると思います [o-tsuri ga machigatte iru to omoimasu]; **The bill is wrong** 請求書が間違っています [seikyuusho ga machigatte imasu]

W

X

Xmas [ɛksməs] *n* クリスマス [kurisumasu]

X-ray [ɛksreɪ] *n* X線 [ekkususen] ▸ *v* X線写真 を撮る [x-sen shashin-o toru]

xylophone [zaɪləfoun] *n* シロホン [shirohon]

Y

yacht [yɒt] *n* ヨット [yotto]

yard [yɑrd] *n (enclosure)* 庭 [niwa], *(measurement)* ヤード [yaado]

yawn [yɔn] *v* あくびをする [akubi-o suru]

year [yɪər] *n* 年 [nen, toshi]; **academic year** *n* 学年 [gakunen]; **financial year** *n* 会計年度 [kaikeinendo]; **leap year** *n* うるう年 [uruudoshi]; **New Year** *n* 新年 [shinnen]; **last year** 去年 [kyonen]; **next year** 来年 [rainen]; **this year** 今年 [kotoshi]

yearly [yɪərli] *adj* 年に一度の [nen ni ichido no] ▷ *adv* 年に一度 [nen ni ichido]

yeast [yist] *n* 酵母菌 [koubokin]

yell [yɛl] *v* 叫ぶ [sakebu]

yellow [yɛloʊ] *adj* 黄色の [ki iro no]; **Yellow Pages®** *npl* イエローページ® [ieroopeeji]

Yemen [yɛmən] *n* イエメン [iemen]

yes [yɛs] *excl* はい [hai]

yesterday [yɛstərdeɪ, -di] *adv* 昨日 [kinou, sakujitsu]

yet [yɛt] *adv* まだ [mada]

yew [yu] *n* イチイ [ichii]

yield [yild] *v* 生む [umu] *(利益)*

yoga [yoʊgə] *n* ヨガ [yoga]

yogurt [yoʊgərt] *n* ヨーグルト [yooguruto]

yolk [yoʊk] *n* 卵の黄身 [tamago no kimi]

you [yu] *pron* あなた [anata]; **How much do you weigh?** あなたの体重はどのくらいありますか? [anata no taijuu wa dono kurai arimasu ka?]

young [yʌŋ] *adj* 若い [wakai]

younger [yʌŋgər] *adj* 年下の方の [toshishita no hou no]

youngest [yʌŋgɪst] *adj* 一番若い [ichiban wakai]

your [yɔr, yʊər] *adj* あなたの [anata no]

yours [yɔrz, yʊərz] *pron* あなたの [anata no]

yourself [yɔrsɛlf, yʊər-] *pron* あなた自身 [anata jishin]

yourselves [yɔrsɛlvz, yʊər-] *pron* あなた方自身 [anatagata jishin]

youth [yuθ] *n* 青春時代 [seishun jidai]; **youth club** *n* ユースクラブ [yuusukurabu]; **youth hostel** *n* ユースホステル [yuusuhosuteru]

Z

Zambia [zæmbiə] *n* ザンビア [zanbia]

Zambian [zæmbiən] *adj* ザンビアの [Zanbia no] ▷ *n* ザンビア人 [Zanbia jin]

zebra [zibrə] *n* シマウマ [shimauma]; **zebra crossing** (*crosswalk*) *n* 太い白線の縞模様で示した横断歩道 [futoi hakusen no shimamoyou de shimeshita oudanhodou]

zero [ziərou] *n* 零 [rei]

Zimbabwe [zimbɑmbwi] *n* ジンバブウェ [jinbabuue]

Zimbabwean [zimbɑbwiən] *adj* ジンバブウェの [Jinbabuue no] ▷ *n* ジンバブウェ人 [Jinbabuue jin]

zinc [ziŋk] *n* 亜鉛 [aen]

zip [zip] *v* ファスナーを締める [fasunaa-o shimeru]

zip code [zip koud] *n* 郵便番号 [yuubin bangou]

zipper [zipər] *n* ファスナー [fasunaa]

zit [zit] *n* にきび [nikibi]

zodiac [zoudiæk] *n* 十二宮 [juunikyuu]

zone [zoun] *n* 地帯 [chitai]; **time zone** *n* 標準時間帯 [hyoujun jikantai]

zoo [zu] *n* 動物園 [doubutsuen]

zoology [zouplədʒi] *n* 動物学 [doubutsugaku]

zoom [zum] *n* **zoom lens** *n* ズームレンズ [zuumurenzu]

zucchini [zukini] *n* ズッキーニ [zukkiini]

zwieback [zwibæk] *n* **zwieback toast** *n* ラスク [rasuku]